ADVANCES IN THEORY
AND
FORMAL METHODS OF COMPUTING

Proceedings of the Third Imperial College Workshop

ADVANCES IN THEORY AND FORMAL METHODS OF COMPUTING

Christ Church, Oxford
1 – 3 April 1996

Editors

A. Edalat

S. Jourdan

G. McCusker

Imperial College, UK

ICP

Imperial College Press

Published by

Imperial College Press
57 Shelton Street
Covent Garden
London WC2H 9HE

Distributed by

World Scientific Publishing Co. Pte. Ltd.
5 Toh Tuck Link, Singapore 596224
USA office: 27 Warren Street, Suite 401-402, Hackensack, NJ 07601
UK office: 57 Shelton Street, Covent Garden, London WC2H 9HE

British Library Cataloguing-in-Publication Data
A catalogue record for this book is available from the British Library.

ADVANCES IN THEORY AND FORMAL METHODS OF COMPUTING

ISBN-13 978-1-86094-031-6
ISBN-10 1-86094-031-5

Preface

This volume is the proceedings of the third workshop of the Theory and Formal Methods Section of the Department of Computing, Imperial College, London. The papers are contributions from members, ex-members and visitors of the Section.

As the variety of work in these pages shows, the interests of the Section encompass many areas in theoretical computer science, ranging from formal specification and verification of programs through denotational and operational semantics to rarefied areas such as computational measure theory. The aim of our work is to improve both the theory and practice of the design of programs and programming languages; to facilitate efficient implementation of correct programs; to increase understanding and enable fruitful exploitation of computing paradigms such as concurrency or object orientation; and to allow the smooth incorporation of advanced features such as exact real number arithmetic into computation, always with an emphasis on mathematically rigorous development.

Topics addressed by papers in this collection include Formal Specification, Theorem Proving, Concurrency, Operational and Denotational Semantics, Real Number Computation, Abstract Interpretation, Computational Measure Theory and Neural Networks.

The workshop was held at Christ Church, Oxford, between the 1st and 3rd of April 1996. Since the workshop, all the papers have been refereed and revised.

Abbas Edalat
Sofia Jourdan
Guy McCusker
July 1996, Imperial College, London.

Contents

TOPOSES POUR LES VRAIMENT NULS

STEVEN VICKERS
Department of Computing, Imperial College, London SW7 2BZ
email sjv@doc.ic.ac.uk

Restriction to geometric logic can enable one to define topological structures and continuous maps without explicit reference to topologies. This idea is illustrated with some examples and used to explain toposes as generalized topological spaces.

1 Introduction

Last year I wrote a short article[8] "Toposes pour les nuls", with the aim of explaining toposes (and in particular their nature as generalized topological spaces) to those who knew nothing about them. Unfortunately, it seems that I was unsuccessful in that aim, for when I presented the material in a seminar I was told that I should write another article *pour les vraiment nuls*. This is intended to be it.

The "generalized topological space" view is only one aspect of toposes, but it is an aspect that is very easily obscured. My aim here is to plant sufficiently strong intuitions that the reader can then turn to the standard texts and their technical development without losing sight of the generalized spaces.

I shall not give comprehensive references, but simply refer the reader to some standard introductory texts: Johnstone[3] and Vickers[6] for locales, Mac Lane and Moerdijk[4], McLarty[5], Bell[1] and Johnstone[2] for toposes (though the last is hardly recommended for the beginner). The topos books provide a good variety of approaches, but still tend to follow a broadly similar route governed by the view of toposes as generalized categories of sets. A number of my references to Mac Lane and Moerdijk will therefore also apply to the other three.

2 Real numbers

For our leading example, let a *real number* be defined as a Dedekind section of the rationals, i.e. a pair (L, R) of subsets of the rational numbers $\mathbb{Q}$, such that –

- L is inhabited: $\exists q \in \mathbb{Q}.\ q \in L$
- L is "rounded lower": $\forall q \in \mathbb{Q}.\ (q \in L \leftrightarrow \exists q' \in \mathbb{Q}.\ (q < q' \wedge q' \in L))$
- R is inhabited and rounded upper
- L and R are disjoint

- L and R are "arbitrarily close": $\forall q,r \in \mathbb{Q}. (q < r \rightarrow q \in L \vee r \in R)$

(For a real number x, I shall usually write (L_x, R_x) for the corresponding section.)

In a topological development, one would follow this with a definition of the usual *topology* on the set $\mathbb{R}$ of real numbers. If q is rational, let us write (q, ∞) for the set of reals x for which $q \in L_x$ (i.e. $q < x$), and $(-\infty, q)$ for the set of reals x for which $q \in R_x$. These are defined to be "subbasic open" subsets of $\mathbb{R}$, and in general the open subsets are those that can be expressed as unions of finite intersections of subbasics. (The intersection $(-\infty,q+\varepsilon)\cap(q-\varepsilon,\infty)$ gives the rational open ball $B_\varepsilon(q)$, the set of reals strictly between $q-\varepsilon$ and $q+\varepsilon$, and the open sets are usually characterized as the unions of these.)

However, there is a good sense in which this topology is already inherent in the definition of the real numbers themselves. For the two sets L and R can be described equally well by two $\mathbb{Q}$-indexed families of propositions "$q \in L$" and "$q \in R$", and so we can equivalently present the theory of Dedekind sections as a propositional theory, with propositional symbol schemas (q,∞) and $(-\infty,q)$. The axioms now become the schemas

- $\mathbf{true} \rightarrow \bigvee_q (q,\infty)$ (note the use of an infinitary disjunction here)
- $(q',\infty) \rightarrow (q,\infty)$ $(q < q')$
- $(q,\infty) \rightarrow \bigvee_{q<q'} (q',\infty)$
- $\mathbf{true} \rightarrow \bigvee_q (-\infty,q)$
- $(-\infty,q') \rightarrow (-\infty,q)$ $(q > q')$
- $(-\infty,q) \rightarrow \bigvee_{q>q'} (-\infty,q')$
- $(q,\infty) \wedge (-\infty,q) \rightarrow \mathbf{false}$
- $\mathbf{true} \rightarrow (q,\infty) \vee (-\infty,r)$ $(q < r)$

It should be clear that these two theories are equivalent. Though there are technical differences concerning the precise form of a model (one theory uses subsets of $\mathbb{Q}$, the other uses $\mathbb{Q}$-indexed families of truth values), there should be no doubt that these differences are inessential.

We see now that the subbasic opens correspond exactly to the primitive propositional symbols, and $\cap$, $\cup$ and $\subseteq$ correspond to the logical $\wedge$ (finitary conjunction), $\bigvee$ (arbitrary disjunction) and $\rightarrow$. If we restrict our connectives to $\wedge$ and $\bigvee$ then the propositions we get correspond exactly to the opens. Of course, this appears to depend critically on the presentation of the theory. We could equally well present an equivalent theory using the analogues of the closed subsets $[q,\infty)$ and $(-\infty,q]$ (i.e. $\neg(q \in R)$ and $\neg(q \in L)$) and get a different topology. But plainly the problem there is that negation $\neg$ has crept into the presentation. If we restrict our connectives also in getting equivalences between presentations, then there is no problem – the topology is presentation invariant.

Let us continue by looking at continuous maps, taking as our example the negation map neg: $\mathbb{R} \to \mathbb{R}$, defined by

$$L_{neg(x)} = \{-q: q \in R_x\}, \qquad R_{neg(x)} = \{-q: q \in L_x\}$$

It is easy to show that these give a new Dedekind section. However, this should normally be augmented by proof of continuity, to show that the inverse images of opens (or, sufficiently, subbasic opens) are open:

$neg^{-1}(q,\infty) = (-\infty,-q)$

$(x \in neg^{-1}(q,\infty) \Leftrightarrow neg(x) \in (q,\infty) \Leftrightarrow q \in L_{neg(x)} \Leftrightarrow -q \in R_x \Leftrightarrow x' \in (-\infty,-q))$

$neg^{-1}(-\infty,q) = (-q,\infty)$

But let us study more closely how the equivalence of the two theories works here. A Dedekind section x, i.e. a model of the predicate theory, yields interpretations of all the symbols (q,∞) and $(-\infty,q)$ as truth values. Negation constructs a new Dedekind section neg(x), and, correspondingly, new interpretations $(q,\infty)'$ and $(-\infty,q)'$ (say) of the propositional symbols: e.g. $(q,\infty)'$ is **true** iff $q \in L_{neg(x)}$, i.e. neg(x) is in the open set corresponding to (q,∞). It follows that $(q,\infty)'$, considered as a subset of $\mathbb{R}$ (comprising those models x for which $(q,\infty)'$ is **true**) is exactly $neg^{-1}(q,\infty)$, and similarly for $(-\infty,q)'$.

Now in constructing the new Dedekind section neg(x) from the original one, x, we find that, correspondingly, $(q,\infty)'$ and $(-\infty,q)'$ were constructed from the propositional symbols (q,∞) and $(-\infty,q)$. Hence continuity is obvious if the propositional constructions are constrained to using $\wedge$ and $\bigvee$. It turns out that this will follow, provided that the construction as described on the Dedekind sections also observes certain "geometric" constraints. We shall examine these in the next section.

3 Geometric logic and locales

The example of Section 2 is suggesting that if we restrict our logic suitably, then topological issues are completely implicit: the topology is implicit in the theory presentation that defines the points (as models), and continuity is implicit in the construction of the maps. The appropriate logic is *geometric logic*.

To describe the points geometrically is already to topologize them.

A propositional geometric theory is one presented using axioms of the form $\phi \to \psi$ where the propositions ϕ and ψ are "geometric" – their connectives are restricted to $\wedge$ (finitary conjunction) and $\bigvee$ (arbitrary disjunction). The approach then is to describe the points of a topological space as the models of a propositional geometric theory, and the open sets as the geometric propositions (modulo equivalence). This works even if we replace the propositional theory by an equivalent non-propositional one.

Let us take the word *locale* to have the intuitive meaning of "space of models of a propositional geometric theory", in other words our revised idea of topological space. This is a little vague – what, for instance, is a "space"? But the idea is that if we can present a propositional theory T, then something or other should be the corresponding locale [T], "the space of T-models".

But of course, the word "locale" already has a use, and the link with the intuitions above is via the notion of the *frame* Ω[T], the set of *all* expressible geometric propositions in T, modulo equivalence. The frame is effectively a geometric Lindenbaum algebra, and algebraically it is presented by generators and relations taken from T (Vickers[6]). Moreover, the frame provides a canonical way of presenting the locale, so locales and their properties can be studied through frames and their properties: and of course this has been done extensively (Johnstone[3]).

The next point to make is that these ideas extend to continuous maps. If X and Y are two locales, then to define a map from X to Y, continuous for the implicit topologies, it suffices to give a uniform description of the form, "Let x be a point of X. Then f(x) is defined [geometrically] to be ...."

Continuity = uniformity + geometricity

If we cheerfully accept the restrictions of geometric logic, then topology appears much simpler, much closer to sets and functions:

- To define the topological space, just give a geometric description of its points (no separate topology needed).
- To define a continuous map, just give a uniform, geometric description of how the result f(x) is constructed from x (no continuity proof needed).

An example of these two ideas in application is Vickers[11].

If we refuse to relinquish the power of classical logic, then we enable ourselves to define equivalences between theories without respecting the topologies – so the topology is no longer presentation invariant. We also enable ourselves to define discontinuous functions (examples later) so that a separate continuity proof is needed: this is really an explicit warranty that we haven't misused the extra power. To put it another way, classical point-set topology is a complicated (and only partially successful) machinery whose purpose is to correct for the errors introduced by classical reasoning principles! To use an image from planetary orbits, geometric logic is ellipses, classical logic is circles and point-set topology is epicycles.

In section 7 we shall consider more critically whether we really can just adopt a geometric logic and find topology doing itself automatically.

Specialization order

Though it's not evident in $\mathbb{R}$, locales automatically bear an ordering. If x and y are two points of a given locale, then it may be that every open (proposition) that is true for x is also true for y. To put it another way, every open containing x also contains y. We then say that y *specializes* x, and write $x \sqsubseteq y$. On $\mathbb{R}$, this ordering is discrete ($x \sqsubseteq y$ iff $x = y$), but for most locales – including the domains used in denotational semantics – it is non-discrete and important. It is also true that for any locale we have directed joins (sups) of points. In denotational semantics, the importance of this is vital.

Any continuous map between locales is monotone with respect to the specialization order, essentially because of the positivity of geometric logic – the map cannot use any negative information about its argument. More subtly, because of the finiteness of conjunctions in geometric logic, the map must preserve directed joins.

This ordering appears quite concretely as an order enrichment on the category of locales. If f and g are two continuous maps from X to Y, then $f \sqsubseteq g$ iff we have a proof of the form, "Let x be a point of X. Then $f(x) \sqsubseteq g(x)$ (geometrically)."

4 More examples

We follow with three more examples. The first illustrates how classical reasoning can lead to discontinuous functions, the second gives a deeper flavour of how the geometric reasoning works in practice, and the third marks a distinction between geometric logic and intuitionistic logic.

4.1 The Heaviside step function

We consider the Heaviside function H: $\mathbb{R} \to \mathbb{R}$, defined by letting H(x) be 0 if $x < 0$, 1 if $x \geq 0$. In terms of Dedekind sections, we have $x < 0$ iff $0 \in R_x$, so

$$q \in R_{H(x)} \text{ (i.e. } q > H(x)) \quad \text{iff} \quad q > 1 \vee (q > 0 \wedge 0 \in R_x)$$
$$q \in L_{H(x)} \text{ (i.e. } q < H(x)) \quad \text{iff} \quad q < 0 \vee (q < 1 \wedge 0 \notin R_x)$$

To prove that $(L_{H(x)}, R_{H(x)})$ is a Dedekind section is largely straightforward, except that in the final axiom we must use excluded middle on the formula $0 \in R_x$. (We also use it on formulae concerning the order of rationals, but that is no problem for that order is decidable.) Suppose $q < r$. If $q < 0$ then $q \in L_{H(x)}$, and if $r > 1$ then $r \in R_{H(x)}$, so the only question is over the case $0 \leq q < r \leq 1$. But then if $0 \in R_x$ we have $r \in R_{H(x)}$, while if $0 \notin R_x$ we have $q \in L_{H(x)}$.

4.2 Addition of reals

This example shows more clearly the influence of the geometric constraints on the reasoning: the influence is often quite algorithmic in nature. We can define addition on $\mathbb{R}$ as follows.

Let $x = (L_x, R_x)$ and $y = (L_y, R_y)$ be two Dedekind sections. Then their sum x+y is defined by

$$L_{x+y} = \{q+r: q \in L_x, r \in L_y\}, \qquad R_{x+y} = \{q+r: q \in R_x, r \in R_y\}$$

It is required to show that x+y is again a Dedekind section. Most of the axioms are easily disposed of, but the final one needs harder work.

Lemma Let (L, R) be a Dedekind section, and let ε be a positive rational. Then there are rationals $q \in L$ and $r \in R$ such that $r-q < \varepsilon$.

Proof L and R are both inhabited, so we can find $q_0 \in L$ and $r_0 \in R$. Certainly $q_0 < r_0$. There is some natural number n such that $2^n\varepsilon > r_0-q_0$; the proof is by induction on n. If $n = 0$, then we are already done.

For the induction step, suppose $2^{n+1}\varepsilon > r_0-q_0$ and let the interval $[q_0, r_0]$ be divided into four equal parts by $q_0 < s < t < u < r_0$. Out of these, we find numbers $q_1 \in L$ and $r_1 \in R$ such that $r_1-q_1 = (r_0-q_0)/2$ and we can then use the induction hypothesis. We have

$$s \in L \vee t \in R \quad \text{and} \quad t \in L \vee u \in R$$

If $t \in R$, we define $q_1 = q_0$, $r_1 = t$. If $t \in L$, then $q_1 = t$, $r_1 = r_0$. The remaining case has $s \in L$ and $u \in R$, and then we can take $q_1 = s$, $r_1 = u$. In all three cases we have q_1 and r_1 as required.

Note the algorithmic flavour of this: we start off with rationals q_0 and r_0 in L and R, and then an iteration replaces these by two closer rationals in L and R. We iterate this until they are close enough, when we can halt with the answer. To be sure, it is highly non-deterministic – the algorithm will usually offer a choice of new numbers. But the logic ensures that the choice is non-empty.]

Returning to the problem of sums, suppose $s < t$. By the Lemma, we can find $q_x \in L_x$ and $r_x \in R_x$ such that $r_x-q_x < t-s$. Then $s-q_x < t-r_x$, so we have either $s-q_x \in L_y$, in which case $s \in L_{x+y}$, or $t-r_x \in R_y$, in which case $t \in R_{x+y}$.

4.3 Upper real numbers

Brouwer maintained that all functions on the real line were continuous: that "constructions" of discontinuous functions must inevitably use some inadmissible principles, for instance of "omniscience". Our previous section can clearly be understood as suggesting that the admissible principles and constructions, that always lead to continuous functions, are the geometric ones. That general argument applies to far more than just the real line. However, Brouwer's ideas led to Heyting's intuitionistic logic, and what I want to present in this section is an example, not quite of the real line, where even intuitionistic reasoning can lead to discontinuous functions.

Let us define an *upper real* to be an inhabited rounded upper subset of $\mathbb{Q}$ – we shall normally write R_x for the subset itself, x for the upper real considered more abstractly. Classically, R_x is either the whole of $\mathbb{Q}$ or the second component of a Dedekind section, so the space of upper reals could be denoted $[-\infty, \infty)$. However, the natural topology has a basis comprising the sets (q, ∞), and its specialization order is numerical $\geq$ (so big numbers are low in the specialization order). To suggest that, let us write it as $\overleftarrow{[-\infty,\infty)}$. (Note the fact that $-\infty$ has appeared. For any locale we have all directed joins of points, so $-\infty$ has to be there as the directed join of the points in $(-\infty, \infty)$ under the specialization order $\geq$.) The example we shall give actually concerns the sublocale $\overleftarrow{[0,\infty)}$, whose points are inhabited rounded subsets of the set of *positive* rationals.

Let x and y be two points of $\overleftarrow{[0,\infty)}$. Then their truncated difference, $x \mathbin{\dot{-}} y$, is defined by

$$q \in R_{x \dot{-} y} \quad \text{iff} \qquad \exists q' \in \mathbb{Q}.\ 0 < q' < q \wedge \forall r \in R_y.\ q'+r \in R_x$$

It is not hard to show that this is rounded upper and contains only positive rationals. As for inhabitedness, let $q' \in R_x$. Then any r in R_y is positive, so $q'+r$ is also in R_x. It follows that $q'+1$ is in $R_{x \dot{-} y}$.

This is truncated difference, i.e. $x \mathbin{\dot{-}} y = \max(0, x-y)$, and in fact it is possible to justify this by proving –

Proposition For any x, y, z in $\overleftarrow{[0,\infty)}$ we have $z \geq x \mathbin{\dot{-}} y$ iff $z+y \geq x$.]

Now the interesting part of this is that all the reasoning – in both the construction and the Proposition – is intuitionistically valid, but truncated minus is *not* continuous. This is obvious, because it is antitone in its second argument – if $y \leq y'$ then $(x \mathbin{\dot{-}} y)+y' \geq (x \mathbin{\dot{-}} y)+y \geq x$, so $x \mathbin{\dot{-}} y \geq x \mathbin{\dot{-}} y'$ – and continuous maps must be monotone (with respect to the specialization order). We can see that the construction is not geometric, because of the universal quantification $\forall r \in R_y$.

5 Predicate theories and toposes

The locales correspond to propositional geometric theories, but there are also more general predicate theories, not all equivalent to propositional ones. The "space of models" for one of these will not in general be a locale. Nonetheless, our programme of accepting the geometric discipline still makes perfect sense, and this is where we shall use the word *topos:* a topos is the "class of models" (its points) for a general geometric theory, and a continuous map is a geometrically constructed transformation of points. (The topos is usually referred to as the *classifying topos* for its theory, and such a continuous map is usually known as a *geometric morphism.*) Very literally, a topos is a generalized locale (a locale is simply a topos whose corresponding geometric theory happens to be propositional), and so, as Grothendieck said, "A topos is a generalized topological space." In accepting the geometric discipline we are therefore again, in some generalized sense, doing topology without being aware of it.

"Geometric mathematics"

I should first say something about the nature of these geometric constructions.

Logically, we get a restriction on the theories presented: a geometric theory is a many-sorted first order theory, with a vocabulary of sorts, predicates and functions, and axioms of the form $\phi \vdash_S \psi$ where ϕ and ψ are geometric formulae (their permitted connectives are $\wedge$, $\bigvee$, $=$ and $\exists$) whose free variables are all taken from the finite set S.

Set theoretically, we get a restriction on the constructions allowed. The general rule is that the geometric constructions are those that can be characterized uniquely up to isomorphism by geometric theories. This includes finite products, arbitrary coproducts (disjoint unions), equalizers and coequalizers, and also free algebra constructions (for finitary algebraic theories). This gives us list types (free monoids), finite powersets (free semilattices) as well as $\mathbb{N}$ (natural numbers) and $\mathbb{Z}$ (integers), from which $\mathbb{Q}$ (rationals) can be constructed. However, certain constructions are *not* geometric, notably power sets, function sets and $\mathbb{R}$. (Geometrically, we can define a theory whose models are the reals, but we cannot define the set of reals: so geometrically, $\mathbb{R}$ is a locale but not a set.)

The practical mathematical effect is to allow finitary constructions, as well as inductive and recursive ones, but not impredicative ones. This gives geometric mathematics a highly algorithmic flavour, building constructions – and often proofs too – "from below".

In presenting theories we might as well presume a geometric type theory, from which we can derive new types from the base types (the sorts). We have already seen this in the theory of Dedekind sections. There were no base types there, but out of nothing we can construct $\mathbb{Q}$, which we used there, and hence $\mathbb{Q}\times\mathbb{Q}$ and so forth. Furthermore, by using the finite power set construction we get a weak 2nd order logic in which finite subsets can appear as terms, and we can universally quantify over finite sets despite the fact that $\forall$ is not in general geometric.

We now have a first view of toposes, based on the analogy with locales:

- A topos is defined by giving a geometric theory of its points.
- To define a geometric morphism f from E to F, just give a uniform, geometric description of how the result f(x) is constructed from x.

Already this is sufficient to do a certain amount of topos theory, and this can be seen quite explicitly in Vickers[10] which reworks certain categories and functors of domain theory as toposes and geometric morphisms.

Homomorphisms

The specialization order on locales generalizes to a category structure on a topos, through the notion of *homomorphism* between two models: it comprises, for each base type, a function between the two corresponding carriers, that respects the functions and relations. (e.g. Suppose the theory has one base type, a unary function f, and a binary relation R. If ϕ is the carrier function for a homomorphism, then we require $f(\phi(x)) = \phi(f(x))$ and $R(x, y) \Rightarrow R(\phi(x), \phi(y))$.) Because of the positivity of the logic, such a homomorphism can be defined at all the derived types too, and the notion of homomorphism is presentation-independent. In the propositional case (no sorts), such a homomorphism is precisely an instance of the specialization order.

The good behaviour of homomorphisms means that every topos has an intrinsic category structure: object = point, morphism = homomorphism. Moreover, any filtered diagram of points (such as a chain $x_0 \to x_1 \to x_2 \to \ldots$) has a colimit. A map (geometric morphism) between toposes is functorial with respect to homomorphisms and preserves the filtered colimits.

The homomorphisms make the category of toposes into a 2-category. For if f and g are two continuous maps (geometric morphisms) between toposes X and Y, then we can define 2-cells (or natural transformations) α: f $\Rightarrow$ g in the form, "Let x be a point of X. Then α_x is a homomorphism from f(x) to g(x) defined [geometrically] as ...."

6 Generalized categories of sets

The connection between propositional geometric theories and topologies was not too strained, and was made all the firmer by the frames. But for the predicate theories there is no pre-existing "generalized topology" we can connect up with, and the best we can do is to find something corresponding to the frames. For a locale D = [T], its frame ΩD comprises all the propositions expressible in T. Now propositional truth values are the points of a locale $\$$ (the *Sierpinski* locale, presented by a single propositional symbol and no axioms), and it follows that the elements of ΩD are the maps from D to $\$$.

For a *topos* D, classifying a predicate theory, the propositions are – unsurprisingly – not enough. We must replace $\$$ by [set], the topos classifying sets, and define $\mathcal{S}D$ to be the class of geometric morphisms from D to [set].

Examples (i) Suppose D is a locale. $\mathcal{S}D$ is the *category of sheaves* over D, and definitions (which can now be understood as structural elucidations) can be found in the standard texts such as Mac Lane and Moerdijk[4]. Other intuitions are in Vickers[8]. By extension, we shall refer to objects of $\mathcal{S}D$ as *sheaves on D* even when D is not a locale. If F is a sheaf on D, and x is a point of D, then F(x) is the *stalk of F at x*.
(ii) Suppose D is the locale classifying the empty theory – no vocabulary, no axioms. This theory has a unique model given by the vacuous interpretation of the empty vocabulary, so the locale has a unique point and is written 1. $\mathcal{S}1$ is the category of sets.
(iii) Suppose D is [set], and write FC for the category of finite cardinals. These are points of [set], so we get a functor from FC×$\mathcal{S}$[set] to **Sets**, and hence one from $\mathcal{S}$[set] to the functor category $\mathbf{Sets}^{FC}$. It turns out (e.g. Mac Lane and Moerdijk[4]) that this is in fact an equivalence: a sheaf on [set] is determined by its stalks at finite cardinals, the essential reason being that an arbitrary set is a filtered colimit of finite cardinals. This behaviour (that $\mathcal{S}D$ is equivalent to $\mathbf{Sets}^{C}$ where C is some restricted category of points) is typical of toposes that classify algebraic theories.

The objects of $\mathcal{S}D$, the sheaves, are essentially parametrized sets, and for this reason $\mathcal{S}D$ behaves in many respects just like a (non-classical) category of sets. It has all the geometric set-theoretic constructions (finite products, arbitrary coproducts, etc.), and indeed it has some non-geometric ones too (principally, function sets and power sets): it is a *generalized category of sets*. It certainly has enough good properties that we can say what it means to find a model in $\mathcal{S}D$ for a geometric theory.

We have now found a wide range of generalized categories of sets (indeed this is the key to the logical applications of topos theory), and in each of these we can discuss models of a theory T. It is important to realise that when we refer to points of the topos [T], we allow ourselves to consider models of T in arbitrary generalized categories of sets, not just some favourite "underlying set theory".

Purely in terms of our definition of $\mathcal{S}$D, it is actually not too hard to see –

Theorem Let D and E be toposes. Then the following are equivalent:

(i) Geometric morphisms from D to E.
(ii) Points of E in $\mathcal{S}$D.
(iii) Functors from $\mathcal{S}$E to $\mathcal{S}$D that preserve geometric constructions.

Proof hint: Use the fact that $\mathcal{S}$D contains a "generic" point of D. For instance, given a sort in a theory T, what is the corresponding carrier for the generic model? It is an object of $\mathcal{S}$[T], a sheaf on [T]: its stalk at point x (model of T) is the corresponding carrier of x.]

A consequence of this is that, just as with locales and frames, toposes and their properties can be studied through the categories of sheaves and their properties, which are moreover interesting in their own right. It has therefore become customary to say that the topos *is* its category of sheaves (and use the phrase "elementary topos" for some even more generalized categories of sets), but this does not harmonize with the idea of generalized spaces. For instance, the category structure of $\mathcal{S}$D – sheaves and sheaf morphisms – is completely different from the category structure of D – points and homomorphisms.

7 How much does geometric mathematics encompass?

The propaganda you've seen above – Do all your mathematics geometrically and you need not think about topology or frames or categories of sheaves – is in many ways delightfully simple. It holds out the promise of a grand encompassing geometric mathematics in which topology and continuity are intrinsic features, not added structure. Let us consider the claim a little more soberly.

It works quite well when defining the spaces and the maps, but it is heuristically naive for anything deeper. As an example, let us consider compactness. There is a good geometric account of this, but it is non-obvious and requires some structural knowledge of geometric mathematics itself. How far similar methods can be applied to other topological concepts such as connectedness and completeness is not entirely clear.

Compactness is known from ordinary topology and can readily be transferred to frames; the question is whether it can be discussed purely in terms of locales, given by theory presentations. The trick is to use the upper powerlocale $P_U D$ (Vickers[7,9]). The points of $P_U D$ are certain compact sublocales of D, with reverse ordering (big sublocales are low in the specialization order), and it turns out that D itself is compact iff $P_U D$ is local (has a bottom point). Now the presentation for $P_U D$ is normally derived from the frame ΩD, but it turns out that it can always be derived, and by geometric constructions, direct from a presentation of D. Hence compactness comes out of a deep structural feature of geometric mathematics, namely the existence of the upper powerlocale construction.

Even in the localic context we have a non-trivial piece of work here. I at least am still far from understanding the analogous structure for toposes.

Acknowledgements

I should like to thank Sofia Jourdan for her careful review of the first draft of this paper, and the EPSRC for their support via the "Foundational Structures in Computer Science" project.

References

1. J.L. Bell, *Toposes and local set theories: an introduction* (Oxford: Clarendon, 1988).
2. P.T. Johnstone, *Topos Theory* (Academic Press, London, 1977).
3. P.T. Johnstone, *Stone Spaces* (Cambridge University Press, 1982).
4. S. Mac Lane and I. Moerdijk, *Sheaves in geometry and logic* (Springer Verlag, 1992).
5. C. McLarty, *Elementary Categories, Elementary Toposes* (Oxford University Press, 1991).
6. S.J. Vickers, *Topology Via Logic* (Cambridge University Press, 1988).
7. S.J. Vickers, "Locales are Not Pointless", Theory and Formal Methods of Computing 94, ed. C.L. Hankin, I.C. Mackie and R. Nagarajan (Imperial College Press, 1995), 199–216.
8. S.J. Vickers, "Toposes Pour les Nuls", *Semantics Society Newsletter* **4** (1995). Also available as Imperial College Research Report DoC 96/4 (1996).
9. S.J. Vickers, "Constructive Points of Power Locales", accepted for *Math. Proc. Cam. Phil. Soc.*, 1997.
10. S.J. Vickers, "Topical Categories of Domains", in preparation. Preliminary notes in *Proceedings of the CLICS workshop, Aarhus,* ed. G. Winskel (Technical report DAIMI PB--397--I, Computer Science Department, Aarhus University, 1992), 261–274.
11. S.J. Vickers, "Localic Completion of Quasimetric Spaces", in preparation.

REAL PCF EXTENDED WITH ∃ IS UNIVERSAL
(EXTENDED ABSTRACT)

Martín Hötzel Escardó
Department of Computing, Imperial College, London SW7 2BZ.

Real PCF is an extension of the programming language PCF with a data type for the real line, introduced elsewhere. We show that Real PCF extended with ∃ is universal, in the sense that all computable elements of all types of its universe of discourse are definable. We also show that ∃ is not necessary to define first order computable functions in Real PCF. In order to obtain our definability results, we consider a domain-equation-like structure on the real numbers data type.
Keywords and phrases: Real number computability, λ-calculus, domain theory.

Introduction

Real PCF is an extension of the programming language PCF [13] with a ground type for the real line [8]. Real PCF has denotational and operational semantics, related by an adequacy relation.

The real numbers data type is interpreted as a domain of compact real intervals, with subspace of maximal elements homeomorphic to the real line. It is natural to effectively present this domain by enumerating its basis of rational intervals in some standard way. Then all Real PCF definable elements are computable. However, as in PCF, the converse fails. For instance, a computable function $\exists : [\mathcal{N} \to \mathcal{T}] \to \mathcal{T}$ is not definable. We show that Real PCF extended with ∃ is *universal*, in the sense that all computable elements and functions of its universe of discourse are definable. We do not need to add parallel-or, because Real PCF already has a parallel conditional.

It is natural to ask if the notion of computability depends on the choice of bases and their enumerations, and indeed this is the case [10]. We say that an effective presentation of the Real PCF domains is *sound* if every Real PCF definable element is computable. The idea is that the definable elements are concretely computable, because Real PCF has an effective operational semantics. We show that any two sound effective presentations of the Real PCF domains induce the same notion of computability. In this sense, Real PCF extended with ∃ is *absolutely universal*.

In order to establish universality, we use a technique due to Thomas Streicher [18], originally used by him to establish that PCF extended with recursive types, parallel-or and ∃ is universal. The technique consists of taking a universal PCF domain $\mathcal{U}$, and showing that (in our case) every Real PCF domain is a definable retract of $\mathcal{U}$. Since PCF extended with parallel-or and ∃ is universal [13], all computable $x \in \mathcal{U}$ and all computable $f : \mathcal{U} \to \mathcal{U}$ are definable, and the universality result follows.

In order to obtain our definability results, we consider a domain-equation-like structure on the real numbers data type.

The Real PCF notion of computability induces classical notions of computability on real numbers and real valued functions of real variables [3, 11, 12, 16, 19, 20], but this material is not included in this extended abstract due lack of space. Also, we only considered the unit interval type of Real PCF, although we indicate how the type for the whole real line can be handled.

1 The real numbers domains

Our main reference to domain theory is [1]; see also [15, 9]. We use several results from [14]. In this paper, a *domain* is a bounded complete, countably based continuous cpo. Domains are implicitly considered as topological spaces under their Scott topology.

Plotkin [14] defines a *coherent domain* to be a domain in which every pairwise consistent subset has a join. Notice that the word *coherence* has been used in several different senses in theoretical computer science and related fields.

We denote by **CDom** the category of coherent domains and continuous maps. This category is cartesian closed, and closed under lifting, amalgamated sum, and smash product. It contains the flat domains and the domains $\mathcal{R}_\perp$ and $\mathcal{I}$, where $\mathcal{R}$ is the continuous dcpo of compact real intervals ordered by superset, and $\mathcal{I}$ is the subdomain of intervals contained in the unit interval $[0, 1]$. Moreover, **CDom** is closed under the formation of retracts and canonical solutions of domain equations involving the above constructions. Thus, **CDom** contains all domains of interest for the purpose of this work.

Let $\mathcal{T} = \{\mathsf{tt}, \mathsf{ff}\}_\perp$ be the domain of truth values. In [14] it is shown that $\mathcal{T}^\omega$ is a *universal coherent domain*, in the sense that a domain is coherent iff it is a retract of $\mathcal{T}^\omega$. Notice that there are two notions of universality in this paper.

The elements of the domains $\mathcal{I}$ and $\mathcal{R}_\perp$ are considered as "partial real numbers", and their maximal elements (singleton intervals) are identified with real numbers. This identification makes sense from a topological view, because the subspace of maximal elements of $\mathcal{R}_\perp$ is homeomorphic to the Euclidean real line. We thus sometimes notationally identify real numbers and singleton intervals.

The reason for introducing partial numbers is similar to the reason for introducing partial functions $\mathbb{N}^k \to \mathbb{N}$ in recursion theory. For instance, the set of computable real numbers is countable but not r.e. [20], whereas the set of computable partial real numbers is r.e., because the set of computable elements of any domain is r.e. [6, 15]. In particular, no programming language with a real numbers data type can define all computable real numbers without having some divergent programs of real number type. As opposed to natural numbers, in which divergence corresponds to $\bot$, divergence is a matter of degree for real numbers; $\bot$ is in the worst possible degree, maximal partial numbers are in the best possible degree (no divergence at all), and the remaining partial real numbers are in between.

Let $f : \mathbb{R} \to \mathbb{R}$ be continuous, and define $\mathbf{I}f : \mathcal{R} \to \mathcal{R}$ by $\mathbf{I}f(x) = f(x)$, for all $x \in \mathcal{R}$. This function is well-defined, because continuous functions preserve compactness and connectedness, so that $f(x)$ is a compact interval if x is a compact interval. Moreover, it is continuous w.r.t. the Scott topology [4]. Similarly, for $f : [0,1] \to [0,1]$ continuous, the above equation also defines a continuous function $\mathbf{I}f : \mathcal{I} \to \mathcal{I}$. The function $\mathbf{I}f$ is an *extension* of f, in the sense that $\mathbf{I}f(\{x\}) = \{f(x)\}$. A continuous function has uncountably many continuous extensions. The extension $\mathbf{I}f$ is characterized as the greatest one. If $f : \mathbb{R} \to \mathbb{R}$ is *non-decreasing* then the greatest extension is given pointwise, in the sense that $\mathbf{I}f(x) = [f(\underline{x}), f(\overline{x})]$, where $\underline{x} = \inf x$ and $\overline{x} = \sup x$ are the left and right end-points of the interval x. When there is no danger of ambiguity, we write f instead of $\mathbf{I}f$ or $\mathbf{I}_\bot f$.

For $x, y \in \mathcal{R}_\bot$, we define $(x < y) \in \mathcal{T}$ by

$$(x < y) = \begin{cases} \mathrm{tt} & \text{if } \overline{x} < \underline{y}, \\ \mathrm{ff} & \text{if } \underline{x} > \overline{y}, \\ \bot & \text{otherwise.} \end{cases}$$

This definition reflects the fact that equality of real numbers is not decidable [20]. The map $(x, y) \mapsto (x < y)$ can be regarded as the best continuous approximation of the characteristic function of the inequality predicate $<$ on real numbers.

Recall that the *parallel* conditional $\mathrm{pif} : \mathcal{T} \times D \times D \to D$ is defined by

$$\mathrm{pif}\ t \text{ then } y \text{ else } z \quad = \quad \begin{cases} y & \text{if } t = \mathrm{tt}, \\ z & \text{if } t = \mathrm{ff}, \\ y \sqcap z & \text{if } t = \bot. \end{cases}$$

Proposition 1.1 *Let R be any domain with* $\mathrm{Max}(R)$ *homeomorphic to the real line or the unit interval, let D be a domain, let $p : R \to \mathcal{T}$ be a continuous predicate, let $g, h : R \to D$ be continuous functions, and define a function f :*

$R \to D$ *by* $f(x) = \text{if } p(x) \text{ then } g(x) \text{ else } h(x)$. *If there are maximal elements* x *and* y *such that* $p(x) = \mathrm{tt}$ *and* $p(y) = \mathrm{ff}$, *then* $f(z) = \bot$ *for some maximal element* z.

Proof The non-empty disjoint sets $U = p^{-1}(\mathrm{tt}) \cap \mathrm{Max}(R)$ and $V = p^{-1}(\mathrm{ff}) \cap \mathrm{Max}(R)$ are open in $\mathrm{Max}(R)$, because p is continuous, and $\{\mathrm{tt}\}$ and $\{\mathrm{ff}\}$ are open in $\mathcal{T}$. Hence $U \cup V \neq \mathrm{Max}(R)$, because $\mathrm{Max}(R)$ is connected. Therefore there is some maximal element z such that $p(z) = \bot$. □

Thus, the sequential conditional is not appropriate for definition by cases of total functions on the real numbers domains, because it produces non-total functions for non-trivial continuous predicates.

In most definitions by cases of the form $f(x) = \text{pif } p(x) \text{ then } g(x) \text{ else } h(x)$ which occur in practice, one has that $g(x) = h(x)$ for all maximal x with $p(x) = \bot$. In such a situation, if x is maximal and $p(x) = \bot$, then $f(x) = g(x) \sqcap h(x) = g(x) = h(x)$. An example is given by the following definition of the absolute value function: $|x| = \text{pif } x < 0 \text{ then } -x \text{ else } x$. For the case $x = 0$ one has $|0| = \text{pif } \bot \text{ then } -0 \text{ else } 0 = 0 \sqcap 0 = 0$. Hence, the parallel conditional is also useful to overcome the fact that equality of real numbers is not decidable.

A domain-equation-like structure for the real numbers domains Define continuous non-decreasing functions $\mathrm{cons}_L, \mathrm{cons}_R, \mathrm{tail}_L, \mathrm{tail}_R : [0,1] \to [0,1]$ by

$$\begin{aligned} \mathrm{cons}_L(x) &= x/2, & \mathrm{tail}_L(x) &= \min(2x, 1), \\ \mathrm{cons}_R(x) &= (x+1)/2, & \mathrm{tail}_R(x) &= \max(0, 2x-1), \end{aligned}$$

and define $\mathrm{head} : \mathcal{I} \to \mathcal{T}$ by $\mathrm{head}(x) = (x < 1/2)$, where the inequality map was defined in Section 1. For motivation and a detailed discussion about these functions see [8, 7, 5], where effective computation rules for them are given.

The main property of the functions $\mathrm{cons}_L, \mathrm{cons}_R, \mathrm{tail}_L, \mathrm{tail}_R : \mathcal{I} \to \mathcal{I}$ and $\mathrm{head} : \mathcal{I} \to \mathcal{T}$ is given by the following lemma:

Lemma 1.2 *The identity of* $\mathcal{I}$ *is the unique continuous function* $f : \mathcal{I} \to \mathcal{I}$ *such that* $f(x) = \text{pif } \mathrm{head}(x) \text{ then } \mathrm{cons}_L(f(\mathrm{tail}_L(x))) \text{ else } \mathrm{cons}_R(f(\mathrm{tail}_R(x)))$.

Proof (Outline) That $f = \mathrm{id}$ satisfies the above equation is routinely checked by cases on the value of $\mathrm{head}(x)$ (see [8]). Let $A = \{m/2^n \in [0,1] | m, n \in \mathbb{Z}\}$ be the set of dyadic numbers in the unit interval. In order to prove that a property holds for every $x \in A$, it suffices to prove that it holds for 0 and 1, and that it holds for $x/2$ and $(x+1)/2$ whenever it holds for x. We call this principle *dyadic induction* [7]. Let B be the basis of $\mathcal{I}$ consisting of intervals with dyadic end-points. By dyadic induction on the end-points of x, we see that for any f satisfying the above equation, $f(x) = x$ for every $x \in B$. It follows that if f is continuous then f is the identity. □

The above lemma gives rise to domain-equation-like structure on $\mathcal{I}$. Recall that a *section-retraction* pair between objects X and Y of a category $\mathbf{X}$ consists of morphisms $X \underset{s}{\overset{r}{\leftrightarrows}} Y$ with $r \circ s = id_X$. In this case $s \circ r$ is an idempotent on Y and X is called a *retract* of Y.

Definition 1.1 Let $\mathbf{X}$ be a category and $\mathbf{F} : \mathbf{X} \to \mathbf{X}$ be a functor. A section-retraction pair $X \underset{s}{\overset{r}{\leftrightarrows}} \mathbf{F}X$ is $\mathbf{F}$-*stable* if $f = r \circ \mathbf{F}f \circ s$ implies $f = \mathrm{id}_X$. □

Lemma 1.3 *Define* $\mathbf{F} : \mathbf{CDom} \to \mathbf{CDom}$ *by* $\mathbf{F}D = \mathcal{T} \times D \times D$, *and define* $\mathrm{cons} = \mathrm{pif} \circ \mathbf{F}(\mathrm{id}, \mathrm{cons}_L, \mathrm{cons}_R)$ *and* $\mathrm{destr} = [\mathrm{head}, \mathrm{tail}_L, \mathrm{tail}_R]$. *Then* $\mathcal{I} \underset{\mathrm{destr}}{\overset{\mathrm{cons}}{\leftrightarrows}} \mathbf{F}\mathcal{I}$ *is an* $\mathbf{F}$*-stable section-retraction pair.*

Proof $f = \mathrm{cons} \circ \mathbf{F}f \circ \mathrm{destr}$ holds iff the equation in Lemma 1.2 holds. □

The domain $\mathcal{R}_\perp$ is treated similarly, by showing that its identity is the unique continuous function satisfying an appropriate equation.

Let $\mathbf{X}$ be a category and $\mathbf{F} : \mathbf{X} \to \mathbf{X}$ be a functor. Recall that an $\mathbf{F}$-*algebra* is a morphism $\alpha : \mathbf{F}X \to X$, and that an $\mathbf{F}$-*algebra homomorphism* from an algebra $\alpha : \mathbf{F}X \to X$ to an algebra $\beta : \mathbf{F}Y \to Y$ is a morphism $h : X \to Y$ such that $h \circ \alpha = \beta \circ \mathbf{F}h$. Dually, an $\mathbf{F}$-*coalgebra* is a morphism $\alpha : X \to \mathbf{F}X$, and an $\mathbf{F}$-*coalgebra homomorphism* from a coalgebra $\alpha : X \to \mathbf{F}X$ to a coalgebra $\beta : X \to \mathbf{F}X$ is a morphism $h : X \to Y$ such that $\mathbf{F}h \circ \alpha = \beta \circ h$. Algebras (resp. coalgebras) compose in the obvious way and form a category. Let $\mathbf{F} : \mathbf{CDom} \to \mathbf{CDom}$ be a functor. Recall that a *canonical solution* for a domain equation $D \cong \mathbf{F}D$ is given by an initial algebra $i : \mathbf{F}C \to C$, which is necessarily an isomorphism. A functor $\mathbf{F} : \mathbf{CDom} \to \mathbf{CDom}$ is *locally continuous* if for all D and E, the map $f \mapsto \mathbf{F}f : [D \to E] \to [\mathbf{F}D \to \mathbf{F}E]$ is continuous. For every locally continuous functor $\mathbf{F} : \mathbf{CDom} \to \mathbf{CDom}$, the domain equation $D \cong \mathbf{F}D$ has a canonical solution $i : \mathbf{F}C \to C$, and $i^{-1} : C \to \mathbf{F}C$ is a final coalgebra.

Proposition 1.4 *Let* $\mathbf{F} : \mathbf{CDom} \to \mathbf{CDom}$ *be a locally continuous functor,* $\mathbf{F}C \xrightarrow{i} C$ *be an initial algebra, and let* $D \underset{\beta}{\overset{\alpha}{\leftrightarrows}} \mathbf{F}D$ *be an* $\mathbf{F}$*-stable section-retraction pair. If* r *is the unique algebra homomorphism from* i *to* α*, and* s *is the unique coalgebra homomorphism from* β *to* i^{-1}*, then* $D \underset{s}{\overset{r}{\leftrightarrows}} C$ *is a section-retraction pair.*

Proof By hypothesis, $r \circ i = \alpha \circ \mathbf{F}r$ and $i^{-1} \circ s = \mathbf{F}s \circ \beta$. Hence $r \circ s = r \circ i \circ i^{-1} \circ s = \alpha \circ \mathbf{F}r \circ \mathbf{F}s \circ \beta = \alpha \circ \mathbf{F}(r \circ s) \circ \beta$. By stability, $r \circ s = \mathrm{id}_D$. □

Proposition 1.5 *Let* $\mathbf{F} : \mathbf{CDom} \to \mathbf{CDom}$ *be a locally continuous functor, and* $D \underset{\psi}{\overset{\phi}{\leftrightarrows}} \mathbf{F}D$ *be an isomorphism. Then* ϕ *is an initial algebra iff the isomorphism pair is* $\mathbf{F}$*-stable.*

2 Effectively given coherent domains

Algebraic domains have a relatively simple theory of effectivity [6, 15]. Unfortunately, this is not the case for continuous domains. Smyth [17] defines three notions of effectivity for continuous domains, namely effectively given *domain*, effectively given *M-domain*, and effectively given *A-domain*. The notions are not strictly equivalent, but they are essentially equivalent, in the sense that they can be effectively translated to each other. The notion of effectively given A-domain gives rise to a simple notion of effectively given coherent domain, as shown below. We slightly modify Smyth's definition in order to make effective presentations explicit, as Kanda and Park [10] show that it is possible to effectively present some domains in essentially different ways:

Definition 2.1 An *effective presentation of an algebraic domain* D consists of an enumeration of the finite elements of D such that (1) it is decidable whether $a \sqsubseteq b$ for finite $a, b \in D$; (2) it is decidable whether A is consistent, for an arbitrary finite set A of finite elements of D; (3) for A ranging over consistent finite sets of finite elements, the map $A \mapsto \bigsqcup A$ is recursive. An *effectively given algebraic domain* is an algebraic domain D together with an effective presentation. Let D and E be effectively given algebraic domains. An element $d \in D$ is *computable* if it is it the join of an r.e. directed set of finite elements. A continuous function $f : D \to E$ is *computable* if the relation $b \sqsubseteq f(a)$ is r.e. for a and b finite. An *effectively given A-domain* is a list (D, E, s, r) where D is a domain, E is an effectively given algebraic domain, $(s : D \to E, r : E \to D)$ is a section-retraction pair, and the idempotent $s \circ r : E \to E$ is computable. □

Notice that this definition of effectively given algebraic domain coincides with the one given in [6] and discussed in detail in [15].

An element $p \in \mathcal{T}^\omega$ is finite iff $p^{-1}(\mathrm{tt})$ and $p^{-1}(\mathrm{ff})$ are finite subsets of ω. Plotkin [14] considers the following effective presentation of $\mathcal{T}^\omega$: b_n is the unique finite $p \in \mathcal{T}^\omega$ such that $n = \sum_{i \in p^{-1}(\mathrm{tt})} 2 \cdot 3^i + \sum_{i \in p^{-1}(\mathrm{ff})} 3^i$. Then $p \in \mathcal{T}^\omega$ is computable iff $p^{-1}(\mathrm{tt})$ and $p^{-1}(\mathrm{ff})$ are r.e. subsets of ω. We call this effective presentation the *standard effective presentation of* $\mathcal{T}^\omega$, and from now on we implicitly assume the standard effective presentation of $\mathcal{T}^\omega$, unless otherwise stated. This induces effective presentations on the product $\mathcal{T}^\omega \times \mathcal{T}^\omega$ and the function space $[\mathcal{T}^\omega \to \mathcal{T}^\omega]$ (see [6, 17, 14, 15]).

It is natural to define effectivity for coherent domains as follows:

Definition 2.2 An *effective presentation of a coherent domain* D is a section-retraction pair $(s : D \to \mathcal{T}^\omega, r : \mathcal{T}^\omega \to D)$ such that $s \circ r : \mathcal{T}^\omega \to \mathcal{T}^\omega$ is computable. An *effectively given coherent domain* is a list (D, s, r) where D is a coherent domain and (s, r) is an effective presentation of D. Let (D, s_D, r_D) and (E, s_E, r_E) be effectively given coherent domains. An element $x \in D$ is *computable* if $s_D(x) \in \mathcal{T}^\omega$ is computable. A continuous function $f : D \to E$ is *computable* if $(r_D \to s_E)(f) : \mathcal{T}^\omega \to \mathcal{T}^\omega$ is computable. □

Since coherent domains form a cartesian closed category and $\mathcal{T}^\omega$ is a universal domain, we know that $\mathcal{T}^\omega \times \mathcal{T}^\omega$ and $[\mathcal{T}^\omega \to \mathcal{T}^\omega]$ are retracts of $\mathcal{T}^\omega$. In fact, $\mathcal{T}^\omega \times \mathcal{T}^\omega$ is isomorphic to $\mathcal{T}^\omega$. An isomorphism is given by $\mathrm{Pair} : \mathcal{T}^\omega \to \mathcal{T}^\omega \times \mathcal{T}^\omega$ defined by $\mathrm{Pair}(p) = \langle n \mapsto p(2n), n \mapsto p(2n+1)\rangle$. Then $(\mathcal{T}^\omega, \mathrm{Pair}^{-1}, \mathrm{Pair})$ is an effectively given coherent domain. We assume the section-retraction pair $(\mathrm{Pred} : [\mathcal{T}^\omega \to \mathcal{T}^\omega] \to \mathcal{T}^\omega, \mathrm{Fun} : \mathcal{T}^\omega \to [\mathcal{T}^\omega \to \mathcal{T}^\omega])$ constructed in [14]. Since Pred and Fun are computable, so is $\mathrm{Pred} \circ \mathrm{Fun} : \mathcal{T}^\omega \to \mathcal{T}^\omega$. Therefore $([\mathcal{T}^\omega \to \mathcal{T}^\omega], \mathrm{Pred}, \mathrm{Fun})$ is an effectively given coherent domain.

Theorem 2.1 *Effectively given coherent domains and computable functions form a cartesian closed category.*

We denote by **ECDom** the category of effectively given coherent domains and computable functions. From now on, given effective presentations of D and E, we implicitly assume the effective presentations of $D \times E$ and $[D \to E]$ constructed in the above theorem, unless otherwise stated. Let D be any effectively given coherent domain. Then fixed-point combinator $\mathrm{fix}_D : [D \to D] \to D$, and the conditionals $\mathrm{if}, \mathrm{pif} : \mathcal{T} \times D \times D \to D$ are computable. In particular, the least fixed-point of a computable function is computable.

Equivalence of effectively given coherent domains A coherent effective presentation of $\mathcal{T}^\omega$ is given by $(\mathrm{id}_{\mathcal{T}^\omega}, \mathrm{id}_{\mathcal{T}^\omega})$. Let $f : \omega \to \omega$ be a non-recursive permutation of ω, and define $\phi : \mathcal{T}^\omega \to \mathcal{T}^\omega$ by $\phi(p) = p \circ f$. Since $\phi \circ \phi^{-1} = \mathrm{id}_{\mathcal{T}^\omega}$, (ϕ, ϕ^{-1}) is an effective presentation of $\mathcal{T}^\omega$. But this effective presentation is intuitively not "really" effective, by construction. The same phenomenon takes place for the usual notion of effectively given algebraic domain. If we define $b'_n = b_{f(n)}$, where b is the standard algebraic effective presentation of $\mathcal{T}^\omega$, it is easy to check that the axioms for effectively given algebraic domains given in definition 2.1 are satisfied for b'.

Moreover, $(\mathcal{T}^\omega, \mathrm{id}, \mathrm{id})$ and $(\mathcal{T}^\omega, \phi, \phi^{-1})$ are isomorphic objects of **ECDom**, and this is also not intuitive. In fact, ϕ, considered as a morphism $(\mathcal{T}^\omega, \mathrm{id}, \mathrm{id}) \to (\mathcal{T}^\omega, \phi, \phi^{-1})$ and as a morphism $(\mathcal{T}^\omega, \phi, \phi^{-1}) \to (\mathcal{T}^\omega, \mathrm{id}, \mathrm{id})$ gives the desired isomorphism. Again, in the category of effectively given algebraic domains and computable maps, $(\mathcal{T}^\omega, b)$ and $(\mathcal{T}^\omega, b')$ are isomorphic objects, with isomorphism also given by ϕ.

On the other hand, the identity of $\mathcal{T}^\omega$ is not computable as a morphism $(\mathcal{T}^\omega, \mathrm{id}, \mathrm{id}) \to (\mathcal{T}^\omega, \phi, \phi^{-1})$ or as a morphism $(\mathcal{T}^\omega, \phi, \phi^{-1}) \to (\mathcal{T}^\omega, \mathrm{id}, \mathrm{id})$. This *is* reasonable, and shows us that we cannot access within $\mathcal{T}^\omega$ "correctly presented" the computable elements of $\mathcal{T}^\omega$ "incorrectly presented", which are not computable in $\mathcal{T}^\omega$ "correctly presented".

We can summarize the above remarks by saying that effective domain theory does not give an absolute notion of effectivity. In this section we show that additional structure on effectively given coherent domains can be used to achieve absoluteness.

We recall the following definitions from [2], and we make explicit a notion which we call representability:

Definition 2.3 A *concrete category* over a category $\mathbf{X}$ is a category $\mathbf{A}$ together with a faithful functor $U : \mathbf{A} \to \mathbf{X}$, called the *underlying functor*. Let $(\mathbf{A}, U)$ be a concrete category over $\mathbf{X}$. If A and B are $\mathbf{A}$-objects, then an $\mathbf{X}$-morphism $f : UA \to UB$ is *(A,B)-representable* if there is a (necessarily unique) $\mathbf{A}$-morphism $\bar{f} : A \to B$ such that $U(\bar{f}) = f$, called the *(A,B)-representation* of f. The *fibre* of an $\mathbf{X}$-object X is the preordered class consisting of all $\mathbf{A}$-objects A with $U(A) = X$, ordered by: $A \leq B$ iff id_X is (A,B)-representable. Two $\mathbf{A}$-objects A and B are *equivalent*, written $A \equiv B$, if $A \leq B$ and $B \leq A$. □

Clearly, **ECDom** is concrete over **CDom**, with the underlying functor given by the forgetful functor that forgets effective presentations. Using the language of the above definition, we have that $(\mathcal{T}^\omega, \mathrm{id}, \mathrm{id})$ and $(\mathcal{T}^\omega, \phi, \phi^{-1})$ are isomorphic objects of the category **ECDom**, but inequivalent objects of the concrete category $(\mathbf{ECDom}, U)$.

Definition 2.4 We say that two effective presentations (s_1, r_1) and (s_2, r_2) of a coherent domain D are *equivalent* if (D, s_1, r_1) and (D, s_2, r_2) are equivalent objects of the concrete category $(\mathbf{ECDom}, U)$. □

It is immediate that (s_1, r_1) and (s_2, r_2) are equivalent iff $s_1 \circ r_2$ and $s_2 \circ r_1$ are computable. Notice that these two functions are inverses of each other, and hence they are automorphisms of $\mathcal{T}^\omega$.

Clearly, a morphism $f : UD \to UE$ in **CDom** is (D,E)-representable iff it is computable.

Proposition 2.2 *Let $(\mathbf{A}, U)$ be a concrete category over $\mathbf{X}$, let Y be an $\mathbf{X}$-object, and let B and B' be $\mathbf{A}$-objects in the fibre of Y. Then the following are equivalent:* (1) $B \leq B'$. (2) *For every $\mathbf{A}$-object A, if a morphism $f : UA \to Y$ is (A,B)-representable then it is (A,B')-representable.* (3) *For every $\mathbf{A}$-object C, if a morphism $f : Y \to UC$ is (B',C)-representable then it is (B,C)-*

representable.

Proof (1) $\Rightarrow$ (2): Assume that $f : UA \to Y$ is (A,B)-representable, and let $\bar{f} : A \to B$ be the (A,B)-representation of f, and $\bar{\mathrm{id}}_Y : B \to B'$ be the (B,B')-representation of id_Y. Then $f' = \bar{\mathrm{id}}_Y \circ \bar{f}$ is a (B,B')-representation of f, because $U(f') = U(\bar{\mathrm{id}}_Y \circ \bar{f}) = U(\bar{\mathrm{id}}_Y) \circ U(\bar{f}) = \mathrm{id}_Y \circ f = f$. (1) $\Rightarrow$ (3): Similar. (2) $\Rightarrow$ (1): Take $A = B$ and $f = \mathrm{id}_Y$. (3) $\Rightarrow$ (1): Similar. □

This can be expressed by saying that two effective presentations of a coherent domain are equivalent iff they induce the same notion of computability on the domain. The following definition is also taken from [2]:

Definition 2.5 A concrete category $(\mathbf{A}, U)$ over $\mathbf{X}$ is called *concretely cartesian closed* provided that $\mathbf{A}$ and $\mathbf{X}$ are cartesian closed and that U preserves finite products, exponentials, and evaluation. □

Clearly, $(\mathbf{ECDom}, U)$ is concretely cartesian closed.

Proposition 2.3 *Let $(\mathbf{A}, U)$ be a concretely cartesian closed category over $\mathbf{X}$. If 1 and $1'$ are terminal objects of $\mathbf{A}$ in the same fibre then $1 \leq 1'$, and if $A \leq A'$ and $B \leq B'$ are $\mathbf{A}$-objects then $A \times B \leq A' \times B'$ and $[A' \to B] \leq [A \to B']$.*

We can thus say that equivalence is a "cartesian closed congruence".

Proposition 2.4 *Let $(\mathbf{A}, U)$ be a concretely cartesian closed category over $\mathbf{X}$, and let A and B and be equivalent $\mathbf{A}$-objects. Then any two products of A and B are equivalent, and any two exponentials of B to the power A are equivalent.*

Corollary 2.5 *Let D and E be effectively given coherent domains. Then any two effective presentations of $D \times E$ which make the projections $D \times E \to D$ and $D \times E \to E$ computable are equivalent, and any two effective presentations of $[D \to E]$ which make the evaluation map $[D \to E] \times D \to E$ computable are equivalent.*

Thus, as soon as effective presentations of D and E are specified, the effective presentations of $D \times E$ and $[D \to E]$ are implicitly specified up to equivalence. Clearly, any two effective presentations of a finite coherent domain are equivalent.

Proposition 2.6 *Define continuous maps* $\mathrm{cons} : \mathcal{T} \times \mathcal{T}^\omega \to \mathcal{T}^\omega$, $\mathrm{head} : \mathcal{T}^\omega \to \mathcal{T}$, $\mathrm{tail} : \mathcal{T}^\omega \to \mathcal{T}^\omega$, *by* $\mathrm{cons}(t,p)(0) = t$, $\mathrm{cons}(t,p)(n+1) = p(n)$, $\mathrm{head}(p) = p(0)$, *and* $\mathrm{tail}(p)(n) = p(n+1)$. *Then any two effective presentations of $\mathcal{T}^\omega$ which make* cons, head, *and* tail *computable are equivalent.*

Proof Similar to the proof of Proposition 3.1 below. □

This can be expressed by saying that there is a unique notion of computability for $\mathcal{T}^\omega$ such that cons, head, and tail are computable. A similar holds for $\mathcal{N}$ w.r.t the test-for-zero and successor functions.

3 Computability and definability

Proposition 3.1 *Any two effective presentations of $\mathcal{I}$ which make* cons_L, cons_R, head, tail_L, *and* tail_R *computable are equivalent.*

Proof By Lemma 1.2, the identity of $\mathcal{I}$ is the least fixed point of the map $F : [\mathcal{I} \to \mathcal{I}] \to [\mathcal{I} \to \mathcal{I}]$ defined by $F(f)(x) = \mathrm{pif\ head}(x)\ \mathrm{then\ cons}_L(f(\mathrm{tail}_L(x)))$ $\mathrm{else\ cons}_R(f(\mathrm{tail}_R(x)))$. If D and E are effectively given coherent domains in the fibre of $\mathcal{I}$ such that cons_L, cons_R, head, tail_L, and tail_R are computable w.r.t. each of the corresponding effective presentations, then F is both $([D \to E], [D \to E])$-representable and $([E \to D], [E \to D])$-representable. Since the fixed point combinator is computable, $\mathrm{id}_{\mathcal{I}} = \mathrm{fix}(F)$ is both (D, E) and (E, D)-representable. Therefore D and E are equivalent. □

A similar fact holds for $\mathcal{R}_\perp$.

Lemma 3.2 *Define* $\mathbf{F} : \mathbf{CDom} \to \mathbf{CDom}$ *by* $\mathbf{F}D = \mathcal{T} \times D \times D$. *Then there is a computable initial algebra* $\phi : \mathbf{F}\mathcal{T}^\omega \to \mathcal{T}^\omega$.

Proof $\mathcal{T}^\omega$ is the canonical solution of the domain equation $D \cong \mathcal{T} \times D$. An initial algebra is given by $\mathrm{cons} : \mathcal{T} \times \mathcal{T}^\omega \to \mathcal{T}^\omega$. Since $\mathrm{Pair} : \mathcal{T}^\omega \to \mathcal{T}^\omega \times \mathcal{T}^\omega$ is an isomorphism, so is $\phi(t, p, q) = \mathrm{cons}(t, \mathrm{Pair}^{-1}(p, q))$. This isomorphism is clearly computable. A routine verification shows that (ϕ^{-1}, ϕ) is an $\mathbf{F}$-stable isomorphism pair. By Proposition 1.5, ϕ is an initial algebra. □

Proposition 3.3 *There is an effective presentation of $\mathcal{I}$ which makes* cons_L, cons_R, head, tail_L, *and* tail_R *computable.*

Proof (Sketch) Let $\mathbf{F} : \mathbf{CDom} \to \mathbf{CDom}$ and $\mathcal{I} \underset{\mathrm{destr}}{\overset{\mathrm{cons}}{\leftrightarrows}} \mathbf{F}\mathcal{I}$ be defined as in Lemma 1.3, $\phi : \mathbf{F}\mathcal{T}^\omega \to \mathcal{T}^\omega$ be a computable initial algebra, r be the unique algebra homomorphism from ϕ to cons, s be the unique coalgebra homomorphism from destr to ϕ^{-1}. Then (s, r) is an effective presentation of $\mathcal{I}$. □

Propositions 3.1 and 3.3 can be interpreted by saying that there is a unique notion of computability for $\mathcal{I}$ such that cons_L, cons_R, head, tail_L, and tail_R are computable. A similar fact holds for $\mathcal{R}_\perp$.

Real PCF is an extension of PCF with ground types interpreted as $\mathcal{R}_\perp$ and $\mathcal{I}$, and new constants. In this extended abstract we only consider the unit interval type of Real PCF. The type for the whole real line is treated similarly. The constants for the unit interval type include constants for the primitive operations defined in Section 3 and used to recursively define the identities of $\mathcal{I}$ and $\mathcal{R}_\perp$. For more details see [8]. By Propositions 3.1 and 3.3, and Theorem 2.1, we can say that there is a unique notion of computability for Real PCF such that every Real PCF definable element is computable.

Proposition 3.4 *$\exists$ is computable but not Real PCF definable.*
Proof The inductive proof given in [13] for the fact that $\exists$ is not definable in PCF extended with parallel-or goes through for Real PCF, by adding obvious inductive steps for the Real PCF constants. □

Theorem 3.5 *Real PCF extended with $\exists$ is universal.*
Proof $\mathcal{T}^\omega$ can be identified with the domain of strict functions $\mathcal{N} \to_\perp \mathcal{T}$. Hence $\mathcal{U} = [\mathcal{N} \to \mathcal{T}]$ is a universal domain too. Since PCF extended with $\exists$ is universal and $\mathcal{U}$ is a PCF domain, it suffices to show that every ground domain D is a definable retract of $\mathcal{U}$, in the sense that there is a section-retraction pair $(r : D \to \mathcal{U}, s : \mathcal{U} \to D)$ with s and r definable. This is immediate for $\mathcal{T}$ and $\mathcal{N}$. For $\mathcal{I}$, let s and r be defined as in Proposition 3.3, with $\phi : \mathbf{F}\mathcal{T}^\omega \to \mathcal{T}^\omega$ as defined in Lemma 3.2. Call ψ the inverse of ϕ, and define $[\psi_H, \psi_L, \psi_R] = \psi$. Then

$$\begin{aligned} r(p) &= \mathrm{cons} \circ \mathbf{F}r \circ \phi^{-1}(p) = \mathrm{cons} \circ (\mathrm{id} \times r \times r) \circ (\psi_H(p), \psi_L(p), \psi_R(p)) \\ &= \mathrm{pif}\ \psi_H(p)\ \mathrm{then}\ \mathrm{cons}_L(r(\psi_L(p))\ \mathrm{else}\ \mathrm{cons}_R(r(\psi_R(p)), \\ s(x) &= \phi \circ \mathbf{F}s \circ \mathrm{destr}(x) = \phi \circ (\mathrm{id} \times s \times s) \circ (\mathrm{head}(x), \mathrm{tail}_L(x), \mathrm{tail}_R(x)) \\ &= \phi(\mathrm{head}(x), s(\mathrm{tail}_L(x)), s(\mathrm{tail}_R(x))). \end{aligned}$$

Since s and r are the unique continuous maps which satisfy the above equations, we can use the fixed-point combinator to recursively define them. It is easy to see that

$$\begin{aligned} \phi(t,p,q)(n) &= \mathrm{if}\ n = 0\ \mathrm{then}\ t\ \mathrm{else\ if\ odd}(n)\ \mathrm{then}\ p((n-1)/2)\ \mathrm{else}\ q((n-2)/2), \\ \psi_H(p) &= p(0), \qquad \psi_L(p)(n) = p(2n+1), \qquad \psi_R(p)(n) = p(2n+2). \end{aligned}$$

In order to get into the Real PCF universe of discourse, define $\Phi : \mathcal{T} \to \mathcal{U} \to \mathcal{U} \to \mathcal{U}$, $\Psi_H : \mathcal{U} \to \mathcal{T}$ and $\Psi_L, \Psi_R : \mathcal{U} \to \mathcal{U}$ by (almost the same equations)

$$\begin{aligned} \Phi(t)(p)(q)(n) &= \mathrm{if}\ n = 0\ \mathrm{then}\ t\ \mathrm{else\ if\ odd}(n)\ \mathrm{then}\ p((n-1)/2)\ \mathrm{else}\ q((n-2)/2) \\ \Psi_H(p) &= p(0), \qquad \Psi_L(p)(n) = p(2n+1), \qquad \Psi_R(p)(n) = p(2n+2). \end{aligned}$$

Then these functions are clearly PCF definable. Now recursively define $\alpha : \mathcal{U} \to \mathcal{I}$ and $\beta : \mathcal{I} \to \mathcal{U}$ by

$$\begin{aligned} \alpha(p) &= \mathrm{pif}\ \Psi_H(p)\ \mathrm{then}\ \mathrm{cons}_L(\alpha(\Psi_L(p))\ \mathrm{else}\ \mathrm{cons}_R(\alpha(\Psi_R(p)), \\ \beta(x) &= \Phi(\mathrm{head}(x), \beta(\mathrm{tail}_L(x)), \beta(\mathrm{tail}_R(x)). \end{aligned}$$

Then α and β are Real PCF definable too, and they clearly (co)restrict to r and s. Therefore $\alpha \circ \beta = \mathrm{id}_\mathcal{I}$. □

Acknowledgements

I am grateful to Thomas Streicher for letting me know his proof technique, which allowed me to fully solve the universality problem for Real PCF. I have been supervised by Mike Smyth. I have had endless discussions with him and Abbas Edalat. This work has been supported by an ARC project "A Computational Approach to Measure and Integration Theory" and the Brazilian agency CNPq.

1. S. Abramsky and A. Jung. Domain theory. In S. Abramsky, D.M. Gabbay, and T.S.E Maibaum, editors, *Handbook of Logic in Computer Science*, volume 3, pages 1–168. Clarendon Press, Oxford, 1994.
2. J Adamek, H Herrlich, and G.E. Strecker. *Abstract and Concrete Categories*. John Wiley & Sons, Inc., 1990.
3. E. Bishop and D. Bridges. *Constructive Analysis*. Springer-Verlag, Berlin, 1985.
4. A. Edalat. Dynamical systems, measures and fractals via domain theory. *Information and Computation*, 120(1):32–48, July 1995.
5. A. Edalat and M.H. Escardó. Integration in Real PCF. In *Proceedings of the Eleventh Annual IEEE Symposium on Logic In Computer Science*, New Brunswick, New Jersey, USA, July 1996.
6. H. Egli and Constable R.L. Computability concepts for programming languages. *Theoretical Computer Science*, 2:133–145, 1976.
7. M.H. Escardó. Induction and recursion on the real line. In C. Hankin, I. Mackie, and R. Nagarajan, editors, *Theory and Formal Methods 1994: Proceedings of the Second Imperial College Department of Computing Workshop on Theory and Formal Methods*, pages 259–282, Møller Centre, Cambridge, UK, 11–14 September 1994. IC Press. 1995.
8. M.H. Escardó. PCF extended with real numbers. *Theoretical Computer Science*, 162, To appear in 1996.
9. G. Gierz, K.H. Hofmann, K. Keimel, J.D. Lawson, M. Mislove, and D.S. Scott. *A Compendium of Continuous Lattices*. Springer-Verlag, New York, 1980.
10. A. Kanda and D. Park. When are two effectively given domains identical? In K. Weihrauch, editor, *Theoretical Computer Science* 4th *GI Conference*, LNCS, 1979.
11. Ker-I Ko. *Complexitity Theory of Real Functions*. Birkhauser, Boston, 1991.
12. P. Martin-Lof. *Notes on Constructive Mathematics*. Almqvist & Wiksell, Stockholm, 1970.
13. G. Plotkin. LCF considered as a programming language. *Theoretical Computer Science*, 5(1):223–255, 1977.
14. G. Plotkin. T^{ω} as a universal domain. *Journal of Computer and System Sciences*, 17:209–236, 1978.
15. G. Plotkin. Domains. Post-graduate Lectures in advanced domain theory, University of Edinburgh, Department of Computer Science, 1980.
16. M.B. Pour-el and I. Richards. Computability and non-computability in classical analysis. *Trans. Am. Math. Soc.*, pages 539–560, 1983.
17. M.B. Smyth. Effectively given domains. *Theoretical Computer Science*, 5(1):256–274, 1977.
18. T. Streicher. A universality theorem for PCF with recursive types, parallel-or and $\exists$. *Mathematical Structures for Computing Science*, 4(1):111 – 115, 1994.
19. K. Weihrauch. *Computability*. Springer-Verlag, Berlin, 1987.
20. K. Weihrauch. A simple introduction to computable analysis. Technical Report 171 – 7/1995, FernUniversitat, 1995.

A SMOOTH APPROXIMATION ON THE EDGE OF CHAOS

P. J. POTTS
Department of Computing, Imperial College, London SW7 2BZ.

It is known that for almost all starting points the non-deterministic dynamical system corresponding to a hyperbolic iterated function system with probabilities generates orbits whose frequency of visits to any given Borel subset of the domain is described by the unique invariant measure of the iterated function system with probabilities. In this paper, we will show that under certain conditions this chaotic probability measure can be approximated by a smooth probability density. We apply this result to forgetful neural networks.

1 Introduction

The study of iterated function systems has been an active area of research since the seminal work of Mandelbrot [11] on fractals and self-similarity in nature.

1.1 Iterated Function System

An *iterated function system* (IFS) $\{X; f_1, f_2, \ldots, f_N\}$ on a topological space X is given by a finite set of continuous maps $f_i : X \to X$ $(i = 1, 2, \ldots, N)$. If X is a complete metric space [15] and the maps f_i are all contracting, then the IFS is said to be *hyperbolic*.

A hyperbolic IFS induces a contracting map [10] on the complete metric space $\mathbf{H}X$ of all non-empty compact subsets of X with a unique fixed point called the *attractor* of the IFS.

For graphical applications, X is usually the plane $\mathbb{R}^2$, f_i are contracting *affine* transformations and the attractor is a *fractal.*

1.2 IFS with Probabilities

A hyperbolic IFS with probabilities $\{X; f_1, f_2, \ldots, f_N; p_1, p_2, \ldots, p_N\}$ is a hyperbolic IFS $\{X; f_1, f_2, \ldots, f_N\}$, with X a compact metric space, such that each f_i $(i = 1, 2, \ldots, N)$ is assigned a probability p_i with $0 < p_i < 1$ and $\sum_{i=1}^{N} p_i = 1$.

A hyperbolic IFS with probabilities induces a contracting map [3] on the set of normalized Borel measures $\mathbf{M}X$ on X with a unique fixed point described as a *multifractal* whose support is the attractor of $\{X; f_1, f_2, \ldots, f_N\}$.

In the extreme case where all the maps f_i $(i = 1, 2, \ldots, N)$ are the same, the unique invariant measure has the Dirac delta function [5] as its density and its support is a single point corresponding to the unique fixed point of the map.

In this paper, we show that for a certain class of hyperbolic IFS with probabilities, close to the extreme case, the unique invariant measure can be approximated by a smooth probability density.

1.3 Non-Deterministic Dynamical System

Given a hyperbolic IFS with probabilities $\{X; f_1, f_2, \ldots, f_N; p_1, p_2, \ldots, p_N\}$ the corresponding ***non-deterministic dynamical system*** is the iterative orbit of a single point in X, in which at each iteration a map f_i is selected with probability p_i.

In 1986, Elton [7] made the important observation that the frequency of visits to any given Borel subset of X is described by the unique invariant measure of $\{X; f_1, f_2, \ldots, f_N; p_1, p_2, \ldots, p_N\}$.

Using this observation, we are able to demonstrate computationally, by considering ordits of length 10^9, that the unique invariant measure gets closer to the formulated smooth probability density.

We then proceed to formulate the average Lyapunov exponent for the non-deterministic dynamical system and apply it to the problem of evaluating the storage capacity of forgetful neural networks using the smooth learning scheme.

2 The Approximate Probability Density

Consider the non-deterministic dynamical system with small ϵ corresponding to the hyperbolic iterated function system with probabilities $\{[x_-, x_+]; \phi_+, \phi_-; \frac{1}{2}, \frac{1}{2}\}$ where $\phi_\pm(x;\epsilon) = \phi(x \pm \epsilon)$, $\phi : \mathbb{R} \to \mathbb{R}$, ϕ is smooth, odd, monotonically increasing, strictly concave for $x > 0$, $\phi'(0) = 1$, $\epsilon > 0$ and $x_\pm$ is the fixed point of $\phi_\pm$. This prescription determines the function ϕ as having the form

$$\phi(x) = x - ax^r + O(x^{r+2}), \tag{1}$$

where $r \geq 3$ is an odd number and $a > 0$.

In general, the *order* notation $f(x) = O(g(x))$ means that for all $\delta > 0$, there exists a $C > 0$ such that $|x| < \delta$ implies $|f(x)| < C\,|g(x)|$.

Strictly speaking, the above IFS needs to be folded once to make it hyperbolic. In other words, we ought to consider

$$\left\{[x_-, x_+]; \phi_+ \circ \phi_+, \phi_+ \circ \phi_-, \phi_- \circ \phi_+, \phi_- \circ \phi_-; \frac{1}{4}, \frac{1}{4}, \frac{1}{4}, \frac{1}{4}\right\}$$

because there exists $c(\epsilon) < 1$ such that $\frac{d}{dx}\phi_\alpha \circ \phi_\beta(x) \leq c$ for all $\alpha, \beta \in \{+, -\}$, $x \in [x_-, x_+]$ and $\epsilon > 0$.

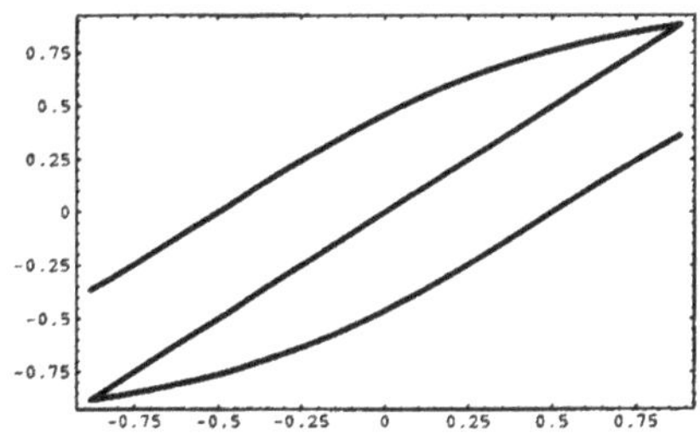

Figure 1: Plot of $y = \phi_+(x)$, $y = \phi_-(x)$ and $y = x$ from $x = x_-$ to $x = x_+$ where $\phi(x) = \tanh(x)$ and $\epsilon = \frac{1}{2}$

The unique invariant measure μ of the above IFS with probabilities is a fixed point of the *Frobenius-Peron equation*,

$$\begin{aligned} F : \mathbf{M}X &\rightarrow \mathbf{M}X \\ F(\nu) &= \frac{1}{2}\nu \circ \phi_+^{-1} + \frac{1}{2}\nu \circ \phi_-^{-1}. \end{aligned} \tag{2}$$

In other words,

$$\mu(B) = \frac{1}{2}\mu\left(\phi_+^{-1}(B)\right) + \frac{1}{2}\mu\left(\phi_-^{-1}(B)\right)$$

for all Borel sets $B \subseteq [x_-, x_+]$.

It is known that the shape of the invariant measure when represented by its value over certain narrow partitions of $[x_-, x_+]$ becomes gradually smoother [4] as $\epsilon \rightarrow 0$. However, it also becomes narrower. In fact, it tends to the Dirac delta function [5].

Let us change variables according to the prescription

$$y = \left(\frac{a^{\frac{1}{r+1}}}{\epsilon^{\frac{2}{r+1}}}\right) x \text{ and } h = a^{\frac{1}{r+1}} \epsilon^{\frac{r-1}{r+1}}. \tag{3}$$

This leads to a new IFS with probabilities $\{[y_-, y_+]; \psi_+, \psi_-; \frac{1}{2}, \frac{1}{2}\}$ where $\psi_\pm(y; h) = \psi(y \pm h)$, $y_\pm$ is the fixed point of $\psi_\pm$,

$$\begin{aligned} \psi : \mathbb{R} &\rightarrow \mathbb{R} \\ \psi(y; h) &= y - y^r h^2 + O(h^s) \end{aligned}$$

and $s = 2\left(\frac{r+1}{r-1}\right) > 2$.

It can be shown that for small ϵ, $x_\pm \approx \pm\sqrt{\frac{\epsilon}{a}}$ and therefore that for small h, $y_\pm \approx \pm\sqrt[r]{\frac{1}{h}}$, which tends to $\pm\infty$ as $h \to 0$.

Another view of the invariant measure is the following. Imagine that we begin with an infinite number of starting points distributed according to a smooth probability density $p_0(x)$. The relation evolving the probability density forward in time is

$$p_{n+1}(y) = \int_{y_-}^{y_+} \left(\frac{1}{2}\delta(y - \psi_+(z)) + \frac{1}{2}\delta(y - \psi_-(z))\right) p_n(z)\mathrm{d}z$$

where $\delta(y)$ is the Dirac delta function [5]. The unique invariant probability density $p(y)$ is the fixed point of the above iterative prescription.

Using the identity

$$\int_{-\infty}^{\infty} f(z)\delta(y - g(z))\mathrm{d}z = \frac{f(g^{-1}(y))}{g'(g^{-1}(y))}$$

we have

$$2p(y) = \frac{p(\psi_+^{-1}(y))}{\psi'_+(\psi_+^{-1}(y))} + \frac{p(\psi_-^{-1}(y))}{\psi'_-(\psi_-^{-1}(y))} \tag{4}$$

assuming that we can ignore that part of the integral where $y > y_+$ and $y < y_-$, which we certainly can do if $\phi(x)$ is bounded.

Furthermore, it can be shown that

$$\begin{aligned} \psi_\pm(y;h) &= y \pm h - y^r h^2 + O(h^q) \\ \psi'_\pm(y;h) &= 1 - ry^{r-1}h^2 + O(h^q) \\ \psi_\pm^{-1}(y;h) &= y \mp h + y^r h^2 + O(h^s) \end{aligned}$$

where $q = \min\{3, s\}$ and the differentiation and inversion are with respect to y.

Finally, by considering Taylor's expansion for the main parts on the right hand side of Eq. 4

$$\begin{aligned} p(\psi_\pm^{-1}(y)) &= p(y) + (\mp h + y^r h^2)p'(y) + \frac{h^2}{2}p''(y) + O(h^s) \\ \psi'_\pm(\psi_\pm^{-1}(y)) &= 1 - ry^{r-1}h^2 + O(h^q) \end{aligned}$$

and dividing through by h^2, we arrive at

$$p''(y) + 2y^r p'(y) + 2ry^{r-1}p(y) = O(h^\lambda) \tag{5}$$

where $\lambda = \frac{4}{r-1} > 0$.

Remarkably, this linear, second-order, differential equation has the exact solution

$$p(y) = K \exp\left(-\frac{2}{r+1}y^{r+1}\right) \tag{6}$$

as $h \to 0$ where K is an arbitrary constant. This solution goes to zero exponentially fast as $y \to \pm\infty$, perhaps justifying the earlier assumption about ignoring the far reaches of the integral range in the unbounded $\phi(x)$ case.

In order to satisfy the normalizing constraint for a probability density, we have to set

$$K = \frac{\left(\frac{r+1}{2}\right)^{\frac{r}{r+1}}}{\Gamma\left(\frac{1}{r+1}\right)} \tag{7}$$

where $\Gamma(x)$ is the gamma function [5], which can be defined by

$$\Gamma(x) = \int_0^\infty t^{x-1} \exp(-t)\ dt.$$

3 The Experimental Evidence

We backed up our careful mathematical analysis with computer simulations for a few cases of r and ϵ.

We considered $r = 3$ and $r = 5$. For each case, we started with $\epsilon = \frac{1}{2}$ and then halve it at each step until we reached $\epsilon = \frac{1}{32}$. For each step, we plotted the chaotic probability measure in black and the corresponding smooth probability density given by Eq. 6 in grey. The convergence of the two as ϵ decreases is striking.

The chaotic probability measure has been represented by partitioning the interval where the theoretical density is greater than one thousandth its value at zero into 500 equal sub-intervals and considering the frequency with which the orbit of the point starting at the origin visits each sub-interval over an excessive sequence of 10^9 iterations of the non-deterministic dynamical system.

Fig. 2 shows some of the plots for $\phi(x) = \tanh(x) = x - \frac{1}{3}x^3 + O(x^5)$ and Fig. 3 shows some of the plots for $\phi(x) = x - x^5$ with the horizontal axis representing x. Observe that the black lines are bounded exactly by x_- and x_+ as expected, while the grey lines are clearly not.

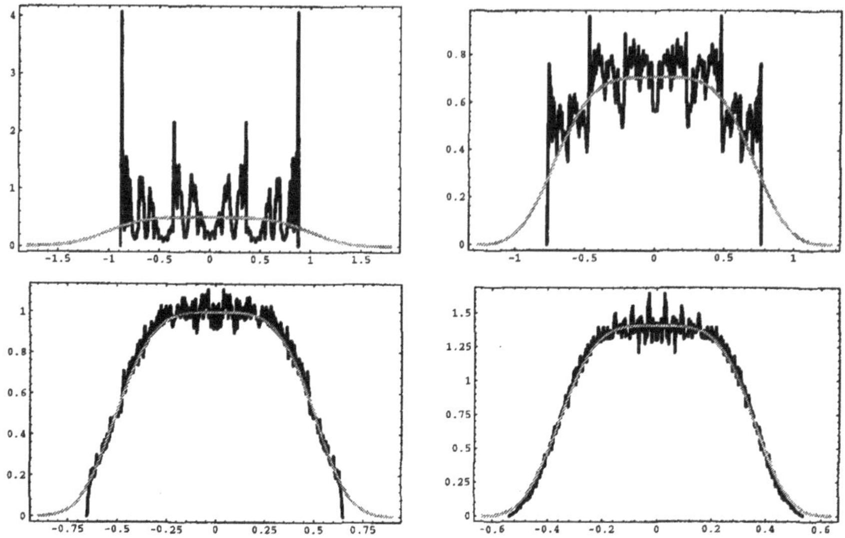

Figure 2: Plots of experimental measure (black) and theoretical density (grey) generated by IFS with $\phi(x) = \tanh(x)$ and $\epsilon = \frac{1}{2}, \frac{1}{4}, \frac{1}{8}$ and $\frac{1}{16}$

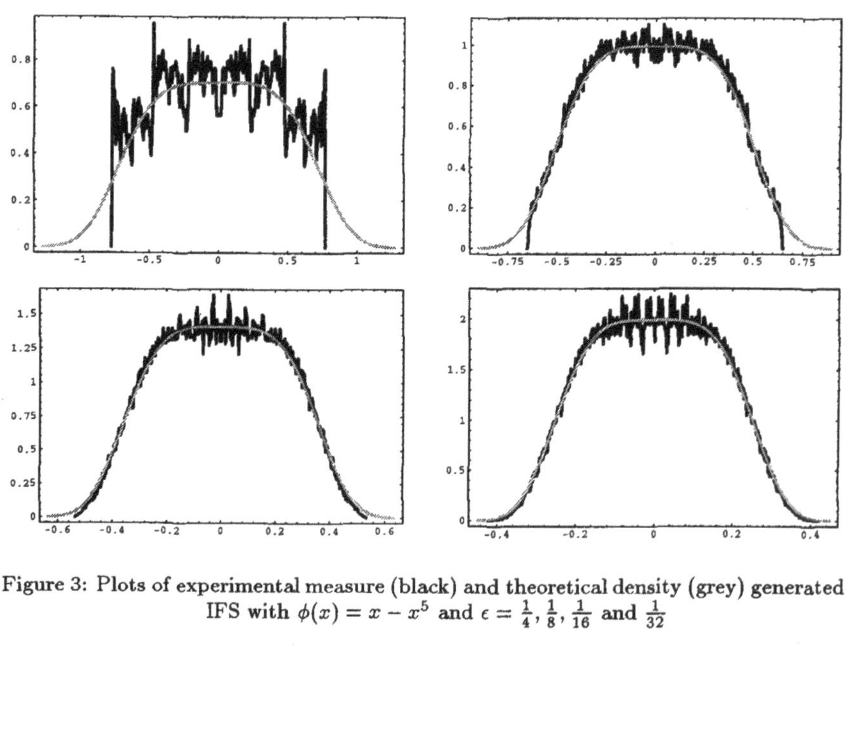

Figure 3: Plots of experimental measure (black) and theoretical density (grey) generated by IFS with $\phi(x) = x - x^5$ and $\epsilon = \frac{1}{4}, \frac{1}{8}, \frac{1}{16}$ and $\frac{1}{32}$

4 Analytical Expression for the Integral of any Smooth Function

Consider the integral

$$\int_{[x_-, x_+]} g(x)\ \mathrm{d}\nu(x) \tag{8}$$

where $g(x)$ is smooth and there exists n even such that the nth derivative of $g(x)$ is its first non-zero derivative at the origin. There is no constructive technique for computing this integral [17] in general.

In the specific case, where ν is the unique invariant measure of a hyperbolic IFS with probabilities, a constructive technique, called *generalized Riemann integration*, by Edalat [6] can be used to compute the integral.

However, for the extreme case that we are considering in this paper the technique becomes impractical. In any case, it gives a numerical rather than an analytical answer.

Using the change of variable given in Eq. 3, we get

$$\begin{aligned}\int_{[x_-, x_+]} g(x)\ \mathrm{d}\mu(x) &\approx \int_{-\infty}^{\infty} p(y) g\left(\left(\frac{\epsilon^{\frac{2}{r+1}}}{a^{\frac{1}{r+1}}}\right) y\right)\ \mathrm{d}y \\ &\approx \frac{g^{(n)}(0)}{n!} \frac{\Gamma\left(\frac{n+1}{r+1}\right)}{\Gamma\left(\frac{1}{r+1}\right)} \left(\frac{r+1}{2a}\epsilon^2\right)^{\frac{n}{r+1}} .\end{aligned} \tag{9}$$

5 Analytical Expression for the Average Lyapunov Exponent

Consider two orbits, one starting at x and another starting at $x + \delta x$ where δx is small. The exponential rate at which these two orbits repel each other is known as the *Lyapunov exponent* γ_r at x. However, for the case in question, we have exponential attraction, therefore we would expect a negative Lyapunov exponent. In other words,

$$|\phi_{i_n} \circ \cdots \circ \phi_{i_2} \circ \phi_{i_1}(x + \delta x) - \phi_{i_n} \circ \cdots \circ \phi_{i_2} \circ \phi_{i_1}(x)| \approx \delta x \exp(\gamma_r n).$$

where $i_1, i_2, \ldots, i_n \in \{+, -\}$, n is large and δx is small.

It follows that

$$\gamma_r = \lim_{n \to \infty} \frac{1}{n+1} \sum_{m=0}^{n} g(\phi_{i_m} \circ \cdots \circ \phi_{i_2} \circ \phi_{i_1}(x)) \tag{10}$$

where $g(x) = \ln \phi'_+(x)$ and $\phi(x)$ is odd.

The average Lyapunov exponent of a physical system quantifies its chaotic behavior. It has been found to be an extremely useful quantity to predict the macroscopic properties of many complex systems.

Elton's Ergodic Theorem [7] states:

For a non-deterministic dynamical system corresponding to an IFS with probabilities $\{X; f_1, \ldots, f_N; p_1, \ldots, p_N\}$, where X is a compact metric space, the corresponding time average of a continuous function g for almost all initial points $x \in X$ and for almost all sequences $i_1, i_2, \ldots \in \{1, \ldots, N\}$ tends with probability one to its integral with respect to the unique invariant measure of the IFS

$$\lim_{n\to\infty} \frac{1}{n+1} \sum_{m=0}^{n} g(f_{i_m} \circ \cdots \circ f_{i_2} \circ f_{i_1}(x)) = \int g \, \mathrm{d}\nu \tag{11}$$

provided that there exists $r < 1$ such that

$$\prod_{i=1}^{N} d(f_i(x), f_i(y))^{p_i} \le r d(x, y) \tag{12}$$

for all $x, y \in X$ where d is the metric on X.

The condition for Elton's Ergodic Theorem is met in our case because $\phi_\pm$ are contracting maps and therefore the average Lyapunov exponent is given by

$$\gamma_r = \int g(x) \, \mathrm{d}\mu(x). \tag{13}$$

For small x, we have $g(x) \approx -arx^{r-1}$, and so, using Eq. 9, we have

$$\gamma_r \approx -ra^{\frac{2}{r+1}} \frac{\Gamma\left(\frac{r}{r+1}\right)}{\Gamma\left(\frac{1}{r+1}\right)} \left(\frac{r+1}{2}\epsilon^2\right)^{\frac{r-1}{r+1}}. \tag{14}$$

In particular, for $\phi(x) = \tanh(x)$, we have $\gamma_3 = -0.827901\epsilon$ and for $\phi(x) = x - x^5$, we have $\gamma_5 = -2.10909\epsilon^{\frac{4}{3}}$.

6 An Application to Forgetful Neural Networks

Neural networks [8] are the study of idealized systems containing very large numbers of connected neurons deliberately constructed to make use of organizational principles found in the human brain.

Forgetting in neural networks has a useful stabilizing role. Using the results above, we will derive an analytical expression for the optimal rate of forgetting. Optimal in the sense of maximizing its storage capacity for memorizing patterns.

Firstly, we need to consider the Hopfield model[9] with N fully connected neurons. Each neuron is a processing unit with one output $x_i \in \{-1, 1\}$.

The symmetric synaptic coupling parameter J_{ij} characterizes the connection from neuron j to neuron i.

Each neuron updates its output asynchronously according to

$$x_i \text{ becomes } \begin{cases} 1 & \text{if } \sum_{j=1}^{N} J_{ij} x_j > 0 \\ -1 & \text{otherwise} \end{cases} .$$

If we define the energy of the model as

$$H = -\frac{1}{2} \sum_{i,j=1}^{N} J_{ij} x_i x_j$$

it can be shown that it decreases monotonically to the local minimum.

We want to store binary patterns in the neural network. The obvious approach is to make the the required stored patterns correspond to local minima. This way when the neural network is set in motion close a local minimum, it should make it way down the energy mountain to this local minimum and hence act out a form of pattern recognition.

So, we require J_{ij} such that there are local minima corresponding to the required stored patterns. Given M patterns $\{\mathbf{X}^m \mid 1 \leq m \leq M\}$, the simplest storage prescription is

$$J_{ij} = \frac{1}{N} \sum_{m=1}^{M} X_i^m X_j^m .$$

Unfortunately, this prescription leads to *catastrophic forgetting*[1,2] for $M > 0.14N$.

Hopfield suggested alternative learning schemes in his original paper[9] that avoided this catastrophic forgetting. In these learning schemes, new patterns are learned at the expense of gradually forgetting previously stored patterns. These models are called *forgetful neural networks.* However, there is a price to pay for this more desirable behavior. Namely, the storage capacity is lower than that for the Hopfield model.

The forgetful storage prescription is given by the local iterative procedure

$$J_{ij}^m = \frac{1}{N} \phi(N J_{ij}^{m-1} + \epsilon X_i^m X_j^m) \tag{15}$$

where $J_{ij}^0 = 0$ and $J_{ij} = J_{ij}^M$.

Let us consider the synaptic couplings. If we set $x_m = NJ_{ij}^m$ and $h_m = X_i^m X_j^m$ [4] then Eq. 15 reduces to

$$x_{m+1} = \phi(x_m + \epsilon h_m)$$

where $x_0 = 0$.

Assuming that the stored patterns are random, this means that h_m is a random variable, which is equal to 1 or -1 with equal probability. Therefore, in the limit as $M \to \infty$, this is a non-deterministic dynamical system corresponding to the IFS [10] with probabilities $\{[x_-, x_+]; \phi_+, \phi_-; \frac{1}{2}, \frac{1}{2}\}$ where $\phi_\pm(x) = \phi(x \pm \epsilon)$ and $x_\pm$ is the fixed point of $\phi_\pm$.

The nature of ϕ determines the properties of the neural network.

In 1986, Nadal et al. [13] explored various learning schemes for forgetful neural networks including the *marginalist* scheme and the *smooth* scheme.

The marginalist learning scheme specifies that the contribution of each pattern to the synaptic couplings decays exponentially with age.

$$\phi(x) = \Lambda\left(\frac{1}{N}\right) x \text{ where } \Lambda(z) = \epsilon \exp\left(-\frac{1}{2} z \eta^2\right). \tag{16}$$

In 1986, Mézard et al. [12] formulated and solved a general learning scheme that incorporated both the Hopfield model and the marginalist learning scheme in the thermodynamic limit as $N \to \infty$. It was shown that the maximum storage capacity is attained with $\eta_{\text{opt}} = 4.10812$ to 6 significant figures.

The smooth learning scheme specifies a general iterative procedure for the synaptic couplings using a restricted class of functions $\phi : \mathbb{R} \to \mathbb{R}$ such that ϕ is odd, monotonically increasing, strictly concave for $x > 0$ and $\phi'(0) = 1$. Notice that this prescription determines the function ϕ as having the form in Eq. 1.

The *embedding strength* of a stored pattern is a measure of how well represented it is in the synaptic couplings. Given M patterns $\{\mathbf{X}^m \mid 1 \leq m \leq M\}$, the embedding strength e_m of pattern $\mathbf{X}^m$ is defined by

$$e_m = \frac{1}{N} \sum_{i,j=1}^{N} J_{ij} X_i^m X_j^m. \tag{17}$$

We know that the embedding strengths of all stored patterns decay to zero as further patterns are subsequently stored by virtue of the properties of a forgetful neural network. Also, it would seem reasonable that this decay is exponential on average when large numbers of patterns have been previously stored because all patterns are homogeneous in character. This leads effectively to investigating the Lyapunov stability of the neural network, where the decay rate corresponds to the *Lyapunov exponent* [16,4].

Therefore, in the limiting case as $n \to \infty$, we have the following approximation up to scaling

$$e_m \sim \exp(\gamma_r n) \tag{18}$$

where $n = M + 1 - m$ and γ_r is the average Lyapunov exponent.

It can be shown [14] that for the marginalist learning scheme

$$e_m \approx \Lambda\left(\frac{n}{N}\right).$$

Comparing this with Eq. 18 up to scaling, we deduce that the optimal value of ϵ for a forgetful neural network with large N is

$$\epsilon_{\text{opt}} = \frac{\eta^2_{\text{opt}}}{2N\sqrt{6}} \frac{\Gamma\left(\frac{1}{4}\right)}{\Gamma\left(\frac{3}{4}\right)} \approx \frac{10.19}{N} \tag{19}$$

for the canonical case where $\phi(x) = \tanh(x)$. Remember, it is not the actual values of the embedding strengths that count, but rather their values relative to each other.

Note that the optimal ϵ is only inversely proportional to N in the cases where $r = 3$. This is in contrast to that proposed in previous literature [16,4].

For the general case

$$\epsilon_{\text{opt}} \sim N^{-\frac{(r+1)}{2(r-1)}} \tag{20}$$

7 Conclusion

We have derived a smooth analytical expression Eq. 9 to approximate the integral of any smooth function over multifractal measures generated by iterated function systems with probabilities on the edge of chaos.

We have backed this up with experimental evidence and also applied it to the problem of calculating the storage capacity of forgetful neural networks.

There ought to be applications for this technique in statistical physics, and in particular to the Ising model.

References

1. D. J. Amit, H. Gutfreund, and H. Sompolinsky. Information storage in neural networks with low levels of activity. *Phys. Rev. A*, 35:2293–2303, 1987.

2. Daniel J. Amit. *Modelling Brain Function.* Cambridge University Press, 1992.
3. M. F. Barnsley and S. Demko. Iterated function systems and the global construction of fractals. *The proceedings of the Royal Society of London*, A399:243–275, 1985.
4. U. Behn, J. L. van Hemmen, R. Kühn, A. Lange, and V. A. Zagrebnov. Multifractality in forgetful memories. *Physica D*, 68:401–415, 1993.
5. R. Creighton Buck. *Advanced Calculus.* McGraw-Hill Book Company, 1965.
6. A. Edalat. Domain theory and integration. *Theoretical Computer Science*, 151:163–193, 1995.
7. John H. Elton. Ergodic theorem for iterated maps. *Ergod. Th. & Dynam. Sys.*, 7:481–488, 1987.
8. John Hertz, Anders Krogh, and Richard G. Palmer. *Introduction to the Theory of Neural Computation.* Addison-Wesley Publishing Company, 1993.
9. J. J. Hopfield. Neural networks and physical systems with emergent collective computational abilities. *Proc. Natl. Acad. Sci. USA*, 79:2554–2558, 1982.
10. J. E. Hutchinson. Fractal and self-similarity. *Indiana University Mathematics Journal*, 30:713–747, 1981.
11. B. Mandelbrot. *The Fractal Geometry of Nature.* W. H. Freeman and co., San Francisco, 1982.
12. M. Mézard, J. P. Nadal, and G. Toulouse. Solvable models of working memories. *J. Phys.*, 47:1457–1462, 1986.
13. J. P. Nadal, G. Toulouse, J. P. Changeux, and S. Dehaene. Networks of formal neurons and memory palimpsests. *Europhys. Lett.*, 1:535, 1986.
14. Peter Potts. The storage capacity of forgetful neural networks. Master's thesis, Department of Computing, Imperial College, Sept. 1995.
15. W. A. Sutherland. *Introduction to Metric and Topological Spaces.* Oxford University Press, 1993.
16. J. L. van Hemmen, G. Keller, and R. Kühn. Forgetful memories. *Europhys. Lett.*, 5:663–668, 1988.
17. Alan J. Weir. *Lebesgue Integration & Measure.* Cambridge University Press, 1994.

LOGICAL RELATIONS AND λ-THEORIES

A. BUCCIARELLI
LIENS-DMI, Ecole Normale Supérieure,
45, rue d'Ulm 75230 Paris, France

A natural way of comparing two models of a given typed λ-calculus is to compare their theories. We describe a method for proving inclusions of λ-theories, based on particular logical relations that we call *extensional collapses*, and show some applications.

1 Introduction

Two phrases of a programming language are operationally equivalent if, when plugged in any context, they both produce the same result, if any.

Proving operational equivalences by syntactic means is usually difficult. Any model provides a theory ($M =_{\mathcal{M}} N$ if $[\![M]\!]^{\mathcal{M}} = [\![N]\!]^{\mathcal{M}}$) which approximates the operational equivalence. From this point of view the natural way of comparing different models of a given language is to compare their theories: the closer the theory is to the operational theory, the better the model is.

On the other hand if we want to use models in order to prove operational equivalences, they should be effective.

An example of this trade-off is provided by the state of the art in the study of the finitary fragment of Scott's PCF ([12], see example 1): there exist fully abstract models [a] ([1, 7, 10]), but the decidability of their theory is an open problem. On the other hand there exist several models whose theory is decidable ([12, 5, 2] ,the list is not exaustive see [5] for a survey), but each of them gives us only an approximation of the operational equivalence.

Surprisingly enough, not much attention seems to have been paid to the developement of methods allowing to prove that, for two given models $\mathcal{M}$ and $\mathcal{N}$, $Th(\mathcal{M}) \subseteq Th(\mathcal{N})$. A way of getting this result would be to provide a homomorphism from $\mathcal{M}$ to $\mathcal{N}$, *i.e* a family of mappings $\{h_\sigma\}_{\sigma \in Types}$ such that, for any term $M : \sigma$, $h_\sigma([\![M]\!]^{\mathcal{M}}) = [\![M]\!]^{\mathcal{N}}$. The problem is that most often (and in particular in all the cases we deal with in section 4), such a homomorphism does not exist.

Alternatively one can get $Th(\mathcal{M}) \subseteq Th(\mathcal{N})$ as a corollary of a full abstraction result for $\mathcal{N}$, but again in many cases the models we deal with are not fully abstract.

[a] A model is fully abstract when its theory coincide with the operational one.

Two proofs of inclusion of theories I am aware of, which do not fall in one of the categories cited above, are those of [4] and [13], which are based on the following idea: given $\mathcal{M}$ and $\mathcal{N}$, one shows that for any element f of $\mathcal{N}$ there exists an element g of $\mathcal{M}$ which "behaves like f" with respect to definable elements, in the sense that if $[\![M]\!]^{\mathcal{N}} f_1 f_2 \ldots f_k = [\![c]\!]^{\mathcal{N}}$ where c is a ground constant, then $[\![M]\!]^{\mathcal{M}} g_1 g_2 \ldots g_k = [\![c]\!]^{\mathcal{M}}$. As a corollary one gets that if $[\![M]\!]^{\mathcal{N}} \neq [\![N]\!]^{\mathcal{N}}$ then $[\![M]\!]^{\mathcal{M}} \neq [\![N]\!]^{\mathcal{M}}$, and hence $Th(\mathcal{M}) \subseteq Th(\mathcal{N})$.

We show that a synthetic way of expressing the relation existing between the f's and the g's is to define an appropriate logical relation $\mathcal{E}$, that we call *extensional collapse* of $\mathcal{M}$ and $\mathcal{N}$, such that $g_i \mathcal{E} f_i$. This allows us to provide new proofs, which do not make any reference to syntax, of the cited results of [4] and [13], and to obtain a new result of inclusion of theories in a simple and quite unexpected way.

In section 2 we introduce the syntax and semantics of applied λ-calculi; section 3 deals with logical relations, ending up with the definition of extensional collapses. Section 4 presents some applications.

2 Applied typed λ-calculi

Following [9] we adopt the term *applied λ-calculus* to designate a simply typed λ-calculus endowed with a set of ground types, a set of typed constants and a set of rules (often called δ-rules) stipulating the operational behaviour of the constants. Constants may be first-order (*e.g.* arithmetical operations or conditional statements) or higher-order (*e.g.* fixpoint operators).

Models of applied λ-calculi can be presented in several ways. Here we use the notion of *environment models*, which is general enough for our purposes, and refer to [9] for a comprehensive discussion on the relations between this and other approaches (combinatorial, categorical).

2.1 Syntax

Given a set K of ground types, the set of types of the corresponding applied calculus is defined by the following BNF-expression:

$$T ::= \; K \mid T \rightarrow T$$

Given a family $\{C_\sigma\}_{\sigma \in T}$ of typed constants, and for any type σ a denumerable set Var^σ of variables, the set of terms of the corresponding applied calculus is inductively defined by stipulating that constants and variables are terms, and that (typed) applications and λ-abstractions on terms produce terms.

The operational semantics of the language is provided by the usual β rule, combined with the δ-rules specific to the constants.

A *program* P is a closed term of ground type, and it *converges* to a ground constant c if there exists a reduction path $P \rightarrow^* c$.

example 1: As an example of applied λ-calculus, we define a finitary version of Scott's PCF ([12]), PCF_{fin}.

PCF_{fin} has a unique ground type, B, and four constants: $\{\Omega, true, false\} = C_B$ and $\{if\} = C_{B\rightarrow(B\rightarrow(B\rightarrow B))}$.

The δ-rules define if as a conditional statement and Ω as the undefined boolean value:

$$if\ true\ M\ N \rightarrow M \qquad if\ false\ M\ N \rightarrow N \qquad if\ \Omega\ M\ N \rightarrow \Omega$$

∎

Two programs are *operationally equivalent* if they converge to the same ground constant, and two terms $M, N : \alpha$ are operationally equivalent if for any program context $P[\,]$, $P[M]$ and $P[N]$ are.

2.2 Models

A *typed applicative structure* $\mathcal{A}$ for an applied calculus L is a tuple

$$< \{\mathcal{A}^\sigma\}, \{App^{\sigma,\tau}\}, Const >$$

such that:

- $\mathcal{A}^\sigma$ is a set.
- $App^{\sigma,\tau}$ is a set-theoretic map $App^{\sigma,\tau} : \mathcal{A}^{\sigma\rightarrow\tau} \rightarrow (\mathcal{A}^\sigma \rightarrow \mathcal{A}^\tau)$.
- $Const$ maps each constant of L onto an element of the appropriate $\mathcal{A}^\sigma$.

An applicative structure $\mathcal{A}$ is *extensional* if for any $\sigma, \tau \in T$, $f, g \in \mathcal{A}^{\sigma\rightarrow\tau}$, if for any $x \in \mathcal{A}^\sigma$ $App^{\sigma,\tau} f x = App^{\sigma,\tau} g x$ then $f = g$.

An *environment* ρ for an applicative structure $\mathcal{A}$ is a type-respecting mapping from variables of L to the union of $\mathcal{A}^\sigma$.

An *environment model* is an extensional applicative structure such that the clauses below define a total meaning function $[\![.]\!]$. which maps terms and environments to elements of the appropriate $\mathcal{A}^\sigma$. The clauses concerning constants are required to validate the δ-rules.

- $[\![x]\!]\rho = \rho(x)$,
- $[\![c]\!]\rho = Const(c)$,
- $[\![MN]\!]\rho = App^{\sigma,\tau}[\![M]\!]\rho[\![N]\!]\rho$ for the appropriate σ and τ,
- $[\![\lambda x\ M]\!]\rho = f \in \mathcal{A}^{\sigma\to\tau}$ such that for all $d \in \mathcal{A}^{\sigma}$ $App^{\sigma,\tau} fd = [\![M]\!]\rho[d/x]$, for the appropriate σ and τ.

It is easy to prove by structural induction that if M is closed then for all ρ, ρ', $[\![M]\!]\rho = [\![M]\!]\rho'$. Hence the interpretation of a closed term M will be noted just $[\![M]\!]$.

The *theory* of an environment model $\mathcal{M}$, $Th(\mathcal{M})$ is the set of closed equation $M = N$ such that $[\![M]\!] = [\![N]\!]$.

example 2: We define the well-known continuous model of PCF_{fin}: let $\mathcal{C}^B$ be the flat domain of boolean values:

$$\mathcal{C}^B = < \{\bot, tt, ff\}, x \leq y \ \text{ if and only if } \ x = \bot \quad \text{or} \quad x = y >$$

and $\mathcal{C}^{\sigma\to\tau}$ be the cpo of monotone functions from $\mathcal{C}^{\sigma}$ to $\mathcal{C}^{\tau}$ ordered pointwise:

$$\mathcal{C}^{\sigma\to\tau} = < \{f : \mathcal{C}^{\sigma} \to \mathcal{C}^{\tau} \mid f \text{ monotone }\}, f \leq g \ \text{ if for all } d \in \mathcal{C}^{\sigma}\ f(d) \leq g(d) >$$

In $\mathcal{C}$ *App* is simply functional application, that is $App^{\sigma,\tau} fd = f(d)$.

The ground constants of PCF_{fin} are interpreted as follows:

$$[\![\Omega]\!]^{\mathcal{C}} = \bot,\ [\![true]\!]^{\mathcal{C}} = tt,\ [\![false]\!]^{\mathcal{C}} = ff$$

and the constant *if* by the corresponding monotone function. ∎

3 Logical relations

Logical relations have been extensively used in the study of both syntactic and semantic properties of typed λ-calculi (see [9] for a survey).

Here we just need a particular kind of binary logical relations, establishing a correspondence between two given models of a given applied λ-calculus. Throughout this section the application $App^{\sigma,\tau} fx$ in an applicative structure will be abbreviated by $f(x)$.

Definition 1 *Let $\mathcal{A}$ and $\mathcal{B}$ be models of an applied calculus L;* a logical relation *between $\mathcal{A}$ and $\mathcal{B}$ is a family $\{R^{\sigma}\}_{\sigma\in T}$ such that:*

- $\forall \sigma \in T\ R^{\sigma} \subseteq \mathcal{A}^{\sigma} \times \mathcal{B}^{\sigma}$.
- $\forall \sigma, \tau \in T\ \forall f \in \mathcal{A}^{\sigma\to\tau}\ \forall g \in \mathcal{B}^{\sigma\to\tau}$:

$$fR^{\sigma\to\tau} g \ \textit{ if and only if } \ \forall x \in \mathcal{A}^{\sigma}\ \forall y \in \mathcal{B}^{\sigma}\ [\ xR^{\sigma} y \Rightarrow f(x)R^{\tau} g(y)\ ]$$

- *for any constant* $c \in C_\sigma$ *of* L, $[\![c]\!]^{\mathcal{A}} R^\sigma [\![c]\!]^{\mathcal{B}}$.

We will denote the fact that $\{R^\sigma\}_{\sigma \in T}$ is a logical relation between $\mathcal{A}$ and $\mathcal{B}$ by $R \subseteq \mathcal{A} \times \mathcal{B}$.

The following is the basic lemma of logical relations:

Lemma 1 *If* $R \subseteq \mathcal{A} \times \mathcal{B}$ *then for any closed term* $M : \sigma$ *of* L $[\![M]\!]^{\mathcal{A}} R^\sigma [\![M]\!]^{\mathcal{B}}$.

Logical relations with certain properties are particularly well suited for studying L-theories:

Definition 2 *A logical relation* $R \subseteq \mathcal{A} \times \mathcal{B}$ *is a* logical partial function *if*

$$\forall \sigma \in T\ \forall x \in \mathcal{A}^\sigma\ \forall y, y' \in \mathcal{B}^\sigma\ (xR^\sigma y \text{ and } xR^\sigma y') \Rightarrow y = y'$$

Lemma 2 *If* $R \subseteq \mathcal{A} \times \mathcal{B}$ *is a logical partial function, then* $Th(\mathcal{A}) \subseteq Th(\mathcal{B})$.

Proof: Let $M, N : \sigma$ be closed terms such that $[\![M]\!]^{\mathcal{A}} = [\![N]\!]^{\mathcal{A}}$. By the basic lemma we have that $[\![M]\!]^{\mathcal{A}} R^\sigma [\![M]\!]^{\mathcal{B}}$ and $[\![N]\!]^{\mathcal{A}} R^\sigma [\![N]\!]^{\mathcal{B}}$. Hence, since R is a logical partial function, we conclude that $[\![M]\!]^{\mathcal{B}} = [\![N]\!]^{\mathcal{B}}$ ∎

In practical cases, proving directly that a given logical relation is a logical partial function seems to be hard. The following lemma provides sufficient conditions for a logical relation to be a logical partial function, which turn out to be quite easily checkable in some cases:

Definition 3 *A logical relation* $R \subseteq \mathcal{A} \times \mathcal{B}$ *is* surjective *if*

$$\forall \sigma \in T \forall y \in \mathcal{B}^\sigma \exists x \in \mathcal{A}^\sigma\ xR^\sigma y$$

Lemma 3 *If* $R \subseteq \mathcal{A} \times \mathcal{B}$ *is surjective, and if for any ground type* k R^k *is a logical partial function, then* R *is a logical partial function.*

Proof: Easy induction on types. ∎

Hence, a way to prove that for two given models $\mathcal{A}$ and $\mathcal{B}$, $Th(\mathcal{A}) \subseteq Th(\mathcal{B})$, is to define a logical relation $R \in \mathcal{A} \times \mathcal{B}$ which is a logical partial function at ground types, and to prove that it is surjective. We are left with the problem of deciding which particular logical relation to pick, which we deal with in the next section.

3.1 The extensional collapse

The term "extensional collapse" has been used in literature ([6, 1]) to designate the operation which consists in extracting an extensional applicative strucure $\mathcal{M}^{ext}$ from an arbitrary one $\mathcal{M}$. The idea is to consider the logical relation $R \subseteq \mathcal{M} \times \mathcal{M}$ which is the identity at ground types. This logical relation defines a partial equivalence relation on $\mathcal{M}^\sigma$, for any σ, and the extensional collapse of $\mathcal{M}$ is the applicative structure obtained by quotienting any $\mathcal{M}^\sigma$ by R^σ.

We simply generalise this idea to the case of two different models $\mathcal{A}$ and $\mathcal{B}$. Our aim is not to define quotient models but to obtain a logical relation which is a good candidate to be proved to be a logical partial function, hence proving $Th(\mathcal{A}) \subseteq Th(\mathcal{B})$.

Of course we can no longer define the extensional collapse of $\mathcal{A}$ and $\mathcal{B}$ to be the logical relation which is the identity at ground types, since the interpretation of ground types may be different in different models.

Definition 4 *Let $\mathcal{A}$, $\mathcal{B}$ be models of a given applied calculus L, and define for any ground type k of L*

$$\mathcal{E}_L(\mathcal{A},\mathcal{B})^k = \bigcap_{R \subseteq \mathcal{A} \times \mathcal{B}} R^k$$

If $\{\mathcal{E}_L(\mathcal{A},\mathcal{B})^\sigma\}_{\sigma \in T}$ is a logical relation, then it is the extensional collapse *of $\mathcal{A}$ and $\mathcal{B}$, noted $\mathcal{E}_L(\mathcal{A},\mathcal{B})$.*

The extensional collapse of $\mathcal{A}$ and $\mathcal{B}$ is the logical relation which, at ground types, is the intersection of all logical relations between $\mathcal{A}$ and $\mathcal{B}$. We have not made enough assumptions on constants of L in order to be able to prove that $\mathcal{E}_L(\mathcal{A},\mathcal{B})$ always exists. However in practical cases, as we shall see, it will be easily shown that the extensional collapse does exist. A first remark is that, for any ground type k,

$$\{([\![c]\!]^\mathcal{A}, [\![c]\!]^\mathcal{B}) \mid c \in C_k\} \subseteq \mathcal{E}_L(\mathcal{A},\mathcal{B})^k$$

since any logical relation relates the interpretations of constants of L, by definition.

In the next two sections we show that for finitary PCF

$$\mathcal{E}_{\text{PCF}_{fin}}(\mathcal{A},\mathcal{B})^B = \{([\![c]\!]^\mathcal{A}, [\![c]\!]^\mathcal{B})\}_{c=\Omega,true,false}$$

whereas for the full PCF, relating ground constants is not enough.

3.2 Extensional collapse for PCF_{fin}

Proposition 1 *Let $\mathcal{A}$ and $\mathcal{B}$ be models of PCF_{fin}. The relation defined by*

$$R^B = \{([\![\Omega]\!]^\mathcal{A}, [\![\Omega]\!]^\mathcal{B}), ([\![true]\!]^\mathcal{A}, [\![true]\!]^\mathcal{B}), ([\![false]\!]^\mathcal{A}, [\![false]\!]^\mathcal{B})\}$$

is logical, and it is $\mathcal{E}_{PCF_{fin}}(\mathcal{A},\mathcal{B})$.

Proof: R is trivially a logical relation. In order to show that $R = \mathcal{E}_{\text{PCF}_{fin}}(\mathcal{A},\mathcal{B})$ it is enough to remark that for any logical relation $S \subseteq \mathcal{A} \times \mathcal{B}$, $R^B \subseteq S^B$. ∎

3.3 Extensional collapse for PCF

PCF has two ground types, B and N. The ground constants are

$$C_B = \{true, false\}$$

and

$$C_N = \{\underline{0}, \underline{1}, \ldots, \underline{n}, \ldots\}$$

Other constants are $succ, pred : N \to N$, $Z : N \to B$ (the "test for zero"), $if : B \to (B \to (B \to B))$ (boolean conditional statement) $intif$: $B \to (N \to (N \to N))$ (integer conditional statement), and, for any type σ, $Y_\sigma : (\sigma \to \sigma) \to \sigma$ (fixpoint operators). The δ-rules concerning these constants are the usual ones, in particular $Y_\sigma M \to^\delta M(Y_\sigma M)$.

Given two models $\mathcal{M}$ and $\mathcal{N}$ of PCF, it is easy to see that the relation defined by

$$R^B = \{([\![true]\!]^{\mathcal{M}}, [\![true]\!]^{\mathcal{N}}), ([\![false]\!]^{\mathcal{M}}, [\![false]\!]^{\mathcal{N}})\}$$

$$R^N = \{[\![\underline{0}]\!]^{\mathcal{M}}, [\![\underline{0}]\!]^{\mathcal{N}}), \ldots, ([\![\underline{n}]\!]^{\mathcal{M}}, [\![\underline{n}]\!]^{\mathcal{N}}), \ldots\}$$

is not logical, since, for instance, it does not relate the interpretations in $\mathcal{M}$ and $\mathcal{N}$ of the closed PCF-term $Y_B(\lambda x\ x)$. Quite naturally, it turns out that by adding to R^B and R^N the pairs composed by the fixed points of the identity, we get the extensional collapse for PCF. In order to prove it, we have to make some "minimal" assumptions on $\mathcal{M}$ and $\mathcal{N}$, which turn out to be satisfied in all the examples of the next section, namely:

- $\mathcal{M}$ and $\mathcal{N}$ are least fixpoint models, *i.e.* $\mathcal{M}^\sigma$'s and $\mathcal{N}^\sigma$s are domains, and Y_σ is interpreted in both model by $\underline{\lambda} f \bigvee_{n\in\omega} f^n(\bot_\sigma)$.
- The least upper bounds of directed set of functions are defined pointwise, in both $\mathcal{M}$ and $\mathcal{N}$.
- $\mathcal{M}^B$, $\mathcal{M}^N$, $\mathcal{N}^B$, $\mathcal{N}^N$ do not contain infinite increasing chains.

Proposition 2 *Given two models $\mathcal{M}$ and $\mathcal{N}$ of PCF, the relation defined by*

$$R^B = \{([\![Y_B(\lambda x\ x)]\!]^{\mathcal{M}}, [\![Y_B(\lambda x\ x)]\!]^{\mathcal{N}}), ([\![c]\!]^{\mathcal{M}}, [\![c]\!]^{\mathcal{N}})\}_{c=true,false}$$

$$R^N = \{([\![Y_N(\lambda x\ x)]\!]^{\mathcal{M}}, [\![Y_N(\lambda x\ x)]\!]^{\mathcal{N}}), [\![\underline{0}]\!]^{\mathcal{M}}, [\![\underline{0}]\!]^{\mathcal{N}}), \ldots, ([\![\underline{n}]\!]^{\mathcal{M}}, [\![\underline{n}]\!]^{\mathcal{N}}), \ldots\}$$

is logical, and it is $\mathcal{E}_{PCF}(\mathcal{M}, \mathcal{N})$.

Proof: R does relate the interpretations of ground constants by definition. Easy by-cases arguments prove that the interpretations of first-order constants are also related. It remains to prove that, for any type σ, $[\![Y_\sigma]\!]^{\mathcal{M}} R^{(\sigma\to\sigma)\to\sigma} [\![Y_\sigma]\!]^{\mathcal{N}}$. It is enough to prove that R is *directed complete* (see [9]), *i.e.* that for any σ, if $D \subseteq R^\sigma$ is directed in $\mathcal{M}^\sigma \times \mathcal{N}^\sigma$, then $\bigvee D \in R^\sigma$. We prove this by induction on types: if σ is ground and $D \subseteq R^\sigma$ is directed then $\bigvee D \in D$, by our third assumption, and we are done. Let $D \subseteq R^{\sigma\to\tau}$ be directed, and let $\bigvee D = (f,g)$. If $(x,y) \in R^\sigma$ then $D' = \{(f'(x), g'(y)) \mid (f',g') \in D\}$ is a directed set included in R^τ, hence by hypothesis $\bigvee D' \in R^\tau$. By our second assumption above, $\bigvee D' = (f(x), g(y))$, hence $f R^{\sigma\to\tau} g$ and we are done.

In order to show that $R = \mathcal{E}_{\text{PCF}}(\mathcal{M},\mathcal{N})$ it is enough to remark that for any logical relation $S \subseteq \mathcal{M} \times \mathcal{N}$, $R^B \subseteq S^B$. ∎

Moreover $\mathcal{E}_{\text{PCF}}(\mathcal{M},\mathcal{N})$ is clearly a logical partial function at B, hence:

Corollary 1 *Let $\mathcal{M}$ and $\mathcal{N}$ be models of PCF. If $\mathcal{E}_{PCF}(\mathcal{M},\mathcal{N})$ is surjective then $Th(\mathcal{M}) \subseteq Th(\mathcal{N})$.*

Remark that the same corollary does hold for PCF_{fin}.

4 Applications

In this section we show how, in some cases, one can use extensional collapses and prove their surjectivity to prove inclusions of theories. Our examples are based on PCF.

4.1 Extensionally embedded domains

We have already described the continuous model $\mathcal{C}$ of PCF_{fin}. Extending it to PCF simply amounts to interpreting N by the flat domain of natural numbers, additional first order constants by the corresponding continuous functions and fixpoint constants by domain-theoretic least fixpoint operators.

The model $\mathcal{D}$ of *extensionally embedded dI-domains with coherence* and *extensionally strongly stable functions* is defined in [4]. Both in $\mathcal{C}$ and in $\mathcal{D}$ application is simply functional application. For our purposes it is enough to know that for any PCF-type σ, $\mathcal{D}^\sigma$ is a domain with a built-in continuous injection $i_\sigma : \mathcal{D}^\sigma \to \mathcal{C}^\sigma$, which is the identity function at ground types (hence $\mathcal{D}^B = \mathcal{C}^B$ and $\mathcal{D}^N = \mathcal{C}^N$), and which is defined as follows at higher types:

$$\forall f \in \mathcal{D}^{\sigma\to\tau}\ \forall x \in \mathcal{C}^\sigma\ (i_{\sigma\to\tau}(f))(x) = \bigvee_{z\in\mathcal{D}^\sigma\ i_\sigma(z)\leq x} i_\tau(f(z))$$

If we prove that, for any σ and any $x \in \mathcal{D}^\sigma$, $i_\sigma(x)\mathcal{E}_{\text{PCF}}(\mathcal{C},\mathcal{D})^\sigma x$ then we conclude by corollary 1 that $Th(\mathcal{C}) \subseteq Th(\mathcal{D})$.

Proposition 3 *The extensional collapse* $\mathcal{E}_{PCF}(\mathcal{C},\mathcal{D})$ *is surjective.*

Proof: We show that for any type σ and any $s \in \mathcal{D}_\sigma$, $i_\sigma(s)\mathcal{E}^\sigma(\mathcal{C},\mathcal{D})s$. Throghout the proof $\mathcal{E}_{PCF}(\mathcal{C},\mathcal{D})$ will be abbreviated by $\mathcal{E}$, and the σ in $\mathcal{E}^\sigma$ and i_σ will be omitted whenever no confusion can arise.

Actually we will prove by simultaneus induction on types three properties relating the extensional collapse $\mathcal{E}^\sigma$ and the extensional embedding i_σ; the third one implies that $\mathcal{E}$ is surjective:

$$P_1(\sigma) \equiv \forall s \in \mathcal{D}^\sigma \forall e \in \mathcal{C}^\sigma \quad e\mathcal{E}s \Rightarrow i(s) \leq e$$

$$P_2(\sigma) \equiv \forall s, s' \in \mathcal{D}^\sigma \forall e \in \mathcal{C}^\sigma \quad (e\mathcal{E}s \text{ and } i(s') \leq e) \Rightarrow i(s') \leq i(s)$$

$$P_3(\sigma) \equiv \forall s \in \mathcal{D}^\sigma \quad i(s)\mathcal{E}s$$

To start with, $P_i(B)$ and $P_i(N)$ for $1 = 1,2,3$ are insured by the fact that i_B and i_N are the identity function on the flat domain of boolean and integer values.

Let now suppose that for two given types σ and τ, $P_i(\sigma)$ and $P_i(\tau)$ do hold for $i = 1,2,3$, and let us show that in this case $P_i(\sigma \to \tau)$ also holds for $i = 1,2,3$:

- P_1: given $f \in \mathcal{D}^{\sigma\to\tau}$, $g \in \mathcal{C}^{\sigma\to\tau}$ such that $g\mathcal{E}f$, we have to show that $i(f) \leq g$. Since elements of $\mathcal{C}^{\sigma\to\tau}$ are ordered pointwise, we just have to prove that $i(f)(a) \leq g(a)$ for any given $a \in \mathcal{C}^\sigma$. Now $i(f)(a) = \bigvee_{i(s)\leq a} i(f(s))$, hence it is enough to prove that, for any $s \in \mathcal{D}^\sigma$ such that $i(s) \leq a$, $i(f(s)) \leq g(a)$. Now by $P_3(\sigma)$ we have that $i(s)\mathcal{E}s$, hence $g(i(s))\mathcal{E}f(s)$. By $P_1(\tau)$ we get $i(f(s)) \leq g(i(s)) \leq g(a)$ and we are done.

- P_2: given $f, f' \in \mathcal{D}^{\sigma\to\tau}$, $g \in E^{\sigma\to\tau}$ such that $g\mathcal{E}f$ and $i(f') \leq g$, we have to show that $i(f') \leq i(f)$. It is enough to show that, for any $s \in \mathcal{D}^\sigma$, $i(f'(s)) \leq i(f(s))$. For any $s \in \mathcal{D}^\sigma$ we have by $P_3(\sigma)$ that $i(s)\mathcal{E}s$, so that $g(i(s))\mathcal{E}f(s))$. Moreover $i(f'(s)) = i(f')(i(s)) \leq g(i(s))$, [b] hence by $P_2(\tau)$ we get $i(f'(s)) \leq i(f(s))$ and we are done.

- P_3: given $f \in \mathcal{D}^{\sigma\to\tau}$ we have to show that $i(f)\mathcal{E}f$. Let $s \in \mathcal{D}^\sigma$, $e \in \mathcal{C}^\sigma$ be such that $e\mathcal{E}s$. We have to show that $i(f)(e)\mathcal{E}f(s)$. If we prove that $i(f)(e) = \bigvee_{i(z)\leq e} i(f(z)) = i(f(s))$ we are done by $P_3(\tau)$.

[b] $i(f'(s)) = i(f')(i(s))$ since any extensionally strongly stable function h verifies the following property: $i(a) \leq i(a') \Rightarrow i(h(a)) \leq i(h(a'))$

- $i(f(s)) \leq i(f)(e)$ is immediate since by hypothesis $e\mathcal{E}s$, hence by $P_1(\sigma)$ $i(s) \leq e$.
- $i(f(s)) \geq i(f)(e)$: let $z \in \mathcal{D}^\sigma$ be such that $i(z) \leq e$; then by $P_2(\sigma)$ we get $i(z) \leq i(s)$, hence $i(f(z)) \leq i(f(s))$ and we are done.

■

4.2 Event structures and extended bistructures

In [13] the models of PCF $\mathcal{S}$ (of event structures) and $\mathcal{B}$ (of extended bistructures) are defined.

$\mathcal{S}$ is isomorphic to $\mathcal{C}$, and in particular $Th(\mathcal{S}) = Th(\mathcal{C})$.

It is possible to rephrase the proof of proposition 3 in this framework. Here we just state our main result. The proof and further details are included in the full paper [3].

Proposition 4 *The extensional collapse* $\mathcal{E}_{\ PCF}\ (\mathcal{S}, \mathcal{B})$ *is surjective.*

Both the inclusions proved so far, $Th(\mathcal{C}) \subseteq Th(\mathcal{D})$ and $Th(\mathcal{S}) \subseteq Th(\mathcal{B})$, are in fact strict, and this can be proved by using Plotkin's example ([11]), showing that Scott's continuous model is not fully abstract for PCF. It turns out that both $\mathcal{D}$ and $\mathcal{B}$ do equate Plotkin's terms, which are not equated in $\mathcal{C}$ and $\mathcal{S}$.

4.3 Lattice model of PCF

The last application of our method based on extensional collapses is somehow surprising, since in this case the proof of surjectivity of $\mathcal{E}$ comes for free, as a corollary of the basic lemma of logical relations and of a full-abstraction result due to Plotkin ([11]). Having defined the lattice model of PCF $\mathcal{L}$, the proof goes as follows: in order to show that $\mathcal{E}_{\ \mathrm{PCF}}\ (\mathcal{L}, \mathcal{C})$ is surjective, we use a well known extension of PCF, PCF_{por}, which has the property that any (finite) element of the continuous model $\mathcal{C}$, at any types, is PCF_{por}-definable. Then we realize that the extensional collapse for PCF_{por} coincides with the one for PCF, and we conclude by the basic lemma that $\mathcal{E}_{\ \mathrm{PCF}}\ (\mathcal{L}, \mathcal{C})$ is surjective.

This example suggests a general method for proving inclusions of L-theories when one of the models we deal with is fully abstract for a super-language of L.

Let us start by describing $\mathcal{L}$: $\mathcal{L}^B$ and $\mathcal{L}^N$ are the "topped" flat domains of booleans and integers, respectively. $\mathcal{L}^{\sigma\to\tau}$ is the lattice of all continuous functions from $\mathcal{L}^\sigma$ to $\mathcal{L}^\tau$. Application in $\mathcal{L}$ is function application, and the constants of PCF are interpreted by the appropriate continuous functions. For instance:

$$[\![if]\!]^{\mathcal{L}}xyz = \begin{cases} \top & \text{if } x = \top \\ y & \text{if } x = true \\ z & \text{if } x = false \\ \bot & \text{if } x = \bot \end{cases}$$

In order to prove that $\mathcal{E}_{\text{PCF}}(\mathcal{L}, \mathcal{C})$ is surjective, let us consider the language PCF_{por} obtained by adding to PCF the constant $por : B \to (B \to B)$ and the rules: $por\ true\ M \to^{\delta} true$, $por\ M\ true \to^{\delta} true$ and $por\ false\ false \to^{\delta} false$. $\mathcal{L}$ and $\mathcal{C}$ are both models of PCF_{por}, the interpretations of the new constant being the minimal monotone functions validating the δ-rules listed above.

The following proposition is due to Plotkin ([11]):

Proposition 5 *For any type σ and any (finite) $x \in \mathcal{C}^{\sigma}$ there exists a closed term of PCF_{por} M_x such that $[\![M_x]\!]^{\mathcal{C}} = x$.*

It is easy to see that the extensional collapses of $\mathcal{L}$ and $\mathcal{C}$ relative to PCF and PCF_{por} coincide. In fact it is enough to check that the extensional collapse for PCF described in section 3.3, does provide a logical relation for PCF_{por}.

This is all we need in order to conclude that:

Proposition 6 *The extensional collapse $\mathcal{E}_{PCF}(\mathcal{L}, \mathcal{C})$ is surjective.*

Proof: Since $\mathcal{E}$ is directed complete, it is enough to prove the statement above for finite elements of $\mathcal{C}$.

Given σ and a finite $f \in \mathcal{C}^{\sigma}$, let M_f the PCF_{por} term given by proposition 5. By the basic lemma

$$[\![M_f]\!]^{\mathcal{L}} \mathcal{E}_{\text{PCF}}(\mathcal{L}, \mathcal{C})^{\sigma} [\![M_f]\!]^{\mathcal{C}} = f$$

and we are done. ∎

In order to prove that the inclusion $Th(\mathcal{L}) \subseteq Th(\mathcal{C})$ is strict, let us consider the following PCF-terms of type $B \to B$:

$$M_1 = \lambda x\ \Omega$$

$$M_2 = \lambda x\ if\ x\ \Omega\ \Omega$$

where Ω abbreviates $Y_B(\lambda x\ x)$.

$M_1 = M_2 \notin Th(\mathcal{L})$, since $[\![M_1]\!]^{\mathcal{L}}\top = \bot$ and $[\![M_2]\!]^{\mathcal{L}}\top = \top$, whereas it is easy to check that $[\![M_1]\!]^{\mathcal{C}} = [\![M_2]\!]^{\mathcal{C}} = \underline{\lambda} d\ \bot$.

Acknowledgements

This paper has been written during the author's stay at the Departement of Computing (Theory and Formal Methods section) of the Imperial College, funded by the projects Foundational Structures of Computer Science (EPSRC) and Categorical Logic in Computer Science II (CEE).

References

1. S. Abramsky, R. Jagadeesan, P. Malacaria. *Full abstraction for PCF (Extended Abstract).* Proc. of TACS 94, Lecure Notes in Computer Science 789, Springer, 1994.
2. G. Berry. *Stable models of typed lambda-calculi.* Proc. 5th Int. Coll. on Automata, Languages and Programming, Lecure Notes in Computer Science 62, Springer, 1978. LNCS 62, 1978.
3. A. Bucciarelli. *Logical relations and λ-theories.* Technical Report LIENS, Ecole Normale Supérieure. To appear.
4. A. Bucciarelli, T. Ehrhard. *Sequentiality in an extensional framework.* Information and Computation, Volume 110, Number 2, 1994.
5. P.L. Curien. *Categorical Combinators, Sequential Algorithms and Functional Programming.*Revised edition, Birkhäuser, 1993.
6. R. O. Gandy. *On the axiom of extensionality, part I.* J. of Symbolic Logic 21, 1956.
7. J.M.E. Hyland, L. Ong. *On full abstraction for PCF: I, II and III* (preliminary version, september 1995).
8. R. Milner. *Fully abstract models of typed lambda-calculi.* Theoretical Computer Science 4, 1-23, 1977.
9. J.C. Mitchell. *Type Systems for Programming Languages* Handbook of Theoretical Computer Science, edited by J. van Leeuwen, Elsevier, 1990.
10. P. O'Hearn, J. Riecke. *Kripke Logical Relations and PCF.* To appear in Information and Computation.
11. G. Plotkin. *LCF considered as a programming language.* Theoretical Computer Science 5, 223-256, 1977.
12. D. Scott. *A type theoretic alternative to OWHY, CHUC, ISWIM.* 1969, published in the special issue of Theoretical Computer Science dedicated to Professor C. Böhm's 70th birthday, 1993.
13. G. Winskel. *Stable Bistructure Models of PCF.* BRICS Report Series 94-13, Departement of Computer Science, University of Aarhus, 1994.

GAMMA AND THE LOGIC OF TRANSITION TRACES

S. J. GAY
Department of Computer Science,
Royal Holloway, University of London,
Egham, Surrey TW20 0EX, UK

C. L. HANKIN
Department of Computing,
Imperial College of Science, Technology and Medicine,
180 Queen's Gate, London SW7 2BZ, UK

Gamma is a language of conditional multiset rewrites, which can be seen either as a parallel programming language or as a specification language for parallel algorithms. Taking the latter view, we are interested in program refinement and formal techniques for reasoning about it. In the present paper we apply Abramsky's framework of ***domain theory in logical form***, to systematically develop a program logic for Gamma from a denotational semantics. Our semantics is a domain-theoretic reformulation of the ***transition trace semantics***, which was defined for Gamma by Sands and based on earlier work by Brookes. We obtain a logic and proof system which is sound for our chosen notion of operational approximation or refinement.

1 Introduction

The programming language Gamma was originally introduced by Banâtre and Le Métayer[2] and has been developed further by Hankin, Le Métayer and Sands.[5,6] Computation in Gamma consists of the application of conditional rewriting rules to a multiset of data elements. Such a rule takes the form

$$x_1, \ldots, x_n \rightarrow A(x_1, \ldots, x_n) \Leftarrow R(x_1, \ldots, x_n),$$

in which the *reaction condition* R is a predicate, and the *action* A maps a collection of data elements to the multiset of elements which will replace them. An application of this rule consists of finding, if possible, elements $x_1, \ldots, x_n$ of the multiset such that $R(x_1, \ldots, x_n)$ is true, and replacing them by the elements of $A(x_1, \ldots, x_n)$. This process is repeated until it is no longer possible to find suitable $x_1, \ldots, x_n$, at which point the computation ceases and the resulting multiset represents the answer. A single rewriting rule of this form, which may also be written $(A \Leftarrow R)$, is called a *basic reaction*. Compound programs can be built from basic reactions by means of sequential and parallel composition operators. In the parallel composition $P+Q$, reactions from either P or Q can be applied at any time, and the program terminates when a state is reached in which neither P nor Q can perform a rewrite. The sequential

$$\frac{a_1,\ldots,a_n \in M \qquad R(a_1,\ldots,a_n)}{\langle (A \Leftarrow R), M\rangle \to \langle (A \Leftarrow R), (M - \{\!|a_1,\ldots,a_n|\!\}) \uplus A(a_1,\ldots,a_n)\rangle}$$

$$\frac{\neg\exists a_1,\ldots,a_n \in M.R(a_1,\ldots,a_n)}{\langle (A \Leftarrow R), M\rangle \to M}$$

$$\frac{\langle Q, M\rangle \to M}{\langle P \circ Q, M\rangle \to \langle P, M\rangle} \qquad \frac{\langle Q, M\rangle \to \langle Q', M'\rangle}{\langle P \circ Q, M\rangle \to \langle P \circ Q', M'\rangle}$$

$$\frac{\langle P, M\rangle \to \langle P', M'\rangle}{\langle P + Q, M\rangle \to \langle P' + Q, M'\rangle} \qquad \frac{\langle Q, M\rangle \to \langle Q', M'\rangle}{\langle P + Q, M\rangle \to \langle P + Q', M'\rangle}$$

$$\frac{\langle P, M\rangle \to M \quad \langle Q, M\rangle \to M}{\langle P + Q, M\rangle \to M}$$

Figure 1: Operational Semantics of Gamma.

composition $Q \circ P$ behaves as P until a terminal state for P is reached, and then behaves as Q. Examples of programming using these operators can be found elsewhere.[2,4,5,6]

The version of Gamma considered in this paper only makes use of these operators, so that programs are defined by the grammar

$$P ::= (A \Leftarrow R) \mid P \circ P \mid P + P.$$

Other papers[5,6] have defined combinators called *tropes* which capture common styles of basic reaction, but the present study concentrates on the pure language.

The operational semantics of Gamma is defined in Figure 1. A nonterminal configuration $\langle P, M\rangle$ consists of a program P and a multiset M; a terminal configuration is simply a multiset M. We write $\to^*$ for the transitive closure of $\to$, and say that the configuration $\langle P, M\rangle$ *diverges*, written $\langle P, M\rangle \uparrow$, if there is an infinite sequence of transitions

$$\langle P, M\rangle \to \langle P_1, M_1\rangle \to \langle P_2, M_2\rangle \to \ldots$$

If Gamma is considered as a specification language, the question of program refinement becomes interesting: a program which is very abstract and close to a specification, can be refined into a program which captures a more detailed description of an algorithm and is closer to an implementation. For example, it may be desirable to refine a program containing a great deal of parallel composition into one which contains more sequential composition. For this reason, previous work on Gamma has studied various operational approximation relations with the aim of formulating general rules for program refinement.[5,6,7] The approximation relation which we will consider in this paper is defined as follows. First define, for any program P,

$$\begin{aligned} \mathcal{B}(P) &= \{(M,N) \mid \langle P,M\rangle \rightarrow^* N\} \\ &\cup \{(M,\bot) \mid \langle P,M\rangle\uparrow\}. \end{aligned}$$

This leads to an approximation relation on programs (the $\leqslant_R$ relation of Hankin *et al.* [5]) defined by $P \leqslant Q \iff \mathcal{B}(P) \subseteq \mathcal{B}(Q)$. Equivalently, $P \leqslant Q$ if and only if $\forall M,N.\langle P,M\rangle \rightarrow^* N \Rightarrow \langle Q,M\rangle \rightarrow^* N$. This is used in the standard way to define an observational precongruence, by demanding approximation in all program contexts $\mathbf{C}$: $P \sqsubseteq_o Q \iff \forall \mathbf{C}.\mathbf{C}[P] \leqslant \mathbf{C}[Q]$. The corresponding congruence is denoted by $\equiv_o$.

The purpose of the present paper is to study a formal system for reasoning about operational approximation and equivalence in Gamma—a program logic. This logic is derived systematically from a denotational semantics of Gamma, by means of Abramsky's framework of *domain theory in logical form*.[1] The semantics in question is the transition trace semantics, defined for Gamma by Sands[7] and based on earlier work by Brookes.[3] In fact, we need to work with a domain-theoretic reformulation of this semantics. According to Abramsky's theory, soundness of the logic follows from the fact that denotational approximation is sound for operational approximation.

2 The Transition Trace Semantics

The denotational semantics which has been defined for Gamma[5,6,7] is based on ideas of Brookes[3] relating to the semantics of shared-variable parallel languages. The meaning of a program P is a set of sequences of pairs of multisets:

$$(M_1,N_1)(M_2,N_2)\ldots$$

representing possible sequences of state transitions. Both finite and infinite sequences are included, to cater for terminating and nonterminating computations. The presence of the pair (M_1,N_1) indicates that there is a possible sequence of transitions $\langle P,M_1\rangle \rightarrow^* \langle P',N_1\rangle$; similarly there is a possible sequence of transitions $\langle P',M_2\rangle \rightarrow^* \langle P'',N_2\rangle$. The key feature of this style of semantics is that in general the states N_1 and M_2 are different, to allow for the fact that in between two applications of a rewrite from P, another program which has been placed in parallel with P may perform a rewrite of its own.

For the transition trace semantics to be useful, it should not distinguish between behaviours which only differ in trivial ways. For Gamma, this means considering sets of traces T which are closed under the following operations. Here, α ranges over finite sequences of multiset pairs, and β ranges over finite and infinite sequences.

$$\frac{\alpha\beta \in T \quad \beta \neq \epsilon}{\alpha(M,M)\beta \in T}\ \textbf{left-stuttering} \qquad \frac{\alpha(M,N)(N,M')\beta \in T}{\alpha(M,M')\beta \in T}\ \textbf{absorption}$$

Absorption corresponds to the fact that a program may perform an arbitrary sequence of transitions without interference from the environment. Conversely, stuttering corresponds to the fact that there may be arbitrary interference from the environment without any visible actions being performed by the program.

Let $\ddagger T$ denote the left-stuttering and absorption closure (henceforth just closure) of a set T. We now define the function $\mathsf{T}[\![\cdot]\!]$ which yields the finite and infinite sequences of pairs of multisets which can arise from a program. In the terminology of Hankin *et al.*[6] these are the *atomic* traces.

$$\begin{aligned} \mathsf{T}[\![P]\!] &= \{(M_0,N_0)(M_1,N_1)\ldots(M_k,N_k) \mid \langle P,M_0\rangle \to \langle P_1,N_0\rangle \\ &\qquad \&\langle P_1,M_1\rangle \to \langle P_1,N_1\rangle\&\ldots\&\langle P_k,M_k\rangle \to N_k\} \\ &\cup\ \{(M_0,N_0)(M_1,N_1)\ldots(M_i,N_i)\ldots \mid \\ &\qquad \langle P,M_0\rangle \to \langle P_1,N_0\rangle\&\langle P_i,M_i\rangle \to \langle P_{i+1},N_i\rangle, i \geq 1\}. \end{aligned}$$

The *transition traces* are then given by the closure of the atomic traces: $\ddagger\mathsf{T}[\![P]\!]$. This is the semantic function which we will use. It can be defined compositionally as follows.

$$\begin{aligned} \ddagger\mathsf{T}[\![(A \Leftarrow R)]\!] &= \ddagger((\mathsf{mediators}_{(A\Leftarrow R)})^* \mathbin{;} \mathsf{terminals}_{(A\Leftarrow R)} \\ &\quad \cup\ \ddagger(\mathsf{mediators}_{(A\Leftarrow R)})^\omega) \\ \ddagger\mathsf{T}[\![P \circ Q]\!] &= \ddagger(\ddagger\mathsf{T}[\![Q]\!] \mathbin{;} \ddagger\mathsf{T}[\![P]\!]) \\ \ddagger\mathsf{T}[\![P + Q]\!] &= \ddagger(\ddagger\mathsf{T}[\![P]\!] \oplus \ddagger\mathsf{T}[\![Q]\!]) \end{aligned}$$

The sets $\mathsf{mediators}_{(A\Leftarrow R)}$ and $\mathsf{terminals}_{(A\Leftarrow R)}$ are defined by

$$\begin{aligned} \mathsf{mediators}_{(A\Leftarrow R)} &= \{(M,N) \mid \langle (A \Leftarrow R), M\rangle \to \langle (A \Leftarrow R), N\rangle\} \\ \mathsf{terminals}_{(A\Leftarrow R)} &= \{(M,N) \mid \langle (A \Leftarrow R), M\rangle \to N\}. \end{aligned}$$

The operation $;$ on trace sets is defined by

$$T_1 \mathbin{;} T_2 = \{\alpha\beta \mid \alpha \in T_1, \beta \in T_2\}.$$

When α is infinite, $\alpha\beta = \alpha$. The definition of $\oplus$ is more complicated:

$$T_1 \oplus T_2 \quad = \quad \{\gamma \mid \alpha \in T_1, \beta \in T_2, \gamma \in \alpha \sharp \beta\}$$

where $\alpha \sharp \beta = \bigcup\{\mathbf{m}(\alpha, \beta) \mid \mathbf{m}$ is an ESM$\}$ and an *end-synchronised merger* (ESM) is a function $\mathbf{m}$ from pairs of non-empty traces to sets of non-empty traces such that

1. if $(M, N) \in \mathbf{m}(\beta, \gamma)$ then $\beta = \gamma = (M, N)$
2. if $\alpha \in \mathbf{m}(\beta, \gamma)$ then $(M, N)\alpha \in \mathbf{m}((M, N)\beta, \gamma)$ and $(M, N)\alpha \in \mathbf{m}(\gamma, (M, N)\beta)$.

Finally, the justification for this sequence of definitions is the following result.[6]

Proposition 2.1 $\ddagger\mathsf{T}[\![P]\!] \subseteq \ddagger\mathsf{T}[\![Q]\!] \Rightarrow P \sqsubseteq_o Q$.

We do not know whether the implication can be reversed, i.e. whether the transition trace semantics is fully abstract. Although Brookes has established full abstraction for transition trace semantics of other parallel languages,[3] his methods do not apply to Gamma. His proofs make essential use of the fact that for every state transition, there is a program which can perform that transition and no other. This is not true in the case of Gamma, because any multiset rewrite can also take place in the context of any larger multiset. More work is required to determine whether there is a different proof strategy which will apply to Gamma.

3 Domain Theory in Logical Form

Abramsky[1] has developed a very general framework for connecting denotational semantics and program logic. This framework will be described briefly here, before going on to apply it to Gamma.

Consider a typed language with a denotational semantics expressed in terms of some variety of domain: perhaps Scott domains or SFP domains. This means that for each type σ there is a domain $D(\sigma)$, and for each typed term $t : \sigma$ there is a corresponding element $[\![t]\!]$ of $D(\sigma)$. The language may have several type constructors, such as products or function spaces, and for each one there is a matching domain construction. This situation is very standard. The new dimension introduced by Abramsky's work is the association of a propositional theory $\mathcal{L}(\sigma)$ with each type σ. The formulae of $\mathcal{L}(\sigma)$ are the possible assertions about terms of type σ. Each theory has meets, joins and an ordering, giving it the structure of a distributive lattice. For each type constructor there is a construction on the propositional theories, and so this gives an alternative *logical* semantics of types. These constructions give extra formula constructions to the propositional theories. The logical view extends to the terms as well: for each type σ there is a satisfaction relation between terms of type σ and formulae in $\mathcal{L}(\sigma)$, and this satisfaction relation is axiomatised by a proof system. To make the framework as general as possible, Abramsky works with a typed metalanguage, which is a simply typed λ-calculus with additional term constructions for each type construction. The propositional theories relate to this metalanguage, and the proof system axiomatises satisfaction of properties by terms of the metalanguage. For any particular computational situation, the general theory is applied by expressing the desired denotational semantics in terms of a translation into the metalanguage and then specialising the logic to construct formulae relating to the particular combinations of constructions which have been used.

Of course, the whole point of this theory is that there is a very strong connection between the denotational semantics and the program logic. In addition to the notion of property arising from the logic, there is a semantic notion of property: a compact open subset of a domain. The set of terms whose denotations lie in a given compact open set is interpreted as the set of terms satisfying the corresponding property. Motivation for this view of compact open sets as properties can be found elsewhere[1] and comes primarily from notions of observability.

A similar shift of view on the logical side leads to consideration of the set of properties satisfied by a given term. Such a set X is closed under conjunction and implication ($\leq$) and inaccessible by joins: if $a \vee b \in X$ then either $a \in X$ or $b \in X$. This latter property expresses the fact that the logic is constructive. In terms of distributive lattices, such a set X is a prime filter.

Now for the connection between the denotational and logical views. For any domain D, the set of compact open sets ordered by inclusion forms a lattice $K\Omega(D)$. For any distributive lattice $\mathcal{L}$, the set of prime filters ordered by inclusion forms a domain $\mathsf{Spec}(\mathcal{L})$. For each type σ, the domain $D(\sigma)$ and the theory $\mathcal{L}(\sigma)$ are related in this way: $\mathcal{L}(\sigma) = K\Omega(D(\sigma))$ and $D(\sigma) = \mathsf{Spec}(\mathcal{L}(\sigma))$. This relationship is an instance of Stone duality.

This means that the set of all properties satisfied by a term corresponds to the denotation of the term, and this gives a logical characterisation of denotational equivalence. In fact, the logical characterisation operates at the level of the denotational order: $[\![t]\!] \sqsubseteq [\![u]\!]$ if and only if every property satisfied by t is satisfied by u. The full benefit of this correspondence is obtained when the denotational order coincides with an operational approximation relation, because then the logical system can be used to deduce facts about the operational behaviour of programs.

4 The Domain of Transition Trace Sets

We will now present a domain-theoretic reformulation of the transition trace semantics. For the remainder of the paper we will restrict attention to Gamma programs which operate on multisets of natural numbers; it will be clear that the theory can be generalised to multisets of any type.

The first requirement is a domain of sets of transition traces, that is, a domain whose elements are sets of finite and infinite sequences of pairs of multisets of natural numbers. This leads to the first problem—we do not know of a general construction of a domain of multisets over a given domain. Our solution is to observe that there is a countable set of finite multisets of natural numbers, assume some fixed enumeration of that set, and replace multisets by naturals in our domain. When we consider basic reactions, we will assume that the reaction conditions and actions are given in terms of the enumeration, and the proof system for our logic will assume the existence of a proof system for satisfaction of reaction conditions. The development of our logic will concentrate on features intrinsic to Gamma rather than the particular state space.

We will use the flat domain $\mathbb{N}$ of strict natural numbers, defined by $\mathbb{N} = \mathsf{rec}\, t.\mathbf{0} \oplus t$, where $\mathbf{0} = \mathbf{1}_\perp$, $\mathbf{1}$ is the one-point domain, and $\oplus$ is coalesced sum. Corresponding to this domain are the expected term constructions in the metalanguage: two introduction rules and an elimination rule. In all of the term construction rules in this section, variables should be explicitly typed; for convenience, we have omitted these types.

$$\frac{}{0 : \mathbb{N}} \qquad \frac{M : \mathbb{N}}{\mathsf{succ}(M) : \mathbb{N}} \qquad \frac{M : \mathbb{N} \quad N_1, N_2 : \nu}{\mathsf{case}\, M\, \mathsf{of}\, 0 \Rightarrow N_1\,;\, \mathsf{succ}(x) \Rightarrow N_2\, \mathsf{end} : \nu}$$

We also need the domain of booleans, defined by $\mathbb{B} = \mathbf{0} \oplus \mathbf{0}$, with the following term constructions.

$$\frac{}{\mathsf{true} : \mathbb{B}} \qquad \frac{}{\mathsf{false} : \mathbb{B}} \qquad \frac{M : \mathbb{B} \quad N_1, N_2 : \nu}{\mathsf{if}\, M\, \mathsf{then}\, N_1\, \mathsf{else}\, N_2\, \mathsf{end} : \nu}$$

The type constructor $\times$ is available, with these term constructions.

$$\frac{M : \sigma \quad N : \tau}{(M, N) : \sigma \times \tau} \qquad \frac{M : \sigma \times \tau \quad N : \nu}{\mathsf{let}\, M\, \mathsf{be}\, (x, y).N\, \mathsf{end} : \nu}$$

We will be interested in the type $\mathbb{N} \times \mathbb{N}$, representing state transitions.

Because the transition trace semantics involves both finite and infinite sequences of transitions, we use a domain constructor for lazy lists. In general,

$\mathsf{List}(\sigma)$ is defined by $\mathsf{List}(\sigma) = \mathsf{rec}\, t.\mathbf{1} + (\sigma \times t)$, where $+$ is separated sum. There are three term constructions.

$$\frac{}{\mathsf{nil} : \mathsf{List}(\sigma)} \qquad \frac{M : \sigma \quad N : \mathsf{List}(\sigma)}{M :: N : \mathsf{List}(\sigma)} \qquad \frac{M : \sigma \quad N_1, N_2 : \nu}{\mathsf{case}\, M\, \mathsf{of}\, \mathsf{nil} \Rightarrow N_1 \,;\, x :: y \Rightarrow N_2\, \mathsf{end} : \nu}$$

Finally, we use the Hoare (lower) powerdomain to give sets of transition traces. We will need the following metalanguage term constructions for $\mathcal{P}_l(\sigma)$.

$$\frac{M : \sigma}{\{M\}_P : \mathcal{P}_l(\sigma)} \qquad \frac{M, N : \mathcal{P}_l(\sigma)}{M \cup_P N : \mathcal{P}_l(\sigma)} \qquad \frac{M : \mathcal{P}_l(\sigma) \quad N : \mathcal{P}_l(\tau)}{\mathsf{over}\, M\, \mathsf{extend}\, x.N\, \mathsf{end} : \mathcal{P}_l(\tau)}$$

The domain of transition trace sets is $\mathsf{T} = \mathcal{P}_l(\mathsf{List}(\mathbb{N} \times \mathbb{N}))$.

Following Abramsky[1] we interpret types as SFP domains, and metalanguage terms as functions on these domains. The behaviour of these functions is as expected; one which may be unfamiliar is $\mathsf{over}\, M\, \mathsf{extend}\, x.N\, \mathsf{end}$, whose meaning is essentially $\bigcup\{N[a/x] \mid a \in M\}$.

Now that the metalanguage is available, defining the domain-theoretic semantics becomes a matter of programming the operations used in the original definitions. For sequential composition we need to extend the append function (defined as usual) to sets of lists. Note that the behaviour of append with an infinite first argument is to ignore the second argument, which is precisely what we need for the sequential composition of an infinite trace with a finite trace. For parallel composition we need the function syncmerge, which does end-synchronised merging. For a basic reaction $(A \Leftarrow R)$ we need to assume the existence of functions $\bar{R} : \mathbb{N} \to \mathbb{B}$, which tests the reaction condition, and $\bar{A} : \mathbb{N} \to \mathcal{P}_l(\mathbb{N})$, which returns the set of possible rewritten states. Then the functions mediators and terminals can be programmed, along with omega which computes all finite and infinite iterations of lists from a given set. For all the cases, stuttering and absorption closure (functions stutter and absorb) are also needed; it can be shown that applying stutter and absorb separately is sufficient to give the stuttering and absorption closure.

Defining these functions is an exercise in functional programming, and we have omitted the details. The final definition of the domain-theoretic transition trace semantics is

$$\begin{aligned}
[\![(A \Leftarrow R)]\!] &= \mathsf{stutter}\,(\,\mathsf{absorb}\,(\,\mathsf{seq}\,(\,\mathsf{omega}\,(\,\mathsf{mediators}\,(\bar{A}, \bar{R})),\\
&\qquad \mathsf{terminals}\,(\bar{R}))))\\
[\![Q \circ P]\!] &= \mathsf{stutter}\,(\,\mathsf{absorb}\,(\,\mathsf{seq}\,([\![P]\!], [\![Q]\!])))\\
[\![P + Q]\!] &= \mathsf{stutter}\,(\,\mathsf{absorb}\,(\,\mathsf{par}\,([\![P]\!], [\![Q]\!]))).
\end{aligned}$$

5 Extracting the Domain Logic

According to the framework of domain theory in logical form, each type σ generates a corresponding language of formulae $L(\sigma)$, which is then made into a logical theory $\mathcal{L}(\sigma)$ by imposing an order $\leqslant$, corresponding to implication, and subjecting it to certain axioms. We can now describe the steps leading to the definition of the theory $\mathcal{L}(\mathsf{T})$. Rather than present the fully general definitions of $\mathcal{L}(\sigma)$ for each type constructor,[1] we specialise them to our situation.

First of all, there are formulae at each type corresponding to truth, falsity, conjunction and disjunction.

$$t, f \in L(\sigma) \qquad \frac{\phi, \psi \in L(\sigma)}{\phi \wedge \psi, \phi \vee \psi \in L(\sigma)}$$

In $L(\mathbb{N})$ there are formulae corresponding to the properties of "being zero" and "being successor of something satisfying a given property".

$$0 \in L(\mathbb{N}) \qquad \frac{\phi \in L(\mathbb{N})}{\mathsf{succ}(\phi) \in L(\mathbb{N})}$$

Note that we use, for example, $\mathsf{succ}(0)$ for both the metalanguage term denoting 1 and the formula representing the property of being equal to 1. Which meaning is intended should always be clear from the context.

In $L(\mathbb{N} \times \mathbb{N})$ there are formulae corresponding to properties of the form "being a pair whose components satisfy given properties".

$$\frac{\phi, \psi \in L(\mathbb{N})}{\phi \times \psi \in L(\mathbb{N} \times \mathbb{N})}$$

Similarly, $L(\mathsf{List}(\mathbb{N} \times \mathbb{N}))$ has formula constructions corresponding to the metalanguage term constructions.

$$\mathsf{nil} \in L(\mathsf{List}(\mathbb{N} \times \mathbb{N})) \qquad \frac{\phi \in L(\mathbb{N} \times \mathbb{N}) \quad \psi \in L(\mathsf{List}(\mathbb{N} \times \mathbb{N}))}{\phi :: \psi \in L(\mathsf{List}(\mathbb{N} \times \mathbb{N}))}$$

If $\phi, \psi \in L(\mathsf{List}(\sigma))$ we will write $\phi\psi$ for the formula obtained by concatenating ϕ and ψ.

The Hoare powerdomain introduces the *may* modality $\Diamond$.

$$\frac{\phi \in L(\mathsf{List}(\mathbb{N} \times \mathbb{N}))}{\Diamond\phi \in L(\mathcal{P}_l(\mathsf{List}(\mathbb{N} \times \mathbb{N})))}$$

If $\phi \in L(\mathsf{List}(\mathbb{N} \times \mathbb{N}))$, i.e. ϕ is a property which a list could satisfy, then $\Diamond\phi \in L(\mathcal{P}_l(\mathsf{List}(\mathbb{N} \times \mathbb{N})))$ is a property which a set of lists could satisfy: namely, the property of containing at least one element satisfying ϕ.

In each case, more general formulae can be constructed by means of conjunction and disjunction.

For each σ there is a relation $\leqslant$ on $L(\sigma)$, which is to be thought of as logical consequence. Various axioms are imposed, and $\mathcal{L}(\sigma)$ consists of equivalence classes of formulae under the equivalence defined by $\phi = \psi \iff (\phi \leqslant \psi$ and $\psi \leqslant \phi)$. The first group of axioms, present for every σ, give $\mathcal{L}(\sigma)$ a distributive lattice structure with t, f as top and bottom elements and $\wedge$, $\vee$ as meet and join. There are also various type-specific axioms, which describe how the distributive lattice structure interacts with formula constructors such as $\mathsf{succ}(\cdot)$ and $\Diamond$. They can be summarised as follows: each constructor is monotonic with respect to $\leqslant$, and each constructor commutes with arbitrary joins.

6 The Proof System

The general framework of domain theory in logical form includes, for each type σ, a proof system for a satisfaction relation between metalanguage terms of type σ and properties in $\mathcal{L}(\sigma)$. This means that the proof system for our Gamma logic can be derived systematically by specialising the general proof rules to the particular metalanguage terms used to define the semantics. Not surprisingly, the derivations are rather long and involved. An easier approach is to take a higher-level look at our metalanguage programs, formulate the proof rules which we expect to obtain, and then check that they really are valid. In the present paper we are omitting the detailed verifications, for reasons of space.

Because the transition trace sets are closed under stuttering and absorption, we obtain proof rules for stuttering and absorption, as follows.

$$\frac{P \vdash \Diamond(\theta\psi)}{P \vdash \Diamond(\theta(\phi,\phi)\psi)}\ \psi \neq \mathsf{nil} \qquad\qquad \frac{P \vdash \Diamond(a(\phi,\psi)(\psi,\theta)b)}{P \vdash \Diamond(a(\phi,\theta)b)}$$

To formulate the proof rules for parallel and sequential composition, it is convenient to define operations of parallel and sequential composition on formulae.

$$\frac{P \vdash \phi \quad Q \vdash \psi}{Q \circ P \vdash \psi \circ \phi} \qquad\qquad \frac{P \vdash \phi \quad Q \vdash \psi}{P + Q \vdash \phi \parallel \psi}$$

To define the formula $\psi \circ \phi$, first assume without loss of generality that $\phi =$

$\bigvee_i \diamond\phi_i$ and $\psi = \bigvee_j \diamond\psi_j$ with each ϕ_i, ψ_j a list of pairs of formulae. Then

$$\psi \circ \phi \quad = \quad \bigvee_{i,j} \diamond\psi_j \circ \phi_i \qquad\qquad \phi \parallel \psi \quad = \quad \bigvee_{i,j} \bigwedge_\theta \diamond\theta$$

where $\psi_j \circ \phi_i$ is defined by appending lists of pairs and θ ranges over end-synchronised merges of ϕ and ψ.

For a basic reaction there are two rules, the first corresponding to the **terminals** part of the semantic definition, and the second allowing any number of steps corresponding to **mediators** to be added.

$$\frac{\phi \Rightarrow \neg R}{(A \Leftarrow R) \vdash \diamond(\phi, \phi)} \qquad\qquad \frac{\phi \Rightarrow R \quad A(\phi) \Rightarrow \psi \quad (A \Leftarrow R) \vdash \diamond\theta}{(A \Leftarrow R) \vdash \diamond((\phi, \psi)\theta)}$$

The hypothesis $\phi \Rightarrow \neg R$ means $\forall M.M \vdash \phi \Rightarrow \neg\exists\bar{x} \subseteq M.R(\bar{x})$, where M ranges over multisets. The combined hypothesis $\phi \Rightarrow R, A(\phi) \Rightarrow \psi$ means $\forall M.[M \vdash \phi \Rightarrow \exists\bar{x} \subseteq M.[R(\bar{x}) \wedge M[A(\bar{x})/\bar{x}] \vdash \psi]]$. We need to assume the existence of a proof system for establishing such assertions. Given a sound and complete proof system for these assertions, Abramsky's general results on domain logic yield the following.

Proposition 6.1 $\forall\phi.[P \vdash \phi \Rightarrow Q \vdash \phi] \iff \ddagger\mathsf{T}[\![P]\!] \subseteq \ddagger\mathsf{T}[\![Q]\!]$.

Combined with Proposition 2.1, we obtain:

Proposition 6.2 $\forall\phi.[P \vdash \phi \Rightarrow Q \vdash \phi] \Rightarrow P \sqsubseteq_o Q$.

7 Conclusions

Starting with a domain-theoretic reformulation of the transition trace semantics of Gamma, we have applied Abramsky's framework of domain theory in logical form to obtain a program logic. This logic is sound for our chosen notion of operational approximation or refinement, for quite general reasons. Our only assumption is the existence of a proof system for establishing appropriate properties of multisets, in particular the existence or non-existence of collections of elements satisfying given reaction conditions.

It would be very satisfying to eliminate this assumption, by deriving a logic of multisets in the same systematic way. This would require a general domain constructor for multisets; if such a constructor could be developed, we would be able to modify our domain of transition traces to include the details of the multiset level. However, there is another potential difficulty: in the proof rule which establishes the termination of a basic reaction, there is a negative hypothesis (the non-existence of a reacting collection of elements). This negative hypothesis appears to be at odds with the generally intuitionistic nature of domain logic; it remains to be seen whether or not it would be a genuine problem. In any case, our present technique of working with an enumeration of the set of finite multisets seems to yield a convenient level of generality; it also means that we may be able to adapt our logic to other languages which have been given transition trace semantics.

Another open question is that of full abstraction of the transition trace semantics. In situations where the semantics is fully abstract, domain theory in logical form produces stronger results, i.e. the exact logical characterisation of operational approximation. More work is needed in order to settle the full abstraction question for Gamma.

Acknowledgements

The research described in this paper was supported by Esprit Basic Research Project 9102 (Coordination). The authors would like to thank Dusko Pavlović and Sebastian Hunt for their comments and suggestions.

References

1. S. Abramsky. Domain theory in logical form. *Annals of Pure and Applied Logic*, 51:1–77, 1991.
2. J.-P. Banâtre and D. Le Métayer. The GAMMA model and its discipline of programming. *Science of Computer Programming*, 15:55–77, 1990.
3. S. D. Brookes. Full abstraction for a shared variable parallel language. In *Proceedings, Eighth Annual IEEE Symposium on Logic in Computer Science*, pages 98–109. IEEE Computer Society Press, 1993.
4. L. Errington, C. L. Hankin, and T. P. Jensen. Reasoning about Gamma programs. In G. L. Burn, S. J. Gay, and M. D. Ryan, editors, *Theory and Formal Methods 1993: Proceedings of the First Imperial College Department of Computing Workshop on Theory and Formal Methods*, Workshops in Computing. Springer-Verlag, 1993.
5. C. L. Hankin, D. Le Métayer, and D. Sands. A calculus of Gamma programs. Technical Report 672, INRIA-RENNES, October 1992.
6. C. L. Hankin, D. Le Métayer, and D. Sands. The coordination language Gamma: Semantics and transformation. Submitted, 1995.
7. D. Sands. Laws of parallel synchronised termination. In G. L. Burn, S. J. Gay, and M. D. Ryan, editors, *Theory and Formal Methods 1993: Proceedings of the First Imperial College Department of Computing Workshop on Theory and Formal Methods*, Workshops in Computing. Springer-Verlag, 1993.

HOW LINEAR IS HOWE?

ROY L. CROLE

Department of Mathematics and Computer Science, University of Leicester, University Road, LEICESTER, LE1 7RH, United Kingdom.

In recent years there has been much progress in the use of operationally based methods for reasoning about programs. Notions such as contextual equivalence and bisimilarity, which are historically more usually associated with functional programming and concurrency respectively, have been shown to be very closely connected, and such connections can be seen throughout the functional, concurrent and indeed imperative paradigms. In this paper we show that operational techniques from these three settings also apply in a *linear* functional setting, by proving that in a simple linear type theory involving function types and tensor types, one can establish *linear* contextual equivalences by coinductive techniques.

1 Introduction

During the past five or so years, many advances in the theory and practice of operational methods for proving program equivalences have been made. Many of the fundamental ideas which are employed in the underlying theory originated in the world of concurrency [1]. Abramsky [2] was the first person to investigate such ideas in the setting of functional programming. A technique which underpins the work in this paper originated with Howe[3]. This technique has been significantly refined and adapted by Gordon [4], Pitts [5], Sands [6] and others, and the results presented in this paper have been developed using ideas from those in loc. cit.

In this paper we study a linear type theory whose equational theories correspond to autonomous categories. Here we shall not be concerned with such equational theories, but instead with an operational semantics for the expressions of the linear type theory. Such operational notions are discussed by Abramsky [7]. In this work, Abramsky notes that the expressions of a linear type theory have a natural operational evaluation strategy, which possesses a mixture of both lazy and eager computations. While his observations are very persuasive, there are no absolute reasons for utilising the strategies he suggests. Ironically, for the fragment of linear type theory considered in this paper, the "natural" evaluation strategy would be eager (see Abramsky [7]), but we shall only study lazy evaluations, as this simplifies the technical details of many of the proofs. However, our results remain true for eager evaluations.

Why are we studying a linear system? Linearity has proved to be a useful framework for discussions of resource control and optimisation in Computer Science. As such it seems sensible to think about methods for reasoning about linear systems. That is our aim here, and on the way to our result, it is interesting to note many of the more delicate technical issues which arise due to linearity constraints.

The structure of the paper is as follows: In Section 2 we define the linear type theory we wish to study. In Section 3 we define a linear contextual preorder. In Section 4 we define similarity for the linear type theory. In Section 5 we show that similarity is a linear precongruence, and prove our main theorem, namely that the linear contextual preorder contains similarity. In the final section we draw our conclusions. Finally, note that due to shortage of space, many ideas and proofs are only sketched; unfortunately one of the points of this paper is to illustrate technical problems due to linearity, and these too are only sketched.

2 A Linear Type Theory

We shall specify a linear type theory by giving its types, expressions, a type assignment relation, and a (lazy) evaluation semantics. The set of (linear) types is given by the grammar $\sigma ::= I \mid \sigma \multimap \sigma \mid \sigma \otimes \sigma$. The set of **terms** is defined by the following grammar:

$$M ::= x \mid \lambda x.M \mid M\,M \mid * \mid M \otimes M \mid \mathsf{split}\ M\ \mathsf{as}\ x \otimes x\ \mathsf{in}\ M$$

We define the notion of a *bound* or *binding* occurrence of any variable v in any term T as follows: Let M and S range over expressions, and v and x over variables. An occurrence of a variable v in a term T is **binding** if the occurrence is in a subterm of the form $\lambda v.S$ or $\mathsf{split}\ M\ \mathsf{as}\ v \otimes x\ \mathsf{in}\ S$ or $\mathsf{split}\ M\ \mathsf{as}\ x \otimes v\ \mathsf{in}\ S$ and moreover the occurrence is not in M or S. In each case, S is the **scope** of v. An occurrence of a variable v in a term T is **bound** if it occurs in a subterm of the form $\lambda v.S$ or $\mathsf{split}\ M\ \mathsf{as}\ v \otimes x\ \mathsf{in}\ S$ or $\mathsf{split}\ M\ \mathsf{as}\ x \otimes v\ \mathsf{in}\ S$, and v is not a binding occurrence. An occurrence of v in T is **free** if it is neither binding nor bound.

The terms described in this paper require a very careful treatment of variable binding and substitution. We could adopt a Martin-Löf style metalanguage[8] for the presentation of the expressions of our type theory, but the details are omitted due to space constraints. Using such a metalanguage it is standard to define a **simultaneous substitution function** whose action is denoted by

$$(N, M_1, \ldots, M_n, x_1, \ldots, x_n) \mapsto N[M_1, \ldots, M_n/x_1, \ldots, x_n]$$

where $N[M_1, \ldots, M_n/x_1, \ldots, x_n]$ is a term described as "the term N with the (finite list) of terms $M_1, \ldots, M_n$ simultaneously replacing the (finite list) of variables $x_1, \ldots, x_n$". We shall sometimes write $N[M_i/x_i]$ when the meaning is clear. Given the existence of the substitution function, one can then inductively define $\sim_\alpha$**-equivalence** of terms (see for example Pitts [9] or Crole [10]).

As usual, an **environment** Γ is a list of (variable, type) pairs in which each of the variables is required to be distinct. A typical environment will be written $x_1 : \sigma_1, \ldots, x_n : \sigma_n$. We shall define a **type assignment** relation which takes the form $\Gamma \vdash M : \sigma$. The (obvious/usual) rules are omitted from this report—see for example [7]. We shall let $Exp_\sigma(\Gamma)$ denote the set of terms which can be assigned the type σ in the environment Γ, identified up to $\sim_\alpha$-equivalence. We shall write $M : \sigma$ instead of $[\,] \vdash M : \sigma$ and we write Exp_σ instead of $Exp_\sigma([\,])$. Given that Γ and Δ are environments, we shall write Γ, Δ to mean that the latter is indeed a valid environment (so in particular that $var(\Gamma) \cap var(\Delta) = \varnothing$). We shall write M for both a term and the expression which it represents, as is the usual practice. The following is crucial for the results in this paper, and its proof requires the use of simultaneous substitution. The proof is also quite delicate due to linearity, but space prevents a detailed exposition.

Theorem 2.1 If Γ, Δ is an environment, then there is a well-defined function of the form $Exp_\tau(\Gamma, x : \sigma) \times Exp_\sigma(\Delta) \longrightarrow Exp_\tau(\Gamma, \Delta)$ whose action is written $(M, N) \mapsto M[N/x]$.

Lemma 2.2 For any type assignment $\Gamma \vdash M : \sigma$, $fv(M) = var(\Gamma)$.

We shall now define a notion of a *program*, *value* and an evaluation relation style *operational semantics*. The intuition and motivation for these concepts is now quite standard (see for example Abramsky [7] or Crole [10]) and so we just give the definitions. A **program** (of type σ) is an element of Exp_σ for some type σ; P and Q range over programs. The set of **values** is given by those V generated by the grammar $V ::= * \mid P \otimes Q \mid \lambda x.M$ which are themselves programs (of some type σ). We define the lazy evaluation relation $\Downarrow$ between the set of all programs and the set of all values, with typical relationships denoted by $P \Downarrow V$, by the usual rules which are omitted.

3 Contextual Equivalence

We introduce a notion of contextual equivalence in a linear setting. The fundamental notion of a program context as some code with a hole is used here, but contexts are required to possess a single hole. However, because of the constraints linearity imposes on the occurrences of variables in expressions, we

Table 1: Examples of Rules for Generating Linear Contexts $\Gamma \vdash^{\beta}_{\eta} C : \sigma$

$$\frac{}{[\,] \vdash^{[\,]}_{[\,]} -_{\rho} : \rho} \qquad \frac{\Delta, x{:}\sigma_1, y{:}\sigma_2 \vdash^{\beta}_{\eta} C : \sigma}{\Gamma, \Delta \vdash^{\beta}_{\eta, x:\sigma_1, y:\sigma_2} \mathsf{split}\ M\ \mathsf{as}\ x \otimes y\ \mathsf{in}\ C : \sigma}\ [\Gamma \vdash M : \sigma_1 \otimes \sigma_2]$$

$$\frac{\Delta \vdash^{\beta}_{\eta} C : \sigma}{\Gamma, \Delta \vdash^{\beta, x:\sigma_1, y:\sigma_2}_{\eta} \mathsf{split}\ M\ \mathsf{as}\ x \otimes y\ \mathsf{in}\ C : \sigma}\ [\Gamma \vdash M : \sigma_1 \otimes \sigma_2,\ x, y \notin \Delta,\ x, y \notin \eta](\dagger)$$

$$\frac{\Gamma \vdash^{\beta}_{\eta} C : \sigma}{\Gamma, \Delta \vdash^{\beta}_{\eta} \mathsf{split}\ C\ \mathsf{as}\ x \otimes y\ \mathsf{in}\ M : \sigma}\ [\Delta, x{:}\sigma_1, y{:}\sigma_2 \vdash M : \sigma]$$

have to be extremely careful in our definition of an "expression with a hole". We first define *pre-contexts* which are un-typed templates for typed contexts: A **pre-context** is given by the grammar

$$C ::= -_{\rho} \mid \lambda x.C \mid C\,M \mid M\,C \mid C \otimes M \mid M \otimes C \mid \mathsf{split}\ C\ \mathsf{as}\ x \otimes y\ \mathsf{in}\ M \mid \mathsf{split}\ M\ \mathsf{as}\ x \otimes y\ \mathsf{in}\ C$$

where ρ ranges over the linear types, and M over terms. A **linear context** is one which takes the form $\Gamma \vdash^{\beta}_{\eta} C : \sigma$ and is generated by rules such as those in Table 1. In reading the rules, they apply only when any Γ or β is an environment. Each η is a list of (variable,type) pairs, but need not be an environment. The intended meaning of a linear context $\Gamma \vdash^{\beta}_{\eta} C : \sigma$ is that C denotes a linear expression with one hole (denoted by $-_{\rho}$) whose free variables are exactly those appearing in Γ. For each $\Gamma \vdash^{\beta}_{\eta} C : \sigma$ the following statements hold:

• β is an environment which lists exactly those binding variables whose scope includes $-_{\rho}$ but whose scope does not include any occurrence of the binding variable. We call the variables in β **context binding variables**.

• Each η is a list of (variable, type) pairs which lists each binding variable v whose scope includes $-_{\rho}$ *and* one bound occurrence of the binding variable v.

Each η only plays a role in the construction of linear contexts, ensuring that under appropriate conditions we can substitute a (representative of) a linear expression for a hole and guarantee that a linear type assignment results. Each β lists those variables which, if they occur free in an expression and the expression is substituted for $-_{\rho}$, will become bound in the resulting expression.

These ideas are made precise in the next lemma, in which if $\mathcal{C}$ is a pre-context with a hole $-_\rho$, which we denote by $\mathcal{C}[-_\rho]$, and $M = [T]_{\sim_\alpha}$ is an expression of type ρ, $\mathcal{C}[M]$ denotes the expression given by $[\mathcal{C}[T]]_{\sim_\alpha}$ where $\mathcal{C}[T]$ means "replace the hole $-_\rho$ by the term T".

Lemma 3.1 For any linear context of the form $\Gamma \vdash^\beta_\eta \mathcal{C}[-_\rho] : \tau$ and expression $M \in \mathit{Exp}_\rho(\beta, \Delta)$, where Γ, Δ and η, Δ, we have $\mathcal{C}[M] \in \mathit{Exp}_\tau(\Gamma, \Delta)$.

Proof Induction on the derivation of the linear context. We illustrate for the rule (†). Let us suppose that we have

$$\beta, x{:}\, \sigma_1, y{:}\, \sigma_2, \Theta \vdash M' : \rho \qquad (\Gamma, \Delta), \Theta \ \ldots (1) \qquad \eta, \Theta$$

It follows from the well-formedness of the environments, and the assumption that $x, y \notin \mathit{var}(\Delta)$ and $x, y \notin \mathit{var}(\eta)$ for each instance of (†), that

$$\Delta, (x{:}\, \sigma_1, y{:}\, \sigma_2, \Theta) \qquad \eta, (x{:}\, \sigma_1, y{:}\, \sigma_2, \Theta)$$

Thus by induction we have $\Delta, x{:}\, \sigma_1, y{:}\, \sigma_2, \Theta \vdash \mathcal{C}[M'] : \sigma$, and so using (1), and the rules for linear type assignments (including exchange) we may deduce

$$\Gamma, \Delta, \Theta \vdash \mathsf{split}\ M\ \mathsf{as}\ x \otimes y\ \mathsf{in}\ \mathcal{C}[M'] : \sigma$$

□

Corollary 3.2 For any linear context of the form $[\,] \vdash^\beta_\eta \mathcal{C}[-_\rho] : \tau$ and type assignment of the form $\beta \vdash M : \rho$, we have $\mathcal{C}[M] : \tau$.

For any program P, $P \Downarrow$ means $\exists V. P \Downarrow V$. We now write $\Gamma \vdash M \leq M' {:}\, \sigma$ just in case

(i) $\Gamma \vdash M : \sigma$ and $\Gamma \vdash M' : \sigma$; and

(ii) for all linear contexts of the form $[\,] \vdash^\Gamma_\eta \mathcal{C}[-_\sigma] : \tau$, we have $\mathcal{C}[M] \Downarrow$ implies $\mathcal{C}[M'] \Downarrow$.

We have thus defined a family of relations $(\leq_{\Gamma,\sigma} \subseteq \mathit{Exp}_\sigma(\Gamma) \times \mathit{Exp}_\sigma(\Gamma) \mid \Gamma, \sigma)$ which we refer to as the **linear contextual preorder**. If $(M, M') \in \leq_{\Gamma,\sigma}$ we say that M is **contextually below** M'. We now aim to give an alternative, coinductive method for establishing instances of the linear contextual preorder.

4 Similarity

We can define a notion of **similarity**, denoted by $\preccurlyeq$, which is a type indexed family of binary relations between programs of the same type:

$$\preccurlyeq \ = (\ \preccurlyeq_\sigma \ \mid \sigma) \in \Pi_\sigma \mathcal{P}(\mathit{Exp}_\sigma \times \mathit{Exp}_\sigma)$$

Note that when the powerset is given the inclusion partial order, it becomes a complete lattice, and thus the product set is a complete lattice with the pointwise partial order—we use $\lhd$ to denote the order on the product. The definition of $\precsim$ is given by the greatest pre-fixed point of a certain monotone function of the form $\Phi : \Pi_\sigma \mathcal{P}(Exp_\sigma \times Exp_\sigma) \longrightarrow \Pi_\sigma \mathcal{P}(Exp_\sigma \times Exp_\sigma)$ and as usual such a pre-fixed point exists by the Knaster-Tarski theorem. Given any $R \in \Pi_\sigma \mathcal{P}(Exp_\sigma \times Exp_\sigma)$, we define $\Phi(R)$ by the following clauses:

- $P\Phi(R)_I P' \iff P \Downarrow * \Longrightarrow P' \Downarrow *$.
- $P\Phi(R)_{\sigma \multimap \sigma'} P' \iff$

$$(\exists M.P \Downarrow \lambda x.M) \Longrightarrow ((\exists N.P' \Downarrow \lambda x.N) \text{ and } (\forall Q.\ M[Q/x]\ R_{\sigma'}\ N[Q/x])).$$

- $P\Phi(R)_{\sigma_1 \otimes \sigma_2} P' \iff (\exists P_1, P_2.P \Downarrow P_1 \otimes P_2) \Longrightarrow (\exists P_1', P_2'.P' \Downarrow P_1' \otimes P_2'$ and $P_1\ R_{\sigma_1}\ P_1'$ and $P_2\ R_{\sigma_2}\ P_2')$.

This kind of definition is becoming standard—see for example Crole and Gordon [11], Gordon [4], or Pitts [5]. It is easy to verify that Φ is monotone, and thus we can define $\precsim \stackrel{\text{def}}{=} \nu R.\Phi(R)$. We thus have a principle of **coinduction**: in order to prove that for any set A we have $A \lhd \precsim$, all we need to prove is that $A \lhd \Phi(A)$.

Proposition 4.1 For every type σ, $\precsim_\sigma$ is a preorder.

Proof We can prove that $Id_{\Pi_\sigma \mathcal{P}(Exp_\sigma \times Exp_\sigma)} \lhd \precsim$ and $(\precsim \circ \precsim) \lhd \precsim$ by coinduction, which is precisely that $\precsim$ is a preorder. □

We write $\Gamma \vdash M \precsim^\circ M' : \sigma$ just in case

(i) $\Gamma \vdash M : \sigma$ and $\Gamma \vdash M' : \sigma$; and

(ii) $\forall P_i \in Exp_{\sigma_i}.\ M[P_i/x_i] \precsim_\sigma M'[P_i/x_i]$, where the types σ_i are those appearing in Γ.

We have thus defined a family of relations $(\precsim^\circ_{\Gamma,\sigma} \subseteq Exp_\sigma(\Gamma) \times Exp_\sigma(\Gamma) \mid \Gamma, \sigma)$ which we refer to as **open similarity**. If $(M, M') \in \precsim^\circ_{\Gamma,\sigma}$ we say that M is **similar** to M'.

The main theorem is that the linear contextual preorder contains open similarity:

Theorem 4.2 For all Γ, M, M' and σ, we have $\Gamma \vdash M \precsim^\circ M' : \sigma$ implies $\Gamma \vdash M \leq M' : \sigma$.

We prove this by: Defining linear precongruence; defining a Howe relation; proving some properties of the Howe relation; deducing that the Howe relation and open similarity coincide; finally deducing that similarity is a linear precongruence and thus that the linear contextual preorder contains open similarity (at each type). *Note: Proofs are only sketched, or even omitted when routine.*

5 Linear Precongruence of Similarity

The major step in proving Theorem 4.2 in a non-linear setting involves a proof that similarity is a precongruence using methods due to Howe[3], [12] and Gordon[13]. However, the usual definition of precongruence is intimately tied to the properties of weakening, substitution and strengthening (the latter is usually derivable—see page 36 of[5]). In a linear setting we shall work with *linear precongruence.* This is similar to the usual notion of precongruence, but the weakening and strengthening requirements are dropped, and the usual substitution properties are modified.

Remark 5.1 In a non-linear setting the strengthening property is crucial to the proof that similarity is a precongruence—it amounts to the inductive base case in the proof of (the non-linear analogue of) Lemma 5.8. In such systems in which not all types are inhabited, strengthening is included as an explicit property in the definition of precongruence. (If all types are inhabited, it happens to be a derivable property.) In this paper, not all types are inhabited. However, the lack of strengthening is not a problem in the non-linear setting because linear contexts explicitly list their binding variables. Thus strengthening is not required in the base case of the proof of Lemma 5.8.

A family of binary relations of the form $(R_{\Gamma,\sigma} \subseteq Exp_\sigma(\Gamma) \times Exp_\sigma(\Gamma) \mid \Gamma, \sigma)$, for which we shall write $\Gamma \vdash M \; R \; M' : \sigma$ instead of $(M, M') \in R_{\Gamma,\sigma}$ and $M \; R_\sigma \; M'$ instead of $(M, M') \in R_{[\,],\sigma}$, is called a **linear precongruence** if:

(a) For any type assignment $\Gamma \vdash M : \sigma$ and relationship $\Delta, x{:}\,\sigma \vdash N \; R \; N' : \sigma'$ where Γ, Δ, we have $\Gamma, \Delta \vdash N[M/x] \; R \; N'[M/x] : \sigma'$.

(b) For any type assignment of the form $\Delta, x{:}\,\sigma \vdash N : \sigma'$ and relationship $\Gamma \vdash M \; R \; M' : \sigma$ where Γ, Δ, we have $\Gamma, \Delta \vdash N[M/x] \; R \; N[M'/x] : \sigma'$.

(c) For any $\Gamma \vdash M : \sigma$ we have $\Gamma \vdash M \; R \; M : \sigma$.

(d) For any $\Gamma \vdash M \; R \; M' : \sigma$ and $\Gamma \vdash M' \; R \; M'' : \sigma$ we have $\Gamma \vdash M \; R \; M'' : \sigma$.

(e) For any $\Gamma, x{:}\,\sigma \vdash M \; R \; M' : \sigma'$ we have $\Gamma \vdash \lambda x.M \; R \; \lambda x.M' : \sigma \multimap \sigma'$.

(f) For any $\Gamma \vdash M \; R \; M' : \sigma_1 \otimes \sigma_2$ and $\Delta, x{:}\,\sigma_1, y{:}\,\sigma_2 \vdash N \; R \; N' : \sigma$ where Γ, Δ we have $\Gamma, \Delta \vdash \mathsf{split}\ M\ \mathsf{as}\ x \otimes y\ \mathsf{in}\ N \; R \; \mathsf{split}\ M'\ \mathsf{as}\ x \otimes y\ \mathsf{in}\ N' : \sigma$.

(g) The remaining properties of being a precongruence hold (see page 35 of[5]) but modified for linear environments.

Table 2: Examples of Rules Generating the Howe Relation $\Gamma \vdash M \precsim^{\bullet} M' : \sigma$

$$\frac{}{[\,] \vdash * \precsim^{\bullet} M : I}\,[\,[\,] \vdash * \precsim^{\circ} M : I] \qquad \frac{}{x{:}\sigma \vdash x \precsim^{\bullet} M : \sigma}\,[x{:}\sigma \vdash x \precsim^{\circ} M : \sigma]$$

$$\frac{\Gamma \vdash M_1 \precsim^{\bullet} M_1' : \sigma_1 \quad \Delta \vdash M_2 \precsim^{\bullet} M_2' : \sigma_2}{\Gamma, \Delta \vdash M_1 \otimes M_2 \precsim^{\bullet} N : \sigma_1 \otimes \sigma_2}\,[\Gamma, \Delta \vdash M_1' \otimes M_2' \precsim^{\circ} N : \sigma_1 \otimes \sigma_2]$$

$$\frac{\left\{\begin{array}{l} \Gamma \vdash M_1 \precsim^{\bullet} M_1' : \sigma_1 \otimes \sigma_2 \\ \Delta, x{:}\sigma_1, y{:}\sigma_2 \vdash M_2 \precsim^{\bullet} M_2' : \sigma \end{array}\right.}{\Delta, \Gamma \vdash \mathsf{split}\ M_1\ \mathsf{as}\ x \otimes y\ \mathsf{in}\ M_2 \precsim^{\bullet} N : \sigma}\,[\Delta, \Gamma \vdash \mathsf{split}\ M_1'\ \mathsf{as}\ x \otimes y\ \mathsf{in}\ M_2' \precsim^{\circ} N : \sigma]$$

In order to prove that similarity is a linear precongruence, we adopt a linearised version of Howe's method. We inductively define a family of binary relations of the form $(\precsim^{\bullet}_{\Gamma,\sigma} \subseteq \mathit{Exp}_\sigma(\Gamma) \times \mathit{Exp}_\sigma(\Gamma) \mid \Gamma, \sigma)$. The definition is quite similar to that found in[4], except for the "linearisation of contexts", and example rules appear in Table 2.

Lemma 5.2 The family of relations $(\precsim^{\bullet}_{\Gamma,\sigma} \mid \Gamma, \sigma)$ satisfy the linear precongruence substitution clauses (a) and (b).

Proof This follows from the definition of open similarity, together with the properties of the environments. Suppose that $\Gamma \vdash M : \sigma$ and $\Delta, x{:}\sigma \vdash N \precsim^{\circ} N' : \sigma'$ where Γ, Δ. Let us write x_i for the variables appearing in Γ, and y_j for those in Δ. Thus $\forall j. x \neq y_j$ (though possibly $\exists i. x = x_i$). Pick arbitrary programs P_i and Q_j whose types match those of the variables x_i and y_j, for each i and j. We have $\vdash M[P_i/x_i] : \sigma$. Thus by definition of open similarity, we have

$$N[Q_j, M[P_i/x_i] \;/\; y_j, x] \precsim_{\sigma'} N'[Q_j, M[P_i/x_i] \;/\; y_j, x]$$

which on re-arranging is

$$N[M/x][P_i, Q_j \;/\; x_i, y_j] \precsim_{\sigma'} N'[M/x][P_i, Q_j \;/\; x_i, y_j]$$

As the programs were arbitrary, we have shown that

$$\Gamma, \Delta \vdash N[M/x] \precsim^{\circ} N'[M/x] : \sigma'$$

This shows substitution clause (a); the verification of (b) is similar.

□

Lemma 5.3

(i) For all $\Gamma \vdash M \preccurlyeq^{\bullet} M' : \sigma$ and $\Gamma \vdash M' \preccurlyeq^{\circ} M'' : \sigma$ we have $\Gamma \vdash M \preccurlyeq^{\bullet} M'' : \sigma$.

(ii) For all $\Gamma \vdash M : \sigma$ we have $\Gamma \vdash M \preccurlyeq^{\bullet} M : \sigma$.

(iii) For all $\Gamma \vdash M \preccurlyeq^{\circ} M' : \sigma$ we have $\Gamma \vdash M \preccurlyeq^{\bullet} M' : \sigma$.

(iv) For all $\Delta, x : \sigma \vdash N \preccurlyeq^{\bullet} N' : \sigma'$ and $\Gamma \vdash M \preccurlyeq^{\bullet} M' : \sigma$, where Γ, Δ, we have $\Gamma, \Delta \vdash N[M/x] \preccurlyeq^{\bullet} N'[M'/x] : \sigma'$.

Lemma 5.4

(i) $* \preccurlyeq^{\bullet}_{I} P$ implies $P \Downarrow *$.

(ii) $\lambda x.M \preccurlyeq^{\bullet}_{\sigma \multimap \sigma'} P$ implies $\exists N.P \Downarrow \lambda x.N$ and $\forall Q.M[Q/x] \preccurlyeq^{\bullet}_{\sigma'} N[Q/x]$.

(iii) $P_1 \otimes P_2 \preccurlyeq^{\bullet}_{\sigma_1 \otimes \sigma_2} Q$ implies $\exists Q_1, Q_2.Q \Downarrow Q_1 \otimes Q_2$ and moreover $P_1 \preccurlyeq^{\bullet}_{\sigma_1} Q_1$ and $P_2 \preccurlyeq^{\bullet}_{\sigma_2} Q_2$.

Proof In each of (i), (ii) and (iii) one unravels the definition of $\preccurlyeq^{\bullet}_{\sigma}$ in the hypothesis of each implication, and then applies Lemma 5.3 to the resulting data. □

Lemma 5.5 If $P \preccurlyeq^{\bullet}_{\sigma} Q$ and $P \Downarrow V$ then $V \preccurlyeq^{\bullet}_{\sigma} Q$.

Proof We use Rule Induction for $\Downarrow$, with subsidiary case analyses. We look at the rule

$$\frac{P \Downarrow P_1 \otimes P_2 \quad M[P_1, P_2/x, y] \Downarrow V}{\mathsf{split}\ P\ \mathsf{as}\ x \otimes y\ \mathsf{in}\ M \Downarrow V} \Downarrow\text{SPLIT}$$

Let us suppose that $\mathsf{split}\ P\ \mathsf{as}\ x \otimes y\ \mathsf{in}\ M \preccurlyeq^{\bullet}_{\sigma} Q$. It follows that $\exists P', M'$ such that

$$P \preccurlyeq^{\bullet}_{\sigma_1 \otimes \sigma_2} P' \qquad (1)$$

$$x : \sigma_1, y : \sigma_2 \vdash M \preccurlyeq^{\bullet} M' : \sigma \qquad (2)$$

$$\mathsf{split}\ P'\ \mathsf{as}\ x \otimes y\ \mathsf{in}\ M' \preccurlyeq_{\sigma} Q \qquad (3)$$

By the induction hypothesis and (1) we have $P \Downarrow P_1 \otimes P_2 \preccurlyeq^{\bullet}_{\sigma_1 \otimes \sigma_2} P'$ and hence $\exists P_1', P_2'$ such that

$$P_1 \preccurlyeq^{\bullet}_{\sigma_1} P_1' \qquad P_2 \preccurlyeq^{\bullet}_{\sigma_2} P_2' \qquad P_1' \otimes P_2' \preccurlyeq_{\sigma_1 \otimes \sigma_2} P' \qquad (4)$$

From (4) we have $\exists P_1'', P_2''$ such that

$$P' \Downarrow P_1'' \otimes P_2'' \quad P_1' \preccurlyeq_{\sigma_1} P_1'' \quad P_2' \preccurlyeq_{\sigma_2} P_2'' \qquad (5)$$

From (2), (4), and (5), plus Lemma 5.3 (i) and (iv) we have $M[P_1, P_2/x, y] \precsim^{\bullet}_{\sigma} M'[P_1'', P_2''/x, y]$. We must also have $M[P_1, P_2/x, y] \Downarrow V$, and so from the induction hypotheses $V \precsim^{\bullet}_{\sigma} M'[P_1'', P_2''/x, y]$ $(*)$. We now consider cases for V:

(*Case* $V \equiv Q_1 \otimes Q_2$): From $(*)$ we must have $\exists Q_1', Q_2'$ such that

$$Q_1 \precsim^{\bullet}_{\sigma_1} Q_1' \qquad Q_2 \precsim^{\bullet}_{\sigma_2} Q_2' \tag{6}$$

$$Q_1' \otimes Q_2' \precsim_{\sigma_1 \otimes \sigma_2} M'[P_1'', P_2''/x, y] \tag{7}$$

Note that given (6), to prove that $V \precsim^{\bullet}_{\sigma} Q$ all we need to show is

$$Q_1' \otimes Q_2' \precsim_{\sigma_1 \otimes \sigma_2} Q \tag{8}$$

From (7) we have

$$M'[P_1'', P_2''/x, y] \Downarrow Q_1'' \otimes Q_2'' \tag{9}$$

and this together with (5) gives split P' as $x \otimes y$ in $M' \Downarrow Q_1'' \otimes Q_2''$. From the definition of similarity, we must therefore have $Q \Downarrow Q_1''' \otimes Q_2'''$, where $Q_1'' \precsim_{\sigma_1} Q_1'''$ and $Q_2'' \precsim_{\sigma_2} Q_2'''$. From (7) and (9) we have $Q_1' \precsim_{\sigma_1} Q_1''$ and $Q_2' \precsim_{\sigma_2} Q_2''$. These facts, together with Proposition 4.1 and the definition of similarity, prove (8).
□

Proposition 5.6 For all Γ, M, M' and σ, we have $\Gamma \vdash M \precsim^{\circ} M' : \sigma$ iff $\Gamma \vdash M \precsim^{\bullet} M' : \sigma$.

Proof

($\Longrightarrow$): This is Lemma 5.3 part (iii).

($\Longleftarrow$): From Lemma 5.3 parts (ii) and (iv) and the fact that any program is a closed expression, it is enough to prove that we have $P \precsim^{\bullet}_{\sigma} P' \Longrightarrow P \precsim_{\sigma} P'$ for all types and programs, which is precisely that $\precsim^{\bullet} \lhd \precsim$. To prove this, we use coinduction (which involves a case analysis on types): the details are omitted.

□

Theorem 5.7 The family $(\preceq^{\circ}_{\Gamma,\sigma} \mid \Gamma, \sigma)$ is a linear precongruence.

Proof

Clauses (a) and (b) are shown in Lemma 5.2. Clauses (c) and (d) follow from Proposition 4.1 that similarity is a preorder, together with the definition of open similarity. Clauses (e) and (f) hold due to the definition of $\precsim^{\bullet}$, plus clause (c): for (e), suppose that $\Gamma, x{:}\,\sigma \vdash M \precsim^{\circ} M' : \sigma'$. By (c) we have $\Gamma \vdash \lambda x.M' \precsim^{\circ} \lambda x.M' : \sigma \multimap \sigma'$. By Proposition 5.6 we have $\Gamma, x{:}\,\sigma \vdash M \precsim^{\bullet} M' : \sigma'$. From the definition of the Howe relation, and the latter two deductions, one has $\Gamma \vdash \lambda x.M \preccurlyeq^\bullet \lambda x.M' : \sigma \multimap \sigma'$. We are done by appeal to Proposition 5.6. Clause (f) is similar.

□

Lemma 5.8 For any open similarity relationship $\beta, \Delta \vdash M \preccurlyeq^\circ M' : \rho$ and linear context $\Gamma \vdash^\beta_\eta \mathcal{C}[-_\sigma] : \sigma$, we have $\Gamma, \Delta \vdash \mathcal{C}[M] \preccurlyeq^\circ \mathcal{C}[M'] : \sigma$.

Proof We use induction on the derivation of the linear contexts; here are two example induction steps:

(*Case* $\overline{[\,] \vdash^{[\,]}_{[\,]} -_\rho : \rho}$): In this case, $\beta = [\,]$. Hence $\Delta \vdash M \preccurlyeq^\circ M' : \rho$, and as $\Gamma = [\,]$ the conclusion is immediate.

(*Case* $\dfrac{\Gamma \vdash^\beta_\eta \mathcal{C} : \sigma'}{\Gamma \vdash^{\beta, x:\sigma}_\eta \lambda x.\mathcal{C} : \sigma \multimap \sigma'}$ $[x \notin var(\Gamma), x \notin var(\eta)]$):

Suppose that $\beta, x{:}\sigma, \Delta \vdash M \preccurlyeq^\circ M' : \rho$. By the induction hypothesis we have $\Gamma, x{:}\sigma, \Delta \vdash \mathcal{C}[M] \preccurlyeq^\circ \mathcal{C}[M'] : \sigma'$, and thus $\Gamma, \Delta \vdash \lambda x.\mathcal{C}[M] \preccurlyeq^\circ \lambda x.\mathcal{C}[M'] : \sigma'$ using Theorem 5.7 and clause (e) of linear precongruence.

□

Proof [*Of Theorem* 4.2] Follows from Lemma 5.8 and $\preccurlyeq_\tau = \Phi(\preccurlyeq)_\tau$. □

6 Conclusions and Further Work

We have defined a notion of contextual preorder in a typed linear setting, and shown that preorder relationships can be established using coinductive techniques. This result hinges on the fact that similarity is a (linear) precongruence, and this can be shown using an adaptation of Howe's method. Many of the techniques used here are similar to those which appear in the corresponding non-linear setting, but the proofs of results are very delicate, arising from the fact that linearity forces an extremely controlled use of variables.

We plan to write a further paper, based on the work here, which gives examples of the contextual preorder established via coinduction, details of the exact relationship between the linear contextual preorder and open similarity, and which expands significantly on the complexity of the linear system under study.

Acknowledgements

Thanks to Lindsay Errington and Guy McCusker for comments on a draft of the paper.

References

1. R. Milner. *Communication and Concurrency.* Prentice-Hall International, 1989.
2. S. Abramsky. The lazy lambda calculus. In David Turner, editor, *Research Topics in Functional Programming*, pages 65–116. Addison-Wesley, 1990.
3. D. J. Howe. Equality in lazy computation systems. In *Proceedings of the 4th IEEE Symposium on Logic in Computer Science*, pages 198–203, 1989.
4. A. D. Gordon. Bisimilarity as a theory of functional programming. *Electronic Notes in Theoretical Computer Science*, 1, 1995.
5. A. M. Pitts. Operationally based theories of program equivalence. Technical report, Cambridge University Computer Laboratory, 1995. Notes to accompany lectures given at the Summer School on Semantics and Logics of Computation, Isaac Newton Institute for Mathematical Sciences, Cambridge, UK.
6. D. Sands. Operational theories of improvement in functional languages. In *Glasgow Functional Programming Workshop*, 1991.
7. S. Abramsky. Computational interpretations of linear logic, 1990.
8. B. Nordström, K. Petersson, and J.M. Smith. *Programming in Martin-Löf's Type Theory*, volume 7 of *Monographs on Computer Science.* Oxford University Press, 1990.
9. A. M. Pitts. Some notes on inductive and coinductive techniques in the semantics of functional programs. Technical Report BRICS-NS-94-5, BRICS, Department of Computer Science, University of Aarhus, Denmark, December 1994 1994.
10. R. L. Crole. Functional programming theory. Lecture notes, 1996.
11. R. L. Crole and A. D. Gordon. Relating operational and denotational semantics for input/output effects. Technical Report 1996/5, Department of Mathematics and Computer Science, University of Leicester, 1996. Submitted to the Journal of Mathematical Structures in Computer Science.
12. D. J. Howe. Proving congruence of simulation orderings in functional languages. 1993.
13. Andrew D. Gordon. *Functional Programming and Input/Output.* Cambridge University Press, 1994. Distinguished dissertations in Computer Science.

THE GENERALIZED RIEMANN INTEGRAL ON LOCALLY COMPACT SPACES
Extended Abstract

A. EDALAT, S. NEGRI
Department of Computing, Imperial College, London SW7 2BZ.

We extend the basic results on the theory of the generalized Riemann integral to the setting of locally compact second countable Hausdorff spaces with bounded or locally finite measures, the latter being measures which are finite on compact subsets of the space. We show that the correspondence between Borel measures on X and continuous valuations on the upper space UX gives rise to a topological embedding between the space of locally finite measures and locally finite continuous valuations, both endowed with the Scott topology. We construct an approximating chain of simple valuations on the upper space of a locally compact space, whose least upper bound is the given locally finite measure. We define the generalized Riemann integral for bounded functions with respect to bounded and unbounded measures. Also in this setting generalized R-integrability for a bounded function is proved to be equivalent to the condition that the set of its discontinuities has measure zero. Finally we prove that if a bounded function is R-integrable then it is also Lebesgue integrable and the two integrals coincide.

1 Introduction

Domain theory was introduced by Dana Scott in 1970 ([11]) as a foundational basis for the semantics of computation.

In [3], a basic connection between domain theory and some main branches of mathematics has been established, giving rise, in particular, to a novel computational approach to measure theory and integration.

A domain-theoretic framework for measure and integration has been provided in [4], by proving that any bounded Borel measure on a compact metric space X can be obtained as the least upper bound of simple valuations on the dcpo given by the upper space UX.

Simple valuations approximating the given measure play the role of partitions in Riemann integration and are used to obtain increasingly better approximations of the integral of a bounded real-valued function on a compact metric space. This idea leads to a new notion of integration, called generalized Riemann integration, R-integration for short, similar in spirit to Riemann integration but more general.

All the basic results of the theory of Lebesgue integration can be extended to this setting. For instance, it is proved in [4] that a bounded real-valued function on a compact metric space is R-integrable w.r.t. a bounded Borel measure if and only if its set of discontinuities has measure zero and that if it is R-integrable then it is also Lebesgue integrable and the two integrals coincide.

This theory has had applications in exact computation of integrals [5], in the 1-dimensional random fields Ising model in statistical physics [6], in forgetful neural networks [7], in stochastic processes [2] and in chaos theory [5].

In order to apply the generalized Riemann integration to a wider range of problems, we look for a generalization of the results in [4] and [5] to the more general setting of locally compact second countable Hausdorff spaces with bounded or locally finite measures, the latter being measures which are finite on compact subsets of the space.

We stress the fact that these more general hypotheses cover some central fields of application. For instance, probability distributions on the real line are examples of bounded measures on a locally compact space, whereas the Lebesgue measure on the real line is an example of a locally finite measure on a locally compact space.

In this paper we face the problem *ab initio*, from the correspondence between Borel measures on X and continuous valuations on the upper space UX (as given in [3]). We start with showing, in section 2, that such correspondence also holds between locally finite measures and locally finite continuous valuations.

In the fourth section we show how to approximate a locally finite valuation on a locally compact space by means of an increasing sequence of simple valuations on the upper space, that is built up from any given presentation of the locally compact space as a union of increasing regular compact subsets.

We proceed with the definition of the generalized Riemann integral of a bounded real-valued function defined on a locally compact space with respect to a bounded Borel measure. As in the case of compact spaces [4], generalized R-integrability for a bounded function f is seen to be equivalent to the condition that the set of discontinuities of f has measure zero.

Finally, we define the R-integral for a real-valued function on a locally compact space with respect to a locally finite measure. In the case of functions with compact support, R-integrability reduces to R-integrability in compact spaces with respect to the restriction of the measure to the support of the function. In the case of functions with unbounded support, R-integrability is defined in a way similar to improper Riemann integrability and it is proved, also in this more general case, that if a function is R-integrable then it is also Lebesgue integrable and the two integrals coincide.

All the proofs can be found in the full version of this paper ([8]).

2 Locally finite measures and locally finite continuous valuations

All throughout the paper X will denote a second countable locally compact Hausdorff space. We will use the decomposition $X = \bigcup_{i \in \mathbb{N}} X_i$, where $\langle X_i \rangle_{i \in \mathbb{N}}$ is an increasing sequence of relatively compact subsets of X such that $\overline{X_i} \subseteq X_{i+1}$.

In this section we will prove that the correspondence stated in [3] between Borel measures on X and valuations on the upper space supported in $s(X)$ gives rise, when X is a locally compact topological space, to an equivalence between locally finite Borel measures on X and locally finite continuous valuations on the upper space supported in $s(X)$ (defined below).

Definition 2.1 *Let X be a second countable locally compact Hausdorff space. Then we define $M^l(X)$ to be the set of* locally finite *Borel measures μ on X, i.e., of Borel measures with the property that $\mu(C) < \infty$ for all compact subsets C of X.*

We recall from [3] that the upper space UX of a topological space is the set of all non-empty compact subsets of X, with the base of the *upper topology* given by $\Box a = \{C \in UX \mid C \subseteq a\}$ $(a \in \Omega(X))$. When X is a second countable locally compact Hausdorff space, then the upper space UX of X is an ω-continuous dcpo and the Scott topology of $(UX, \supseteq)$ coincides with the upper topology.

Definition 2.2 *Let X be a second countable locally compact Hausdorff space. A* locally finite *continuous valuation on UX is a mapping*

$$\nu : \Omega(UX) \to [0, \infty]$$

satisfying, for all $U, V \in \Omega(UX)$ and for any directed family A in $\Omega(UX)$, the following conditions:

1. $\nu(U) + \nu(V) = \nu(U \cup V) + \nu(U \cap V)$;

2. $\nu(\emptyset) = 0$;

3. $U \subseteq V \Rightarrow \nu(U) \leq \nu(V)$;

4. $\nu(\bigcup_{O \in A} O) = \sup_{O \in A} \nu(O)$;

5. $\nu(V) < \infty$ *for* $V \ll UX$.

We will denote with $P^l(UX)$ the set of all such valuations.

Proposition 2.3 *Let $s : X \to UX$ be the singleton map. Then the map*

$$\begin{array}{rcl} e : M^l(X) & \to & P^l(UX) \\ \mu & \mapsto & \mu \circ s^{-1} \end{array}$$

is well defined, i.e., whenever μ is a locally finite Borel measure on X, then $\mu \circ s^{-1}$ is a locally finite continuous valuation.

By a result from [10] (theorem 3.9), if P is a continuous poset with its Scott topology, then every continuous valuation extends uniquely to a measure. Thus, in particular, $\mu \circ s^{-1}$ extends to a unique measure on UX, which we will denote by μ^*. Such a measure satisfies $\mu^*(UX - s(X)) = 0$, that is we have:

Proposition 2.4 *The valuation $\mu \circ s^{-1}$ is supported in $s(X)$.*

Adapting the notation from [3], we will denote with $S^l(X)$ the locally finite valuations on UX which are supported in $s(X)$. We have:

Theorem 2.5 *The map*

$$\begin{array}{rcl} e : M^l(X) & \to & S^l(X) \\ \mu & \mapsto & \mu \circ s^{-1} \end{array}$$

is a bijection with inverse given by

$$\begin{array}{rcl} j : S^l(X) & \to & M^l(X) \\ \nu & \mapsto & \nu^* \circ s \, . \end{array}$$

The following lemma is used in the proof and elsewhere in the paper:

Lemma 2.6 *Let X be a second countable locally compact Hausdorff space and suppose that μ and ν are locally finite Borel measures which have the same restriction to $\Omega(X)$. Then $\mu = \nu$.*

We recall from [3] that, given a topological space Y, the *point valuation* based at $b \in Y$ is the valuation

$$\delta_b : \Omega(Y) \to [0, \infty)$$

defined by

$$\delta_b(O) = \begin{cases} 1 & \text{if } b \in O \\ 0 & \text{otherwise} \end{cases} .$$

Any finite linear combination

$$\sum_{i=1}^{n} r_i \delta_{b_i} \quad (r_i \in [0, \infty), i = 1, \ldots, n)$$

of point valuations is called a *simple valuation*.

When considering locally finite valuations closure under directed joins does not hold anymore. However, it is still true that locally finite valuations can be approximated by simple valuations, since the results holds in general for (unbounded) valuations (cf. theorem 5.2, page 46 in [9]), and simple valuations are in particular locally finite. So we have:

Proposition 2.7 *For all $\mu \in P^l(UX)$, μ is the supremum of the (directed) set of simple valuations way-below it.*

3 The Scott topology on $M^l(X)$

This section is devoted to prove that the map

$$e : M^l(X) \to P^l(UX)$$

is a topological embedding when both spaces are endowed with the Scott topology.

We can define a partial order on $M^l(X)$ by putting, for $\mu_1, \mu_2 \in M^l(X)$

$$\mu_1 \leq \mu_2 \equiv (\forall O \in \Omega(X))(\mu_1(O) \leq \mu_2(O)) .$$

The relation $\leq$ is clearly reflexive and transitive, and it is antisymmetric by lemma 2.6. Observe that the space $(M^l(X), \leq)$ is not a dcpo since, for instance, the $\langle n \cdot \delta_x \rangle_{n>0}$ is an increasing sequence in M^lX whose least upper bound is not a locally finite measure.

We proceed by characterizing those directed subsets of M^lX having least upper bound in M^lX. We have:

Proposition 3.1 *A directed subset D of M^lX has least upper bound in M^lX if and only if for all open sets O such that $O \ll X$ in $\Omega(X)$ the set $\{\mu(O) : \mu \in D\}$ is bounded in $\mathbb{R}$.*

It is immediate to check that the map e is continuous with respect to the Scott topologies on M^lX and P^lUX. The map e is a topological embedding since also its inverse j is continuous with respect to the Scott topologies on $M^l(X)$ and $S^l(X)$ (cf. [8] for the details).

4 Approximation of locally finite measures

Given a measure on a compact metric space it is possible to construct a chain of simple valuations on the upper space with the measure as its least upper bound (cf. [5]). In this section we will generalize this construction to the case of locally finite measures on a locally compact space.

The relatively compact subsets X_i will serve as a basis to construct a sequence of simple valuations on UX approximating any given locally finite measure on X, thus generalizing the procedure which is worked out in [5]. We assume as in [5] that the measure is given by its values on a given countable basis closed under finite unions and finite intersections.

Since the spaces X_i are relatively compact, for all $i \in \mathbb{N}$ there exists an ordered finite covering $\mathcal{C}_i$ of X_i made of open sets of the basis with diameter $\leq \frac{1}{i}$. Moreover such coverings can be chosen satisfying the additional requirement $\bigcup\mathcal{C}_i \subseteq \bigcup\mathcal{C}_{i+1}$. These hypotheses are needed in order to obtain an increasing sequence of simple valuations. We will assume in this section (and the rest of the paper) that open covers are always constructed from the given countable base satisfying the above property.

For each $i \in \mathbb{N}$ we define inductively a finite open cover $\mathcal{D}_i$ for X_i in the following way:

$\mathcal{D}_1 \equiv \mathcal{C}_1$;

$\mathcal{D}_2 \equiv \mathcal{D}_1 \wedge \mathcal{C}_2 \cup \{O \in \mathcal{C}_2 : O \not\subseteq \ \bigcup\mathcal{C}_1\}$;

$D_3 \equiv \mathcal{D}_2 \wedge \mathcal{C}_3 \cup \{O \in \mathcal{C}_3 : O \not\subseteq \ \bigcup\mathcal{C}_2\}$;

...

$\mathcal{D}_{i+1} \equiv \mathcal{D}_i \wedge \mathcal{C}_{i+1} \cup \{O \in \mathcal{C}_{i+1} : O \not\subseteq \ \bigcup\mathcal{C}_i\}$;

...

where for given covers $\mathcal{A}$ and $\mathcal{B}$, $\mathcal{A} \wedge \mathcal{B}$ denotes the cover

$$\{O_1 \cap O_2 : O_1 \in \mathcal{A}, O_2 \in \mathcal{B}\}.$$

Assume the covers $\mathcal{D}_i$ to be ordered with the lexicographic order for the first part $(\mathcal{D}_{i-1} \wedge \mathcal{C}_i)$, and with the order induced by the order on $\mathcal{C}_i$ for the second part.

We recall from [5] that given an ordered cover $\mathcal{A} = \{O_1, \ldots, O_n\}$, the simple valuation $\mu_{\mathcal{A}}$ associated with $\mathcal{A}$ is given by

$$\mu_{\mathcal{A}} \equiv \sum_{i=1}^{n} r_i \delta_{\overline{O_i}}\ , \quad \text{where} \quad r_i = \mu(O_i - \bigcup_{j<i} O_j).$$

We will denote with μ_i the simple valuation $\mu_{\mathcal{D}_i}$ associated with $\mathcal{D}_i$.

We are now going to prove that the μ_i's constitute a chain of simple valuations with least upper bound μ.

The following lemma is proved as proposition 3.1 in [5].

Lemma 4.1 *Let $\mathcal{A} = \{O_1, \ldots, O_n\}$ be a covering of X_i and let μ be a locally finite measure on X. Then for all open subsets O of X_i we have*

$$\sum_{O_i \subseteq O} r_i \leq \mu(O) \leq \sum_{\overline{O_i} \cap O \neq \emptyset} r_i \ .$$

Then we have:

Proposition 4.2 *For all $i \in \mathbb{N}$ the following hold*

1. $\mu_i \sqsubseteq \mu$ *in* $P^l(UX)$;
2. $\mu_i \sqsubseteq \mu_{i+1}$ *in* $P^l(UX)$;
3. $\mu = \bigsqcup_{i \in \mathbb{N}} \mu_i$.

5 The generalized Riemann integral

Let X be a second countable locally compact Hausdorff space. Let μ be a Borel measure on X such that $0 < \mu(X) < \infty$. By rescaling we can suppose that μ is normalized, i.e. that $\mu(X) = 1$. The continuous dcpo UX does not have a bottom element, so that for practical purposes we will adjoin a bottom element $\bot$ and denote the dcpo with bottom thus obtained with $(UX)_\bot$. By corollary 3.3 in [4], $P^1(UX)_\bot$, the set of normalized valuations of the probabilistic power domain of $(UX)_\bot$, is an ω-continuous dcpo with a basis of normalized simple valuations. There exists an embedding

$$\begin{array}{ccc} M^1X & \to & P^1(UX)_\bot \\ \mu & \mapsto & \mu \circ s^{-1} \end{array}$$

and by the result of the previous section we also know that there exists an increasing chain of simple valuations $\langle \mu_i \rangle_{i \geq 0}$ in $P(UX)_\bot$ such that $\mu \circ s^{-1} = \sup_{i \geq 0} \mu_i$,

If we consider the valuations

$$\mu_i^+ \equiv \mu_i + (1 - \mu_i((UX)_\bot))\delta_\bot$$

then the μ_i^+'s are in $P^1(UX)_\bot$. Moreover, for any proper open subset O of $(UX)_\bot$, we have $\mu_i^+(O) = \mu_i(O)$ and $\mu \circ s^{-1} = \sup_{i \geq 0} \mu_i^+$, where $\langle \mu_i^+ \rangle_{i \geq 0}$ is again an increasing chain of simple valuations.

Let f be a bounded real-valued function defined on X and let μ be a bounded Borel measure on X. For a simple valuation $\nu \equiv \sum_{b \in B} r_b \delta_b$, define, as in [4],

$$S^l_X(f, \nu) \equiv \sum_{b \in B} r_b \inf f[b], \qquad S^u_X(f, \nu) \equiv \sum_{b \in B} r_b \sup f[b]$$

and observe that, since f is bounded, $S^l_X(f,\nu)$ and $S^u_X(f,\nu)$ are well-defined real numbers. By proposition 4.2 in [4] we have:

Proposition 5.1 *Let $\mu_1, \mu_2 \in P^1(UX)_\perp$ be simple valuations with $\mu_1 \sqsubseteq \mu_2$. Then $S^l_X(f,\mu_1) \le S^l_X(f,\mu_2)$ and $S^u_X(f,\mu_2) \le S^u_X(f,\mu_1)$.*

Corollary 5.2 *If $\mu_1, \mu_2 \in P^1(UX)_\perp$ are simple valuations with $\mu_1, \mu_2 \ll \mu$, then $S^l_X(f,\mu_1) \le S^u_X(f,\mu_2)$.*

Therefore we have, for all $i, j \in \mathbb{N}$,

1. $S^l_X(f,\mu_i^+) \le S^l_X(f,\mu_{i+1}^+)$;
2. $S^u_X(f,\mu_{i+1}^+) \le S^u_X(f,\mu_i^+)$;
3. $S^l_X(f,\mu_i^+) \le S^u_X(f,\mu_j^+)$.

Using the notation introduced above we define the lower and upper R-integral as follows:

Definition 5.3 $\mathbf{R}\underline{\int} f d\mu \equiv \sup_{\nu \ll \mu} S^l_X(f,\nu)$ *(lower R-integral);*

$\mathbf{R}\overline{\int} f d\mu \equiv \inf_{\nu \ll \mu} S^u_X(f,\nu)$ *(upper R-integral).*

By proposition 5.2 we have

$$\mathbf{R}\underline{\int} f d\mu \le \mathbf{R}\overline{\int} f d\mu \ .$$

Definition 5.4 *We say that f is R-integrable w.r.t. μ (and write $f \in R_X(\mu)$) if $\mathbf{R}\underline{\int} f = \mathbf{R}\overline{\int} f$.*

If f is R-integrable then the integral of f can be calculated by using the increasing sequence of simple valuations $\langle \mu_i^+ \rangle_{i \ge 0}$ (cf. proposition 4.9 in [4]):

Proposition 5.5 *If f is R-integrable w.r.t. μ, and $\langle \mu_i \rangle_{i \ge 0}$ is an increasing sequence of simple valuations on UX with least upper bound μ, then*

$$\int_X f d\mu = \sup_{i \ge 0} S^l_X(f,\mu_i^+) = \inf_{i \ge 0} S^u_X(f,\mu_i^+).$$

6 Lebesgue criterion for R-integrability

We are now going to generalize the Lebesgue criterion for Riemann integration of a bounded function on a compact real interval to R-integration of a bounded real-valued function on a locally compact space, by generalizing the result in [4], that is the analogous criterion for R-integration on compact spaces.

We first recall some definitions.

Definition 6.1 *Let $T \subseteq X$ and $r > 0$ and define*

$\Omega_f(T) \equiv \sup\{f(x) - f(y) \mid x, y \in T\}$, *called* oscillation of f at T;

$\omega_f(x) \equiv \lim_{h \to 0^+} \Omega_f(B(x,h))$, *where $B(x,h)$ is the open ball of radius h centred at x;*

$D_r \equiv \{x \in X \mid \omega_f(x) \geq \frac{1}{r}\}$.

Then we have (cf. [1], p. 170 and [4]):

Proposition 6.2 *The following statements hold:*

(i) f is continuous at x iff $\omega_f(x) = 0$.

(ii) If X is compact and $\omega_f(x) < \epsilon$ for all $x \in X$, then there exists $\delta > 0$ such that for all compact subsets $b \subseteq X$ with $|b| < \delta$ we have $\Omega_f(b) < \epsilon$.

(iii) For any $r > 0$, the set D_r is closed.

If D is the set of discontinuities of f, we have $D = \bigcup_{n \geq 1} D_n$ where $D_1 \subseteq D_2 \subseteq D_3 \subseteq \ldots$ is an increasing chain of closed sets. Hence D is an F_δ and therefore a Borel set. In the following, X will be a second countable locally compact metric space and $\mu \in M^1(X)$. We have (cf. lemma 6.4 in [4] for the proof):

Lemma 6.3 *Let d be a compact subset of X and let $\nu = \sum_{b \in B} r_b \delta_b \in P^1 UX$. Then we have:*

1. *If $\nu \sqsubseteq \mu$ then $\sum_{b \cap d \neq \emptyset} r_b \geq \mu(d)$.*
2. *If $\nu \ll \mu$ then $\sum_{b^\circ \cap d \neq \emptyset} r_b \geq \mu(d)$, where b° denotes the interior of b.*

Then Lebesgue criterion follows:

Theorem 6.4 *A bounded real-valued function on a locally compact second countable Hausdorff space is R-integrable with respect to a bounded Borel measure μ on X iff its set of discontinuities has measure zero.*

7 R-integration and Lebesgue integration

In this section we will prove that the result in [4] connecting R-integration and Lebesgue integration for bounded real-valued functions defined on a compact space extends to the case of bounded functions defined on a locally compact second countable Hausdorff space.

Theorem 7.1 *If a bounded real-valued function f is R-integrable with respect to a bounded Borel measure μ on a locally compact second countable Hausdorff space, then it is also Lebesgue integrable and the two integrals coincide.*

8 The improper R-integral

8.1 Functions with compact support

In this section we define the R-integral for a real-valued function with compact support defined on a locally compact space w.r.t. a locally finite measure.

Basically, our definition will be obtained by cutting down the construction of the chain of simple valuations approximating a given locally finite measure that we gave in section 4 to the compact support of the function.

Let f be a real-valued function on a locally compact space X with compact support C and let μ be a locally finite measure on X. Recall from section 4 that $\mu = \sqcup \mu_i$, where μ_i is the simple valuation, associated with the covering $\mathcal{D}_i$ of X_i, given by $\sum_{j=1}^{n} r_j \delta_{\overline{O_j}}$, with $r_j = \mu(O_j - \bigcup_{k<j} O_k)$. Since C is compact, there exists $k \in \mathbb{N}$ such that $C \subseteq X_i$ for all $i > k$. For $i > k$, define

$$\mu_i^C = \sum_{j=1}^{n} r_j^C \delta_{\overline{O_j} \cap C}, \text{ where } r_j^C = \mu(O_j \cap C - \bigcup_{k<j} O_k \cap C)\ .$$

Moreover define, for all open subsets O of X, $\mu^C(O) = \mu(O \cap C)$.

In order to prove that the integral of f can be defined by means of the chain of simple valuations $\langle \mu_i^C \rangle_i$, some properties which are easily derived as in section 4 are needed. We observe that it is enough to know the value of μ on the induced topology of C.

Lemma 8.1 $\sum_{O_j \cap C \subseteq O} r_j^C \leq \mu(O \cap C) \leq \sum_{\overline{O_j} \cap C \cap O \neq \emptyset} r_j^C$.

Then we have

Proposition 8.2 *Let μ^C and μ_i^C be defined as above. Then:*

1. *For all $i > k$, $\mu_i^C \sqsubseteq \mu^C$;*
2. *For all $i > k$, $\mu_i^C \sqsubseteq \mu_{i+1}^C$;*
3. *$\mu^C = \sqcup_{i>k} \mu_i^C$.*

The R-integrability of f w.r.t. μ thus reduces to the R-integrability of $f|_C$ w.r.t. μ^C.

8.2 Functions with unbounded support

Let X be a locally compact second countable Hausdorff space, μ a locally finite measure on X and $f : X \to \mathbb{R}$ a bounded positive function. Given a subset A of X let χ_A denote the characteristic function of A. In order to extend the theory of generalized Riemann integration to this setting we make the following:

Definition 8.3 *The function f is improper R-integrable on X w.r.t. μ if for all $i \in \mathbb{N}$ the function with compact support $f \cdot \chi_{X_i}$ is R-integrable and there exists*

$$\lim_{i\to\infty} \mathbf{R}\int_X f \cdot \chi_{X_i} d\mu \; .$$

In this case we put

$$\mathbf{R}\int_X f d\mu = \lim_{i\to\infty} \mathbf{R}\int_X f \cdot \chi_{X_i} d\mu \; .$$

The above definition of improper R-integrability does not depend on the choice of the increasing sequence of relatively compact subsets X_i's such that $X = \bigcup_i X_i$. Indeed, if $\langle Y_i \rangle_{i\in\mathbb{N}}$ is another such sequence then it is clear that for all i, $f \cdot \chi_{X_i}$ is R-integrable if and only if for all i, $f \cdot \chi_{Y_i}$ is R-integrable and

$$\lim_{i\to\infty} \mathbf{R}\int_X f \cdot \chi_{X_i} d\mu = \lim_{i\to\infty} \mathbf{R}\int_X f \cdot \chi_{Y_i} d\mu$$

since for all i there exists j such that $X_i \subseteq Y_j$, hence

$$\mathbf{R}\int_X f \cdot \chi_{X_i} d\mu \leq \mathbf{R}\int_X f \cdot \chi_{Y_i} d\mu$$

and conversely.

If we release the assumption on f being positive, then we can use the decomposition

$$f = f^+ - f^-$$

where $f^+ = max(f, 0)$ and $f^- = max(-f, 0)$, and say that f is improper R-integrable if both f^+ and f^- are improper R-integrable and put

$$\mathbf{R}\int_X f d\mu = \mathbf{R}\int_X f^+ d\mu - \mathbf{R}\int_X f^- d\mu \; .$$

The following result connects improper R-integration with Lebesgue integration, generalizing theorem 7.1.

Theorem 8.4 *If a bounded real-valued function f is improper R-integrable with respect to a locally finite Borel measure μ on a locally compact second countable Hausdorff space, then it is also Lebesgue integrable and the two integrals coincide.*

Acknowledgments

This work has been funded by EPSRC project "Foundational Structures in Computer Science".

References

1. T. M. Apostol. *Mathematical Analysis*, Addison-Wesley, 1974.
2. A. Edalat. *Domain Theory in Stochastic Processes*, to appear in the Proceedings of Logic in Computer Science, Tenth Annual IEEE Symposium, 26-19 June, 1994, San Diego, IEEE Computer Society Press, 1995.
3. A. Edalat. *Dynamical systems, Measures and Fractals via Domain Theory*, Information and Computation, vol 120, no. 1, pp. 32-48, 1995.
4. A. Edalat. *Domain Theory and Integration*, Theoretical Computer Science 151, pp. 163-193, 1995.
5. A. Edalat. *The Scott topology induces the weak topology*, Proceedings of LICS '96.
6. A. Edalat. *Domain of computation of a random field in statistical physics*, in Proc. 2nd Imperial College, Department of Computing, Theory and Formal Methods Workshop, 1994.
7. A. Edalat. *Domain Theory in Learning Processes*, in Proceedings of MFPS, S. Brookes and M. Main and A. Melton and M. Mislove eds, Electronic Notes in Theoretical Computer Science, vol. 1, Elsevier, 1995.
8. A. Edalat, S. Negri. *The generalized Riemann Integral on Locally Compact Spaces*, available at `http://theory.doc.ic.ac/forum/comprox`.
9. O. Kirch. *Bereiche und Bewertungen*, Master Thesis, Technischen Hochschule Darmstadt, 1993.
10. T. Norberg. *Existence theorems for measures on continuous posets, with applications to random set theory*, Math. Scand. 64, pp. 15-51, 1989.
11. D. S. Scott, *Outline of a mathematical theory of computation*, in 4th Annual Princeton Conference on Information Sciences and Systems, pp. 169-176, 1970.

FINITE APPROXIMATION OF FUNCTIONS USING INVERSE SEQUENCES OF GRAPHS

M. B. Smyth and J. Webster
Department of Computing, Imperial College, London SW7 2BZ.

Various topological spaces may be approximated by inverse sequences of finite (discrete topological) graphs. When multi-functions are considered, a wide class of mappings between such spaces may be approximated by mappings between the respective approximating graphs. 'Upper power graphs' are introduced to accommodate multi-functions as single-valued functions.

1 Introduction

Topological graphs were introduced in [9, 10] as a generalization of both graphs and topological spaces in order to provide a way in which various spaces may be approximated by graphs. This method of approximation involves the derivation of spaces from limits of *inverse sequences* of (discrete topological) graphs. Thus a formal and reasonably natural link is obtained between classical topology and related areas of discrete mathematics such as graph theory, tolerance geometry and digital topology. Moreover, when the spaces involved are compact, the approximating graphs may be taken as finite, thus increasing the computational relevance of the theory.

Our general programme is the development of the above framework by the relation of various intuitively similar discrete and continuous concepts. Thus the topological and graph-theoretic definitions of 'line' are related in [12]. In this work we discuss the approximation of topologically continuous functions by relation-preserving functions between graphs. The use of single-valued relation-preserving functions, however, precludes in general the construction of some continuous functions as 'limit functions'. We therefore use *multi-valued* relation-preserving functions, which does then allow the construction of all (and only all) continuous functions as limit functions.

'Upper graphs' are introduced in order to treat multi-valued functions as single-valued functions.

2 Inverse sequences of spaces

This section contains the basic topological results to be used in the rest of the work.

Categorically, inverse sequences are ω-op sequences, which are diagrams of the form $\Delta = X_1 \xleftarrow{f_1} X_2 \xleftarrow{f_2} \cdots$. The mappings (f_i) are called *bonding* maps. The category **Top** has inverse limits. The limit in **Top** of the inverse sequence Δ may be characterized as the set $X = \{(x_1x_2\ldots) \mid \forall i.\ x_i \in X_i,\ x_i = f_i(x_{i+1})\}$, together with the projection mappings (p_i) where, for all i, $p_i : X \to X_i$, $(x_1x_2\ldots) \mapsto x_i$, together with the topology on X having as base the collection $\{p_i^{-1}(U) \mid U \text{ open in } X_i\}$. This topology is the least such that each projection mapping is continuous. The elements $(x_1x_2\ldots) \in X$ are called the *threads* of Δ. Limits are of course only unique up to isomorphism. For a comprehensive account of the theory of inverse sequences, the reader is referred to [3, 4].

We define a *decreasing sequence* in Δ to be a sequence of compact sets $(A_i \subseteq X_i)$ such that, for all i, $f_i(A_{i+1}) \subseteq A_i$. The *limit* of this sequence is the meet of the sequence $p_1^{-1}(A_1) \supseteq p_2^{-1}(A_2) \supseteq \ldots$. The decreasing sequence (A_i) is said to be *canonical* if $f_i(A_{i+1}) = A_i$ for all i. Each thread is a canonical decreasing sequence. The relevant properties of inverse sequences of spaces in this work are:

Lemma 2.1 *Let $\Delta = X_1 \xleftarrow{f_1} X_2 \xleftarrow{f_2} \cdots$ be an inverse sequence of compact Hausdorff spaces with limit $(X, (p_i))$. Let (A_i) be a decreasing sequence in Δ with limit A. Then:*

(1) A is a compact subset of X;

(2) A is non-empty iff each A_i is non-empty;

(3) For any open $U \subseteq X$, $A \subseteq U$ implies there is some open $V \subseteq X_i$ such that $A_i \subseteq V$ and $p_i^{-1}(V) \subseteq U$;

(4) If (A_i) is canonical then, for all i, $p_i(A) = A_i$;

(5) Any compact $B \subseteq X$ is the limit of the canonical decreasing sequence $(p_i(B))$.

Proof (1) As is well-known [3], X is a compact Hausdorff space. A is the meet of compact sets in X; (2) Finite intersection property; (3) For each i, let U_i be the largest open set in X_i such that $p_i^{-1}(U_i) \subseteq U$. Then $(A_i - U_i)$ is a decreasing sequence with (empty) limit $A - U$; (4) For $a \in A_i$ there exists some thread $(a_1a_2\ldots)$ with $a = a_i$ and $a_j \in A_j$ for all j; (5) Any $x \in X$ is the limit of the decreasing sequence $(p_i(x))$. If $x \notin B$ then there is some open $V \subseteq X_i$ with $p_i(x) \in V$ and $p_i^{-1}(V) \subseteq X - B$. □

Results 4. and 5. of the lemma give an obvious bijection between the compact subsets of X and the canonical decreasing sequences in Δ.

3 Inverse sequences of topological graphs

This section is a brief outline of the approximation of various topological spaces by inverse sequences of finite (discrete topological) graphs. More details can be found in [9, 10]

Definition 3.1 *A topological graph, $G = (X, R)$, is a topological space X endowed with a relation R.*

Topological graphs will usually be referred to simply as 'graphs'. We will not discuss here any connection which should be required between the space and the relation in a topological graph. Typically, the graphs we deal with are those in which the relation is *closed* (as a subset of the product space). G is called a *tolerance graph* if R is a tolerance (reflexive and symmetric) relation. Tolerance graphs are also known as tolerance *spaces* [6, 13]. G is called *finite* (*discrete*) if X is finite (discrete). Discrete graphs are essentially ordinary graphs (which we consider as *sets* endowed with relations). Thus discrete tolerance graphs are, in terms of standard graph theory, undirected graphs with loops.

For graphs (X, R) and (Y, S), a mapping $f : X \to Y$ is *relation-preserving* if, for all $x, y \in X$, $x \; R \; y$ implies $f(x) \; S \; f(y)$.

Definition 3.2 *A* graph morphism *from the graph (X, R) to the graph (Y, S) is a continuous relation-preserving map $f : X \to Y$. The* category of topological graphs and graph morphisms *is denoted* **TopGr**.

Proposition 3.3 **TopGr** *has ω-op limits.*

Proof Let $\Delta = (X_1, R_1) \xleftarrow{f_1} (X_2, R_2) \xleftarrow{f_2} \cdots$ be an inverse sequence in **TopGr**. Let $(X, (p_i))$ be the limit of the sequence $X_1 \xleftarrow{f_1} X_2 \xleftarrow{f_2} \cdots$ in **Top**. The *inverse limit relation* on X with respect to the relations (R_i) is: $x \; R \; y \Leftrightarrow \forall i.\; p_i(x) \; R_i \; p_i(y)$. R is the greatest relation on X for which each p_i is relation-preserving. It follows that $((X, R), (p_i))$ is the limit of Δ in **TopGr**. □

A *Stone graph* is a graph in which the underlying space is a 2nd countable Stone space, and in which the relation is closed. (Recall that a Stone space is a compact Hausdorff totally disconnected space.) The following two results may be found in, respectively, [10, 9], though it is instructive to outline their proofs here.

Notation. For a graph (X, R) and for $x \in X$, $R(x)$ denotes the set $\{y \mid x \; R \; y\}$; for $A \subseteq X$, $R(A)$ denotes the set $\bigcup\{R(x) \mid x \in A\}$.

Proposition 3.4 *A graph is a Stone graph iff it is the limit of an inverse sequence of finite discrete graphs.*

Proof It is shown in [9] that a space X is a 2nd countable Stone space iff it is the limit of an inverse sequence $X_1 \xleftarrow{f_1} X_2 \xleftarrow{f_2} \cdots$ of finite discrete spaces. Where R is a relation on X, for $x, y \in X_i$ let: $x \; R_i \; y \Leftrightarrow R(p_i^{-1}(x)) \cap p_i^{-1}(y) \neq \emptyset$. Each f_i is relation-preserving w.r.t. R_{i+1}, R_i. The relation R is closed iff for all x, y, $\neg(x \; R \; y)$ implies there is some open U, V with $x \in U$, $y \in V$ and $R(U) \cap V = \emptyset$. Given that any $x \in X$ has the neighbourhood base $\{p_i^{-1}(p_i(x))\}$

we have that: R is closed iff $\forall x, y \in X.(\neg(x\ R\ y) \Rightarrow \exists i.\neg(p_i(x)\ R_i\ p_i(y)))$, which is the case iff R is the limit of the relations (R_i). □

If Δ is an inverse sequence of graphs with limit graph (X, R), and R is an equivalence relation, the sequence Δ may reasonably be said to *approximate* the quotient space X/R: Δ contains all the information sufficient to recover the space X/R from its limit.

Recall that a compact metrizable space is a compact Hausdorff 2nd countable space.

Theorem 3.5 *A space is compact metrizable iff it can be approximated by an inverse sequence of finite discrete graphs.*

Proof (Outline) The result follows from Proposition 3.4 and the fact that a space is compact metrizable iff it is the quotient of a 2nd countable Stone space (indeed, of Cantor space [4]) by a closed equivalence relation. □

The above theorem is the main motivation for our work. It provides the connection between classical topology and various areas of discrete mathematics discussed in the introduction. Although we are concerned essentially with inverse sequences of finite discrete graphs, most of the results and definitions to follow will be about obvious generalizations such as 'compact Hausdorff graphs'; the reason being partly to show the theory in its generality, and partly because the proofs are more topologically satisfying.

Example 3.6 The Unit Interval. *For each k let I_k be the set $\{1, 2, \ldots, k\}$ taken with the discrete topology. For $x, y \in I_k$, let $x\ R_k\ y$ if $|x - y| \leq 1$. The graph $\mathbb{I}_k = (I_k, R_k)$ is the standard representation in digital topology of the unit interval, I. For each i let $f_i : \mathbb{I}_{2^{k+1}} \rightarrow \mathbb{I}_{2^k}$, $x \mapsto x/2$ if x is even, $x \mapsto x/2 + 1$ if x is odd. Then each f_i is a graph morphism and I is approximated by the inverse sequence $\mathbb{I}_2 \xleftarrow{f_1} \mathbb{I}_4 \xleftarrow{f_2} \cdots$.*

The category **TopGr** has binary products. The product graph of the graphs (X, R) and (Y, S) is the graph $(X, R) \times (Y, S) = (X \times Y, R \times S)$, where $X \times Y$ is the product space of X and Y and $(x, y)\ R \times S\ (x', y') \Leftrightarrow x\ R\ x'\ \&\ y\ S\ y'$.

Example 3.7 The Unit Square. *For each k, the graph $\mathbb{I}_k \times \mathbb{I}_k$ is the standard '8-connectivity' representation of the unit square, I^2, in digital topology. I^2 is approximated by the inverse sequence $\mathbb{I}_2 \times \mathbb{I}_2 \xleftarrow{f_1 \times f_1} \mathbb{I}_4 \times \mathbb{I}_4 \xleftarrow{f_2 \times f_2} \ldots$*

4 Mappings between inverse sequences of spaces

In this section is discussed the approximation of mappings between limits of inverse sequences of spaces by mappings between the spaces contained in the sequences.

Let $\Delta_X = X_1 \xleftarrow{f_1} X_2 \xleftarrow{f_2} \cdots$, $\Delta_Y = Y_1 \xleftarrow{g_1} Y_2 \xleftarrow{g_2} \cdots$ be inverse sequences of spaces with respective limits $(X, (p_i))$ and $(Y, (q_i))$. A *mapping* from Δ_X to Δ_Y is a sequence of $(h_i : X_i \rightarrow Y_i)$ of continuous maps such that, for all i, $f_i \circ h_{i+1} = h_i \circ g_i$ [3]. The *limit* of the mapping (h_i) is unique map h from X to Y such that, for all i, $q_i \circ h = h_i \circ p_i$. h is continuous and, in terms of threads, h maps the thread $(x_1 x_2 \ldots)$ to the thread $(h_1(x_1)h_2(x_2)\ldots)$.

Despite its simplicity, however, the approach has certain quite severe limitations, especially when the spaces involved are finite. There will, in general, be continuous maps from X to Y which do not arise as limits of functions from Δ_X to Δ_Y. For example, if each of the spaces *is* finite, and each of the bonding maps is onto, then if, for some i, the cardinality of Y_i is greater than that of X_i, the limit mapping h cannot be onto: $y \in Y_i - h_i(X_i)$ implies that $q_i^{-1}(y) \cap h(X) = \emptyset$.

A solution to such limitations is to allow the mappings involved to be *multi-functions*. Rather than extend **Top** to include multi-functions, multi-functions will be regarded as single-valued functions with range some *power space*. The appropriate space to use is the so-called *upper space*. The upper space UX over a space X is the set $\mathcal{C}X$ of non-empty compact subsets of X, with topology having as base the collection $\{\Box U \mid U \text{ open in } X\}$, where $\Box U = \{K \in \mathcal{C}X \mid K \subseteq U\}$. For any continuous map $f : X \rightarrow Y$, the map $Uf : UX \rightarrow UY,\ K \mapsto f(K)$, is well-defined and continuous. The upper space construction may be regarded as a functor from **Top** to itself.

The relationship between multi-functions and single-valued functions with range some upper space is as follows. A multi-function $f : X \rightarrow Y$ is *bounded non-deterministic* if each point in X is mapped to a compact subset of Y. f is *upper semi-continuous* if, for each open $U \subseteq Y$, the set $f^+(U) = \{x \mid f(x) \subseteq U\}$ is open in X. If f is bounded non-deterministic it may obviously be considered as a single-valued function with range UY, and this single-valued function is then continuous if and only if f is upper semi-continuous. The single-valued continuous maps from X to Y are in an obvious one-to-one correspondence with the continuous maps from X to UY which map each point in X to a singleton subset of Y.

An important property of the upper space construction here is that it preserves limits of relevant inverse sequences:

Proposition 4.1 *Let* $\Delta = X_1 \xleftarrow{f_1} X_2 \xleftarrow{f_2} \cdots$ *be an inverse sequence of compact Hausdorff spaces, with limit* $(X, (p_i))$. *Then* $(UX, (Up_i))$ *is the limit of the sequence* $U\Delta = UX_1 \xleftarrow{Uf_1} UX_2 \xleftarrow{Uf_2} \cdots$.

Proof (Outline) The threads of $U\Delta$ are precisely the canonical decreasing sequences of non-empty sets in Δ. Then, by Lemma 2.1, we may identify the set of threads with the set $\mathcal{C}X$. The projections are then the mappings

(Up_i), and the continuity of these mappings gives that the upper topology on $\mathcal{C}X$ is finer than the inverse limit topology. For any $A \in \mathcal{C}X$ and any open $U \subseteq X$ containing A, there is, by Lemma 2.1 (3), some open $V \subseteq X_i$ with $A \in (Up_i)^{-1}(\Box V) \subseteq \Box U$. The inverse limit topology is therefore finer than the upper topology. $\Box$

It will be necessary in what follows to make use of the following mappings:

Lemma 4.2 *For any spaces X, Y, and any continuous map $f : X \to UY$, the map $f^u : UX \to UY$, $K \mapsto \bigcup\{f(x) \mid x \in K\}$ is well-defined and continuous.*

Lemma 4.3 *For compact metrizable spaces X, Y and for any onto continuous map $f : X \to Y$, the restriction of the pre-image of f to the map $f^{-1} : Y \to UX$, $y \mapsto f^{-1}(y)$ is well-defined, and continuous.*

Proof f^{-1} is clearly well-defined. $y \in Y$ is the meet of a sequence $A_1 \supseteq A_2 \supseteq \ldots$ of compact sets, each of which contains y in its interior. For U open in X, $f^{-1}(y) \in \Box U$ implies, by the finite intersection property, that $f^{-1}(A_i) \in \Box U$ for some i. Then $y \in int(A_i) \subseteq (f^{-1})^{-1}(\Box U)$. $\Box$

In defining a 'multi-function between inverse sequences of spaces', Lemma 4.3 makes it necessary to consider each bonding map in one of the sequences as being onto. No generality is lost by this restriction, however, as the limit space of an inverse sequence of spaces is the limit space of an inverse sequence of subspaces in which each bonding map is onto (see [3]). For the remainder of this section we assume that $\Delta_X = X_1 \xleftarrow{f_1} X_2 \xleftarrow{f_2} \cdots$ and $\Delta_Y = Y_1 \xleftarrow{g_1} Y_2 \xleftarrow{g_2} \cdots$ are inverse sequences of compact metrizable spaces with respective limits $(X, (p_i))$ and $(Y, (q_i))$, and that each bonding map f_i is onto.

Definition 4.4 *A* multi-function *from Δ_X to Δ_Y is a sequence of mappings $(h_i : X_i \to UY_i)$ such that, for all i, $h_i = Ug_i \circ (h_{i+1})^u \circ f_i^{-1}$. The* limit *of (h_i) is the map $h : X \to UY$, where, for all $x \in X$, $h(x)$ is the limit of the decreasing sequence $(h_i \circ p_i(x))$.*

If each map h_i is the definition maps each point in X_i to a singleton subset of UY_i (in which case each h_i is essentially a continuous single-valued map from X_i to Y_i) then the sequence (h_i) is in essence an ordinary function (defined at the beginning of this section) from Δ_X to Δ_Y. Multi-functions give the full range of continuous functions as limits:

Proposition 4.5 *A mapping from X to UY is continuous iff it is the limit of a multi-function from Δ_X to Δ_Y.*

Proof ($\Leftarrow$): Let h be the limit of the multi-function (h_i). For $x \in X$ and U open in Y, if $h(x) \in \Box U$ then, by Lemma 2.1 (3), there is some open $V \subseteq X_i$ with $h_i \circ p_i(x) \subseteq V$ and $q_i^{-1}(V) \subseteq U$. Then $x \in (h_i \circ p_i)^{-1}(\Box V) \subseteq h^{-1}(\Box U)$. ($\Rightarrow$): Let $h : X \to UY$ be continuous. For each i let $h_i = Uq_i \circ h^u \circ p_i^{-1}$. Then (h_i) is a multi-function with limit, say, h'. Then $y \in h'(x)$ iff

$\forall i.(q_i(y) \in Uq_i \circ h^u \circ p_i^{-1} \circ p_i(x))$ iff (by Lemma 2.1 (5)) $\forall i.(y \in h^u \circ p_i^{-1} \circ p_i(x))$ iff $y \in h(x)$. □

Corollary 4.6 *The limit h of a multi-function (h_i) is the unique continuous map from X to UY such that, for all i, $h_i = Uq_i \circ h^u \circ p_i^{-1}$.*

5 Mappings on inverse sequences of graphs

The aim of this section is to extend the definitions and results of the previous section to topological graphs. First is required a suitable definition of 'upper graph'.

Definition 5.1 *Let $G = (X, R)$ be a topological graph. The corresponding* upper relation *on UX is the set $UR = \{(A, B) \mid R(A) \cap B \neq \emptyset\}$. The* upper topological graph *over G is the graph $UG = (UX, UR)$.*

The definition of 'upper relation' bears a strong resemblance to that of a (symmetric) *semi-proximity* relation [7]. Semi-proximity spaces (weaker than the more standard *proximity* spaces in that the 'Strong Axiom' in [5] is dropped) are, like topological graphs, introduced as generalizations of both discrete graph structures and continuous topological structures. If (X, R) is a tolerance graph, then the upper relation UR, extended to the powerset of X in the obvious way, is a symmetric semi-proximity relation. Moreover, the upper relation provides a one-to-one correspondence between finite tolerance graphs and finite symmetric semi-proximity spaces.

Relations on upper spaces employed in the domain-theoretic approaches (the upper power order is used in [14]; the Egli-Milner order is used in [2]) are not useful for our purposes, due principally to the fact that the relations we deal with are typically non-transitive.

For any relation-preserving map $f : G \to H$, the map $Uf : UG \to UH$ is also relation-preserving, and the upper graph construction may be regarded as a functor from **TopGr** to itself.

A *compact Hausdorff graph* is a compact Hausdorff space endowed with a closed relation. A *compact metrizable graph* is a compact metrizable space endowed with a closed relation. If (X, R) is a compact Hausdorff graph, then for any compact $A \subseteq X$ it may be verified that $R(A)$ is also compact. It may also be verified that the limit of an inverse sequence of compact Hausdorff (metrizable) graphs is itself a compact Hausdorff (metrizable) graph. The upper graph construction preserves limits of inverse sequences of compact Hausdorff graphs:

Lemma 5.2 *Let $\Delta = (X_1, R_1) \xleftarrow{f_1} (X_2, R_2) \xleftarrow{f_2} \cdots$ be an inverse sequence of compact Hausdorff graphs, with limit $((X, R), (p_i))$. Let (A_i) and (B_i) be decreasing sequences in Δ with respective limits A and B. Then $A\ UR\ B$ if and only if $A_i\ UR_i\ B_i$ for all i.*

Proof We claim that $R(A)$ is the limit of the decreasing sequence $(R_i(A_i))$. This follows from the fact that for any $x \in X$, the set $\{a \in A \mid a\ R\ x\}$ is the limit of the decreasing sequence $(\{a \in A_i \mid a\ R_i\ p_i(x)\})$. It then follows that the set $R(A) \cap B$ is the limit of the decreasing sequence $(R_i(A_i) \cap B)$, from which (by Lemma 2.1 (2)) the result follows. □

Proposition 5.3 *Let* $\Delta = G_1 \xleftarrow{f_1} G_2 \xleftarrow{f_2} \cdots$ *be an inverse sequence of compact Hausdorff graphs with limit* $(G, (p_i))$. *Then* $(UG, (Up_i))$ *is the limit of the sequence* $U\Delta = UG_1 \xleftarrow{Uf_1} UG_2 \xleftarrow{Uf_2} \cdots$.

Proof Let $G = (X, R)$, $G_i = (X_i, R_i)$. Given Proposition 4.1, all that needs to be shown is that UR is the inverse limit relation on UX with respect to the relations (UR_i), which follows immediately from Lemma 5.2. □

For any graph morphism $f : G \to UH$, the map $f^u : UG \to UH$ (Lemma 4.2) is also a graph morphism. However, for a graph morphism $f : G \to H$ between compact metrizable graphs, the map $f^{-1} : H \to UG$ (Lemma 4.3) is not necessarily relation-preserving. We therefore make use of the following definition.

Definition 5.4 *For graphs* (X, R), (Y, S) *and a mapping* $f : X \to Y$, *the relation* S *is* final *with respect to* f *and* R *if:* $\forall y, y' \in Y.(y\ S\ y' \Rightarrow \exists x \in f^{-1}(y).\exists x' \in f^{-1}(y').\ x\ R\ y)$.

S is final w.r.t. f and R if and only if it is the smallest relation on Y for which the map f is relation-preserving. It is easily checked that if S is final with respect to R and f, the mapping f^{-1} above is relation-preserving. An inverse sequence of graphs $\Delta = (X_1, R_1) \xleftarrow{f_1} (X_2, R_2) \xleftarrow{f_2} \cdots$ will be called *minimal* if each R_i is final w.r.t. R_{i+1} and f_i. Informally, where $((X, R), (p_i))$ is the limit of Δ, minimality means that none of the relations R_i can be made smaller without making R smaller. It is then the case that each relation R_i is final with respect to R and p_i. No generality is lost by restricting our attention to minimal inverse sequences: the set of relations (R_i) in the proof of Proposition 3.4 yields a minimal inverse sequence.

For the following definition, we assume that $\Delta_G = G_1 \xleftarrow{f_1} G_2 \xleftarrow{f_2} \cdots$, $\Delta_H = H_1 \xleftarrow{g_1} H_2 \xleftarrow{g_2} \cdots$ are inverse sequences of compact metrizable graphs with respective limits $(G, (p_i))$ and $(H, (q_i))$, and that Δ_G is minimal.

Definition 5.5 *A* multi-function *from* Δ_G *to* Δ_H *is a sequence of graph morphisms* $(h_i : G_i \to UH_i)$ *such that, for all* i, $h_i = Ug_i \circ (h_{i+1})^u \circ f_i^{-1}$. *The* limit *of the sequence* (h_i) *is the map* $h : X \to UY$, *where, for all* $x \in X$, $h(x)$ *is the limit of the decreasing sequence* $(h_i \circ p_i(x))$.

Proposition 5.6 *A mapping from* G *to* UH *is a graph morphism iff it is the limit of a multi-function from* Δ_G *to* Δ_H.

Proof ($\Leftarrow$): Let (h_i) be a multi-function with limit h. Given Proposition 4.5, all that needs to be shown is that h is relation-preserving, which follows from Lemma 5.2. ($\Rightarrow$): For any graph morphism $h : G \to UH$, all that needs to be shown is that each map h_i (defined in the proof of Proposition 4.5) is relation-preserving, which follows from the fact that, for each i, the relation in G_i is final with respect to p_i and the relation in G. □

6 Passing to the quotient

Where Δ_X and Δ_Y are inverse sequences of graphs approximating the spaces X and Y respectively, we discuss in this section the derivation from multi-functions from Δ_X to Δ_Y of continuous mappings from X to UY.

Notation. If R is an equivalence relation on the space X, then for $x \in X$, $[x]_R$ denotes the equivalence class of x with respect to R, and ϕ_R denotes the canonical quotient map from X to X/R.

Suppose (X, R) and (Y, S) are topological graphs where R and S are equivalence relations. For any graph morphism $f : (X, R) \to (Y, S)$, the map $f^* : X/R \to Y/S$, $[x]_R \mapsto [f(x)]_S$, is well-defined, continuous and is the unique map from X/R to Y/S such that $f^* \circ \phi_R = \phi_S \circ f$. f^* is called f *passed to the quotient* [3]. Conversely, given a continuous map $g : X/R \to Y/S$, any continuous map $f : X \to Y$ such that $g \circ \phi_R = \phi_S \circ f$ is called a *representation* of g [15] (if $g \circ \phi_R = \phi_S \circ f$ then f is relation-preserving w.r.t. R, S and therefore $g = f^*$). g does not necessarily have a representation.

Even when the relation R in a graph (X, R) is an equivalence relation, the upper relation UR is not, in general, an equivalence relation on UX. We will quotient UX by the relation: $A \ \widehat{UR}\ B \Leftrightarrow UR(A) = UR(B)$. If (X, R) is a compact Hausdorff graph, it is easily checked that $A \ \widehat{UR}\ B \Leftrightarrow R(A) = R(B)$. Theoretical motivation for the relation $\widehat{UR}$ and for quotienting graphs in which the relation is not an equivalence relation can be found in [9], though we will not discuss this here.

At this point it is convenient to give the following notation and definitions. For a graph (X, R), and for $A \subseteq X$, $int_R(A)$ denotes the set $\{x \mid R(x) \subseteq A\}$. (X, R) is *continuous* if $int_R(U)$ is open for all open $U \subseteq X$. A compact Hausdorff graph is easily checked to be continuous. $A \subseteq X$ is *R-saturated* if $A = R(A)$. If R is an equivalence relation, the significance of R-saturated open sets is that their images are open under the map ϕ_R. If (X, R) is a compact Hausdorff graph, with R an equivalence relation, let $\psi_R : U(X/R) \to UX$, $A \mapsto \phi_R^{-1}(A)$.

Proposition 6.1 *Let (X, R) be a compact Hausdorff graph, with R an equivalence relation. Then $UX/\widehat{UR}$ is homeomorphic to $U(X/R)$.*

Proof We first claim that ψ_R is a continuous open mapping. For any U open in X, $int_R(U)$ is open and R-saturated, therefore $\phi_R(int_R(U))$ is open in X/R. $\psi_R^{-1}(\Box U) = \Box(\phi_R(int_R(U)))$, therefore ψ_R is continuous. ψ_R is open because for U open in X/R, $\psi_R(\Box U) = \Box(\phi_R^{-1}(U))$. We claim that the map $\phi_{\widehat{UR}} \circ \psi_R$ is a homeomorphism. It is the composition of continuous maps and is easily checked to be a bijection. For U open in X/R, $\psi_R(\Box U)$ is $\widehat{UR}$-saturated and open. $\phi_{\widehat{UR}}(\psi_R(\Box U))$ is then open in $UX/\widehat{UR}$. □

Corollary 6.2 *If Δ is an inverse sequence of compact Hausdorff graphs approximating the space X, then $U\Delta$ approximates the space UX.*

The corollary follows from Propositions 6.1 and 5.3. It also follows from Proposition 6.1 that if (X, R) and (Y, S) are compact Hausdorff graphs, with R and S equivalence relations, then from any graph morphism $f : (X, R) \to (UY, \widehat{US})$ there may, by passing to the quotient, be derived a continuous map $f^* : X/R \to U(Y/S) \cong UY/\widehat{US}$. Conversely:

Proposition 6.3 *If (X, R) and (Y, S) are compact Hausdorff graphs, with R and S equivalence relations, then any continuous map $f : X/R \to U(Y/S)$ has a (canonical) representation $f_* : X \to UY$.*

Proof Let $f_* = \psi_S \circ f \circ \phi_R$. Then f_* is continuous by continuity of each of the maps ψ_S, f, ϕ_R. That $f = (f_*)^*$ follows from the fact that for any $A \in U(Y/S)$, $A = \phi_S(\psi_S(A))$. □

The above result may have some relevance to the theory of representations in [15]:

Example 6.4 Multiplication by 3. *Where $\Sigma = \{0, 1, \ldots 9\}$, let $X = \Sigma^\omega$ and let $R = \{(a09^\omega, a10^\omega), \ldots, (a89^\omega, a90^\omega) \mid a \in \Sigma^*\}$. Let $\phi_1 : X \to [0, 1]$, $a_1a_2 \ldots \mapsto 0 \cdot a_1a_2 \ldots$; $\phi_2 : X \to [0, 10]$, $a_1a_2 \ldots \mapsto a_1 \cdot a_2 \ldots$ (ϕ_1 and ϕ_2 are quotient mappings). As is well-known, the mapping $f : [0, 1] \to [0, 10], x \mapsto 3x$ has no representation by a map from X to itself. If, however, f is considered as a mapping from $[0, 1]$ to $U[0, 10]$, then it is represented by the map $f_* : X \to UX$, $(a_1a_2 \ldots) \mapsto R(b_1b_2 \ldots)$, where $b_1 \cdot b_2 \ldots = 3(0 \cdot a_1a_2 \ldots)$.*

For the following result, assume that Δ_X and Δ_Y are inverse sequences of compact metrizable graphs approximating the spaces X and Y respectively, and that Δ_X is minimal. We say that a multi-function (h_i) from Δ_X to Δ_Y *approximates* a function f from X to UY if $f = h^*$, where h is the limit of (h_i). Thus, where (X, R) and (Y, S) are the respective limits of Δ_X and Δ_Y, we are interested in those multi-functions from Δ_X to Δ_Y whose limits are relation-preserving w.r.t. R and $\widehat{US}$. By reflexivity of S, $\widehat{US} \subseteq US$ and therefore any graph morphism from (X, R) to $(UY, \widehat{US})$ is a graph morphism from (X, R) to (UY, US). It is, at present, an embarassment to our theory that we do not make use of those multi-functions from Δ_X to Δ_Y whose limits are not relation-preserving w.r.t. $\widehat{US}$.

Theorem 6.5 *A function from X to UY is continuous if and only if it can be approximated by a multi-function from Δ_X to Δ_Y.*

Proof ($\Rightarrow$): If $f : X \rightarrow UY$ is continuous, let h be the canonical representation of f (Proposition 6.3), and let (h_i) be a multi-function with limit h (Proposition 5.6). Then (h_i) approximates f. ($\Leftarrow$): The limit of each multi-function from Δ_X to Δ_Y is continuous (Proposition 5.6), and any continuous function passed to the quotient is continuous. □

The theorem is our main result. It gives that, in the context of the approximation of spaces by graphs, any continuous mapping may be constructed from graph morphisms between the graphs, although multi-functions and minimal inverse sequences have to be employed in doing so.

7 Applications/Further work

An obvious theoretical extension to the material presented is that of developing a theory of 'function space graphs' and of inverse sequences of such. Such a theory has been developed (the definition of 'function space graph' makes use of the relation of *indistinguishability* between functions in [6]), though for reasons of space we have not presented it here. If the objects in **TopGr** are restricted to the compact metrizable graphs, and the morphisms restricted to those graph morphisms $f : G \rightarrow H$ for which the relation in H is final w.r.t. f and the relation in G, then the function space graph construction may be considered as a functor which is covariant in both arguments, and which preserves limits of inverse sequences.

The upper graph contruction may be considered as part of a monad on **TopGr**. The corresponding Kleisli category does not have products, so is not cartesian closed. It is, however, monoidal, and is monoidal closed when the objects in **TopGr** are restricted to those graphs in which the space is compact and the relation is reflexive.

Locally compact spaces may be approximated by *finitary* (each point has finite valency) discrete graphs, and the theory of mappings presented here may be extended to this more general case.

In the context of digital topology, the work here presented may be viewed as a theory of mappings between digital images which is in some sort of harmony with the theory of continuous mappings on topological spaces. In the use of multi-functions, our approach is in contrast to the theory of mappings between digital images in [8, 1], where only single-valued maps are considered. Our main conjecture in this regard, based on the limitations of single-valued maps discussed in Section 4, is that single-valued maps do not provide an adequate theory of mappings between digital images, whereas multi-functions do. A particular application might be the expression of thinning algorithms in terms of multi-functions; we envisage developing a theory along the lines of that in [7].

1. L. Boxer, Digitally continuous functions, *Pattern Recognition Letters* **15** (1994).
2. C. Brink, *Power structures and their applications*, Technical report, University of Cape Town (1992).
3. J. Dugundji, *Topology*, Allyn and Bacon, 1966.
4. G. Hocking and J. Young, *Topology*, Addison-Wesley, 1961.
5. S. Naimpally and B. Warrack, *Proximity Spaces*, CUP, 1970.
6. T. Poston, Fuzzy geometry, Ph.D. thesis, Warwick (1971).
7. L. Latecki and F. Prokop, Semi-proximity continuous functions in digital images, Preprint.
8. A. Rosenfeld, 'Continuous' functions on digital pictures, *Pattern Recognition Letters* **4** (1986).
9. M. Smyth, Semi-Metrics, closure spaces and digital topology, *Theoretical Computer Science* **151** (1995) 257-276.
10. M. Smyth, Inverse limits of graphs, *Theory and Formal Methods 1994: Proceedings of the Second Imperial College Department of Computing Workshop on Theory and Formal Methods*, IC Press, 1995.
11. M. Smyth, Topology, *Handbook of Logic in Computer Science*, OUP, 1992.
12. M. Smyth, Lines as topological graphs, to appear.
13. A. Sossinsky, Tolerance space theory and some applications, *Acta Appl. Math.*, **5** (1986).
14. P. Sünderhauf, Discrete approximation of spaces, Ph.D. thesis, Darmstadt (1994).
15. Weihrauch, K, Kreitz, C, Theory of Representations, *Theoretical Computer Science* **38** (1985).

Specifications as spans of geometric morphisms (Extended abstract)

Till Plewe
Department of Computing, Imperial College, London SW7 2BZ.

Abstract

We give a semantics interpreting Hoare triples $\{\mathbb{S}\}\mathbf{P}\{\mathbb{T}\}$ as maps in the 2-category $\mathcal{TOP}/\mathcal{S}$ of toposes over $\mathcal{S}$ and bounded geometric morphisms, and specifications as spans in $\mathcal{TOP}/\mathcal{S}$. Here $\{\mathbb{S}\}$ and $\{\mathbb{T}\}$ are presentations of geometric theories, and $\mathbf{P}$ is a program in either a simple imperative language, or in a non-deterministic extension in the sense of Dijkstra. The topos $\mathcal{S}$ is the classifying topos for a geometric theory which gives a formal description of the computing environment.

The command structures of the programming language can then be lifted first to arbitrary geometric morphisms and then to spans, hence to specifications. This uniform interpretation of command structures for programs and specifications allows us to introduce the idea of stepwise refinement into this context.

Introduction

This paper is intended to be one step in the program initiated by S. Vickers to use geometric logic to design a specification language. This program is based on the theses that a specification language should build a bridge between (a formalization of) the real world and the formal world of computing, that geometric logic provides a suitable formalization of the real world (as a logic of observational classes)[7], that schemas can be interpreted as presentations of geometric theories[9,10], and finally that topos theory is rich enough to provide all the theoretical tools needed to describe the interplay between specifications and programs.

Here we will deal only with the question of whether topos theory provides sufficiently many tools. Our starting point is the idea that a schema should be the same thing as a presentation of a (geometric) theory[10]. Using this idea and identifying geometric theories with their classifying toposes we arrive at the problem of interpreting programs and specifications in the category $\mathcal{TOP}$ of Grothendieck toposes and geometric morphisms (to be more precise, in the 2-category $\mathcal{TOP}/\mathcal{S}$ of toposes and bounded geometric morphisms over a base topos $\mathcal{S}$). Programs will be considered here only together with given pre- and post-conditions. Departing slightly from standard convention we will assume that a Hoare triple $\{\mathbb{S}\}\mathbf{P}\{\mathbb{T}\}$ includes the assertion that $\mathbf{P}$ terminates if the input satisfies $\{\mathbb{S}\}$[8]. Hoare triples will be interpreted as geometric morphisms whose domain is the classifying topos for the theory generated by the pre-conditions, and whose codomain classifies the corresponding theory for the post-conditions. As suggested by S. Vickers[10], we will interpret specifications as spans in $\mathcal{TOP}$, i.e. as a pair of geometric morphisms with common domain. (The domain should be thought of as the topos of models for the theory generated by the relations binding input and output together, while the respective codomains correspond to pre- and post-conditions.)

A summary of this paper follows. In the first section we give a semantics for Hoare triples over a simple imperative language. The second section contains an extension to an imperative language which includes guarded commands. In the third section we sketch how to view specifications as spans of geometric morphisms and how to extend the operations on geometric morphisms induced by the various command structures considered in the first sections to operations on specifications.

We assume that the reader is familiar with basic facts concerning geometric morphisms[2,4] and classifying toposes[2,4,5]. An introduction for computer scientists is given in[9].

1 Semantics for Hoare triples with deterministic programs

We start by giving the inference rules for the Hoare logic we are going to use. A Hoare triple $\{\mathbb{S}\}\mathbf{P}\{\mathbb{T}\}$ consists of a program $\mathbf{P}$ and pre- respectively post-conditions $\{\mathbb{S}\}$ and $\{\mathbb{T}\}$. $\mathbf{P}$ is a program in a simple imperative language including guarded commands a la Dijkstra[1]. Unlike Dijkstra we assume that one of the guarded commands in the generalized while loop is the command which terminates the loop. This does not change the expressive power if all truth values are Boolean. But in the topos theoretic context it seems more natural (and is also less restrictive) than restricting to Boolean guards. A simplifying assumption we will make throughout this paper is that all numerical and logical expressions are simple, i.e. their evaluation has no side effects.

$\{\mathbb{S}\}$ and $\{\mathbb{T}\}$ are schemas describing pre- and post-conditions for the program $\mathbf{P}$. "Schema" is used here synonymously with "presentation of a geometric theory"[10].

Finally, the inference rules we are going to use for Hoare triples $\{\mathbb{S}\}\mathbf{P}\{\mathbb{T}\}$ are intended to capture not only that, if $\mathbf{P}$ terminates and the input satisfies $\mathbb{S}$, then the output satisfies $\mathbb{T}$, but also that $\mathbf{P}$ terminates whenever the input satisfies the pre-conditions.

Notation: $Bool([\mathbb{S}])$ will denote the set of Boolean truth values in $[\mathbb{S}]$.

$\{\mathbb{S}, R\}$ will be used as an abbreviation for the schema given by $\mathbb{S}$ with the additional axiom $\top \vdash R$. If U and V are subobjects of the terminal object $1_{\mathcal{E}}$ of some topos $\mathcal{E}$, and $U \leq V$, then we will use ι as the generic name for inclusion $\mathcal{E}/U \longrightarrow \mathcal{E}/V$ induced by the inclusion $U \leq V$. In composites we will sometimes omit to name such inclusions altogether.

The inference rules for Hoare triples

composition

$$\frac{\{\mathbb{S}\}\mathbf{P}\{\mathbb{T}\}, \{\mathbb{T}\}\mathbf{Q}\{\mathbb{U}\}}{\{\mathbb{S}\}\mathbf{P};\mathbf{Q}\{\mathbb{U}\}}$$

if-then-else

$$\frac{\{\mathbb{S}, B\}\mathbf{P}\{\mathbb{T}\}, \{\mathbb{S}, \neg B\}\mathbf{Q}\{\mathbb{T}\}, B \in Bool([\mathbb{S}])}{\{\mathbb{S}\}\mathbf{if}\ B\ \mathbf{then\ P\ else\ Q\ fi}\{\mathbb{T}\}}$$

skip

$$\frac{}{\{\mathbb{S}\}\mathbf{skip}\{\mathbb{S}\}}$$

while

$$\frac{\{\mathbb{S}, B\}\mathbf{P}\{\mathbb{S}\}, \{\mathbb{S}, R(n+1), B\}\mathbf{P}\{\mathbb{S}, R(n)\}, R(0) \wedge B \vdash \bot, B \in Bool([\mathbb{S}])}{\{\mathbb{S}, (\exists n : R(n)) \vee \neg B\}\mathbf{while}\ B\ \mathbf{do\ P\ od}\{\mathbb{S}, \neg B\}}$$

weakening/strengthening

$$\frac{\mathbb{S}' \Rightarrow \mathbb{S}, \{\mathbb{S}\}\mathbf{P}\{\mathbb{T}\}, \mathbb{T} \Rightarrow \mathbb{T}'}{\{\mathbb{S}'\}\mathbf{P}\{\mathbb{T}'\}}$$

Here we have to say what we mean by an implication $\mathbb{S}' \Rightarrow \mathbb{S}$ between presentations of geometric theories. For now we will just use it as an abbreviation for a fixed translation of the language $L(\mathbb{S})$ of the schema $\{\mathbb{S}\}$ into $L(\mathbb{S}')$ for which all axioms of $\{\mathbb{S}\}$ become valid in the theory generated by $\{\mathbb{S}'\}$. But more general interpretations of such an implication are also possible.

assignments

$$\frac{x \in \mathbf{Add}, e \in \mathbb{N}[Def]}{\{\mathbb{S}[e/x]\}\mathbf{x} := \mathbf{e}\{\mathbb{S}\}}$$

Here $\mathbb{N}[Def]$ denotes the free $\mathbb{N}$-algebra generated by Def, i.e. the free polynomial rig (= commutative ring without negatives) over Def, and Def is a type symbol representing the subset of the set (type) of all possible storage locations Add which consists precisely of those addresses which have values assigned to them. For more details see below.

The two rules introducing non-deterministic programs are a modified if-then-else rule, and a modified while rule.

if ... fi

$$\frac{\{\mathbb{S}, b_1\}\mathbf{P_1}\{\mathbb{T}\}, \ldots, \{\mathbb{S}, b_n\}\mathbf{P_n}\{\mathbb{T}\}}{\{\mathbb{S}, \bigvee b_i\}\mathbf{if}\ b_1 \rightarrow \mathbf{P_1} [\!] \ldots [\!] b_n \rightarrow \mathbf{P_n}\ \mathbf{fi}\{\mathbb{T}\}}$$

do ... od

$$\frac{\{\mathbb{S}, b_j\}\mathbf{P_j}\{\mathbb{S}\}, \{\mathbb{S}, b_j, R(n+1)\}\mathbf{P_j}\{\mathbb{S}, R(n)\}, R(0) \vdash b_1 (j = 2, \ldots, k)}{\{\mathbb{S}, \exists n : R(n), \bigvee_{i=1}^{n} b_i\}\mathbf{do}\ b_1 \rightarrow \mathbf{exit} [\!] \ldots [\!] b_k \rightarrow \mathbf{P_k}\ \mathbf{od}\{\mathbb{S}, b_1\}}$$

In this section we will give semantics for Hoare triples in which $\mathbf{P}$ is deterministic. For deterministic programs $\mathbf{P}$ a sequent $\{\mathbb{S}\}\mathbf{P}\{\mathbb{T}\}$ will be interpreted as a geometric morphism $[\mathbb{S}] \xrightarrow{[\mathbf{P}]} [\mathbb{T}]$. Here $[\mathbb{S}]$ and $[\mathbb{T}]$ are the classifying toposes for the geometric theories presented by $\{\mathbb{S}\}$ and $\{\mathbb{T}\}$ respectively. $[\![\mathbf{P}]\!]$ is constructed via structural induction.

The interpretation of composition and if-then-else is straightforward.

$$[\![\{\mathbb{S}\}\mathbf{P}; \mathbf{Q}\{\mathbb{U}\}]\!] = [\![\{\mathbb{S}\}\mathbf{P}\{\mathbb{T}\}]\!]; [\![\{\mathbb{T}\}\mathbf{Q}\{\mathbb{U}\}]\!]$$

$$[\![\{\mathbb{S}\}\mathbf{if}\ B\ \mathbf{then}\ \mathbf{P}\ \mathbf{else}\ \mathbf{Q}\ \mathbf{fi}\{\mathbb{T}\}]\!] = \langle [\mathbb{S}]/B \xrightarrow{[\mathbf{P}]} [\mathbb{T}], [\mathbb{S}]/\neg B \xrightarrow{[\mathbf{Q}]} [\mathbb{T}] \rangle$$

Here $[\mathbb{S}]/B$ is the part of $[\mathbb{S}]$ where B is true, equivalently the classifying topos for the theory generated by $\{\mathbb{S}\}$ augmented by the additional axiom $\top \vdash B$, and $\langle [\![\mathbf{P}]\!], [\![\mathbf{Q}]\!] \rangle$ is a map $[\mathbb{S}] \longrightarrow [\mathbb{T}]$ because $[\mathbb{S}]$ is the coproduct of $[\mathbb{S}]/B$ and $[\mathbb{S}]/\neg B$ in $\mathcal{TOP}$. (The underlying category of the topos coproduct is just the product of the underlying categories.)

While loops require a bit more work. As usual, the denotation of a sequent $\{\mathbb{S}, \exists n : R(n) \vee \neg B\}$**while** B **do P od**$\{\mathbb{S}, \neg B\}$ will be the least (actually the unique) fixpoint of the operation Γ which assigns to a map $([\mathbb{S}]/(\bigvee R(n) \vee \neg B) \xrightarrow{g} [\mathbb{S}]/\neg B)$ the map $([\mathbb{S}]/(\bigvee R(n) \wedge B) + [\mathbb{S}]/\neg B \xrightarrow{\langle g[\mathbf{P}], \iota \rangle} [\mathbb{S}]/\neg B)$. There are two ways to construct this fixpoint. One consists of replacing the topos $[\mathbb{S}]/\neg B$ by its lift $([\mathbb{S}]/\neg B)_\perp$ [3] $((-, ([\mathbb{S}]/\neg B)_\perp)$ represents the functor which maps a topos $\mathcal{E}$ to the set of all partial maps $\mathcal{E} \longrightarrow [\mathbb{S}]/\neg B$ whose domain is an open subtopos of $\mathcal{E}$) and then constructing the fixpoint by taking the colimit of all finite iterations of the map which corresponds to the identity on $[\mathbb{S}]/\neg B$ considered as a partial map $[\mathbb{S}] \rightharpoonup [\mathbb{S}]/\neg B$. Here we will choose the second, more straightforward method of taking the various iterations and gluing them together. Put

$$f_n = [\mathbb{S}]/(R(n+1) \wedge B) + [\mathbb{S}]/\neg B \xrightarrow{\langle \alpha_n, \beta_n \rangle} [\mathbb{S}]/(R(n) \wedge B) + [\mathbb{S}]/\neg B$$

where

$$\alpha_n = [\mathbb{S}]/(R(n+1) \wedge B) \xrightarrow{[\mathbf{P}]} [\mathbb{S}]/R(n) \simeq$$

$$[\mathbb{S}]/(R(n) \wedge B) + [\mathbb{S}]/(R(n) \wedge \neg B) \xrightarrow{id+\iota} [\mathbb{S}]/(R(n) \wedge B) + [\mathbb{S}]/\neg B$$

and

$$\beta_n = [\mathbb{S}]/\neg B \xrightarrow{\iota} [\mathbb{S}]/(R(n) \wedge B) + [\mathbb{S}]/\neg B.$$

The summand $[\mathbb{S}]/\neg B$ has been added to ensure composability of the f_n. Put $g_n = f_0 f_1 \ldots f_n$ ($f_{-1} = g_{-1} = id_{[\mathbb{S}]/\neg B}$). If all $R(n) \wedge B$ are pairwise disjoint then

$$[\![\{\mathbb{S}, (\exists n : R(n)) \vee \neg B\}\textbf{while } B \textbf{ do P od}\{\mathbb{S}, \neg B\}]\!]$$

is obtained from $\coprod [\mathbb{S}]/((R(n) \wedge B) \vee \neg B) \xrightarrow{\langle g_n \rangle} [\mathbb{S}]/\neg B$ by identifying the subtoposes $[\mathbb{S}]/\neg B \xrightarrow{\iota} [\mathbb{S}]/((R(n) \wedge B) \vee \neg B)$ for each n. In the general case we will also obtain the denotation of the while loop by gluing the g_n together, but since we are working in a 2-category we have to use the following slightly unsightly diagram in which the unique arrow γ which makes the triangle on the right commute is equal to $[\![\{\mathbb{S}, \exists n : R(n) \vee \neg B\}\textbf{while } B \textbf{ do P od}\{\mathbb{S}, \neg B\}]\!]$.

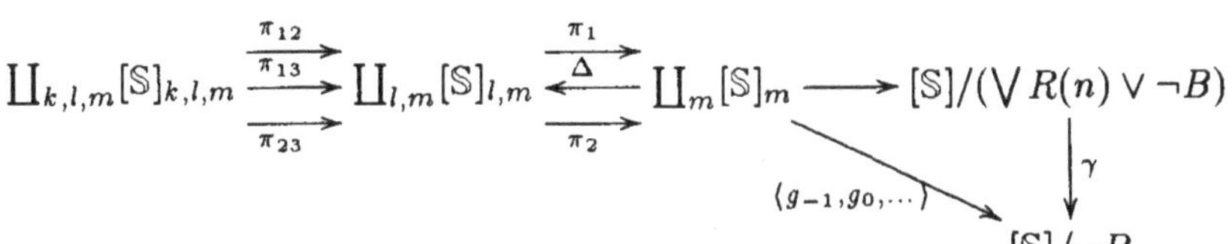

($[\mathbb{S}]_m$ is an abbreviation for $[\mathbb{S}]/(R(m) \vee \neg B)$, $[\mathbb{S}]_{l,m}$ for $[\mathbb{S}]/((R(l) \wedge R(m)) \vee \neg B)$ and similarly for $[\mathbb{S}]_{k,l,m}$.)

The necessity of using the extended kernel pair is essentially due to coherence conditions on the specified 2-isomorphisms which we have suppressed so far. To be able to glue the given family $\{[\mathbb{S}]_n \xrightarrow{g_n} [\mathbb{S}]/\neg B\}$ together, we need to know, not only that there exists a family $\{\eta_{n,m} : g^*_{n,m} \Rightarrow g^*_{m,n}\}$ of 2-isomorphisms (here $g_{n,m}$ stands for the restriction of g_n to $[\mathbb{S}]/((R(n) \wedge R(m)) \vee \neg B)$), but also that this family is compatible in the sense that $\eta_{n,m,k}\eta_{m,k,n} = \eta_{n,k,m}$ and $\eta_{n,n} = id$ (here $\eta_{n,m,k} = \iota^* \eta_{n,m}$ for the obvious inclusion $[\mathbb{S}]_{n,m,k} \xrightarrow{\iota} [\mathbb{S}]_{n,m}$). These compatibility conditions are precisely what is provided by the fact that a given morphism is a cocone over the extended kernel pair, because a 2-isomorphism $\pi_1^*\eta \colon \langle g_{-1}, g_0, \ldots\rangle \Rightarrow \pi_2^*\langle g_{-1}, g_0, \ldots\rangle$ which satisfies $\pi_{2,3}^*\eta \circ \pi_{1,2}^*\eta = \pi_{1,3}^*\eta$ and $\Delta^*\eta = id$ gives rise to such a family by precomposing with all coproduct inclusions.

The necessity of using these compatibility conditions can be seen more easily if $[\mathbb{S}]$ is the category of sheaves over a topological space or locale X. In this case the inverse image maps can be glued together only if for each object A in $[\mathbb{S}]/\neg B$, the families $\{g_n^*(A)\}$ can be glued together. But an object $h_n = g_n^*(A)$ is a local homeomorphism whose codomain is the open subspace corresponding to $U_n = R_n \vee \neg B$, and a family $\{h_n\}$ of maps can be glued together along their codomains only if there exist isomorphisms $h_n \mid_{U_m} \xrightarrow{i_{n,m}} h_m \mid_{U_n}$ which satisfy $i_{n,n} = id$ and $i_{n,m} \mid_{U_k} i_{m,k} \mid_{U_n} = i_{n,k} \mid_{U_m}$.

To show that there exists such a family $\{\eta_{n,m} \colon g_{n,m}^* \Rightarrow g_{m,n}^* \mid n, m \in \mathbb{N}\}$ of natural isomorphisms, observe first that there exists an isomorphism $\eta_{-1,0} \colon g_{1,0}^* \Rightarrow g_{0,-1}^*$ because $g_{-1,0} = g_{-1}$ and $g_{0,-1} = \beta_0 \simeq id_{[\mathbb{S}]/\neg B}$. Now put

$$\begin{aligned}
\eta_{n,n+1} &= \langle [\![\mathbf{P}]\!] \mid_{[\mathbb{S}]/(R(n+1)\wedge R(n)\wedge B)}, \iota\rangle^* \eta_{n-1,n};\\
\eta_{n,n+m} &= \eta_{n+m-1,n+m} \circ \cdots \circ \eta_{n,n+1} (m \geq 1);\\
\eta_{n+m,n} &= \eta_{n,n+m}^{-1} (m \geq 1);\\
\eta_{n,n} &= id.
\end{aligned}$$

$\{\eta_{n,m}\}$ is a compatible family, essentially because each f_i is a restriction of the map $[\mathbb{S}]/(\bigvee R(n) \wedge B) + [\mathbb{S}]/\neg B \xrightarrow{\langle [\![P]\!], \iota\rangle} [\mathbb{S}]/(\bigvee R(n) \vee \neg B)$.

It remains to show that this denotation is the unique fixpoint of Γ as claimed above. Consider the diagram

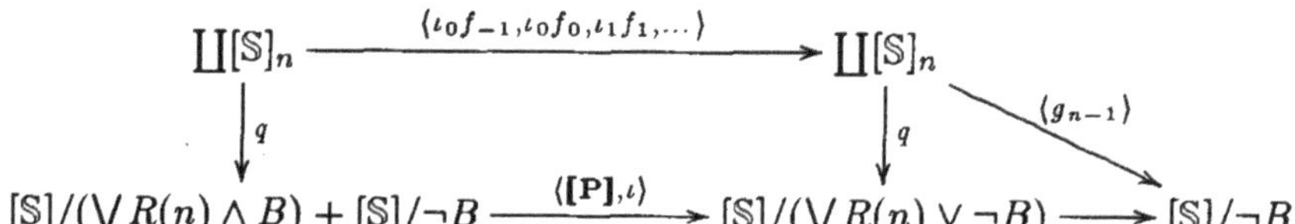

where $\gamma = [\![while \ldots]\!]$. This diagram commutes and a simple calculation shows that $\langle g_{n-1}\rangle \circ \langle f_{-1}, \iota_0 f_0, \iota_1 f_1, \ldots\rangle = \langle g_{n-1}\rangle$ (again ignoring the specified 2-isomorphisms). The universal property of coequalizers implies that $\gamma\langle [\![\mathbf{P}]\!], \iota\rangle = \gamma$. As for the uniqueness, if $[\mathbb{S}]/(\bigvee R(n) \vee \neg B) \xrightarrow{h} [\mathbb{S}]/B$ is any other morphism which satisfies $h\langle [\![\mathbf{P}]\!], \iota\rangle = h$, then, replacing γ in the diagram above by h, we see that $hq\iota_0 = g_{-1}$, and then, using induction, that $hq\iota_n = g_{n-1}$ for all n, hence $h = \langle g_{n-1}\rangle$.

Next we consider the interpretation of the two inference rules which introduce the basic (0-step or 1-step) programs. The interpretation of $\{\mathbb{S}\}$**skip**$\{\mathbb{S}\}$ is just $[\mathbb{S}] \xrightarrow{id_{[\mathbb{S}]}} [\mathbb{S}]$, the identity on the topos classifying $\{\mathbb{S}\}$. Assignments differ from the rules considered so far in that they require the existence of two distinguished types, *Add* and *Val*, in the presentations of both pre- and post-conditions, and that these types are furthermore preserved by all denotations $[\![\mathbf{P}]\!]$. (One of the reasons for this special treatment is that the basic theory does not single out any particular notion of underlying machine. Therefore, the theory of the basic computational steps has to be included into the specifications.)

One way to achieve this is to replace the base topos $\mathcal{S}$ by the topos classifying the theory of these two types, and then considering classifying toposes relative to the new base. Here we will assume that both the type *Add* representing the possible storage locations or identifiers, and also the type *Val* of possible values for a particular address are isomorphic to the natural numbers (together with the usual operations). So we will "replace" our universe of sets by the classifying topos of the theory with types *Add* and *Val*, the function symbols given above and the usual axioms. ("replace", because the natural numbers can be obtained by a geometric construction from the empty theory, so that in effect we have done nothing but introducing names for already existing types. $[Add, Val \mid \ldots] = \mathcal{S}$.)

Besides the two constant types *Add* and *Val* each presentation will contain a type

$$State : \mathbb{F}(Add \times Val),$$

and a predicate

$$isdef : \mathbb{P}(Add);$$

satisfying the axioms

$$(x, m) \in State \wedge (y, n) \in State \wedge x = y \vdash m = n$$

$$isdef(x) \vdash \exists n \in Val : (x, n) \in State$$

$$\exists n \in Val : (x, n) \in State \vdash isdef(x).$$

The type *State* represents a partial function $Add \longrightarrow Val$ whose domain $Def = \{x \in Add \mid isdef(x)\}$ is finite (it is the image of a finite set under an epimorphism) and hence complemented in *Add* (every finite subset of a decidable set is complemented).

Let $\{\mathbb{S}', State', isdef'\}$ be the presentation obtained from $\{\mathbb{S}, State, isdef\}$ by attaching primes to each type, predicate and function symbol. (Here we assume that no symbol in $L(\mathbb{S})$ is primed.) In order to construct maps $[\{\mathbb{S}, State, isdef\}[e/a]] \xrightarrow{[\mathbf{a}:=\mathbf{e}]} [\{\mathbb{S}', State', isdef'\}]$, we define a new type $State''$ and a new predicate $isdef''$ in $[\mathbb{S}, State, isdef]$ as the type, respectively the predicate, uniquely determined by the following geometric axioms:

$$\begin{gathered}
(y, n) \in State'' \vdash (y, n) \in State \vee (y = a \wedge n = eval(e)) \\
\top \vdash (a, eval(e)) \in State'' \\
(y, n) \in State \vdash ((y, n) \in State'' \vee y = a) \\
isdef''(x) \vdash isdef(x) \vee x = a \\
isdef(x) \vee x = a \vdash isdef''(x)
\end{gathered}$$

Here $eval$ is the unique extension of the map $Def \xrightarrow{State} Val$ to the free Val-algebra $Val[Def]$ generated by Def. Now the denotation of an assignment $\{\mathbb{S}[e/a]\}\mathbf{a} := \mathbf{e}\{\mathbb{S}\}$, is simply the geometric morphism obtained interpreting $isdef'$ and $State'$ as $isdef''$ and $State''$, and for the remainder every primed object is interpreted as its unprimed counterpart.

2 Semantics for Hoare triples with non-deterministic programs

If $\mathbf{P}$ is a non-deterministic program, then a sequent $\{\mathbb{S}\}\mathbf{P}\{\mathbb{T}\}$ will be interpreted as a geometric morphism $\coprod_{i\in I}[\mathbb{S}]/U_i \xrightarrow{[\mathbf{P}]} [\mathbb{T}]$, where the U_i are a subobjects of $1_{[\mathbb{S}]}$ whose union is equal to $1_{[\mathbb{S}]}$.

The semantics for deterministic programs is included via those geometric morphisms $\coprod_{i\in I}[\mathbb{S}]/U_i \xrightarrow{[\mathbf{P}]} [\mathbb{T}]$ for which I is the singleton set and $U_i = 1$ for the unique element $i \in I$.

Whereas before two geometric morphisms were considered to be equivalent if and only if they are isomorphic, we use now a slightly weaker form of equivalence. The previous notion of equivalence is sufficient to insure that expressions like $[\![\mathbf{P}; (\mathbf{Q}; \mathbf{R})]\!]$ and $[\![(\mathbf{P}; \mathbf{Q}); \mathbf{R}]\!]$ are equivalent, but it is too strong a notion for allowing us to identify programs like $\mathbf{do}\ b_1 \to \mathbf{P} [\!] \ldots [\!] b_n \to \mathbf{P}\ \mathbf{od}$ and $\mathbf{do}\ \bigvee_{i=1}^{n} b_i \to \mathbf{P}\ \mathbf{od}$. If we want to identify such pairs of programs we have to take the equivalence relation generated by all pairs $(\coprod_{i\in I}[\mathbb{S}]/U_i \xrightarrow{[\mathbf{P}]} [\mathbb{T}], [\mathbb{S}] \xrightarrow{[\mathbf{Q}]} [\mathbb{T}])$ for which the following diagram commutes:

$$\begin{array}{ccc}
\coprod_{i\in I}[\mathbb{S}]/U_i & \xrightarrow{[\mathbf{P}]=\langle[\mathbf{P}]_i\rangle} & [\mathbb{T}] \\
\Big\downarrow{\scriptstyle \langle j_i\rangle} & & \Big\downarrow{\scriptstyle id} \\
[\mathbb{S}] & \xrightarrow{\quad [\mathbf{Q}] \quad} & [\mathbb{T}]
\end{array}$$

Here each $[\mathbb{S}]/U_i \xrightarrow{j_i} [\mathbb{S}]$ is just the obvious inclusion. An equivalent formulation is that $[\![\mathbf{P}]\!]$ is a cocone for the (extended) kernel pair of the open surjection $\coprod_{i\in I}[\mathbb{S}]/U_i \xrightarrow{\langle j_i\rangle} [\mathbb{S}]$. (Note that this means that the interpretation of the while loop was obtained by first giving the interpretation as a non-deterministic program, and then showing that this interpretation can be glued together appropriately.)

The equivalence relation $\approx$ generated by such pairs can be constructed by first extending the relation given by pairs $[\![\mathbf{P}]\!] \sim [\![\mathbf{Q}]\!]$ as above to arbitrary pairs of geometric morphisms whose domains are of the form $\coprod_{i\in I}[\mathbb{S}]/U_i$ as follows:

$$\coprod_{i\in I}[\mathbb{S}]/U_i \xrightarrow{f=\langle f_i\rangle} [\mathbb{T}] \sim \coprod_{j\in J}[\mathbb{S}]/V_j \xrightarrow{g=\langle g_j\rangle} [\mathbb{T}]$$

iff

$$\forall j \in J \exists I_j \subseteq I : V_j \leq \bigvee_{i\in I_j} U_i \text{ and } \coprod_{i\in I_j}[\mathbb{S}]/V_j \wedge U_i \xrightarrow{\coprod \iota_i} \coprod_{i\in I_j}[\mathbb{S}]/U_i \xrightarrow{\langle f_i\rangle} [\mathbb{T}] \sim g_j$$

and then defining $f \approx g \Leftrightarrow f \sim g$ and $g \sim f$.

The interpretations of **skip** and of **assignment** do not change. The interpretation of **composition** has to be slightly modified. Given denotations $\coprod[\mathbb{S}]/U_i \xrightarrow{[\![\mathbf{P}]\!]=\langle[\![\mathbf{P}]\!]_i\rangle} [\mathbb{T}] = [\![\{\mathbb{S}\}\mathbf{P}\{\mathbb{T}\}]\!]$ and $\coprod[\mathbb{T}]/V_j \xrightarrow{[\![\mathbf{Q}]\!]=\langle[\![\mathbf{Q}]\!]_j\rangle} [\mathbb{U}] = [\![\{\mathbb{T}\}\mathbf{Q}\{\mathbb{U}\}]\!]$ we put $[\![\{\mathbb{S}\}\mathbf{P};\mathbf{Q}\{\mathbb{U}\}]\!] = \coprod[\mathbb{S}]/(U_i \wedge [\![\mathbf{P}]\!]^*(V_j)) \xrightarrow{[\![\mathbf{P};\mathbf{Q}]\!]} [\mathbb{U}]$, where each component $[\![\mathbf{P};\mathbf{Q}]\!]_{i,j}$ is given by

$$[\mathbb{S}]/(U_i \wedge [\![\mathbf{P}]\!]^*(V_j)) \xrightarrow{[\![\mathbf{P}_i]\!]|_{[\![\mathbf{P}]\!]^*(V_j)}} [\mathbb{T}]/V_j \xrightarrow{[\![\mathbf{Q}_j]\!]} [\mathbb{U}].$$

(This is just a special instance of the usual composition of spans in any category with pullbacks.)

The interpretation of the generalized if-then-else rule is also straightforward: for given interpretations $[\![\{\mathbb{S}, b_j\}\mathbf{P_j}\{\mathbb{T}\},]\!] = \coprod_{i\in I_j}[\mathbb{S}]/U_i \xrightarrow{[\![\mathbf{P_j}]\!]} [\mathbb{T}]$ we put

$$[\![\{\mathbb{S}\}\mathbf{if}\, b_1 \to \mathbf{P_1} [\!] \ldots [\!] b_n \to \mathbf{P_n}\, \mathbf{fi}\{\mathbb{T}\}]\!] = \coprod_{i\in\coprod I_j}[\mathbb{S}]/U_i \xrightarrow{[\![\mathbf{P_j}]\!]} [\mathbb{T}].$$

Note that under the given assumption $\bigvee_{j=1}^{n} b_j \leq \bigvee_{j=1}^{n}\bigvee_{i\in I_j} U_i$, so that the canonical map $\coprod_{i\in\Sigma I_j}[\mathbb{S}]/U_i \to [\mathbb{S}]/\bigvee_{j=1}^{n} b_i$ is an open surjection.

The interpretation of the generalized while rule is simpler than the interpretation given in the deterministic case. It is just the sum of the various iterations. We omit all details since the construction is similar to the construction used for deterministic programs. The main difference is that here we do not need to glue the various iterations together.

Finally, the question of whether one should include the requirement of termination into the notion of a Hoare triple or, as it is usually done, just require partial correctness, is not central for the approach taken here. In the interpretations given above, termination was included essentially by restricting the domain of an interpretation to an open subtopos on which the program could be proven to terminate. The alternative approach (via the notion of the lifting $\mathcal{E}_\perp$ of a topos $\mathcal{E}$ [3]) avoids these overt restrictions of the domain by mapping the closed complement to the bottom of $\mathcal{E}_\perp$.

3 Specifications as spans

Because of space limitations I can only sketch some of the ideas here. Any pair of pre-conditions $\{\mathbb{S}\}$ and post-conditions $\{\mathbb{T}\}$ gives rise to a span

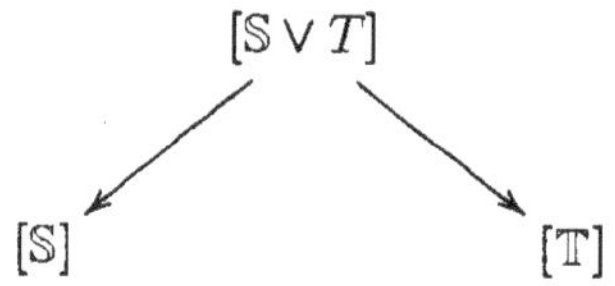

where $\{\mathbb{S} \vee T\}$ is the presentation which is the set theoretic union of the presentations of $\{\mathbb{S}\}$ and $\{\mathbb{T}\}$, and where both legs are given by the obvious translations of $\{\mathbb{S}\}$ and $\{\mathbb{T}\}$ into $[\mathbb{S} \vee T]$. A bit more generally, we will consider arbitrary spans of geometric morphisms. A geometric morphism $\mathcal{F} \xrightarrow{f} \mathcal{G}$ (resp. $\coprod_{i \in I} \mathcal{F}/U_i \xrightarrow{f} \mathcal{G}$ with $\bigvee U_i = 1$) is a (non-)deterministic program satisfying the specification (α, β) below, if there exists a geometric morphism $\mathcal{F} \xrightarrow{s} \mathcal{E}$ (resp.$\coprod_i \mathcal{F}/U_i \xrightarrow{s} \mathcal{E}$) such that

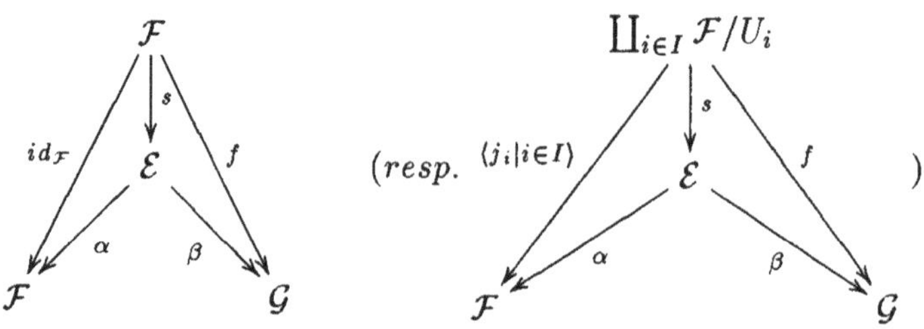

commutes (where the maps j_i are the obvious inclusions $\mathcal{F}/U_i \xrightarrow{j_i} \mathcal{F}$).

Since deterministic and non-deterministic programs can be considered as spans the left leg of which is the identity, respectively an open surjection of type $\coprod_i [\mathbb{S}]/U_i \longrightarrow [\mathbb{S}]$, it is natural to ask whether the operations on geometric morphisms considered in the previous section can be extended to arbitrary spans, so that they restrict to the previously considered operations on spans of the type above. Such extensions to spans do indeed exist, but it is not the mere existence which is important, but the fact that these liftings can be chosen to be functorial, i.e. these liftings are families of functors parametrized by (classifying) toposes, and propositions. For instance, if-then-else can be viewed as a functor

$$\textit{if-then-else}_{B,[\mathbb{S}],[\mathbb{T}]}\colon \mathcal{SP}([\mathbb{S}]/B,[\mathbb{T}]) \times \mathcal{SP}([\mathbb{S}]/\neg B,[\mathbb{T}])) \longrightarrow \mathcal{SP}([\mathbb{S}],[\mathbb{T}])$$

parametrized by a two toposes $[\mathbb{S}]$ and $[\mathbb{T}]$ and a Boolean truth value in $[\mathbb{S}]$. If

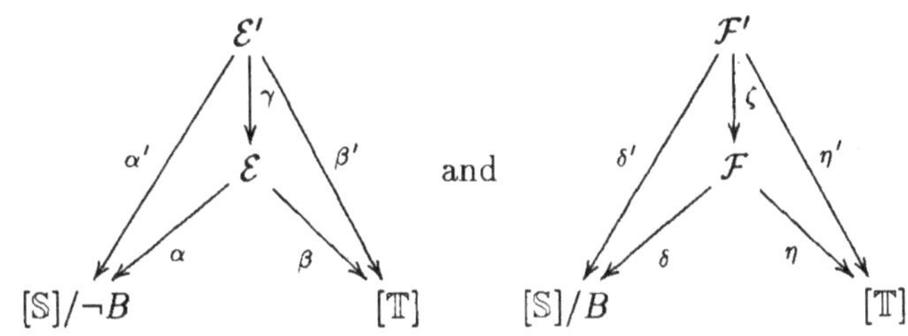

are maps of spans, then there is a corresponding map

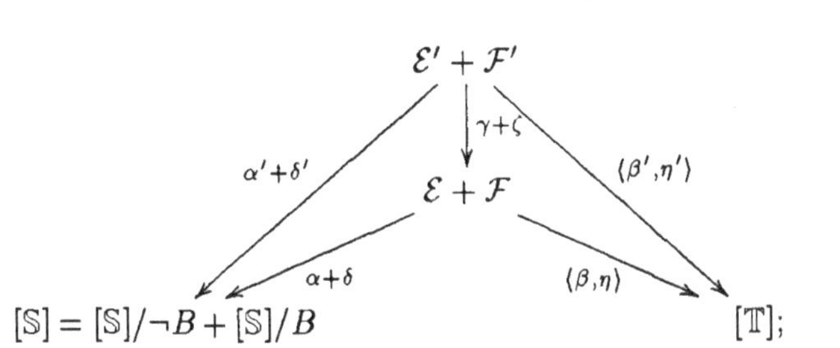

if the primed specifications are (deterministic or non-deterministic) programs then so is their sum $(\alpha' + \delta', \langle\beta', \eta'\rangle)$. Similar statements are true for the other operations, where, of course, **if** ... **fi** and **do** ... **od** do not necessarily preserve determinacy. Functoriality of these operations is essential for introducing the idea of stepwise refinement into this context. If the maps γ and ζ above are sections for α and δ respectively, then $\gamma + \zeta$ is a section of $\alpha + \delta$. So in order to obtain a program satisfying the more complex specification $(\alpha + \delta, \langle \beta, \eta \rangle)$ it suffices to find programs satisfying the simpler specifications (α, β) and (δ, η). Again, analogous statements hold for all other command structures considered here.

4 Acknowledgements

I am indebted for suggestions and illuminating discussions to Steve Vickers.

1. E.W. Dijkstra, *A discipline of programming*, Prentice Hall, 1976.
2. P.T. Johnstone, *Topos Theory*, Academic Press, London 1977.
3. P.T. Johnstone and I. Moerdijk, "Local maps of toposes", *Proc. Lond. Math. Soc.* **(3) 58** (1989), 281-305.
4. S. Mac Lane and I. Moerdijk, *Sheaves in geometry and logic*, Springer-Verlag, Berlin, 1992.
5. M. Makkai and G. Reyes, *First order categorical logic*, Springer LNM 611, Springer-Verlag, Berlin, 1977.
6. I. Moerdijk, "The classifying topos of a continuous groupoid, I", *Trans. Amer. Math. Soc.* **310** (1988), 629-668.
7. S.J. Vickers, "Geometric theories and databases", pp. 288-314 in Fourman, Johnstone and Pitts (eds) *Applicatons of Categories in Computer Science*, Lond. Math. Soc. Lecture Note Series **177** 1991.
8. —, "Formal implementation" in McDermid (ed) *Software Engineers' Reference Book*, Butterworth-Heinemann, 1991.
9. —, "Geometric logic in computer science", pp. 37-54 in Burn, Gay, Ryan (eds) *Theory and Formal Methods 1993* Workshops in Computing, Springer, 1993.
10. —, "Geometric logic as a specification language" pp. 321-340 in Hankin, Mackie, Nagarajan (eds) *Theory and Formal Methods of Computing 94* Proc. of the Second Imperial College Workshop, Imperial College Press, London, 1994.

A COMPUTATIONAL MODEL FOR METRIC SPACES

A. EDALAT
Department of Computing, Imperial College, London SW7 2BZ.

R. HECKMANN
FB 14 - Informatik, Universität des Saarlandes, Postfach 151150, D-66041 Saarbrücken, Germany.

For every metric space X, we define a continuous poset $\mathbf{B}X$ such that X is homeomorphic to the set of maximal elements of $\mathbf{B}X$ with the relative Scott topology. The poset $\mathbf{B}X$ is a dcpo iff X is complete, and ω-continuous iff X is separable. The computational model $\mathbf{B}X$ is used to give domain-theoretic proofs of Banach's fixed point theorem and of a classical result of Hutchinson: on a complete metric space, every iterated function system with probabilities has a unique invariant measure with bounded support. We also show that the probabilistic power domain of $\mathbf{B}X$ provides an ω-continuous computational model for measure theory on a separable complete metric space X.

1 Introduction

In this paper, we establish new connections between the theory of metric spaces and domain theory. For every metric space X, we define a continuous poset $\mathbf{B}X$ of *formal balls*. The space X is homeomorphic with the subset of maximal elements of $\mathbf{B}X$. The order-theoretic properties of $\mathbf{B}X$ are closely related with the metric properties of X. In particular, $\mathbf{B}X$ is a dcpo iff X is complete, which gives a simple connection between completeness of a partial order and that of a metric space. Furthermore, $\mathbf{B}X$ is ω-continuous iff X is separable. Thus if X is a separable complete metric space, then $\mathbf{B}X$ is an ω-continuous dcpo.

These results extend earlier ones of Edalat[1] for a locally compact Hausdorff space. They present a considerably simpler framework than that of an ω-algebraic cpo with distance and weight used by Weihrauch and Schreiber[2] to embed a complete separable metric space into a domain. Our construction is also much simpler than Lawson's recent construction of an MP hull for a Polish space[3]. Furthermore, our results lead to a simple computational model for Hilbert and Banach spaces. In fact, for a normed vector space X, $\mathbf{B}X$ is isomorphic to the poset of closed balls ordered by reverse inclusion. It follows that for a separable Banach space and in particular for a Hilbert space X, $\mathbf{B}X$ is an ω-continuous dcpo.

Using $\mathbf{B}X$, we give a domain-theoretic proof of the Banach fixed point theorem. Our framework also provides a simple domain-theoretic model for measure theory on Polish spaces, the basic structures used in probability theory and stochastic processes. We show that the probabilistic power domain of $\mathbf{B}X$ provides an ω-continuous computational model for measure theory on a separable complete metric space X. As an application we give a domain-theoretic proof of Hutchinson's classical result without the need for the Hutchinson metric: We use the space of formal balls to show that an iterated function system with probabilities on a complete metric space has a unique invariant measure. As in the case of locally compact Hausdorff spaces [4], our domain-theoretic framework can be used to derive algorithms for generating invariant measures and for computing expected values of functions w.r.t. these measures.

Some Notation

Let $f : X \to Y$ be a function. For $A \subseteq X$, we write f^+A for $\{fa \mid a \in A\}$, and for $B \subseteq Y$, we write f^-B for $\{x \in X \mid fx \in B\}$. The set $\mathbf{R}_+$ is the set of real numbers r with $0 \leq r < \infty$. In a metric space, we write $O(x,r)$ for the open ball around x with radius r, and $C(x,r)$ for the closed ball.

2 The Poset $\mathbf{B}X$ of Formal Balls

For every metric space X, we define a continuous poset $\mathbf{B}X$ whose subspace of maximal elements is homeomorphic to X. This poset is directed complete iff the metric space is complete.

2.1 Closed Balls and Formal Balls

In Edalat's earlier work [1], for every locally compact Hausdorff space X, a continuous bounded complete dcpo $\mathbf{U}X$ was constructed which consists of the non-empty compact subsets of X, ordered by reverse inclusion. The space X equipped with the metric topology was shown to be homeomorphic to the space of maximal elements of $\mathbf{U}X$. These results do not directly extend to all metric spaces since the poset $\mathbf{U}X$ is not continuous in general.

If (X,d) is a metric space, one may consider the poset of closed balls $C(x,r)$ of X ordered by reverse inclusion '$\supseteq$'. The points x of X can be identified with the maximal closed balls $C(x,0)$. Thus we have found a poset whose set of maximal elements is in one-to-one correspondence with X. However, even if X is complete, the poset of closed balls may be not complete.

From the triangle inequality, it follows that $C(x,r) \supseteq C(y,s)$ holds if $d(x,y) \leq r - s$; the converse implication is not always true (but see Theorem 2.10). This observation is taken as the basis of the following definition:

A *formal ball* in a metric space X is a pair (x, r) with x in X and r in $\mathbf{R}_+$ (i.e., $0 \leq r < \infty$). The set of formal balls in X is called $\mathbf{B}X$. Formal balls are ordered by

$$(x, r) \sqsubseteq (y, s) \iff d(x, y) \leq r - s.$$

Hence $(x, r) \sqsubseteq (y, s)$ implies $C(x, r) \supseteq C(y, s)$, and also $r \geq s$. For every metric space X, $\mathbf{B}X$ is a poset. Its maximal elements are the formal balls $(x, 0)$, which obviously are in one-to-one correspondence with the points of X.

Formal balls were first introduced by Weihrauch and Schreiber[2]. However, they did not consider the poset of formal balls itself, but completed it to a bounded complete ω-algebraic cpo. They also embed the metric space in the cpo, but not simply as the set of maximal points. In contrast, they have to impose additional non-order structures on their cpo in order to characterise the image of the embedding. Compared with their work, our approach is much simpler and more direct.

2.2 Ascending Sequences in $\mathbf{B}X$

In a metric space X, it is not necessary to study limits of general nets; it suffices to consider sequences. The poset $\mathbf{B}X$ has an analogous property: when considering least upper bounds of directed sets, it suffices to look at ascending sequences.

Proposition 2.1 *For every directed subset D of $\mathbf{B}X$, there is an ascending sequence $(x_1, r_1) \sqsubseteq (x_2, r_2) \sqsubseteq \cdots$ of elements of D which has the same upper bounds as D.*

Proof: Let $s = \inf\{r \mid (x, r) \in D\}$. For every n in $\mathbf{N}$, there is (y_n, s_n) in D such that $s_n \leq s + 1/n$. Let $(x_1, r_1) = (y_1, s_1)$, and for every $n > 1$, let (x_n, r_n) be an upper bound of (x_{n-1}, r_{n-1}) and (y_n, s_n) in D.

Let (z, t) be an upper bound of all (x_n, r_n), and let (a, u) be an element of D. Since D is directed, there are upper bounds (b_n, v_n) of (a, u) and (x_n, r_n) in D. Then for all n in $\mathbf{N}$,

$$\begin{aligned} d(a, z) &\leq d(a, b_n) + d(b_n, x_n) + d(x_n, z) \leq (u - v_n) + (r_n - v_n) + (r_n - t) \\ &\leq u - t + 2(r_n - s) \leq u - t + 2/n \end{aligned}$$

Hence $(a, u) \sqsubseteq (z, t)$ as required. □

In the sequel, we compare ascending sequences in $\mathbf{B}X$ with sequences in X.

Proposition 2.2 *If $(x_1, r_1) \sqsubseteq (x_2, r_2) \sqsubseteq \cdots$ is an ascending sequence in $\mathbf{B}X$, then the sequence $(r_n)_{n \in \mathbf{N}}$ is descending and converging, and the sequence $(x_n)_{n \in \mathbf{N}}$ is a Cauchy sequence in X.*

Least upper bounds in $\mathbf{B}X$ are closely related with limits in X.

Proposition 2.3 *An element (y, s) of $\mathbf{B}X$ is the least upper bound of an ascending sequence $(x_n, r_n)_{n \in \mathbf{N}}$ if and only if $\lim_{n \to \infty} x_n = y$ and $\lim_{n \to \infty} r_n = s$.*

Proof: Let $(x_n, r_n)_{n \in \mathbf{N}}$ be ascending with least upper bound (y, s). Then $(r_n)_{n \in \mathbf{N}}$ is descending with lower bound s. Assume there is $\epsilon > 0$ such that $r_n \geq s + \epsilon$ for all n in $\mathbf{N}$. Since $(x_n)_{n \in \mathbf{N}}$ is a Cauchy sequence (Prop. 2.2), there is N in $\mathbf{N}$ such that $d(x_n, x_m) < \epsilon/2$ for all $n, m \geq N$. Hence for all $n \geq N$, $d(x_n, x_N) < \epsilon/2 \leq r_n - (s + \epsilon/2)$, or $(x_n, r_n) \sqsubseteq (x_N, s + \epsilon/2)$. Since the sequence is ascending, $(x_N, s + \epsilon/2)$ is an upper bound of the whole sequence. Thus $(y, s) \sqsubseteq (x_N, s + \epsilon/2)$, whence $s \geq s + \epsilon/2$, a contradiction. This proves $\lim_{n \to \infty} r_n = s$. Using this and $(x_n, r_n) \sqsubseteq (y, s)$, i.e., $d(x_n, y) \leq r_n - s$, for every n in $\mathbf{N}$, $\lim_{n \to \infty} x_n = y$ follows.
For the opposite direction, assume $\lim_{n \to \infty} x_n = y$ and $\lim_{n \to \infty} r_n = s$. For every $m \geq n$, $(x_n, r_n) \sqsubseteq (x_m, r_m)$ holds, whence $d(x_n, x_m) \leq r_n - r_m$. Increasing m to infinity, we obtain $d(x_n, y) \leq r_n - s$, whence $(x_n, r_n) \sqsubseteq (y, s)$. Thus (y, s) is an upper bound of the sequence. If (z, t) is an arbitrary upper bound of the sequence, then $d(x_n, z) \leq r_n - t$ holds for all n in $\mathbf{N}$. Increasing n to infinity, $d(y, z) \leq s - t$ follows, i.e., $(y, s) \sqsubseteq (z, t)$. □

From Prop. 2.3, we may conclude a direct connection between metric completeness and dcpo completeness.

Theorem 2.4 *For a metric space X, the following are equivalent:*

1. *X is a complete metric space, i.e., every Cauchy sequence has a limit.*
2. *In $\mathbf{B}X$, every ascending sequence has a least upper bound.*
3. *$\mathbf{B}X$ is a dcpo, i.e., every directed set has a least upper bound.*

Proof: The equivalence between (2) and (3) follows from Prop. 2.1. To prove (2) from (1), use Prop. 2.2 and 2.3. For the proof of (1) from (2), let $(x_n)_{n \in \mathbf{N}}$ be a Cauchy sequence in X. Let $n_0 = 0$. For every k in $\mathbf{N}$, there is $n_k > n_{k-1}$ in $\mathbf{N}$ such that $d(x_i, x_j) \leq 2^{-(k+1)}$ for all $i, j \geq n_k$. Hence in particular, $d(x_{n_k}, x_{n_{k+1}}) \leq 2^{-(k+1)} = 2^{-k} - 2^{-(k+1)}$, i.e., $(x_{n_k}, 2^{-k}) \sqsubseteq (x_{n_{k+1}}, 2^{-(k+1)})$. By (2), this sequence has a least upper bound (y, s). By Prop. 2.3, $\lim_{k \to \infty} x_{n_k} = y$, whence $\lim_{n \to \infty} x_n = y$. □

2.3 Continuity of $\mathbf{B}X$

In this subsection, we show that for every metric space X, the poset $\mathbf{B}X$ is *continuous*. Usually, this notion and related ones are defined for dcpo's only, but they can easily be generalised to arbitrary posets; one only has to replace quantifications such as 'for every directed set' by 'for every directed set which has a least upper bound'.
First, we characterise the way-below relation on $\mathbf{B}X$.

Proposition 2.5 $(x, r) \ll (y, s)$ *iff* $d(x, y) < r - s$

Proof: First assume $(x, r) \ll (y, s)$. Consider the sequence $a_n = (y, s + 1/n)$ which is obviously ascending. By Prop. 2.3, (y, s) is its least upper bound.

From the hypothesis, there is some n such that $(x,r) \sqsubseteq (y, s+1/n)$, whence $d(x,y) \leq r-s-1/n < r-s$.

For the opposite direction, assume $d(x,y) < r-s$. Hence, there is $\epsilon > 0$ such that $d(x,y) < r-s-\epsilon$. Let S be a directed subset of $\mathbf{B}X$ such that $\bigsqcup S = (z,t)$ exists and $(y,s) \sqsubseteq (z,t)$ holds. By Prop. 2.1, there is an ascending sequence $(z_n, t_n)_{n\in\mathbf{N}}$ in S with least upper bound (z,t). By Prop. 2.3, $\lim_{n\to\infty} z_n = z$ and $\lim_{n\to\infty} t_n = t$ holds. Hence, there is some n in $\mathbf{N}$ such that $d(z_n, z) < \epsilon/2$ and $t_n < t + \epsilon/2$. The estimation

$$\begin{aligned} d(x, z_n) \;&\leq\; d(x,y) + d(y,z) + d(z,z_n) \;<\; (r-s-\epsilon) + (s-t) + \epsilon/2 \\ &=\; r - (t+\epsilon/2) \;<\; r - t_n \end{aligned}$$

shows $(x,r) \sqsubseteq (z_n, t_n)$. □

We now come to the continuity theorem. We prove that $\mathbf{B}X$ is continuous, and also show how a basis of $\mathbf{B}X$ can be obtained from dense subsets of X and $\mathbf{R}_+$. Recall that a subset B of a poset P is a basis of P iff for all x in P, the set $\Downarrow_B x = \{b \in B \mid b \ll x\}$ is directed with least upper bound x. In case of $P = \mathbf{B}X$, Prop. 2.1 implies that B is a basis iff for all x in P, the set $\Downarrow_B x$ contains an ascending sequence with least upper bound x.

Theorem 2.6 *Let X be a metric space with a dense subset A, and let Q be a dense subset of $\mathbf{R}_+ = [0,\infty)$. Then $A \times Q$ is a basis of $\mathbf{B}X$.*

Proof: Consider (x,r) in $\mathbf{B}X$. For every n in $\mathbf{N}$, there is a_n in A such that $d(a_n, x) < 4^{-n}$, and q_n in Q such that $r + 2\cdot 4^{-n} < q_n < r + 3\cdot 4^{-n}$. Then $(a_n, q_n) \ll (x,r)$, and $(a_{n-1}, q_{n-1}) \sqsubseteq (a_n, q_n)$ for $n > 1$. Clearly, $\lim_{n\to\infty} a_n = x$ and $\lim_{n\to\infty} q_n = r$, whence (x,r) is the least upper bound of $(a_n, q_n)_{n\in\mathbf{N}}$ by Prop. 2.3. □

With Prop. 2.3, it is easy to show that $\{a \in X \mid (a,r) \in B\}$ is dense in X if B is a basis of $\mathbf{B}X$.

Corollary 2.7 *For every metric space X, $\mathbf{B}X$ is a continuous poset. It is ω-continuous iff X is separable.*

2.4 Embedding X into $\mathbf{B}X$

Clearly, the function $\mathsf{i} : X \to \mathbf{B}X$ with $\mathsf{i}x = (x,0)$ is a one-to-one correspondence between X and the subset $X \times \{0\}$ of $\mathbf{B}X$, which we call X^+.

Proposition 2.8 *The set X^+ is the set of maximal elements of $\mathbf{B}X$. It is a (Scott) G_δ-subset of $\mathbf{B}X$.*

For (x,r) in $\mathbf{B}X$, $\mathsf{i}^-(\Uparrow(x,r)) = O(x,r)$ holds. Hence, i is a topological embedding, which makes X homeomorphic to the subspace X^+ of $\mathbf{B}X$ in the relative Scott topology.

The complements of the sets $\uparrow(x,r)$ together with the sets $\Uparrow(x,r)$ form a subbasis of the Lawson topology on $\mathbf{B}X$. Since $\mathsf{i}^-(\uparrow(x,r))$ is $C(x,r)$, i is also a topological embedding w.r.t. the Lawson topology. Summarising, we obtain:

Theorem 2.9 *On the subset $X^+ = Max(\mathbf{B}X)$, the relative Scott and the relative Lawson topology agree. The function $\mathsf{i} : X \to \mathbf{B}X$ with $\mathsf{i}x = (x,0)$ is a homeomorphism from X with the metric topology onto X^+ with the relative Scott or Lawson topology.*

If X is a separable complete metric space, then $\mathbf{B}X$ is an ω-continuous dcpo by Cor. 2.7. Thus, $\mathbf{B}X$ can be given an effective structure[5]. This structure can be used to derive an effective structure for X via the homeomorphism between X and X^+.

Several authors studied the subspace of maximal points of a domain with the relative Scott topology (MP space). Kamimura and Tang[6] considered MP spaces of bounded complete ω-continuous domains. In the algebraic case, these spaces are shown to be Polish spaces, i.e., topological spaces with a separable complete metric.

This result is generalised by Lawson[3]. He shows that for all ω-continuous domains where the relative Scott and relative Lawson topologies agree on the maximal points, the MP spaces are Polish spaces. He also provides a complicated construction for the opposite direction which shows that every Polish space can be obtained as the MP space of such an ω-continuous domain. The construction presented in the paper at hand proves the same in a much simpler fashion. Furthermore, as we will see in the following, we obtain new results for Banach spaces and a functorial construction; we are also able to prove Banach's fixed point theorem domain-theoretically.

2.5 Normed Vector Spaces

In Subsection 2.1, we mentioned that $C(x,r) \supseteq C(y,s)$ does not in general imply $d(x,y) \leq r - s$. Here, we prove that the equivalence does hold in non-trivial normed vector spaces. Normed vector spaces $(X, \|\,.\,\|)$ (over $\mathbf{R}$) form a special class of metric spaces where the distance is given by $d(x,y) = \|x - y\|$. A normed vector space is non-trivial if it contains elements different from 0.

Theorem 2.10 *In a non-trivial normed vector space, $C(x,r) \supseteq C(y,s)$ holds iff $d(x,y) \leq r - s$.*

Proof: Let $t = d(x,y) + s$. We construct an element z with $d(x,z) = t$ and $d(y,z) = s$. In the case $x = y$, let u be an element of X different from x, which exists by non-triviality, and in case of $x \neq y$, we choose $u = y$. In both cases, $z = x + \frac{t}{d(x,u)}(u - x)$ has the desired properties. Hence z is in $C(y,s) \subseteq C(x,r)$. Thus, $d(x,y) + s = t = d(x,z) \leq r$ holds. □

Corollary 2.11 *For a non-trivial normed vector space, the poset of formal balls is isomorphic with the poset of closed balls ordered by reverse inclusion.*

Corollary 2.12 *For a separable Banach or Hilbert space, the poset of closed balls ordered by reverse inclusion is an ω-continuous dcpo.*

2.6 Completion

Starting from an arbitrary metric space (X, d), we may first construct its *metric completion* $(\overline{X}, \overline{d})$, and then the poset $\mathbf{B}\overline{X}$, which is a continuous dcpo by Theorem 2.4. On the other hand, we may construct $\mathbf{B}X$, which is a continuous poset, consider $(\mathbf{B}X, \ll)$ as an abstract basis and construct its *rounded ideal completion* [7] $\mathcal{I}(\mathbf{B}X)$, which is a continuous dcpo. We claim that the two continuous dcpo's $\mathbf{B}(\overline{X})$ and $\mathcal{I}(\mathbf{B}X)$ are isomorphic.

We may consider X as a subset of $\overline{X}$ such that $\overline{d}$ restricted to X is d. By Theorem 2.6, the set $\mathbf{B}X = X \times \mathbf{R}_+$ is a basis of $\mathbf{B}\overline{X}$. By Prop. 2.5, the way-below relation of $\mathbf{B}\overline{X}$ restricts to that of $\mathbf{B}X$. By the theory of continuous domains, $\mathbf{B}\overline{X}$ is isomorphic to the rounded ideal completion of its basis $\mathbf{B}X$.

With these results, the metric completion can be constructed domain-theoretically. Starting from an arbitrary metric space X, construct the continuous poset $\mathbf{B}X$ and use rounded ideal completion to obtain $D = \mathcal{I}(\mathbf{B}X)$. Since we know $D \cong \mathbf{B}\overline{X}$, Theorem 2.9 tells us that $\overline{X}$ is (homeomorphic to) *Max* D, the space of maximal elements of D in the relative Scott topology. Thus, we obtain $\overline{X}$ as a topological space. In a future paper, the metric of X will be extended to a partial metric on $\mathbf{B}X$ and D, whose restriction to *Max* D will recover the metric on $\overline{X}$.

3 Fixed Point Theorems

Using $\mathbf{B}X$, Banach's fixed point theorem can be derived from the dcpo fixed point theorem. First, we have to extend functions defined on metric spaces to formal balls.

Let $f : X \to Y$ be a function between two metric spaces with a Lipschitz constant $c \in \mathbf{R}_+$, i.e., $d(fx, fx') \leq c \cdot d(x, x')$ holds for all x, x' in X. Define $\mathbf{B}(f, c)(x, r) = (fx, c \cdot r)$ for every (x, r) in $\mathbf{B}X$. It is straightforward to check that $\mathbf{B}(f, c)$ is Scott continuous from $\mathbf{B}X$ to $\mathbf{B}Y$. Therefore $\mathbf{B}$ is a functor from the category of metric spaces and maps with a Lipschitz constant to the category of continuous posets and continuous functions.

Theorem 3.1 *A contracting map on a non-empty complete metric space has a unique fixed point which is the limit of the orbit of any point in the space.*

Proof: Let (X, d) be a complete metric space and $f : X \to X$ a contracting map. This means f has a Lipschitz constant $c < 1$. The function $g = \mathbf{B}(f, c) : \mathbf{B}X \to \mathbf{B}X$ is Scott continuous.
Let x be an arbitrary point of X, and let $r_x = d(x, fx)/(1-c)$. For every $r \geq r_x$, we obtain $d(x, fx) \leq r - cr$, whence $(x, r) \sqsubseteq g(x, r)$. Using monotonicity, this relation implies that g maps $\uparrow(x, r)$ into itself.
Since $\uparrow(x, r)$ is a dcpo with least element (x, r), the dcpo fixed point theorem implies that $(f^n x, c^n r)_{n \in \mathbf{N}}$ is an ascending sequence whose least upper bound (y, s) is the least fixed point of g on $\uparrow(x, r)$. By Prop. 2.3, $s = \lim_{n \to \infty} c^n r = 0$ and $y = \lim_{n \to \infty} f^n x$ holds. Since $(y, 0)$ is maximal in $\mathbf{B}X$ by Prop. 2.8, it is not only the least, but also the unique fixed point of g on $\uparrow(x, r)$.
Clearly, $(y, 0) = (\lim_{n \to \infty} f^n x, 0)$ is independent from $r \geq r_x$. We show that it is the unique fixed point of g not only in $\uparrow(x, r)$, but in the whole of $\mathbf{B}X$. Let (z, t) be an arbitrary fixed point of g. Let $r \geq \max(r_x, d(x, z) + t)$. Then (z, t) is in $\uparrow(x, r)$ and thus must equal $(y, 0)$.
So far, we have shown that $(y, 0)$ is the unique fixed point of g in $\mathbf{B}X$. Hence, y is independent from x, i.e., $y = \lim_{n \to \infty} f^n x$ for all x in X. Since $z \in X$ is a fixed point of $f : X \to X$ iff $(z, 0)$ is a fixed point of $g : \mathbf{B}X \to \mathbf{B}X$, it follows that y is the unique fixed point of f. □

With the domain-theoretic method as exhibited in the proof above, it is easy to estimate the distance from the fixed point y. For every n, $g^n(x, r) \sqsubseteq (y, 0)$ holds, whence $d(f^n x, y) \leq c^n r$. Thus, the iteration can be stopped once $c^n r < \epsilon$, if the fixed point y is to be computed with accuracy $\epsilon > 0$.

The fixed point theorem can be extended to systems $(X; f_1, \ldots, f_N)$ of several contracting maps $f_i : X \to X$. Such systems are called *(hyperbolic) iterated function systems (IFS)*. In the classical work of Hutchinson [8], one considers the space $\mathbf{H}X$ of non-empty compact subsets of X with the *Hausdorff metric* d_H. One shows that $(\mathbf{H}X, d_H)$ is a complete metric space and that the map $f : \mathbf{H}X \to \mathbf{H}X$ defined by $f(K) = \bigcup_{1 \leq i \leq N} f_i^+(K)$ is contracting. It will therefore have a unique fixed point in $\mathbf{H}X$, the so-called *attractor* of the IFS.

With the techniques used in the proof of Theorem 3.1, a domain-theoretic proof of this result can be given which completely avoids the Hausdorff metric. This extends the corresponding result for a compact metric space [9,4]. The proof is performed in the Plotkin power domain [7] of the domain $\mathbf{B}X$. It is similar to the proof of Theorem 5.1 below.

4 A Computational Framework for Measure Theory

By a *measure* on a metric space X, we mean a Borel measure with $\mu(\bigcup_{i \in I} U_i) = \sup_{i \in I} \mu U_i$ for every directed family $(U_i)_{i \in I}$ of opens. This continuity assumption is very mild (see Theorem 2.2.16 in Federer's book [10]), and holds anyway in separable metric spaces.

The computational framework for measure theory will be defined in terms of valuations on $\mathbf{B}X$. A *valuation* on a topological space Y is a function from the opens of Y to $\mathbf{R}_+$ which is strict, modular, and Scott continuous.

From the definitions, it is obvious that every measure yields a valuation when restricted to the opens. On a metric space, every valuation μ extends uniquely to a measure by defining $\mu B = \inf\{\mu O \mid O \text{ open} \supseteq B\}$ for Borel sets B. Hence, measures and valuations can be identified on metric spaces. A corresponding result is known for ω-continuous dcpo's [11,12]. The extension problem for general continuous dcpo's is still open.

For a complete metric space X, let $\mathbf{M}^1 X$ be the set of normalised measures on X. We embed $\mathbf{M}^1 X$ into $\mathbf{PB}X$, the *probabilistic power domain* [13,14] of $\mathbf{B}X$. It consists of all valuations ν on $\mathbf{B}X$ with $\nu(\mathbf{B}X) \leq 1$, ordered by their values on Scott open sets, and forms a continuous dcpo.

Let $\mathbf{S}X$ be the set of all ν in $\mathbf{PB}X$ with $X^+ \subseteq O \Rightarrow \nu O = 1$ for opens O.

Theorem 4.1 *The elements of* $\mathbf{S}X$ *are maximal in* $\mathbf{PB}X$.

Theorem 4.2 *For every complete metric space* X*, the function* $\bar{\mathsf{i}} : \mathbf{M}^1 X \to \mathbf{S}X$ *with* $\bar{\mathsf{i}}\mu(V) = \mu(\mathsf{i}^- V)$ *for opens* V *of* $\mathbf{B}X$ *is a bijection.*

Proof: Clearly, $\bar{\mathsf{i}}\mu$ is in $\mathbf{S}X$. For the opposite direction, let ν be in $\mathbf{S}X$. Since $\mathsf{i} : X \to \mathbf{B}X$ is a topological embedding, every open U of X can be written as $U = \mathsf{i}^- V$ for some open V of $\mathbf{B}X$. Let U^* be the union of these V, and define $\nu' U = \nu(U^*)$ for opens U of X. The assignment $\nu \mapsto \nu'$ is the inverse of $\bar{\mathsf{i}}$. □

We can obtain much stronger results when we restrict ourselves to *separable* complete metric spaces X. In this case, $\mathbf{B}X$ is an ω-continuous dcpo, and $\mathbf{PB}X$ is ω-continuous as well [13,14]. Thus it admits an effective treatment [5]. This generalises earlier results for locally compact spaces [1,15].

The correspondence $\bar{\mathsf{i}}$ of Theorem 4.2 is a homeomorphism if $\mathbf{M}^1 X$ is equipped with the weak topology and $\mathbf{PB}X$ with the relative Scott topology [16]. By ω-continuity, every valuation ν on $\mathbf{B}X$ extends uniquely to a Borel measure [11,12]; for convenience this unique extension will be denoted by ν as well. Since X^+ is a G_δ-subset of $\mathbf{B}X$ (Prop. 2.8), the defining condition of $\mathbf{S}X$ can be simplified to $\nu(X^+) = 1$. Using the measure extension, we can prove the converse of Theorem 4.1.

Theorem 4.3 *If* X *is a separable complete metric space, then every maximal element of* $\mathbf{PB}X$ *is in* $\mathbf{S}X$.

Corollary 4.4 *For any complete separable metric space* X*, the space* $\mathbf{M}^1 X$ *of normalised measures on* X *is homeomorphic with the space of maximal elements of the* ω*-continuous dcpo* $\mathbf{PB}X$*. These maximal elements are characterised by* $\mu(X^+) = 1$.

This domain-theoretic framework for measure theory can be used to do generalised Riemann integration theory on complete separable metric spaces or indeed on Polish spaces as in the case of compact metric spaces [15].

5 Iterated Function Systems with Probabilities

An *IFS with probabilities* is an IFS $(X; f_1, \ldots, f_N)$, i.e., a system of N contracting functions f_i on X, together with a vector $(p_1, \ldots, p_N)$ of real numbers $p_i > 0$ with $\sum_{i=1}^{N} p_i = 1$. For every $f_i : X \to X$, there is a function $\mathbf{M}f_i : \mathbf{M}^1 X \to \mathbf{M}^1 X$ with $\mathbf{M}f_i(\mu)(B) = \mu(f_i^{-} B)$ for Borel sets B. Using these functions, one can define $f = \sum_{i=1}^{N} p_i \cdot \mathbf{M}f_i : \mathbf{M}^1 X \to \mathbf{M}^1 X$. Hutchinson [8] showed that f has a unique fixed point with bounded support, the so-called *invariant measure* of the IFS. The *support* of a measure μ is the closed set of all x such that $\mu O > 0$ for all opens O containing x. Hutchinson proved his result by defining a complete metric on the set of normalised measures with bounded support with respect to which f is contracting. He also showed that the invariant measure has compact support.

Edalat [1] found a domain-theoretic proof of this result for compact metric spaces. Here, we will use the domain-theoretic framework of the previous section to extend the above result to any complete (not necessarily separable) metric space. Thus we obtain Hutchinson's theorem in its full generality.

Theorem 5.1 *A hyperbolic IFS with probabilities on a complete metric space has an invariant measure which is unique among the normalised measures with bounded support. The invariant measure has compact support.*

Proof: Given the probabilistic IFS $(X; f_i; p_i)_{i \in \Sigma}$ where $\Sigma = \{1, \ldots, N\}$, let $f = \sum_{i \in \Sigma} p_i \cdot \mathbf{M}f_i : \mathbf{M}^1 X \to \mathbf{M}^1 X$. Let $c_i < 1$ be Lipschitz constants for f_i. The functions $g_i = \mathbf{B}(f_i, c_i) : \mathbf{B}X \to \mathbf{B}X$ are continuous. They induce continuous functions $\mathbf{P}g_i : \mathbf{PB}X \to \mathbf{PB}X$ with $\mathbf{P}g_i(\nu)(O) = \nu(g_i^{-} O)$. Hence $g = \sum_{i \in \Sigma} p_i \cdot \mathbf{P}g_i : \mathbf{PB}X \to \mathbf{PB}X$ is continuous. The equality $g \circ \bar{\mathsf{i}} = \bar{\mathsf{i}} \circ f$ is easily verified. With injectivity of $\bar{\mathsf{i}}$, it follows that μ is a fixed point of f iff $\bar{\mathsf{i}}\mu$ is a fixed point of g.

For a in $\mathbf{B}X$, let $\delta(a)$ be the valuation with $\delta(a)(O) = 1$ if a in O, and $= 0$ otherwise. The function $\delta(.)$ is an order embedding. Obviously, $\mathbf{P}g_i(\delta(a)) = \delta(g_i a)$ holds.

The following is similar to the proof of Theorem 3.1. Fix any x in X, let $r_x = \max_{i \in \Sigma} d(x, f_i x)/(1 - c_i)$, and consider an arbitrary $r \geq r_x$. For $a = (x, r)$, $g_i a \sqsupseteq a$ holds for all i, whence $g(\delta(a)) \sqsupseteq \delta(a)$. Therefore, g maps the subdomain $\uparrow\delta(a)$ to itself and thus has a least fixed point $\nu_a = \bigsqcup_{n \in \mathbf{N}} \nu_{n,a}$ on it where $\nu_{n,a} = g^n(\delta(a))$.

We introduce some abbreviating notations. For $\sigma = (i_1, \ldots, i_n)$ in Σ^n, let

$\sigma i = (i_1, \ldots, i_n, i)$, $p_\sigma = p_{i_1} \cdot \ldots \cdot p_{i_n}$ and $g_\sigma = g_{i_1} \circ \ldots \circ g_{i_n}$. The notations c_σ and f_σ are defined analogously.
For every n in $\mathbf{N}$, $\nu_{n,a} = \sum_{\sigma \in \Sigma^n} p_\sigma \cdot \delta(g_\sigma a)$ holds. This can be shown by induction using linearity of g. Let $F_n = \{g_\sigma a \mid \sigma \in \Sigma^n\}$.
Since $g_i a \sqsupseteq a$ for all i in Σ, and all the g_σ are monotonic, $g_\sigma a \sqsubseteq g_{\sigma i}\, a$ follows. Consider the tree with node set $\Sigma^* = \bigcup_{n \in \mathbf{N}} \Sigma^n$ and edges $\sigma \to \sigma i$. This is an infinite tree with constant degree N at every node. If node σ is labeled by $g_\sigma a$, then infinite paths in the tree correspond to ascending sequences in $\mathbf{B}X$. Let K be the set of least upper bounds of all these sequences. If $K \subseteq O$ for some open set O, then $F_n \subseteq O$ for some n by König's Lemma. This property suffices to show compactness of K. Since $F_n \subseteq O$ implies $\nu_{n,a} O = 1$, we conclude:
(1) If $K \subseteq O$ open, then $\nu_a O = 1$.
If some x in K is contained in an open set O, then some F_n meets O. Since $p_i > 0$ for all i in Σ, $\nu_{n,a} O > 0$ follows. Thus, we obtain:
(2) If K meets an open set O, then $\nu_a O > 0$.
Since $g_\sigma a = (f_\sigma x, c_\sigma \cdot r)$ and $c_i < 1$, set K is a subset of X^+. Therefore, property (1) implies $\nu_a \in \mathbf{S}X$. By Theorem 4.1, ν_a is maximal in $\mathbf{PB}X$ and thus the unique fixed point of g in $\uparrow\delta(a)$. Since $r' > r$ implies $\uparrow\delta(x, r') \supseteq \uparrow\delta(x, r)$, $\nu_{(x,r)}$ does not depend on r. Hence, we may write ν_x for it.
By Theorem 4.2, there is a normalised measure μ_x on X with $\nu_x = \bar{\mathsf{i}}\mu_x$. Properties (1) and (2) imply that $\mathsf{i}^- K$ is the support of μ_x. Since i is an embedding, $\mathsf{i}^- K$ is a compact subset of X.
So far, we have shown the existence of invariant normalised measures μ_x for every x in X. These measures are continuous with compact support. For uniqueness, let μ be an arbitrary invariant normalised measure with bounded support. Then there is some $r \geq r_x$ such that the support is contained in $\mu(O(x, r))$. By continuity, μ maps the complement of the support to 0. Thus $\mu(O(x, r)) = 1$ holds, whence $\delta(x, r) \sqsubseteq \bar{\mathsf{i}}\mu$ follows. Since ν_x is the unique fixed point of g on $\uparrow\delta(x, r)$, $\bar{\mathsf{i}}\mu = \nu_x$ follows whence $\mu = \mu_x$ by injectivity of $\bar{\mathsf{i}}$. □

6 Future Work

To obtain a full domain-theoretic treatment of metric completion, the metric of X will be extended to a *partial metric* on $\mathbf{B}X$. This partial metric should be easily extendible to the rounded ideal completion of $\mathbf{B}X$, to obtain the metric completion $\overline{X}$.

A major area for further work is in developing the domain-theoretic measure and integration theory on Polish spaces. Given a Borel measure on a complete separable metric space X, we need to explicitly construct an increasing chain of simple valuations on $\mathbf{B}X$ whose least upper bound is the given measure. One should then be able to use the generalised Riemann integration theory to compute the expected value of well-behaved continuous functions with respect to the Borel measure to any degree of accuracy. This can provide new computational techniques in probability theory and stochastic processes.

References

1. A. Edalat. Dynamical systems, measures and fractals via domain theory. *Information and Computation*, 120:32–48, July 1995.
2. K. Weihrauch and U. Schreiber. Embedding metric spaces into cpo's. *Theoretical Computer Science*, 16:5–24, 1981.
3. J. D. Lawson. Spaces of maximal points. Preprint, 1995.
4. A. Edalat. Power domains and iterated function systems. *Information and Computation*, 1995. To appear.
5. A. Edalat. Continuous information categories. Technical Report Doc 91/41, Imperial College, 1991.
6. T. Kamimura and A. Tang. Total objects of domains. *Theoretical Computer Science*, 34:275–288, 1984.
7. S. Abramsky and A. Jung. Domain theory. In S. Abramsky, D. M. Gabbay, and T. S. E. Maibaum, editors, *Handbook of Logic in Computer Science, Vol. III.* Oxford University Press, 1994.
8. J. E. Hutchinson. Fractals and self-similarity. *Indiana University Mathematics Journal*, 30:713–747, 1981.
9. S. Hayashi. Self-similar sets as Tarski's fixed points. *Publications of the Research Institute for Mathematical Sciences*, 21:1059–1066, 1985.
10. H. Federer. *Geometric Measure Theory.* Springer-Verlag, 1969.
11. J. D. Lawson. Valuations on continuous lattices. In R.-E. Hoffmann, editor, *Continuous Lattices and Related Topics.* Volume 27 of *Mathematik Arbeitspapiere*, Universität Bremen, 1982.
12. T. Norberg. Existence theorems for measures on continuous posets, with applications to random set theory. *Math. Scand.*, 64:15–51, 1989.
13. C. J. Jones. *Probabilistic Non-Determinism.* PhD thesis, University of Edinburgh, 1990.
14. C. J. Jones and G. D. Plotkin. A probabilistic powerdomain of evaluations. In *LICS '89*, pages 186–195. IEEE Computer Society Press, 1989.
15. A. Edalat. Domain theory and integration. *Theoretical Computer Science*, 151:163–193, 1995.
16. A. Edalat. When Scott is weak on the top. Preprint, 1995.

A SEMANTIC VIEW ON DISTRIBUTED COMPUTABILITY AND COMPLEXITY

E. GOUBAULT
CNRS & Ecole Normale Supérieure
45 rue d'Ulm, 75005 PARIS, FRANCE

Abstract

This paper intends to give a semantical perspective on the recent work by Herlihy, Shavit and Rajsbaum on computability and complexity results for t-resilient and wait-free protocols for distributed systems. It is an extended abstract[a] of a talk given at the Imperial College Workshop, Oxford, Christ Church on the 2nd of April 1996.

1 Introduction

In this article we address some computability and complexity problems which have most often arisen in the area of protocols for distributed systems and concurrent databases. The essence of these problems is to decide whether we can compute a certain kind of *function* in a distributed - yet *robust* - manner. Let us take our first example from the concurrent database theory. Imagine that we have a database that can be shared by n concurrent transactions $T_1, \cdots, T_n$ asynchronously. We suppose that the network linking the transactions to the shared database is not reliable in the sense that any wire can be cut unexpectedly, and no transaction can test the failure of a wire - or equivalently, the processors supporting each transaction may fail without prior notice to any of the others. So we would like our transactions to be managed by a protocol, that is by a program on each processor, which can handle all sorts of failure and still ensure some basic properties on the transactions which have not failed. This means that we want the transactions to be as loosely coupled as possible so that a failure of one processor will not prevent others that might wait for an answer from deadlocking. What functions can these transactions compute then? Let us make precise what sort of function we are interested in. Suppose all transactions T_i want to change the value of the same item x to (maybe) different values x_i. Can all transactions agree on a common value, taken from the set $x_1, \cdots, x_n$? A classic result is that as soon as we ask for a certain robustness to failure, this cannot be computed on ordinary atomic read/write register machines[4]. We will derive a new proof of this result and other similar

[a]Many thanks to Sergio Rajsbaum and Patrick Cousot for useful discussions. I have used Paul Taylor's macro package for drawing diagrams.

ones in an entirely semantic framework, giving another perspective on recent work[1,2,10,11,12,13,14,17].

In section 2 we define formally the class of *functions* we are interested in computing, then define the class of distributed *machines* that we are considering for the computation. We relate this class to the geometric considerations of E. Goubault[6,8] and in Section 3 and 4 we derive the main decidability (or computability) results, giving examples in a toy language. In Section 4 we generalize these questions in order to define the complexity of the computation of functions allowed on some machines.

2 The framework

2.1 The functions

We will actually try to compute *relations* and not just functions. To account for the distributed nature of their computation, we will consider that the input arguments and output values of the relations are tuples $(x_1, \cdots, x_n)$ of integers. The idea is that each x_i is the local view of the input (or of the output) on processor i, on a system which might use at most n processors (that is at most n independent threads of execution). So the class of relations $\mathcal{R}_n$ we are interested in is just the set of binary relations on $\mathbb{Z}^n$. Let us give a few examples. The relation considered in the introduction is the relation *consensus* Γ defined by $(x_1, \cdots, x_n)\Gamma(x_i, \cdots, x_i)$ for any tuple $(x_1, \cdots, x_n) \in \mathbb{Z}^n$ and $i \in \{1, \cdots, n\}$. This means that the n processors can elect any of them, and choose thier local value as the common local view of the result. The *binary consensus* relation Γ_b is defined in a similar manner, except its domain is restricted to $\{0,1\}^n \subseteq \mathbb{Z}^n$. Suppose now that we equip $\mathbb{Z}^n$ with the lattice structure induced by the order $(x_1, \cdots, x_n) \leq (y_1, \cdots, y_n)$ if and only if $x_1 \leq y_1$ and$\cdots x_n \leq y_n$. The ordered consensus relation Δ represents the fact that the election takes the greatest input value as the result, $(x_1, \cdots, x_n)\Delta(x_i, \cdots, x_i)$ where $x_i = \vee_{1 \leq j \leq n} x_j$. Notice that the *ordered binary consensus* is nothing but the *parallel or* (on n booleans). Pseudo-consensus is a weak version of the consensus in the sense that we allow some errors in the agreement between the transactions: the first processor might agree on the the common value plus one (so that the error is at most one on the agreement). Formally, this is the relation Ψ such that, $(x_1, \cdots, x_n)\Psi(x_i, \cdots, x_i)$, $(x_1, \cdots, x_n)\Psi(x_i+1, x_i, \cdots, x_i)$

2.2 The machines

Suppose we have a machine with n processors. Then the machine (or a program on the machine) is t-resilient ($t \leq n-1$) if it can terminate any computation even if t among its n processors fail. This means not only that the whole system will terminate in case of t failures but also that the "partial result" computed by the remaining $n-t$ processors will be a partial view of the result that one would have obtained if ever the n processors would have completed their executions. When $t = n-1$ we say that the machine (or the program) is wait-free. In some way, we are just asking for the processors to be as loosely coupled as possible so that no one has actually to wait for another. This obviously limits the amount of information one process can have from the others at any moment of the execution. When you look at the possible schedulings of actions, all permutations of actions are allowed in a wait-free program since there should be no waiting between processors. The amount of permutation allowed for t-resilient programs is less in general. This will motivate the approach using a characterization of the possible schedulers of the machines (Section 4).

These requirements on the machines will also slightly change the formulation we had on the relations we wish to compute (Section 2). If we use the most famous symbol $\perp$ to denote failure or non-termination, then all relations R we wish to compute on a t-resilient machine should actually be extended over $(\mathbb{Z} \cup \{\perp\})^n$ so that they satisfy, $(\cdots, x_{i-1}, \perp, x_{i+1}, \cdots) R (\cdots, y_{i-1}, \perp, y_{i+1}, \cdots)$ and $(x_1, \cdots, x_n) R (y_1, \cdots, \perp, y_{i_1}, \cdots, \perp, y_{i_2}, \cdots)$ where there could be at most t $\perp$ in the right-hand side of the last equation.

Example of a machine

An interesting case is a shared memory machine with atomic read/write registers[14]. The shared memory is formalized by a collection of registers x_i in a set V. Each processor P_i has got a local memory composed of registers r^i_j in a set V_i. All reads and writes are done in an asynchronous manner on the shared memory. There is no conflict in reads, nor in writes since we ensure that the writes of distinct processors are made on distinct parts of the shared memory (P_i is only allowed to write on x_i). We will use the following syntax for our machine; first we have a grammar for instructions I, and then one for processes P,

$$I := \mathbf{nil} \mid scan \mid write(u) \mid r = f(r_1, \cdots, r_n)$$

where u is a local register or a value (in $\mathbb{Z}$), $r, r_1, \cdots, r_n$ are the local registers and f is any partial recursive function.

$$P := I \mid branch(r, I, I) \mid P; P$$

where r is any local register. Programs are $Prog := (P \mid Prog)$.

nil is the instruction that writes the local value of processor P_i (i.e. r^i_i) in the shared variable x_i. an action). It is used as one of the branches of the if statement (called *branch* here) if we do not need to do anything in the alternative case. *scan* reads the shared array in one round and stores it into some of the local registers of the process in which it is executed. If $x_1, \cdots, x_k$ is the shared array in the shared memory, and r^i_j is the jth local register of process P_i, then *scan* executed in P_i stores $x_1, \cdots, x_k$ in $r^i_1, \cdots, r^i_k$. We suppose (for convenience) that it also writes its local value (r^i_i for processor i) in the shared variable x_i. $write(u)$ executed in P_i writes u in x_i. $r = f(r_1, \cdots, r_n)$ computes the partial recursive function f with arguments $r_1, \cdots, r_n$ and stores the result in r. $branch(r, i_1, i_2)$ where i_1 and i_2 are two instructions, tests whether r is strictly positive or not (it is an "instant decision", see the semantics). If it is strictly positive then it executes i_1 otherwise it executes i_2. ; is the sequential composition of processes. | is the parallel composition of processes.

Let us step back for a second, and look at a sample program in our language.

$$\begin{array}{rcl} Prog & = & P \mid Q \\ P & = & scan; \\ & & branch(r_2, write(1), \mathbf{nil}) \end{array} \qquad \begin{array}{rcl} Q & = & scan; \\ & & branch(r_1, \mathbf{nil}, write(0)) \end{array}$$

This program achieves binary pseudo-consensus (look at the formal semantics of next section). Remark that there is indeed no waiting (i.e. synchronisation) between processes. Therefore, if a processor was shut down in the middle of the computation, the others could carry on their respective computations. More generally, we can see that in this language, even if t processors fail ($1 \leq t \leq n-1$), the remaining processes can carry on their computations. Now, what relations can we compute in that language?

The concrete semantics

We model the concurrent execution of sequential processes by using Higher-Dimensional Automata (HDA[16,5]). Let us first explain informally the geometric ideas underlying the formalization with HDA. If we had a local clock with continuous time on each processor[7], sequential observations of concurrent executions of our system could be viewed as 1-dimensional curves, or trajectories, parameterized by the local time of each processor taking part in the execution. In general we associate one coordinate in the Euclidean space R^n, say x_i to each processor p_i in the set of available processors $p_1, p_2, \cdots, p_n$. For instance, in (i) of Figure 1, two processors are firing actions a, b concurrently, each of them with a local time in $[0,1]$. So the possible trajectories will be paths inside the square $[0,1] \times [0,1]$. As we suppose that our processors "consume" time for computation, paths should also be strictly increasing in every coordinate. In our example, none of the processors interfere in any manner, so the sequential

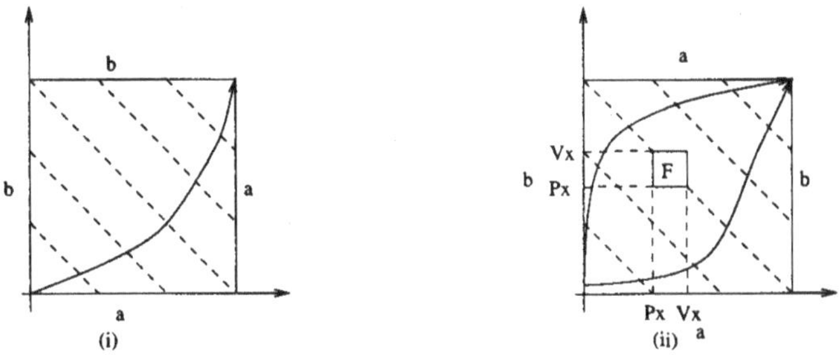

Figure 1: Difference between non-interfering (i) and interfering (ii) parallel composition.

observer might observe any of the trajectories within the square $[0,1] \times [0,1]$. Notice that we are not knowing the exact computations made by the actions of the two processors. Thus the fact that they are non-interfering, therefore the fact that any sequential *schedule* of the two actions give the same result (terminates in the same global state) is reflected by the *geometric* fact that all the paths from the initial to the final state (and in particular the two interleavings of the two actions) are *homotopic*. This means that one can always be continuously deformed through the surface of the square into the other. The idea is that any action a is actually made up of many more subactions, which, by commutation transform "a then b" into "b then a" (see (i) of Figure 1). Conversely, if actions a and b interfere (typically because of a mutual exclusion on a variable accessed by both a and b as in (ii) of Figure 1), then there is a *hole* or forbidden region, in which paths cannot enter, and then through which paths cannot be deformed. This view was first introduced by E. W. Dijkstra[3], reintroduced in a somewhat different way by V. Pratt[16] then used by J. Gunawardena[9] and after by E. Goubault[6].

Now, let us suppose we can simultaneously observe two processes acting concurrently. We are observing a *surface* now and not just a path when we were just a sequential observer, since now, our path is parameterized by two local times (see (i) of Figure 2). In some sense we are observing a schedule of the allocation of pairs of actions to pairs of processors. The "interleaving" of the three (unordered) pairs of actions (taken from the set $\{a, b, c\}$) is the boundary of the cube shown in (ii) of Figure 2, and represents the possible allocations in time of two of the three actions a, b and c on two processors, i.e. the implementation of $a \mid b \mid c$ on two processors, whereas the interior of the cube represents the purely asynchronous execution of the three actions.

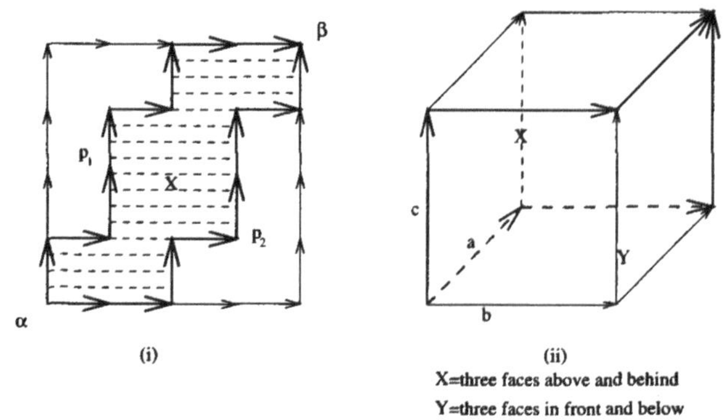

Figure 2: A concurrent execution of two processes (i) and two equivalent surfaces (ii)

There again, the two 2-schedules are homotopic if one can be deformed into the other through cubes. This can be generalized to any sequence of hypercubes. Semi-regular HDA are just amalgamated sums of points, segments, cubes and hypercubes glued along their boundaries. Basically they are just collections of n-transitions (n-cubes, i.e. asynchronous executions of n actions, abstraction of the unit hypercube $[0,1]^n$) together with two series of boundary operators. One is the series "start boundary operators" d_i^0 $(0 \le i \le n-1)$ which to any n transition gives one of the n $(n-1)$-transitions which can start its execution. The other one is the series of "end boundary operators" d_i^1, the obvious complement to the start boundary operators. Formally,

Definition 1 *An unlabeled semi-regular HDA is a collection of sets* $M_{p,q}$ $(p, q \in \mathbb{Z})$ *together with functions* $d_i^0 : M_{p,q} \rightarrow M_{p-1,q}$ *and* $d_j^1 : M_{p,q} \rightarrow M_{p,q-1}$ *for all* $p, q \in \mathbb{Z}$ *and* $0 \le i, j \le p+q-1$ *($p+q$ is the dimension of the transition), such that* $d_i^k \circ d_j^l = d_{j-1}^l \circ d_i^k$ *($i < j$ and $k, l = 0, 1$) and* $\forall n, m\ n \neq m, \quad M_n \cap M_m = \emptyset$.

2.3 Schedules, input, output and protocol complexes

The main idea is to describe the schedulers[6] that a language or a machine can implement. Then using the detailed semantics of the shared data structures or the communication network through which the information is exchanged, we determine what amount of information might be different when we go from one schedule to another. This can then be used to decide whether a decision task can be implemented under the constraints of architecture and language. Other considerations (again of a topological nature) will be used for giving lower bounds on the complexity of the computation when shown possible.

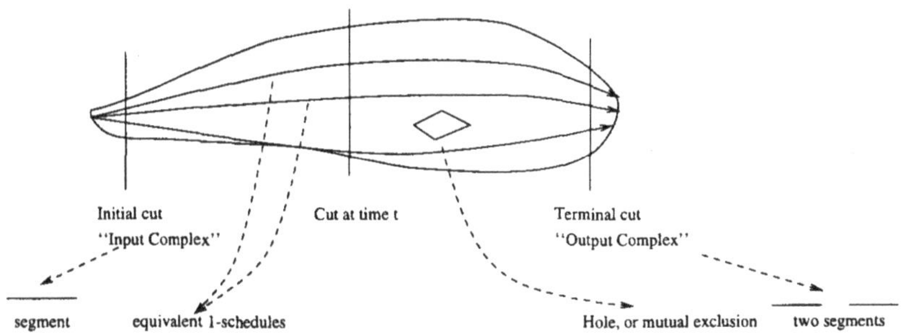

Figure 3: Geometry of schedules and cuts

The n-schedules are just the sequences of hypercubes of dimension n in an HDA. If they are homotopic then they define equivalent schedules in the sense that they will compute the same function. When we want to know whether we can implement some relation then we just know the cuts at initial time and terminal time of the HDA semantics. The equivalence of schedules induces an equivalence (a homotopy) on the different cuts. So if we can characterize geometrically the schedulers of our machine, then we will know if we can implement some relation (see Figure 3).

The problem for implementing some relations will be that the topology of the cut can never change enough. If we suppose that a relation can be computed then the new question is now, "how much time do we need to compute it?". The basic idea here is to determine at which time the topological obstruction to computing the relation is no longer here. Therefore, we need to see from what time on the topology of the cuts match the output complex.

3 Application to our asynchronous machine

We denote both the shared and local stores by ρ which is a function from $V \cup (\cup_i V_i)$ to D, the domain of values. We then extend ρ to denote all the homotopies[5] between environments. In order to retain some complexity measure on computation, we add an ordinal counter to the environment denoted by $\rho(t)$ (we suppose t is not the name of a local nor shared variable). Then, for processor i the standard denotational semantics for instructions is,

$$\begin{array}{lcl}
[\![\mathbf{nil}]\!]_d\ \rho & = & \rho[x_i \leftarrow r^i_i, t \leftarrow t+1] \\
[\![scan]\!]_d\ \rho & = & \rho[r^i_j \leftarrow x_j (j \neq i), x_i \leftarrow r^i_i, t \leftarrow t+1] \\
[\![write\ u]\!]_d\ \rho & = & \rho[x_i \leftarrow u, t \leftarrow t+1] \\
[\![r^i_j = f(r^i_{j_1}, \ldots, r^i_{j_n})]\!]_d\ \rho & = & \rho[r^i_j \leftarrow f(r^i_{j_1}, \ldots, r^i_{j_n}), t \leftarrow t+1]
\end{array}$$

This semantics can be extended to a truly-concurrent semantics $[\![.]\!]$ using HDA by letting $[\![I]\!]\ \rho = [\rho, [\![I]\!]_d\rho]$ to be the higher-dimensional transition from ρ to $[\![I]\!]_d\rho$. Then for processes the truly-concurrent semantics is given by,

$$\begin{array}{lcl} [\![branch(r, I_1, I_2)]\!]\ \rho & = & tt^*(\rho(r))[\![I_1]\!]\ \rho + (ff^* + \bot^*)(\rho(r))[\![I_2]\!]\ \rho \\ [\![P_1; P_2]\!]\ \rho & = & [\![\hat{P_2}]\!]([\![P_1]\!]\ \rho) \end{array}$$

The equation for branch[5] is just the union of the true (tt), false (ff) and undefined ($\bot$) branches. The sequential composition is just the composition of the homotopy $[\![P_2]\!]$ with the final states of $[\![P_1]\!]\rho$, together with those of $[\![P_1]\!]\rho$. We refer to E. Goubault[5] for details of the construction of the sequentialization (via the operator $\hat{}$). Finally the semantics of the whole system is

$$[\![Prog]\!]\ \rho = \sum_{\sigma \in \mathcal{S}_n} [\![P_{\sigma(1)}]\!] \circ [\![P_{\sigma(2)}]\!] \circ \cdots \circ [\![P_{\sigma(n)}]\!]\rho$$

where $Prog = P_1 \mid \cdots \mid P_n$ and $\mathcal{S}_n$ is the group of permutations on $\{1, \cdots, n\}$.

3.1 Herlihy/Shavit/Rajsbaum's approach in a semantic framework

Notice that all equivalent schedules, or homotopic n-paths compute the same function. In order to compute a relation we need to have one schedule associated with each possible outcome from a given set of arguments. This implies that there is a direct relation between the possible schedules that a machine can express and the relations it can compute. This was used by E. Goubault[6] for the automatic verification of protocols for distributed systems. Here we want to know, given a specification of the relation we need to compute, if there is a program in $\mathcal{L}$ which implements it.

In order to do so, we will use a compact representation (which defines the simplicial complex of the decision task[10]) of the relation induced by the schedules. Actually, this could be shown to be an abstract interpretation of the concrete semantics[b]. Let X be a non-cyclic semi-regular HDA where all 1-paths from the initial states (all in $X_{0,0}$) to the final states are of the same length k. This implies that $X_{k,-k}$ is the set of final states and $X_{0,0}$ is the set of initial states. Then the cuts of X at time 0 and at time k are the codomain and domain of the relation that X computes (called respectively input and output complexes of X). More formally, if l_I is the labelling morphism which retains only the name of the process firing the transition and the value of the local variable at the source of the transition and l_O only retains the name of the process and the value of the shared variable belonging to that process

[b]It was shown[6] that the schedulers in dimension k are an abstract interpretation of the concrete HDA semantics.

then the input complex of X is the sequence $\mathcal{I} = l_I(X_{p,0}, (d_i^0)_i)_p$. The output complex of X is the sequence $\mathcal{O} = l_O(X_{k,q}, (d_i^1)_i)_q$. Notice that $\mathcal{I}$ and $\mathcal{O}$ are semi-simplicial sets.

Let $p_I : X \rightarrow \mathcal{I}$ and $p_O : X \rightarrow \mathcal{O}$ be the projections onto the initial and terminal cuts respectively (see Figure 3). The relation induced by the schedules of a program whose semantics is given by a HDA, X, is the sequence $- >= (- >_n \in \mathcal{I}_n \times \mathcal{O}_n)_n$ with $s- > s'$ if and only if, $s \in \mathcal{I}_n$ and $s' \in \mathcal{O}_n$ for some n, and there is a n-schedule u such that $p_I(u) = s$ and $p_O(u) = s'$.

4 Some results and examples on asynchronous protocols

All terms P of $\mathcal{L}$ are non-cyclic and all 1-paths from an initial state to a final state in P are of the same length, so we can use the definitions of the last section to study $\mathcal{L}$.

In the following, we will consider only protocols written in $\mathcal{L}$ such that the global store is undefined at the beginning of execution, i.e. such that the first environment is $\rho(x_i) = \bot$, $(\rho(r_i^i))_i$ being the initial tuple, argument of the program. This means that we are considering $X = [\![P_1 \mid \cdots \mid P_n]\!]\ \rho$ for which for all $s \in I_0$, $s(x_i) = \bot$. We now relate executions of the n processes with the executions of only a subset of these processes (the "solo executions"[10]). If $S = \{i_1, \cdots, i_j\} \subset \{1, \cdots, n\}$ then we write X^S, $\mathcal{I}^S$, $\mathcal{O}^S$, $- >^S$ for the HDA semantics of $P_{i_1} \mid \cdots \mid P_{i_j}$, its input complex, its output complex and its relation respectively. There are obvious inclusions between the $\mathcal{I}^S$ and $\mathcal{I}^{S'}$ when $S \subseteq S'$ (by just adding some extra local variables). Equality of states will then mean the equality on the intersection of the set of variables defined in each case. We also write $- >^{\{i\}} (s)$, $s \in \mathcal{I}_0^{\{i\}}$ for <u>the</u> point s' in $\mathcal{O}_0^{\{i\}}$ such that $s- >^{\{i\}} s'$. By induction on the semantics,

Lemma 1 *For any $S \subseteq \{1, \cdots, n\}$ such that $i, j \in S$, $i \neq j$ and any $s = \{s_i, s_j\} \in \mathcal{I}_1^{\{i,j\}}$, if $\{s_1, \cdots, s_k\}$ is the set of s' such that $s- >^S s'$ then $s_1 + \cdots + s_k$ is a 1-simplex from $- >^{\{i\}} (s_i)$ to $- >^{\{j\}} (s_j)$.*

This 1-simplex is denoted by $p(s, s')$. The different segments comprising this 1-simplex are due to the different interactions between the two processes each corresponding to different 2-schedules. These differences in the interactions can only come from *branch* instructions in the processes.

Proposition 1 *For any $S \subseteq \{1, \cdots, n\}$ such that $i_1, \cdots, i_l \in S$, the i_j being all distinct and any $s \in \mathcal{I}_l^S$, if $\{s_1, \cdots, s_k\}$ is the set of s' such that $s- >^S s'$ then $s_1 + \cdots + s_k$ is a $(l-1)$-simplex[15] whose boundaries are the l $(l-2)$-simplexes defined by the subsets $\{i_1, \cdots, \hat{i_j}, \cdots, i_l\}$.*

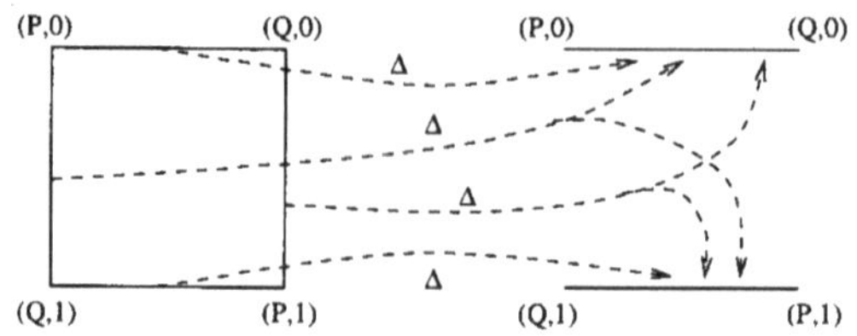

Figure 4: The specification for the binary consensus.

Theorem 1 *The image of any k-connected component of $\mathcal{I}$ ($k \leq n$) is k-connected*[15] *in $\mathcal{O}$.*

4.1 The consensus problems

The binary consensus problem will be our first example. The specification relation and input, output complexes are shown in Figure 4. An easy inpection shows that the image of the 1-simplex $((P,0),(Q,1))$ is a set of two disconnected 1-simplexes, thus violating Lemma 1. Therefore, binary consensus cannot be implemented in a wait-free manner. The intuition behind this result is quite simple. Consensus requires that a process can tell whether it is the first or last to choose, because otherwise there is no way to be sure that the two processes will agree on any value. This means it needs a synchronisation, a break of the connexity of the cuts of the dynamics. This is of course impossible in a wait-free language. Similarly, parallel or (or ordered binary consensus) cannot be implemented in a wait-free manner if the input is given locally to the processes (though there is a wait-free solution for parallel or if the input is stored in the shared memory right from the beginning).

4.2 Boolean binary relations

We first suppose that all relations R we are interested in in this section are such that $(r,\perp)R(r,\perp)$ and $(\perp,s)R(\perp,s)$. In fact, we can handle all other situations by code transformations (implementing the symmetries between processes and between values). By the theorem of the last section we know that all four segments of the input complex must be mapped onto 1-paths of the output complex, between the respective images of the vertices. We also know that the output complex must be a subcomplex of the binary 2-sphere (which is the complex left of Figure 4 for instance).

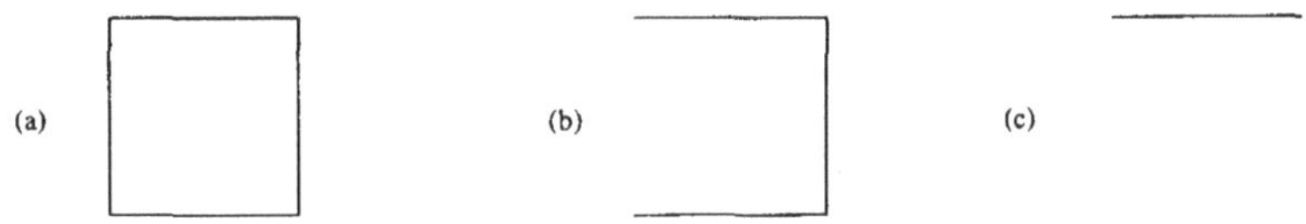

Figure 5: The three possible output complexes for wait-free binary relations

Therefore we have the three possibilities (a), (b), and (c) of Figure 5 for the output complexes. There are actually many more possibilities for the allowed relations between the input and output complexes. A typical "type (a)" program is the identity for processes P and Q. The relation in this case is therefore the identity relation on the binary 2-sphere. Notice that there are other kinds of programs of "type (a)". For instance the relation $\{(P,0),(Q,0)\}R\{(P,0),(Q,0)\}$, $\{(P,0),(Q,0)\}R\{(P,0),(Q,1)\}$, $\{(P,0),(Q,1)\}$ $R\{(P,0),(Q,1)\}$, $\{(P,0),(Q,1)\}R\{(P,0),(Q,0)\}$, $\{(P,1),(Q,1)\}R\{(P,1),(Q,1)\}$ and $\{(P,1),(Q,0)\}R\{(P,1),(Q,0)\}$ can be implemented as follows,

$$\begin{array}{lllllll} Prog & = & P \mid Q & & Q & = & scan; \\ P & = & scan; & & & & branch(r_1, write(1), \mathbf{nil}) \end{array}$$

A typical "type (b)" program is pseudo-consensus. A typical "type (c)" program is composed of two constant processes in parallel.

4.3 Some complexity results

As such, we are not interested in the cost of any sequential function in particular, they are all abstracted by a single action in the semantic framework. We are in fact much more interested in the number of successive choices (i.e. *branch* statements) we have to make before reaching the solution.

Let l be the length function of 1-paths in output complexes, i.e. the number of 1-simplices which compose the 1-paths. Then we can prove that $l_{max} = max_{s,s' \in \mathcal{I}_0} l(p(s,s'))$ is the maximum number of *branch* statements. For instance, in the pseudo-consensus example, we see that the image of the 1-simplex $((P,0),(Q,1))$ is the sum of the three 1-simplexes $((P,0),(Q,0))$, $((Q,0),(P,1))$ and $((P,1),(Q,1))$. It results from an interaction of two *branch* statements.

Now, suppose that the set of possible values that each process (P or Q) can deal with is $[0,M] \cap \mathbb{Z}$ ($M \in \mathbb{Z}$). Then the input complex is the graph (V,E) with vertices $V = \{P\} \times [0,M] \cap \mathbb{Z} \cup \{Q\} \times [0,M] \cap \mathbb{Z}$ and edges $E = \{(v_1,v_2)/v_1 = (P,r), v_2 = (Q,s)\}$ with the obvious boundaries. The wait-free binary relations on that domain are actually quite constrained: all wait-free relations in $[0, M]^2$ can be computed in at most M^2 steps.

References

[1] E. Borowsky and E. Gafni. Generalized FLP impossibility result for t-resilient asynchronous computations. In *Proc. of the 25th STOC.* ACM Press, 1993.

[2] S. Chaudhuri. Agreement is harder than consensus: set consensus problems in totally asynchronous systems. In *Proc. of the 9th Annual ACM Symposium on Principles of Distributed Computing*, pages 311–334. ACM Press, August 1990.

[3] E.W. Dijkstra. *Cooperating Sequential Processes.* Academic Press, 1968.

[4] M. Fisher, N. A. Lynch, and M. S. Paterson. Impossibility of distributed commit with one faulty process. *Journal of the ACM*, 32(2):374–382, April 1985.

[5] E. Goubault. Domains of higher-dimensional automata. In *Proc. of CONCUR'93*, Hildesheim, August 1993. Springer-Verlag.

[6] E. Goubault. Schedulers as abstract interpretations of HDA. In *Proc. of PEPM'95*, La Jolla, June 1995. ACM Press.

[7] E. Goubault. Durations for truly-concurrent actions. In *Proceedings of ESOP'96*, number 1058. Springer-Verlag, 1996.

[8] E. Goubault. *The Geometry of Concurrency.* PhD thesis, Ecole Normale Supérieure, to be published, 1996.

[9] J. Gunawardena. Homotopy and concurrency. In *Bulletin of the EATCS*, number 54, pages 184–193, October 1994.

[10] M. Herlihy. A tutorial on algebraic topology and distributed computation. Technical report, presented at UCLA, 1994.

[11] M. Herlihy and S. Rajsbaum. Set consensus using arbitrary objects. In *Proc. of the 13th Annual ACM Symposium on Principles of Distributed Computing.* ACM Press, August 1994.

[12] M. Herlihy and S. Rajsbaum. Algebraic topology and distributed computing, a primer. Technical report, Brown University, 1995.

[13] M. Herlihy and N. Shavit. The asynchronous computability theorem for t-resilient tasks. In *Proc. of the 25th STOC.* ACM Press, 1993.

[14] M. Herlihy and N. Shavit. A simple constructive computability theorem for wait-free computation. In *Proceedings of STOC'94.* ACM Press, 1994.

[15] J. P. May. *Simplicial objects in algebraic topology.* D. van Nostrand Company, inc, 1967.

[16] V. Pratt. Modeling concurrency with geometry. In *Proc. of the 18th ACM Symposium on Principles of Programming Languages.* ACM Press, 1991.

[17] M. Saks and F. Zaharoglou. Wait-free k-set agreement is impossible: The topology of public knowledge. In *Proc. of the 25th STOC.* ACM Press, 1993.

REDUCTIONS OF SEARCH SPACE IN RUE-RESOLUTION THEOREM PROVING

D. RAPTIS
Department of Computing, Imperial College, London SW7 2BZ.

Abstract

RUE resolution is a natural extension of resolution that replaces the substitutivity axioms of equality. The major drawback of it is that it generates a lot of irrelevant negative equality literals. To relieve this problem, a simple and easy to apply criterion that can be used to characterise some negative equality literals as pure, in the sense that the clause they belong to can be removed from a clause set without affecting satisfiability, is identified. Furthermore, two restrictions on the application of the RUE resolution rules on equality literals that reduce the number of derived resolvents are presented.

1 Introduction

The predicate of equality has a special role in logic. The formulation of most problems in first order logic require the use of the equality predicate. In theorem proving, when the predicate of equality appears in the formulation of a problem, the properties of equality need to be included. The equality substitutivity property however makes theorem proving more cumbersome and inefficient by generating a lot of irrelevant clauses.

In proofs of unsatisfiability by resolution, the explicit addition of domain specific equality axioms in a clause set can be replaced with the extension of the normal resolution rules (or the addition of new ones like paramodulation [WR69]).

RUE resolution [DH86] is a natural extension of resolution to replace the substitutivity axioms of equality from a clause set. The major drawback is that a lot of irrelevant negative equality literals are generated. So it is very helpful to identify as many as possible of them as irrelevant for a proof, or identify restrictions on the application of the RUE resolution rules that avoid generating useless clauses reducing the search space while preserve completeness.

In [DH86], the notion of *viability* is used to identify certain inequalities as irrelevant and avoid generating the clause they belong to. However, the use of this notion is shown in [LS93] to be sometimes non-terminating. A different notion of viability that is guaranteed to terminate is presented [DLS89] but this is difficult to apply in practice.

Here instead, a criterion that some negative equality literals can be characterised as *pure inequalities* is presented. This criterion is very easy to apply in practice and it is proved that clauses that contain pure inequalities can be removed from a clause set without affecting satisfiability.

Further, two restrictions on the way that the RUE-resolution rule can be applied in (in)equality literals are presented. The first one allows the derivation of only a single resolvent when one of the arguments of the equality and complementary inequality literals are identical. The second one requires that at least one argument in each of the equality and complementary inequality literals has a term with the same leading function symbol. Furthermore, the RUE unification algorithm is appliedto the arguments of this function symbol.

Section 2 gives a brief description of RUE resolution. Section 3 describes the notion of pure inequalities is and explains why removal of the corresponding clauses preserves unsatisfiability. The two restrictions on the RUE resolution rules can be applied on equality literals are discussed on section 4. Section 5 concludes the paper.

2 RUE Resolution

RUE resolution [1] can be considered as a generalisation of resolution in the sense that, from the clauses

$$P(r) \vee C$$

$$\neg P(s) \vee D$$

we can infer the clause, $C \vee D$ if $r = s$, or in clausal form

$$r \neq s \vee C \vee D$$

If the terms r and s can be unified with $\theta = mgu\{r, s\}$, then the standard resolvent $(C \vee D)\theta$ can also be derived. But if r and s are not unifiable, these may be proved equal by the other clauses of a clause set.

Note Unless otherwise stated, variables will be represented either with capital letters or with letters from the end of the alphabet u, v, w, x, y. Constants will be represented as letters from the begin of the alphabet $a, b, c, \ldots$.

A *disagreement pair*, $t_1 : t_2$, is a pair of non-identical terms, t_1, t_2, where neither of them is a variable, or the variable term occurs inside the other term.

[1] RUE stands for Resolution with Unification and Equality.

The RUE resolution rules do not use the standard unification algorithm but a different one [2] called *RUE unification*. The differences are that, the RUE unification is not recursive, and it never fails (hence all term lists of the same size are RUE unifiable) but forms disagreement pairs instead. The result of RUE unification on two, same size, lists of terms tl_1 and tl_2, is the pair (θ, d) of variable substitutions θ and disagreement pairs d sets, of the corresponding terms in the lists. For example, the result of the left-right RUE unification algorithm on the term lists $[x, f(x,a), f(a,x), x]$ and $[y, f(a,y), y, a]$ is the substitutions $\{x \mapsto a, y \mapsto a\}$ and the disagreement pair $\{f(a,a) : a\}$. The operation of RUE unifying two expressions (terms or atoms) E and E' is denoted by $rueu\{E, E'\}$.

In the RUE resolution set of rules, the RUE rule captures the predicate substitutivity property, while the NRF rule captures the function substitutivity and reflexivity properties of equality. The RUE rule applies to two literals in a different clause, the RUE-Factoring rule applies to two literals in the same clause, while the NRF rule is unary in that it applies to a single (inequality) literal only.

Definition 2.1 Assuming that: (1) A, A' are atoms and L, L' are literals with the same predicate symbol, (2) The $A \vee C$ and $\neg A \vee D$ clauses have no variables in common, (3) The $\bigvee_{\neq}$ operator forms the clause with an inequality literal for each disagreement pair in a disagreement set, (4) C, D are any clauses, then the *RUE resolution* set of rules comprises the following three rules:

1.
$$\text{RUE}\ \frac{\begin{array}{c} A \vee C \\ \neg A' \vee D \end{array}}{\bigvee_{\neq}(d) \vee (C \vee D)\theta} \qquad (\theta, d) = rueu\{A, A'\}$$

   When the predicate of the atom A (and A') is the equality, A is $s = t$ and A' is $s' = t'$, two resolvents derived. One by RUE unifying $s = t$ with $s' = t'$, and one by RUE unifying $s = t$ with $t' = s'$.

   The $\bigvee_{\neq}(d) \vee (C \vee D)\theta$ is called *RUE resolvent*.

2. If s, t are terms, with the same leading function symbol:

$$\text{NRF}\ \frac{s \neq t \vee C}{} \qquad (\theta, d) = rueu\{s, t\}$$

[2] In fact, it is not exactly unification because no terms have to become identical.

$$\bigvee_{\neq}(d) \vee C\theta$$

If s is a variable (respectively for t) that occurs inside the term t that is of the form $f(t_1, t_2, \ldots, t_n)$, then the rule is applied after replacing s with $f(x_1, x_2, \ldots, x_n)$ (for new variables $x_1, x_2, \ldots, x_n$) everywhere in $s \neq t \vee C$.

If s (respectively for t) is a variable that does not occur inside the term t, then $(\theta, d) = (s \mapsto t, \emptyset)$ (respectively $(\theta, d) = (t \mapsto s, \emptyset)$)[3].

The $\bigvee_{\neq}(d) \vee C\theta$ is called *NRF resolvent.*[4]

3. RUE-Factoring $$\frac{L \vee L' \vee C}{\bigvee_{\neq}(d) \vee (L' \vee C)\theta} \quad (\theta, d) = rueu\{L, L'\}$$

No variable renaming is performed on the literal L and L'. When the predicate in the literal L (and L') is the equality (positive or negative), L is $s = t$ and L' is $s' = t'$, two factors are derived. One by RUE unifying $s = t$ with $s' = t'$, and one by RUE unifying $s = t$ with $t' = s'$.

The $\bigvee_{\neq}(d) \vee (L \vee C)\theta$ is called *RUE factor.*

where (θ, d) is the result of the RUE unification of the respective expressions in each rule.

3 Pure Inequalities

We start from the observation that, using resolution with equality axioms, the literals that appear in the resolvents or factors of clauses are *instances* of their parent literals. In particular, in standard resolution using equality axioms, new positive equality literals are generated only from the symmetry and transitivity axioms of equality.

Take a clause set S that contains a clause of the form $f(t) \neq g(t') \vee C$ and in which no positive equality literal occurs that has as argument either a variable, or exactly one term with leading function symbol f. Then $f(t) \neq g(t')$ can not be resolved with any clause in S except from the positive equality literals of the symmetry and transitivity axioms of equality. In other words, the function symbol f makes the inequality literal unifiable only with the symmetry and

[3] That requirement was overlooked in [DH86].

[4] NRF stands for **N**egative **R**eflexive **F**unction.

transitivity clauses. But these clauses alone (and the substitutivity axiom for f) can not resolve away the function symbol f from an inequality literal. New resolvents will have as arguments inequalities with leading function symbol f that in turn can only unify with the symmetry and transitivity property of equality.

For example, resolving the inequality in the clause

$$f(t) \neq g(t') \vee C$$

with the transitivity clause

$$x \neq y \vee y \neq z \vee x = z$$

we get as resolvent

$$f(t) \neq y \vee y \neq g(t') \vee C$$

Still the literal $f(t) \neq y$ can only be resolved with the same literals in S that $f(t) \neq g(t')$ can. In addition, this can be resolved with the substitutivity axiom as well

$$u \neq v \vee f(u) = f(v)$$

to get

$$t \neq v \vee f(v) \neq g(t') \vee C$$

This clause also has the $f(v) \neq g(t')$ literal with f as leading function symbol.

This process (resolving with the symmetry and transitivity clauses only) can be repeated ad infinitum, but obviously all resolvents will have an inequality literal that has a term with leading function symbol f as one of the arguments. So none of these clauses can contribute to a derivation of the empty clause.

Further, even if there is a clause of the form

$$f(t) = f(r) \vee D$$

in S, resolving for example with the

$$f(t) \neq y \vee y \neq g(t') \vee C$$

above, we get

$$f(r) \neq g(t') \vee C \vee D$$

Now it is the $f(r)$ term in the inequality literal that can not be resolved away.

The only way to resolve away the $f(t)$ term in the inequality literal above is to have an equality literal of the form $f(r) = s$ (with s *not* having f as leading function symbol), or $x = s'$ (in a clause other that equality axiom) in the clause set.

So, under these conditions, a clause that has such negative equality literals can be removed without affecting the satisfiability of the clause set. The definition and theorem below express this property formally.

Definition 3.1 (Pure inequality) Let f and g be any different function symbols, t and t' be (possibly empty) term lists of size equal to the arity of f and g respectively, and C be any (possibly empty) disjunction of literals. Then, the negative equality literal $f(t) \neq g(t')$ (or $g(t') \neq f(t)$) in the clause $f(t) \neq g(t') \vee C$ (or $g(t') \neq f(t) \vee C$) in a clause set S is called a *pure inequality on* f iff there is no positive equality literal in $S \setminus \{f(t) \neq g(t') \vee C\}$ with arguments, either a variable (or two) or exactly one term with leading function symbol f.

Note The inequality in the clause $f(t) \neq g(t') \vee C$ is pure even if there is a positive equality in C, that has as arguments a variable or exactly one term with leading function symbol f. So, for example, the clause $a \neq t \vee a = x \vee C$ can be pure (on a) in a clause set S.

Example 3.2 The literal $f(a) \neq g(c)$ is a pure inequality on f in the clause set

$$\{a = b, f(x) = f(b), g(x) = a, f(a) \neq g(c)\}$$

The literal $f(a) \neq g(c)$ is not a pure inequality on g because the equality $g(x) = a$ has as arguments exactly one term with leading function symbol g. □

It should be noted here that, this notion of pure inequality literals does not coincide exactly with the usual notion of purity in resolution where a literal is called pure in clause set iff it has no complement in this clause set. In the context of RUE resolution however, all literals with the same predicate symbol and opposite signs are RUE complementary. The reason however for calling such literals pure, is that the clause they belong to, can be removed from the clause set without affecting the satisfiability of the set, as it is demonstrated by the following theorem.

Theorem 3.3 (Pure inequality) A clause set S that contains a clause of the form $f(t) \neq g(t') \vee C$, where $f(t) \neq g(t')$ is a pure inequality literal in S, is unsatisfiable iff $S \setminus \{f(t) \neq g(t') \vee C\}$ is unsatisfiable.

Only the outline of the proof is presented here. A detailed proof can be found in [Rap96]. The difficult part in the proof of this theorem is to show that if $S \setminus \{f(t) \neq g(t') \vee C\}$ is satisfiable then S is also satisfiable. That is done by taking a normal[5] model $\mathcal{I}$ of $S \setminus \{f(t) \neq g(t') \vee C\}$ and constructing an identity interpretation $\mathcal{I}'$ that is model of S.

The domain D' of $\mathcal{I}'$ is constructed by "doubling" the domain D of $\mathcal{I}$ to $D' = D \cup M(D)$ where M is any one-to-one mapping. Then, $\mathcal{I}'$ is defined over D' in such a way that the value (image) of all predicates and function symbols, except f, is the same for all arguments from D and their corresponding element in $M(D)$ (and coincide with their value in $\mathcal{I}$), except for the image of f which is in $M(D)$. Under $\mathcal{I}'$, all terms have the same value as under $\mathcal{I}$, except from the terms of the form $f(t)$, where their value is in $M(D)$, and therefore literals of the form $f(t) \neq g(t')$ are always be true under $\mathcal{I}'$. Hence, $\mathcal{I}'$ satisfy $f(t) \neq g(t') \vee C$ and, under the given assumptions of the theorem and the way $\mathcal{I}'$ is constructed, all other literals have the same truth value under $\mathcal{I}'$ as under $\mathcal{I}$. Therefore $\mathcal{I}'$ is a model of S.

The requirements on the pure inequalities in the theorem are minimal, in the sense that if any one of them is not met, the theorem does not hold and therefore an unsatisfiable set of clauses may become satisfiable if the inequality clause is removed. This is demonstrated by the following examples.

- In case the function symbols f and g are the same, the above theorem does not hold because the clause $f(t) \neq f(t') \vee C$ has an NRF resolvent that may be needed to derive the empty clause. So the $f(a) \neq f(b)$ unit can not be removed from the clause set $\{a = b, f(a) \neq f(b)\}$ preserving unsatisfiability, although it satisfies the rest of the requirements of the theorem.

- If one of the arguments of an inequality is a variable, the inequality is not pure no matter of whether this variable appears inside the other argument or not. The $f(g(x)) \neq x$ is not pure on f in the[6]

  $$\{g(x) = c, f(g(x)) \neq x\}$$

  and the $a \neq x$ is not pure on a in $\{a \neq x\}$ If either of these two inequalities is removed, the remaining clause set (singleton and empty respectively) becomes satisfiable.

- The $a \neq b$ in $\{x = c, a \neq b\}$ is not pure on a because a variable appears in a positive equality literal. Removing the $a \neq b$ the remaining clause set becomes satisfiable.

[5] A normal model of a formula is model where the predicate of equality is interpreted to the identity relation.

[6] This clause set is unsatisfiable because substituting x with $f(c)$ in $f(g(x)) \neq x$ we get $f(g(f(c))) \neq f(c)$ which from $g(x) = c$ becomes $f(c) \neq f(c)$.

- The $a \neq b$ in $\{a = b, a \neq b\}$ is not pure on a because there is a positive equality literal that has exactly one argument with leading function symbol (constant) a. Removing the $a \neq b$ the remaining clause set becomes satisfiable.

The pure inequalities theorem is independent of the theorem proving mechanism employed. It can be applied even when the equality axioms, or paramodulation is used. However, it is most useful when the RUE resolution rules are applied because they generate a lot of irrelevant inequalities.

The pure inequalities theorem is weaker than the notion of viability in [DH86]. So no pure inequality is viable, whereas non pure inequlities are not necessarily viable. But on the other hand, the application of the pure inequalities theorem is by far easier.

4 Restrictions of the RUE Rule on Equality Literals

There are two simple restrictions that can be applied to RUE resolution rules when these are applied on (in)equality literals. These restrictions allow the derivation of fewer resolvents than the standard rules while preserving completeness.

Identical arguments restriction When applying the RUE rule on equality atoms $t \neq r$ (or $r \neq t$) and $t' = s$ (or $s = t'$) where t and t' are *identical*, only the resolvent that comes from the RUE unification of the terms r and s need be derived.

When applying the RUE-Factoring rule on (positive or negative) equality literals $t = r$ (or $t \neq r$) and $t' = s$ (or $t' \neq s$) where t and t' are *identical*, only the factor that comes from the RUE unification of the terms r and s need be derived.

In the case of the RUE rule, the second resolvent would be subsumed by the clause that has the negative equality literal. So, assume that t and t' are identical. Then, RUE resolving the clauses

$$t \neq r \vee D$$

and

$$s = t' \vee C$$

only the clause

$$r \neq s \vee C \vee D$$

need be derived. The resolvent $t \neq s \vee r \neq t' \vee C \vee D$ is subsumed by the parent clause $t \neq r \vee C$. If however t and t' are not identical, this subsumption does not necessarily hold.

In the case of the RUE-Factoring rule, factoring positive equality literals, the second factor would be a tautology. So, RUE-Factoring the clause

$$t = r \vee t' = s \vee C$$

only the clause

$$r \neq s \vee t = r \vee C$$

need be derived. The second factor $t \neq s \vee r \neq t' \vee t = r \vee C$ is a tautology.

When RUE-Factoring negative equality literals, the second factor is subsumed by the first. So, RUE-Factoring the clause

$$t \neq r \vee t' \neq s \vee C$$

only the clause

$$r \neq s \vee t \neq r \vee C$$

need be derived. The second factor $t \neq s \vee r \neq t' \vee t \neq r \vee C$ is subsumed by the previous one.

The second restriction takes into account the leading function symbols of terms in (in)equality literals.

Equality restriction Assume that tl, tl' are any term lists, t and t' are any terms, f is any function symbol and x is any variable.

When applying the RUE rule to a negative equality literal of the form $f(tl) \neq t$, the complementary positive equality literal should be, either of the form $f(tl') = t'$ (or $t' = f(tl')$), or of the form $x = t'$ (or $t' = x$). In the first case, their RUE resolvent is formed by RUE unifying the term lists $[t|tl]$ and $[t'|tl']$, and in the second case, it is formed by RUE unifying the term lists $[f(tl), t]$ and $[x, t']$.

The same condition should hold when applying the RUE-Factoring rule to any (positive or negative) equality literal. If the term t is of the form $f(tl')$, the NRF rule is applied as usual.

The only way to make the terms $f(tl)$ and t equal, is through the use of a sequence of equalities and the transitivity property. So, if these terms can be proved equal, they can be proved by resolving with equalities that have as an argument either a variable, or a term with leading function symbol f only. In addition, in the latter case, these terms will become equal because their arguments become equal, and so it is needed to RUE unify directly their arguments omitting the leading symbols.

The resolvents derived applying the equality restriction can also be derived by applying the usual RUE rule followed by the NRF rule. So this restriction preserves soundness.

This restriction (as presented here) is weaker than the corresponding one in [DH86]. The difference is that there is no requirement for the disagreement set formed by RUE unifying $[t|tl]$ and $[t'|tl']$ to be viable. Instead, all disagreements are allowed to be formed, and then they are removed by the pure inequality property (if it is applicable).

Example 4.1 Applying the equality restriction, the only RUE resolvents of $f(b) \neq g(d)$ in the clause set

$$\{a=b, c=d, f(a)=f(c), f(c)=g(c), f(b) \neq g(d)\}$$

are the clauses

1 $a \neq b \vee f(c) \neq g(d)$ with $f(a)=f(c)$ by RUE unifying $[a, f(c)]$ and $[b, g(d)]$

2 $c \neq b \vee f(a) \neq g(d)$ with $f(c)=f(a)$ by RUE unifying $[c, f(a)]$ and $[b, g(d)]$

3 $c \neq b \vee g(c) \neq g(d)$ with $f(c)=g(c)$ by RUE unifying $[c, g(c)]$ and $[b, g(d)]$

4 $c \neq d \vee f(c) \neq f(b)$ with $f(c)=g(c)$ by RUE unifying $[c, f(c)]$ and $[d, f(b)]$

The $a=b$ and $c=d$ do not resolve at all with the $f(b) \neq g(c)$.

Further, applying the identical arguments restriction as well, the only resolvent of the literal $a \neq b$ in clause 1 above is the unit

5 $f(c) \neq g(d)$ with $a=b$ by RUE unifying $[b]$ and $[b]$

because of the identical arguments restriction on the identical term, say a.

The resolvents of the literal $f(c) \neq g(d)$ in clause 1 are:

6 $a \neq b \vee f(a) \neq g(d)$ with $f(a) = f(c)$ by RUE unifying $[f(a)]$ and $[g(d)]$ applying the identical arguments restriction.

7′ $a \neq b \vee g(c) \neq g(d)$ with $f(c)=g(c)$ by RUE unifying $[g(c)]$ and $[g(d)]$ applying the identical arguments restriction, or

7″ $a \neq b \vee c \neq d$ with $f(c)=g(c)$ by RUE unifying $[c, f(c)]$ and $[d, f(c)]$ applying the equality restriction.

□

What the resolvent 7 above will be, depends on the restriction that is preferred. In this particular case, the resolvent $7''$, applying the equality restriction, is better that the $7'$ applying the identical arguments restriction, because it is the clause $7''$ that is needed for the derivation of the empty clause. However, in a developed implementation, the identical arguments restriction is given higher priority.

This property can be extended further in that the resolvents of only one term in an inequality need be derived at any time. So, when applying purity reductions to a negative equality literal in a clause of the form $r \neq s \vee C$, it is sufficient to derive all the RUE resolvents and factors with complementary equality literals that have as argument a variable, or a term with the same leading function symbol with only one of the two terms, r or s. But if r and s have the same leading function symbol, the NRF resolvent needs to be derived as well.

Example 4.2 In the clause set

$$\{\ \mathbf{1}\ a=c, \quad \mathbf{2}\ a=c, \quad \mathbf{3}\ a=b \vee c=d, \quad \mathbf{4}\ a \neq b \vee c \neq d\ \}$$

In order to "resolve away" the $a \neq b$, it is sufficient to resolve it with equalities that a is (or can be) equal to, until the term b is reached.

The resolvents of the inequality $a \neq b$ on the argument a are only the clauses

5 $c \neq b \vee c \neq d$ from 4(1)-1(1), **6** $c=d \vee c \neq d$ from 4(1)-3(1)

and on the argument b are only the

7 $d \neq a \vee c \neq d$ from 4(1)-2(1), **8** $c=d \vee c \neq d$ from 4(1)-3(1)

In both cases, no RUE factors need be formed. The second resolvents (6 and 8 respectively) are tautologies so, either of the clauses 5 or 7 can replace clause 4 in this clause set preserving satisfiability. □

5 Conclusion

RUE resolution is a simple and natural extension of resolution that can replace the substitutivity axioms of equality in a clause set. The major drawback however is that generates a lot of irrelevant negative equality literals.

This work attempts to alleviate this problem by identifying criteria that some negative equality literals can be characterised as pure (in the sense that the clause they belong to can be removed from a clause set without affecting satisfiability). Further, two restrictions on the application of the RUE resolution rules on equality literals that reduce the search space and preserve completeness are presented.

The methods presented here to reduce the irrelevancy in the search space of the RUE resolution are implemented, incorporated and tested in a prototype automatic theorem prover that uses RUE resolution as described here [Rap96]. This prover demonstrated good performance compared to other state of the art theorem provers.

However, more criteria to identify redundancy or further restrictions on the applicability of the RUE resolution rules are required, in order to achieve a satisfactory performance of automatic theorem provers on hard problems.

Although the restrictions of RUE resolution on equality literals are clear, intuitive and tested on large number on data, the formal proof that they preserve completeness is left as further work. Other topics that are left for further study include restrictions on the use of RUE factoring on equality literals (normal factoring seems sufficient), and identification and special treatment of skolem functions.

Acknowledgements

I am grateful to Dr Krysia Broda for her valuable corrections, comments and suggestions she made during the course of this research.

This work has been partially supported from the State Scholarships Foundation (SSF) of Greece by grant 73086-2699.

References

[DH86] Vincent J. Digricoli and Malcolm C. Harrison. Equality-based binary resolution. *Journal of the Association for Computing Machinery*, 33(2):253–289, April 1986.

[DLS89] Vincent J. Digricoli, James J. Lu, and V. S. Subrahmanian. AND-OR graphs applied to RUE resolution. In N. S. Sridharan, editor, *11th International Joint Conference on Artificial Intelligence (August 1989)*, volume 1, pages 354–358. Morgan Kaufmann Publishers, Inc., 1989.

[LS93] James J. LU and V. S. Subrahmanian. Completeness issues in RUE-NRF deduction: The undecidability of viability. *Journal of Automated Reasoning*, 10:371–388, 1993.

[Rap96] Dimitris Raptis. Reduction rules for resolution-based theorem proving. Draft PhD Thesis. Imperial College, University of London, 1996.

[WR69] L. A. Wos and G. A. Robinson. Paramodulation and theorem proving in first-order theories with equality. *Machine Intelligence*, 4:135–150, 1969.

Process Algebra for Object-Oriented Specification – an extended abstract

S. J. Liebert
Department of Computing, Imperial College, London SW7 2BZ.

Abstract

This paper explores methods of specifying problems in a language designed to emphasize the links between process algebra and object oriented methodologies. First we discuss the features of object-oriented specification to be modelled in process algebra and the design decisions taken. Priority is added to an algebra with process mobility to enable encapsulation. There follows an example of the use of such a language to handle resource scheduling.

1 Introduction

Firstly, what is "object-oriented" design for? According to Booch [3], specifications at the object level should be considered before algorithms for individual methods because this approach best enables us to reason about the complexity of a problem. We learn to use abstraction (thinking about the relevant aspects of an object or problem and disregarding the parts which are temporarily not our concern) when processing all kinds of information about the outside world. There is a certain natural way of reasoning about the world as though it were composed of objects of certain classes.

If object-oriented design is concerned with classes and objects, what are the basic components of the paradigm of concurrency and what do they have in common? Work in process algebra concentrates on entities called processes and their means of communication. If an object in the object-oriented paradigm is a parcel of data and some functions for manipulating it, suitably encapsulated so that it can be seen as an entity in its own right, a concurrent process is a more ephemeral being identified by the traces of its actions/communications (equivalences such as trace equivalence or bisimilarity). (Data storage can easily be added to these pure processes).

Objects typically come with the extra baggage of being identified as members of a certain class, which is rather like telling us what type they have. Structuring objects into classes enables us to deduce things about the behaviour of an entire class at once, or take for granted that all the members of the class have the same ability or behaviour. With languages such as Smalltalk which allow inheritance it also allows us to have a hierarchy of more and less general objects, e.g. an object of type "whale" will inherit a lot of general behaviour of objects of type "mammal", plus some extra quirks peculiar to its own species.

Various authors have attempted to reflect this in process algebra with differing degrees of success[15, 5, 2] [17, Chapter 6]. In practice the advantages of hierarchy and typing in an object oriented specification are that there exists a clear structure of objects (usually a tree, although some languages permit diamond-shaped inheritance patterns, i.e. D inherits from B and C, which both inherit from A) in a diagram in some formalism somewhere, and at the programming level hierarchy enables re-use of code. For the purposes of this paper it is assumed that this tree-diagram can be orthogonal to any process algebra specification of individual objects, and that there will be no typing information attached directly to a process. In the same way, sorts of a process are usually considered separately from the process's "program code".

The structure of the paper is as follows:–

First there is a review of some important standard concepts in object oriented design, and a comparison of some existing approaches to object-oriented concurrency. We then make some design decisions about defining a new process language, set up its operational semantics, and discuss an example of scheduling to motivate the new language. The resulting language will be prioritised to enable simple encapsulation of objects, and dynamics to allow easy reconfiguration of objects.

2 Object-oriented concepts

2.1 Abstraction

Abstraction of an object consists of defining its essential characteristics and providing it with clear conceptual boundaries [3]. An ideal abstraction is an entity abstraction, in which an object represents a useful model of a whole clearly delineated problem or solution domain entity.

Abstraction in concurrency is similar to abstraction in the object oriented paradigm, what we are looking for in a neatly defined process and a neatly defined object is the same.

2.2 Encapsulation and modularization

Encapsulation is about hiding information which should be private to an object, usually information about its internal data structure or the implementation of methods.

For a discussion of modularization in CCS_σ, a variant of CCS, and $2L$, another two-level priority language, see a previous paper [8].

In concurrency we can define special parallel operators which mediate the way in which processes can communicate so that we can implement modules. The operators in the paper above are isolating parallel for CCS_σ and interface parallel for $2L$. They both essentially hide priority information from the environment of a process so that its internal actions can continue unimpeded by, and without in turn influencing, all outside events which we decide to screen off.

It is clear how this method can enable us to have a two-level interface and implementation module concept like in Modula-2. More complicated structures like C++ with its public, private, protected and friend statuses might be representible, but this is as yet unknown.

Very large systems would need both encapsulation of individual objects and physical division of the whole code into separate files, the traditional module structure. It is doubtful that there are any key differences in the type of operators required for encapsulation versus modularization in concurrent languages.

2.3 Concurrency

Concurrency is a relatively minor component of OO compared to issues such as modularity. Nevertheless, when we think of objects we typically think of them existing concurrently so that they can perform tasks which do not interfere with each other at the same time, and send each other messages.

3 Comparison of existing approaches to object-oriented concurrency

3.1 The π-calculus

This is an extension of the "standard" or monadic π-calculus. The central notion of the π-calculus [11] is that to create new processes and connect existing processes in new ways we pass names of links along existing links. It is possible to create new processes in CCS but in a more cumbersome way. This has obvious applications in designing semantics for object-oriented languages, as such languages usually allow objects to create new objects with their own new methods.

3.2 An intermediate calculus

Sangiorgi in [14] creates an intermediate language between CCS and the π-calculus, called πI. In this language internal and external mobility are distinguished. Internal mobility occurs when a bound output meets an input, and external when a free output meets an input. Thus in the internal case a local name becomes identified with an external name. πI only allows internal mobility as this makes defining bisimulations, axiomatizations and canonical normal forms much simpler than in π-calculus. Nevertheless the language is still powerful as Sangiorgi argues that few practical examples require the full power of external mobility and π-calculus. It is also suficient for modelling objects.

3.3 Actors

This is a concurrent programming language (see [1]) which combines the object paradigm with functional programming style methods for the "inside" implementation of individual objects. Actors are activated by receiving messages from other actors. They can send communications to themselves or other actors, create new actors, or specify replacement behaviours to handle subsequent communications received. A central mail system buffers communications until the objects specified in the "targets" or mail addresses can receive them. Communications are thus asynchronous and the order of receipt is nondeterministic. The system is dynamically reconfigurable. Actors accept communications by pattern-matching them with the templates in their methods.

3.4 ABCL/1 - an object-oriented concurrent system

ABCL/1 combines the advantages of the object-oriented and functional approaches. The authors have developed a computation model ABCM/1 and a programming language ABCL/1 [1, 17]. Objects pass messages to each other, but in this formalism there are three kinds of message:- past, now and future types, allowing more flexibility in writing specifications. For example, when an object sends a now type message it stops executing itself at that point until it receives the reply. Message passing also occurs in two modes, ordinary and express. The express mode is used for higher priority messages such as interrupts, giving a two-level priority message structure between objects. Once again the object paradigm is used for transmissions between objects, and the internal working of objects is a mixture of functional and imperative features. Objects' method code is functional with some imperative features such as internal stores or states updated by assertions. Simple data types like numbers are not objects.

3.5 Jones' $\pi o\beta\lambda$

Jones [4, 6, 5] is concerned with development methods for concurrent programs, and particularly with overcoming the interference problem for objects accessing shared data. Inheritance has been made to work in practice but it is not very well thought out as a theoretical concept, so it is hard to reason about the existing object-oriented languages or write specifications. He discusses limiting interference by starting from a sequential program and introducing only "safe" concurrency. This results in a language called $\pi o\beta\lambda$ developed through examples, particularly setting up objects to perform prime number sieving. [4] then gives a mapping from $\pi o\beta\lambda$ to a version of the polyadic π-calculus (concretions and abstractions are not separated out as in [11] , but apart from that the language is as usual). Classes have methods; only one method can be active at a time for each instance of the class. Methods start running when the object synchronises with another, but they can return before they have finished processing, releasing the object which invoked them. This is like making a promise to the calling process that the work will be done, in the case when the calling process does not need to be told a value immediately.

3.6 POOL-T : A parallel object-oriented language

Pierre America's POOL-T [2] is an object-oriented language designed for building large systems in a systematic, incremental way. Because of this focus on large systems POOL-T has a module structure as well as objects and classes. Modules collect together definitions related to the same data type. POOL-T associates a process with every object and starts by considering a system in which only one process is active at a time. Concurrency is then introduced where possible without disrupting the correctness reasoning about the system obtained so far. POOL-T objects have a body, i.e. an activity of their own which is active without the need for an external message to be received, and contains explicit declaration of the points at which outside messages can be accepted (synchronously).

4 Adding OO to concurrent languages

In order to define a new process language, some design decisions will have to be made. Among the things which must be chosen are the method of communication between processes, the way in which parallelism (or several types of parallelism) is to be implemented, the means of encapsulation, use of priority, and whether dynamic reconfiguration and creation of new processes are to be implemented.

The flavour of the language chosen in this paper is like π-calculus with priorities added. Priorities are used directly in message-passing and more implicitly in modularization.

- Processes will communicate in synchronised pairs of actions like CCS. This makes for simplicity and enables us to use existing results from other CCS-like languages. We have channel names as in π-calculus and CCS so that we can refer to the data routes used between processes by name. Priorities could enable several levels of message passing, rather like express and ordinary modes in ABCL/1, [17].

- We shall use the regular CCS parallel operator and also the interface parallel developed in [8].

- Considering the sequential activity of processes, we will be using pure processes, i.e. processes will have object-oriented/process calculus method bodies and other internal workings. (This is distinct from such languages as Actors, which mix OO external behaviour and functional programming in internal workings). This should lead to a smaller language and simpler semantics, and implementation is not a consideration at present.

- Priority will exist both in the method bodies of individual objects and also in the operators to separate objects. This distinguishes the approach in this paper from others considered so far.

- Dynamic reconfiguration is desirable in an OO specification language, and the method of achieving this is borrowed from π-calculus.

- Note that typing or inheritance information is not included at the moment.

5 The syntax

The basic syntax follows that of the π-calculus, see [11].

There are two levels of priority, and if a pair of higher priority actions is available these occur and pre-empt any lower priority pairs.

Rules for communication:–

Definition 1 *stab(P)* $\longleftrightarrow P \stackrel{\tau}{\not\rightarrow}$

$$\textbf{COMM1}\ \frac{...+\underline{x}(y).P+...|...+\overline{\underline{x}}(z).Q+...}{P\{z/y\}Q}$$

$$\textbf{COMM2}\ \frac{...+x(y).P+...|...+\overline{x}(z).Q+...}{P\{z/y\}Q}\quad \nexists\underline{a} : \ldots + x(y).P + \ldots \overset{a}{\rightarrow} \wedge \ldots + \overline{x}(z).Q + \ldots \overset{\overline{a}}{\rightarrow}$$

The remainder of the operational semantics rules are like those of π-calculus, i.e.:–

$$\textbf{PAR}\ \frac{P \rightarrow P'}{P|Q \rightarrow P'|Q}$$

$$\textbf{RES}\ \frac{P \rightarrow P'}{(\nu x)P \rightarrow (\nu x)P'}$$

$$\textbf{STRUCT}\ \frac{Q{\equiv}Q'|\vee P \rightarrow P' \vee P' \equiv}{Q \rightarrow Q'|Q}$$

6 First example - scheduling printing

This initial example does not require priorities.

A collection of printers $P_1 \ldots P_n$ is to be managed by a resource allocator R. Users U_i who wish to print data contact R and when a printer is available will receive a channel name on which to send their data to a waiting printer. This makes use of the π-calculus feature of sending channel names so that the users do not need to know in advance what channel to send to the printer, and they cannot jump the queue by interacting with the printers directly before R has told them which printer to use.

R maintains a queue of available printers, and when it is necessary to wait users are also queued. The two queues are controlled by separate modules, QP for the printer queue and QU for the user queue, attached to the main resource manager R.

The specification for a FIFO queue is:–

$$\begin{aligned}
Q &\equiv Queue(\varepsilon)\\
Queue(\varepsilon) &= queue(x).Queue(x) + \overline{dequeue}(empty).Queue(\varepsilon)\\
Queue(s:(v_1)) &= queue(x).Queue(x:s:(v_1)) + \overline{dequeue}(v_1).Queue(s)
\end{aligned}$$

The queue module will be implemented using two varieties of process: regular nodes storing data and a special head element which maintains pointers to the first and last regular nodes. Initially we have a head element with two nil pointers. When we add the first value we create a new node and both the first and last pointer point to this node. Nodes contain a value and a pointer to the next node. Then for a general queue we use the following procedures for adding or removing values:–

To add an element n:–

- use the last-pointer of $Head$ to find the old last node L.
- tell the old last node L to change its next-pointer from nil to L_{new}.
- put n in a new node L_{new}.
- change the last-pointer to L_{new}.

To remove an element n:–

- suppose the $Head$'s first-pointer points to F
- output F's first field (its value)
- find F's second field, its next-pointer, and set $Head$'s first-pointer to this value

$$\begin{aligned} Init &= Head(nil, nil) \\ Head(nil, nil) &= in(x).(Head(N, N)|N(x, nil)) \end{aligned}$$

for any $X \neq nil$

$$\begin{aligned} Head(X,Y) &= in(x).(Head(X,Y')|Y'(x,X)) \\ &+ out(x).first(X).\overline{X}(x).second(X).\overline{X}(M).\overline{ch}(x)Head(M,Y) \\ N(x,M) &= first(ch).\overline{ch}(x).N(x,M) + second(ch).\overline{ch}(M).N(x,M) \end{aligned}$$

To initialise an empty queue we define

$$Queue \equiv Init$$

Thus

$$QU \equiv Base$$

and the printer queue, which initially contains all the printers:–

$$QP \equiv (Init|P_1|\ldots|P_n|Q)\text{after } in(P_1).\ldots.in(P_n)$$

$$\begin{aligned}
P_i &= out_{QP}(P_i).printchan(data).\overline{in}_{QP}(P_i) \\
U &= \overline{in}_{QU}(myname).out_{QU}(myname).myname(printchan).\overline{printchan}(data).0 \\
R &= in_{QU}(myname).R + \overline{out}_{QP}(printchan).R'(printchan) \\
&+ in_Q P(printname).R \\
R'(printchan) &= \overline{out}_Q U(somename).\overline{somename}(printchan).R \\
&+ in_Q U(myname).R'(printchan) + in_Q P(printname).R'(printchan)
\end{aligned}$$

7 Second example - scheduling with priorities

Now suppose we have two types of customer for our printers. Some people/ processes are to be served as soon as possible and have a higher priority attached to their requests. We can handle this by placing customers in the low or high priority people's queue as appropriate when they arrive, and servicing the low priority queue,called $Q2$ only when there is nobody waiting on the other queue $Q1$ (disregarding fairness for the moment).

$$\begin{aligned}
R &= in_{Q2}(name).R + \overline{out}_{Q2}(name).R'(name) + \overline{out}_{Q2}(name).R'(name) \\
R'(name) &= in_{Q1}(newname).R'(name) + in_{Q2}(newname).R'(name) \\
&+ \overline{out}_{QP}(printer).\overline{name}(printer).R
\end{aligned}$$

8 Equivalences

Strong reduction equivalence $\dot{\sim}_r$ is defined as the largest equivalence R over processes such that:–

$PRQ \Rightarrow$

(i) $P \to P' \Rightarrow Q \to Q', P'RQ'$ for some Q'

(ii) $\forall \alpha. P{\downarrow}\alpha \Rightarrow Q{\downarrow}\alpha$

There is also an analogous weak reduction equivalence $\dot{\approx}_r$, which is the largest equivalence R over processes such that:–

$PRQ \Rightarrow$

(i) $P \rightarrow P' \Rightarrow Q \rightarrow *Q', P'RQ'$ for some Q'

(ii) $\forall \alpha . P{\downarrow}\alpha \Rightarrow Q \rightarrow * {\downarrow}\alpha$

9 Conclusions

This is a preliminary exploration of the links between object-oriented design and process algebra. The similarities in the two approaches to specification make it possible that a process algebra with appropriate constructs and operators could be used as a layer of formal specification for an object-oriented methodology. Modularization and prioritization are useful constructs in a process algebra designed for such a purpose. Future work may include some kind of typing system for processes to facilitate modelling hierarchies of classes with inheritance. The axiomatization of the current language and its relationship to other CCS-variants also remain to be seen.

1. Gul Agha and Carl Hewitt. Concurrent programming using actors. In *Object-oriented Concurrent Programming*, 1987.
2. Pierre America. Pool-T: a parallel object-oriented language. In *Object-oriented Concurrent Programming*, 1987.
3. Grady Booch. *Object-oriented analysis and design with applications.* Cummings, 1994.
4. C.B.Jones. Constraining interference in an object-based design method. In Gaudel and Jouannaud, editors, *TAPSOFT 1993*, 1993.
5. C.B.Jones. A pi-calculus semantics for an object-based design notation. In *CONCUR 1993*, 1993.
6. C.B.Jones. Reasoning about interference in an object-based design method. In Woodcock and Larsen, editors, *FME 1993*, 1993.
7. R. Cleaveland and M. Hennessy. Priorities in process algebra. Technical report, University of Sussex, 1988.
8. Sarah Liebert. Modularization and priorities. In *Second Imperial College Dept. of Theory and Formal Methods Workshop*, 1995.
9. Huimin Lin. Complete inference systems for weak bisimulation equivalences in the π-calculus. In *TAPSOFT 1995*, 1995.
10. Robin Milner. *Communication and Concurrency.* Prentice Hall, 1989.
11. Robin Milner. The polyadic pi-calculus: a tutorial. Technical report, Edinburgh, 1991.
12. Iain Phillips. CCS with broadcast stability. Technical report, Imperial College, 1988.

13. Benjamin Pierce and Davide Sangiorgi. Typing and subtyping for mobile processes. In *LICS 1993*, 1993.
14. Davide Sangiorgi. πI: a symmetric calculus bsed on internal mobility. In *TAPSOFT 1995*, 1995.
15. Vasco Vasconcelos. Typed concurrent objects. Technical report, Keio, 1994.
16. David Walker. Objects in the π-calculus. Technical report, University of Warwick, 1992.
17. Akinori Yonezawa, editor. *ABCL: an object-oriented concurrent system*. MIT Press, 1989.

Convenient categories of asynchronous processes and simulations

Duško Pavlović

COGS, University of Sussex, Brighton, England; e-mail: **duskop@cogs.susx.ac.uk**

Abstract

In [9] we have argued for a representation of processes taking into account computationally relevant morphisms. It has been shown that the category of synchronous processes, modulo strong bisimulation, with the bisimilarity preserving simulations, is isomorphic with a particular subcategory of transition systems with graph morphisms.

In the present paper, we extend this representation to asynchronous processes, modulo the weak and the branching bisimulations and congruences. They are shown to correspond to further interesting subcategories of the category of transition systems. The form of the representatives in the case of the branching bisimilarity suggests possible connections with game theory. An abstract construction of a category of processes in a general setting is presented in the appendix.

1 Introduction

As a first approximation, processes are presented as directed graphs of states and transitions: a computation is a directed path of transitions, a *run* from state to state, starting from the initial one. The transitions are labelled by the actions taken.

However, many different graphs remain indistinguishable when only such runs are observed. The computationally irrelevant properties of graphs are factored out by defining processes as classes of observationally equivalent, *bisimilar* graphs. But large classes of graphs are not very convenient to work with, and one tries to pick a canonical representative from each of them. This boils down to extracting a class of graphs that display only the computational behaviour of a process, free of geometric redundancies. In [9], we have described a category of *irredundant* transition systems, which couniversally represent synchronous processes, i.e. strong bisimilarity classes. The treatment is now extended to asynchronous processes, induced by weaker notions of bisimilarity. Such representations are necessary for logical studies of processes [10]. The new task will be reduced to the previously solved one. In each weaker bisimilarity class we shall find a strong subclass, in fact a retract, for which we already have a representative. This retraction is worked out in section 3, after the categorical framework needed for it has been introduced in section 2 (based on a universal construction frome the appendix). The actual representation of asynchronous processes is in 4, while 5 outlines modifications needed for capturing processes with respect to the generated congruences.

2 From graphs to processes

We begin with the category of *reachable transition systems*, as described in [9]. The only additional feature is the distinguished label $\tau \in \Sigma$, denoting *silent* actions [7, sec. 2.3]. It has no reprecussions for the category, but allows conceptual refinements, leading to richer notions of (bi)simulation and of process. While the strong bisimulations [8, 7] take all actions into account, the weak (or observational) equivalence [4, 7] discards the silent actions from the output, and only takes their power to preempt other actions into account. However, it evens out different trees of silent actions, and remains too crude for some situations. The suitable refinement is the notion of branching bisimulation [3, ch. 3], which fully respects the branching structure of a process, including its silent parts. We shall now align the three notions formally, and derive three categories of processes.

To analyse them in categories, we shall treat bisimulations as *internal full* binary relations in various categories of transition systems. An *internal* relation between transition systems P and Q consists of a binary relation on their states and a binary relation on their transitions. The former always relates the initial states. The latter only relates transitions with the same label. Finally, whenever two transitions are related, their source states must also be related, as well as their target states. An internal relation is *full* if the converse holds as well: two transitions are related if and only if they have the same label, and related sources and targets. Obviously, such a relation is completely determined by its state component. Our categorical bisimulations are thus equivalent to the original ones, which are just relations on states (given in terms of transitions).

As usually, $x \xrightarrow{a} x'$ denotes a transition, or the statement that it exists; $x_0 \overset{*}{\twoheadrightarrow} x_n$ abbreviates a silent run $x_0 \xrightarrow{\tau} x_1 \xrightarrow{\tau} x_2 \xrightarrow{\tau} \cdots \xrightarrow{\tau} x_n$ of length $n \geq 0$. An empty run $x_0 \overset{*}{\twoheadrightarrow} x_0$.

Definition 2.1 An internal relation $P \leftarrow R \rightarrow Q$ in the category of transition systems is a *strong simulation* if it satisfies

$$x \xrightarrow{a} x' \wedge xRy \implies \exists y'.\, y \xrightarrow{a} y' \wedge x'Ry' \tag{1}$$

$$\left.\begin{array}{r} x \xrightarrow{a} x' \wedge xRy \\ \wedge y \xrightarrow{a} y' \wedge x'Ry' \end{array}\right\} \implies \left(x \xrightarrow{a} x'\right) R \left(y \xrightarrow{a} y'\right) \tag{2}$$

for all states $x, x' \in P$ and $y \in Q$. It is a *weak [resp. branching]* simulation if it satisfies (2) and

$$x \xrightarrow{a} x' \wedge xRy \implies \exists uu'y'.\, y \overset{*}{\twoheadrightarrow} u \xrightarrow{a} u' \overset{*}{\twoheadrightarrow} y' \wedge x'Ry' \quad [\wedge xRu \wedge x'Ru']$$

$$\vee \left(a = \tau \wedge x' R y\right) \tag{3}$$

A strong (resp. weak, branching) *bi*simulation is a strong (weak, branching) simulation $P \leftarrow R \rightarrow Q$ such that the dual $Q \leftarrow R^o \rightarrow P$ is a strong $(\ldots)$ simulation too. The transition systems P and Q are strongly $(\ldots)$ *bisimilar* if there is a strong $(\ldots)$ bisimulation between them. The strong, weak and branching bisimilarities are respectively denoted by $\sim$, $\approx$ and $\approxeq$.

In pictures, the above definitions say that each span

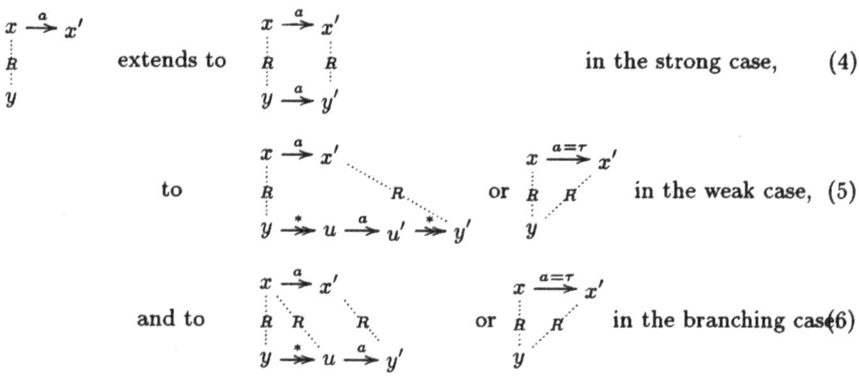

Note that omitting u' in the branching case does not change anything: one can always take $u' = y'$.

These notions now induce three poset-enriched categories, with the reachable transition systems as objects and the simulations as morphisms. Restricting to the sober simulations, we get the categories $\mathcal{C}^{\sim}$, $\mathcal{C}^{\approx}$ and $\mathcal{C}^{\approxeq}$, to which we apply the construction from the appendix, and get the categories of processes $\mathcal{P}_{\sim}$, $\mathcal{P}_{\approx}$ and $\mathcal{P}_{\approxeq}$. The components of the families $\sim$, $\approx$ and $\approxeq$ are in each case the largest bisimulations.

Let us sumarize what the obtained categories of processes look like. For any family of arrows/equivalence relation $\psi \in \{\sim, \approx, \approxeq\}$, the objects of $\mathcal{P}_\psi$ are the ψ-bisimilarity classes of reachable transition systems. Given two such classes, Π and Θ, a morphism $\Pi \leftarrow \Xi \rightarrow \Theta$ in $\mathcal{P}_\psi$ will be a class

$$\Xi \quad = \quad \{P \leftarrow R \rightarrow Q | P \in \Pi, Q \in \Theta\},$$

of ψ-simulations, such that for any $P \leftarrow R \rightarrow Q$ and $P' \leftarrow R' \rightarrow Q'$ holds

$$x\psi x' \wedge xRy \wedge y\psi y' \quad \Longrightarrow \quad x'R'y' \tag{7}$$
$$x\psi x' \wedge xRy \wedge x'R'y' \quad \Longrightarrow \quad y\psi y' \tag{8}$$

for all $x \in P, y \in Q, x' \in P', y' \in Q'$. Respectively, these conditions say that Ξ is *saturated* and *sober*. The latter says that the components of Ξ jointly preserve the

ψ-bisimilarity, i.e. take the computationally equivalent states to the computationally equivalent ones. The saturation condition, on the other hand, says that if x and y are related, then everything equivalent to x must be related to everything equivalent to y. The formal consequences of these conditions are explained in the appendix. See also section 2.3 of the first part.

The obvious implications (4)$\Rightarrow$(6)$\Rightarrow$(5), induce the quotient functors $\mathcal{P}_\sim \to \mathcal{P}_{\approxeq} \to \mathcal{P}_{\approx}$. Note however, that the morphisms will fit only if the implications $\sim$-sober$\Rightarrow$ $\approxeq$-sober$\Rightarrow$ $\approx$-sober are valid as well. This is not immediate, but it will follow from proposition 3.2.

3 Relating simulations

In [9], we have described a subcategory $\mathcal{I}$ of *irredundant* transition systems, and shown that it is strongly equivalent with $\mathcal{P}_\sim$. In fact, its skeleton is even isomorphic with $\mathcal{P}_\sim$. By definition, an irredundant transition system must be reachable, and such that $x \sim x'$ implies $x = x'$ for any pair x, x' of states. This irredundant representation, known in many forms, is actually universal in a formal sense [9, sec. 5].

This picture of $\mathcal{P}_\sim$ will now be used for representing $\mathcal{P}_\approx$ and $\mathcal{P}_{\approxeq}$. A transition system P will be transformed into transition systems WP and BP, weakly resp. branching bisimilar to P, and such that the weak resp. the branching simulations to and from P exactly correspond to the strong ones on WP resp. BP. The idea how for such WP and BP follows from (4), (5) and (6). To reduce (5) to (4), we must add in WP a transition $x \stackrel{a}{\to} x'$ whenever a path $x \stackrel{*}{\twoheadrightarrow} v \stackrel{a}{\to} v' \stackrel{*}{\twoheadrightarrow} x'$ occurs in P; and a transition $x \stackrel{\tau}{\to} x$ for every state x. The obtained transition system WP is thus the closure of P under the "composition" with τ-transitions.

The construction of BP is bound to be more complicated, since it must expand the trapezoid from (6) into *two* squares (4). The idea is that the transition $x \stackrel{c}{\to} x'$, $c \neq \tau$, should be expanded in two new transitions, corresponding to $y \stackrel{*}{\twoheadrightarrow} u$, and $u \stackrel{c}{\to} y'$ respectively. Moreover, τ should be "closed under composition" with itself. The construction B itself will thus be the composite of the constructions C and D, where

- C replaces each $x \stackrel{c\neq\tau}{\longrightarrow} x'$ with $x \stackrel{\tau}{\to} \begin{pmatrix} x \\ c\downarrow \\ x' \end{pmatrix} \stackrel{c}{\to} x'$, where $\begin{pmatrix} x \\ c\downarrow \\ x' \end{pmatrix}$ is a new state; while
- D adds $x \stackrel{\tau}{\to} x'$ whenever there is a path $x \stackrel{*}{\twoheadrightarrow} x'$.

All the described constructions induce endofunctors on the category of reachable transition systems. W and D are moreover idempotent monads, while C extends a comonad G, which for all $x \stackrel{c\neq\tau}{\longrightarrow} x'$ adds $\begin{pmatrix} x \\ c\downarrow \\ x' \end{pmatrix} \stackrel{c}{\to} x'$ but not $x \stackrel{\tau}{\to} \begin{pmatrix} x \\ c\downarrow \\ x' \end{pmatrix}$. The units $\eta : P \to WP$ and $\eta : P \to DP$ are given by the identity maps on the states, and the inclusions on the transitions. The counit $\varepsilon : GP \to P$ maps both x and $\left(\begin{smallmatrix} x \\ c\downarrow \\ x' \end{smallmatrix}\right)$ to x, the transitions $\left(\begin{smallmatrix} x \\ c\downarrow \\ x' \end{smallmatrix}\right) \xrightarrow{c} x'$ to $x \xrightarrow{c} x'$, and each τ-transition to itself. These data now provide a weak bisimulation $P \xleftarrow{\mathrm{id}} P \xrightarrow{\eta} WP$ and a branching bisimulation $P \xleftarrow{\varepsilon} GP \hookrightarrow CP \xrightarrow{\eta} DCP = BP$. This is proved simply by the inspection of definitions.

Proposition 3.1 For every reachable transition system P, the equality relation on the states yields a weak bisimulation between P and WP. A branching bisimulation between P and BP is obtained by extending the equality on the states of P with the pairs of the form $\left\langle x, \left(\begin{smallmatrix} x \\ c\downarrow \\ x' \end{smallmatrix}\right)\right\rangle$.

Since a simulation is determined by its state component, and W does not change the states, the W-image of a full relation $P \leftarrow R \to Q$ can be defined as the full relation $WP \leftarrow WR \to WQ$ induced by the state component of the original. The B-image, on the other hand, will be the full relation $BP \leftarrow BR \to BQ$ spanned by the state component of $P \leftarrow R \to Q$ *extended* on the new states by

$$\left(\begin{smallmatrix} x \\ c\downarrow \\ v \end{smallmatrix}\right) BR \left(\begin{smallmatrix} y \\ d\downarrow \\ u \end{smallmatrix}\right) \quad \Longleftrightarrow \quad c = d \wedge xRy \wedge vRu. \tag{9}$$

In this way, we get enriched functors $W : \mathcal{C}^{\approx} \longrightarrow \mathcal{C}^{\sim}$ and $B : \mathcal{C}^{\cong} \longrightarrow \mathcal{C}^{\sim}$, which turn out to be full and faithful, as a consequence of the following proposition.

Proposition 3.2 A full relation $P \leftarrow R \to Q$ on reachable transition systems is a weak simulation if and only if $WP \leftarrow WR \to WQ$ is a strong simulation. It is a branching simulation if and only if $BP \leftarrow BR \to BQ$ is a strong simulation.

Proof. We only prove the second statement, since the weak case is straightforward.

($\Rightarrow$) Assuming that $P \leftarrow R \to Q$ satisfies (6) we derive that $BP \leftarrow BR \to BQ$ satisfies (4). In BP, there are clearly three kinds of transitions to be simulated:

(i) $x \xrightarrow{\tau} x'$, or

(ii) $x' \xrightarrow{\tau} \left(\begin{smallmatrix} x \\ c\downarrow \\ v \end{smallmatrix}\right)$, or

(iii) $\left(\begin{smallmatrix} x \\ c\downarrow \\ v \end{smallmatrix}\right) \xrightarrow{c} v$,

where x, x' and v are old states, coming from P, while $c \neq \tau$.

To discuss (i), suppose xRy. Since R is a branching simulation, there is $y \overset{*}{\twoheadrightarrow} y'$ in Q, with $x'Ry'$. Hence $y \xrightarrow{\tau} y'$ in BQ.

Towards case (ii), note that in CP, the state $\left(\begin{smallmatrix} x \\ c\downarrow \\ v \end{smallmatrix}\right)$ can only be reached through x. The transition $x' \xrightarrow{\tau} \left(\begin{smallmatrix} x \\ c\downarrow \\ v \end{smallmatrix}\right)$ thus comes in BP from a path $x' \overset{*}{\twoheadrightarrow} x \xrightarrow{\tau} \left(\begin{smallmatrix} x \\ c\downarrow \\ v \end{smallmatrix}\right)$ in CP. On the other hand, $x \xrightarrow{\tau} \left(\begin{smallmatrix} x \\ c\downarrow \\ v \end{smallmatrix}\right)$ comes from $x \xrightarrow{c} v$ in P. So there must have been $x' \overset{*}{\twoheadrightarrow} x \xrightarrow{c} v$ in P. Given $x'Ry'$, the assumption that R is a branching simulation yields $y' \overset{*}{\twoheadrightarrow} y \overset{*}{\twoheadrightarrow} u \xrightarrow{c} w$ in Q, with xRy, xRu and vRw. But the transition $u \xrightarrow{c} w$ from Q becomes $u \xrightarrow{\tau} \left(c{\downarrow}^{u}_{w}\right) \xrightarrow{c} w$ in CQ. The path $y' \overset{*}{\twoheadrightarrow} y \overset{*}{\twoheadrightarrow} u \xrightarrow{\tau} \left(c{\downarrow}^{u}_{w}\right)$ in CQ now induces $y' \xrightarrow{\tau} \left(c{\downarrow}^{u}_{w}\right)$ in BQ. This transition simulates $x' \xrightarrow{\tau} \left(c{\downarrow}^{x}_{v}\right)$, since by (9), xRu and vRw imply $\left(c{\downarrow}^{x}_{v}\right) BR \left(c{\downarrow}^{u}_{w}\right)$.

Finally, for case (iii), suppose $\left(c{\downarrow}^{x}_{v}\right) BR\, z$. By the definition of BR again, the state z must be in the form $\left(c{\downarrow}^{u}_{w}\right)$, for some u, w with xRu and vRw. The transition $\left(c{\downarrow}^{x}_{v}\right) \xrightarrow{c} v$ is thus simulated by $\left(c{\downarrow}^{u}_{w}\right) \xrightarrow{c} w$.

($\Leftarrow$) Now assume that $BP \leftarrow BR \rightarrow BQ$ is a strong simulation, and take $x \xrightarrow{a} x'$ in P, with xRy. If $a = \tau$, (4) gives $y \xrightarrow{\tau} y'$ in BQ, with $x'Ry'$. Hence $y \overset{*}{\twoheadrightarrow} y'$ in Q. If this is an empty path, and $y = y'$, we have the triangle from (6); otherwise we have the trapezoid.

If $a = c \neq \tau$, the transition $x \xrightarrow{c} x'$ becomes $x \xrightarrow{\tau} \left(c{\downarrow}^{x}_{x'}\right) \xrightarrow{c} x'$ in BP. Since BR is a strong simulation, this is simulated by $y \xrightarrow{\tau} z \xrightarrow{c} y'$ in BQ, with $\left(c{\downarrow}^{x}_{x'}\right) BR\, z$ and $x'BRy'$. By the definition of BR, y' must be a state from Q, such that $x'Ry'$, while z must be in the form $\left(c{\downarrow}^{u}_{y'}\right)$, for some Q-state u with xRu. As pointed out before, the transition $x' \xrightarrow{\tau} \left(c{\downarrow}^{u}_{y'}\right)$ in BQ must have originated from $x' \overset{*}{\twoheadrightarrow} u \xrightarrow{\tau} \left(c{\downarrow}^{u}_{y'}\right)$ in CQ. In Q, there is thus $x' \overset{*}{\twoheadrightarrow} u \xrightarrow{c} y'$, with xRu and $x'Ry'$, just as required by (6). This completes the proof. □

The construction W induces a poset isomorphism between the weak simulations from P to Q and the strong simulations from WP to WQ, because the state component of $WP \leftarrow WR \rightarrow WQ$ is the same as the state component of $P \leftarrow R \rightarrow Q$ again. Therefore, W is a full and faithful enriched functor from the category of weak simulations to the category of strong simulations. Since two states in P are weakly bisimilar if and only if they are strongly bisimilar in WP, the functor W preserves and reflects the sobriety, and thus restricts to a full and faithful enriched functor $W : \mathcal{C}^{\approx} \rightarrow \mathcal{C}^{\sim}$.

A similar reasoning leads to the same conclusion for $B : \mathcal{C}^{\cong} \rightarrow \mathcal{C}^{\sim}$. The fullness may seem not as obvious this time, though. But note that the sources of the transitions labelled by $c \neq \tau$ in BP are always the new states $\left(c{\downarrow}^{x}_{x'}\right)$; and that all of them appear as such sources. Hence, a strong simulation from BP to BQ must relate the new states among themselves. It must further satisfy (9) — and thus appear in the form BR for some $P \leftarrow R \rightarrow Q$.

4 The representation

The described functors on the categories of simulations now induce the full and faithful functors $W : \mathcal{P}_{\approx} \to \mathcal{P}_{\sim}$ and $B : \mathcal{P}_{\approxeq} \to \mathcal{P}_{\sim}$. Proposition 3.1 implies that they are right inverse, respectively, to the quotient functors $\mathcal{P}_{\sim} \twoheadrightarrow \mathcal{P}_{\approx}$ and $\mathcal{P}_{\sim} \to \to \mathcal{P}_{\approxeq}$. Although the construction B on transition systems was not idempotent, the endofunctor that it induces on $\mathcal{P}_{\approx}$ is. $\mathcal{P}_{\approxeq}$ and $\mathcal{P}_{\approx}$ are thus retracts of $\mathcal{P}_{\sim}$; the latter is even a reflective subcategory. They are thus also retracts of the category of reachable transition systems and sober morphisms, since $\mathcal{P}_{\sim}$ can be viewed as its reflective category (cf. sec. 5 of the first part [9, sec. 5]). This is based on presenting $\mathcal{P}_{\sim}$ as the skeleton of the category $\mathcal{I}$ of irredundant transition systems [9, thm. 4.4].

Our next task is characterising the retracts of $\mathcal{I}$ corresponding to $\mathcal{P}_{\approx}$ and $\mathcal{P}_{\approxeq}$. They are spanned by the images of the constructions W and B on $\mathcal{I}$. The scheme of the representation is:

$$
\begin{array}{ccccc}
P & \longleftarrow & R & \longrightarrow & Q \\
\updownarrow \approx & & & & \updownarrow \approx \\
WP & \leftarrow & WR & \rightarrow & WQ \\
\updownarrow \sim & & & & \updownarrow \sim \\
\widetilde{WP} & = & \widetilde{WR} & \rightarrow & \widetilde{WQ}
\end{array}
\qquad
\begin{array}{ccccc}
P & \longleftarrow & R & \longrightarrow & Q \\
\updownarrow \approxeq & & & & \updownarrow \approxeq \\
BP & \leftarrow & BR & \rightarrow & BQ \\
\updownarrow \sim & & & & \updownarrow \sim \\
\widetilde{BP} & = & \widetilde{BR} & \rightarrow & \widetilde{BQ}
\end{array}
\tag{10}
$$

The upper squares depict the contents of the previous section: the vertical bisimulations are those from proposition 3.1, while 3.2 relates the horizontal sober simulations. The lower squares are from [9, sec. 5]. The functor $\widetilde{(-)}$ assigns to each reachable transition system its irredundant quotient, and to each sober $\sim$-simulation a graph morphism. Although $\mathcal{I}$ is not closed under W or B, direct inspection of the definitions of W and B shows that their images are closed under $\widetilde{(-)}$. The representatives $\widetilde{WP}$ and $\widetilde{BP}$ will thus be in the following forms.

Definition 4.1 A transition system is *τ-replete* if whenever there is a path $x \overset{*}{\twoheadrightarrow} y$, there is also a transition $x \overset{\tau}{\to} y$ in it. It is *c-replete*, for $c \neq \tau$ if every path $x \overset{*}{\twoheadrightarrow} u \overset{c}{\to} v \overset{*}{\twoheadrightarrow} y$ in it can be "shortcut" by a transition $x \overset{c}{\to} y$. The *replete* transition systems are a-replete for all $a \in \Sigma$. The irredundant replete transition systems span the subcategory $\mathcal{I}_{\approx}$ of $\mathcal{I}$.

A *τ-strategy* is a transition system in which the source of a visible transition is always the target of exactly one transition, necessarily silent. In other words, if $y \overset{c\neq\tau}{\longrightarrow} z$, then there is $x \overset{\tau}{\to} y$, and no other transitions to y. Irredundant, τ-replete τ-strategies span the subcategory $\mathcal{I}_{\approxeq}$ of $\mathcal{I}$.

Theorem 4.2 $\mathcal{P}_{\psi} \cong \mathcal{I}_{\psi}$, where $\psi \in \{\approx, \approxeq\}$.

Remarks. In a way, the repleteness embodies asynchrony: any action action can be delayed by idling, and any action that can be taken after some idling can also be taken immediately. However, such "shortcuts" may erase a part of the branching structure. In a τ-strategy, this is prevented by separating visible actions from each other by silent actions. The idea behind its name is that each visible move is given a unique silent response. The game is played *towards* the initial state, which can be thought of as the final position. The side which plays a last move, wins. The silent side wins using the τ-strategies.

Regardless of the relevance of this game theoretic picture, the point of the τ-replete τ-strategies is to allow waiting to be extended at will, or reduced to one silent step — but not completely eliminated. The branching structure is protected from these deformations by keeping the visible and the silent layers of actions separated.

5 Congruences

Finally, let us turn to a conceptual shortcoming of the weak and the branching bisimilarities: they are not congruences with respect to all of the process operations. In particular, the nondeterministic sum + does not preserve them [7]. Fortunately, the reason for this turns out to be localized at the initial state. Bergstra and Klop [2] have observed that *rooted* bisimulations — where the initial states are *only* related with each other — are always preserved under +. The following lemma is probably folklore.

Lemma 5.1 A (strong, weak, branching) simulation $P \leftarrow R \rightarrow Q$ is rooted if and only if the relations $P + M \longleftarrow R + M \longrightarrow Q + M$ are $(\ldots)$ simulations for all transition systems M.

Although simple and elegant, the root condition is not well suited for categorical treatment. However, there is a weaker condition, due to Milner [7, ch. 7, def. 2], which yields the same processes as the rooted bisimulations, and is easily captured in categories. It requires that a transition in the form $\iota \stackrel{\tau}{\rightarrow} x'$ is never simulated by an empty path. The simulations satisfying this requirement may not be rooted, hence they are not stable under sums; but *if* there is a bisimulation between P and Q satisfying Milner's requirement, *then* a rooted one must exist as well. Roughly, the *only* reason why it may be impossible to simply drop a pair $\langle x, \iota\rangle$ (or $\langle \iota, y\rangle$) from a bisimulation is that the only transition simulating $\iota \stackrel{\tau}{\rightarrow} x$ (or $\iota \stackrel{\tau}{\rightarrow} y$) may be $\iota \stackrel{\tau}{\rightarrow} \iota$. The following definition thus yields processes as the rooted bisimulations. Similarly, the induced process morphisms do not consist of rooted simulations, but each of them contains rooted components (e.g., the tree morphisms), and this suffices for +-stability.

Definition 5.2 A relation $P \leftarrow R \rightarrow Q$ in $\mathcal{A}_\Sigma$ is a *ι-weak [ι-branching]* simulation if it satisfies

$$x \xrightarrow{a} x' \wedge xRy \implies \exists uu'y'.\ y \stackrel{*}{\twoheadrightarrow} u \xrightarrow{a} u' \stackrel{*}{\twoheadrightarrow} y' \wedge x'Ry' \quad [\wedge xRu \wedge x'Ru']$$
$$\vee \left(\underline{\underline{x \neq \iota}} \wedge a = \tau \wedge x'Ry\right) \qquad (11)$$

and (2). A weak [branching] congruence is a ι-weak [ι-branching] simulation, the dual of which is ι-weak [ι-branching] simulation as well.

The ι-weak and ι-branching simulations differ from the weak and the branching ones only by the underlined part of (11); the rest is exactly like (3). The ι-simulations can thus be analyzed along the same lines as the ordinary ones — just slightly modifying the constructions W and B. Namely, everything remains the same, but *no* τ-cycles $x \xrightarrow{\tau} x$ must be added at $x = \iota$. On the representatives, this exception is expressed simply by restricting the τ-repleteness at the root.

6 Future work

The main point of our approach is to capture processes dynamically, in a category, with computation preserving morphisms. Concurrency may have sailed well without such morphisms, but the forest of its operations looks more and more like tensor calculus in the time when it was based on bright physical intuitions, but the universal property of the tensor product had not yet been understood.

1. P. Aczel, *Non-Well-Founded Sets*, Lecture Notes 14 (CSLI 1988)
2. J.A. Bergstra and J.W. Klop, Algebra of communicating processes with abstraction, *Theoret. Comput. Sci.* 37(1985) 77–121
3. R.J. van Glabbeek, *Comparative Concurrency Semantics and Refinement of Actions*, thesis (CWI, 1990)
4. M. Hennessy and R. Milner, On observing nondeterminism and concurrency, *in:* J. de Bakker and J. van Leeuwen, eds., *Proceedings of ICALP 80*, Lecture Notes in Computer Science 85 (Springer 1980) 299–309
5. A. Joyal, M. Nielsen and G. Winskel, Bisimulation and open maps, *Proceedings of the Eight Symposium on Logic in Computer Science* (IEEE 1993) 418–427
6. R. Milner, *A Calculus of Communicating Systems*, Lecture Notes in Computer Science 92 (Springer 1980)
7. R. Milner, *Communication and Concurrency*, Internat. Ser. in Comp. Sci. (Prentice Hall, 1989)
8. D. Park, *Concurrency and Automata on Infinite Sequences*, Lecture Notes in Computer Science 104 (Springer 1980)
9. D. Pavlovic, Convenient category of synchronous processes and simulations, *in:* D. Pitt et al. (eds.), *Category Theory in Computer Science '95*, Lecture Notes in Computer Science 953 (Springer 1995) 3–24

10. D. Pavlovic, Categorical logic of concurrency and interaction I: Synchronous processes, *in:* C. Hankin et al. (eds.), *Proceedings of the Second TFM Workshop* (World Press 1995) 105–141

Appendix A: Quotient of a poset-enriched category

Let $\mathcal{C}$ be a poset-enriched category and Ψ a composition closed family of arrows in it, at most one from each hom-poset. Write $P\psi Q$ for the Ψ-arrow from P to Q. It is further required that Ψ contains for each $P \in \mathcal{C}$ an endomorphism $P\psi P$, greater than id_P; and also an arrow $Q\psi P$ whenever there is $P\psi Q$ in it. The family Ψ can thus be construed as an equivalence relation ψ on the objects of $\mathcal{C}$, *realized* by its arrows.

We want to form a quotient category $\mathcal{P} = \mathcal{C}/\Psi$. The objects should be the ψ-equivalence classes of objects from $\mathcal{C}$, the morphisms — the families of ψ-equivalent arrows between their elements. Here the equivalence boils down to the requirement that all components of such a family of arrows can be obtained by extending any of them along ψ, just like any element of an equivalence class determines all of it. This seems to be a precondition of the existence of the quotient map, a functor $\mathcal{C} \to \mathcal{P}$. But it is not hard to satisfy.

Let Π, Θ be some ψ-equivalence classes of objects. A morphism $\Pi - \Xi \rightarrowtail \Theta$ in $\mathcal{P}$ will now be a class Ξ of arrows $P - R \rightarrowtail Q$ in $\mathcal{C}$, one for each pair $P \in \Pi$, $Q \in \Theta$, such that for any $R, R' \in \Xi$ holds $\psi R \psi \subseteq R'$, or diagrammatically

$$\begin{array}{ccc} P & \leftarrow \psi - & P' \\ | & & | \\ R & \subseteq & R' \\ \downarrow & & \downarrow \\ Q & - \psi \rightarrow & Q' \end{array} \tag{12}$$

This is the *saturation* condition. Using the above assumptions about Ψ, we get $R' \subseteq \psi R' \psi = \psi\psi R' \psi\psi \subseteq \psi R \psi$, so that for all components any $\mathcal{P}$-morphism actually holds

$$R' \quad = \quad \psi R \psi. \tag{13}$$

In particular, each of them is *saturated*, i.e. $R = \psi R \psi$. At any rate, each component pins down a $\mathcal{P}$-morphism by formula (13).

The quotient map $\mathcal{C} \to \mathcal{P}$ will, of course, take each object P to its equivalence class Π, and each arrow $P - R \rightarrowtail Q$ to the family of arrows $P' - R' \rightarrowtail Q'$, one for each $P' \in \Pi$ and $Q' \in \Theta$, which are obtained as in (13). Clearly, this family will consist of *saturated* morphisms, satisfying $\overline{R} = \psi \overline{R} \psi$. In fact, the image of each morphism R along $\mathcal{C} \to \mathcal{P}$ is determined by the *saturation* $\overline{R} = \psi R \psi$. Clearly, saturation can be viewed as a functor $\mathcal{C} \to \overline{\mathcal{C}}$, where $\overline{\mathcal{C}}$ is the subcategory of $\mathcal{C}$, consisting of the same objects but only the saturated morphisms. $\overline{\mathcal{C}}$ is the *saturation* of $\mathcal{C}$.

To spell out the universal properties of the quotient $\mathcal{P}$ and the saturation $\mathcal{C}$, we shall say that a functor *annihilates* ψ *on objects* if it takes any two ψ-related objects to the same image; that it *annihilates* ψ *on arrows* if each R has the same image as its saturation $\overline{R} = \psi R \psi$; and that it *annihilates* ψ if it does so both on objects and arrows.

Proposition A.1 The quotient $\mathcal{C} \to \mathcal{P}$ is initial among those that annihilate ψ. The saturation $\mathcal{C} \to \overline{\mathcal{C}}$ is initial among those that annihilate ψ on arrows. The induced functor $\overline{\mathcal{C}} \to \mathcal{P}$ is full and faithful, and surjective on objects — hence a weak equivalence.

Appendix B: Categories of processes, abstractly

Now we want to focus on situations when $\mathcal{C}$ is a category of simulations, while Ψ consists of maximal bisimulations. The quotient construction should thus yield the corresponding category of processes.

In order to be able to express some special properties of simulations, one additional operation will be needed, namely the dualising

$$\Big(P - R \rightarrowtail Q \Big) \quad \longmapsto \quad \Big(Q - R^o \rightarrowtail P \Big). \tag{14}$$

A relation can always be dualized, but the dual of a simulation need not be a simulation. The category $\mathcal{C}$ will thus not be closed under dualizing, but we shall assume that it is couched a "category of relations", providing the needed operation. For instance, $\mathcal{C}$ can be viewed as a poset-enriched subcategory of an allegory or of a cartesian bicategory.

There are two additional requirements that need to be imposed on the arrows of $\mathcal{C}$. Firstly, each of them should be *total*, or formally:

$$\mathrm{id} \subseteq RR^o. \tag{15}$$

Furthermore, they should all preserve the bisimilarity: indeed, a sound computational morphism should preserve computational equivalence [9, sec. 2.3]. Formally, this means that all $R \in \mathcal{C}$ should satisfy the *sobriety* condition

$$R^o \psi R \subseteq \psi. \tag{16}$$

But this is easily enforced: in specific cases, we simply restrict consideration to the *sober* simulations.

A poset-enriched category $\mathcal{C}$ with total and sober morphisms can be construed as an *abstract category of simulations.* Remarkably, the enrichment of such a category degenerates under saturation: $\overline{\mathcal{C}}$ turns out to be an *ordinary* category.

Lemma B.2 If $P \multimap R \twoheadrightarrow Q$ is a sober morphism, its saturation $\overline{R} = \psi R \psi$ is sober too. If, furthermore, all morphisms from P to Q are total, the saturation $\overline{R}$ is the largest among them which is both sober and contains R.

Proof. $\overline{R}$ is sober because $\overline{R}^o \psi \overline{R} = \psi R^o \psi \psi \psi R \psi = \psi R^o \psi R \psi \subseteq \psi \psi \psi = \psi$. For the second statement, suppose that $\hat{R} \supseteq R$ is sober. The totality now yields $\hat{R} \subseteq RR^o \hat{R} \subseteq R\hat{R}^o \hat{R} \subseteq R\hat{R}^o \psi \hat{R} \subseteq R\psi \subseteq \psi R \psi$. □

Corollary B.3 The saturation $\overline{\mathcal{C}}$ of an abstract category of simulations $\mathcal{C}$ is an ordinary category.

Proof. If $R \subseteq \hat{R}$, and $\hat{R}$ is sober, lemma yields $\hat{R} \subseteq \overline{R}$. When R is saturated, this yields $\hat{R} \subseteq R$. □

The quotient $\mathcal{P}$, constructed from a category of simulations by the method from appendix A, is an *abstract category of processes.* The universal properties described in proposition A.1 remain valid. The additional properties make $\mathcal{P}$ into an ordinary category, though, since it is weakly equivalent to $\overline{\mathcal{C}}$. Another point worth emphasizing about $\mathcal{P}$ is that the bisimilarity is preserved not just by the individual components of its morphisms, but also jointly, which renders an apparently stronger, global notion of sobriety.

Proposition B.4 If each component of a $\mathcal{P}$-morphism $\Pi \multimap \Xi \twoheadrightarrow \Theta$ is sober, then any two of them $R, R' \in \Xi$ satisfy $R^o \psi R' \subseteq \psi$.

$$\begin{array}{ccc} P & \leftarrow R^o - & Q \\ | & & | \\ \psi & \subseteq & \psi \\ \downarrow & & \downarrow \\ P' & - R' \rightarrow & Q' \end{array} \qquad (17)$$

Proof. $R^o \psi R' = R^o \psi \psi R \psi = R^o \psi R \psi \subseteq \psi \psi = \psi$ □

Conditon (17) is the naturality requirement more suitable for a relational setting than the ordinary one. When the relations involved in it are total ($\mathrm{id} \subseteq RR^o$) and single-valued ($R^o R \subseteq \mathrm{id}$), this condition is equivalent with the usual lax naturality $\psi R' \subseteq R\psi$. In general, though, the two are incomparable, and (17) captures the ψ-preservation. Conditions (12) and (17), fulfilled in each category of processes, were explained from a computational point of view in [9, sec. 2.3]. A morphism satisfying them actually induces a partial map between the bisimilarity classes of states at its domain and codomain. Since all simulations are total by assumption (15), this map yields an honest morphism of transition systems.

TYPE INFERENCE FOR A TYPED PROCESS CALCULUS

RUSSELL HARMER
Department of Computing, Imperial College, London SW7 2BZ.

An explicitly typed process calculus is considered and a type inference scheme presented—thereby allowing the use of implicit typing—which deduces a principal type for a process term together with appropriate substitutions. We have soundness and completeness results for this inference with respect to the calculus: any valid substitution applied to the principal type of a process yields a correct typed process term and conversely, any typed process term derivable in the calculus can be recovered from the term's inferred principal type with an appropriate choice from the permitted substitutions.

1 Introduction

The merits of types are well-known in functional computation both from a theoretical and a practical perspective. However, it is often more convenient, when working in a typed framework, to be able to dispense with typing information and work with raw—*i.e.* untyped—terms. A good example of this is the writing of (functional) programs where it is cumbersome to be obliged to make all types explicit. In such a situation however, we often require the capability of reconstructing a type from the raw term. In this paper, we consider this issue in the context of the explicitly typed process calculus developed by Simon Gay and Rajagopal Nagarajan [6, 7] which is based on Abramsky's synchronous *interaction category* **SProc** [1–3]. In fact, our type inference deduces a principal type [5] for a raw process term together with substitutions which we can then apply to determine particular concrete instances of a typed process term.

1.1 The Typed Process Calculus

The calculus we present here is essentially the same as in [7]. It consists of a number of rules for the manipulation of process terms and is parametrised by a *process signature.* We shall first define the latter. A process signature specifies the basic types and actions of the calculus.

A process signature is a collection of *ground types*, a collection of *ground actions* and a collection of *ground prefixes.* Given the ground types, we define *types* with a grammar α where

$$\mathcal{L}_T ::= \gamma \mid \gamma^{\perp} \quad \text{and} \quad \alpha ::= \mathcal{L}_T \mid \circ\mathcal{L}_T \mid \alpha \otimes \alpha \mid \alpha \mathbin{⅋} \alpha$$

where γ is any ground type in the collection and the $\circ(\cdot)$ operator is a one time-step delay. Note that we restrict the $(\cdot)^{\perp}$ operator to ground types only. This is because we restrict the Axiom rule of the process calculus to ground types only. Similarly, given the ground actions, we define *actions* with a grammar

$$\pi ::= \sigma \mid * \mid (\pi, \pi)$$

where σ is any ground action in the collection and $*$ is the explicit *idle* action, distinct from all ground actions. A ground prefix then consists of a ground action σ and two ground types γ, γ' and is written Pre $\sigma : \gamma \rightarrow \gamma'$. There is a functional restriction that if Pre $\sigma : \gamma \rightarrow \gamma'$ and Pre $\sigma : \gamma \rightarrow \gamma''$ then $\gamma' = \gamma''$ which ensures that when an action is performed, the process's type evolves in a predictable manner. Note however that having Pre $\sigma : \gamma' \rightarrow \gamma$ and Pre $\sigma : \gamma'' \rightarrow \gamma$ is permitted. It is precisely this fact which enables a given process term to have more than one possible type. We then use the following inference rules to determine the *prefixes* generated by a signature.

Prefixes

$$\frac{\text{Pre } \pi_1 : \alpha \rightarrow \alpha' \qquad \text{Pre } \pi_2 : \beta \rightarrow \beta'}{\text{Pre } (\pi_1, \pi_2) : \alpha \otimes \beta \rightarrow \alpha' \otimes \beta'}\ \otimes$$

$$\frac{}{\text{Pre } * : \circ\gamma \rightarrow \gamma}\ \circ_1 \qquad \frac{}{\text{Pre } * : \circ\gamma^{\perp} \rightarrow \gamma^{\perp}}\ \circ_2 \qquad \frac{\text{Pre } \sigma : \gamma \rightarrow \gamma'}{\text{Pre } \sigma : \gamma^{\perp} \rightarrow \gamma'^{\perp}}\ \perp$$

$$\frac{\text{Pre } \pi_1 : \alpha \rightarrow \alpha' \qquad \text{Pre } \pi_2 : \beta \rightarrow \beta'}{\text{Pre } (\pi_1, \pi_2) : \alpha \mathbin{⅋} \beta \rightarrow \alpha' \mathbin{⅋} \beta'}\ ⅋$$

We now define the *raw process terms*—untyped process terms—upon which the type inference will be performed.

$$P ::= \pi : P \mid ⅋_z^{x,y}(P) \mid P \otimes_z^{x,y} P \mid P \cdot_x P \mid P\backslash_{x,y} \mid I_{u,v} \mid P + P \mid \mathsf{nil}(\tilde{x})$$

Finally, we present the *proved processes*. These are the expressions of the form $P \vdash x_1 : \alpha_1, \ldots, x_n : \alpha_n$ which can be derived by the manipulative rules of the calculus given below. Notice that they correspond precisely to the form suggested by the "proofs as processes" paradigm [4]; the x_i are port names and the α_i are types. The ordering of these is unimportant—they simply determine the *port interface* of the process. Note that a port is where an action may take place; these two notions are clearly separated. Further, the form of an action is independent of input and output; this is now represented by the types.

Prefixing

$$\frac{P \vdash x : \beta \quad \text{Pre } \pi : \alpha \to \beta}{\pi : P \vdash x : \alpha}\text{Prefix}$$

Multiplicatives

$$\frac{P \vdash A, x : \alpha \quad Q \vdash B, y : \beta}{P \otimes_z^{x,y} Q \vdash A, B, z : \alpha \otimes \beta}\text{Tensor} \qquad \frac{P \vdash A, x : \alpha, y : \beta}{⅋_z^{x,y}(P) \vdash A, z : \alpha ⅋ \beta}\text{Par}$$

Connecting

$$\frac{}{I_{x,y} \vdash x : \gamma^{\perp}, y : \gamma}\text{Axiom}$$

$$\frac{P \vdash A, x : \alpha^{\perp}, y : \alpha}{P\backslash_{x,y} \vdash A}\text{Cycle} \qquad \frac{P \vdash A, x : \alpha^{\perp} \quad Q \vdash B, y : \alpha}{P \cdot_{x,y} Q \vdash A, B}\text{Cut}$$

Additives

$$\frac{}{\mathsf{nil}_{\tilde{\gamma}}(\tilde{x}) \vdash x_1 : \gamma_1, \ldots, x_n : \gamma_n}\text{Nil}$$

$$\frac{P \vdash x_1 : \alpha_1, \ldots, x_n : \alpha_n \quad Q \vdash y_1 : \alpha_1, \ldots, y_n : \alpha_n}{P +_{\tilde{z}}^{\tilde{x},\tilde{y}} Q \vdash z_1 : \alpha_1, \ldots z_n : \alpha_n}\text{Sum}$$

The development of type inference presented here has been only partially extended to cover recursive processes, as defined with the standard style of fix notation (see [6,7]) and consequently we do not, at this stage, present our type inference for these kinds of processes. The completion of this extension to the work presented here is clearly an area for immediate future research.

1.2 Some Preliminaries

We use γ and δ as metavariables ranging over ground types and α and β ranging over types. We use the notation $i \in [n]$ as a shorthand for $1 \leq i \leq n$. Since a process term may be assigned more than one type, we must have a mechanism in the type inference to cope with this. Define a grammar Φ of *type expressions* as

$$\mathcal{L}_{\mathcal{TE}} ::= \Gamma \mid \Gamma^{\perp} \mid \Gamma^{\dagger} \text{ and } \Phi ::= \mathcal{L}_{\mathcal{TE}} \mid \circ \mathcal{L}_{\mathcal{TE}} \mid \Phi \otimes \Phi \mid \Phi ⅋ \Phi$$

where Γ is a *ground type variable* ranging over ground types. The negation operator $(\cdot)^{\perp}$ is extended to the binary type expressions in the usual manner, but note that we define $(\circ\Phi)^\perp =_{\mathrm{df}} \circ(\Phi^\perp)$. The intuition is for the type of a given port x to be represented by a type expression Φ (its principal type) and for a port interface to be represented by a set of pairs of the form (x_i, Φ_i) together with a *substitution* $\mathcal{S}$. This substitution is a partial function from ground type variables to *sets* of ground types. It is defined on the ground type variables occuring in the Φ_i and assigns to each such Γ_i a set $\mathcal{S}(\Gamma_i)$ of ground types—*i.e.* the set of ground types that may be substituted for Γ_i in this port interface. We denote this domain of definedness by $\mathtt{dom}(\mathcal{S})$. Thus, a given process may have, in general, many possible instantiations of the ground type variables representing its interface—*i.e.* many possible types. We can make this formal as follows. Note that this, as with all other inductive definitions, is defined only for the cases explicitly listed; any other case is to be regarded as undefined—a failure.

Definition 1 *Given a type expression Φ and a substitution $\mathcal{S}$ where the ground type variables in Φ are $\Gamma_1, \ldots, \Gamma_n$ and $\{\Gamma_1, \ldots, \Gamma_n\} \subseteq \mathtt{dom}(\mathcal{S})$ then for an instantiation $\gamma_i \in \mathcal{S}(\Gamma_i)$ for $i \in [n]$, $\Phi[\gamma_i/\Gamma_i]$ gives the set of types that Φ can represent.*

- GROUND TYPE: If Φ is a ground type variable Γ and $\gamma \in \mathcal{S}(\Gamma)$ then

$$\Gamma[\gamma/\Gamma] = \{\gamma\},\ \Gamma^\perp[\gamma/\Gamma] = \{\gamma^\perp\} \text{ and } \Gamma^\dagger[\gamma/\Gamma] = \{\gamma, \gamma^\perp\}.$$

- IDLE: If Φ is of the form $\circ\Phi'$ then Φ' is of the form Γ, $\Gamma^\perp$ or $\Gamma^\dagger$. Let $\gamma \in \mathcal{S}(\Gamma)$ and then

$$\circ\Phi'[\gamma/\Gamma] = \{\circ\alpha' \mid \alpha' \in \Phi'[\gamma/\Gamma]\}.$$

- TENSOR: If Φ is of the form $\Phi_1 \otimes \Phi_2$ with $\Gamma_1, \ldots, \Gamma_n$ the ground type variables in Φ_1 and $\Delta_1, \ldots, \Delta_m$ the ground type variables in Φ_2 then let $\gamma_{i_1} \in \mathcal{S}(\Gamma_{i_1})$ for $i_1 \in [n]$ and $\delta_{i_2} \in \mathcal{S}(\Delta_{i_2})$ for $i_2 \in [m]$ and then

$$(\Phi_1 \otimes \Phi_2)[\gamma_{i_1}/\Gamma_{i_1}, \delta_{i_2}/\Delta_{i_2}] = \{\alpha \otimes \beta \mid \alpha \in \Phi_1[\gamma_{i_1}/\Gamma_{i_1}], \beta \in \Phi_2[\delta_{i_2}/\Delta_{i_2}]\}.$$

- PAR: Similar to TENSOR.

Thus, the $(\cdot)^\dagger$ operator allows us to postpone the decision of whether an instance of a ground type variable occurs under a negation or not.

It is reasonable to ask what a type inference might be capable of producing given an arbitrary raw process term. We know already that, in general, more than one type is possible. The first reason for this, namely the potential overloading of prefix names, is a fundamental feature of the process calculus. The second, which is related to the use of the $(\cdot)^{\dagger}$ operator, is not. A better question might therefore be under what circumstances do we retain this operator in a given type inference. We see, shortly, that the process of unification which is required for some raw process terms removes occurences of $(\cdot)^{\dagger}$. However, in other cases these may remain. Perhaps the archetypal example of a persistent $(\cdot)^{\dagger}$ is the type inference of just a simple nil process. Since we have no way of knowing whether its type should have a $(\cdot)^{\perp}$ or not, we must must retain the $(\cdot)^{\dagger}$ until such time as it is unified (*e.g.* in a Cut or Cycle).

2 A Type Inference Scheme

The type inference is defined inductively on the structure of raw process terms with straightforward base cases for Axiom and Nil. Of the remaining rules, only Tensor and Par are immediate; the others require more complex machinery. We examine this before giving the full definition.

2.1 Cuts and Cycles

We need to take care when inferring the types of process terms that contain connections—*i.e.* Cut or Cycle rules. The reason for this lies in the form of these rules: when we connect two ports, their respective communicating types must be de Morgan duals. Thus, we must ensure that we amend the substitutions for the new composite process in such a way that for any instantiation of the principal type of either of the communicating ports, there is a valid instantiation for the other which is the de Morgan dual of the first. Further, we must ensure that any dependencies that exist between the ground type variables in either of the principal types in question are properly reflected in the composite process. For instance, if there are multiple occurences of a ground type variable in one of the principal types, there may be a need to amend the other to preserve de Morgan duality.

The essential observation is that the process of checking whether or not two type expressions can be de Morgan duals naturally pairs up occurences of ground type variables—this is the meaning of the second component of the result of `resolve`. We can then determine all dependencies between ground type variables by calculating a suitable transitive closure.

Definition 2 *The definition of* `resolve`. *This tranforms type expressions* Φ *and* Ψ *so that any occurences of the* $(\cdot)^{\dagger}$ *operator are resolved and checks that they are de Morgan duals. It is symmetric in its arguments.*

- Ground Types: If Φ is of the form $\Gamma^{\perp}$ and Ψ is of the form Γ' then
$$\texttt{resolve}(\Phi, \Psi) = ((\Gamma^{\perp}, \Gamma'), \{\{\Gamma, \Gamma'\}\}).$$
- Dagger (1): If Φ is of the form $\Gamma^{\dagger}$ and Ψ is of the form Γ' then
$$\texttt{resolve}(\Phi, \Psi) = ((\Gamma^{\perp}, \Gamma'), \{\{\Gamma, \Gamma'\}\}).$$
- Dagger (2): If Φ is of the form $\Gamma^{\dagger}$ and Ψ is of the form $\Gamma'^{\perp}$ then
$$\texttt{resolve}(\Phi, \Psi) = ((\Gamma, \Gamma'^{\perp}), \{\{\Gamma, \Gamma'\}\}).$$
- Dagger (3): If Φ is of the form $\Gamma^{\dagger}$ and Ψ is of the form $\Gamma'^{\dagger}$ then
$$\texttt{resolve}(\Phi, \Psi) = ((\Gamma^{\perp}, \Gamma'), \{\{\Gamma, \Gamma'\}\}) \text{ or } ((\Gamma, \Gamma'^{\perp}), \{\{\Gamma, \Gamma'\}\}).$$
- Idle: If Φ is of the form $\circ\Phi'$ and Ψ is of the form $\circ\Psi'$ then provided $\texttt{resolve}(\Phi', \Psi') = ((\Phi'', \Psi''), S)$ then
$$\texttt{resolve}(\Phi, \Psi) = ((\circ\Phi'', \circ\Psi''), S).$$
- Compound Types: If Φ is of the form $\Phi_1 \otimes \Phi_2$, Ψ is of the form $\Psi_1 \wp \Psi_2$, $\texttt{resolve}(\Phi_1, \Psi_1) = ((\Phi_1', \Psi_1'), S_1)$ and $\texttt{resolve}(\Phi_2, \Psi_2) = ((\Phi_2', \Psi_2'), S_2)$ then
$$\texttt{resolve}(\Phi, \Psi) = ((\Phi_1' \otimes \Phi_2', \Psi_1' \wp \Psi_2'), S_1 \cup S_2).$$

Note that we make an entirely arbitrary choice in Dagger (3). So, given type expressions Φ and Ψ which are to appear on either end of a Cut or Cycle connection, we construct $\texttt{resolve}(\Phi, \Psi) = ((\Phi', \Psi'), S)$. Define a relation $\approx$ by $s \approx s'$ iff $s \equiv s'$ or $s, s' \in P \in S$. Then the transitive closure S^* of S under $\approx$ partitions the ground type variables occuring in Φ and Ψ, capturing precisely any dependencies between variables. Then for each equivalence class E, we can introduce a new ground type variable Ω_E and define a textual transformation taking each variable in the class to Ω_E. The substitution function can easily be defined on Ω_E by taking the intersection of the permitted substitutions on each variable in the equivalence class. Note that if this intersection is empty for *any* equivalence class, the type inference fails as de Morgan duality is vacuously violated. We define

$$\texttt{update}(\Gamma, S) = \begin{cases} \Gamma & \text{if } \Gamma \notin \bigcup S^* \\ \Omega_{[\Gamma]} & \text{otherwise} \end{cases}$$

where $\Omega_{[\Gamma]}$ is a new ground type variable for the equivalence class $[\Gamma]$. There is then a natural extension, $\texttt{update}^{\star}$, defined on type expressions. We also define

$$\texttt{subst}(\Gamma, S, \mathcal{S}) = \begin{cases} \mathcal{S}(\Gamma) & \text{if } \Gamma \notin \bigcup S^* \\ \bigcap_{\Delta \in [\Gamma']} \mathcal{S}(\Delta) & \text{if } \Gamma' \in \bigcup S^* \text{ and } \texttt{update}(\Gamma', S) = \Gamma. \end{cases}$$

2.2 Sums

In some ways, the inference for the Sum rule is a generalisation of that for the Cut and Cycle rules since we have to match each pair of corresponding types in the two interfaces. However, in this case we are interested not in ensuring de Morgan duality but equality of types. This has the consequence that occurences of $(\cdot)^\dagger$ are not always removed, unlike for Cut and Cycle; consider resolving two occurences: $\Gamma^\dagger$ and $\Gamma'^\dagger$. Once again, we must capture all dependencies between ground type variables and we shall employ the same general technique as before.

Definition 3 *The definition of* `resolve'`.

- GROUND TYPE: If Φ is of the form Γ and Ψ is of the form Γ' *or* Φ is of the form $\Gamma^\perp$ and Ψ is of the form $\Gamma'^\perp$ *or* Φ is of the form $\Gamma^\dagger$ and Ψ is of the form $\Gamma'^\dagger$ then

$$\texttt{resolve'}(\Phi, \Psi) = ((\Phi, \Psi), \{\{\Gamma, \Gamma'\}\}).$$

- DAGGER (1): If Φ is of the form Γ and Ψ is of the form $\Gamma'^\dagger$ then

$$\texttt{resolve'}(\Phi, \Psi) = ((\Gamma, \Gamma'), \{\{\Gamma, \Gamma'\}\}).$$

- DAGGER (2): If Φ is of the form $\Gamma^\perp$ and Ψ is of the form $\Gamma'^\dagger$ then

$$\texttt{resolve'}(\Phi, \Psi) = ((\Gamma^\perp, \Gamma'^\perp), \{\{\Gamma, \Gamma'\}\}).$$

- IDLE: If Φ is of the form $\circ\Phi'$ and Ψ is of the form $\circ\Psi'$ then provided $\texttt{resolve'}(\Phi', \Psi') = ((\Phi'', \Psi''), S)$ then

$$\texttt{resolve'}(\Phi, \Psi) = ((\circ\Phi'', \circ\Psi''), S).$$

- TENSOR: If Φ is of the form $\Phi_1 \otimes \Phi_2$ and Ψ is of the form $\Psi_1 \otimes \Psi_2$ then provided $\texttt{resolve'}(\Phi_1, \Psi_1) = ((\Phi_1', \Psi_1'), S_1)$ and $\texttt{resolve'}(\Phi_2, \Psi_2) = ((\Phi_2', \Psi_2'), S_2)$ then

$$\texttt{resolve'}(\Phi, \Psi) = ((\Phi_1' \otimes \Phi_2', \Psi_1' \otimes \Psi_2'), S_1 \cup S_2).$$

- PAR: Similar to TENSOR.

So, given two collections of type expressions $\Phi_1, \ldots, \Phi_n$ and $\Psi_1, \ldots, \Psi_n$ we construct $\texttt{resolve'}(\Phi_i, \Psi_i) = ((\Phi_i', \Psi_i'), S_i)$ for $i \in [n]$. Let $S = \bigcup_{i \in [n]} S_i$. Then we use the same relation $\approx$ as before to partition S as the transitive closure S^* and then `update` and `subst` are defined exactly as before. Of course, it turns out that the cases for $\Gamma \notin \bigcup S^*$ are not needed, but the definitions still suffice. However, note that there is no need for the non-empty condition on the intersection of permitted substitutions. This is precisely because Sum does not hide any types; *cf.* Cut and Cycle.

2.3 Prefixes

Type inference for prefixed processes is largely routine. It involves checking that the prefix π being applied is "compatible with" the process P it is prefixed to; *i.e.* there must be appropriate ground prefixes which can be combined to form π which also match up with permitted types of P. The possible types for the new process $\pi : P$ are then immediately obtained.

Definition 4 *The definition of* `prefix`. *This takes as arguments a prefix and a type expression and ensures that the two are compatible*—i.e. *that there is a bijection between the ground type variables and ground actions—and constructs a set useful for the later type inference.*

- GROUND ACTION: If π is a ground action σ and Φ is a ground type variable Γ, a negated ground type variable $\Gamma^\perp$ or of the form $\Gamma^\dagger$ then

$$\texttt{prefix}(\pi, \Phi) = (\Phi, \{(\Gamma, \sigma)\}).$$

- IDLE: If π is the idle action $*$ and Φ is either a ground type variable Γ, a negated ground type variable $\Gamma^\perp$ or of the form $\Gamma^\dagger$ then

$$\texttt{prefix}(\pi, \Phi) = (\circ\Phi, \{(\Gamma, *)\}).$$

- TENSOR: If π is of the form (π_1, π_2) and Φ is of the form $\Phi_1 \otimes \Phi_2$ such that $\texttt{prefix}(\pi_1, \Phi_1) = (\Phi'_1, S_1)$ and $\texttt{prefix}(\pi_2, \Phi_2) = (\Phi'_2, S_2)$ then

$$\texttt{prefix}(\pi, \Phi) = (\Phi'_1 \otimes \Phi'_2, S_1 \cup S_2).$$

- PAR: Similar to TENSOR.

2.4 Type Inference

We can now proceed to the definition of `type`. Although it is presented as an inductive definition, we intuitively think of type inference as a procedure being applied to a raw process term P according to the rules of `type`. One consequence of this is that we consider a particular inference as an isolated procedure. Thus, the meaning of "new" in the clauses of the definition for AXIOM and NIL is that we introduce a ground type variable which is new to this particular inference. One significant consequence of this is that when two processes are combined by another operator of the calculus, they have come from entirely disjoint derivations and therefore have no ground type variables in common.

Definition 5 *The definition of* **type** *which deduces the structure of a given raw process term's port interface and the ground type variables contained within it, plus the valid substitutions which can be applied to them.*

- AXIOM: If P is of the form $I_{x,y}$ then for a new ground type variable Γ,

  $$\mathtt{type}(P) = (\{(x, \Gamma^{\perp}), (y, \Gamma)\}, \mathcal{S}_P)$$

  where $\mathtt{dom}(\mathcal{S}_P) = \{\Gamma\}$ and $\mathcal{S}_P(\Gamma) = \{\gamma \mid \gamma \text{ is a ground type}\}$.

- TENSOR: If P is of the form $Q \otimes_z^{x,y} R$ then let $\mathtt{type}(Q) = (\mathcal{PI}_Q, \mathcal{S}_Q)$ and $\mathtt{type}(R) = (\mathcal{PI}_R, \mathcal{S}_R)$ and provided $(x, \Phi) \in \mathcal{PI}_Q$ and $(y, \Psi) \in \mathcal{PI}_R$

  $$\mathtt{type}(P) = ((\mathcal{PI}_Q - \{(x, \Phi)\}) \cup (\mathcal{PI}_Q - \{(y, \Psi)\}) \cup \{(z, \Phi \otimes \Psi)\}, \mathcal{S}_Q \cup \mathcal{S}_R).$$

- PAR: Similar to TENSOR.

- CUT: If P is of the form $Q \cdot_{x,y} R$ then let $\mathtt{type}(Q) = (\mathcal{PI}_Q, \mathcal{S}_Q)$ and $\mathtt{type}(R) = (\mathcal{PI}_R, \mathcal{S}_R)$ and provided $(x, \Phi) \in \mathcal{PI}_Q$, $(y, \Psi) \in \mathcal{PI}_R$ and $\mathtt{resolve}(\Phi, \Psi) = ((\Phi', \Psi'), S)$ then $\mathtt{dom}(\mathtt{update}) = \mathtt{dom}(\mathcal{S}_Q) \cup \mathtt{dom}(\mathcal{S}_R)$ and

  $$\mathtt{type}(P) = (\mathtt{update}^{\star}((\mathcal{PI}_Q - \{(x, \Phi)\}) \cup (\mathcal{PI}_R - \{(x, \Psi)\}), S), \mathcal{S}_P)$$

  provided $\mathtt{subst}(\Gamma, S, \mathcal{S}_Q \cup \mathcal{S}_R) \neq \emptyset$ for $\Gamma \in \mathtt{dom}(\mathcal{S}_P) = \mathtt{range}(\mathtt{update})$ and where $\mathcal{S}_P(\Gamma) = \mathtt{subst}(\Gamma, S, \mathcal{S}_Q \cup \mathcal{S}_R)$.

- CYCLE: Similar to CUT.

- NIL: If P is of the form $\mathsf{nil}(x_1, \ldots, x_n)$ then for new ground type variables $\Gamma_1, \ldots, \Gamma_n$,

  $$\mathtt{type}(P) = (\{(x_i, \Gamma_i^{\dagger}) \mid x_i \in \tilde{x}\}, \mathcal{S}_P)$$

  where $\mathtt{dom}(\mathcal{S}_P) = \{\Gamma_1, \ldots, \Gamma_n\}$ and $\mathcal{S}_P(\Gamma_i) = \{\gamma \mid \gamma \text{ is a ground type}\}$ for $i \in [n]$.

- SUM: If P is of the form $Q +_{\tilde{z}}^{\tilde{x},\tilde{y}} R$ then let $\mathtt{type}(Q) = (\mathcal{PI}_Q, \mathcal{S}_Q)$ and $\mathtt{type}(R) = (\mathcal{PI}_R, \mathcal{S}_R)$ and then provided $\mathcal{PI}_Q = \{(x_1, \Phi_1), \ldots, (x_n, \Phi_n)\}$ $\mathcal{PI}_R = \{(y_1, \Psi_1), \ldots, (y_n, \Psi_n)\}$ and $\mathtt{resolve}'(\Phi_i, \Psi_i) = ((\Phi_i', \Psi_i'), S_i)$ for $i \in [n]$ then $\mathtt{dom}(\mathtt{update}) = \mathtt{dom}(\mathcal{S}_Q) \cup \mathtt{dom}(\mathcal{S}_R)$ and $S = \bigcup_{i \in [n]} S_i$ and

$$\mathtt{type}(P) = (\mathtt{update}^\star(\{(z_1, \Phi_1'), \ldots, (z_n, \Phi_n')\}), \mathcal{S}_P)$$

  where $\mathtt{dom}(\mathcal{S}_P) = \mathtt{range}(\mathtt{update})$ and $\mathcal{S}_P(\Gamma) = \mathtt{subst}(\Gamma, S, \mathcal{S}_Q \cup \mathcal{S}_R)$.

- PREFIX: If P is of the form $\pi : Q$ then let $\mathtt{type}(Q) = (\mathcal{PI}_Q, \mathcal{S}_Q)$ where $\mathcal{PI}_Q = \{(x, \Phi)\}$ and $\mathtt{prefix}(\pi, \Phi) = (\Psi, S)$ and then

$$\mathtt{type}(P) = (\{(x, \Psi)\}, \mathcal{S}_P)$$

  where $\mathtt{dom}(\mathcal{S}_P) = \mathtt{dom}(\mathcal{S}_Q)$ and $\mathcal{S}_P(\Gamma) = \bigcap_{(\Gamma,s) \in S} \{\gamma \mid (s = \sigma \wedge \text{Pre } \sigma : \gamma \rightarrow \gamma') \vee (s = * \wedge \text{Pre } * : \circ\gamma \rightarrow \gamma'), \gamma' \in \mathcal{S}_Q(\Gamma)\}$.

There is a mild abuse of notation here; $\mathtt{update}^\star$ is being applied to a set of type expressions. Of course, we mean this to apply the function element-wise; since we are dealing with sets, there could be difficulties, but each type expression is paired up with a (unique) port name so we always know where we are.

3 Soundness and Completeness

3.1 The Main Results

We now turn our attention to the first of the two major results concerning our type inference, namely soundness. This property ensures that if $\mathtt{type}(P) = (\mathcal{PI}, \mathcal{S})$ then any substitution from $\mathcal{S}$ to $\mathcal{PI}$ does indeed yield a proved process.

Theorem 1 (Soundness) *Suppose* $\mathtt{type}(P) = (\{(x_1, \Phi_1), \ldots, (x_n, \Phi_n)\}, \mathcal{S})$, $\mathtt{dom}(\mathcal{S}) = \{\Gamma_1, \ldots, \Gamma_k\}$ *and* $C_i \in \mathcal{S}(\Gamma_i)$ *for* $i \in [k]$. *Let* $\alpha_j \in \Phi_j[C_i/\Gamma_i]$ *for* $j \in [n]$ *and then* $P \vdash x_1 : \alpha_1, \ldots, x_n : \alpha_n$ *is a proved process.*

The second major property is the completeness of $\mathtt{type}$. This ensures that for any proved process $P \vdash A$, $\mathtt{type}(P) = (\mathcal{PI}, \mathcal{S})$ and there exists an appropriate substitution in $\mathcal{S}$ so that $\mathcal{PI}$ can be instantiated to A.

Theorem 2 (Completeness) *Suppose* $P \vdash x_1 : \alpha_1, \ldots, x_n : \alpha_n$ *is a proved process. Then* $\mathtt{type}(P) = (\{(x_1, \Phi_1), \ldots, (x_m, \Phi_n)\}, \mathcal{S})$ *for some* $\Phi_1, \ldots, \Phi_n, \mathcal{S}$ *where* $\mathtt{dom}(\mathcal{S}) = \{\Gamma_1, \ldots, \Gamma_k\}$ *and there exist* $C_i \in \mathcal{S}(\Gamma_i)$ *for* $i \in [k]$ *such that* $\alpha_j \in \Phi_j[C_i/\Gamma_i]$ *for* $j \in [n]$.

Both are lengthy inductions on the structure of raw process terms.

4 Examples

We conclude by showing some examples of the type inference in action. Consider the process signature where $\mathcal{GT} = \{\mathcal{B}, \mathcal{N}\}$ is the specified set of ground types (representing, say, booleans and natural numbers respectively) and where Pre $\mathbf{tt} : \mathcal{B} \to \mathcal{B}$ and Pre $1 : \mathcal{N} \to \mathcal{N}$ are the ground prefixes. Let $Q =_{\mathrm{df}} \mathbf{tt} : \mathsf{nil}(z)$, $R =_{\mathrm{df}} I_{x,y}$ and $R' =_{\mathrm{df}} (I_{a,x} \otimes_e^{a,c} I_{c,y}) \cdot_{e,w} (1,1) : \wp_w^{b,d}(I_{b,d})$.

Example 1 *Let* $P =_{\mathrm{df}} Q \cdot_{z,x} R$. *Then* $\mathsf{type}(\mathsf{nil}(z)) = (\{(z, \Gamma^{\dagger})\}, \{(\Gamma, \mathcal{GT})\})$ *and* $\mathsf{type}(I_{x,y}) = (\{(x, \Delta^{\perp}), (y, \Delta)\}, \{(\Delta, \mathcal{GT})\})$ *for new ground type variables* Γ *and* Δ. *So,* $\mathsf{type}(Q) = (\{(z, \Gamma^{\dagger})\}, \{(\Gamma, \{\mathcal{B}\})\})$.

Now we apply the rule for Cut *which unifies* Γ *and* Δ *to some new variable* Ω. *So,* $\mathsf{type}(P) = (\{(z,\Omega),(x,\Omega^{\perp}),(y,\Omega)\} - \{(z,\Omega),(x,\Omega^{\perp})\}, \{(\Omega, \{\mathcal{B}\} \cap \mathcal{GT})\}) = (\{(y,\Omega)\}, \{(\Omega, \{\mathcal{B}\})\})$, *as expected:*

$$\dfrac{\dfrac{\mathsf{nil}(z) \vdash z : \mathcal{B} \qquad \text{Pre } \mathbf{tt} : \mathcal{B} \to \mathcal{B}}{\mathbf{tt} : \mathsf{nil}(z) \vdash z : \mathcal{B}} \qquad I_{x,y} \vdash x : \mathcal{B}^{\perp}, y : \mathcal{B}}{\mathbf{tt} : \mathsf{nil}(z) \cdot_{z,x} I_{x,y} \vdash y : \mathcal{B}}$$

Example 2 *Now let* $P' =_{\mathrm{df}} Q \cdot_{z,x} R'$. *Clearly, we infer the type of* Q *exactly as before. Now,* $\mathsf{type}(R') = (\{(x, \Delta^{\perp}), (y, \Delta)\}, \{(\Delta, \{\mathcal{N}\})\})$ *and so we can infer the type of* P' *as before.*

However, we have $\mathsf{type}(P') = (\{(y,\Omega)\}, \{(\Omega, \emptyset)\})$. *But this violates the side conditions for the* Cut *rule since one (indeed, in this simple case, the only) ground type variable being "cut" cannot be instantiated to anything. Compare*

$$\dfrac{\mathsf{nil}(z) \vdash z : \mathcal{B} \qquad \text{Pre } \mathbf{tt} : \mathcal{B} \to \mathcal{B}}{\mathbf{tt} : \mathsf{nil}(z) \vdash z : \mathcal{B}}$$

and

$$\dfrac{\dfrac{\dfrac{I_{b,d} \vdash b : \mathcal{N}^{\perp}, d : \mathcal{N}}{\wp_w^{b,d}(I_{b,d}) \vdash w : \mathcal{N}^{\perp} \wp \mathcal{N}} \qquad \dfrac{\text{Pre } 1 : \mathcal{N}^{\perp} \to \mathcal{N}^{\perp} \qquad \text{Pre } 1 : \mathcal{N} \to \mathcal{N}}{\text{Pre } (1,1) : \mathcal{N}^{\perp} \wp \mathcal{N} \to \mathcal{N}^{\perp} \wp \mathcal{N}}}{(1,1) : \wp_w^{x,y}(I_{x,y}) \vdash w : \mathcal{N}^{\perp} \wp \mathcal{N}}}{(I_{a,x} \otimes_e^{a,c} I_{c,y}) \cdot_{e,w} (1,1) : \wp_w^{b,d}(I_{b,d}) \vdash x : \mathcal{N}^{\perp}, y : \mathcal{N}}$$

and clearly, these two processes cannot be cut together.

So, even a simple change can have a considerable effect; the unification performed at Cut, Cycle and Sum rules and the matching needed for Prefix rules are the essense of the type inference, where the unrestricted possibilities allowed by the freedom of the axiom and nil processes are curtailed.

Acknowledgments

I would like to thank David Walker for his helpful supervision during my MSc dissertation project [8] which contained the original formulation of this work. I would also like to thank Simon Gay, Guy McCusker, Pasquale Malacaria and Martin Berger for useful comments on the production of this final version.

References

1. S. Abramsky, S. J. Gay, and R. Nagarajan. Interaction categories and foundations of typed concurrent programming. In M. Broy, editor, *Deductive Program Design: Proceedings of the 1994 Marktoberdorf International Summer School*, NATO ASI Series F: Computer and Systems Sciences. Springer-Verlag, 1995.
2. S. Abramsky, S. J. Gay, and R. Nagarajan. Specification structures and propositions-as-types for concurrency. In G. Birtwistle and F. Moller, editors, *Logics for Concurrency: Structure vs. Automata—Proceedings of the VIIIth Banff Higher Order Workshop*, Lecture Notes in Computer Science. Springer-Verlag, 1995.
3. S. Abramsky. Interaction Categories (Extended Abstract). In G. L. Burn, S. J. Gay, and M. D. Ryan, editors, *Theory and Formal Methods 1993: Proceedings of the First Imperial College Department of Computing Workshop on Theory and Formal Methods*, pages 57–70. Springer-Verlag Workshops in Computer Science, 1993.
4. S. Abramsky. Proofs as processes. *Theoretical Computer Science*, 135:5–9, 1994.
5. L. Damas and R. Milner. Principal type schemes for functional programs. In *Conference Record of the Ninth Annual ACM Symposium on the Principles of Programming Languages*, pages 207–212, 1982.
6. S. J. Gay. *Linear Types for Communicating Processes*. PhD thesis, University of London, 1995.
7. S. J. Gay and R. Nagarajan. A typed calculus of synchronous processes. In *Proceedings, Tenth Annual IEEE Symposium on Logic in Computer Science*. IEEE Computer Society Press, 1995.
8. R. S. Harmer. A logical perspective on concurrency. Master's thesis, University of Warwick, 1995.
9. R. Milner. Calculi for synchrony and asynchrony. *Theoretical Computer Science*, 25:267–310, 1983.
10. R. Nagarajan. *Typed Concurrent Programs: Specification & Verification*. PhD thesis, University of London, 1995. To appear.

CATEGORIES OF PROCESSES WITH STATE (Extended Abstract)

LINDSAY ERRINGTON
Department of Computing, Imperial College, London SW7 2BZ.

Abstract

We define an interaction category of processes having explicit internal state. It is constructed using spans in a category of diagrams. Such a category has applications in defining the semantics of concurrent imperative languages and value-passing process calculi and as a basis for program analysis of such languages.

1 Introduction

Interaction categories have been proposed by Abramsky [1,2] as a basis for a theory of typed concurrency. In interaction categories, types (objects) are specifications, morphisms are processes which satisfy the specifications and composition is interaction. Types in these categories define the interface between processes and also constraints and obligations on the behaviour of processes. Examples of interaction categories include the categories of synchronous processes SProc and asynchronous processes ASProc. Further examples of interaction categories and on the use of types for specification and verification and to control interaction can be found in the cited literature.

This paper describes the interaction category StProc(C) over an extensive, finitely complete category C. Morphisms in this category are processes with internal imperative state. By this we mean that processes have variables (or memory locations) and record all possible variable assignments in their structure. This makes StProc(C) appropriate for giving semantics to value-passing process calculi and concurrent imperative languages. Our goal is to use this category as a basis for the development of program analyses based on abstract interpretation [10].

It could be argued that SProc and ASProc are already sufficient for defining the semantics of languages with state. Morphisms in both are synchronisation trees labelled with symbols from an alphabet. Since a position in a tree indicates the observations made up to that point and all possible future behaviours, processes are already equipped with a notion of state. This is the reasoning by which the semantics of value passing CCS is expressed by expansion into basic CCS.

Our application, however, is static analysis. Amongst other things, we wish to be able to infer and express properties of variables at particular points in a program, for example, the property that a variable x is even or that it depends on an earlier input. We might also wish to infer that there are no variable assignments for which a particular point is reachable. These properties are difficult to express if variables and variable assignments have been discarded in the semantics. Similarly, it is difficult to reason about the effect of an action, an assignment for example, if that action is represented by all of its instantiations.

The remainder of the paper is structured as follows. The next section discusses the use of diagrams in a category as a way of giving operational semantics to sequential languages. After a review of categories of diagrams and processes as spans we introduce our category of processes. Morphisms in the category are spans in a category of diagrams. We conclude by relating it with SProc.

2 Diagrams and operational semantics

For a simple imperative language with assignment, conditionals, loops and simple types, the meaning of a program can be given by a diagram $D : F(G) \to \mathsf{Part}$ in the category of sets and partial functions. Here G is a graph and $F : \mathsf{Grph} \to \mathsf{Cat}$ gives the free category over G. Figure 1 gives an example for the factorial program. We have omitted the identities and the composites.

Each vertex in the graph is mapped to a product of sets. This is the type of the state at that point in the program. Tuples in a product are variable assignments. Each path in the graph maps to a partial function, essentially a conditional rewrite, which describes the effect on the state and the set of variable assignments for which that path can be taken.

Since diagrams are in Part, the map associated with a transition can be empty in which case there are no variable assignments which satisfy the precondition and the transition can never take place. A similar situation arises with event structures where an event e in an event structure $(E, \vdash, \#)$ may be enabled by $\vdash$ but cannot "happen" since it is inconsistent with all other events[17].

In the case of loops, the image of the functor is a collection of morphisms each of which is an approximation to the meaning of the loop. This is in contrast with a denotational semantics where the meaning of the loop would be the limit of a similar set.

To summarise, diagrams of this form express the meaning of a program in terms of schedules of operations and can be seen as defining an operational

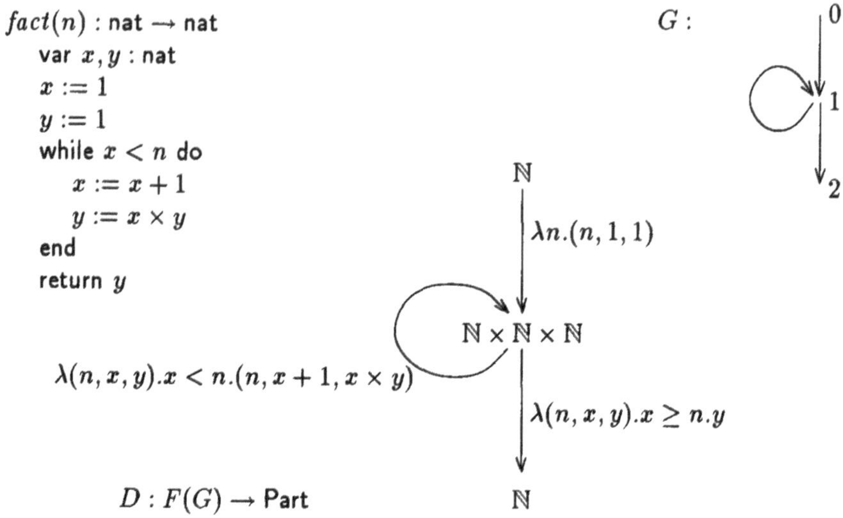

Figure 1: A graph and diagram in Part for the factorial program

semantics. In a forthcoming paper we show that expressing operational semantics in this way is more amenable to program analysis than when given by a relation between states.

3 Categories of diagrams

Definition 1. Let Shp be a category of shapes (*ie.* small categories) and let C be a category. Define the category of diagrams Diag(Shp, C) as follows.

- Objects are pairs (I, D) where I is in Shp and $D : \mathsf{I} \to \mathsf{C}$ is a functor.
- A morphism $(\mathsf{I}, D_1) \to (\mathsf{J}, D_2)$ is a pair (F, η) where $F : \mathsf{I} \to \mathsf{J}$ is a functor and $\eta : D_1 \Rightarrow F ; D_2$ is a natural transformation.
- Given $f = (F, \eta) : (\mathsf{I}, D_1) \to (\mathsf{J}, D_2)$ and $g = (G, \xi) : (\mathsf{J}, D_2) \to (\mathsf{K}, D_3)$, the composition $f ; g = (F ; G, \eta ; (F\xi))$ [a].

[a] This is a variant of a category defined by Makkai and Paré[15]. Goguen[12] defines a similar category of diagrams which is the same as Mac Lane's "super comma" category[14]. All are obtained by applying the Grothendieck construction to appropriate indexed categories.

The following comes from results of Goguen [12] and Tarlecki *et al.* [16].

Proposition 2. *If* Shp *and* C *have all (finite) limits and if* C *is small then* Diag(Shp, C) *has all (finite) limits.*

We focus on shapes freely generated from graphs resembling transition systems.

Definition 3. A *T-graph* is a directed graph having a designated root vertex, 0, at least one other vertex and such that all vertices are reachable from 0 except 0 itself.

T-graphs form a category, TGrph, where morphisms are graph homomorphisms which preserve the root. We write FG for the finitely complete category whose objects are free categories of T-graphs and $\imath : \mathsf{FG} \hookrightarrow \mathsf{Cat}$ for the obvious injection. Also, we write G for the free category over a T-graph G. Hence, the diagram interpreting the factorial program is an object in Diag(FG, Part).

We are particularly interested in diagrams in extensive categories [4,9].

Definition 4. A category with coproducts is *extensive* if every commutative diagram of the form

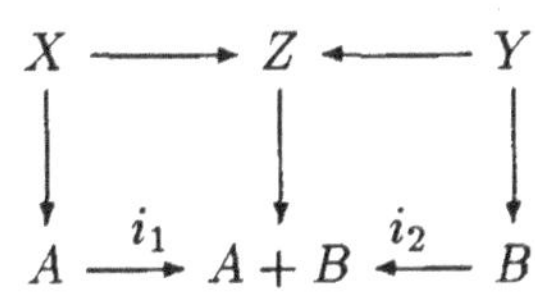

is a pair of pullbacks if and only if the top row is a coproduct diagram.

Proposition 5. *If* Shp *and* C *are extensive then* Diag(Shp, C) *is extensive.*

4 Processes as spans

Spans, *ie.* diagrams of the form $\cdot \leftarrow \cdot \rightarrow \cdot$, play a large part in the discussion which follows. See Bénabou [3] for an introduction to bicategories and in particular the bicategory of spans.

Using spans Cockett and Spooner [6,7] have given abstract definitions of some interaction categories including SProc and ASProc. They construct processes as spans in a category of transition systems. Rather than using 2-isomorphisms, they quotient processes using a span of retractions, f, g:

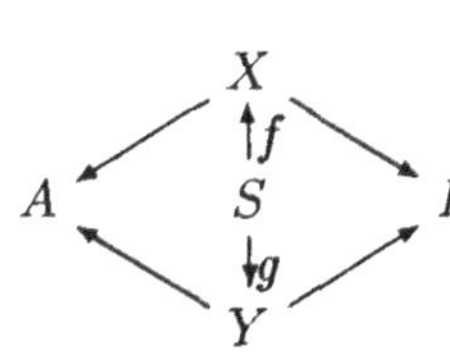

They show that quotienting this way realises strong or weak bisimulation generalising results of Joyal, Nielsen and Winskel [13].

5 Categories of processes with state

In this section we return to the theme of using diagrams to describe operational behaviour and extend it to accommodate concurrency and interaction.

We assume we are given a base category C which is small, has finite limits, finite coproducts and is extensive. From C we will construct a category of processes with internal state, StProc(C). The objects and morphisms of C provide the types for states and the basic operations for manipulating state in the process category.

As in SProc, processes in StProc(C) interact through typed channels. Consequently, objects in the process category are built on top of objects of C. The intuition is that when processes communicate at a transition, they do more than simply agree on a particular symbol in the alphabet - they communicate data. So, for example, if C is Set, then one might define a process type in which a natural number is passed in one transition and a real in the next.

To construct the category we follow the strategy set out by Cockett and Spooner [6,7] and define processes to be spans, but, rather than working in a category of transition systems, we start from a category of diagrams.

Recall that the factorial program was interpreted by a diagram in the category of sets and partial functions. At this point we substitute Sp(C) for Part so, as a first approximation, diagrams will be of the form $D : \mathsf{G} \to \mathsf{Sp(C)}$.

It is important to keep in mind that spans are being used in two ways. Having diagrams in Sp(C) means that each transition is labelled by a span in C and processes will be spans in a category of diagrams.

The figure below illustrates a single transition from a process. The vertical spans (in C) are transitions where those on the left and right are transitions in objects. Between them is a fragment of the span relating them (in the category of diagrams) where the dashed lines are the components of the natural transformation.

Unfortunately, spans over diagrams $D : \mathsf{G} \to \mathsf{Sp(C)}$ do not give us this structure. It fails for two reasons. First, since the diagrams are in Sp(C), the components of the natural transformations would themselves be spans. This is not a serious problem since we can easily impose restrictions on the natural transformations. More serious however, is that the natural transformations between these diagrams do not have components relating the apex of transitions. In the example, this means there are no maps $Y \to B$ and $Y \to E$ and these maps are needed to realise interaction.

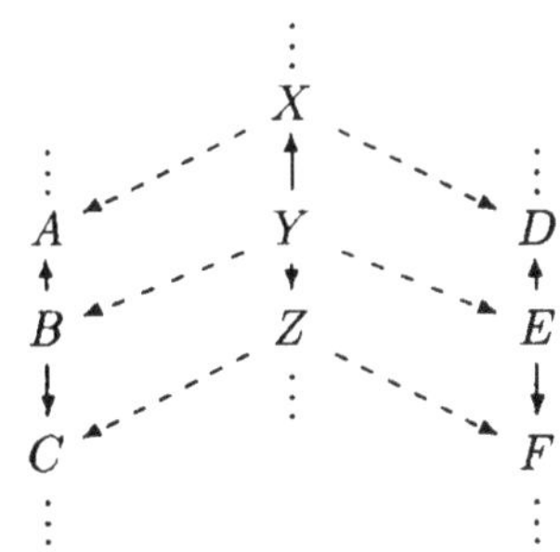

Figure 2: Process fragment

The solution is to work with different shapes. We incorporate the spans for transitions directly into the shapes so rather than working with diagrams $D : \mathsf{G} \to \mathsf{Sp}(\mathsf{C})$, we work with diagrams $D' : \widehat{\mathsf{G}} \to \mathsf{C}$. Here, $\widehat{\mathsf{G}}$ is a category derived from G having spans where G has maps. See figure 3 for an example. Note that $\widehat{\mathsf{G}}$ has a limit object $\widehat{h}$ for each morphism h in G such that if $h = f;g$, then $\widehat{h}$ is the limit for the diagram induced by $\widehat{f}$ and $\widehat{g}$.

Given a small category C define the *twisted arrow category*, $\widehat{\mathsf{C}}$, as follows (see page 223 of Mac Lane [14]):

Definition 6. An object, $\widehat{f}$, of $\widehat{\mathsf{C}}$ is an arrow, f, of C. A morphism $\widehat{f} \to \widehat{g}$ is a pair of morphisms (l, m) in C such that $f = l\,;g\,;m$. Informally, there is a morphism from $\widehat{f}$ to $\widehat{g}$ for each way in which g "divides" f.

Proposition 7. $\widehat{\cdot} : \mathsf{Cat} \to \mathsf{Cat}$ *is a functor.*

Now we define the category of shapes.

Definition 8. The category TFG is the image of $\imath\,;\widehat{\cdot} : \mathsf{FG} \to \mathsf{Cat}$.

We are interested only in those diagrams $D' : \widehat{\mathsf{G}} \to \mathsf{C}$ "induced" by diagrams $D : \mathsf{G} \to \mathsf{Sp}(\mathsf{C})$ in the following sense. If $f : A \to B$ is a map in G and $D(f) = D(A) \leftarrow C_f \to D(B)$ then $D'(\widehat{f}) = C_f$. Also if the image of $f = l\,;g\,;m$ is the limit diagram

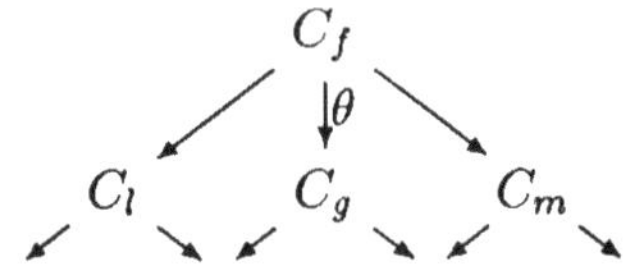

then $D'((l,m) : \widehat{f} \to \widehat{g}) = \theta$. Another way to look at it is that all diagrams D' in $\mathsf{Diag}(\mathsf{TFG}, \mathsf{C})$ must preserve limits.

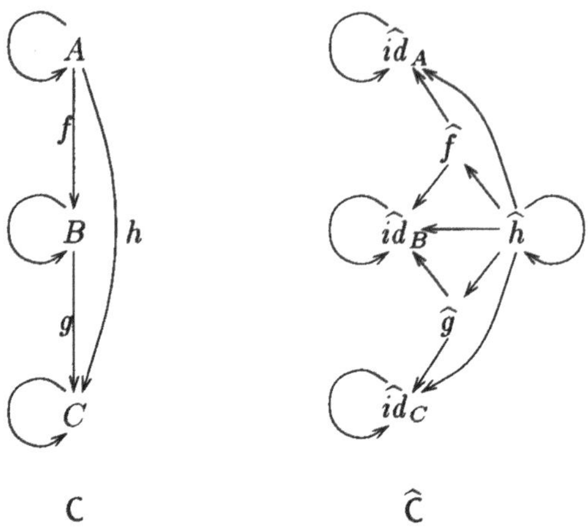

Figure 3: A twisted arrow category

Definition 9. Define $\mathsf{Diag}'(\mathsf{TFG}, \mathsf{C})$ to be the subcategory of $\mathsf{Diag}(\mathsf{TFG}, \mathsf{C})$ such that every diagram $D' : \widehat{\mathsf{G}} \to \mathsf{C}$ is induced by a diagram $D : \mathsf{G} \to \mathsf{Sp}(\mathsf{C})$

Proposition 10. $\mathsf{Diag}'(\mathsf{TFG}, \mathsf{C})$ *is finitely complete, has finite coproducts and is extensive.*

Processes will be spans in the category $\mathsf{Diag}'(\mathsf{TFG}, \mathsf{C})$. We need to show, however, that composition by pullback in the category realises parallel composition with value passing.

To give some intuition we will use an informal CCS-like calculus to describe processes. For syntax we assume an underlying "value" language – an algebraic or functional theory – extended with the usual CCS primitives for prefixing choice *etc.* We also assume the value language can be interpreted in C. Using standard notation, we write $\Gamma \vdash t : \sigma$ for a term t of type σ in a context $\Gamma = [x_1 : X_1, \ldots, x_n : X_n]$ containing the free variables of t. The familiar categorical interpretation of t in C is a morphism $[\![X_1]\!] \times \ldots \times [\![X_n]\!] \xrightarrow{[\![t]\!]} [\![\sigma]\!]$.

Now consider the left side of figure 4. The vertical spans on the left and right are transitions in two processes to be composed. The vertical span in the middle is a transition in the type (interface) between the two processes. The maps into $[\![Y]\!]$ show how each transition participates in the interaction. As in SProc there is no formal distinction between input and output though a direction is often implied.

The process on the left, p, is receiving a value from the process on the right, q. In our informal calculus, p is described by $\Gamma \vdash a(y:Y).p'$ where Γ is the list of free variables in p. If we assume y is a new variable, then after the transition the context is extended with $[y : Y]$. The process q writes the value of the term t, and is described by $\Delta \vdash \bar{a}(t:Y).q'$.

Note the use of the terminal object of C in the interface between p and q. The indicates the absence of imperative/internal state. This seems consistent with our intuition for what an interface is and we will stipulate that objects in the process category have no internal state. This means that if we ignore the limits, then the diagrams for objects are essentially graphs with edges labelled with the objects of C. We refer to these as *state-less* diagrams or *SL*-diagrams. Formally they are characterised by the property that if $D : \widehat{\mathsf{G}} \to \mathsf{C}$ is an object in the process category, then for every object A in G, $D(\widehat{id}_A) = 1$. In other words, these are diagrams where the original vertices of G are mapped to the terminal object of C.

The right side of the figure shows the transition in the composed process where the objects in the diagram are obtained by pulling back the respective components of the natural transformations. As might be expected, the types associated with the state of the composed process are the products of the types associated with the states of the individual processes.

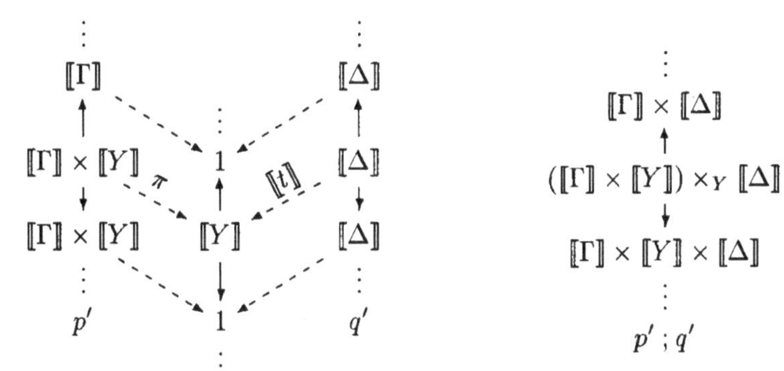

Figure 4: Composing transitions

It is useful to compare this with parallel composition in CCS. In CCS, when an input action in a process p binds an expression t to a variable x, the substitution $[x \mapsto t]$ is applied to all occurrences of x in the remainder of p. Here, values are not explicitly propagated. Instead the constraints on variables and relationships between variables are recorded by the internal maps in the diagram of the process.

Finally we define the interaction category of processes with internal state.

Definition 11. Let C be a small category with finite limits and finite coproducts and which is extensive. The category StProc(C) is the subcategory of Sp(Diag′(TFG, C)) modulo 2-isomorphism such that the objects are SL-diagrams.

We have chosen to quotient by 2-isomorphisms. An obvious alternative would be to quotient by bisimulation, however, this seems inappropriate for program analysis applications since it would identify processes which have the same input/output behaviour but realise that behaviour in different ways.

5.1 Examples

Figure 5 depicts two example processes. On the left is a simple process which receives a value of type A on one port, and on its next transition writes a function of that value on its other port. Using our informal notation, the process would be described by $[] \vdash a(x:A).\bar{b}(f(x):B).\mathsf{nil}$.

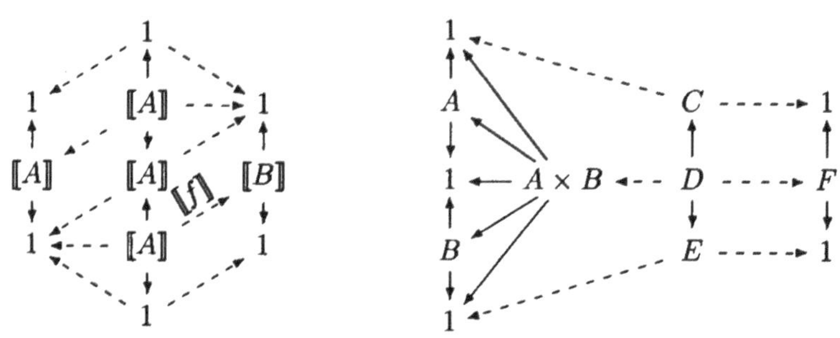

Figure 5: Two examples

As before, the spans on the left and right are process types and the diagram in the middle describes the two transitions of the process. Dashed lines are components of natural transformations and unlabelled maps are either identities or the unique map into the terminal object. The composite map (limit) for the process has been omitted as have the identities.

Note that a process need not participate at a port in a transition. This is indicated when the functor maps a transition to the "idle" transition in the type. This is analogous to τ transitions in Gay's characterisation of ASProc[11]. Hence StProc(C) exhibits asynchrony in a natural way.

The example helps to illustrate the different rôles of the functor and natural transformation in a morphism between diagrams. The functor maps one shape to another and carries the synchronisation information. The data is carried by the components of the natural transformations.

What might be considered a dual form of asynchrony is depicted in the the process on the right where in this case the limit object, $A \times B$, for the type is shown. Here, in a single transition, the process receives a pair of values from its left. However, the interface is such that a correspondent may send the two values in separate transitions.

5.2 Relating StProc(C) *and* SProc

StProc(C) has the same linear type structure as SProc. This includes a symmetric monoidal (tensor) product $A \otimes B$ for all objects A and B. The tensor is the artifact in the span category of the product $A \times B$ in the category of diagrams. If G is the T-graph $\circlearrowleft$ then the tensor unit, I, is the diagram $D : \widehat{F(G)} \to C$ which maps all the objects to the terminal object of C.

Again, because we are working in a category of spans, for each object B there is a right adjoint to the functor $(- \otimes B)$ denoted $(B \multimap -)$ and a dualizing object $\bot \cong I$ giving $A \multimap B = A \otimes B = A \mathbin{⅋} B$. This is summarised as follows:

Proposition 12. StProc(C) *is compact closed.*

Coproducts in the category of diagrams become biproducts in the category of processes[8]:

Proposition 13. StProc(C) *has all biproducts.*

Hence, like SProc, StProc(C) can model the CCS nondeterministic sum operator.

To characterise the relationship with SProc more precisely we have the following:

Proposition 14. *There is a coreflection* StProc(C) $\underset{E}{\overset{i}{\underset{\bot}{\rightleftarrows}}}$ SProc.

If we choose C to be Set, for example, then the functor E discards the imperative state in a process and replaces it with branching structure. This corresponds with the expansion of a value-passing calculus into a basic calculus.

In the case where $C = 1$ we obtain a category very similar to SProc. In fact, had we chosen to quotient processes by bisimulation, we would get an equivalent category.

6 Conclusions

We have described an interaction category of processes with internal state and with the same type structure as other interaction categories. Work is under way on applying this category to give semantics to a typed process calculus and on a static analysis of the calculus using abstract interpretation. The analysis extends work by Clark *et al.* [5] and involves determining dependencies between variables and ports.

Thus far we have not mentioned prefixing or delay. The unit delay functor in particular features prominently in most papers on interaction categories. Prefixing of processes with internal state is subtle because one must take into consideration the types on states. The prefix to a process must provide the same type of state as the initial state of the process which follows. Similarly, sequential composition must respect the types of state and in fact sequential composition is categorical. This brings us to an unusual situation in which each morphism has two types (with objects from two categories) for which there are two distinct notions of composition. A process is typed in one direction for parallel composition and in another for sequential composition. In effect, we have two categories which share the same morphisms. We call these "ortho"-categories and they are the subject of further investigation.

Acknowledgements

Thanks to Chris Hankin, Duško Pavlović, Till Plewe, Samson Abramsky and Steve Vickers for help at various points along the way. Simon Gay kindly reviewed an earlier version of this paper. Special thanks to François Lamarche for his technical assistance and his consistent encouragement.

1. S. Abramsky, S. J. Gay, and R. Nagarajan. Interaction categories and foundations of typed concurrent programming. In M. Broy, editor, *Deductive Program Design: Proceedings of the 1994 Marktoberdorf International Summer School*, NATO ASI Series F: Computer and Systems Sciences. Springer-Verlag, 1995.
2. S. Abramsky, S. J. Gay, and R. Nagarajan. Specification structures and propositions-as-types for concurrency. In F. Moller, editor, *Proceedings of the 1994 Banff Higher-Order Workshop*, Lecture Notes in Computer Science. Springer-Verlag, 1995.
3. Jean Bénabou. Introduction to bicategories. *Lecture Notes in Mathematics*, 47, 1967.
4. Aurelio Carboni, Steve Lack, and Robert F.C. Walters. Introduction to extensive and distributive categories. *Journal of Pure and Applied*

Algebra, 84:145–158, 1993.

5. David Clark, Lindsay Errington, and Chris Hankin. Static analysis of value-passing process calculi (extended abstract). In *Proceedings of the 1994 Theory and Formal Methods Section Workshop*. Imperial College Press, 1995.
6. J. R. B. Cockett and D. A. Spooner. SProc categorically. In *CONCUR 94: Fifth Internation Conference on Concurrency*, Lecture Notes in Computer Science, Uppsala, Sweden, 1994. Springer-Verlag.
7. J. R. B. Cockett and D. A. Spooner. Categories for synchrony and asynchrony. *Electronic Notes in Computer Science*, 1, 1995.
8. J. R. B. Cockett and D. A. Spooner. Constrcuting process categories. To appear.
9. Robin Cockett. Introduction to distributive categories. *Mathematical Structures in Computer Science*, 3:277–307, 1993.
10. Patrick Cousot and Radhia Cousot. Abstract interpretation: A unified lattice model for static analysis of programs by construction or approximation of fixpoints. In *Fourth ACM POPL*, pages 238–252, 1977.
11. Simon J. Gay. *Linear Types for Communicating Processes*. PhD thesis, University of London, 1995.
12. Joseph A. Goguen. Sheaf semantics for concurrent interacting objects. *Mathematical Structures in Computer Science*, 2:159–191, 1992.
13. André Joyal, Mogens Nielsen, and Glynn Winskel. Bisimulation and open maps. In *Proceedings of the Eighth IEEE Symposium on Logic in Computer Science*. IEEE Computer Society Press, 1993.
14. Saunders Mac Lane. *Categories for the Working Mathematician*. Springer-Verlag, Berlin, 1971.
15. Michael Makkai and Robert Paré. *Accessible Categories: The Foundations of Categorical Model Theory*, volume 104 of *Contemporary Mathematics*. American Mathematical Society, 1989.
16. Andrzej Tarlecki, Rod Burstall, and Joseph Goguen. Some fundamental algebraic tools for the semantics of computation, part 3: Indexed categories. *Theoretical Computer Science*, 91:239–264, 1991.
17. G. Winskel and M. Nielsen. Models for concurrency. In S. Abramsky, D. Gabbay, and T.S.E. Maibaum, editors, *Handbook of Logic in Computer Science*. Oxford University Press. To appear.

ON AN ALGEBRAIC FLAVORING OF THE LOGICAL APPROACH

THEODOSIS DIMITRAKOS
Department of Computing, Imperial College, London SW7 2BZ.

Abstract

The logical approach to specification has been successfully used to exploit the foundations of software development in terms of theory manipulations, employing the formalism of many-sorted first order logic. When dealing with constructions inspired from the category theoretic overview, though, or when mechanical support for synthesis, composition and refinement is considered, it seems necessary to augment this approach with features that facilitate the specification, reasoning and manipulation of complex entities.

Such an augmentation is initiated in this paper. Similar augmentations may be applicable to specifications in other logics (e.g. temporal or multi-valued logics).

1 Introduction

The process of software development consists of theory manipulations. This assertion is able to provide an overview of software development (describing what *does* happen) while establishing a viewpoint (explaining what *should* happen). Convincing arguments on the truthfulness of the resulting overview and the usefulness of the particular viewpoint are given in [19] and [17]. In addition, some recent tools for formal software development (e.g. [13]) and composition (e.g. [16]) seem to spring from a similar initiative. The logical approach to specification emanates from this initiation, employing the formalism of (many sorted) first order logic ([19, 17]). Our interest in the logical approach is motivated by its closeness to concepts and methods used in program development / verification and the flexibility it provides for specifying, avoiding over-specification. But, still, when constructions that stem from the category theoretic overview or when mechanical support for synthesis composition and refinement are considered, one needs to augment this approach with mechanisms that facilitate the specification, reasoning and manipulation of complex entities. Such an augmentation is initiated in this paper.

This demonstration aims, among others, to achieve a finitely cocomplete category of theories, to ease the rewriting and manipulation of predicates throughout the refinement process, to support the coexistence and combination of deductive program synthesis mechanisms ([11]), with stepwise refinement and composition techniques ([17, 19, 1]).

The structure of the paper is as follows: First, we review the categoric encapsulation of many sorted first order logic, and exploit the relation between the classes of equivalent formulae (sentences) over a first order language and the underlying boolean algebras (*Section 2*). Then we augment the logical alphabet with a boolean sort and axioms which force all of its model interpretations to designate some 2-element boolean algebra (*Section 3*). We also demonstrate how predicates / formulae could be generated by boolean functions / terms . The resulting logic, which we call $\mathfrak{B}$-logic, is only superficially stronger than many sorted first order logic but presents some interesting advantages which are useful for applications in computing. Some of these advantages are presented in *Section 4*, where we emphasize the following: The finite co-completeness of the category of theories in $\mathfrak{B}$-logic (*paragraphs 4.1* and *4.2*) , the advantages of having a maximally consistent, monomorphic[a] theory as an initial object (*paragraphs 4.1 and 4.2*) and the establishment of unifying versions for Skolemization, Unskolemization (*paragraph 4.3*) and Polarity Analysis of expressions in $\mathfrak{B}$-logic (*paragraph 4.4*).

2 Background

A many sorted signature $\mathbf{\Sigma}$ is a triple $\langle S, P, F\rangle$ such that: S is a non empty set of (sort) symbols, P is the union of a family P_u with u in S^n, for $n \geq 1$, where P_u is the set of *predicate* symbols of rank $\langle u\rangle$. F is the union of a family $F_{u,s}$ with $\langle u, s\rangle \in S^n \times S$, for $n \geq 0$, where $F_{u,s}$ is the set of *function* symbols of rank $\langle u, s\rangle$.

A signature morphism (translation) from a many sorted signature $\mathbf{\Sigma}_1$ to a many sorted signature $\mathbf{\Sigma}_2$ is a map $\sigma : \mathbf{\Sigma}_1 \rightarrow \mathbf{\Sigma}_2$ that preserves the kind and the arity of the symbols. That is, a predicate $p : u_1 \ldots u_n$ is mapped to a predicate $\sigma(p) : \sigma(u_1) \ldots \sigma(u_n)$ and a function $f : u_1 \ldots u_n \rightarrow s$ is mapped to a function $\sigma(f) : \sigma(u_1) \ldots \sigma(u_n) \rightarrow \sigma(s)$.

Given a signature $\mathbf{\Sigma} \equiv \langle S, P, F\rangle$, $\mathbf{\Sigma}$-structure, $\mathfrak{A}$, consists of an S-indexed collection of *non-empty* sets $[s^{\mathfrak{A}}]_{s\in S}$, a relation $p^{\mathfrak{A}}$ on $u^{\mathfrak{A}}$ for each predicate symbol in P_u and a function $f^{\mathfrak{A}} : u^{\mathfrak{A}} \rightarrow s^{\mathfrak{A}}$ for each function symbol $f : u \rightarrow s$ in $\Omega_{u,s}$. If $u \equiv u_1 \ldots u_n$ then $u^{\mathfrak{A}} \equiv u_1^{\mathfrak{A}} \times \ldots \times u_n^{\mathfrak{A}}$ and, if ϵ denotes the empty string, then $\epsilon^{\mathfrak{A}} \equiv \langle\rangle$.

For the sake of *soundness* a many sorted signature should comprise at least one sort symbol (see [5]). Many sorted signatures with signature morphisms consist a category $\mathbf{Sign}_{MS}$. Every *non-empty* finite diagram in the category

[a] A theory is called monomorphic if it has a unique up to isomorphism model

$\mathcal{S}ign_{MS}$ has a colimit but there is no initial object. So the category $\mathcal{S}ign_{MS}$ is *almost* but *not exactly* finitely cocomplete.

The usual inductive definition of terms and formulae (with the logical equality and the range of the quantifiers restricted over the corresponding sorts) are captured by the *grammar functor* $\mathcal{G}ram_{MS}$: $\mathcal{S}ign_{MS} \to \mathcal{S}et$, where $\mathcal{S}et$ is the category of sets. The symbols $(\neg, \vee, \wedge, \Rightarrow, \Leftrightarrow)$ are used to denote the standard logical connectives and $\approx_s \ : s \times s$ denotes the logical equality over a sort s.

The entailment (logical consequence) $\vdash^{MS}$is a $|\mathcal{S}ign|$-indexed family of relations with $\vdash^{MS}_{\Sigma}$, for each Σ in $\mathcal{S}ign_{MS}$, being a subset of $2^{\mathcal{G}ram_{MS}(\Sigma)} \times \mathcal{G}ram_{MS}(\Sigma)$ such that:

for all $\mathbf{i} : \Sigma_1 \to \Sigma_2$ in $\mathcal{S}ign_{MS}$, φ in $\mathcal{G}ram_{MS}(\Sigma_1)$ and $\Gamma \subseteq \mathcal{G}ram_{MS}(\Sigma_1)$,

$$\text{if } \Gamma \vdash^{MS}_{\Sigma_1} \varphi \text{ then } \mathcal{G}ram_{MS}(\mathbf{i})(\Gamma) \vdash^{MS}_{\Sigma_2} \mathcal{G}ram_{MS}(\mathbf{i})(\varphi).$$

By $\Gamma \vdash^{MS}_{\Sigma} \varphi$ we mean that there is a proof of φ from Γ, ie. there is a *finite* sequence $\mathbb{P} \equiv (\psi_i)_{1 \leq i \leq n}$ so that

(1) ψ_n is φ,

(2) for every $1 \leq i \leq n$ either $\psi_i \in \Gamma$ or there is a (non-empty) subsequence $\mathbb{P}_i$ of $(\psi_j)_{1 \leq j \leq i-1}$ such that $\{\psi_j : \psi_j \in \mathbb{P}_i\} \vdash^{MS}_{\Sigma} \psi_i$,and

(3) the set $\mathcal{A}^{MS}_{\Sigma}$ such that $\emptyset \vdash^{MS}_{\Sigma} \mathcal{A}^{MS}_{\Sigma}$ consists of the logical axioms of many-sorted first order logic for the language generated by Σ.

A set of sentences $\mathcal{G} \subseteq \mathcal{G}ram_{MS}(\Sigma)$ is called a *theory* iff it is closed under $\vdash^{MS}_{\Sigma}$. A theory morphism (theory interpretation) $\mathbf{i}$ from a theory $\mathcal{G}_1 \subseteq \mathcal{G}ram_{MS}(\Sigma_1)$ to a theory $\mathcal{G}_2 \subseteq \mathcal{G}ram_{MS}(\Sigma_2)$ is a signature morphism (translation) $\mathbf{i} : \Sigma_1 \to \Sigma_2$ such that: for every sentence in $\mathcal{G}ram_{MS}(\Sigma_1)$,

$$\text{if } \mathcal{G}_1 \vdash^{MS}_{\Sigma_2} \varphi \text{ then } \mathcal{G}_2 \vdash^{MS}_{\Sigma_2} \mathcal{G}ram_{MS}(\mathbf{i})(\varphi).$$

Many sorted first order theories and their morphisms (theory interpretations) constitute a category, named $\mathcal{T}heo_{MS}$ which is *not* finitely co-complete (no initial object) but where colimits of *finite, non-empty* diagrams always exist.

We say that a theory $\mathcal{G}_2$ *extends* a theory $\mathcal{G}_1$ iff every sentence of $\mathcal{G}_1$ is a sentence of $\mathcal{G}_2$. (ie. there is an inclusion id: $\mathcal{G}_1 \to \mathcal{G}_2$ in $\mathcal{T}heo_{MS}$). The restriction of $\mathcal{G}_2$ in $\mathcal{G}ram_{MS}(\Sigma_1)$ is the set of sentences $\mathcal{G}_2\lfloor_{\Sigma_1}$ such that $\mathcal{G}_2\lfloor_{\Sigma_1} \subseteq \mathcal{G}ram_{MS}(\Sigma_1)$ and for every sentence $\varphi \in \mathcal{G}ram(\Sigma_1)$, if $\mathcal{G}_2 \vdash^{MS}_{\Sigma_2} \varphi$ then $\mathcal{G}_2\lfloor_{\Sigma_1} \vdash^{MS}_{\Sigma_1} \varphi$. Generally, $\mathcal{G}_1 \subseteq \mathcal{G}_2\lfloor_{\Sigma_1}$. That is, the additional properties of $\mathcal{G}_2$ may have more consequences in $\mathbf{L}_1$ than $\mathcal{G}_1$. A theory $\mathcal{G}_2$ is a *conservative* (non-creative) extension of a theory $\mathcal{G}_1$ iff the restriction of $\mathcal{G}_2\lfloor_{\Sigma_1}$ is exactly the theory $\mathcal{G}_1$. That is, all the Σ_1-sentences of $\mathcal{G}_2$ are exactly the sentences of $\mathcal{G}_1$.

A Σ-structure $\mathfrak{A}$ is a model of a theory $\mathcal{G}$ iff all the sentences of $\mathcal{G}$ are satisfied by $\mathfrak{A}$. Since many sorted logic is complete, $\Gamma \vdash^{MS}_{\Sigma} \varphi$ iff φ is satisfied in all Σ-structures that satisfy Γ. Given that id: $\Sigma_1 \to \Sigma_2$ is injective, any Σ_1-structure can be *expanded* to a Σ_2-structure.

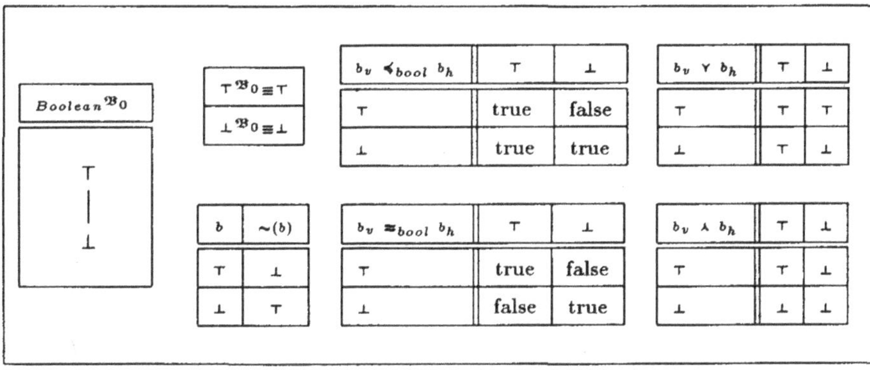

Figure 1: A picture of the $\mathfrak{B}_0$.

2.1 The theory of two element Boolean Algebra

Boolean algebras play a fundamental rôle in logic. In this paragraph we describe the construction of a complete and finitely axiomatizable many-sorted first order theory of the 2-element Boolean algebra. In *Section 3* we use this theory in order to augment the logic itself with an invariant, algebraic encapsulation of the truth constants.

Let $\mathbf{\Sigma}_0 \equiv \langle\{bool\}, \{\preccurlyeq_{bool}\}, \{\curlyvee, \curlywedge, \sim, \bot, \top\}\rangle$, with $\preccurlyeq_{bool} : bool \times bool$, $\bot, \top : \rightarrow bool$, $\sim : bool \rightarrow bool$, $\curlyvee, \curlywedge : bool \times bool \rightarrow bool$, and let $\approx_{bool}$ denote the logical equality (identity) on the sort *bool*. Let $\mathfrak{B}_0$ be the $\mathbf{\Sigma}_0$-structure $\langle\{\bot, \top\}$, $\{\preccurlyeq_{bool}{}^{\mathfrak{B}_0}\}$, $\{\curlyvee^{\mathfrak{B}_0}, \curlywedge^{\mathfrak{B}_0}, \sim^{\mathfrak{B}_0}, \bot^{\mathfrak{B}_0}, \top^{\mathfrak{B}_0}\}\rangle$ of figure 1. Note that $\preccurlyeq_{bool}$ is a partial order over $bool^{\mathfrak{B}_0}$. Now, expand $\mathbf{\Sigma}_0$ to $\mathbf{\Sigma}_0^+$ by adding a unary predicate $\propto$ on *bool*. Expand $\mathfrak{B}_0$ to $\mathfrak{B}_0^+$ by adding a unary relation $\propto^{\mathfrak{B}_0}$ on $\{\bot, \top\}$ such that:

$$\boxed{\propto^{\mathfrak{B}_0} \equiv \{\top\}.}$$

Remark 2.1 Both $\mathfrak{B}_0^+$ and $\mathfrak{B}_0$ can be produced as monomorphic expansions of $\mathfrak{B}\equiv\langle\{\bot, \top\}, \varnothing, \{\curlyvee^{\mathfrak{B}_0}, \sim^{\mathfrak{B}_0}, \bot^{\mathfrak{B}_0}, \top^{\mathfrak{B}_0}\}\rangle$, by defining $\curlywedge^{\mathfrak{B}_0}$ as $(\sim^{\mathfrak{B}} \times \sim^{\mathfrak{B}}); \curlyvee^{\mathfrak{B}_0}; \sim^{\mathfrak{B}}$, $x \preccurlyeq_{bool}{}^{\mathfrak{B}_0} y$ as $(x \curlyvee^{\mathfrak{B}} y) \approx_{bool} y$, and $\propto^{\mathfrak{B}_0^+}(x)$ as $x \approx_{bool} \top^{\mathfrak{B}}$. In $\mathfrak{B}_0$ we have the coexistence of a partially order structure and a (two-element) boolean algebra. Relating po-sets to boolean algebras is quite useful in practice as demonstrated in *paragraphs 2.2 and 4.4*

Let $\mathcal{BOOL}_0$ be the *theory of* $\mathfrak{B}_0^+$. This theory is *maximally consistent* (as the theory of a model), *finitely axiomatizable* and has a unique up-to-isomorphism model. Moreover, $\preccurlyeq_{bool}$ and $\approx_{bool}$ are analogue to $\Rightarrow$ and $\Leftrightarrow$ and

$\sim;\propto$, $\curlyvee;\propto$ and $\curlywedge;\propto$ are analogue to the logical connectives $\neg,\vee$ and $\wedge$ respectively. For convenience the *Boolean* operators $\rightarrow$ and $\leftrightarrow$ are introduced by their usual definition in terms of $\sim, \curlyvee$. The extended signature is denoted by $\mathbf{\Sigma}_{\mathfrak{B}}$ and he resulting theory $\mathcal{BOOL}$ is an extension by external definition of $\mathcal{BOOL}_0$. So $\mathcal{BOOL}$ is maximally consistent and finitely axiomatizable. Moreover it extends $\mathcal{BOOL}_0$ conservatively, it is fully reducible to $\mathcal{BOOL}_0$ and every model of $\mathcal{BOOL}_0$ is monomorphically expanded to some model of $\mathcal{BOOL}$.

2.2 Logical theories and Boolean algebras

Classical logic, as wel as some contemporary logics, are built on the concept of Boolean algebras which are often considered as the obvious mathematical model for our natural intuition of truth. Po-sets on the other hand naturally abstract consequence. This paragraph exploits the interconnection between Boolean algebras, po-sets and logical consequence in classical logic.

Let $\mathbf{\Sigma}$ be any first order signature. Consider the $\vdash_{\mathbf{\Sigma}}\phi\Leftrightarrow\psi$ on the formulae generated by $\mathbf{\Sigma}$. Let $[\varphi]$ denote $\{\psi : \vdash_{\mathbf{\Sigma}}\varphi\Leftrightarrow\psi\}$. Then call $\mathbb{L}$ the set $\{[\varphi] : \varphi$ is a formula in the language generated by $\mathbf{\Sigma}\}$ and let $\mathbf{0}_{\mathbb{L}}$ be $[\neg\varphi\wedge\varphi]$ and $\mathbf{1}_{\mathbb{L}}$ be $[\neg\varphi\vee\varphi]$. Then define the operators $+, *, {}^{c}$ as follows: $[\varphi] + [\psi] \equiv [\varphi\vee\psi], [\varphi] * [\psi] \equiv [\varphi\wedge\psi], [\varphi]^c \equiv [\neg\varphi]$ Then the first order structure $\mathfrak{L} \equiv \langle\mathbb{L}, +, *, {}^{c}, \mathbf{0}_{\mathfrak{L}}, \mathbf{1}_{\mathfrak{L}}\rangle$ is a Boolean algebra, known as the *Lindenbaum algebra* of the language generated by $\mathbf{\Sigma}$. $\mathfrak{L}$ has several important subalgebras. In particular, by letting $\mathbb{L}_n \equiv \{\varphi : \varphi$ has at most $u_0, \ldots, u_n$ variables free$\}$ we can define a subalgebra $\mathfrak{L}_n$ of $\mathfrak{L}$, for each $n < \omega$. The $\mathfrak{L}_0$ subalgebra is the *Lindenbaum algebra of all sentences* of the language generated by $\mathbf{\Sigma}$.

Let $\mathcal{G}\subset\mathcal{G}ram(\mathbf{\Sigma})$ be a first order theory. The quotient algebra $\mathfrak{L}/\mathcal{G}$ is the *Lindenbaum algebra of* $\mathcal{G}$, which is a countable Boolean algebra. The equivalence classes, in this algebra are given by the sets of formulae $[\varphi] \equiv\{\psi : \mathcal{G}\vdash_{\mathbf{\Sigma}}\varphi\Leftrightarrow\psi\}$ its *unit* element $\mathbf{1}_{\mathfrak{L}_{\mathcal{G}}}$ is given by $\mathcal{G}$ and its *zero* element $\mathbf{0}_{\mathfrak{L}_{\mathcal{G}}}$ is given by $\{\varphi : \mathcal{G}\vdash_{\mathbf{\Sigma}}\neg\varphi\}$. Moreover, if the theory of $\mathcal{G}$ is maximally consistent then $\mathfrak{L}/\mathcal{G}$ is exactly[b] the two element algebra $\mathfrak{B}_0$ of *paragraph 2.1*. $\mathfrak{L}/\mathcal{G}$ is the protagonist in a constructive proof of extended completeness for classical logic, given by Rasiowa *&* Sikowski in 1950.

3 An outline of $\mathfrak{B}$-Logic

The use of a *Boolean* sort as an algebraic encapsulation of the truth values, is traditional in the algebraic approach to specifications and has been employed

[b]In general, there is a one-to-one correspondence between the complete extensions of the theory of $\mathcal{G}$ and the ultrafilters on $\mathfrak{L}_0/\mathcal{G}$.

occasionally by the logical approach (e.g. [17, 5, 14, 15]). The problems of a "loose" introduction or treatment of the *Boolean* sort, in both logical and algebraic traditions, may turn out to be destructive. In this section we outline a reformulation of many sorted logic, where the logical alphabet is augmented with the symbols of $\Sigma_{\mathfrak{B}}$ (*paragraph 2.1*) and the logical axioms are augmented by a(ny) finite axiomatisation of the theory $\mathcal{BOOL}$ (*paragraph 2.1*). So, the sort *bool* is included in every language of this logic and all structures have a 2-element Boolean Algebra as a model interpretation for *bool*. We call the resulting logic $\mathfrak{B}$-logic.

Intuitively, $\mathfrak{B}$-logic can be viewed as the part of many-sorted first order logic which concentrates on the extensions by sorts and function symbols of the theory $\mathcal{BOOL}$. From a classical perspective, all theories in $\mathfrak{B}$-logic can be viewed as extensions of the theory $\mathcal{BOOL}$. A basic characteristic of these extensions is that all new symbols are either sort or function symbols. As we will see $\mathfrak{B}$-logic is as expressive as full many-sorted first order logic, in the sense that there is a (natural) transformation from any many-sorted first order theory to some theory in $\mathfrak{B}$-logic.

The logical alphabet of $\mathfrak{B}$-logic is the logical alphabet of many-sorted first order logic augmented with the symbols of $\Sigma_{\mathbf{BOOL}}$ (ie. the sort *bool*, the partial order $\preccurlyeq_{bool}$ and the logical equality $\approx_{bool}$ over *bool*, the monadic predicate $\propto$, the constants $\bot, \top$ and the functions $\sim, \curlyvee, \curlywedge, \rightarrow, \leftrightarrow$)

A $\mathfrak{B}$-signature Σ is a tuple $\langle S, \Omega \rangle$ where S is a non empty set of (sort) symbols, F is the union of a family $F_{u,s}$ with $\langle u, s \rangle \in S^n \times (S \cup \{bool\})$, for $n \geq 0$, where $F_{u,s}$ is the set of *function* symbols of rank $\langle u, s \rangle$. A $\mathfrak{B}$-signature morphism (translation) from a $\mathfrak{B}$-signature Σ_1 to $\mathfrak{B}$- signature Σ_2 is a map $\sigma : \Sigma_1 \rightarrow \Sigma_2$ that preserves the kind and the arity of the signature symbols. That is, a function $f : u_1 \dots u_n \rightarrow s$, with $s \neq bool$, is mapped to a function $\sigma(f) : \sigma(u_1) \dots \sigma(u_n) \rightarrow \sigma(s)$; a function $f : u_1 \dots u_n \rightarrow bool$ is mapped to the function $\sigma(f) : \sigma(u_1) \dots \sigma(u_n) \rightarrow bool$. The empty $\mathfrak{B}$-signature $\mathcal{E}_{\mathfrak{B}} = \langle \emptyset, \emptyset \rangle$ is an acceptable $\mathfrak{B}$-signature. $\mathfrak{B}$-signatures and their morphisms consist a category $\mathit{Sign}_{\mathfrak{B}}$ which is finitely co-complete with $\mathcal{E}_{\mathfrak{B}}$ being its initial element.

$\mathfrak{B}$-signatures are related to many-sorted first order signatures via a functor $\mathbf{C}$: $\mathit{Sign}_{\mathfrak{B}} \rightarrow \mathit{Sign}_{MS}$ such that $\mathbf{C}(\langle S, \Omega \rangle) = \langle S \cup \{bool\}, \{\preccurlyeq_{bool}, \propto\}, \Omega \rangle$ The grammar functor $\mathcal{G}ram_{\mathfrak{B}}$: $\mathit{Sign}_{\mathfrak{B}} \rightarrow \mathit{Set}$, can be induced from $\mathcal{G}ram_{MS}$ and $\mathbf{C}$ as follows: For every $\mathfrak{B}$-signature Σ, $\mathcal{G}ram_{\mathfrak{B}}(\Sigma) = \mathcal{G}ram_{MS}(\mathbf{C}(\Sigma))$. This means that φ is a Σ-expression (Σ-term or Σ-formula) in $\mathfrak{B}$-logic iff it is a $\mathbf{C}(\Sigma)$-expression ($\mathbf{C}(\Sigma)$-term or $\mathbf{C}(\Sigma)$-formula respectively) in many-sorted first order logic.

The entailment $\vdash^{\mathfrak{B}}$ relation over $\mathfrak{B}$-logic, can be explained in terms of $\vdash^{MS}$and $\mathbf{C}$: $\Gamma \vdash^{\mathfrak{B}}_{\Sigma} \varphi$ iff $\Gamma, \mathcal{BOOL} \vdash^{MS}_{\mathbf{C}(\Sigma)} \varphi$.

A set of sentences $\mathcal{G} \subseteq \mathcal{G}ram_{\mathfrak{B}}(\Sigma)$ is called a *theory* iff it is closed under $\vdash_{\Sigma}^{MS}$. A theory morphism (theory interpretation) $\mathbf{i}$ from a theory $\mathcal{G}_1 \subseteq \mathcal{G}ram_{\mathfrak{B}}(\Sigma_1)$ to a theory $\mathcal{G}_2 \subseteq \mathcal{G}ram_{\mathfrak{B}}(\Sigma_2)$ is a signature morphism (translation) $\mathbf{i} : \Sigma_1 \rightarrow \Sigma_2$ such that $\mathcal{G}_2 \vdash_{\Sigma_2}^{\mathfrak{B}} \mathcal{G}ram_{\mathfrak{B}}(\mathbf{i})(\varphi)$, for every sentence $\mathcal{G}_1 \vdash_{\Sigma_1}^{\mathfrak{B}} \varphi$. Theories in $\mathfrak{B}$-logic and their morphisms (theory interpretations) constitute a category, named $\mathit{Theo}_{\mathfrak{B}}$, which is finitely co-complete with $\mathcal{BOOL}$ as an initial element. (Notice that $\mathcal{BOOL}$ is the closure of $\varnothing$ under $\vdash_{\mathcal{E}_{\mathfrak{B}}}^{\mathfrak{B}}$). Extensions (creative and not) in $\mathit{Theo}_{\mathfrak{B}}$ are defined as in *Section 2*.

$\mathfrak{B}$-logic is as expressive as full many sorted first order logic in the sense that there is a (natural) transformation from any theory in Theo_{MS} to some theory in $\mathit{Theo}_{\mathfrak{B}}$:

Consider a functor $\mathbf{tr}$: $\mathit{Sign}_{MS} \rightarrow \mathit{Sign}_{\mathfrak{B}}$ that maps each many sorted first order signature $\Sigma = \langle S, P, F\rangle$ to $\mathbf{tr}(\Sigma) = \langle S, \Omega_P \cup F\rangle$, where $\Omega_P = \{f_p : u \rightarrow bool \mid p : u \in P\}$. Notice that $\mathbf{tr}$ gives rise to a functor $\mathbf{tr}^+$: $\mathcal{G}ram_{MS}[\mathit{Sign}_{MS}] \rightarrow \mathcal{G}ram_{\mathfrak{B}}[\mathit{Sign}_{\mathfrak{B}}]$ that is defined inductively, on the operation of the grammar functor: For any many sorted signature Σ any sort, predicate and function symbols s, p, f, respectively, and any $\varphi[s, p, f] \in \mathcal{G}ram_{MS}(\Sigma)$, $\mathbf{tr}^+(\varphi) = \varphi[s \mapsto \mathbf{tr}(s), p \mapsto (\mathbf{tr}(p); \propto), f \mapsto \mathbf{tr}(f)]$. Intuitively, all occurrences of each predicate symbol p in each Σ-formula φ are simultaneously substituted by $\mathbf{tr}(p); \propto$ and all other symbols remain unchanged. The resulting formula, is a well formed $\mathbf{tr}(\Sigma)$-formula.

The functor $\mathbf{tr}^+$ associates faithfully with $\vdash$: For every $\Gamma \subseteq \mathcal{G}ram_{MS}(\Sigma)$ and every $\varphi \in \mathcal{G}ram_{MS}$, $\Gamma \vdash_{\Sigma}^{MS}$ iff $\mathbf{tr}_{\Sigma}^+[\Gamma] \vdash_{\mathbf{tr}(\Sigma)}^{\mathfrak{B}} \mathbf{tr}_{\Sigma}^+(\varphi)$. So there is a functor $\mathbf{Tr}$ from Theo_{MS} to $\mathit{Theo}_{\mathfrak{B}}$ that preserves logical consequence.

An alternative presentation of the above transformation of many-sorted theories into theories in $\mathfrak{B}$-logic (and its inverse) could be in terms of structures: Any Σ-structure $\mathfrak{A}_{\mathfrak{B}}$ in $\mathfrak{B}$-logic can be transformed to a $\mathbf{tr}^{-1}(\Sigma)$-structure $\mathfrak{A}$ by introducing a relation $p^{\mathfrak{A}} : u^{\mathfrak{A}_{\mathfrak{B}}}$ for each $f_p : u \rightarrow bool$ in Σ, so that $p^{\mathfrak{A}} \equiv (f^{\mathfrak{A}_{\mathfrak{B}}})^{-1}[\{\top^{\mathfrak{A}_{\mathfrak{B}}}\}]$ and then eliminating $\mathfrak{B}_0^+$ from $\mathfrak{A}_{\mathfrak{B}}$ together will all these $f_p^{\mathfrak{A}_{\mathfrak{B}}}$. Similarly, any many sorted Σ-structure $\mathfrak{A}$ can be expanded to a $\mathbf{tr}(\Sigma)$-B structure $\mathfrak{A}_{\mathfrak{B}}$ for $\mathfrak{B}$-logic by appending $\mathfrak{B}_0^+$ in the collection of (sort-)domains for $\mathfrak{A}$, then designating *bool* to $\{\perp^{\mathfrak{B}_0^+}, \top^{\mathfrak{B}_0^+}\}$, introducing, for every predicate symbol p of Σ, a new function $f_p : u^{\mathfrak{A}} \rightarrow \{\perp^{\mathfrak{B}_0^+}, \top^{\mathfrak{B}_0^+}\}$ such that $f_p[p^{\mathfrak{A}}] = \{\top^{\mathfrak{B}_0^+}\}$ and $f_p[(p^{\mathfrak{A}})^c] = \{\perp^{\mathfrak{B}_0^+}\}$, and, finally, eliminating all $p^{\mathfrak{A}}$.

4 Some advantages of reasoning in $\mathfrak{B}$-logic

$\mathfrak{B}$-logic can be viewed as a part of many-sorted first order logic, which is as expressive as the whole logic. In particular, the category $\mathit{Theo}_{\mathfrak{B}}$ of theories in

$\mathfrak{B}$-logic corresponds to a finitely co-complete subcategory of *Theo*$_{MS}$ in which the whole category is reflected. So the $\mathfrak{B}$-logic inherits all the nice properties of first order logic, such as sufficient expressibility, completeness, compactness, semi-decidability and clear distinction between finitude and infiniteness (via the Löwenheim-Skolem theorems). In addition it presents some important advantages related to the applications of Logic in Computing. These advantages comprise a simpler and clearer categoric representation, a nice association of faithfulness and consistency, support for a unifying, extended version of processes like Skolemization and Unskolemization (reverse-Skolemization) and a uniform assignment of polarity values for *all* signature symbols. Each of these advantages are outlined below. For a further, extensive discussion refer to [5].

4.1 Finite cocompleteness, faithfulness and consistency

Finite cocompleteness of the category of theories over one's logical system becomes quite important when viewing software development in terms of theory manipulation ([6, 7, 3]). The very basic operation of theories that we wish to support is amalgamation. That is, to put together theories that share some common subtheories ([1]). Amalgamation is explained in terms of finite colimits in the category of theories, and categories for which colimits of finite diagrams always exist are called finitely cocomplete.

The category of many sorted theories *Theo*$_{MS}$ is not finite cocomplete. Every *non-empty* finite diagram in *Theo*$_{MS}$ has a colimit but there is no initial object (the empty diagram *does not* have a colimit). On the contrary, *Theo*$_{\mathfrak{B}}$ is finitely cocomplete with initial object the theory $\mathcal{BOOL}$. In addition, $\mathcal{BOOL}$ is maximally consistent and monomorphic (it has a unique up-to-isomorphism model). Therefore the unique morphism from $\mathcal{BOOL}$ to any other object of *Theo*$_{\mathfrak{B}}$ is *faithful*, if and only if that object is a consistent theory. This is an exceptional characteristic which lacks even from quite nicely behaved logics such as classical first order logic[c].

A common illusion among researchers in computing is to consider the empty signature as being an initial object in *Sign*$_{MS}$ and the induced theory as the initial object of *Theo*$_{MS}$. This violates the soundness of the resulting logic as indicated in [4] and [5]. As variables in many sorted first order logic range over sorts, the introduction of an empty signature would induce the an empty language and then an empty theory as an object *Theo*$_{MS}$. The empty theory would, then, be both consistent and inconsistent, satisfiable and not

[c]Classical first order logic with equality has a finitely cocomplete category of theories with initial object the theory of logical equality which is not maximally consistent. It is a trivial task to find consistent but not conservative extensions of this theory.

satisfiable. If such a theory existed then it could not be converted to classical first order logic with equality, whereas all many sorted theories can.

4.2 Clear diagrammatic representation

One could suggest that finite cocompleteness is a rather strong requirement. Indeed, when software development is explained in terms of theory manipulation, empty diagrams (and their colimits) are rarely, if ever, met. The ability of computing colimits for any not empty, finite diagram is more that enough for our purposes. On the other hand, one would like the diagrammatic (in the sense of category theory) presentation of relations between theories to be as clear as possible. When the initial elements are missing from the category of theories in some logical system, colimit computations hide some slippery paths.

Consider, for example, the direct sum (co-product) $\mathcal{G}_1 \oplus \mathcal{G}_2$ of two *consistent* theories in Theo_{MS}. The result of this operation is *not* the disjoint union of the two theories, as one might think, but something larger -as a logician should expect. The difference is that there are always some sentences in $\mathcal{G}ram_{MS}(\Sigma_1 \oplus \Sigma_2)$ which are derivable from $\mathcal{G}_1 \oplus \mathcal{G}_2$ via $\vdash^{MS}_{\Sigma_1 \oplus \Sigma_2}$ but cannot be derived from neither $\mathcal{G}_1$ via $\vdash^{MS}_{\Sigma_1}$ nor $\mathcal{G}_2$ via $\vdash^{MS}_{\Sigma_2}$. On the other hand, since logical equality is restricted over the corresponding sorts and both $\mathcal{G}_1$ and $\mathcal{G}_2$ are consistent, the co-product theory $\mathcal{G}_1 \oplus \mathcal{G}_2$ is a conservative extension of both $\mathcal{G}_1$ and $\mathcal{G}_2$. Therefore, the study of this simple construction from a logical perspective becomes a bit more complicated: There are sentences in $\mathcal{G}_1 \oplus \mathcal{G}_2$ which are not derivable from $\mathcal{G}_1$ or $\mathcal{G}_2$ but these sentences are all in $\mathcal{G}ram_{MS}(\Sigma_1 \oplus \Sigma_2)$. The restriction of $\mathcal{G}_1 \oplus \mathcal{G}_2$ in $\mathcal{G}ram_{MS}(\Sigma_1)$ and $\mathcal{G}ram_{MS}(\Sigma_1)$ is exactly $\mathcal{G}_1$ and $\mathcal{G}_2$, respectively.

Now notice the clear presentation and the simplicity of the same construction n $\mathit{Theo}_{\mathfrak{B}}$: The sum of $\mathcal{G}_1$ and $\mathcal{G}_2$ in $\mathcal{G}ram_{\mathfrak{B}}(\Sigma_1 \oplus \Sigma_2)$ consists a pushout construction with respect to $\mathcal{BOOL}$. This shows (in a clear, diagrammatic fashion) that one should expect some new properties derivable from the sum of $\mathcal{G}_1$ and $\mathcal{G}_2$ over $\mathcal{G}ram_{\mathfrak{B}}(\Sigma_1 \oplus \Sigma_2)$ since they share the Boolean values. This piece of information is hidden in the classical approach since the co-domain of the extra-logical predicate symbols remains at the meta-level and lacks any reflection in the syntax. On the other hand, pushouts in (many sorted) first order logic, preserve conservative extensions ([17, 18]). Theories in $\mathfrak{B}$-logic trivially inherit this property. So the sum of $\mathcal{G}_1$ and $\mathcal{G}_2$ in $\mathcal{G}ram_{\mathfrak{B}}(\Sigma_1 \oplus \Sigma_2)$ is a conservative extension of both $\mathcal{G}_1$ and $\mathcal{G}_2$.

4.3 Unifying versions of Skolemization & Unskolemization

Consider a *prenex* sentence $\mathcal{F}$ where an existentially quantified variable $(y : s)$ occurs in the scope of the universally quantified variables $(x_1 : u_1) \ldots (x_n : u_n)$. Skolemisation is the process of replacing all occurrences of the existentially quantified variable by a new function symbol $f : u_1 \ldots u_n \mapsto s$ (then deleting $(y : s)$ from the quantifiers' prefix) The new symbol g is called a *skolem* symbol. The principal property of skolemisation is that it *preserves unsatisfiability.*

Skolemisation is widely used in first-order theorem proving and automated deduction systems, frequently as a preprocessing step. The absence of existentially quantified variables enables the use of particularly simple (complete) inference rules and contributes to the overall effectiveness. Skolemization is traditionally used for classical frist order logic; its application on many sorted logic is straightforward (see *Section 3 of [12]*, for example).

Skolemization is straightforwardly lifted to $\mathfrak{B}$-logic. In the cases that universal quantifiers range over the sort *bool* no particular problem seems to be caused as demonstrated below:
Case 1: $(y : s)$, with $s \neq bool$, depends on some $(b : bool)$. Any prenex formula $Q[x, b, y]\mathcal{F}[x, b, y]$ is rewritten as $Q^{<1>}[x, y]\mathcal{F}^{<1>}[x, y]$ where $\mathcal{F}^{<1>}[x, y] \equiv (\mathcal{F}[x, b \mapsto \top, y] \wedge \mathcal{F}[x, b \mapsto \bot, y])$ and the universally quantified variable $(b : bool)$ is eliminated from the quantifiers prefix. The original formula will take a skolemizable form after a finite set of such equivalence preserving transformations.

Additionally, if the existentially quantified variable y ranges over *bool* then the introduction of a skolem function will produce a new "predicate" symbol:
Case 2: $(y : bool)$ occurs in the scope of $(x : u)$ where $u \in S^*$. A new skolem symbol $p : u \rightarrow Boolean$ can be introduced. This would correspond to the introduction of a new predicate in the traditional notation.
Case 3: $(y : bool)$ occurs in the scope of $(x : u)$ where $u \in (SU\{bool\})^*$. The sentence is stepwisely transformed as in Case1 to a from that is skolemizable as in Case2.

Unskolemization is the reverse process of Skolemization:

Given a well formed formula $\mathcal{F}$ (without existential quantifiers) and a set of constant or function symbols $\mathcal{K}$ that occur in $\mathcal{F}$, one attempts to produce a formula $\mathcal{F}'$ by replacing the expressions which use symbols in $\mathcal{K}$ and inserting existential quantifiers in the appropriate places. The reader should note that *Unskolemization preserves unsatisfiability.*

When the symbols to be eliminated were introduced by Skolemisation, unskolemization is almost trivial. If the symbols to be eliminated were not produced by Skolemisation, then unskolemization is not always simple. A sound (but not complete) solution to this problem is given in [9]. The presence of a *Boolean* sort enables the unskolemization of "predicate" symbols as well.

Some results on the methodological extension of logical specifications have been published in [20], focusing on conditions under which some particular extension by function symbols were conservative. When reasoning in $\mathfrak{B}$-logic, these results are generalised to all signature symbols and Unskolemization supports the automatic derivation of conservativity requirements for any finite chain of such extensions ([5]). Being able to construct conservative extensions is fundamental for the refinement of both logical and algebraic specifications.

4.4 Unifying framework for polarity analysis

Operations in a $\mathfrak{B}$-logic relate elements of their domain to elements of their codomain in a functional manner. Analysing the effect of domain disturbances on the codomain of an operator, one may come to useful results about the behaviour of this operator under syntactic changes. The purpose of Polarity Analysis is to study and code how a change of a subexpression affects the semantics of the whole expression. Positive sentences are known to be preserved under structure homomorphisms and theories with positive axioms are known to be extensible. The (top-down) Polarity Analysis [10] originally consisted of assigning positive polarity values to each axiom and deriving polarity values (positive, negative, or neutral) for its subformulae. Manna and Waldinger [10] use Polarity Analysis over formulae to enrich the resolution format with special inference rules for various relations. As we explain in *section 2*, implication can be considered as a partial order over the algebra of Σ-formulae. In $\mathfrak{B}$-logic, the sort *bool* comes with a natural partial order and equality and formulae are (inductively) generated by terms over *bool*. That way, it supports a unifying application of Polarity Analysis in all expressions as in [14].

A dual (bottom up) Analysis of Polarity values of the propositional structure in axioms is well known in mathematical logic. Lyndon's Interpolation theorem [8],[2] is a classic result based on this dual Polarity Analysis. This approach is out of the scope of this paper and, hence, will not be discussed hereafter. It might be interesting, though, to know whether there is an analogue to Lyndon's Interpolation theorem that is based on the top-down polarity analysis. Recall that Lyndon's Interpolation theorem ([8],[2]) holds for first order logic without function symbols and equality. Any analogue that is based on our top-down polarity analysis would cover all signature symbols.

1. R.M. Burstall and J.A. Goguen. Putting theories together to make specifications. In *Proceedings of the Fifth International Joint Conference on Artificial Inteligence*, pages 1045–1058, 1977.

2. C.C. Chang and H.J. Keisler. *Model Theory*, volume 73 of *Studies in Logic (and the foundations of Mathematics)*. North-Holland publishing company, 1973.
3. T. Dimitrakos. Characterising implementations in the framework of (π)-institutions. Submitted to CSL'96.
4. T. Dimitrakos. On the finite cocompleteness of the category of many-sorted theories. In preparation.
5. T. Dimitrakos. *A formal aproach to software design and implementation.* PhD thesis, Imperial College, 1996. DRAFT.
6. J.L. Fiadeiro and T.S.E. Maibaum. Stepwise program development in π-institutions. Technical report, Imperial College, 1990.
7. J.L. Fiadeiro and T.S.E. Maibaum. Generalising interpretations between Theories in the Context of (π-)institutions. In S. Gay G. Burn and M. Ryan, editors, *Theory and Formal Methods*, pages 126–147. Springer-Verlag, 1993.
8. R. C. Lyndon. Properties preserved under homomorphism. *Pacific Journal of Mathematics*, 1959.
9. W. W. MacCune. Un-skolemizing clause sets. *Information Processing Letters*, 29, 1988.
10. Z. Manna and R. Waldinger. Special relations in automated deduction. *Journal of the ACM*, pages 1–59, January 1986.
11. Z. Manna and R. Waldinger. Fundamentals of deductive program synthesis. In F.L. Bauer, editor, *Logic, Algebra and Computation*, volume F79 of *NATO ASI Series*. Springer-Verlag, 1991.
12. Hans Jürgen Ohlbach and Christoph Weidenbach. A note on assumptions about skolem functions. *Journal of Automated Reasoning*, 15:267–295, 1995.
13. D. R. Smith. KIDS: A semiautomatic program development system. *IEEE Transactions on Software Engineering*, 16(9):1024–1043, September 1990.
14. D. R. Smith. Constructing specification morphisms. *Symbolic Computation*, 15(5-6):571–606, May-June 1993.
15. D. R. Smith and M. R. Lowry. Algorithm theories and design tactics. *Science of Computer programming*, 14(2-3):305–321, September 1990.
16. Y.V. Srinivas and R. Jullig. Diagrams for software synthesis. Technical report, Kestrel Institute, Paolo Alto, California, 1993. Appeared also in KBSE'93.
17. Władysław M. Turski and Thomas S. E. Maibaum. *The Specification of Computer Programs*. Addison-Wesley, 1987.
18. P.A.S. Veloso and T.S.E. Maibaum. On the modularisation theorem for logical specifications. *Information Processing Letters 53*, pages 287–293, 1995.
19. P.A.S. Veloso, T.S.E. Maibaum, and M.R. Sadler. Program development and theory manipulation. In *3rd International Workshop on Software Specification and Design*, 1985.
20. P.A.S. Veloso and S. Veloso. On extensions by function symbols: coservativeness and comparison. Technical report, COPPE , Univ. Federal do Rio de Janeiro, July 1990.

STRUCTURED DATABASES: A FRAMEWORK TO REASON ABOUT BELIEF CHANGE
(Preliminary Abstract)

DOV GABBAY, ODINALDO RODRIGUES
Imperial College, Department of Computing,
London SW7 2BZ, UK
dg@doc.ic.ac.uk, O.Rodrigues@doc.ic.ac.uk

In this paper we present Structured Databases (SDBs), a framework to reason about beliefs. We consider a structured belief base approach in which the base is provided together with a total ordering on its components. The components of the base are allowed to be structured bases as well, so that complex inference patterns can be represented. The ordering determines priorities among components. New beliefs can be accepted by incorporating them into the base with highest priority. Each component is resolved into a sentence via a revision operator and the underlying ordering is used to solve conflicts when they arise. The revision operator provided complies with the AGM postulates [4], supports iteration and can be efficiently implemented.

1 Introduction

In [6], Katsuno and Mendelzon provided a semantic characterisation of all belief revision operators satisfying the AGM postulates for belief revision. They consider finite knowledge bases represented as a conjunction of sentences in propositional logic. Even though the postulates do capture the intuitions about a belief revision process, when the belief base is simplified into a single sentence some information is lost, because it is not possible to distinguish the derived beliefs from the basic ones. This is one of the criticisms against the *standard* AGM approach and whether or not the distinction is important corresponds to the two paradigms: coherence and foundations. The coherence theory asserts that the beliefs in the belief state do not need any support other than *coherence* w.r.t. the inference system, whereas the foundations theory claims that some beliefs are held only as a consequence of more basic beliefs, their *justifications*, and thus have a weaker status in the belief state. There are advantages and shortcomings in both theories and we intend to combine their good features in this formalism.

Another issue is that eventually some beliefs will have to be given up (when new contradictory information is to be accepted), but the decision about what beliefs to retract cannot be made based on logical grounds only. One of the alternatives is to use an ordering on the beliefs (epistemic entrenchment) to help make this choice [3, 8]. If we adopt the coherence view, then this means that an ordering on all sentences in the theory corresponding to the belief set is necessary. The problem is that whenever a revision is performed a new ordering to the new (revised) belief state has to be generated. OTPs [9] offer an alternative solution to this problem by ordering the sentences in the base instead. In this formalism, the belief base is as a list of sentences, where those sentences appearing later in the list are assumed to have higher priority than the ones appearing earlier. A Revision is performed by appending a sentence to the previous base and thus giving it highest priority. The ordering ultimately results in a ordering on interpretations of the language, from where the preferred models of the theory are taken. This provides a semantical approach to the problem.

In this work, we present structured databases (SDBs), which offer a syntactical approach to Belief Revision, by using a similar idea to that of OTPs. That is, the Belief Base is a set of components together with a total ordering on them. We allow the components to be nested structured bases as well, so that more complex inference patterns can be represented. Sentences of propositional logic are expressed in Disjunctive Normal Form (DNF). A revision operator provides revisions of sentences which comply with the AGM postulates for Belief Revision. We show that this operator is not associative and discuss the plausibility or not of associativity for revision operators in Section 3. New information can be accepted in the belief state by simply incorporating it into the base with highest priority.

2 Motivation - Why structure is important

In the Introduction we mentioned briefly the difference between the coherence and foundations theories. In this section we go into deeper detail by analysing an example to discuss the importance of structure in achieving rational changes of belief.

Suppose in the current belief state we have the information that `tweety is a penguin`, represented by pt and that `penguins cannot fly`, whose particular instance in which we are interested is `if tweety is a penguin, it does not fly`. This can be represented by $pt \to \neg ft$.

When the two sentences are combined we get the conjunction $pt \wedge \neg ft$:

$$\frac{pt \quad pt \to \neg ft}{pt \wedge \neg ft}$$

Now suppose the agent receives the information that tweety can in fact fly: ft. Intuitively, there are only two possibilities of consistently accepting this sentence if we consider the information previously available:

① either by rejecting pt. That is, `since penguins cannot fly, tweety cannot be a penguin`.

② or by rejecting the fact that penguins cannot fly (`tweety is a penguin and it does fly, so some penguins can fly`).

However, if the belief state is represented solely by the sentence $pt \wedge \neg ft$ (and its logical consequences), it seems to be condensed into the beliefs `tweety is a penguin` and `it cannot fly`. The previous beliefs $pt \rightarrow \neg ft$ are pt are still accepted (they are logical consequences of $pt \wedge \neg ft$), but we have lost, for instance, the information that $\neg ft$ is only a consequence of the initial beliefs pt and $pt \rightarrow \neg ft$.

When the new information arrives, that is, ft, we just keep the belief in pt and reject the belief in $\neg ft$, resulting in $pt \wedge ft$. This seems the minimal change to accommodate the new information into that belief state and is what most formalisms for belief revision would yield given the flat theory presentation $\{pt \wedge \neg ft\}$ [9, 2, 1].

The example also suggests that there are other reasons to adopt a Belief Base approach apart from the fact that it is the only way to store and represent a belief system in a computer. With this view, we have the beliefs in the base providing *justifications* for the beliefs held in the belief state, namely, the set of logical consequences derived from the base.

However, a belief base on its own is not enough to solve the problem, because there is still the issue of choosing between ① and ②. When we have to change our beliefs in light of new contradictory information, we make this choice based on implicit degrees of confidence we associate with the beliefs. One reason for this is because we may trust more in some sources of information than in others. In any case, this extra information does not represent the beliefs in question themselves, but rather it provides information *about* them. We could consider the extra-logical information as beliefs as well (and revise them !), but for the time being we will use this information only to guide the revision process. One way of representing these degrees of confidence is to specify priorities among the beliefs in the base as in [9].

3 Revisions of sentences

In this and the following sections it is more convenient to consider the sentences in a PDB as sets of disjuncts (conjunctions of literals). Thus, a sentence $P_1 \vee P_2 \vee \ldots P_k$ in DNF, will be identified with the set $\{P_1, P_2, \ldots, P_k\}$.

Remark 3.1 *We assume that* **L** *is the language of propositional logic over some finite set of propositional variables* $\mathcal{P}^a$. *A* literal *is a propositional variable or the negation of a propositional variable. The satisfaction and derivability relations* ($\Vdash$ *and* $\vdash$, *resp.) for* **L** *are assumed to have their usual meanings. An interpretation is a function from* $\mathcal{P}$ *to* $\{\mathbf{tt}, \mathbf{ff}\}$, *and* $\mathcal{I}$ *represents the set of all interpretations of* **L**.

Notation 3.2 *We will use letters from the middle of the alphabet, p, q, r, ... to represent propositional variables; capital letters from the middle of the alphabet, P, Q,R, ... to represent disjuncts of propositional logic, and the letter l (possibly subscripted), to represent literals.*

Let's start with the simplest case: we have only two disjuncts P and Q, where Q has higher priority than P. If we want to accept Q, we have to keep its literals. To maintain consistency and keep some of the informative content of P, we *add* the literals in it which are consistent with Q:

Definition 3.3 (Prioritised Revision of Disjuncts) *Let* $P = \bigwedge_i l_i$ *and* Q *be two disjuncts.*

The prioritised revision of P by Q, denoted $\widehat{PQ}^*$, *is a new disjunct* R, *such that*

$$R = \begin{cases} Q, & \Rightarrow \textit{ if } P \textit{ is contradictory} \\ Q \bigwedge \{l_i \mid l_i \textit{(or the literal opposite in sign} \\ \qquad\qquad \textit{to } l_i\textit{) doesn't appear in } Q\}, & \Rightarrow \textit{ otherwise} \end{cases}$$

Notice that the first condition in Definition 3.3 is the only consistency check necessary to achieve (consistent) revisions. It can be easily performed since it amounts to check whether a disjunct has both positive and negative literals of the same propositional variable.

Proposition 3.4 $\widehat{PQ}^* \vdash Q$ *and* $\widehat{PQ}^*$ *is contradictory iff* Q *is contradictory.*

Proof These follow immediately from Definition 3.3, since all literals in Q are preserved and because of the conditions on which literals in P are kept. □

So far we have defined how to resolve disjuncts of sentences, but this is not enough to achieve revisions of *whole sentences*. One thing that still remains to be done is to provide a means of evaluating the degree of information change during the resolution of disjuncts. The idea is to choose those combinations of disjuncts which cause minimum change to the disjunct with lower priority.

If we think semantically, and for the case of propositional logic, this change can be measured by analysing the truth-values of propositional variables of interpretations. One possibility is to consider the "distance" between two

[a]This is required by [6], whose results we use.

interpretations as the number of propositional variables which are assigned different truth-values.

Definition 3.5 *Let M and N be two elements of $\mathcal{I}$. The* distance d between M and N *is the number of propositional variables p_i for which $M(p_i) \neq N(p_i)$.*

Proposition 3.6 *The function d is a metric on $\mathcal{I}$.*

Proof Omitted. See [7, 2] for details. □

Definition 3.7 (Models of a sentence) *Let φ be a sentence of propositional logic. The models of φ,* mod(φ) *are the elements of the following set:* $\text{mod}(\varphi) = \{M \in \mathcal{I} \mid M \Vdash \varphi\}$.

The function d represents essentially the same distance notion defined in [1]. d can be used to evaluate the "distance" between two sentences ψ and φ by analysing the interpretations in the classes of models satisfying them (if any). Since in a Revision of ψ by φ one always tries to accommodate the information in φ and ψ in the best possible way (that is, by choosing models of φ which are closest to models of ψ), we can define the distance *dist* between ψ and φ as the minimum distance d between any two elements of mod(ψ) and mod(φ). The cases when one of the sentences is contradictory (and thus has no models) correspond to the extremes of the revision process and will be treated accordingly.

Definition 3.8 *Let ψ and φ, be two sentences of propositional logic. The* distance *dist* between ψ and φ, *in symbols $dist(\psi, \varphi)$, is defined as*

$$dist(\psi,\varphi) = \begin{cases} \textit{the minimum } d(M,N), \textit{ for } M \in \text{mod}(\psi) \textit{ and } N \in \text{mod}(\varphi), & \Rightarrow \textit{if } \text{mod}(\psi) \textit{ and } \text{mod}(\varphi) \textit{ are both non-empty} \\ \infty, & \Rightarrow \textit{otherwise} \end{cases}$$

If the formulae are only disjuncts, *dist* can be more easily computed:

Proposition 3.9 *Let P and Q be disjuncts.*

$$dist(P,Q) = \begin{cases} \infty, & \Rightarrow \textit{if either } P \textit{ or } Q \textit{ is contradictory (or both)} \\ \textit{number of literals } l_i \textit{ with opposite signs in } P \textit{ and } Q, & \Rightarrow \textit{otherwise} \end{cases}$$

Proof Straightforward. □

Proposition 3.10 *Let φ and ψ be two formulae of propositional logic:*

$$dist(\varphi,\psi) = 0 \textit{ iff } \text{mod}(\varphi) \cap \text{mod}(\psi) \neq \emptyset$$

Proof ($\Rightarrow$) If $\text{mod}(\varphi) \cap \text{mod}(\psi) \neq \emptyset$, then $\exists M \in \mathcal{I}$ such that $M \Vdash \varphi$ and $M \Vdash \psi$. By Definition 3.5, $d(M,M) = 0$. ($\Leftarrow$) If $dist(\varphi,\psi) = 0$, then $\exists M \in \text{mod}(\varphi)$ and $\exists N \in \text{mod}(\psi)$, such that $d(M,N) = 0$. By Proposition 3.6, $M = N$, and then $M \in \text{mod}(\varphi) \cap \text{mod}(\psi)$. □

Now, as expected, the next step is to choose those combinations of disjuncts in ψ and φ with minimum distance. This will ultimately result in choosing the models in $\text{mod}(\psi)$ and $\text{mod}(\varphi)$ with minimum distance.

Definition 3.11 (Choosing disjuncts with minimum distance) *Let ψ and φ be two sentences in DNF. The* disjuncts which correspond to a minimum change of information to ψ or φ, $\text{best\_fit}(\psi, \varphi)$, *are in the following set:*

$$\text{best\_fit}(\psi, \varphi) = \{(P, Q) \mid P \in \psi, Q \in \varphi, \text{ and } dist(P, Q) \text{ is minimum}\}$$

Notice that the order of the disjuncts in the pairs above is important, as it identifies where each disjunct in the pair came from. Remember that in a revision, the sentence which revises has priority over the revised one.

Definition 3.12 (Revisions of sentences) *Let ψ and φ be two sentences in DNF. The* revision of ψ by φ, $\psi \circ_r \varphi$, *is a sentence γ such that:*

$$\gamma \leftrightarrow \bigvee_{(P,Q) \in \text{best\_fit}(\psi,\varphi)} \overset{\curvearrowleft}{PQ}{}^{*}$$

That is, to compute the revision of sentence ψ by φ in DNF, consider the cartesian product of the disjuncts in ψ and φ, then choose those pairs with minimum distance *dist*, and finally take the disjunction of the revision of disjuncts in all such pairs.

Remark 3.13 *Definition 3.12 does not uniquely define a sentence in DNF, since we can take the pairs in* $\text{best\_fit}(\psi, \varphi)$ *in any order. However, all such sentences will be equivalent modulo $\vdash$.*

Example 3.14

$$\begin{array}{ccl} p \wedge q & & dist(p \wedge q, \neg p) = 1 \\ \uparrow & \Rightarrow & dist(p \wedge q, \neg q) = 1 \\ \neg p \vee \neg q & & \text{best\_fit}(p \wedge q, \neg p \vee \neg q) = \{(p \wedge q, \neg p), (p \wedge q, \neg q)\} \\ \hline \multicolumn{3}{c}{p \wedge q \circ_r (\neg p \vee \neg q) \Rightarrow (\neg p \wedge q) \vee (p \wedge \neg q)} \end{array}$$

Theorem 3.15 *The revision operator defined above verifies the AGM postulates for Belief Revision.*

Proof The proof can be done via Katsuno and Mendelzon's semantical characterisation of revision operators [6], and can be found in [2]. □

Corollary 3.16 *If* $\text{mod}(\psi) \cap \text{mod}(\varphi) \neq \emptyset$, *then* $\text{mod}(\psi \circ_r \varphi) = \text{mod}(\varphi \circ_r \psi)$.

Proof By assumption, $\psi \wedge \varphi$ is satisfiable. By one of the postulates ((R2),[6]), it follows that $\text{mod}(\psi \circ_r \varphi) = \text{mod}(\psi) \cap \text{mod}(\varphi) = \text{mod}(\varphi \circ_r \psi)$. □

Obviously, $\circ_r$ has the properties implied by the postulates. We cannot state them here for space limitations. However, we show some other properties of $\circ_r$:

Proposition 3.17 *If* $\text{mod}(\psi) = \emptyset$, *then* $\text{mod}(\psi \circ_r \varphi) = \text{mod}(\varphi)$.

Proof If $\text{mod}(\psi) = \emptyset$, then all disjuncts in ψ are contradictory, and then by Definition 3.3, $\widehat{PQ}^* = Q$, for all $P \in \psi$, $Q \in \varphi$. It follows that $\psi \circ_r \varphi \leftrightarrow \varphi$, and hence $\text{mod}(\psi \circ_r \varphi) = \text{mod}(\varphi)$. □

It could be argued that the revision operator is then too restrictive in the cases where ψ is contradictory, but we believe that without extra structural information about ψ, no information can be reasonably "recovered" from it. As we said, we intend to regard the belief base as a sequence of sentences. Those which are contradictory will be ignored, unless if it is the one with highest priority, in which case compliance with the *success postulate* ((R1)) forces it to be accepted.

Proposition 3.18 *Suppose that* $\text{mod}(\psi)$ *and* $\text{mod}(\varphi)$ *are both non-empty. If* $\text{mod}(\psi \circ_r \varphi) = \text{mod}(\varphi \circ_r \psi)$, *then* $\text{mod}(\psi) \cap \text{mod}(\varphi) \neq \emptyset$.

Proof If $\text{mod}(\psi) \neq \emptyset$, then $\exists M \in \text{mod}(\varphi \circ_r \psi)$ (postulate (R3),[6]). By (R1) $M \in \text{mod}(\psi)$. Since $\text{mod}(\varphi \circ_r \psi) \subseteq \text{mod}(\psi \circ_r \varphi)$, it follows that $M \in \text{mod}(\psi \circ_r \varphi)$. By (R1) again, $M \in \text{mod}(\varphi)$, and hence $M \in \text{mod}(\psi) \cap \text{mod}(\varphi)$. □

Thanks to the two previous results about commutativity of $\circ_r$, we can perceive any set of sentences Γ, such that $\text{mod}(\Gamma) \neq \emptyset$, as a series of revisions of its elements in any order. The models of the series of revisions will be exactly the models of Γ obtained classically. However, $\circ_r$ is not associative:

Proposition 3.19 $\circ_r$ *is not associative.*

Proof We give a simple example as proof, which we use to discuss the subject briefly.

① $(p \circ_r p \to q) \circ_r \neg q$:

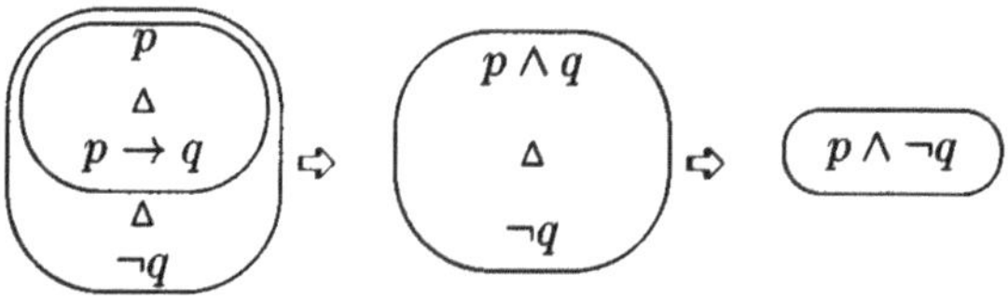

② $p \circ_r (p \to q \circ_r \neg q)$:

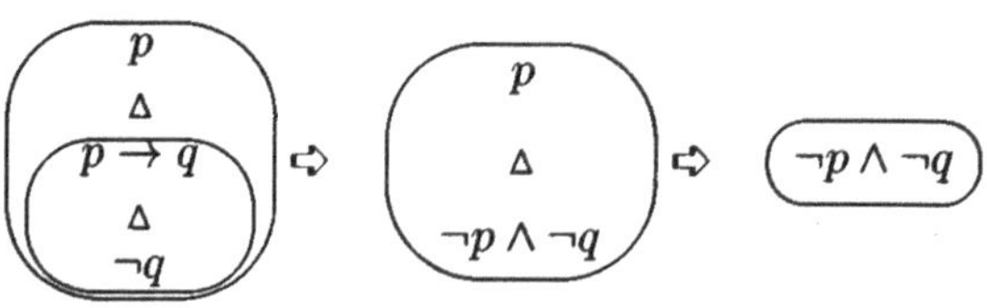

□

In ① above, the agent initially believes in p and $p \to q$, which results in a belief state in which he believes in both propositions p and q. When new information $\neg q$ arrives, he gives up the belief in q, but keeps the belief in p. On the other hand, in ② above, the agent reasons backwards. His priority is to believe in $\neg q$, and subject to this, in $p \to q$. He then is led to believe in $\neg p$ (if he believed in p, he would have to believe in q, which he does not). As he proceeds in his reasoning, he realises that he cannot keep the belief in p, because it contradicts with the other two beliefs.

Even though in the right associative interpretation new information does require a complete recomputation of the belief state, we will advocate for its use, as it leads to a reflection upon the agent's own beliefs.

4 PDBs - Prioritised databases

PDBs were devised having three principles in mind: conservativity, prioritisation and consistency. Conservativity requires that whenever a sentence is inconsistent with sentences having higher priority, as much as possible of its informative content is kept, according to some fixed criterion. Prioritisation ensures that sentences with higher priority have precedence over those with lower priority; and Consistency requires that some mechanism is provided to solve conflicts when they arise. The superimposition of literals provides an efficient way to preserve Consistency and ensure Conservativity at the same time.

Definition 4.1 *A* Prioritised Database (PDB) *is finite list of sentences* $\Gamma = [\varphi_1, \dots, \varphi_k]$*, where each* φ_i *is in DNF.*

As we mentioned before, the order in which the sentences appear in the list is associated with their priority in the PDB. Sentences appearing later in the list have priority over those appearing earlier.

In the previous section, we showed that $\circ_r$ is not associative. Therefore, there are two immediate ways of interpreting the sequence of sentences in a PDB Δ: either perceiving the revision process as a left associative operation or as a right associative one.

We will refer to the first one as *left Delta*, in symbols, $^*\Delta$, and to the second one as *right Delta*, in symbols, Δ^*. Formally,

Definition 4.2 *Let* $\Delta = [\varphi_1, \varphi_2, \dots, \varphi_k]$ *be a PDB.*

$^*\Delta =$	$\Delta^* =$
$\begin{cases} \varphi_k & \Rightarrow \text{ if } k = 1 \\ ((\varphi_1 \circ_r \varphi_2) \circ_r \dots) \circ_r \varphi_k & \Rightarrow \text{ if } k > 1 \end{cases}$	$\begin{cases} \varphi_k & \Rightarrow \text{ if } k = 1 \\ \varphi_1 \circ_r (\dots \circ_r (\varphi_{k-1} \circ_r \varphi_k)) & \Rightarrow \text{ if } k > 1 \end{cases}$

In either case, the last sentence in a PDB is always accepted:

Proposition 4.3 *Let* $\Delta = [\varphi_1, \varphi_2, \ldots, \varphi_k]$ *be a PDB.* $^*\Delta \vdash \varphi_k$ *and* $\Delta^* \vdash \varphi_k$.

Proof By (R1), $\varphi \circ_r \psi \vdash \psi$. Thus, $^*\Delta = ((\varphi_1 \circ_r \varphi_2) \circ_r \ldots) \circ_r \varphi_k \vdash \varphi_k$. On the other hand, $\vdash$ is transitive. Remember that $\varphi_{k-1} \circ_r \varphi_k \vdash \varphi_k$, and $\varphi_1 \circ_r (\ldots \circ_r (\varphi_{k-1} \circ_r \varphi_k)) \vdash (\ldots \circ_r (\varphi_{k-1} \circ_r \varphi_k))$ □

Thus, in order to *accept* new information in a PDB Γ all we have to do is to append the new sentence in DNF, say φ, to Γ.

As suggested in the proof of Proposition 3.19, PDBs could be extended to allow for more complex structures of revisions in a given point. This is the main motivation for the definition of Structured Databases.

5 Structured databases

Definition 5.1 (Structured Databases) *An* structured database (SDB) *is a finite list of objects each of which is either a sentence in DNF; or a list of sentences in DNF, or another SDB.*

Definition 5.2 (Perceiving the information in an SDB) *Let* $\Gamma = [\Delta_1, \Delta_2, \ldots, \Delta_k]$ *be an SDB. The interpretation of the information in* Γ *is a sentence in DNF (denoted* val(Γ)*) and is obtained in the following way:*

$$\text{val}(\Gamma) = \begin{cases} \Delta_k & \Rightarrow \textit{if } k = 1 \textit{ and } \Delta_k \textit{ is a sentence in DNF} \\ \text{val}(\Delta_1) \circ_r (\ldots \circ_r (\text{val}(\Delta_{k-1}) \circ_r \text{val}(\Delta_k))) & \Rightarrow \textit{otherwise} \end{cases}$$

The idea is to reduce each non-terminal element in the SDB to a sentence in DNF, when then the SDB is reduced to a PDB and the right associative interpretation used. Since substructures are allowed, the left associative interpretation can also be obtained if desired by using an appropriate grouping.

Example 5.3 (Obtaining the left associative interpretation) *Let* $\Delta = [\varphi_1, \ldots, \varphi_k]$ *be a PDB. The SDB* $\Gamma = [[[[\varphi_1, \varphi_2], \ldots], \varphi_{k-1}], \varphi_k]$ *corresponds to* $^*\Delta$:

val$(\Gamma) =$

$$\text{val}([[[\varphi_1, \varphi_2], \ldots], \varphi_{k-1}]) \circ_r \text{val}(\varphi_k) = (\text{val}([[\varphi_1, \varphi_2], \ldots]) \circ_r \text{val}(\varphi_{k-1})) \circ_r \varphi_k =$$
$$((\text{val}([\varphi_1, \varphi_2]) \circ_r \ldots) \circ_r \varphi_{k-1}) \circ_r \varphi_k = \ldots = (((\varphi_1 \circ_r \varphi_2) \circ_r \ldots) \circ_r \varphi_{k-1}) \circ_r \varphi_k$$

6 Applications and examples

The extra structure available in a SBD allows for the definition of different classes of priorities among its substructures. This is very useful to represent components with different status in a belief base, as can be seen in the following examples.

Example 6.1 (Extra-logical information for Belief Revision) *We suppose the belief base is represented as the SDB* $\Gamma = [Default, KB, PF]$, *where* $Default$ *represents information with least priority in* Γ, KB *represents general beliefs and* PF *contains protected formulae to be verified in all belief states.*

1. Initially, $Default = [bt \rightarrow ft]$, *representing the sentence* `if tweety is a bird, then it flies`*;* $KB = [bt]$, *representing the information that tweety is a bird; and* $PF = [pt \rightarrow \neg ft]$, *representing the integrity constraint that* `if tweety is a penguin, then it does not fly`. *The integrity constraint is given the highest priority and the default the lowest one.*

The information in KB *is subjected to the protected formulae and then submitted to the defaults. This is to be understood as extracting from the defaults only the information compatible with the knowledge base. Also, only the information in* KB *consistent with the protected formulae is used in the reasoning.*

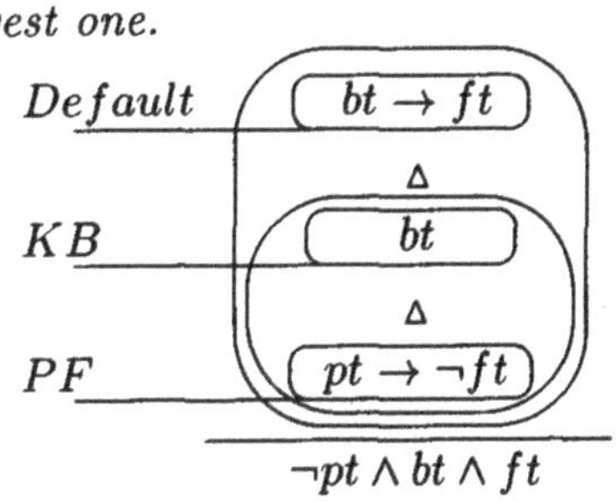

Since he does not know whether or not tweety is a penguin, he assumes that it is not, in order to accept the information represented in the defaults. The result is `tweety is a bird, it is not a penguin and it can fly`.

It can be verified that the three sentences are consistent and the result is exactly the conjunction of all of them.

2. If later on the agent finds out that tweety is in fact a penguin, he can add this information to the knowledge base by appending it to the corresponding list (KB*). This guarantees that it will be accepted in* KB*, but not necessarily in the SDB, as* KB *itself is subject to* PF*. We get the picture on the righ hand side. It is also possible to reject the new information completely if it is found inconsistent with the protected formulae.*

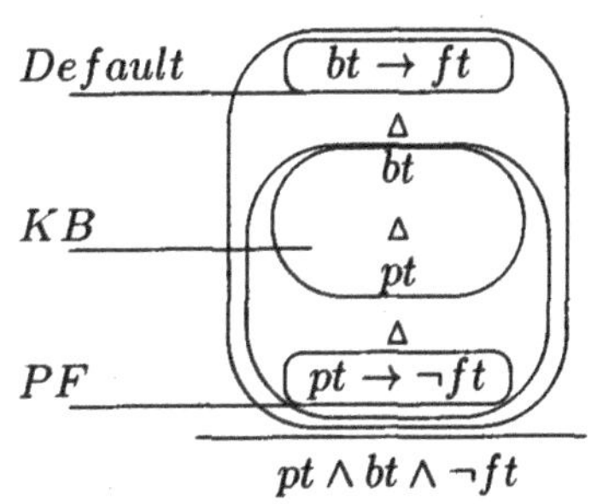

In this case, it is not a matter of verifying or not the principle of primacy of update, but of choosing to decline the revision process *itself when appropriate. Information conveyed by the defaults which is consistent with the belief state would also be incorporated. It is possible to avoid this, by requiring that the revision of the defaults is declined when the defaults are inconsistent with the*

rest of KB. *This can be easily performed:* $\text{mod}(\psi) \cap \text{mod}(\varphi) \neq \emptyset$ *iff there are disjuncts* $P \in \psi$ *and* $Q \in \varphi$, *such that* $dist(P, Q) = 0$.

The final conclusion is `tweety is a bird, it is a penguin and it cannot fly.`

7 Related work

This work has some similarities with Mark Ryan's OTPs [9]. In the general case, OTPs are sets of sentences together with a partial order on them. For Belief Revision, the ordering is required to be total and the set of sentences finite.

The main differences are based on the approach to the problem and the way conflicts are solved. For instance, OTPs are evaluated semantically whereas SDBs offer a syntactical view to the problem. The *conclusions* that can be obtained from a OTP are obtained through preferred models of the theory, whereas in SBDs they are obtained via successive applications of the revision operator.

Moreover, the notion of change is based on natural consequences in OTPs, whereas in SDBs it is based on a distance function (see Section 3). This has some important implications, because as shown in [5], there is a correspondence between revision operators satisfying the AGM postulates and orderings representing "closeness" to the previous belief state. The orderings are required to be total. The ordering resulting from the concept of natural consequence and used in OTPs is partial, whereas the distance function in SDBs generates a total ordering on interpretations. Thus, unlike OTPs, SDBs verify the postulates.

We have also allowed for the definition of another structured base in any given point of the SDB.

8 Conclusions and future work

In this paper we presented a framework to reason about belief change. We outlined the importance of structure to achieve rational changes of belief and provided an initial account to the problem by considering the belief base as an structured set of components. Conflicts among components are solved by a revision operator which complies with the AGM postulates for Belief Revision. The components are hierarchically ordered so that complex priorities among them can be represented.

A straightforward extension to the work may be obtained by allowing other operations among components. These might be of an epistemic nature, such as contraction, or adequate to reasoning about change, e.g. update, which would make the framework suitable to reason about a changing world as well. Such operations have already been defined in a similar way to the revision one shown here and can be found in [2, 7].

As mentioned previously, the distance function results in a total ordering on interpretations of the language w.r.t. to a given theory. Given a sentence ψ, we can obtain the following semantical ordering $\leq_\psi$ on $\mathcal{I}$ w.r.t. to ψ:
$M \leq_\psi N$ iff $M = N$ or $\exists I \in \text{mod}(\psi)$ s.t. $\forall J \in \text{mod}(\psi).dist(M, I) \leq d(N, J)$.

It would be interesting to analyse the relation between such an ordering and the postulates for Epistemic Entrenchment, as well as the consequences resulting from the interaction between it and the ordering on the sentences in the belief base.

Acknowledgements

Odinaldo Rodrigues is supported by CNPq – Conselho Nacional de Desenvolvimento Científico e Tecnológico/Brasil. Dov Gabbay is supported by EPSRC, GR/K57268 (Proof Methods for Temporal Logics of Knowledge and Belief).

References

1. M. Dalal. Investigations into a theory of knowledge base revision: Preliminary report. *Proceedings of the 7th National Conference on Artificial Intelligence*, pages 475–479, 1988.
2. Dov Gabbay and Odinaldo Rodrigues. A methodology for iterated theory change. In Dov M. Gabbay and Hans Jürgen Ohlbach, editors, *Practical Reasoning - First International Conference on Formal and Applied Practical Reasoning, FAPR'96*, Lecture Notes in Artifical Intelligence. Springer Verlag, 1996.
3. P. Gärdenfors and D. Makinson. Revisions of knowledge systems using epistemic entrenchment. In Moshe Y. Vardi, editor, *Proceedings of the Second Conference on Theoretical Aspects of Reasoning About Knowledge*, pages 83–95, Monterey, California, March 1988. Morgan Kaufmann.
4. Peter Gärdenfors. *Knowledge in Flux: Modeling the Dynamics of Epistemic States.* A Bradford Book - The MIT Press, Cambridge, Massachusetts - London, England, 1988.
5. Hirofumi Katsuno and Alberto O. Mendelzon. Propositional knowledge base revision and minimal change. *Artificial Intelligence*, 52:263–294, 1991.
6. Hirofumi Katsuno and Alberto O. Mendelzon. On the difference between updating a knowledge base and revising it. *Belief Revision*, pages 183–203, 1992.
7. Odinaldo Rodrigues. Transfer report: Mphil/phd. Imperial College of Science, Technology and Medicine, December 1995. Department of Computing.
8. Hans Rott. Preferential belief change using generalized epistemic entrenchment. *Journal of Logic, Language and Information*, 1:45–78, 1992.
9. Mark Ryan. *Ordered Presentation of Theories - Default Reasoning and Belief Revision.* PhD thesis, Department of Computing, Imperial College, U.K., 1992.

A CATEGORICAL WORKSPACE FOR SYSTEM CONFIGURATION

GILLIAN HILL

Department of Computer Science, City University Northampton Square, London, EC1V OHB and

Department of Computing, Imperial College, London SW7 2BZ.

System configuration describes the construction of a system from its component parts. This involves keeping the history of system construction and is carried out by applying combinators to recursively defined system components. Diagrams represent specifications and express the history of each construction within a general categorical workspace that is based on the structure of a KZ-monad. A new and simple module concept is presented as a reusable part of a system.

1 Introduction

We are designing a language for the configuration of complex systems [1], and have already suggested a categorical framework for configuration [2]. The possible relationships between the component parts of systems have been identified at an intuitive level by us in order to choose appropriate high-level combinators for configuration [3]. Each high-level combinator is formally defined on recursively defined configured objects of sorts in the set {specification, module}; each configured object is a named theory presentation within a logical framework for systems configuration [4]. Specifications of configured objects are represented in a categorical workspace by recursively defined and structured diagrams, whereas modules are represented by the singleton diagrams created by colimit formation from the diagrams of their specifications. We have already presented the construction of diagrams for specifications and modules in the categorical structure of a KZ-monad [5]. In this paper we define the operations of the combinators and provide further justification for the use of a powerful categorical framework to express precisely the configuration of complex systems.

Our paper is arranged as follows. In Section 2 we present an intuitive view of system configuration, before we define, in Section 3, the logic for configuration. We define the combinators that operate on configured objects in Section 4 and explain how configuration is expressed by formal diagrams. Finally conclusions are drawn in Section 5.

2 An Intuitive View of System Configuration

The building of a system takes place within a development space for configuration in which the architecture of that system, and of each component of the system, is represented by a configured object.

2.1 Configuration

Definition 2.1.1 (A System Configuration) A *system configuration* is a description of how a system is built from its component parts. □

Definition 2.1.2 (A Configured Object) A *configured object* describes the architecture of a system or of a component of a system within a particular system configuration. There are two kinds of configured object : either it is a textual specification or it is a module instance. We express this by saying that each configured object has a sort in the set {specification, module}. An object of sort 'specification' records the history of its configuration; an object of sort 'module' loses that history when the module is created from its specification. The sort of the final configured system object is a module. Because each configured object may be configured in several different ways, the history of an object's configuration may be recorded by several different specifications. Also many module instances may be created from each specification. Each configured object is defined recursively within the uniform development space by means of the combinators of the language for configuration. □

2.2 The Development Space

The *development space* for each system configuration allows the history of the configuration to be expressed diagrammatically. The set of configured objects that describe a particular final configured system object are represented in a three-dimensional development space for that configuration. Objects within the development space are connected to other objects by arrows that lie along the three dimensions of the space, as shown in Figure 1.

The arrows form a series of connected steps from the top left hand corner of the back face of the development space to the bottom right hand corner of the front face. Because each system configuration can be made in several different ways, with the history of each configuration recorded by different specifications, there will be several different series of connected steps within the development space for each system. The arrows that form the steps represent operations to configure objects by the single application of one of the high-level combinators, which are part of the configuration language, and are defined in Section 4.3.

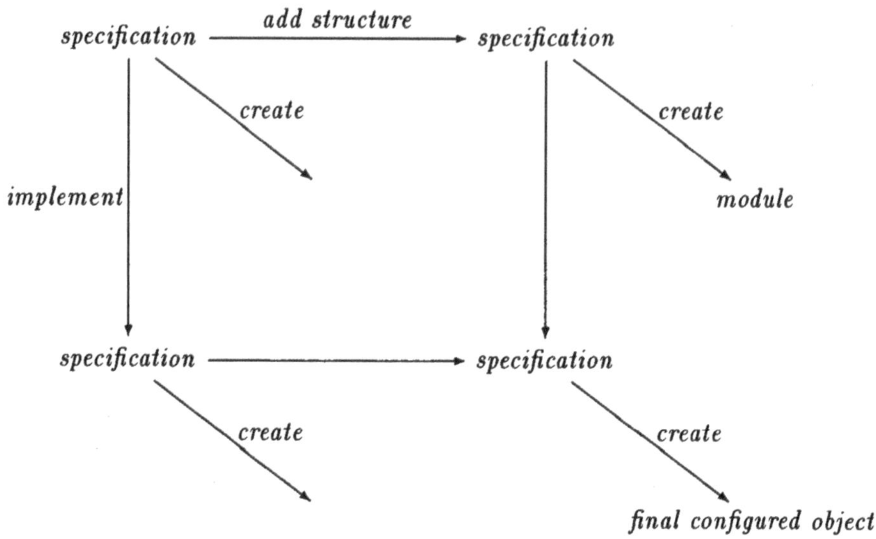

Figure 1: A Three-Dimensional Development Space

Structure is added to a configured object within the space by horizontal development steps; configured objects are implemented by vertical development steps. The specification of each configured object that represents a component part of a system is configured on the back face of its development space; the module is created from a specification by a step in the third dimension to the front face of the space.

The development space for each configured system has a recursive structure that reflects the recursive definition of the final configured object that represents the system. Each configured object that represents a component part of the system has a development space that is nested inside the space for the configuration of the final system. Modules, created in the third dimension of a development space, may themselves be structured and implemented within specifications on the back wall of the 'larger' space within which a more complex specification is configured.

Diagrams in the development space describe the static dependencies between configuration objects by dependency-hierarchies, and the dynamic relationship of actual use in configuration by use-hierarchies. The arrows in the informal hierarchical diagrams represent the high-level combinators.

2.3 The Language for Configuration

The *configuration language* is used to describe the history of the configuration of each configured object. The language uses high-level combinators to express descriptions of configured objects and is at a meta-level to any specification, design or programming language in which descriptions of system components may be expressed.

Within the development space for configuration a system is built by a sequence of individual applications of *high-level combinators* to either a pair of objects or a single configured object. Structure is added to the specifications and modules of configured objects by the application of the high-level combinators for extension and parameterization; vertical development steps are carried out by the high-level combinator for implementation. Modules are created as uniquely named instances from their specifications in the third dimension of the development space by the high-level 'create' combinator. The application of the high-level combinators to configure a particular object is described in the specification for that configured object. Each high-level combinator is defined in terms of low-level (primitive) combinators between configured objects as logical objects. Formal diagrams, with arrows that represent the primitive combinators, express the semantics of the configuration of objects within the formally defined categorical workspace.

We give simple examples of configuration expressed by textual specifications of objects. The advantage of the module concept is illustrated when objects are structured by the high-level combinators for extension and parameterisation. By choosing to extend or to parameterise an object by a module, we ensure that only one module instance is included structurally within that object. If alternatively we extend or parameterise an object by a specification, we allow the possibility that more than one instance of the specification may be created to add structure to that object. Structuring by including specifications provides the potential for data abstraction, therefore, whereas structuring by modules merely gains data encapsulation for the included component part. In order to preserve this choice for structuring objects within the development space for configuration we ensure that vertical development steps are defined within the configuration language only between specifications or between modules.

Example 2.3.1 A house structured by rooms may be represented by the object 'housestructure'. The textual specification for this object will express the high-level structuring by parameterization as **spec house[spec room]**. In terms of the primitive combinators the object is structured by conservatively extending the specification for a room as the parameter to the specification for a house. Instantiation of a room (a generic parameter) requires the addition of more concrete detail and is expressed by the primitive combinator for interpretation. The expression **spec** house $_{\textbf{spec}\ \text{room}}$ [**spec** bedroom] is the result of instantiating a room by a bedroom. The name of the specification that contains this expression in the configuration language could be **spec** house_with_bedroom. □

Example 2.3.2 The number of rooms in the house is specified by creating the required number of module instances of a room as the parameters to a house. It follows that **obj** house_with_one_room is fixed in its structure by applying the create combinator to **spec** room to form a single module instance of a room and then conservatively extending this module to configure the parameterized structure **spec** house[**module** room1]. Instantiation of the module instance of a room by a module instance of a bedroom is recorded by the expression **spec** house $_{\textbf{module}\ \text{room1}}$ [**module** bedroom1]. The name of the specification that contains this expression in the configuration language could be **spec** house_with_one_bedroom. This would make explicit the restriction of this structure to only one bedroom. The objects **obj** house_with_bedroom and **obj** house_with_one_bedroom have the same structure but are configured by their different specifications. The naming scheme used requires them to have different names. □

3 The Logic for Configuration

We present the underlying definitions for many-sorted first-order theory presentations in a linguistic system.

3.1 Many-Sorted First-Order Languages

Definition 3.1.1 (A Linguistic System) A *linguistic system* is a pair $LS = (L, \vdash)$ where

L is a family of first-order *languages*

$\vdash$ is the *consequence relation* over the set *Form* of formulae for L □

Definition 3.1.2 (A Many-Sorted Similarity Type) A *many-sorted similarity type* is the triple (S, ar_r, ar_f) where S is a non-empty set of *sorts* and ar_r and ar_f are *arity functions*. The elements in the domains of ar_r and ar_f are the *relation symbols* and the *function symbols* respectively. If the similarity type is called σ then we denote the domains by *rel* σ and *func* σ. The arity functions assign the sorts of the arguments to each symbol in *rel* $\sigma \cup$ *func* σ and, in addition, for symbols in *func* σ the result sort.

If σ is a many-sorted similarity type,

$$\begin{array}{rcl} sort\ \sigma & \rightleftharpoons & S \\ rel\ \sigma & \rightleftharpoons & dom\ ar_r \\ func\ \sigma & \rightleftharpoons & dom\ ar_f \\ \mid A \mid & \rightleftharpoons & cardinality\ of\ the\ set\ A \\ A^+ & \rightleftharpoons & the\ set\ of\ all\ non\text{-}empty\ finite\ sequences\ of\ elements\ of\ A \\ \langle s_1, \ldots, s_n \rangle & \rightleftharpoons & sequence\ of\ elements\ of\ A\ of\ length\ n \\ \lambda & \rightleftharpoons & the\ empty\ sequence\ of\ length\ 0 \\ A^* & \rightleftharpoons & A^+ \cup \{\lambda\} \end{array}$$

where $\rightleftharpoons$ means 'is equal by definition'. □

Definition 3.1.3 (The Arity Functions for a Many-Sorted Similarity Type) Let σ be a similarity type and let $t = \langle s_1, \ldots, s_n \rangle$ be a non-empty finite sequence, where $s_i \in S$ for $i = 1, \ldots, n$. Then $t \in S^+$ is a finite sequence of sort symbols of the similarity type σ. All the relations on the specific sequence, t, are described as being of the same *arity*. Similarly, any function symbols whose domains are the sequence t and whose ranges are a unique sort $s \in S$, are of the same arity. The *arity functions* for σ are defined so that

$$\begin{array}{lcl} rng\ ar_r & \subseteq & S^* \\ rng\ ar_f & \subseteq & (S^* \setminus \{\lambda\}) = S^+ \text{where } \setminus \text{ is set difference} \\ dom\ ar_r \cap dom\ ar_f & = & \emptyset \\ \text{If } r \in\ rel\ \sigma \text{ then } ar_r(r) & = & \langle s_1, \ldots, s_n \rangle = t \text{ denoted by } r^t \\ \text{If } f \in\ func\ \sigma \text{ then } ar_f(f) & = & \langle s_1, \ldots, s_n\ ;\ s_{n+1} \rangle = t\ ;\ s_{n+1} \text{ denoted } f^{t;s_{n+1}} \end{array}$$

where $s_i \in\ sort\ \sigma,\ i = 1, \ldots, n+1,$ and $n + 1 < \omega_0$.

We use the notation ; to separate the ordered n-tuple of sorts in the domain of a function from the sort in its range. A function symbol c with $ar_f(c) = \langle s \rangle$ is called an s-sorted constant symbol. □

3.2 The Logic

The definition of a many-sorted theory presentation will be used to define a configured object within the logic for configuration. We define a theory by its own presentation in order to distinguish sentences that are the basic axioms from sentences that are the derived theorems. In our view a theory presentation is closer to the notion of a configured object, either as a textual specification or its module instance, than its underlying theory. We therefore choose to identify a specification with a theory presentation within a system configuration.

Definition 3.2.1 (A Many-Sorted First-Order Theory Presentation and its Theory in a Linguistic System) Let σ be a many-sorted similarity type and LS be a many-sorted linguistic system over a family of first-order languages. Then a *many-sorted first-order theory presentation in* LS and over σ is the pair $T = (\sigma, \Gamma)$ where $\Gamma \subseteq Form_\sigma$ is the set of non-logical axioms. The theory presented by T is the pair (σ, Γ°) where Γ° is the closure of the non-logical axioms under the consequence relation and is defined by $\{\varphi \in Form_\sigma \mid \Gamma \vdash_\sigma \varphi\}$. □

The *logic* chosen to express our configuration theory is many-sorted first-order logic. We have already defined the operations of interpretation, extension and conservative extension between many-sorted first-order theory presentations in detail [4]. First-order logic is chosen for configuration because it possesses the Craig interpolation property. This ensures that the structure of objects that have been extended conservatively is preserved if subsequently operated on via interpretations.

Example 3.2.2 The simple specification for a stack as a 'first-in-last-out' structure is given by its theory presentation.

spec stack is
stack[element]
$T_{\text{stack,filo}} = (\sigma_{\text{stack}}, \Gamma_{\text{stack,filo}})$ where

$$\sigma_{\text{stack}} = (S, ar_r, ar_f)$$

and

$$\begin{array}{lcl} S & = & \{s, e\} \\ rel\ \sigma_{\text{stack}} & = & \{stack^s, elem^s\} \\ func\ \sigma_{\text{stack}} & = & \{\lambda^s, push^{s,e;s}, delete^{s;s}, top^{s;e}\} \end{array}$$

The set $\Gamma_{\text{stack,filo}}$ is the set of axioms for a stack.
endspec □

4 The Combinators For System Configuration

We define the application of high-level combinators to configure objects that are in the form either of textual specifications or their module instances. Each high-level combinator is defined notationally in terms of primitive combinators that are based on the meta-logical operation of interpretation between many-sorted first-order theory presentations. Each configured object is defined in its primitive form by giving a unique name to a many-sorted first-order theory presentation. The actual configuration of each primitive object is expressed within its textual specification, and is represented precisely by a formal diagram in the configuration workspace.

4.1 Primitive Combinators Operate on Theory Presentations

First we define the primitive combinators for configuration as functions on the space of theory presentations, **Theor**. The elements of **Theor** belong to the same equivalence class if and only if they have the same underlying theory modulo the renaming of symbols in the similarity type.

Definition 4.1.1 (The Primitive Combinator for Interpretation) Let $T_1 = (\sigma_1, \Gamma_1)$, and $T_2 = (\sigma_2, \Gamma_2)$ be elements in **Theor**. The *primitive combinator for interpretation* is defined as an interpretation $i : T_1 \rightarrow T_2$. The result of the interpretation is the theory $i(T_1)$. □

Definition 4.1.2 (The Primitive Combinator for Extension) Let $T_1 = (\sigma_1, \Gamma_1)$, $T_2 = (\sigma_2, \Gamma_2)$ and $T_3 = (\sigma_3, \Gamma_3)$ be elements in **Theor**. The *primitive combinator for extension* is defined as the extension T_2 of T_1 and denoted by T_1 *e to* T_2. If T_1 is extended by T_2 to form T_3 then the result of the primitive combinator for extension is defined as the extension T_3 of T_1 by T_2. If T_3 is a conservative extension of T_1 this defines the primitive combinator for conservative extension and is denoted by T_1 *c . e to* T_3. □

4.2 The Primitive Objects are Named Theory Presentations

Before we define the high-level combinators on configured objects we need to add names to theory presentations in order to identify the configured objects and also to use some notation to define the high-level combinators on objects in terms of the primitive combinators that operate on theory presentations.

We define the primitive objects as elements in the space of named theory presentations, **Primobj**. The elements of **Primobj** belong to the same equivalence class if and only if they have the same underlying theory modulo the naming of the theory presentation. The elements of **Primobj** are two-sorted elements that are either in the form of textual specifications, that contain no information about configuration, or are in the form of uniquely named module instances of a specification.

4.3 Defining the High-Level Combinators

We define the high-level combinators on the elements in the space **Primobj**. Since the vertical development steps in the three-dimensional development space are defined only between specifications or between modules, the primitive combinator for interpretation must be restricted in its definition. This ensures that a specification cannot be instantiated or implemented by a module, and also that a module cannot be instantiated or implemented by a specification.

Definition 4.3.1 (The High-level Combinator for Extension) The high-level combinator for extension expresses the inclusion of a set of properties, or an entire object, in another object. This inclusion may be made conservatively or non-conservatively and is defined by either the conservative or non-conservative primitive combinators for extension. Let O_1 and O_2 be elements in **Primobj** such that O_1 is *extended to* O_2 by the high-level combinator. Then we denote this by O_1 *ext. to* O_2, and define the extension by O_1 *e to* O_2 or O_1 *c . e to* O_2. □

Definition 4.3.2 (The High-level Combinator for Parameterization) Let O_1 and O_2 be elements in **Primobj**. Then the *parameterization* of O_1 by O_2 expresses the use of O_2, identified as a parameter to the object O_1, to give extra properties to O_1. Parameterization of O_1 by more than one parameter, can also express the composition of those parameters to form the structured object O_1. The parameterization of O_1 by O_2, denoted by $O_1[O_2]$, is the object O_3 that is defined by O_2 *c . e to* O_1. If the object O_2 is a generic parameter to the object O_1, it may be replaced in a later configuration by *instantiation* using the object $i(O_2) = O_4$. The instantiated parameter to O_1 is now part of the configured object O_5, denoted by ${O_1}_{O_2}[O_4]$ to express the instantiation of O_2 by O_4. □

Definition 4.3.3 (The High-level Combinator for Implementation) Let O_1 and O_2 be elements in **Primobj**. The *implementation* of O_1 by the object O_2, denoted by O_1 *impl. by* O_2, is expressed by the object O_4. It is defined by the pair of primitive combinators i and $c\ .\ e$ and the result is denoted by $(i,\ c\ .\ e)O_1 = O_2$. The pair $(i,\ c\ .\ e)$ is well-defined if there exists an object O_3 such that O_1 *i to* O_3 and O_2 *c . e to* O_3. □

The Craig interpolation property is shown by Maibaum *et al*[6] to be a necessary and sufficient condition for the correct composition of implementation steps.

Definition 4.3.4 (The High-level Combinator for Creating Modules) Let O_1 be an object formed by giving a unique name to the theory presentation $T_1 = (\sigma_1, \Gamma_1)$. The *creation* of a module from O_1 by the high-level combinator is defined by *create*(**spec** $\mathsf{O_1}$, (**module** $\mathsf{O_1 1} \ldots$ **module** $\mathsf{O_1 n}$)) = **module** $\mathsf{O_1(n+1)}$) where $n \geq 0$. The second argument to the combinator is the possibly empty string formed by concatenating the names of the n modules that have been created previously as instances of the specification of the object and used within the particular configuration. □

4.4 Configured Objects are Specifications and Modules

Those two-sorted objects that are configured by structuring and by implementation belong to the set **Obj**. They are configured within the three-dimensional development space by the application of the high-level combinators. The specifications are textual in form and express the history of configuration.

Example 4.4.1 (from Example 2.3.2) The specification for a one-bedroomed house may express the following sequence of configurations.

spec house_with_one_bedroom is
create(**spec** room, λ) = **module** room1;
spec house[**module** room1];
create(**spec** bedroom, λ) = **module** bedroom1;
i(**module** room1)= **module** bedroom1;
spec house $_{\textbf{module}\ \text{room1}}$ [**module** bedroom1].
endspec

In **spec** house_with_one_bedroom it is explicitly stated that the only parameter is a module. A two-roomed bungalow could be configured from a house by creating two module instances of a room and instantiating these by creating module instances for a kitchen and a bedroom. □

4.5 Configured Objects are Represented by Formal Diagrams

The operation of the high-level combinators on the configured objects is represented in a space of named diagrams, **Diag**. The elements of the space **Primobj** are represented in this space by diagrams with a single node. Configured objects, as elements of **Obj**, are represented in **Diag** by flat diagrams that express the entire history of the objects configuration. The elements of **Diag** belong to the same equivalence class if and only if they have the same shape but are named differently at the nodes.

Definition 4.5.1 (The Formal Diagrams for Configuration) The *formal diagrams for configuration* are elements in the space **Diag** and represent the specifications and modules of the configured objects. The diagrams are constructed in two-dimensions as single nodes or by drawing arrows between nodes. The horizontal arrows express the operation of the primitive combinators for extension, that are denoted either by e or by c . e. Vertical arrows express the primitive combinator for interpretation, that is denoted by i. Each arrow in a diagram is labelled by the symbol for the primitive combinator as well as by the diagrams that are the source and target of the arrow. The formal diagrams have the same names as the objects whose specifications or modules they represent and are labelled by sorts in the set {s,m}. □

Structured diagrams are built from components that share sub-components by the pushout construction in category theory.

Example 4.5.2 (from Example 4.4.1)

$$\begin{array}{ccc} room1^{m} & \xrightarrow{c\,.\,e^{room1^{m}}_{house\_with\_one\_room^{s}}} & house\_with\_one\_room^{s} \\ \Big\downarrow i^{room1^{m}}_{bedroom1^{m}} & & \Big\downarrow i^{house\_with\_one\_room^{s}}_{house\_with\_one\_bedroom^{s}} \\ bedroom1^{m} & \xrightarrow{c\,.\,e^{bedroom1^{m}}_{house\_with\_one\_bedroom^{s}}} & house\_with\_one\_bedroom^{s} \end{array}$$

is the pushout diagram representing the instantiation of a room by a bedroom in the specification of a one-bedroomed house. □

Flat diagrams do not express the recursive structuring of systems from their component parts, however. Although a KZ-monad, characterised by Kock [7], is itself a complicated structure, we have shown that it will represent specifications at different levels of configuration, as well as provide the mappings that both build the categorical diagrams and also flatten out the complexity of the diagrams, and finally compute their colimits [5]. The creation of uniquely named module instances from the specification of an object is represented by the construction of isomorphic colimits for the specification diagram.

The KZ-workspace for configuration consists of the categories $\mathcal{C}, \mathcal{C}_{\mathcal{D}}, \ldots \mathcal{C}_{\mathcal{D}^n}$ and the adjoint functors between them. The base category $\mathcal{C}$ is the category of objects in **Primobj**. Diagrams in $\mathcal{C}$ are the objects in $\mathcal{C}_{\mathcal{D}}$, and diagrams in $\mathcal{C}_{\mathcal{D}^{n-1}}$ are the elements in $\mathcal{C}_{\mathcal{D}^n}$. The property of adjointness in the KZ-monad provides the functors between the categories that 'make' the diagrams and also flatten the structured diagrams into $\mathcal{C}_{\mathcal{D}}$, which represents the space **Diag**. The colimit objects of diagrams in $\mathcal{C}_{\mathcal{D}}$, are constructed in $\mathcal{C}$.

$$\mathcal{C} \; \underset{lim_{\rightarrow}}{\overset{make-diagram_{\mathcal{C}}}{\rightleftarrows}} \; \mathcal{C}_{\mathcal{D}} \; \underset{flatten-diagram}{\overset{make-diagram_{\mathcal{C}_{\mathcal{D}}}}{\rightleftarrows}} \; \mathcal{C}_{\mathcal{D}\mathcal{D}} \cdots \mathcal{C}_{\mathcal{D}^n}$$

5 Conclusions

We have shown how foundational work from logic and category theory can be applied to the practical problem of constructing complex software engineering systems from their component parts. The powerful framework of a KZ-monad expresses precisely the recursive structuring of complex systems.

Acknowledgments

The many discussions with Tom Maibaum have been very stimulating. Dimitris Raptis provided useful comments on a final draft of the paper. Paul Taylor's macros were used for the diagrams.

1. G. Hill. *A Language for System Configuration*. PhD thesis, Department of Computing, Imperial College, University of London, 1996. draft.
2. G. Hill. Category theory for the configuration of complex systems. In T. Rus M. Nivat, C Rattray and G. Scollo, editors, *Algebraic Methodology and Software Technology, Entschede, 1993*, pages 193–200. Proceedings of the Third International Conference on Algebraic Methodology and Software Technology, University of Twente, The Netherlands, 21–25 June 1993, Springer-Verlag, 1994. Workshops in Computing series.
3. G. Hill. The configuration of complex systems. In T. Ören, editor, *CAST '94 Lecture Notes*. Fourth International Workshop on Computer Aided Systems Technology, University of Ottawa, Ottawa, Ontario, Canada, 16–20 May, 1994. to be published in 1996 by Springer-Verlag.
4. G. Hill. A logical approach to systems construction. In Rudolph Albecht and Franz Pichler, editors, *Proceedings of EUROCAST '95 LNCS 1030*, pages 30–47. Fifth International Workshop on Computer Aided Systems Theory, Innsbruck, May 1995, Springer-Verlag, January 1996.
5. G. Hill. Constructing specifications and modules in a KZ-doctrine. In C. L. Hankin, I. Mackie, and R. Nagarajan, editors, *Theory and Formal Methods '94*, pages 219–236. Proceedings of the Second Imperial College, Department of Computing, Workshop on Theory and Formal Methods, Imperial College Press, distributed by World Scientific Publishing Co. ISBN 1-86094-003-X, September 1995.
6. T. Maibaum, J. Fiadeiro, and M. Sadler. Stepwise program development in Π institutions. Technical report, Imperial College, November 1990.
7. A. Kock. Monads for which structures are adjoint to units, (version 3). *Aarhus Preprint Series*, pages 1–24, June 1993.

EXTENDING B AMN WITH CONCURRENCY

K. LANO
Department of Computing, Imperial College, London SW7 2BZ.

J. FIADEIRO
Dept. of Informatics, Faculty of Sciences, University of Lisbon

J. DICK
B-Core (UK) Ltd., Oxford Science Park, Oxford OX4 4GA

This paper outlines an approach to concurrent specification in B Abstract Machine Notation (AMN), using a combination of linear temporal logic and Ada style task definitions.

1 Introduction

The B Abstract Machine Notation (AMN) is a formal specification and development language which is related to VDM [11] and Z [17], and incorporates modularity mechanisms which support the construction of large systems. It has been used to develop automatic train control systems [2,4,3], medical information systems and modules of the CICS software [10]. B is a sequential specification language in that operations are regarded as single atomic actions, and it is not possible, at the implementation level, for two or more machines to be executing concurrently. The extensions described in this paper will allow concurrent execution between machine implementations, but not concurrent execution within a machine.

Industrial users of B have identified the lack of treatment of concurrency as the major outstanding problem with the language [10]. Although reactive systems have been developed using B AMN, the lack of support for concurrency has limited the general application of the language in this domain, and the extent to which industrial users can benefit from the language.

2 B Abstract Machine Notation

2.1 Syntax

B AMN uses a mathematical notation and logic which is similar to that of Z. A major distinction between B and Z is in the use of 'abstract machines' or specification modules, rather than schemas, as the means of decomposing a system description. These modules have the schematic form:

```
MACHINE M(p)
SETS St
CONSTANTS k
PROPERTIES B
VARIABLES v
INVARIANT I
INITIALISATION T
OPERATIONS
  y ← op(x) =
      PRE P
      THEN
         S
      END
  ....
END
```

The modules encapsulate constant data (described in the SETS, CONSTANTS and PROPERTIES clauses), varying data (described in the VARIABLES and INVARIANT clauses), and provide a public interface consisting of a set of OPERATIONS with inputs **x** and outputs **y**. The INITIALISATION describes how the module is to be initialised. Operations are defined using a mathematical programming language termed the 'generalised substitution notation'. A *generalised substitution* is an abstract mathematical programming construct, built up from basic substitutions **x** := **e**, corresponding to assignments to state variables, via the following constructs:

SKIP	No-op
CHOICE $\mathbf{S}_1$ OR $\mathbf{S}_2$ END	Bounded choice
PRE **P** THEN **S** END	Preconditioning
SELECT **P** THEN **S** END	Guarding
ANY **v** WHERE **P** THEN **S** END	Unbounded non-determinism
$\mathbf{S}_1$; $\mathbf{S}_2$	Sequential composition
$\mathbf{S}_1$ || $\mathbf{S}_2$	Multiple generalised substitution
WHILE **E** DO **S** INVARIANT **I** VARIANT **v** END	Looping

where **S**, $\mathbf{S}_1$ and $\mathbf{S}_2$ represent generalised substitutions, e an expression, **I**, **E** and **P** predicates, and **v** a variable or list of variables.

Machines can import features from other machines by means of the SEES, INCLUDES, EXTENDS and IMPORTS clauses, and others. Operations with input variables **x** and output variables **y** can be invoked with actual parameters **a** and **b**, in machines that access a machine in which **op** is defined, by statements of the form

$$\mathbf{b} \longleftarrow \mathbf{op(a)}$$

More details on the notation are given in [12]. As in the object calculus [7], the *locality principle* is used in B AMN: it is not possible for operations of a machine directly to update variables which have been imported from another machine. Instead, these variables can only be updated by invoking an operation of the machine in which they were declared. This is termed the principle of *semi-hiding* in B. It needs further restriction however once we allow two machines to concurrently execute: any machine **M** containing a thread must only allow access to its variables via enquiry operations, since otherwise machines that INCLUDE or otherwise access it could concurrently read its data whilst an update operation of **M** is in progress.

Sequential composition can only be used in REFINEMENT and IMPLEMENTATION components (representing intermediate and final development steps, respectively), and WHILE loops only in IMPLEMENTATIONs. Abstract constructs (PRE, CHOICE, ANY, SELECT and ||) cannot be used in an IMPLEMENTATION.

The semantics of substitutions **S** is specified by means of weakest preconditions, [S]**P**, for predicates **P**, defined as follows:

$$
\begin{array}{lcl}
[\mathbf{x} := \mathrm{e}]\mathbf{P} & \equiv & \mathbf{P}[\mathrm{e}/\mathbf{x}] \\
[\mathrm{SKIP}]\mathbf{P} & \equiv & \mathbf{P} \\
[\mathrm{CHOICE}\ \mathbf{S}_1\ \mathrm{OR}\ \mathbf{S}_2\ \mathrm{END}]\mathbf{P} & \equiv & [\mathbf{S}_1]\mathbf{P} \land [\mathbf{S}_2]\mathbf{P} \\
[\mathrm{PRE}\ \mathbf{E}\ \mathrm{THEN}\ \mathbf{S}\ \mathrm{END}]\mathbf{P} & \equiv & \mathbf{E} \land [\mathbf{S}]\mathbf{P} \\
[\mathrm{SELECT}\ \mathbf{E}\ \mathrm{THEN}\ \mathbf{S}\ \mathrm{END}]\mathbf{P} & \equiv & \mathbf{E} \Rightarrow [\mathbf{S}]\mathbf{P} \\
[\mathrm{ANY}\ \mathbf{v}\ \mathrm{WHERE}\ \mathbf{E}\ \mathrm{THEN}\ \mathbf{S}\ \mathrm{END}]\mathbf{P} & \equiv & \forall \mathbf{v}.(\mathbf{E} \Rightarrow [\mathbf{S}]\mathbf{P}) \\
[\mathbf{S}_1;\ \mathbf{S}_2]\mathbf{P} & \equiv & [\mathbf{S}_1][\mathbf{S}_2]\mathbf{P} \\
[\mathrm{WHILE}\ \mathbf{E}\ \mathrm{DO}\ \mathbf{S} & & \\
\quad \mathrm{INVARIANT}\ \mathbf{I} & & \\
\quad \mathrm{VARIANT}\ \mathbf{v}\ \mathrm{END}]\mathbf{P} & \Leftarrow & \mathbf{I}\ \land \\
 & & \forall \ell.(\mathbf{I} \land \mathbf{E} \Rightarrow [\mathbf{S}]\mathbf{I})\ \land \\
 & & \forall \ell.(\mathbf{I} \land \neg\, \mathbf{E} \Rightarrow \mathbf{P})\ \land \\
 & & \forall \ell.(\mathbf{I} \land \mathbf{E} \Rightarrow \mathbf{v} \in \mathbb{N})\ \land \\
 & & \forall \ell.(\mathbf{I} \land \mathbf{E} \land \mathbf{v} = \gamma \Rightarrow [\mathbf{S}](\mathbf{v} < \gamma))
\end{array}
$$

In the case of ANY, **v** is not free in **P**, and in the last case, γ is a new variable not free in the WHILE substitution or the predicates concerned, and ℓ is the list of variables modified within the loop.

The semantics of || is defined partly by the requirement:

$$\mathbf{prd}_{\mathbf{x},\mathbf{y}}(\mathbf{S}_1 \mid\mid \mathbf{S}_2) \equiv \mathbf{prd}_{\mathbf{x}}(\mathbf{S}_1) \land \mathbf{prd}_{\mathbf{y}}(\mathbf{S}_2)$$

where $\mathbf{x}$ is the list of variables updated in $\mathbf{S_1}$, and $\mathbf{y}$ those in $\mathbf{S_2}$. $\mathbf{prd_v}$ converts a generalised substitution $\mathbf{S}$ on variables $\mathbf{v}$ into a predicate on $\mathbf{v}$ and $\mathbf{v'}$ which expresses the effect of the substitution as a relation between initial states $\mathbf{v}$ and final states $\mathbf{v'}$:

$$\mathbf{prd_x(S)} \equiv \neg [\mathbf{S}] \neg (\mathbf{x'} = \mathbf{x})$$

$[\mathbf{S}]\mathbf{P}$ means "**S** establishes **P**" or, that every execution of **S** terminates in a state satisfying **P**. As a result, we can interpret SELECT **P** THEN **S** END as meaning "wait for **P** to become true, and then execute **S**". That is, the only execution paths through the guarded statement are those beginning in a state satisfying **P**. (In contrast, PRE **P** THEN **S** END may execute when the prestate does not satisfy **P**, however there is then no guarantee over its behaviour: it may block, fail to terminate or produce an arbitrary result).

3 Extending B with Concurrency

The advantage of B over other formal languages such as Z and RSL[9] is primarily its emphasis on a small, easily learnt, set of notations (which also makes tool development for the language more practicable). Thus care has to be taken in extending B not to change this property. In particular, we want to add concurrency in an orthogonal manner, with as little modification to the original language as possible in the case of sequential specifications (cf. the Eiffel approach[14]).

Thus we do not take the approach of RSL and closely integrate concurrent and sequential language elements. Instead we propose four new notations, based on elements of the VDM^{++} language[6], but given a uniform semantics in the object calculus[7]. These are traces, permission guards, histories, and threads.

There is a close relationship between B AMN and the object calculus, both in terms of the (object-based) modularity approach of both formalisms, their refinement concepts, and in terms of their mathematical basis. Integration of these formalisms provides a means to specify safety properties, permission constraints on operations, and many other constraints on the possible sequences of operations which a module can execute.

Sections 3.1, 3.2, 3.3 and 3.4 introduce these notations and give illustrative examples of their use. Section 4 describes the semantics of these extensions.

3.1 Trace Specifications

A *trace* specification describes in a concise manner the allowed histories of a B module. It consists of a list of trace set definitions and an overall history specification of the possible histories.

A trace set definition has the form

Identifier = **TraceSetExpression**

where a trace set expression is either an explicit definition

(**trace**, **alphabet**)

of a trace and an alphabet, or is built up from trace set identifiers and explicit trace set definitions using operators such as **w** (weave, or synchronised interleaving[16]).

An alphabet is a set of operation names from the machine and a trace is a regular expression in operation names, built using the operators ; (sequence), * (iteration zero or more times), + (iteration one or more times) and | (binary choice). By default the **alphabet** is the set of operation names mentioned in the **trace**, and only needs to be explicitly written if this is not the case.

Thus a machine with cyclic behavior could be specified as:

```
MACHINE Cyclic
OPERATIONS
    opa;
    opb;
    opc
TRACES
     GENERAL (opa; opb; opc)*
END
```

The GENERAL clause defines the overall machine trace set. An operation name listed without a definition defaults to the completely non-deterministic operation on the state.

An example of the effect of the **w** operator is the following combination, corresponding to the concurrent composition of two binary statecharts which share the **opb** transition:

(**opa**; **opb**)* **w** (**opb**; **opc**)* =
opa; (**opb**; ((**opa**; **opc**) | (**opc**; **opa**)))*

3.2 Permission Guards

A permission guard **G** on an operation **op** is a condition which must be satisfied before execution of **op** can proceed. In the case that **G** refers only to the current values of machine variables this form of specification is already available in B via select statements: we simply define **op** using the construct SELECT **G** THEN **S** END.

In the case that **G** refers to a previous history of actions however it is not so direct to express guarding by a SELECT statement, and so a separate part of a machine definition giving permission guards is useful. This has the form

```
GUARDS
    op  ⇒  Guard;
    ⋮
```

where each **op** is an operation name (possibly with input parameters), and **Guard** is a condition involving the state variables, operation parameters, and counts **count**(**op**′) of the number of completed executions of operations **op**′ of the machine.

For example, the condition that there can be a lag of at most **del** between each occurrence of **opa** and a "responding" occurrence of **opb** is specified using:

```
MACHINE Delay(del)
OPERATIONS
  opa;
  opb
GUARDS
  opa  ⇒  count(opa) < count(opb) + del
END
```

A history ⟨**opa**, **opa**, **opb**, **opa**, **opb**⟩ would be allowed by this specification in the case that **del** = 2, whilst a history ⟨**opa**, **opa**, **opb**, **opa**, **opa**⟩ would not.

3.3 Threads

A *thread* is a new clause of a refinement or implementation, written as

```
THREAD
   statement
```

where **statement** usually consists of an unbounded loop WHILE **true** DO **body** INVARIANT **I** END, and **body** is a select statement. We extend the syntax of select statements to include ANSWER clauses (akin to **accept** in Ada):

```
SELECT
        cond1  ANSWER op1
         THEN stat1
     WHEN
        cond2  ANSWER op2
         THEN stat2
     WHEN
        ⋮
END
```

If a guarded command within a select statement contains an ANSWER $\mathbf{op_i}$ clause, then it cannot proceed to execute the corresponding $\mathbf{stat_i}$ until an external caller attempts to call $\mathbf{op_i}$, and $\mathbf{cond_i}$ must also be true at this point in time. The guarded command is executed by executing $\mathbf{op_i}$ and then executing $\mathbf{stat_i}$ (without interruption from other operations of the machine). It is possible to mix guarded commands without ANSWER clauses with guarded commands with such clauses within the same select statement. If more than one guarded command can be executed, then the choice between them remains non-deterministic. This form of statement is essentially the same as that described in [8], where the labels of guarded commands are the names of actions.

Concurrency is introduced by a thread because the caller of an operation $\mathbf{op_i}$ is only blocked waiting for $\mathbf{op_i}$ to return whilst the ANSWER clause (and code of $\mathbf{op_i}$ in the OPERATIONS list) is executing – once the code of the operation is completed, the thread of the called machine can then execute $\mathbf{stat_i}$ concurrently with the caller.

A thread defines exactly what external operation calls can be accepted by the machine: any such call must correspond with the execution of an ANSWER statement for that operation. The thread of a machine is initiated at the start of the execution of the system. No operation which occurs in an ANSWER statement in the thread can be invoked in the remainder of the thread code, since otherwise deadlock could occur. The operations that appear in ANSWER statements are a subset of the external services of the machine, whilst those that appear in the remainder of the code should usually be internal operations of the machine.

Threads are used to implement permission guards and trace specifications in a procedural manner, and are suitable for translation into Ada or OCCAM code.

3.4 Histories

Finally *histories* are used to describe behaviours which concern liveness or fairness constraints which cannot be expressed using the other constructs. Here we use temporal logic operators $\diamond$ (eventually), $\Box$ (henceforth) and $\bigcirc$ (next) to describe temporal constraints in a more abstract manner than via regular expressions. For example, to assert that after any occurrence of **opa** there will eventually be an occurrence of **opb**, we could write:

```
MACHINE Liveness
OPERATIONS
    opa;
    opb
HISTORY
    □(opa ⇒ ◇opb)
END
```

4 Semantics of Extended B

In this section we will describe how the semantics of extended B can be given in terms of object calculus theories, and how the concept of refinement arising from this semantics relates to that of conventional B.

4.1 The Object Calculus

An object calculus theory consists of a set of type and constant symbols, *attribute symbols* (denoting time-varying data) *action symbols* (denoting atomic operations) and axioms describing the types of the attributes and the effects, permission constraints and other dynamic properties of the actions. The axioms are specified using linear temporal logic operators $\bigcirc$ (next), $\bullet$ (in the previous state), $\mathcal{U}$ (strong until), $\mathcal{S}$ (strong since), $\square$ (always in the future) and $\diamond$ (sometime in the future). There is assumed to be a first moment, the predicate **BEG** is true exactly at this time point. We add the least fixed point operator μ and greatest fixed point operators ν [15]: this means that if φ is a formula both $\mu\mathbf{x} : \varphi$ and $\nu\mathbf{x} : \varphi$ are formulae, denoting the least and greatest fixed point solutions of the equation $\mathbf{x} \equiv \varphi$. All occurrences of $\mathbf{x}$ in φ must be within an even number of negation symbols (including implicit negations).

$\bigcirc$ and $\bullet$ are also expression constructors. If **e** is an expression, $\bigcirc\mathbf{e}$ denotes the value of **e** in the next time interval, whilst $\bullet\mathbf{e}$ denotes the value of **e** in the previous time interval.

A **count** operator which gives the number of completed occurrences of an action symbol can also be defined. We have

$$\mathbf{BEG} \;\Rightarrow\; \mathbf{count(op)} = 0$$

and

$$\mathbf{op} \;\Rightarrow\; \bigcirc\mathbf{count(op)} = \mathbf{count(op)} + 1$$
$$\neg\,\mathbf{op} \;\Rightarrow\; \bigcirc\mathbf{count(op)} = \mathbf{count(op)}$$

for any action **op**.

An important element of the object calculus is the *locality principle*. This asserts that the attributes may only change in value over an interval in which at least one of the actions of the module are executing:

$$\mathbf{att} = \bigcirc\mathbf{att} \;\vee\; \mathbf{op_1} \;\vee\; \ldots \;\vee\; \mathbf{op_n}$$

where $\mathbf{op_1}, \ldots, \mathbf{op_n}$ are all the actions of the module **M** declaring **att**. This can also be written as

$$\mathbf{idle_M} \;\Rightarrow\; \mathbf{att} = \bigcirc\mathbf{att}$$

where $\mathbf{idle_M}$ abbreviates $\neg(\mathbf{op_1} \vee \ldots \vee \mathbf{op_n})$.

4.2 Interpreting B AMN in the Object Calculus

A B AMN machine can be viewed as describing a particular form of object calculus specification. A machine

MACHINE **M**
SETS **St1**, ...
CONSTANTS **Con1**, ...
PROPERTIES **Prop**
VARIABLES $\mathbf{v_1}$, ...
INVARIANT **Inv**
INITIALISATION **T**
OPERATIONS

$$\mathbf{y_1} \longleftarrow \mathbf{op_1(x_1)} = \mathbf{Def_1};$$
$$\vdots$$
$$\mathbf{y_n} \longleftarrow \mathbf{op_n(x_n)} = \mathbf{Def_n}$$

END

gives rise to a theory with:

- action symbols $\mathbf{op_1}, \ldots, \mathbf{op_n}$ (possibly parameterised), together with an action symbol **init** for the initialisation;
- constant and type symbols for the machine constants and sets;
- attribute symbols for the machine variables $\mathbf{v_i}$ and operation results $\mathbf{y_j}$;
- axioms for the properties and invariant;
- axioms $\mathbf{P} \wedge \mathbf{op_i} \Rightarrow \bigcirc\mathbf{Q}$ for every pair **P**, **Q** of predicates over the machine data items such that $\mathbf{P} \Rightarrow [\mathbf{Def_i}]\mathbf{Q}$.

An alternative (finitary) way of expressing the operation effects is to use axioms

- $\mathbf{Pre_i} \wedge \mathbf{op_i} \Rightarrow (\neg [\mathbf{S_i}](\mathbf{v}' \neq \mathbf{v}))[\bigcirc\mathbf{v}/\mathbf{v}']$ where **v** is the tuple of machine variables, $\mathbf{Def_i}$ is PRE $\mathbf{Pre_i}$ THEN $\mathbf{S_i}$ END and $\chi[\mathbf{e}/\mathbf{v}]$ denotes substitution of **e** for **v** in χ.

The predicate $\neg [\mathbf{S_i}](\mathbf{v}' \neq \mathbf{v})$ expresses the possible state transitions which can be achieved by executions of $\mathbf{S_i}$ in terms of a relation between a pre-state **v** and post-state $\mathbf{v}'$. For example:

$$\neg [\text{CHOICE } \mathbf{x} := 1 \text{ OR } \mathbf{x} := 2 \text{ END}](\mathbf{x} \neq \mathbf{x}') \equiv$$
$$\mathbf{x}' = 1 \vee \mathbf{x}' = 2$$

For a B machine **M**, all operations declared in **M** will be assumed to be mutually exclusive in their execution. At the specification level they can execute concurrently with operations from machines included in **M** since such operations update disjoint sets of variables from those of **M**, and read the variables of **M** only at initiation of the two operations.

A permission constraint is interpreted as an axiom which constrains an action to only be executable under certain conditions. The guard statement **op** $\Rightarrow$ **Guard** is interpreted as the corresponding object calculus formula. Likewise, axioms written in the HISTORY constraint are directly translated into object calculus formulae.

Traces can (only) be interpreted as temporal logic formulae in the object calculus language by using the least-fixed point and greatest fixed-point operators μ and ν. As such, traces are strictly more expressive than the linear temporal logic of Object-Z histories[5]. For example, a trace of the form

GENERAL $\mathbf{op}^*$

in a machine **M** is represented by the formula $\nu \mathbf{x}.(\mathbf{idle_M}\ \mathcal{U}\ (\mathbf{op} \wedge \mathbf{idle_M}\ \mathcal{U}\ \mathbf{x}))$ which has as models all sequences whose only action from the alphabet of **M** is **op**[1].

If the thread code is specified purely in terms of invocations of internal or external operations of the machine and machines it accesses, then it can be treated as a specification of the possible histories of the machine. We can identify these histories in the loop invariant. For example, in a refinement with two operations **aop** and **bop** we could have:

```
WHILE true
DO
    SELECT
        ANSWER aop
        THEN
            SELECT
                ANSWER bop
                THEN  SKIP
            END
    END
INVARIANT history  |=  (aop; bop)*
END
```

The invariant of this thread definition asserts that the sequence **history** of completed operation invocations obeys the trace specification (**aop**; **bop**)* at the execution points beginning and ending each loop iteration. This invariant is proved by weakest precondition reasoning as usual: the key step in this case is the valid inference

$$\mathbf{history} \models (\mathbf{aop};\ \mathbf{bop})^* \quad \Rightarrow \quad \mathbf{history} \frown [\mathbf{aop}, \mathbf{bop}] \models (\mathbf{aop};\ \mathbf{bop})^*$$

As a result, we can infer that the thread implements the trace specification

GENERAL **(aop; bop)***

for this machine.

history $\models$ **trace** is an abbreviation for a formula over sequences of tokens for operation names.

The above semantics is closely related to the standard set-theoretic semantics of B [12], and extends it by making the sequences of states experienced by machine models explicit.

4.3 Refinement Concepts

An important result is that refinement between B AMN modules implies refinement (ie, theory extension) between their translations as object calculus theories. In the language of category theory, this means that the translation can form the basis of a *functor* from the category of B modules with functional refinements as the morphisms, to the category of object calculus specifications with theory interpretations as morphisms.

5 Conclusions

We have described some extensions of the B specification language for the description of properties of concurrent systems, and given a semantics for these in the object calculus.

Future extensions of this work will address how the B Toolkit can be extended to support the definition of refinement as theory extension, and the animation of temporal logic specifications via event checking [13]. Other work will address the specification of semaphores and adaption of the "layered development" approach of B to the concurrent extensions of this paper.

References

1. B Banieqbal and H Barringer. Temporal logic with fixed points. In *Temporal Logic in Specification*, volume 398 of *Lecture Notes in Computer Science*. Springer-Verlag, 1987.
2. J Bowen and V Stavridou. *Safety-critical systems, formal methods and standards*, Software Engineering Journal, 8(4):189–209, July 1993.
3. P Chapront. Vital coded processor and safety related software design. In H H Frey, editor, *Safety of Computer Control Systems 1992 (SAFECOMP '92), Computer Systems in Safety Critical Applications, Proc IFAC Symp.*, pages 141 – 145. Pergamon Press, 1992.

4. C DaSilva, B Dehbonei, and F Mejia. Formal specification in the development of industrial applications: The subway speed control mechanism. In *FORTE '91*, pages 207 – 221. North-Holland, 1991.
5. R Duke, P King, G Smith. Formalising Behavioural Compatibility for Reactive Object-oriented Systems, *Proc 14th Australian Compt. Sci. Conf. (ACSC-14)*, 1991.
6. E Durr and E Dusink. The role of VDM^{++} in the development of a real-time tracking and tracing system. In J Woodcock and P Larsen, editors, FME '93, Lecture Notes in Computer Science. Springer-Verlag, 1993.
7. J Fiadeiro and T Maibaum, *Temporal Theories as Modularisation Units for Concurrent System Specification*, Formal Aspects of Computing 4(3), pp. 239–272, 1992
8. J Fiadeiro and T Maibaum, *Interconnecting formalisms: supporting modularity, reuse and incrementality*, in Proc. 3rd Symposium on the Foundations of Software Engineering, ACM Press, 1996.
9. C George, P Haff, K Havelund, A E Haxthausen, R Milne, C B Nielsen, S Prehn, and K R Wagner. *The RAISE Specification Language*. Prentice Hall, 1992.
10. J Hoare, *The Use of B in CICS*, in **Applications of Formal Methods**, J. Bowen and M. Hinchey (Eds.), Prentice Hall, 1995.
11. C B Jones. *Systematic Software Construction using VDM*. Prentice Hall, 1990.
12. K Lano, H Haughton, *Formal Development in B AMN*, Information and Software Technology, Vol. 37, No. 5–6, 1995, 303–316.
13. K Lano, *Formal Object-oriented Development*, FACIT series, Springer-Verlag, 1995.
14. B Meyer, Systematic concurrent object-oriented programming. *Communications of the ACM*, 36(9):56–80, 1993.
15. A Pnueli, Applications of Temporal Logic to the Specification and Verification of Reactive Systems: A Survey of Current Trends, *Current Trends in Concurrency*, de Bakker J., de Roever W.-P., Rozenberg G. (Eds), Springer-Verlag Lecture Notes in Computer Science, Vol. 224, 1986.
16. J van de Snepscheunt. Trace Theory and VSLI Design, PhD thesis, Technische Logeschool Eindhoven, Eindhoven, The Netherlands, 1983.
17. M Spivey. *The Z Notation: A Reference Manual*. Prentice Hall, 2nd edition, 1992.

Notions of Refinement for a Coordination Language for Gamma

Michel R. V. Chaudron
Departement of Computer Science, Leiden University
P.O. Box 9512, 2300 RA Leiden, Netherlands

Edwin de Jong
Departement ASR, Hollandse Signaalapparaten b.v.
P.O. Box 42, 7550 GD Hengelo, Netherlands

Gamma has shown to be a powerful and expressive formalism that allows the basic computation of an algorithm to be expressed with a minimum of control. In a subsequent stage, the highly nondeterministic behaviour of Gamma can be exploited to impose additional control using a separate coordination language.

Separating computation from coordination facilitates proving correctness of the computation component, because efficiency related operational details need not be taken into account. In this respect it is important that the coordination component does not invalidate the established correctness of the program.

In this paper we propose several notions of refinement that allow the coordination component of a Gamma program to be constructed through a correctness preserving derivation process. We show that these notions can be combined into a hybrid proof method that can be used to reason about different properties of the coordination component.

1 Introduction

From different areas of computer programming, the view has emerged that a program is made up from a computation and a coordination component. A computation component specifies the basic actions to be performed in order to solve a problem. A coordination component determines the way in which the computations are combined into a coherent ensemble [5].

In accordance to this view, we proposed a method for the design of parallel programs where computation and coordination are addressed separately [4]. The main benefit of this approach, is that it leads to a uniform approach for parallel and distributed computing. This results in a greater ease of design, a high degree of portability (of the computation component) and supports collections of heterogeneous computing agents.

It is argued [1] that the Gamma formalism is well suited for expressing the basic computations of an algorithm with a minimum of control. Hence Gamma programs are not biased towards any particular mode of execution.

In a second phase of the design process, we can exploit the highly nondeterministic behaviour of Gamma programs to obtain efficiency. To this end, we proposed a language for coordinating the actions of Gamma programs [3]. This language enables the programmer to determine operational details that are left unspecified by the Gamma program. In this paper we investigate several notions of refinement that allow the construction of a coordination component through a correctness preserving derivation process.

The paper is organized as follows. In Section 2 we briefly describe the Gamma model and its coordination language. In Section 3 we examine various notions of refinement for schedules and illustrate their use in the derivation process. In Section 4 we conclude with some final remarks and directions for future research.

2 Gamma and its Coordination Language

We start with a brief introduction to the components that make up our programming model: the Gamma language, which is used to specify computations, and the coordination language which is used to control Gamma computations.

2.1 The Computation Language Gamma

The Gamma model [1] provides the multiset as the basic data structuring mechanism. Multisets can be formed over arbitrary domains of values, including integers, reals, booleans and tuples. Gamma programs are built from conditional multiset rewrite rules, denoted $\overline{x} \rightarrow m \Leftarrow b$. Here $\overline{x}$ denotes a sequence $x_1, \ldots, x_n$ of variables, m denotes a multiset expression, and b denotes a boolean expression, called the reaction condition. The free variables in m and b are taken from $x_1, \ldots, x_n$.

A rewrite rule may execute if there are values in the multiset that satisfy the rule's reaction condition. These values are then replaced by (transformed into) the elements that result from evaluating the multiset expression (for these values). Execution of a rule proceeds until there are no more matching elements in the multiset.

Individual rewrite-rules maybe composed into so-called "*simple*" programs using the parallel operator "+". Simple programs can in turn be composed using the sequential operator, denoted " $\circ$ ". The meaning of Gamma programs has been defined formally using structured operational semantics [6]. We postpone a treatment of the formal semantics until Section 2.2, where we shall present an alternative definition in terms of our coordination language.

2.2 A Coordination Language for Gamma

Execution in Gamma proceeds in a highly nondeterministic fashion. Therefore, a Gamma program can be seen as the specification of a wide spectrum of (more deterministic) behaviours. The language, to be presented shortly, is designed as a kernel language for coordinating Gamma programs. It provides the means to specify execution plans according to which a Gamma program may be executed. Hence we usually refer to the terms from the coordination language as *schedules*.

Introduction to Schedules

The basic components of the coordination language are the multiset rewrite-rules from a Gamma program. Schedules can be built from these rules according to the following abstract syntax. Here s denotes a schedule, r a multiset rewite-rule, c a boolean expression, S a schedule identifier, and $\overline{v}$ a sequence of values.

$$s \ ::= \ \mathsf{skip} \ \mid \ r \to s[s] \ \mid \ s;s \ \mid \ s \,\|\, s \ \mid \ c \triangleright s[s] \ \mid \ !s \ \mid \ S(\overline{v})$$

skip denotes the empty schedule. The link between schedules and Gamma programs is made by the rule-conditional schedule $r \to s[t]$. This schedule first attempts to execute r. If this succeeds, then execution continues with s; otherwise, if r fails, execution continues with t. As a notational convention, we write $r \to s[\mathsf{skip}]$ as $r \to s$ and $r \to \mathsf{skip}$ as r. More complex schedules can be obtained using ";", which denotes sequential composition, and " $\|$ " which denotes parallel composition. The execution of $s \,\|\, t$ proceeds by a step performed by either s or t, or by a parallel step in which both s and t participate. We write s^k, for $k \geq 0$, to denote k copies of s composed in parallel.

Execution of Gamma programs is such that the number of rules that may be executed in parallel varies dynamically with the number of elements available in the multiset. The replication operator "!" is included to describe this varying degree of parallelism. The schedule $!s$ denotes a dynamically varying number of copies of s executing in parallel.

Each occurrence of a schedule identifier, e.g. $S(\overline{v})$, has a corresponding schedule definition of the form $S(\overline{x}) \mathrel{\widehat{=}} s$ where the free variables in s are taken from $\overline{x}$. Such recursive definitions are typically accompanied by the use of the conditional construct $c \triangleright s[t]$, which serves as a guard to the recursion. Here c represents a boolean expression that is independent from the multiset. If c evaluates to *true*, then execution continues with s, otherwise t is executed. Analogously to the rule conditional, $c \triangleright s[\mathsf{skip}]$ is written as $c \triangleright s$.

The nondeterminism in Gamma arises from the arbitrary selection of rewrite-rules and the arbitrary selection of elements from the multiset. The coordination language as introduced so far is only capable of resolving the first type of nondeterminism. The second type is resolved by *strengthening* the condition of a rewrite-rule. Consider a rule $r = \overline{x} \to m \Leftarrow b$. Rather than scheduling r directly, we can schedule a rule $r' = \overline{x} \to m \Leftarrow b'$, such that $b' \Rightarrow b$. Rule r' exhibits restricted behaviour compared to r, because there are fewer elements from the multiset that satisfy the stronger condition b'.

In general, a rewrite rule may not be replaced by an arbitrary strengthening of that rule because this may invalidate computational correctness. In practice, strengthening is used to restrict the enabling condition of a rewrite rule such that it pin-points the elements to be selected for rewriting. The techniques for refinement, to be presented later on, will enable us to assert the correctness of the strengthenings used.

Operational Semantics of Schedules

Formally, execution of a rule $\overline{x} \to m \Leftarrow b$ in a multiset M takes place if there are elements $\overline{v} \subseteq M$ such that the boolean expression with $\overline{v}$ substituted for $\overline{x}$, denoted $b[\overline{x} := \overline{v}]$, evaluates to *true*. Then the values $\overline{v}$ are removed, and the values from the multiset $M' = m[\overline{x} := \overline{v}]$ are inserted. The effect of a rewrite is formally represented by the multiset substitution $M[M'/\overline{v}]$. More formally, $M[M'/\overline{v}] = (M \ominus \overline{v}) \oplus M'$ where $\ominus$ and $\oplus$ denote multiset difference and union respectively.

A configuration of a schedule s and a multiset M is written $\langle s, M\rangle$. The operational semantics of schedules is defined by the structural congruence relation in Figure 1 and a multistep transition relation $\xrightarrow{\lambda}$ between configurations, defined in Figure 2. The label λ of a transition is either a multiset substitution or the special symbol ε which denotes a transition that does not change the multiset.

$$
\begin{array}{lll}
\mathsf{skip}; s \equiv s & s_1; (s_2; s_3) \equiv (s_1; s_2); s_3 & \\
\mathsf{skip} \parallel s \equiv s & s_1 \parallel (s_2 \parallel s_3) \equiv (s_1 \parallel s_2) \parallel s_3 & s_1 \parallel s_2 \equiv s_2 \parallel s_1 \\
\mathsf{true} \triangleright s[t] \equiv s & \mathsf{false} \triangleright s[t] \equiv t & \\
!\mathsf{skip} \equiv \mathsf{skip} & & \\
S(\overline{v}) \equiv \mathsf{skip} & \text{if } S(\overline{x}) \mathrel{\widehat{=}} s \text{ and } s[\overline{x} := \overline{v}] \equiv \mathsf{skip} &
\end{array}
$$

Figure 1: Structural Congruences of Schedules

if $\neg\exists\overline{v} : \overline{v} \subseteq M : b[\overline{x} := \overline{v}]$ then
$$\langle r \to s[t], M\rangle \xrightarrow{\varepsilon} \langle t, M\rangle$$

if $\exists\overline{v} : \overline{v} \subseteq M : b[\overline{x} := \overline{v}]$ then
$$\langle r \to s[t], M\rangle \xrightarrow{\sigma} \langle s, M[\sigma]\rangle$$
where $\sigma = m[\overline{x} := \overline{v}]/\overline{v}$

$$\frac{\langle s_1, M\rangle \xrightarrow{\lambda} \langle s_1', M'\rangle}{\langle s_1; s_2, M\rangle \xrightarrow{\lambda} \langle s_1'; s_2, M'\rangle}$$

$$\frac{\langle s_1, M\rangle \xrightarrow{\lambda} \langle s_1', M'\rangle}{\langle s_1 \parallel s_2, M\rangle \xrightarrow{\lambda} \langle s_1' \parallel s_2, M'\rangle}$$

$$\frac{\langle s_1, M\rangle \xrightarrow{\lambda} \langle s_1', M'\rangle \quad \langle s_2, M\rangle \xrightarrow{\varepsilon} \langle s_2', M\rangle}{\langle s_1 \parallel s_2, M\rangle \xrightarrow{\lambda} \langle s_1' \parallel s_2', M'\rangle}$$

$$\frac{\langle s_1, M\rangle \xrightarrow{\sigma_1} \langle s_1', M_1\rangle \quad \langle s_2, M\rangle \xrightarrow{\sigma_2} \langle s_2', M_2\rangle}{\langle s_1 \parallel s_2, M\rangle \xrightarrow{\sigma_1 \oplus \sigma_2} \langle s_1' \parallel s_2', M[\sigma_1 \oplus \sigma_2]\rangle}$$
if $M \models \sigma_1 \bowtie \sigma_2$

$$\frac{\langle s, M\rangle \xrightarrow{\lambda} \langle s', M'\rangle}{\langle !s, M\rangle \xrightarrow{\lambda} \langle s', M'\rangle}$$

$$\frac{\langle s \parallel !s, M\rangle \xrightarrow{\lambda} \langle s', M'\rangle}{\langle !s, M\rangle \xrightarrow{\lambda} \langle s', M'\rangle}$$

$$\frac{s \equiv t \quad \langle s, M\rangle \xrightarrow{\lambda} \langle s', M'\rangle \quad s' \equiv t'}{\langle t, M\rangle \xrightarrow{\lambda} \langle t', M'\rangle}$$

$$\frac{\langle s[\overline{x} := \overline{v}], M\rangle \xrightarrow{\lambda} \langle s', M'\rangle}{\langle S(\overline{v}), M\rangle \xrightarrow{\lambda} \langle s', M'\rangle}$$
where $S(\overline{x}) \mathrel{\widehat{=}} s$

Figure 2: Structured Operational Semantics of Schedules

The Most General Schedule

The schedule language allows us to specify behaviours from a wide spectrum of possibilities, ranging from the chaotic execution of Gamma programs to the completely deterministic behaviour of known algorithms. The former can be seen by constructing a schedule that comprises all possible behaviours of a Gamma program. We refer to this schedule as the *most general schedule*, and for a given program, it can be defined as follows.

Definition 1 Let R be a simple program $r_1 + \ldots + r_n$ and let P_1 and P_2 be arbitrary Gamma programs. The most general schedules for R and $P_1 \circ P_2$ are defined as

$$\Gamma_R \mathrel{\widehat{=}} !(r_1 \to \Gamma_R) \parallel \ldots \parallel !(r_n \to \Gamma_R)$$
$$\Gamma_{P_1 \circ P_2} \mathrel{\widehat{=}} \Gamma_{P_2}; \Gamma_{P_1}$$

A Gamma program P and its most general schedule Γ_P were shown to be equivalent with respect to their possible transition sequences[3]. Therefore, Γ_P can be thought of as a model for the operational semantics of P.

The fact that the most general schedule explicitly represents the behaviour that is implicit in Gamma programs, makes it amenable to formal manipulation. Hence, the most general schedule may serve as starting point in the derivation process. A successive series of refinements of the most general schedule should enable the programmer to derive more deterministic execution strategies.

3 Notions of Refinement for Schedules

A coordination component is intended to capture the behavioural aspects of a program. Hence for the refinement of the coordination component, a notion should be used that addresses the issue of behaviour. In our setting, we consider a schedule to be a refinement of another schedule if it constitutes a more deterministic description of the behaviour.

The operational behaviour of computing mechanisms is often defined by means of transition systems. The notion of *bisimulation*[8,7] is widely used for comparing behaviours defined in this way. We will use variants of simulation for our investigations into refinement. In order to apply the theory of simulation, we adapt it to our setting of shared memory. Furthermore, we add a clause which imposes that a refining schedule may terminate only if the schedule that it refines may terminate. This ensures that refinement preserves *total* correctness. Thus we arrive at the following definition where $\mathbb{S}$ denotes the set of schedules and $\mathbb{M}$ denotes the set of multisets.

Definition 2 A relation $\mathcal{R} \subseteq \mathbb{S} \times \mathbb{M} \times \mathbb{S} \times \mathbb{M}$ is a *strong statebased simulation* if, for all $\langle s, M\rangle \mathcal{R} \langle t, M\rangle$

i. $\langle s, M\rangle \xrightarrow{\lambda} \langle s', M'\rangle \Rightarrow \exists t' : \langle t, M\rangle \xrightarrow{\lambda} \langle t', M'\rangle$ such that $\langle s', M'\rangle \mathcal{R} \langle t', M'\rangle$

ii. $s \equiv \mathsf{skip} \Rightarrow t \equiv \mathsf{skip}$

If the most general schedule is used as the starting point of the refinement trajectory, this definition of simulation guarantees that any refinement of the most general schedule terminates in some state only if that is a final state of the most general schedule and hence of the corresponding Gamma program.

In compliance with Milner[7], this notion of simulation is called *strong* simulation because every single transition of the refining schedule can be mimicked by a single corresponding transition of the refined schedule. Below we shall relax this property by introducing a weak notion of refinement. The adjective *statebased* is added, because the current state of a computation is taken into account – this in contrast to the stateless notion presented later on.

We can now define our refinement relation as the maximal strong statebased simulation.

Definition 3 Let s and t be schedules and M a multiset; s is a *strong statebased refinement* of t in M, denoted $\langle s, M\rangle \leqq \langle t, M\rangle$, if $\langle s, M\rangle \mathcal{R} \langle t, M\rangle$, for some strong statebased simulation R.

From the semantic rules in Figure 2 we see that ε-transitions do not change the multiset. So adding or removing ε-transitions in a transition sequence does not change the outcome of a computation. Analogously to [7] this brings us to define a weak notion of refinement, that is insensitive to ε-transitions.

We define the transition relation $\xrightarrow{\overline{\lambda}}{}^*$ as the reflexive transitive closure of the transition relation $\xrightarrow{\lambda}$ from Figure 2. The label $\overline{\lambda}$ denotes the sequence obtained by concatenating, in order, all individual labels of the constituent transitions. Furthermore, we use $\widehat{\lambda}$ to denote the sequence $\overline{\lambda}$ where all occurrences of ε have been removed.

Definition 4 A relation $\mathcal{R}$ is a *weak statebased simulation* if,

$$\text{for all } \langle s, M\rangle \mathcal{R} \langle t, M\rangle \quad i. \quad \langle s, M\rangle \xrightarrow{\lambda} \langle s', M'\rangle \Rightarrow \exists t' : \langle t, M\rangle \xrightarrow{\overline{\lambda'}}{}^* \langle t', M'\rangle$$
$$\text{where } \widehat{\lambda'} = \widehat{\lambda} \text{ and } \langle s', M'\rangle \mathcal{R} \langle t', M'\rangle$$
$$ii. \quad s \equiv \mathsf{skip} \Rightarrow \langle t, M\rangle \xrightarrow{\overline{\lambda'}}{}^* \langle \mathsf{skip}, M\rangle \text{ where } \widehat{\lambda'} = \langle\,\rangle$$

Definition 5 Let s and t be schedules and M a multiset; s is a weak statebased refinement of t in M, denoted $\langle s, M\rangle \lesssim \langle t, M\rangle$, if $\langle s, M\rangle \mathcal{R} \langle t, M\rangle$, for some weak statebased simulation $\mathcal{R}$.

An important aspect of statebased refinement is its ability to exploit properties of the multiset. This is possible because the multiset is an explicit component of the simulation relation. The following example illustrates this idea.

Example 1
Consider the Gamma program for summation: $add \mathrel{\widehat{=}} x, y \rightarrow x+y \Leftarrow true$. The program operates by adding pairs of numbers from the multiset in any order - possibly in parallel. This behaviour is equivalently expressed by the program's most general schedule: $\Gamma_{add} \mathrel{\widehat{=}} !(add \rightarrow \Gamma_{add})$.

A more deterministic schedule may exploit the size N of the initial multiset by performing exactly $N-1$ additions in sequence. For example, let

$Sum(n) \mathrel{\widehat{=}} n > 1 \triangleright (add; Sum(n-1))$. Proving that $Sum(N)$ is refinement of Γ_{add}, i.e. $\langle Sum(N), M\rangle \precsim_{\approx} \langle \Gamma_{add}, M\rangle$ for $\#M = N$, involves the construction of a suitable weak statebased simulation.

Proof Let $\mathcal{R} = \{(Sum(n), M, \Gamma_{add}, M) \mid \#M = n, n \geq 0\}$.
We prove that $\mathcal{R}$ is a weak statebased simulation by induction on n:
If $n \leq 1$ then $Sum(0) \cong \mathsf{skip}$.
From $\#M \leq 1$ we derive $\langle \Gamma_{add}, M\rangle \xrightarrow{\varepsilon} \langle \mathsf{skip}, M\rangle$ and $\widehat{\langle \varepsilon \rangle} = \langle\ \rangle$ as required.
If $n > 1$, then $\langle Sum(n), M\rangle \xrightarrow{\{x+y\}/\{x,y\}} \langle Sum(n-1), M'\rangle$ where $\#M' = n-1$.
Then also $\langle \Gamma_{add}, M\rangle \xrightarrow{\{x+y\}/\{x,y\}} \langle \Gamma_{add}, M'\rangle$.
By induction we have $(Sum(n-1), M', \Gamma_{add}, M') \in \mathcal{R}$. □

The method of statebased simulation in principle suffices for proving any (valid) refinement, but has the practical disadvantage that the induced refinement relation is not a precongruence for schedules. This means that refinement cannot be applied in a modular fashion. Hence schedules need to be considered as a whole, which may result in complex proofs.

Statebased refinement fails to be a precongruence for parallel composition because the context of a schedule may change the multiset in a way that affects the schedule's subsequent behaviour. A solution is to devise a notion of refinement that relates schedules only if they are robust enough that they behave the same regardless of any interfering changes of the multiset.

This is accomplished by dropping the multiset component from the simulation relation and requiring that transitions can be matched for *any* multiset. Hence we refer to this type of simulation as "stateless simulation."

For brevity, we shall only present the weak notion of stateless refinement which is, analogous to weak statebased, indifferent to ε-transitions. Strong stateless refinement and equivalence, denoted $\preccurlyeq$ and $\simeq$, are described in[4].

Definition 6 A relation $\mathcal{R} \subseteq \mathbb{S} \times \mathbb{S}$ is a *weak stateless simulation* if, for all $(s,t) \in \mathcal{R}$, for all $M \in \mathbb{M}$

i. $\langle s, M\rangle \xrightarrow{\lambda} \langle s', M'\rangle \Rightarrow \exists t' : \langle t, M\rangle \xrightarrow{\overline{\lambda'}}{}^{*} \langle t', M'\rangle$
where $\widehat{\lambda'} = \widehat{\lambda}$ and $(s', t') \in \mathcal{R}$

ii. $s \equiv \mathsf{skip} \Rightarrow \langle t, M\rangle \xrightarrow{\overline{\lambda'}}{}^{*} \langle \mathsf{skip}, M\rangle$ where $\widehat{\lambda'} = \langle\ \rangle$

Definition 7 1. $\precsim\ = \bigcup\{\mathcal{R} \mid \mathcal{R}$ is a weak stateless simulation $\}$
2. $\sim\ =\ \precsim \cap \precsim^{-1}$

We see that using stateless simulation, s is a refinement of t, if t can match the transitions made by s, independent of the multiset. This relation cannot be invalidated by some (demonic) modification of the multiset by the environment. This has the beneficial consequence that (strong and weak) stateless refinement can be proven to be precongruent[2].

Theorem 3.1 *Let s_1, s_2, t_1 and t_2 be schedules such that $s_1 \precsim t_1$ and $s_2 \precsim t_2$. Then $r \rightarrow s_1[t_1] \precsim r \rightarrow s_2[t_2]$, $s_1; s_2 \precsim t_1; t_2$, $s_1 \parallel s_2 \precsim t_1 \parallel t_2$, $!s_1 \precsim !t_1$ and $c \triangleright s_1[s_2] \precsim c \triangleright t_1[t_2]$.*

The notion of stateless simulation gives rise to a number of interesting refinement laws. These laws can be applied in an algebraic style of reasoning about schedules, whereas precongruence of stateless refinement enables a modular approach. We present the laws grouped per operator, starting with sequential and parallel composition. The proofs follow either from the structural congruence rules in Figure 1 or by determining appropriate simulation relations[2].

1. $\mathsf{skip}; s \sim s$	5. $\mathsf{skip} \parallel s \sim s$
2. $s; \mathsf{skip} \sim s$	6. $s_1 \parallel s_2 \sim s_2 \parallel s_1$
3. $s_1; (s_2; s_3) \sim (s_1; s_2); s_3$	7. $s_1 \parallel (s_2 \parallel s_3) \sim (s_1 \parallel s_2) \parallel s_3$
4. $r \rightarrow (s_1; t)[s_2; t] \sim (r \rightarrow s_1[s_2]); t$	8. $r \rightarrow (s_1 \parallel t)[s_2 \parallel t] \precsim (r \rightarrow s_1[s_2]) \parallel t$

The following fundamental law relates parallel and sequential composition

$$9. \quad (s_1 \parallel s_3); (s_2 \parallel s_4) \precsim (s_1; s_2) \parallel (s_3; s_4)$$

In essence, law 9 states that parallel composition may be refined by sequential composition, as exemplified by the derived property $s_1; s_2 \precsim s_1 \parallel s_2$, which is a special case of law 9. A number of basic laws involving replication and the conditional operator can be found in[4] and are omitted here.

The essential difference between weak and strong stateless refinement can be expressed algebraically by the following law which enables the elimination of *fail* from schedules.

$$10. \quad \mathit{fail} \rightarrow s[t] \quad \sim \quad t$$

In this law we use the rewrite rule *fail* which represents the class of rules that can only make failing transitions. We can think of it as being defined as: $\mathit{fail} \mathrel{\widehat{=}} \overline{x} \rightarrow m \Leftarrow \mathit{false}$.

This law may seem futile because no sensible program or schedule uses *fail*. However, this may be introduced in the process of refinement by the following strong stateless law which relates the schedule conditional $c \triangleright \_[\_]$ to the reaction condition b of a rewrite rule $r = \overline{x} \rightarrow m \Leftarrow b$.

$$11. \quad r \rightarrow s[t] \quad \simeq \quad c \triangleright (r \rightarrow s[t])[fail; t] \quad \text{if } b \Rightarrow c$$

Hence, using law 10 we derive (from 11) the weak stateless equivalence

$$12. \quad r \rightarrow s[t] \quad \sim \quad c \triangleright (r \rightarrow s)[t] \quad \text{if } b \Rightarrow c$$

Next, we show how the notions of refinement we presented are related and how their use can be combined into a hybrid proof method. Our first result is that strong refinement is contained in weak refinement, for both statebased and stateless variants.

Lemma 3.2 1. $\langle s, M\rangle \leqq \langle t, M\rangle \quad \Rightarrow \quad \langle s, M\rangle \precapprox \langle t, M\rangle \quad$ *for all M*
2. $s \leqslant t \quad \Rightarrow \quad s \precsim t$

Proof Immediately from the definitions of strong and weak refinement, and the fact that $\longrightarrow \subseteq \longrightarrow^*$. □

Secondly, stateless refinement is contained in statebased refinement, for both their strong and weak versions.

Lemma 3.3 1. $s \leqslant t \quad \Rightarrow \quad \langle s, M\rangle \leqq \langle t, M\rangle \quad$ *for all M*
2. $s \precsim t \quad \Rightarrow \quad \langle s, M\rangle \precapprox \langle t, M\rangle \quad$ *for all M*

Proof
1. follows from showing that $\mathcal{R} = \{(s, M, t, M) \mid s \leqslant t, M \in \mathbf{M}\}$ is a statebased simulation. The proof of 2 is analogous. □

The relations between the various notions of refinement show that weak statebased refinement is the most liberal notion and strong stateless is the strictest. Deriving refinements will be an interplay between the methods presented. Typically, the first refinements involve the introduction of ordering on the selection of data. This relates the progress of a schedule to the contents of the multiset. This is clearly a statebased property, hence proving it requires the use of one of the statebased refinement methods. Subsequently, the ordering of actions may be refined using stateless laws. Through precongruence of the stateless notions, these refinements may be obtained in a modular way using the algebraic laws. The containment within statebased methods ensures that these refinement are also valid there.

Example 2
To illustrate, we return to the summation program from Example 1. As in Example 1 we exploit the size of the multiset. To prove $\langle add^{N-1}, M\rangle \lessapprox \langle \Gamma_{add}, M\rangle$ for $\#M = N$ it suffices to show that the relation

$$\mathcal{R} = \{(add^{n-1}, M, \Gamma^{k}_{add}, M) \mid \#M = n, n \geq 1, k \geq 1\}$$

is a weak statebased simulation.

The control structure can be further refined by algebraic reasoning using the stateless refinement laws. For instance, a schedule that performs recursive doubling can be defined as follows.

$$RecDubSum(i) \mathrel{\hat{=}} (i > 1) \triangleright (add^{\lfloor i/2 \rfloor}; RecDubSum(\lceil i/2 \rceil))$$

We prove the stateless refinement $RecDubSum(n) \leqslant add^{n-1}$ by induction.
If $n = 1$, then $RecDubSum(n) \leqslant \mathsf{skip} \leqslant add^{n-1}$ as required.
If $n > 1$, we reason

$$\begin{array}{lll} & RecDubSum(n) & \\ \simeq & add^{\lfloor n/2 \rfloor}; RecDubSum(\lceil n/2 \rceil) & \\ \leqslant & add^{\lfloor n/2 \rfloor}; add^{\lceil n/2-1 \rceil} & \text{induction} \\ \leqslant & add^{n-1} & \text{special case of law 9} \end{array}$$

By Lemma 3.2 and Lemma 3.3 also $\langle RecDubSum(N), M\rangle \precapprox \langle add^{N-1}, M\rangle$ if $\#M = N$. Hence, for $\#M = N$, we arrive at the refinement ordering:

$$\langle RecDubSum(N), M\rangle \quad \precapprox \quad \langle add^{N-1}, M\rangle \quad \precapprox \quad \langle \Gamma_{add}, M\rangle$$

□

4 Conclusions

Our aim is to devise a formal method for the design of (parallel) programs where computation and coordination are addressed separately. In our approach we use Gamma to express the basic computations of a program with only a minimum of control. In a second stage of the design process we exploit the highly nondeterministic behaviour of Gamma to introduce explicit control by using a separate coordination language.

It is desirable that by adding operational detail, the established correctness of a Gamma program remains unaffected. We therefore aim at a correctness preserving derivation process. Starting point is the most general schedule, which can be regarded as a model for Gamma's operational behaviour.

In this paper we discussed different notions of refinement that are based on the concept of simulation. Each of these notions has an associated proof method. Together, these notions can be combined into a hybrid method that can be used effectively for proving refinements between schedules.

The notion of statebased simulation provides the most powerful proof method in the sense that it allows to resolve nondeterminism by using properties of the multiset. However, the entailed refinement relation is not a precongruence. In practice this may result in complex proofs for large programs.

Stateless simulation yields a smaller refinement relation that is precongruent. It induces a number of refinement laws that can be used in an algebraic and hence compositional style of reasoning about schedules. It is less powerful than statebased refinement because of its neglect of the multiset.

By combining both notions of refinement we obtain a hybrid proof method that can be used to reason about different properties of schedules. It would be interesting to learn whether a precongruence relation exists that is larger than stateless refinement but still contained in statebased refinement. Work on this topic is currently in progress.

References

1. J.-P. Banâtre and D. Le Métayer. Programming by multiset transformation. *Communications of the ACM*, 36(1):98–111, January 1993.
2. M. Chaudron. Towards compositional design of schedules for multiset transformer programs. Technical Report CS-95-32, Leiden University, Netherlands, November 1995.
3. M. Chaudron and E. De Jong. Schedules for multiset transformer programs. In *Coordination Programming: Mechanisms, Models and Semantics*. Imperial College Press, 1996.
4. M. Chaudron and E. De Jong. Towards a compositional method for coordinating Gamma programs. In *LNCS 1061, Proceedings Coordination '96*, pages 107–123. Springer Verlag, 1996.
5. D. Gelernter and N. Carriero. Coordination languages and their significance. *Communications of the ACM*, 35(2):97–107, February 1992.
6. C. Hankin, D. Le Métayer, and D. Sands. A calculus of GAMMA programs. In *5th International Workshop on Languages and Compilers for Parallel Computing, LNCS 757*, pages 342–355. Springer-Verlag, 1992.
7. R. Milner. *Communication and Concurrency*. Prentice-Hall, 1989.
8. D. M. R. Park. Concurrency and automata on infinite sequences. In *LNCS 104, Proceedings of the 5th G. I. Conference on Theoretical Computer Science*, pages 167–183. Springer-Verlag, 1980.

FULL ABSTRACTION BY TRANSLATION

G. McCUSKER
Department of Computing, Imperial College, London SW7 2BZ.

This paper shows how a fully abstract model for a rich metalanguage such as *FPC* can be used to prove theorems about other languages. In particular, we use results obtained from a game semantics of *FPC* to show that the natural translation of the lazy λ-calculus into the metalanguage is fully abstract, thus obtaining a new full abstraction result from an old one. The proofs involved are very easy—all the hard work was done in giving the original games model. So far we have been unable to prove the completeness of our translation without recourse to the denotational model; we therefore have an indication of the worth of such fully abstract models.

1 Introduction

Plotkin, in his CSLI notes [13], showed how denotational semantics can be viewed as a two-stage process. First one defines a *metalanguage* which describes elements of the intended semantic model, usually some category of domains. Then to give a semantics to a language $\mathcal{L}$ it suffices to translate it into the metalanguage. While this is really no more than a formalization of the usual method of writing semantic equations, Plotkin demonstrated that it has an important advantage. Suppose that the translation of a term M of $\mathcal{L}$ into the metalanguage is $(\!| M |\!)$, and that the element of the denotational model which an expression e of the metalanguage describes is $[\![e]\!]$. The following *soundness* property is essential.

$$[\![(\!| M |\!)]\!] = [\![(\!| N |\!)]\!] \Rightarrow M \sim N$$

where $\sim$ is the notion of program equivalence of interest for $\mathcal{L}$. By equipping the metalanguage with an operational semantics and hence a syntactic notion of equivalence $\simeq$, this requirement can be split into two.

$$[\![e]\!] = [\![f]\!] \Rightarrow e \simeq f. \tag{1}$$

$$(\!| M |\!) \simeq (\!| N |\!) \Rightarrow M \sim N. \tag{2}$$

In general, proving (1) is a non-trivial task; but if the metalanguage is sufficiently rich, it can be used in the semantics of a large variety of languages $\mathcal{L}$, and for each of these one only needs to prove (2) to establish soundness. What's more, the proof of (2) is essentially routine, so the burden of proof is greatly reduced by the generic soundness result of part (1). This philosophy has also been taken by Crole and Gordon [4,6].

Recent work on game semantics [10] has provided a model of Plotkin's metalanguage, now known as *FPC*, which is not only sound but also *fully abstract*, i.e. it satisfies the following *completeness* condition.

$$e \simeq f \Rightarrow [\![e]\!] = [\![f]\!].$$

It is therefore natural to ask whether full abstraction results may also be factored into two: can one easily prove the following?

$$M \sim N \Rightarrow (\!|M|\!) \simeq (\!|N|\!).$$

Of course, the hope is that when this is possible, it can be done easily and syntactically. Such a result would not only provide a fully abstract model of $\mathcal{L}$, but also the assurance that, even if a model of $\mathcal{L}$ via *FPC* were not fully abstract, the loss of completeness did not occur at the syntactic translation stage.

This paper considers the simple example of the lazy λ-calculus [1, 3, 11]. We give a translation into *FPC* and perform the easy proof of its soundness. However, the completeness half is not so simple without the aid of some results about *FPC* obtained by the use of game semantics. Implicit in the proof of full abstraction in [10] is a strong characterization of program equivalence for *FPC*. We show how this can be used to establish completeness of the translation from lazy λ-calculus to *FPC*, thus arriving at a new full abstraction result bred from an old one. (A fully abstract games model of the lazy λ-calculus has already been described in [2]; but this used a different category of games from the one in which *FPC* is modelled, so we obtain here a genuinely new, if not altogether surprising, full abstraction theorem.) A useful characterization of *FPC* equivalence has been obtained by Gordon without the use of denotational semantics [7], but it is weaker than the one we present here, and in particular not good enough to establish our completeness theorem. In [14], Ritter and Pitts show that a certain translation between SML and a λ-calculus with reference types is fully abstract, again without recourse to a denotational model. This therefore raises two questions.

- Can the characterization of equivalence for *FPC* be obtained without the use of a fully abstract denotational model? This is important because there are many programming language features for which a fully abstract model is lacking.

- Can completeness of the translation perhaps be obtained in some other, more syntactic, way?

2 The metalanguage FPC

This section presents the syntax of *FPC* and equips it with a call-by-name operational semantics very similar to that of lazy functional languages such as Miranda[a]. It should be noted that this is not the same as the semantics used by Plotkin, which is call-by-value. This language has also appeared in [5,8,16]. We define the notion of program equivalence for *FPC*, and give a coinductive characterization of it, due to Gordon [7]. This is then strengthened using results obtained from the fully abstract model of *FPC* in [10].

2.1 Syntax

There are two syntactic classes of variables: $\mathtt{T}$ ranges over type variables, and $\mathtt{x}$ over expression variables. The types τ and expressions M of *FPC* are generated by the following grammar.

$$\begin{array}{rcl} \tau \in \text{Types} & ::= & \mathtt{T} \mid \tau_1 + \tau_2 \mid \tau_1 \times \tau_2 \mid \tau_1 \to \tau_2 \mid \mu\mathtt{T}.\tau. \\ M \in \text{Exp} & ::= & \mathtt{x} \mid \mathtt{inl}_{\tau_1,\tau_2}(M) \mid \mathtt{inr}_{\tau_1,\tau_2}(M) \\ & \mid & \mathtt{case}\ M\ \mathtt{of}\ \mathtt{inl}(\mathtt{x}_1).M_1\ \mathtt{or}\ \mathtt{inr}(\mathtt{x}_2).M_2 \\ & \mid & (M_1, M_2) \mid \mathtt{fst}(M) \mid \mathtt{snd}(M) \\ & \mid & \lambda\mathtt{x} : \tau.M \mid M_1(M_2) \\ & \mid & \mathtt{intro}_{\mu\mathtt{T}.\tau}(M) \mid \mathtt{elim}(M). \end{array}$$

In fact the syntax given above is abbreviated: in general it is useful to have sums of all arities in the language rather than just binary sums. In particular, we will make use of the unary case, which corresponds to *lifting*. Let us introduce some special informal syntax for this type constructor. The lifted version of the type τ will be written as $\tau_\perp$. The injection, corresponding to the unary version of $\mathtt{inl}(-)$ and $\mathtt{inr}(-)$, is $\mathbf{up}(-)$, and the destructor term, corresponding to $\mathtt{case}\ M\ \mathtt{of}\ \mathtt{inl}(\mathtt{x}_1).M_1\ \mathtt{or}\ \mathtt{inr}(\mathtt{x}_2).M_2$, is $\mathbf{conv}\ M\ \mathtt{in}\ \mathtt{x}.N$.

The type- and term-formation rules for *FPC* are standard, and for reasons of space we omit a detailed definition, which can be found in [8] or [10]. A well-formed type $\Theta \vdash \tau$ consists of a type context Θ (a list of distinct type variables) and a type τ. A well-formed expression $\Theta, \Gamma \vdash M : \tau$ consists of a type context Θ, an expression context Γ (a list of distinct expression variables tagged with types) and a typed term $M : \tau$. All the types in such a judgement are well-formed with respect to Θ.

---

[a] When used as the name of a functional programming system, Miranda is a trade mark of Research Software Ltd.

The syntax $\texttt{intro}(-)$ and $\texttt{elim}(-)$ is used to fold and unfold recursive types. The associated term formation rules are as follows.

$$\frac{\Theta, \Gamma \vdash M : \tau[\mathrm{T} \mapsto \mu\mathrm{T}.\tau]}{\Theta, \Gamma \vdash \texttt{intro}_{\mu\mathrm{T}.\tau}(M) : \mu\mathrm{T}.\tau}$$

$$\frac{\Theta, \Gamma \vdash M : \mu\mathrm{T}.\tau}{\Theta, \Gamma \vdash \texttt{elim}(M) : \tau[\mathrm{T} \mapsto \mu\mathrm{T}.\tau]}$$

The rule for the **case** statement is this.

$$\frac{\Theta, \Gamma \vdash M : \tau_1 + \tau_2 \quad \Theta, \Gamma, \mathrm{x}_1 : \tau_1 \vdash M_1 : \tau \quad \Theta, \Gamma, \mathrm{x}_2 : \tau_2 \vdash M_2 : \tau}{\Theta, \Gamma \vdash \textbf{case } M \textbf{ of } \texttt{inl}(\mathrm{x}_1).M_1 \texttt{ or } \texttt{inr}(\mathrm{x}_2).M_2 : \tau}$$

Definition An *FPC* ***program*** is a closed term of closed type. We write Prog for the set of programs, tagged with their types. The notion of ***context*** $C[-]$ with hole of a given type can also be defined; informally, a context is just a term with (possibly several occurrences of) a "hole" in it, and $C[M]$ denotes the result of filling in each hole with the expression M.

Before finishing our discussion of the syntax, it is worth remarking that though there is no explicit recursion combinator in the language, recursion is nonetheless supported. This is because the Curry fixed point combinator Y of the untyped λ-calculus can be encoded in *FPC*, by the power of recursive types. This is left as an exercise for the interested reader; the bored reader can find it in Gunter's book [8]. An important consequence of this is that there is a divergent term of each type, given by $Y(\lambda \mathrm{x} : \tau.\mathrm{x})$. We will denote this term by Ω, or Ω_τ when the type is important.

2.2 Operational semantics

We equip the language *FPC* with an operational semantics. In contrast to the work of Fiore and Plotkin, our semantics is call-by-name. As usual it is given in terms of a "big-step" evaluation relation $\Downarrow$. Again the rules are standard and we just give those for recursive types and one of the two symmetrical rules for the **case** statement.

$$\frac{}{\texttt{intro}_{\mu\mathrm{T}.\tau}(M) \Downarrow \texttt{intro}_{\mu\mathrm{T}.\tau}(M)} \qquad \frac{M \Downarrow \texttt{intro}(M') \quad M' \Downarrow M''}{\texttt{elim}(M) \Downarrow M''}$$

$$\frac{M \Downarrow \texttt{inl}(M') \quad M_1[M'/\mathrm{x}_1] \Downarrow M''}{\textbf{case } M \textbf{ of } \texttt{inl}(\mathrm{x}_1).M_1 \texttt{ or } \texttt{inr}(\mathrm{x}_2).M_2 \Downarrow M''}$$

2.3 Program equivalence in FPC

We are now in a position to define the notion of program equivalence that we are interested in. As usual, this is given in terms of an ***observational preorder***, defined as follows. Given two programs M and N of type τ, define

$$M \precsim N \iff \forall C[-] : \tau_1 + \tau_2\ [C[M]\Downarrow \Rightarrow C[N]\Downarrow]$$

where τ_1 and τ_2 are any closed types, and $M\Downarrow$ means that there exists some N such that $M \Downarrow N$. We then define program equivalence $\simeq$ by

$$M \simeq N \iff M \precsim N \wedge N \precsim M.$$

We have chosen to observe only convergence of programs in contexts of (binary) sum type. Two programs are equivalent if, whatever context of sum type they are put in, either they both converge or they both diverge. A consequence of our decision to observe convergence at sum types alone is that the following equivalences hold.

$$\lambda \mathbf{x} : \tau.\Omega_{\tau'} \simeq \Omega_{\tau \to \tau'} \qquad (\Omega_{\tau}, \Omega_{\tau'}) \simeq \Omega_{\tau \times \tau'}$$

The first would not hold if we allowed observation of convergence at function types; the second would fail if we allowed observation at product types. The decision to observe only convergence at sum types is by no means the only possible one. For example, Haskell allows observation of convergence at product types too. Our notion of equivalence is more like that of Miranda.

It is easy to show that it is equivalent to observe convergence at sum types of any arity, and in particular at lifted types. We will make use of this fact later on.

Andrew Gordon has given a coinductive characterization of $\simeq$ using the technique of *applicative bisimulation*. Applicative bisimulation is the analogue in functional programming of Park's bisimulation [12] from concurrency, and was first used by Abramsky in his work on the lazy λ-calculus. We now review and refine Gordon's work. To make clear the connection with bisimulation as used in concurrency theory, Gordon presents applicative bisimulation in terms of a labelled transition system on *FPC* terms, as follows. It is a family of relations $(\xrightarrow{\alpha} \subseteq \text{Prog} \times \text{Prog} \mid \alpha \in \text{Act})$ indexed by the set Act of ***actions***.

$$\text{Act} = \{\mathtt{inl}, \mathtt{inr}, \mathtt{fst}, \mathtt{snd}, \mathtt{elim}\} \cup \{@M \mid M \in \text{Prog}\}.$$

The labelled transition system is defined inductively as follows.

$$\frac{M \Downarrow \mathtt{inl}(M')}{M \xrightarrow{\mathtt{inl}} M'} \qquad \frac{M \Downarrow \mathtt{inr}(M')}{M \xrightarrow{\mathtt{inr}} M'} \qquad \frac{M : A \to B \quad N : A}{M \xrightarrow{@N} \underline{M}N}$$

$$\frac{M : A \times B}{M \xrightarrow{\texttt{fst}} \texttt{fst}(M)} \qquad \frac{M : A \times B}{M \xrightarrow{\texttt{snd}} \texttt{snd}(M)} \qquad \frac{M : \mu\mathrm{T}.\tau}{M \xrightarrow{\texttt{elim}} \texttt{elim}(M)}$$

Notice the difference in the rules for sum types: there the term is evaluated in order to calculate its transitions, whereas at other types, we merely apply a 'destructor' term. This reflects the fact that we can observe convergence at sum types directly.

Gordon goes on to define bisimulation with respect to this transition system in the usual way, and ***similarity*** $\approx$ to be the largest bisimulation. The following theorem appears in [7].

Theorem 1 (Gordon) Similarity and observational equivalence coincide. That is to say, for any *FPC* programs M and N of the same type,

$$M \simeq N \iff M \approx N.$$

In [10], a fully abstract game semantics is given for *FPC*. This model allows us to prove the above result very easily, although of course it requires a good deal of effort to construct the model in the first place. However, the proof in fact shows a stronger result, namely that in the clause for terms of function type, it suffices to consider transitions $\xrightarrow{@N}$ where N is a program whose denotation in the games model is finite. Fortunately, the finite elements can easily be characterized syntactically, by the following grammar. We will call the terms generated by this grammar the ***compact*** terms.

$$\begin{array}{rcl} K & ::= & \Omega \mid \texttt{inl}(K) \mid \texttt{inr}(K) \\ & \mid & \lambda\texttt{x} : \tau.K \mid (K_1, K_1) \mid \texttt{intro}(K) \\ & \mid & \texttt{case}\ \alpha\ \texttt{of}\ \texttt{inl}(\texttt{x}_1).K_1\ \texttt{or}\ \texttt{inr}(\texttt{x}_2).K_2 \\ \alpha & ::= & \texttt{x} \mid \texttt{fst}(\alpha) \mid \texttt{snd}(\alpha) \\ & \mid & \texttt{outl}(\alpha) \mid \texttt{outr}(\alpha) \mid \texttt{elim}(\alpha) \\ & \mid & \alpha K_1 \ldots K_n \end{array}$$

In the clause for case expressions, the terms K_1 and K_2 are of sum type, K_1 does not contain $\texttt{x}_1$ and K_2 does not contain $\texttt{x}_2$. The term `outl` is shorthand for

$$\lambda\texttt{x} : \tau_1 + \tau_2.\texttt{case x of inl}(\texttt{x}_1).\texttt{x}_1\ \texttt{or}\ \texttt{inr}(\texttt{x}_2).\Omega_{\tau_1}.$$

so that `outl` projects from $\tau_1 + \tau_2$ to τ_1. The term `outr` is defined symmetrically. In the unary case we write dn for this term, dually to up.

This grammar is particularly restricted in its use of application. One can only apply a variable to other compact terms, and only then if the result will be used as the argument to a case expression; having tested for convergence, control then passes to the subterm K_1 or K_2 which makes no further use of the application. This means that the types of subterms of a compact term are much more predictable than for general terms, a fact which facilitates the proof of completeness to follow.

We can now define a new transition system which has the same rules as before except that the rule for function types is replaced by the more restricted rule below.

$$\frac{M : A \to B \quad N : A \quad N \text{ compact}}{M \xrightarrow{@N} MN}$$

We define ***compact bisimulation*** with respect to the new transition system in the same way as before, arriving at ***compact similarity***. We then have the following characterizations of program equivalence for FPC.

Theorem 2

1. Compact similarity, similarity and observational equivalence coincide.

2. Given terms M and N of type τ, $M \simeq N$ if and only if for all compact terms $\mathbf{x} : \tau \vdash f : \tau_1 + \tau_2$ we have $f[M/\mathbf{x}]\Downarrow$ iff $f[N/\mathbf{x}]\Downarrow$.

3 The lazy λ-calculus

We present the form of the lazy λ-calculus which contains the "sequential convergence testing" constant C; this language is known as λl_{C}. After describing the operational semantics and the notion of operational equivalence, we define a translation from λl_{C} into FPC which can be seen as a description of its denotational semantics: the translation induces a model of λl_{C} in any model of FPC, including the games model.

3.1 Syntax and operational semantics

The syntax of λl_{C} is that of untyped λ-calculus with an additional constant C.

$$M ::= x \mid \lambda x.M \mid MM \mid \mathsf{C}.$$

The inductive definition of the well formed terms $x_1, \ldots x_n \vdash M$ is standard, and is omitted.

The operational semantics of λl_{C} is defined as follows.

$$\frac{}{\lambda x.M \Downarrow \lambda x.M} \qquad \frac{}{\mathsf{C} \Downarrow \mathsf{C}} \qquad \frac{M \Downarrow \lambda x.P \quad P[Q/x] \Downarrow N}{MQ \Downarrow N} \qquad \frac{M \Downarrow \mathsf{C} \quad N \Downarrow}{MN \Downarrow \lambda x.x}$$

Again we define observational equivalence in terms of an observational preorder; in this case we can observe convergence of any term, because there are no types (or rather, there is only one type).

$$M \preccurlyeq N \iff \forall C[-].C[M]\Downarrow \Rightarrow C[N]\Downarrow$$

where $C[-]$ denotes a closed context. We write the associated equivalence relation as $\sim$.

3.2 Denotational semantics via FPC

We now give a "denotational semantics" for λl_C by translating it into *FPC*, so using *FPC* as a metalanguage for some semantic category, such as the category of games mentioned previously, or more traditionally a category of domains. Terms of λl_C will be interpreted by terms of *FPC* of type D, where D is the solution to the "domain equation" $D = (D \to D)_\perp$, i.e. D is the type $\mu\mathtt{T}.(\mathtt{T} \to \mathtt{T})_\perp$. For more discussion of the use of this domain equation, see [3].

We now inductively define a translation $(\!|-|\!)$ taking λl_C terms to *FPC* terms. The translation is precisely the semantics that one would ordinarily give to λl_C in a domain satisfying the above equation. The only difference is in the level of formality. First, we associate with each variable x of λl_C a variable $\mathtt{x} : D$ of *FPC*. Given a list Γ of λl_C-variables, $(\!|\Gamma|\!)$ denotes the list of associated *FPC* variables. A term $\Gamma \vdash M$ of λl_C is translated to an *FPC* term $(\!|\Gamma|\!) \vdash (\!|M|\!) : D$ as follows.

$$(\!|x|\!) = \mathtt{x} : D$$

$$(\!|\mathsf{C}|\!) = \mathtt{intro}(\mathtt{up}(\lambda\mathtt{x} : D.\mathtt{conv}\ (\mathtt{elim}(x))\ \mathtt{in}\ \mathtt{y}.\mathtt{intro}(\mathtt{up}(\lambda\mathtt{z} : D.\mathtt{z}))))$$

$$\frac{(\!|M|\!) = m}{(\!|\lambda x.M|\!) = \mathtt{intro}(\mathtt{up}(\lambda\mathtt{x} : D.m))}$$

$$\frac{(\!|M|\!) = m \quad (\!|N|\!) = n}{(\!|MN|\!) = \mathtt{conv}\ (\mathtt{elim}(m))\ \mathtt{in}\ \mathtt{x}.\mathtt{x}n}$$

4 Soundness and completeness

Now that we have defined the metalanguage *FPC*, our object language λl_C and the translation from λl_C into *FPC*, we can set about proving that the translation is fully abstract. The first part of the proof, soundness, follows from a computational adequacy result which is very easy to establish. The second part, completeness, makes essential use of the characterization of program equivalence in *FPC* given in section 2.

4.1 Soundness

The proof of soundness of our translation is completely routine. Similar proofs have appeared in [4,6,13]. We will omit the proof entirely, merely stating the key lemmas: a substitution lemma; the fact that reduction of translated terms mirrors that of the original terms; and the correspondence between convergence of terms and their translations, which is known as computational adequacy. All of these results are proved by a straightforward induction over syntax.

Lemma 3 (Substitution) If $\Gamma \vdash M$ and $\Gamma, x \vdash N$ then $\Gamma \vdash N[M/x]$ and

$$(\!| N[M/x] |\!) = (\!| N |\!)[(\!| M |\!)/\mathbf{x}].$$

Lemma 4 (Reduction is respected) If $M \Downarrow N$ then $(\!| M |\!) \Downarrow (\!| N |\!)$.

Lemma 5 (Computational Adequacy) If $(\!| M |\!) \Downarrow$ then $M \Downarrow$.

Proposition 6 (Soundness) If $(\!| M |\!) \simeq (\!| N |\!)$ then $M \sim N$.

In contrast, the original soundness proof for the metalanguage itself [10]is much longer and relies on the method of "formal approximation relations" used by Plotkin [13]. It is this which makes the methodology of using a metalanguage for denotational semantics attractive. If instead we gave semantics to the lazy λ-calculus directly, much more effort would be required to establish soundness.

4.2 Completeness

In this section we make use of the strong characterization of program equivalence in *FPC* given in section 2.3 to show that the translation from λl_C into *FPC* is not just sound but also complete. As usual for such completeness results, the proof rests on *definability*: we show that sufficiently many *FPC* programs are in fact the denotation of some term of λl_C. Here, "sufficiently many" means enough to distinguish any two distinct *FPC* programs, so that if we have $(\!| M |\!) \not\simeq (\!| N |\!)$ we can find some *FPC* context $C[-]$ such that $C[(\!| M |\!)]\Downarrow$ but not $C[(\!| N |\!)]\Downarrow$, and moreover this *FPC* context is the denotation of a λl_C context $C'[-]$, so we have $C'[M]\Downarrow$ but not $C'[N]\Downarrow$, which allows us to conclude that $M \not\sim N$.

Without the notion of compact terms introduced earlier, such a definability result would be hard to prove. The first temptation is to attempt to prove by structural induction that all *FPC* terms of type D are λl_C definable. This approach fails immediately because in a term MN, the subterms M and N may be of types very different from D. However, for compact terms, this case cannot arise, and as we have seen, the compact terms suffice to distinguish any two distinct *FPC* programs.

Proposition 7 For any compact term $\mathtt{x}_1 : D, \ldots, \mathtt{x}_2 : D \vdash K : D$ there exists a λl_{C}-term $x_1, \ldots, x_n \vdash M$ such that $(\!|M|\!) \simeq K$, that is to say K is *definable.* Similarly, for any compact term K of type $(D \to D)_\perp$ the term $\mathtt{intro}(K)$ is definable, and for any compact term K of type $D \to D$, the term $\mathtt{intro}(\mathtt{up}(K))$ is definable.

Proof By induction on the structure of K. The case of Ω is trivial, since there is the λl_{C}-term $(\lambda x.xx)(\lambda x.xx)$ which diverges and hence has divergent denotation, by computational adequacy. The case of $\mathtt{intro}(K)$ comes directly from the inductive hypothesis, as does the case of $\mathtt{up}(K)$. The cases of (K, K), $\mathtt{inl}(K)$ and $\mathtt{inr}(K)$ are all vacuous. The only case of the form $\lambda\mathtt{x}.K$ which is of interest has type $D \to D$, so we need to show that $\mathtt{intro}(\mathtt{up}(\lambda\mathtt{x} : D.K))$ is definable. But the inductive hypothesis says that $\Gamma, \mathtt{x} \vdash K$ is definable, so this follows by definition of the translation of λ-abstractions. This just leaves the case statement $\mathtt{case}\ \alpha\ \mathtt{of}\ \mathtt{inl}(\mathtt{x}_1).K_1\ \mathtt{or}\ \mathtt{inr}(\mathtt{x}_2).K_2$ (and similar statements for sums of different arities). Note that since all the free variables have type D, the α in question can only be of type $(D \to D)_\perp$. So we in fact have $\mathtt{conv}\ \alpha\ \mathtt{in}\ \mathtt{x}.K$ where K has 'sum' type, which must therefore be $(D \to D)_\perp$. We are to show that $\mathtt{intro}(\mathtt{conv}\ \alpha\ \mathtt{in}\ \mathtt{x}.K)$ is definable, and it can easily be shown that this is equivalent to $\mathtt{conv}\ \alpha\ \mathtt{in}\ \mathtt{x}.\mathtt{intro}(K)$. The inductive hypothesis immediately tells us that $\mathtt{intro}(K)$ is definable by some term M of λl_{C}. Inspection of the grammar for α shown that we must have $\alpha = \mathtt{elim}(\alpha')$ for some α' of type D. Suppose for now that α' is definable, so that $\alpha' = (\!|N|\!)$ for some N. We need to show that $\mathtt{conv}\ \mathtt{elim}((\!|N|\!))\ \mathtt{in}\ \mathtt{x}.(\!|M|\!)$ is definable. But it's easy to show that this is equivalent to $(\!|(\mathsf{C}N)M|\!)$—one converges if and only if the other does, and then to the same value, namely that of $(\!|M|\!)$. Therefore we just need to show that each α' of type D is definable. This we do by induction on the structure of α'. The base case, $\alpha' = \mathtt{x}$, is trivial. For the inductive step, we need only consider the case

$$\alpha' = \mathtt{dn}(\mathtt{elim}(\alpha''))((\!|P|\!))$$

for some λl_{C}-term P, since by the inductive hypothesis each argument we supply to α' is definable. Our inner inductive hypothesis tells us that $\alpha'' = (\!|Q|\!)$ for some Q. We can calculate as follows.

$$\begin{array}{rcl}\alpha' & = & (\mathtt{conv}\ \mathtt{elim}((\!|Q|\!))\ \mathtt{in}\ \mathtt{y}.\mathtt{y})(\!|P|\!) \\ & \simeq & \mathtt{conv}\ \mathtt{elim}((\!|Q|\!))\ \mathtt{in}\ \mathtt{y}.\mathtt{y}((\!|P|\!)) \\ & = & (\!|QP|\!).\end{array}$$

□

Completeness, and hence full abstraction, is now easy to establish.

Theorem 8 The translation from λl_C into *FPC* is fully abstract.

5 Conclusions

We have shown how the metalanguage *FPC* can be used as a stepping stone in giving semantics to a different programming language, and how this facilitates an easy proof of soundness of this semantics. Furthermore, using some results obtained by studying a fully abstract games model of *FPC*, we were able to show that for a particular language, the lazy λ-calculus, the translation into *FPC* is not only sound but fully abstract, so any fully abstract model of *FPC* induces a fully abstract model of λl_C too. In particular, we now know that the games model in [10] contains a fully abstract model of λl_C, subsuming the earlier result of [2]. The proof of this result was extremely simple, thanks to the power of the theorem imported from game semantics.

So far, the search for a self-contained proof of completeness of the translation presented here, that is to say a proof which does not rely on the existence of a fully abstract model, has been unsuccessful. The method of Ritter and Pitts [14] does not seem applicable. It would involve translating back from *FPC* to λl_C and proving terms are invariant under translation to the other language and back. The type system of *FPC* is so rich that it is not at all clear how such a translation might work. In particular, the usual coding of sum and product types in the λ-calculus is not suitable. In their work on using "domain theoretic" properties in a purely operational setting [9], Mason, Talcott and Smith identify the finite elements of a simple functional language syntactically. The connection with our compact terms remains to be seen.

References

1. S. Abramsky. The lazy λ-calculus. In D. A. Turner, editor, *Research Topics in Functional Programming*, chapter 4, pages 65–117. Addison Wesley, 1990.
2. S. Abramsky and G. McCusker. Games and full abstraction for the lazy λ-calculus. In *Proceedings, Tenth Annual IEEE Symposium on Logic in Computer Science*, pages 234–243. IEEE Computer Society Press, 1995.
3. S. Abramsky and C.-H. L. Ong. Full abstraction in the lazy lambda calculus. *Information and Computation*, 105(2):159–267, August 1993.
4. R. Crole and A. Gordon. Factoring an adequacy proof. In C. J. van Rijsbergen, editor, *1993 Glasgow Functional Programming Workshop*, Springer Verlag Workshops in Computing, pages 9–25, 1994.

5. M. P. Fiore. *Axiomatic Domain Theory in Categories of Partial Maps.* PhD thesis, University of Edinburgh, 1994.
6. A. D. Gordon. *Functional programming and Input/Output.* Distinguished Dissertations in Computer Science. Cambridge University Press, 1994.
7. A. D. Gordon. Bisimilarity as a theory of functional programming: minicourse. Notes Series BRICS-NS-95-3, BRICS, Department of Computer Science, University of Aarhus, July 1995.
8. C. A. Gunter. *Semantics of Programming Languages: Structures and Techniques.* Foundations of Computing. MIT Press, 1992.
9. I. A. Mason, S. F. Smith, and C. L. Talcott. From operational semantics to domain theory. Revised version of [15], to appear.
10. G. McCusker. *Games and Full Abstraction for a Functional Metalanguage with Recursive Types.* PhD thesis, Department of Computing, Imperial College, University of London, 1996. To appear.
11. C. H. L. Ong. *The Lazy Lambda Calculus: An Investigation into the Foundations of Functional Programming.* PhD thesis, Imperial College of Science and Technology, 1988.
12. D. Park. Concurrency on automata and infinite sequences. In P. Deussen, editor, *Conference on Theoretical Computer Science*, Berlin, 1981. Springer-Verlag. Lecture Notes in Computer Science Vol. 104.
13. G. Plotkin. Lectures on predomains and partial functions. Notes for a course given at the Center for the Study of Language and Information, Stanford, 1985.
14. E. Ritter and A. M. Pitts. A fully abstract translation between a λ-calculus with reference types and Standard ML. In *2nd Int. Conf. on Typed Lambda Calculus and Applications, Edinburgh, 1995*, volume 902 of *Lecture Notes in Computer Science*, pages 397–413. Springer-Verlag, Berlin, 1995.
15. S. F. Smith. From operational to denotational semantics. In S. B. *et al.*, editor, *7th International Conference on Mathematical Foundations of Programming Semantics, Pittsburgh PA*, pages 54–76, Berlin, 1992. Springer Verlag. Lecture Notes in Computer Science Volume 598.
16. G. Winskel. *The Formal Semantics of Programming Languages.* Foundations of Computing. The MIT Press, Cambridge, Massachusetts, 1993.

UNIFYING FIXED-POINT THEOREMS VIA ENRICHED CATEGORIES

SOFIA JOURDAN
Imperial College, Department of Computing,
London SW7 2BZ, UK
isj@doc.ic.ac.uk

KIM RITTER WAGNER
University of Cambridge, Computer Laboratory,
Cambridge CB2 3QG, UK
Kim.Wagner@cl.cam.ac.uk

We set up a framework for the unification of various fixed-point theorems traditionally used in semantics. We follow Lawvere in using enriched categories as the unifying concept for preorders and generalized metric spaces, and work both at the level of objects inside a given category of domains and at the level of endofunctors on the category itself. It turns out that the methods used at the two levels can both be conveniently expressed in the internal logic of the base category over which we enrich. We thus expose not only a common structure underlying both the metric and the partial order approaches, but also a common structure underlying the methods used at the level of a single domain and those used at the level of recursively defined domains. We relate our work to that of Smyth, Flagg and Kopperman, Adamek and Rutten, Bonsangue et al.

1 Introduction

There have been several attempts at "reconciling domains with metric spaces" ([Smyth 88]). A good summary - and an interesting application - can be found in [Seda 96]. Our approach uses Lawvere's idea of seeing both preorders and (suitably generalized) metric spaces as enriched categories ([Lawvere 73]). It has previously been shown ([Wagner 94]) that both can be seen as categories enriched over a quantale, and that the resulting theory succeeds in unifying many essential notions. For example, increasing chains in preorders correspond to Cauchy sequences in metric spaces, least upper bounds of such chains correspond to metric limits, and the appropriate notions of continuity coincide. In this paper we extend these analogies to the study of various (more or less categorical) versions of the traditional fixed-point theorems: the Kleene fixed-point theorem in the order-theoretic approach and the Banach fixed-point theorem in the metric case.

2 The order-theoretic approach

We begin with a brief outline of the development of fixed-point theory in the order-theoretic approach. We start with Kleene's well-known fixed-point theorem , which is closely related to results by Knaster and Tarski .

Kleene's theorem considers a function $f : D \to D$ where D is a cpo (complete partial order), i.e. a poset with a least element $\bot$ and least upper bounds of ω-chains. Assuming that f is continuous (preserves such least upper bounds), the theorem states that f has a least fixed-point in D which is obtained as the least upper bound of the ω-chain

$$\bot \leq f(\bot) \leq f^2(\bot) \leq \dots$$

The straightforward categorical generalization of this – there was a partial generalization by Adámek a little earlier – is due to Smyth and can be found in [Smyth & Plotkin 82]. It considers a functor $F : K \to K$ where K is an ω-category (a category with an initial element $\bot$ and colimits of ω-chains) and F is ω-continuous (preserves such colimits), and states that F has a least fixed-point (initial algebra) which can be obtained as the colimit object of the ω-chain

$$\bot \xrightarrow{!} F(\bot) \xrightarrow{F(!)} F^2(\bot) \to \dots$$

Scott's well-known "inverse limit" theorem ([Scott 72], also in [Plotkin 83]) can be stated as follows: If $F : CPO^{ep} \to CPO^{ep}$ is a functor on the category of cpo's with embedding-projection pairs as arrows (which category turns out to have an initial object $\{\bot\}$ and colimits of ω-chains of embeddings) and F is ω-continuous (preserves such colimits), then F has a least fixed-point which can be obtained both as the colimit object of the ω-chain of embeddings

$$\{\bot\} \xrightarrow{!} F(\{\bot\}) \xrightarrow{F(!)} F^2(\{\bot\}) \to \dots$$

and as the limit object of the ω-op chain of projections

$$\{\bot\} \xleftarrow{!'} F(\{\bot\}) \xleftarrow{F(!')} F^2(\{\bot\}) \leftarrow \dots$$

If we relax the requirement that the objects of the category actually be cpo's, and demand only that the hom-sets maintain the structure of a cpo, we get the following result ([Adámek 92]): Let $F : K \to K$ be a functor on a cpo-enriched category with an initial object $\bot$ and colimits of ω-chains of embeddings, and assume that F is locally continuous (continuous on the function spaces). Then it can be shown that $\bot$ is also terminal and that F

has a least fixpoint which can be obtained both as the colimit object of the ω-chain

$$\perp \xrightarrow{!} F(\perp) \xrightarrow{F(!)} F^2(\perp) \rightarrow \ldots$$

and as the limit object of the ω-op chain

$$\perp \xleftarrow{!'} F(\perp) \xleftarrow{F(!')} F^2(\perp) \leftarrow \ldots$$

These variations on the Kleene fixed-point theorem are closely mirrored by variations on the Banach fixed-point theorem, which we now turn to.

3 The metric approach

Banach's fixed-point theorem considers a function $f : D \rightarrow D$ where D is a complete non-empty metric space and f is a contraction (i.e. there exists a positive number $c < 1$ such that $d(f(x), f(y)) \leq c \cdot d(x, y))$ for all $x, y \in D$). It states that f then has a unique fixed-point which can be obtained as the limit of the converging sequence

$$a, f(a), f^2(a), \ldots$$

for any choice of a in D.

We note that there cannot be a straightforward categorical generalization of this theorem to mirror Smyth's generalization of the Kleene fixed-point theorem, since that generalization built on the idea that a category can be viewed as a generalized preorder (thus initial objects correspond to least elements, etc).

Now corresponding to Scott's "inverse limit" theorem we have the following result ([America & Rutten 87]): Consider a functor $F : CMS^{ep} \rightarrow CMS^{ep}$ where CMS^{ep} is the category of complete metric spaces with (suitably defined) embedding-projection pairs as arrows. In this category we can define a notion of "converging tower" so that the category has limits of all such converging towers, and suitable notions of contractiveness and hom-contractiveness (as expected, contractiveness on the hom-spaces), so that if F is both contracting and hom-contracting then it has a unique fixed-point which can be obtained as the colimit of the ω-chain

$$D_0 \xrightarrow{(e_0,p_0)} F(D_0) \xrightarrow{F(e_0,p_0)} F^2(D_0) \rightarrow \ldots$$

for any choice of $D_0 \xrightarrow{(e_0,p_0)} F(D_0)$ (and it can be shown that it is always possible to choose such D_0, e_0, p_0).

The analogy with Scott's theorem is clear in that we are using CMS^{ep} in one case and CPO^{ep} in the other, but of course there is nothing in the metric case resembling the most striking feature of Scott's theorem, the limit-colimit coincidence. Surprisingly, that can be remedied at the next step.

Paralleling Adámek's generalization to cpo-enriched categories is his later generalization of the Banach theorem ([Adámek 95]). Here he shows that if we consider a functor $F : K \to K$, with K any cms-enriched category which is connected, has a terminal object 1 and limits of (suitably defined) contracting sequences, and if F is contracting in a fairly strong sense ("uniformly" contracting on the hom-spaces) then F has a unique fixed-point which can be obtained both as the colimit of the ω-chain

$$1 \xrightarrow{a_0} F(1) \xrightarrow{F(a_0)} F^2(1) \to \dots$$

for any choice of $1 \xrightarrow{a_0} F(1)$, and as the limit of the ω^{op}-chain

$$1 \xleftarrow{!} F(1) \xleftarrow{F(!)} F^2(1) \leftarrow \dots$$

(The only condition here which apparently has no parallel in the order-theoretic version, that of K being connected (for any objects a and b, there exists at least one arrow $f : a \to b$), is actually trivially true in the case of cpo-enriched categories.)

Again, this is by no means an exhaustive survey of results in this area. In particular, much attention has focused on ultrametric spaces (in which the triangle inequality $d(x, z) \leq d(x, y) + d(y, z)$ is replaced by the (stronger) requirement that $d(x, z) \leq max\{d(x, y), d(y, z)\}$) (see for example [Rutten 95], [Bonsangue, van Breugel & Rutten 95]).

4 Unification via enriched categories

Most work on the unification of the two theories has focused on the idea of defining a suitable structure to be used as a common generalization of partial orders (or preorders) and metric spaces. The difficulty is that metric spaces, as such, necessarily lead to Hausdorff topologies, whereas the topologies naturally associated with partial orders are not even T_1. (For the reader unfamiliar with these issues of separation in topology, this essentially means that the two frameworks are incompatible.) The solution, as suggested in [Smyth 88], is to weaken the requirements on our metric spaces. In particular, we can drop the symmetry axiom ($d(x, y) = d(y, x)$). Also, we can allow d to take the value ∞. (It is necessary to have a supremum of any set of distances if we wish to be able to define the distance between functions f and g as

$sup\{d(f(a), g(a))|a \in A\}$.) The resulting structure is usually called a quasi-metric space, or simply a generalized metric space. It is easy to see that a cpo can be trivially represented by such a space, and the "quasi-metric" version of the Banach theorem obtained (still in [Smyth 88]) therefore implies, as a special case, the Kleene theorem. Most work on "metric" semantics has in fact centered on (ultra-)quasi-metric spaces.

Smyth's paper also suggests quasi-uniformities as a tool for unification. Although that approach has not proved very popular, we should mention that a "uniform" version of the Banach theorem has been obtained in ([Escardo 95]). An obvious task is to develop the "quasi-uniform" version.

It might seem from the preceding paragraphs that little remains to be done, in that quasi-metric (or quasi-uniform) spaces provide us with the appropriate framework for unification. The truth is that although there is a general agreement about the need to thus tailor our definition of a metric space, it remains unclear what exactly the right definition should be and how far the unification can be extended. Symptomatic of this situation is the fact that the title of one of the most recent papers on this topic ([Flagg & Kopperman 96]) describes its aim as being still, as in [Smyth 88], that of "reconciling domains and metric spaces"– this time via "continuity spaces". (How that work relates to ours is something we shall return to later.)

We concentrate here on an approach via enriched categories, as first suggested in [Lawvere 73]. It is coherent with Smyth's idea of using quasi-metrics, but allows much greater freedom in the choice of our semantic domains, in that the theory contains, as special cases, preorders and (quasi-)metric spaces, but is valid in a more general setting. We begin by recalling the basic concepts of the theory of enriched categories. (For a general introduction, we recommend [Lawvere 73] and [Kelly 82]; here we give only the definitions necessary for our case, which is fairly simple because we enrich only over posets. Much of this – explained in more detail – can be found in [Wagner 94].)

Definition 4.1 A *commutative unital quantale* is a complete lattice Ω equipped with a commutative and associative operation $\otimes$, called *tensor*, such that $\otimes$ has a unit, which we denote by I, and such that $p \otimes \_$ has a right adjoint for every $p \in \Omega$. We denote this right adjoint by $[p, \_]$. □

The adjointness condition says that $p \otimes q \leq r$ if and only if $q \leq [p, r]$, the usual relation between tensor and linear implication in linear logic. In fact the whole approach can with some advantage be formulated internally in a kind of linear logic, but we shall for simplicity refrain from doing that here.

The requirement that $p \otimes \_$ have a right adjoint for every $p \in \Omega$ is equivalent to saying that $\otimes$ distributes over all joins. Essentially, what we have here is a strict symmetric monoidal closed category with additional completeness requirements. These allow us to make the necessary quantifications, e.g. when we define a notion of Cauchy sequence.

In the following Ω will always denote a commutative unital quantale.

Definition 4.2 An Ω-*category* is a small category enriched over Ω, that is, a pair $(A, A[\_,\_])$, where A is a set and $A[\_,\_] : A \times A \to \Omega$, the *hom*, fulfills

(*i*) $I \leq A[a,a]$ (reflexivity) and

(*ii*) $A[a,b] \otimes A[b,c] \leq A[a,c]$ (transitivity).

(For convenience, we often denote an Ω-category $(A, A[\_,\_])$ simply by A.) An Ω-*functor* from an Ω-category $(A, A[\_,\_])$ to an Ω-category $(B, B[\_,\_])$ is a function between the underlying sets, $f : A \to B$, fulfilling

$$A[a,a'] \leq B[f(a), f(a')].$$

We denote by Ω-*Cat* the category of Ω-categories and Ω-functors. □

It is easily shown that if we choose for Ω the two-point lattice then Ω-*Cat* is the category of preorders and monotone functions, and that if we choose $\Omega = [0,\infty]_+$, the non-negative reals extended with infinity, ordered by the reverse numerical ordering and with $+$ as tensor, then Ω-*Cat* is the category of quasi-metric spaces (with possibly infinite distances) and non-expanding functions. Taking *max* for tensor instead of $+$ gives us ultra-quasi-metric spaces.

Proposition 4.3 *The category* Ω-CAT *is symmetric monoidal closed with tensor defined as*

$$(A, A[\_,\_]) \otimes (B, B[\_,\_]) = (A \times B, (A \otimes B)[\_,\_]),$$

where $A \times B$ *is the cartesian product of* A *and* B *and*

$$(A \otimes B)[(a,b),(a',b')] = A[a,a'] \otimes B[b,b']$$

and with linear implication defined as

$$[(A, A[\_,\_]), (B, B[\_,\_])] = ((A \to B), (A \to B)[\_,\_]),$$

where $(A \to B)$ *is the set of* Ω-*functors from* $(A, A[\_,\_])$ *to* $(B, B[\_,\_])$ *and* $(A \to B)[f,g] = \bigwedge_{a \in A} B[f(a), g(a)]$.

Proof: Easy. See e.g. [Borceux 94]. The unit of $\otimes$ is the Ω-category $\mathbb{1}$ with one element, $*$, and $\mathbb{1}[*,*] = I$. □

The pair $(\Omega, [\_,\_])$, where the second component is given by the adjointness condition with $\otimes$, is itself an Ω-category. Given an Ω-category $(A, A[\_,\_])$ and

$a \in A$, we use the notation $A[a, \_]$ for the Ω-functor from A to Ω that maps $a' \in A$ into $A[a, a']$ – the Yoneda embedding. Similarly for $A[\_, a]$.

We introduce the Ω-category $\mathbb{N}$ of natural numbers. It has as objects the natural numbers, and the hom from one natural number to another is $\top$ (the top element of Ω) if the two are equal, otherwise it is $\perp$ (the bottom element of Ω). We still use $\mathbb{N}$ also just for the set of natural numbers. Whether $\mathbb{N}$ is to be regarded as an Ω-category or merely as a set will be clear from the context.

The following has been found to be the most suitable definition of Cauchy sequence, as it leads to a more unified theory than the (slightly simpler) one used by Smyth and others (see [Wagner 95] for details):

Definition 4.4 A *sequence* in an Ω-category A is an Ω-functor $\alpha : \mathbb{N} \to A$. We say that α is *Cauchy* if $I \leq \bigvee_{N \in \mathbb{N}} \bigwedge_{n \geq N} \bigvee_{M \in \mathbb{N}} \bigwedge_{m \geq M} A[\alpha(n), \alpha(m)]$. We say that α *converges* to an object $a \in A$ (which is then called the *liminf* of α) if $A[a, \_] = \bigvee_{N \in \mathbb{N}} \bigwedge_{n \geq N} A[\alpha(n), \_]$. We call an Ω-functor *continuous* if it preserves Cauchy sequences and their liminfs, and an Ω-category *liminf-complete* if every Cauchy sequence in it has a liminf. We denote by *Ω-CCat* the category of liminf-complete Ω-categories and continuous Ω-functors. □

In the case of ordinary metric spaces, this definition of Cauchy reduces to the usual one, liminfs correspond to metric limits, and liminf-completeness is ordinary metric completeness. For posets, a Cauchy sequence is an "essentially increasing" sequence, in the sense that it is allowed to oscillate perpetually as long as the following condition is satisfied: from some point onwards, any value of the sequence will eventually be dominated by the tail of the sequence. Liminfs then specialize to lub's and it can be shown that a poset is liminf-complete iff it is a cpo. It should be noted, however, that liminf-completeness and Cauchy-completeness as defined in [Lawvere 73] are independent. We shall return to this point when we mention the issue of completion.

Definition 4.5 We define *negation* $\neg : \Omega^{op} \to \Omega$ by $\neg p = A[p, \perp]$. We say that Ω *has property* (*) if for every $p, q \in \Omega$, if $I \leq \neg\neg p$ and $I \leq \neg\neg q$ then we also have $I \leq \neg\neg(p \otimes q)$. □

It is easy to see that property (*) is true for the two examples of Ω in which we are particularly interested here. We can now state our candidate for a generalized Kleene-Banach fixed-point theorem in terms of Ω-categories:

Theorem 4.6 *Let A be a liminf-complete Ω-category, $f : A \to A$ be a continuous Ω-functor and assume that Ω has property (*). Assume further that there exists $a \in A$ such that*

(i) $I \leq \neg\neg A[a, f(a)]$ *and*

(ii) $I \leq \bigvee_{N \in \mathbb{N}} \bigwedge_{y \in A} \left[\neg\neg A[a, y], A[f^N(a), f^N(y)]\right]$.

Then f has a fixed-point which is obtainable as the liminf of the sequence

$$a, f(a), f^2(a), \ldots.$$

Proof: If we show that the sequence is Cauchy, liminf-completeness of A then implies that it has a liminf and it is easy to show, just as in the case of preorders or metric spaces, that continuity of f implies that the liminf is a fixed-point of f. To see that the sequence is Cauchy we first observe that $I \leq \neg\neg A[a, f(a)]$ implies (by monotonicity of $\neg\neg$) $I \leq \neg\neg A[f(a), f^2(a)]$ and in general $I \leq \neg\neg A[f^n(a), f^{n+1}(a)]$ for all n. By property (*) and transitivity of the homs we obtain $I \leq \neg\neg A[a, f^n(a)]$. We then calculate as follows:

$$\begin{aligned}
&\bigvee_{N\in\mathbb{N}} \bigwedge_{n\geq N} \bigvee_{M\in\mathbb{N}} \bigwedge_{m\geq M} A[f^n(a), f^m(a)] \\
&= \bigvee_{N\in\mathbb{N}} \bigwedge_{n\geq N} \bigvee_{M\geq n} \bigwedge_{m\geq M} A[f^n(a), f^m(a)] \\
&= \bigvee_{N\in\mathbb{N}} \bigwedge_{n\geq N} \bigvee_{M\geq n} \bigwedge_{m\geq M} A\left[f^n(a), f^n\left(f^{m-n}(a)\right)\right] \\
&\geq \bigvee_{N\in\mathbb{N}} \bigwedge_{n\geq N} \bigvee_{M\geq n} \bigwedge_{m\geq M} \left[\neg\neg A\left[a, f^{m-n}(a)\right], A\left[f^n(a), f^n\left(f^{m-n}(a)\right)\right]\right] \\
&\geq \bigvee_{N\in\mathbb{N}} \bigwedge_{n\geq N} \bigwedge_{m\geq n} \left[\neg\neg A\left[a, f^{m-n}(a)\right], A\left[f^n(a), f^n\left(f^{m-n}(a)\right)\right]\right] \\
&\geq \bigvee_{N\in\mathbb{N}} \bigwedge_{y\in A} \left[\neg\neg A[a, y], A[f^N(a), f^N(y)]\right] \\
&\geq I
\end{aligned}$$

□

Let us pause to see how we can interpret this theorem in the case of preorders and in the case of metric spaces. For preorders, $\neg\neg$ is the identity and *(i)* means that $a \leq f(a)$, whereas *(ii)* means that

$$\exists N \in \mathbb{N}. \forall y \in A. \left[a \leq y \Longrightarrow f^N(a) \leq f^N(y)\right],$$

which is true by monotonicity of f (we can choose $N = 1$). This is as expected: to obtain a fixed-point of f (not necessarily the least such), we need only a point a such that $a \leq f(a)$ to start the process of iteration from. There is no condition on f (other than that it be continuous). For metric spaces, *(i)* means that $d(a, f(a))$ is finite, and *(ii)* means that

$$\forall \epsilon > 0. \exists N \in \mathbb{N}. \forall y \in A. \left[d(a, y) < \infty \Longrightarrow d(f^N(a), f^N(y)) < \epsilon\right].$$

In ordinary metric spaces all distances are finite, hence *(i)* is trivially true i.e. there is no condition on a, and it is easy to see that the second condition is weaker than the Banach condition that f be contracting. (We could say, in line with our comments on the definition of Cauchy sequence, that f merely has to be "essentially" contracting.)

We now turn to the problem of solving domain equations, and of finding an analogue of the categorical versions of the Kleene and Banach theorem that we discussed previously. It is natural to consider Ω-$CCat$ and the corresponding category with embedding-projection pairs (just retracts in the usual categorical sense) Ω-$CCat^{ep}$ as suitable categories for solving such equations. We can define what it means for a sequence of domains to be 'Cauchy' and obtain a generalization of Scott's inverse limit theorem, leading to the following generalized Kleene-Banach theorem for domain equations:

Theorem 4.7 *Given a continuous endofunctor F on Ω-$CCat$, consider the corresponding endofunctor F on Ω-$CCat^{ep}$ and assume that we have an Ω-functor $\phi : \mathbb{1} \to F\mathbb{1}$. If the diagram*

$$\mathcal{D} = \quad \mathbb{1} \underset{!}{\overset{\phi}{\rightleftarrows}} F\mathbb{1} \underset{F!}{\overset{F\phi}{\rightleftarrows}} \cdots$$

is Cauchy, then its limit is a fixed-point, up to isomorphism, of F.

□

This is the approach taken in [Wagner 94], where the missing definitions and the proof can be found. (The general applicability of this theorem is widened by an easy extension to functors of several arguments, some of which may be contravariant (such as $(\_ \to \_)$). For this general technique, see e.g. [Plotkin 83].)An alternative strategy for obtaining a fixed-point theorem for domain equations is to equip Ω-$CCat$ with the structure of a (large) Ω-category and then apply Theorem 4.6 directly to it. We start by defining the hom between two Ω-categories via the notion of 'noise' of an embedding-projection pair (a generalization of the corresponding notion in [America & Rutten 87]):

Definition 4.8 Let A and B be Ω-categories, $\phi : A \to B$ and $\psi : B \to A$ be Ω-functors and assume that $\psi \circ \phi = id_A$. We define the *noise* of (ϕ, ψ) by

$\delta(\phi, \psi) = (B \to B)[\phi \circ \psi, id_B]$. □

The noise of a retraction pair is a measure of how well the retract approximates the other Ω-category. In the case of preorders a retraction pair has noise $\top$ if and only if it fulfills the Scott condition $\phi \circ \psi \leq id_B$, i.e. if it is an embedding-projection pair in the usual sense. Given two Ω-categories we can now measure how well one approximates the other by quantifying over all possible embedding-projection pairs as follows:

Definition 4.9 Let A and B be Ω-categories. We define $\nu[A, B]$ as

$$\bigvee \{ \delta(\phi, \psi) \mid \phi : A \to B,\ \psi : B \to A,\ \psi \circ \phi = id_A \}. \qquad \square$$

It is easy to see that ν is reflexive and transitive, and can thus be seen as a hom on Ω-*CCat*. It should be noted, however, that Ω-*CCat* cannot strictly be seen as an Ω-category, as its objects form a proper class. It is not sufficient to relax our definition of Ω-category: in Theorem 4.6 we actually quantify over all the objects in our Ω-category. This, however, is also easily remedied: it suffices to notice that in the proof of that theorem we use only a and points in the orbit of a (i.e. of the form $f^n(a)$). We can therefore relax condition *(ii)* to:

$$I \leq \bigvee_{N\in\mathbb{N}} \bigwedge_{M\in\mathbb{N}} \left[\neg\neg A\left[a, f^M(a)\right], A\left[f^N(a), f^{N+M}(a)\right]\right],$$

where we quantify only over the natural numbers. Full details of the generalized Kleene-Banach fixed-point theorem for domain equations thus obtained will be given in a separate paper.

5 Conclusion and related work

We have shown that the enriched-category approach provides a unified framework for both order-theoretic and metric fixed-point theory, one that encompasses both functions inside a given category and endofunctors on that category.

Flagg and Kopperman have independently developed a generalized domain theory based on Lawvere's notion of enriched categories, also enriching over commutative unital quantales ([Flagg & Kopperman 94, 96]), but they restrict their quantales to be what they term 'value quantales', which fulfill a kind of continuity requirement. Also they prefer to see a preorder not as a category enriched over the two point lattice, but as a category enriched over a value quantale generated by the compact elements of the original preorder. On the one hand this means that they can give a more topological account of their spaces, since the continuity requirement on Ω means essentially that they can "divide epsilons by 2" mimicking many classical metric arguments. On the other it means that their theory is not parameterized with respect to Ω in the same way as ours – which, for fixed Ω, allows us to use the nice categorical structure of Ω-*Cat*. (For instance, the tensor product of two preorders is simply their tensor as Ω-categories.)

Concerning the issue of completion, we note firstly that Lawvere introduces the concept of Cauchy completion for enriched categories using bimodules (relations valued in the category one enriches over) ([Lawvere 73]). With this definition he shows how the categorical Cauchy completion of a symmetric metric space, seen as an enriched category, coincides with the standard metric completion. In spite of this, however, his is not the right definition for our purposes. The reason is that Lawvere's concept is a direct generalization of the usual notion of Cauchy completion of a category in terms of splitting idempotents, and in a preorder seen as a category all idempotents split, hence every preorder is Cauchy complete according to this definition.

If we insist of basing our completion directly on the notion of Cauchy sequences we can define the Cauchy completion of an Ω-category in the same manner as the completion of a generalized ultrametric space is defined in [Bonsangue, van Breugel & Rutten 95]. This amounts to defining the completion of an Ω-category, A say, to be the intersection of all liminf-complete sub-Ω-categories of $(A^{\text{op}} \to \Omega)$ which contain all representables (Ω-functors of the form $A[\_, a]$ for some $a \in A$.) This definition does yield the completion under Cauchy sequences of an Ω-category, but it is so unconstructive that it is of little use. As an alternative, the notion of ideal completion of Ω-categories has been carried out in some generality in [Wagner 96]. Here ideal completion of preorders is unified with metric completion of generalized metric spaces.

Acknowledgments

This work was partially funded by JNICT, Programa de Formacão de Recursos Humanos e Mobilidade, BD855. We wish to thank Reinhold Heckmann and Dusko Pavlovic for their careful reviewing of an early draft of this paper.

References

[Adámek 92] J. Adámek, **Data types in algebraically ω-complete categories**, Universität Passau, Fakultät für Mathematik und Informatik, MIP-9201, Feb. 1992.

[Adámek 95] J. Adámek, **Banach's fixpoint theorem as a basis for recursive data types**, preprint.

[America & Rutten 87] P. America and J. Rutten, **Solving reflexive domain equations in a category of complete metric spaces**, Centrum voor Wiskunde en Informatica, Report CS-R8709, Feb. 1987. Also in *Journal of Computer and System Science*, 39(3):343–375, 1989.

[Bonsangue, van Breugel & Rutten 95] M. Bonsangue, F. van Breugel and J. Rutten, **Generalized ultrametric spaces: completion, topology and powerdomains via the Yoneda embedding**, Technical Report CS-R9560, Centrum voor Wiskunde en Informatica, Amsterdam, 1995.

[Borceux 94] F. Borceux, **Handbook of Categorical Algebra**, vol. I–III, Encyclopedia of Mathematics and its Applications, Cambridge University Press, 1994.

[Escardo 95] M. Escardo, **Induction and Recursion on the Real Line**, Theory and Formal Methods 1994, IC Press, 1995

[Flagg & Kopperman 94] B. Flagg and R. Kopperman, **Fixed points and reflexive domain equations in categories of continuity spaces**, MFPS XI, New Orleans March–April 1995, ENTCS, vol.1, 1995.

[Flagg & Kopperman 96] B. Flagg and R. Kopperman, **Continuity spaces: reconciling domains with metric spaces**, preprint.

[Kelly 82] F. Kelly, **Basic Concepts of Enriched Category Theory**, London Mathematical Society Lecture Series, vol. 64, Cambridge University Press, 1982.

[Lawvere 73] F.W. Lawvere, **Metric spaces, generalized logic, and closed categories**, Rendiconti Seminario Matematico e Fisico di Milano, vol. 43, pp. 135-166, 1974.

[Plotkin 83] G. Plotkin, **Domains**, Notes from the Department of Computer Science, University of Edinburgh, 1983.

[Rutten 95] J. Rutten, **Elements of generalized ultrametric domain theory**, Technical Report CS-R9507, Centrum voor Wiskunde en Informatica, Amsterdam, 1995.

[Scott 72] Scott, D.S., **Continuous lattices**, in Lawvere (ed.): Toposes, Algebraic Geometry and Logic, Lecture Notes in Mathematics 274, Springer Verlag, Berlin 1972.

[Seda 96] A. Seda, **Quasi-metrics and the semantics of logic programming**, preprint.

[Smyth 88] M. Smyth, **Quasi-uniformities: reconciling domains with metric spaces**, Proceedings of the 3'rd Workshop on the Mathematical Foundations of Programming Language Semantics, Tulane, April 1987, Lecture Notes in Computer Science, Vol. 298, Springer Verlag, 1988.

[Smyth & Plotkin 82] M. Smyth and G. Plotkin, **The category theoretic solution of recursive domain equations**, SIAM Journal of Computing, Vol. 11, No. 4, Nov. 1982.

[Wagner 94] K.R. Wagner, **Solving Recursive Domain Equations with Enriched Categories**, Ph.D. Thesis, Carnegie Mellon University, Technical Report CMU-CS-94-159, July 1994.

[Wagner 95] K.R. Wagner, **Liminf convergence in Ω-categories**, Theoretical Computer Science, *to appear*.

[Wagner 96] K.R. Wagner, **Some ideal completions in categories**, *submitted.*

SYNTACTIC CONTINUITY FROM STRUCTURAL OPERATIONAL SEMANTICS

DAVID SANDS
Department of Computing Science,
Chalmers University of Technology and Göteborg University,
S-412 96 Göteborg, Sweden; dave@cs.chalmers.se

We illustrate how standard properties of recursive constructs in functional languages can be established directly from operational semantics, with very little mathematical overhead. The main property is a syntactic analogy of continuity which relates a recursive function to is finite unwindings. This property forms the basis of Scott-style fixed point induction. We present a rule format for deterministic structural operational semantics, and prove that any language which can be expressed in this rule format satisfies the syntactic continuity property.

1 Summary and Related Work

Methods for reasoning about equivalence in functional languages are often based upon denotational semantics. One characteristic feature of such semantics is that recursion in the language is modelled by the construction of a least fixed point in some suitable ordered domain of interpretations. The meta-theory of denotational semantics—domain theory—guarantees the existence of fixed points, and provides certain reasoning principles for recursion based on this theory.

Operational semantics can also be used as the basis for reasoning about equivalence in functional languages. A notable operationally-based technique is the use of "applicative bisimulation" [Abr90] to reason about equivalence. In this article we illustrate how the properties of recursive definitions usually associated with the trappings of a denotational semantics can be established at the syntactic level from operational semantics, with very little mathematical overhead. The main property that we establish is a syntactic analogy of continuity which forms the basis of Scott-style fixed point induction. The syntactic continuity property says that a recursive constant $\mathbf{f}$ can be characterised in terms of its syntactic finite unwindings, $\{\mathbf{f}^i\}_{i\geq 0}$. More specifically, $\mathbf{f}$ the least term (up to operational equivalence) which is operationally greater than the $\mathbf{f}^i$; moreover, this property is preserved by all syntactic contexts:

$$C\langle \mathbf{f}\rangle \precsim M \iff \forall i.\, C\langle \mathbf{f}^i\rangle \precsim M$$

Proofs of related properties based on operational semantics, for specific languages, are not particularly new. See for example [Tal85, Smi92, Dam94,

MT91, MST99, Pit99]. We have taken the term "syntactic continuity" from [Pit99] although our proof is somewhat more direct, and much more in the spirit of proofs found in [Smi92, MST99, MT91]. The main contribution is to lift these proofs from a particular language to any language whose structural operational semantics fit a certain *rule format*; as well as providing some generality for the proofs, the proofs themselves are actually simplified, since fewer cases need be considered. Such rule formats are well-known in process algebra (e.g., see [GV92] [BIM95]) where the typical theorem established is that bisimulation is a congruence. Howe [How91, How96] defines a rule format for the evaluation relation for functional languages, and proves that a functional analogy of bisimulation is a congruence. Our meta-syntax for defining rules is close to Howe's. Our rule format is based on a single step reduction relation, and appears to be less general, since it seems possible to obtain, from our rule format for reduction, a natural semantics format which is subsumed by Howe's.

2 Preliminaries

2.1 Evaluation, Operational Approximation and Equivalence

The subject of this study will be untyped, typically higher-order functional languages. To define what it means for two programs to be equivalent, or for one program to "approximate" another, we use an evaluation relation as our basic building block. An evaluation relation, $\Downarrow$, is a binary relation between closed terms and values; values are themselves just terms of a particular syntactic form. If $M{\Downarrow}V$ then computation beginning with M terminates with value V.

Given such a relation, we can build, in a standard way, definitions of approximation and equivalence. The operational approximation we use is the standard Morris-style contextual ordering. The notion of "observation" we take is just the fact of convergence, as in the lazy lambda calculus [Abr90]. This choice is not central to the development. Operational equivalence equates two expressions if and only if in all closing contexts they give rise to the same observation - i.e. either they both converge, or they both diverge.

Definition 2.1

(i) M operationally approximates N, $M \sqsubseteq N$, *if for all contexts C such that $C[M]$, $C[N]$ are closed, if $C[M]{\Downarrow}V$ then there exists a W such that $C[N]{\Downarrow}W$.*

(ii) M *is* operationally equivalent *to* N, $M \cong N$, *if* $M \sqsubseteq N$ *and* $N \sqsubseteq M$.

2.2 Structural Operational Semantics

We will consider evaluation relations which are defined in terms of a finer one-step evaluation relation, $\mapsto$; we define $M {\Downarrow} V$ for some value V if $M \mapsto^* V$. The mechanism we consider for defining $\mapsto$ is the well-known *Structural Operational Semantics* (SOS) [Plo81]. SOS is a syntactic style for presenting an inductively defined transition relation between "machine configurations", given by cases according to their syntactic structure. In the our setting, the machine configurations will be simply closed terms. As an example we present the one-step evaluation relation for the lazy lambda calculus [Abr90], together with booleans and conditionals, in Figure 1.

$$\frac{M \mapsto M'}{M\,N \mapsto M'\,N}$$

$$\frac{}{(\lambda x.M)\,N \mapsto M\{{}^{N}/_{x}\}}$$

$$\frac{M \mapsto N}{\textbf{if } M \textbf{ then } N_1 \textbf{ else } N_2 \mapsto \textbf{if } N \textbf{ then } N_1 \textbf{ else } N_2}$$

$$\frac{}{\textbf{if } \textit{true} \textbf{ then } N_1 \textbf{ else } N_2 \mapsto N_1}$$

$$\frac{}{\textbf{if } \textit{false} \textbf{ then } N_1 \textbf{ else } N_2 \mapsto N_2}$$

Figure 1: Example SOS Rules

For this language the values are deemed to be ***true***, ***false***, and any closed lambda-term. It is easy to see that $\mapsto$, and hence $\Downarrow$ are partial functions.

3 A Second Order Abstract Syntax

We introduce an abstract syntax for specifying functional programs, and for specifying a SOS rule format given in the next section. Our syntax follows [How91] very closely, but is fairly standard from the point of view of formal specification of syntax which includes variable binding operators such as lambda abstraction (e.g., see [NPS90, Klo80]).

First we fix a countably infinite set V of ordinary variables. A language **L** is specified by a set of operators O of a fixed arity α. The arity specifies the number of *operands* for each operator. The arity of an operator specifies more than this; each operand is possibly an abstraction, i.e., a list of zero or more distinct variables followed by a term, where the variables are considered bound in the term. The arity of an operator is thus specified by a sequence of natural numbers; the length of the sequence is the number of operands, and the natural numbers are the number of bound variables associated to each operand. For example, the language implicit in the rules of Figure 1 would be represented in this syntax by the set of operators $\{\lambda, \textbf{\textit{apply}}, \textbf{\textit{if}}, \textbf{\textit{true}}, \textbf{\textit{false}}\}$ with arities $\alpha(\lambda) = (1)$, $\alpha(\textbf{\textit{apply}}) = (0,0)$, $\alpha(\textbf{\textit{if}}) = (0,0,0)$, $\alpha(\textbf{\textit{true}}) = \alpha(\textbf{\textit{false}}) = ()$.

Let x, y, etc., range over V, and let p, q range over O. The terms of $\mathbf{L}$, $T(\mathbf{L})$, ranged over by M, N are defined inductively as follows:

$$\frac{}{x \in T(\mathbf{L})} \qquad \frac{M_1 \in T(\mathbf{L}) \cdots M_n \in T(\mathbf{L})}{p((\vec{x_1})M_1, \ldots, (\vec{x_n})M_n) \in T(\mathbf{L})}\ \alpha(p) = (k_1, \ldots k_n)$$

where each $\vec{x_i}$ is a list of k_i distinct variables.

For example, the term $(\lambda x.y)z$ will be written in this abstract syntax as $\textbf{\textit{apply}}(\lambda((x)y), z)$.

3.1 Meta Terms

In order to formalise the rules of a structural operational semantics for such a language we introduce a syntax for *meta terms*. First we fix an infinite set of meta variables $\mathcal{V}$, ranged over by $\mathcal{X}$, $\mathcal{Y}$, etc. Meta variables will range over both terms and operands (abstractions). With each metavariable $\mathcal{X}$, we associate an arity $\alpha(X)$ which is a natural number. The idea is that metavariables of arity 0 will range over terms, while meta variables of higher arity will range over abstractions.

Definition 3.1 *To define the metaterms for a given language* $\mathbf{L}$, *we define an indexed set of meta-abstractions* $\{MT_i\}_{i \geq 0}$, *(ranged over by* $\mathcal{M}$, $\mathcal{N}$, *etc.) inductively according to the following rules.*

$$\frac{}{x \in MT_0} \qquad \frac{}{\mathcal{X} \in MT_n}\ \alpha(\mathcal{X}) = n$$

$$\frac{\mathcal{M} \in MT_0}{(x_1, \ldots, x_n)\mathcal{M} \in MT_n} \qquad \frac{\mathcal{M}_1 \in MT_0 \cdots \mathcal{M}_n \in MT_0}{\mathcal{X} \cdot (\mathcal{M}_1, \ldots, \mathcal{M}_n) \in MT_0}\ \alpha(\mathcal{X}) = n$$

$$\frac{\mathcal{M}_1 \in MT_{k_1} \ldots \mathcal{M}_n \in MT_{k_n}}{p(\mathcal{M}_1, \ldots, \mathcal{M}_n) \in MT_0}\ \alpha(p) = (k_1, \ldots, k_n)$$

Then we define the metaterms to be MT_0.

The construct $\mathcal{X} \cdot (\mathcal{M}_1, \ldots, \mathcal{M}_n)$ is meta-application. Metavariable $\mathcal{X}$ ranges over an abstractions with n variables. When $\mathcal{X}$ is replaced by such an abstraction, the meta-terms $\mathcal{M}_1, \ldots, \mathcal{M}_n$ will be substituted for the abstracted variables. Let σ range over second-order substitutions—finite mappings from metavariables to abstractions of corresponding arity. Thus if $\sigma(\mathcal{X})$ is defined then it has the form $(x_1, \ldots, x_n)M$. The operation of second order substitution is defined as for normal substitution, except that if $\sigma(\mathcal{X}) = (x_1, \ldots, x_n)M$ then

$$\sigma(\mathcal{X} \cdot (\mathcal{M}_1, \ldots, \mathcal{M}_n)) = M\{\sigma(\mathcal{M}_1), \ldots, \sigma(\mathcal{M}_n)/_{x_1, \ldots, x_n}\}.$$

4 The DSOS Rule Format

The purpose of metaterms is to describe the rules of a structural operational semantics. As an example, the application axiom from the operational semantics of Figure 1 can be written as

$$\overline{\boldsymbol{apply}(\lambda\mathcal{X}, \mathcal{Y}) \mapsto \mathcal{X} \cdot \mathcal{Y}}$$

Such a rule schema defines transitions on terms as follows: for all second order substitutions σ whose domain includes $\mathcal{X}$ and $\mathcal{Y}$, and whose range are closed terms, we have that $\sigma(\boldsymbol{apply}(\lambda\mathcal{X}, \mathcal{Y})) \mapsto \sigma(\mathcal{X} \cdot \mathcal{Y})$. Here we use the metaterms to define a particular rule format.

Definition 4.1 (Deterministic Structural Operational Semantics) *A language* **L** *is in* DSOS format *if the one step evaluation relation can be expressed by rules of the following forms. First, each operator of the language is classified as a* type 1 *operator, a* type 2 *operator, or a* canonical operator *(ranged over by* **c**, **c**′*). Now the SOS rules of the operators have the following forms:*

Type 1 *Each type 1 operator has a single axiom of the form*

$$\boxed{\overline{p(\mathcal{X}_1, \ldots, \mathcal{X}_n) \mapsto \mathcal{M}}}$$

where $\alpha(p) = (k_1 \ldots, k_n)$, and the free metavariables of $\mathcal{M}$ are included in $\{\mathcal{X}_1, \ldots, \mathcal{X}_n\}$.

Type 2 *Each type 2 operator* **p** *has an arity of the form $(0, k_2, \ldots k_n)$, and has one inference rule, together with possibly infinitely many axioms of the of the following forms:*

$$\boxed{\begin{array}{c} \dfrac{\mathcal{X}_1 \mapsto \mathcal{Y}_1}{p(\mathcal{X}_1, \mathcal{X}_2, \ldots \mathcal{X}_n) \mapsto p(\mathcal{Y}_1, \mathcal{X}_2, \ldots \mathcal{X}_n)} \\[2em] \left\{ \overline{p(c_i(\vec{\mathcal{Y}}), \mathcal{X}_2, \ldots, \mathcal{X}_n) \mapsto \mathcal{M}_i} \right\}_{i \in I} \end{array}}$$

where the canonical operators c_i *are distinct, and the free metavariables of* $\mathcal{M}_i$ *are included in* $\vec{\mathcal{Y}} \cup \{\mathcal{X}_2, \ldots, \mathcal{X}_n\}$.

There are no rules for the canonical operators.

Examples Here we give some examples of operators which can be expressed in DSOS format. The rules of Fig. 1 can all be written in this format. The interesting example is the application operator, which is a type 2 operator. The associated rules are:

$$\frac{\mathcal{Z} \mapsto \mathcal{Z}'}{\boldsymbol{apply}(\mathcal{Z}, \mathcal{Y}) \mapsto \boldsymbol{apply}(\mathcal{Z}', \mathcal{Y})} \qquad \frac{}{\boldsymbol{apply}(\lambda\mathcal{X}, \mathcal{Y}) \mapsto \mathcal{X} \cdot \mathcal{Y}}$$

As an example of a type-one operator, consider a local recursion construct with concrete syntax **letrec** $x = M$ **in** N, and with a computation rule:

$$\textbf{letrec } x = M \textbf{ in } N \mapsto N\{\textbf{letrec } x = M \textbf{ in } M/_x\}$$

The ***letrec*** operator has arity $(1,1)$, and **letrec** $x = M$ **in** N has abstract syntax $\boldsymbol{letrec}((x)M, (x)N)$. The type 1 rule is

$$\frac{}{\boldsymbol{letrec}(\mathcal{X}, \mathcal{Y}) \mapsto \mathcal{Y} \cdot \boldsymbol{letrec}(\mathcal{X}, \mathcal{X})}$$

Multiple-strict operators cannot be represented directly. Fortunately they can be represented indirectly with the help of additional operators. In this way we can obtain results for e.g., call-by-value languages without considering a more general rule format.

4.1 Convergence and Reduction Contexts for DSOS

The rules of a DSOS induce a one step transition relation on closed terms of the underlying language **L** in the obvious way. Let $\mapsto^*$ denote the reflexive and transitive closure of the one step evaluation relation. Convergence is defined as follows:

Definition 4.2 *The* Weak Head Normal Forms, *WHNF, ranged over by* W, V *are defined to be the set of all closed terms whose outermost operator is canonical.*

Closed term M *converges to* W, *written* $M{\Downarrow}W$ *if and only if* $M \mapsto^* W$.

Proposition 4.3 *Relations* $\mapsto$ *and* $\Downarrow$ *are deterministic (up to* $\equiv$*).*

PROOF. The conditions on the rules guarantee that $\mapsto$ is deterministic (this is shown easily by induction on the formal derivations of transitions), and this in turn establishes that $\Downarrow$ is deterministic. □

4.2 Context Notation and Reduction Contexts

The definition of operational approximation and equivalence involve the notions of a context. The definition of a context is the usual one. In particular the holes in a context occur in place of *terms*, and not arbitrary operands (abstractions). As is also usual, a context may capture free variables in the term placed in its holes. In reasoning directly about the operational orderings for a language in DSOS format we will do some proofs directly involving manipulation of contexts. For this we need a more general form of context in which more than one distinct type of hole may occur. These are sometimes called *polyadic* contexts. In fact we will be able to make do with just two distinct "holes", denoted by $[\,]$ and $\langle\,\rangle$.

Contexts C, C' etc. will now denote contexts containing zero or more occurrences of two distinct types of hole, $[\,]$ and $\langle\,\rangle$. We will adopt the convention that when we write $C\langle\,\rangle$ we are indicating that context C contains no occurrences of the hole $[\,]$, and vice-versa. As an example, if C is the context $(\lambda x.[\,])\langle\,\rangle$ then $C[x]\langle \boldsymbol{true}\rangle$ is the term $(\lambda x.x)\,\boldsymbol{true}$

4.3 Reduction Contexts

An alternative (but equivalent) presentation of the one step evaluation relation is in terms of a simple form of contexts containing a single occurrence of a single hole, known as *reduction context* [FFK87] (or *evaluation contexts*). A reduction context is used to specify the position in a term where the next reduction step can be performed. As an example, for the language in Figure 1 the reduction contexts $\mathcal{R}$ are contexts given inductively by: $\mathcal{R} ::= [\,] \mid \mathcal{R}\ M \mid \textbf{if}\ \mathcal{R}\ \textbf{then}\ M\ \textbf{else}\ N$. We will use a reduction context presentation of the rules to simplify some of our reasoning.

Definition 4.4 *The reduction contexts for a language in DSOS format are defined inductively as follows:*

- $[\,]$ *is a reduction context;*
- *if* $\mathcal{R}$ *is a reduction context, and* $\boldsymbol{p}$ *is a type 2 operator then a well-formed context of the form* $\boldsymbol{p}(\mathcal{R}, (\vec{x}_2)M_2, \ldots, (\vec{x}_n)M_n)$ *is a reduction context.*

Given this definition, it can be seen that the transition relation generated by the rules of a DSOS can be equivalently represented by the collection of axioms

$$\{\mathcal{R}[\mathcal{M}] \mapsto \mathcal{R}[\mathcal{N}] \mid \mathcal{M} \mapsto \mathcal{N} \text{ is an axiom of the DSOS }\}$$

The determinacy of the system guarantees that if $M \mapsto N$ then there exists a unique reduction context $\mathcal{R}$, and unique terms M' and N' such that $M \equiv$

$\mathcal{R}[M']$, $N \equiv \mathcal{R}[N']$, and such that $M' \mapsto N'$ is an instance of an axiom of the DSOS (we say that M' is a *redex*).

4.4 Reduction Contexts with Holes

A reduction step of a term of the form $C\langle M\rangle$, if $M \notin$ WHNF, satisfies the following informal property: either the reduction step does not depend on M (it is uniform in M) or it occurs inside M. This property holds of any language in DSOS format, and captures a common case analysis used (usually informally) when reasoning directly about operational approximation. This property is formalised below.

The following defines a particular set of contexts – namely reduction contexts with additional $\langle\ \rangle$-holes:

Definition 4.5 *Let* $\hat{\mathcal{R}}$, $\hat{\mathcal{R}}'$, *the* reduction contexts with holes, *be defined as follows:*

- $[\,]$ *is a reduction context with holes;*
- *if* p *is a type 2 operator of arity* $(0, k_2, \ldots k_n)$, *and* $\vec{x}_i$, $i \in \{2, \ldots, n\}$ *is a vector of* k_i *distinct variables, then*

  $$p(\hat{\mathcal{R}}, (\vec{x}_2).C_2\langle\ \rangle, \ldots (\vec{x}_n).C_n\langle\ \rangle)$$

  is a reduction context with holes.

Lemma 4.6 *For any DSOS language, for all contexts* $C\langle\ \rangle$, *and all closed expressions* $M \notin$ *WHNF, if* $C\langle M\rangle \mapsto M'$, *then there exit contexts* $\hat{\mathcal{R}}$, $C'\langle\ \rangle$ *such that* $C \equiv \hat{\mathcal{R}}\langle\ \rangle[C']$ *and exactly one of the following two properties hold:*

(i) either the reduction is uniform in M*:*

there exists a context C'', *such that for all closed* N, $C'\langle N\rangle \mapsto C''\langle N\rangle$

(ii) or the reduction is "inside" M*:*

$C' = \langle\ \rangle$ *and* $M \mapsto$.

The proof is by induction on the context C, and by cases according to the outermost operator type.

Example Taking the concrete language of the previous section, if C is the context **if** $(\lambda x.x)\langle\ \rangle$ **then** ***false*** **else** $\langle\ \rangle$ and $M = $ ***true***, then $\hat{\mathcal{R}} = $ **if** $[\,]$ **then** ***false*** **else** $\langle\ \rangle$, $C' = (\lambda x.x)\langle\ \rangle$, and the reduction step of $C\langle$***true***$\rangle$ is uniform in ***true***.

5 Fixed-Point Properties

In this section we present the main result which establishes the "syntactic continuity" property for DSOS languages with recursion.

There are many equivalent forms of recursive definition. In what follows we will consider DSOS languages containing constants as specified by recursion equations. The addition of such constants does not change the expressive power of a DSOS languages[a] but eases the job of proving fixed point properties—in particular since the recursive constants are not variables, so cannot be captured.

A recursion equation $\mathbf{h} \triangleq M$ is taken to be synonymous with a type 1 operator $\mathbf{h}$ of arity (), with DSOS rule $\mathbf{h} \mapsto M$. In particular we consider languages in DSOS format which contain some recursively defined constant

$$\mathbf{f} \triangleq C_{\mathbf{f}}\langle \mathbf{f} \rangle$$

where we assume that the (closed) context $C_{\mathbf{f}}$ does not contain occurrences of $\mathbf{f}$. Now we also assume a set of constants $\{\mathbf{f}^i\}_{i \geq 0}$ defined inductively by

$$\begin{aligned} \mathbf{f}^0 &\triangleq \mathbf{f}^0 \\ \mathbf{f}^{i+1} &\triangleq C_{\mathbf{f}}\langle \mathbf{f}^i \rangle \end{aligned}$$

We will call such a language a *DSOS language with recursion.* The functions $\{\mathbf{f}^i\}_{i \geq 0}$ form a chain, bounded above by $\mathbf{f}$:

Proposition 5.1 *For any DSOS language with recursion,*

(i) $\mathbf{f} \cong C_{\mathbf{f}}\langle \mathbf{f} \rangle$.

(ii) For all $i \geq 0$, $\mathbf{f}^i \precsim \mathbf{f}^{i+1} \precsim \mathbf{f}$.

PROOF. (Sketch) For the first part, we establish more generally that $\mapsto \subseteq \cong$ reasoning directly from the definition of operational approximation, making use of of Lemma 4.6. The second part is proved by induction on i; in the base case show that $\mathbf{f}^0$ is operationally less than any other expression; the induction case then follows easily.

□

The point of the functions $\{\mathbf{f}^i\}_{i \geq 0}$ is that they completely characterise the behaviour of the function $\mathbf{f}$. This is the essence of the fixed point induction principle of Scott-style denotational semantics. The main property which justifies this is the following syntactic continuity property for the chain $\{\mathbf{f}^i\}_{i \geq 0}$; $\mathbf{f}$ the least upper bound of this chain, and contexts preserve this:

[a]More precisely, under the assumption that the language already contains some nonterminating term, then the addition of recursive constants conservatively extends the theory of operational approximation.

Theorem 5.2 (Syntactic Continuity for DSOS with Recursion) *For any DSOS language with recursion, for all closed contexts $C\langle\ \rangle$, and closed expressions M of the language we have*

$$C\langle \mathbf{f} \rangle \underset{\sim}{\sqsubset} M \iff \forall i.\, C\langle \mathbf{f}^i \rangle \underset{\sim}{\sqsubset} M$$

PROOF. ($\Rightarrow$) Follows from Prop 5.1, together with the congruence property of $\underset{\sim}{\sqsubset}$.

($\Leftarrow$) Under the assumption that $\forall i.\, C\langle \mathbf{f}^i \rangle \underset{\sim}{\sqsubset} M$ we will show that for all contexts $C_0[\,]$, and all natural numbers n, if $C_0[C\langle \mathbf{f} \rangle]$ converges in n steps then $C_0[M]$ converges. From the assumption, and the congruence property of $\underset{\sim}{\sqsubset}$, it will be sufficient to show that $C_0[C\langle \mathbf{f}^n \rangle]$ converges, and this we do by induction on n.

Let $C_1\langle\ \rangle$ denote the context $C_0[C]$.

Base: $n = 0$ Then $C_1\langle \mathbf{f} \rangle \in$ WHNF, and hence C_1 must have an outermost canonical operator. Hence $C_1\langle \mathbf{f}^n \rangle \in$ WHNF.

Induction: $n > 0$ In that case we have $C_1\langle \mathbf{f} \rangle \mapsto N$ for some N such that N converges in $n-1$ steps. We proceed by case analysis according to Lemma 4.6. C_1 can be written as $\hat{\mathcal{R}}\langle\ \rangle[C']$ for some $\hat{\mathcal{R}}$ and $C'\langle\ \rangle$. The Lemma gives us two cases, corresponding to whether $\mathbf{f}$ is involved in the reduction step or not. In the first case there exists a C'' such that for all L, $C'\langle L \rangle \mapsto C''\langle L \rangle$ So in particular we have that

$$\begin{aligned} C_1\langle \mathbf{f} \rangle &\equiv \hat{\mathcal{R}}\langle \mathbf{f} \rangle[C'\langle \mathbf{f} \rangle] &&\mapsto \hat{\mathcal{R}}\langle \mathbf{f} \rangle[C''\langle \mathbf{f} \rangle] \equiv N \\ \text{and}\quad C_1\langle \mathbf{f}^n \rangle &\equiv \hat{\mathcal{R}}\langle \mathbf{f}^n \rangle[C'\langle \mathbf{f}^n \rangle] &&\mapsto \hat{\mathcal{R}}\langle \mathbf{f}^n \rangle[C''\langle \mathbf{f}^n \rangle] \end{aligned}$$

Now since $\hat{\mathcal{R}}\langle \mathbf{f} \rangle[C''\langle \mathbf{f} \rangle]$ converges in $n-1$ steps, by the induction hypothesis we conclude that $\hat{\mathcal{R}}\langle \mathbf{f}^{n-1} \rangle[C''\langle \mathbf{f}^{n-1} \rangle]\Downarrow$.

Since $\mathbf{f}^{n-1} \underset{\sim}{\sqsubset} \mathbf{f}^n$ we can conclude by congruence that $\hat{\mathcal{R}}\langle \mathbf{f}^n \rangle[C''\langle \mathbf{f}^n \rangle]\Downarrow$, i.e., that $C_1\langle \mathbf{f}^n \rangle\Downarrow$.

In the second case we have $C' = \langle\ \rangle$ and hence the redex is $\mathbf{f}$ itself. By definition, $\mathbf{f} \mapsto C_{\mathbf{f}}\langle \mathbf{f} \rangle$ and $\mathbf{f}^n \mapsto C_{\mathbf{f}}\langle \mathbf{f}^{n-1} \rangle$. So in this case we have

$$\begin{aligned} C_1\langle \mathbf{f} \rangle &\equiv \hat{\mathcal{R}}\langle \mathbf{f} \rangle[\mathbf{f}] &&\mapsto \hat{\mathcal{R}}\langle \mathbf{f} \rangle[C_{\mathbf{f}}\langle \mathbf{f} \rangle] \equiv N \\ \text{and}\quad C_1\langle \mathbf{f}^n \rangle &\equiv \hat{\mathcal{R}}\langle \mathbf{f}^n \rangle[\mathbf{f}^n] &&\mapsto \hat{\mathcal{R}}\langle \mathbf{f}^n \rangle[C_{\mathbf{f}}\langle \mathbf{f}^{n-1} \rangle] \end{aligned}$$

But $\hat{\mathcal{R}}\langle \mathbf{f} \rangle[C_{\mathbf{f}}\langle \mathbf{f} \rangle]$ converges in $(n-1)$-steps, and so by the induction hypothesis we have $\hat{\mathcal{R}}\langle \mathbf{f}^{n-1} \rangle[C_{\mathbf{f}}\langle \mathbf{f}^{n-1} \rangle]\Downarrow$ which implies that $\hat{\mathcal{R}}\langle \mathbf{f}^n \rangle[C_{\mathbf{f}}\langle \mathbf{f}^{n-1} \rangle]\Downarrow$. Hence we can conclude that $C_1\langle \mathbf{f}^n \rangle\Downarrow$ as required. □

From this we can establish some other standard fixed point properties. We already know that $\mathbf{f}$ satisfies $\mathbf{f} \cong C_{\mathbf{f}}\langle\mathbf{f}\rangle$. The least-fixed-point property asserts that $\mathbf{f}$ is the least expression (up to $\precsim$) satisfying this equation. The following is a slight strengthening:

Theorem 5.3 (Least Pre-fixed Point) *For any DSOS language with recursion, if M is a closed expression satisfying $C_{\mathbf{f}}[M] \sqsubseteq_{\sim} M$ then $\mathbf{f} \sqsubseteq_{\sim} M$.*

PROOF. By Theorem 5.2, it is sufficient to show that $\forall i.\mathbf{f}^i \sqsubseteq_{\sim} M$. This follows by an easy induction on i. The details are left as an exercise. □

It is possible to build up various fixed-point induction principles. The following is a good starting point:

Theorem 5.4 *If for all $n \geq 0$ we have $C[\mathbf{f}^n] \sqsubseteq_{\sim} C'[\mathbf{f}^n]$, then $C[\mathbf{f}] \sqsubseteq_{\sim} C'[\mathbf{f}]$*

PROOF. Assume the condition of the theorem. Then from Proposition 5.1 we have that for all $n \geq 0$ $C[\mathbf{f}^n] \sqsubseteq_{\sim} C'[\mathbf{f}]$. Theorem 5.2 then gives $C[\mathbf{f}] \sqsubseteq_{\sim} C'[\mathbf{f}]$ as required. □

6 Further Work

We can show that applicative (bi)simulation for a language in DSOS format is a congruence, by inducing a natural semantics and showing that it conforms to Howe's lazy computation system format [How91]. Further work includes the development of other theorems for DSOS, and the details of how richer formats including a more direct treatment of call-by-value can be reduced to DSOS, and a uniform treatment of staticly typed languages.

Acknowledgements

A vital contribution to this paper was made by Davide Sangiorgi (INRIA), in the form of the DSOS rule format; Davide proposed the rule format during an earlier joint investigation into proof techniques for functional programs. Thanks to Guy McCusker and Gabrielle Sinnadurai for helpful comments on an earlier draft.

[Abr90] S. Abramsky. The lazy lambda calculus. In D. Turner, editor, *Research Topics in Functional Programming*, pages 65–116. Addison Wesley, 1990.

[BIM95] Bard Bloom, Sorin Istrail, and Albert R. Meyer. Bisimulation can't be traced. *Journal of the ACM*, 42(1):232–268, January 1995.

[Dam94] L. Dami. *Software Composition: Towards and Integration of Functional and Object-Oriented Approaches.* PhD thesis, Faculté des Sciences Économiques et Scociales, Université de Genève, 1994.

[FFK87] M. Felleisen, D. Friedman, and E. Kohlbecker. A syntactic theory of sequential control. *Theoretical Computer Science*, 52(1):205–237, 1987.

[GV92] J.F. Groote and F.W. Vaandrager. Structured operational semantics and bisimulation as a congruence. *Information and Computation*, 100(2):202–260, October 1992.

[How91] D. J. Howe. On computational open-endedness in Martin-Löf's type theory. In *Sixth annual symposium on Logic In Computer Science*, pages 162–172, 1991.

[How96] D. J. Howe. Proving congruence of bisimulation in functional programming languages. *Information and Computation*, 124(2):103–112, February 1996.

[Klo80] J.W. Klop. *Combinatory Reduction Systems*, volume 127 of *Mathematical Centre Tracts*. Mathematischen Centrum, 413 Kruislaan, Amsterdam, 1980.

[MST99] I. A. Mason, S. Smith, and C. L. Talcott. From Operational Semantics to Domain Theory. *Information and Computation*, 199? to appear.

[MT91] I. Mason and C. Talcott. Equivalence in functional languages with effects. *Journal of Functional Programming*, 1(3):287–327, July 1991.

[NPS90] Bengt Nordström, Kent Petersson, and Jan M. Smith. *Programming in Martin-Löf's Type Theory: An Introduction*, volume 7 of *International Series of Monographs on Computer Science*. Oxford University Press, 1990.

[Pit99] A. M. Pitts. Operationally-based theories of program equivalence. In P. Dybjer and A. M. Pitts, editors, *Semantics and Logics of Computation*. Cambridge University Press, 199? Based on lectures given at the CLICS-II Summer School on Semantics and Logics of Computation, Isaac Newton Institute for Mathematical Sciences, Cambridge UK, September 1995.

[Plo81] G. D. Plotkin. A structural approach to operational semantics. Technical Report DAIMI FN–19, Computer Science Department, Aahus University, Denmark, September 1981.

[Smi92] Scott Smith. From operational to denotational semantics. In *Conference on Mathematical Foundations of Programming Language Semantics*, volume 598 of *Lecture Notes in Computer Science*. Springer-Verlag, 1992.

[Tal85] C. L. Talcott. *The Essence of Rum, A Theory of the intensional and extensional aspects of Lisp-type computation*. PhD thesis, Stanford University, August 1985.

A PROOF OF THE COMPLETENESS OF AN INFERENCE SYSTEM FOR STRICTNESS ANALYSIS DEVELOPED BY HANKIN AND LE MÉTAYER

A. P. G. SINNADURAI
Department of Computing, Imperial College, London SW7 2BZ.

This paper gives the interesting part of a proof of the completeness of an inference system for strictness analysis developed by Hankin and Le Métayer.

1 Introduction

In their paper on deriving algorithms from type inference systems [HLM94] Hankin and Le Métayer present an inference system for strictness analysis which they call the *lazy types system*. They claim that this system is complete in the sense that any theorem derivable in a strictness logic developed by Jensen [Jen92] is a theorem of the lazy types system. Unfortunately their proposed method of proof cannot be made to work. In my MSc dissertation [Dol94] I gave semantics for 'lazy types' and simplified Jensen's semantics for his strictness logic, but was unable to give a direct proof of completeness of the lazy types system against the semantics. I now have such a direct proof. The idea is to show first that given any query the inference system terminates then to show that if a query is valid then either it is an axiom or it can be reduced to valid queries. The second part of the proof is routine and will not be presented here. The proof of termination uses a notion similar to that of 'convertible' term introduced by Tait [Tai67] and is presented here. The full proof can be found in my forthcoming PhD thesis [Sin97].

2 Background and Intuitions

The proof of termination of the lazy types system of Hankin and Le Métayer is rather technical. This section gives the background of the system and the idea behind the proof and is intended to illuminate the following sections containing the definitions and proofs.

The programming language on which the strictness analysis is performed is a version of the simply typed λ-calculus with constants including recursion given in Definitions 3.1 and 3.2.

In [BHA86], Burn, Hankin and Abramsky gave an 'abstract interpretation' of the simply typed λ-calculus in a family of 'abstract domains' and showed that it was sound for strictness analysis in the sense that if the abstract interpretation of a λ-term is a strict function in its abstract domain then the λ-term denotes a strict function in the standard lazy semantics.

Because the abstract domains are finite (Definition 3.3) the abstract interpretation of a λ-term is computable so it is decidable whether or not a λ-term denotes a strict function in its abstract domain. Hence we have an algorithm which takes λ-terms as inputs and tells us which are guaranteed to be strict in the standard lazy semantics. Unfortunately this algorithm is rather slow because it follows the abstract semantic definition so that, for example, to compute $[\![e_1 e_2]\!]$ it computes the whole of the abstract function $[\![e_1]\!]$ only to use it at one point in the application $[\![e_1]\!][\![e_2]\!]$.

Now, when strictness information is used in a compiler the full information as to where the abstract interpretation of a λ-term is in its abstract domain is not required. All that is needed is a *'yes'* or *'no'* answer to the question *'is the λ-term strict enough to allow me to make a desired operational change?'*. It is natural to try to answer such questions using an inference system. If the inference system is derived from the abstract interpretation then it will be 'compositional' in the sense that the strictness property of a λ-term will be inferred from the strictness properties of its subterms. That is, it will be a non standard type inference system.

In his PhD thesis Jensen [Jen92] derived a conjunctive non standard type inference system from the abstract interpretation of Burn, Hankin and Abramsky [BHA86] using Abramsky's domain theory in logical form [Abr91].

Since abstract domains are finite their Scott topology is rather simple so Abramsky's powerful machinery is not needed. Instead, we can view Jensen's inference system as though it were derived *directly* from the abstract interpretation given in [BHA86]. Under this pleasantly simple view we see Jensen's conjunctive types (Definition 3.7) as names of elements of the abstract domains. The top and bottom of the base abstract domain are called t and f. At arrow types, the co-step function which has output called ψ for inputs below that called ϕ and for other inputs has the top of the abstract domain as output is called $(\phi \to \psi)$. Conjunction (meet) in the abstract domain is written $\wedge$. For example, $(f \to f)$ means 'when given an undefined input the output will be undefined', that is the property of being strict; $((f \to f) \to (f \to f))$ means 'when given a strict input the output will be strict'; and $(f \to (t \to f)) \wedge (t \to (f \to f))$ means 'if the first input is undefined then the output will be undefined and if the second input is undefined then the output will be undefined', that is the property of a curried function being strict in both arguments.

Jensen's inference system is in two parts. The first part (under our simplified view) formalises the order relation in the abstract domains and has formulae of the form $\phi \leq \psi$, meaning that the conjunctive type ϕ denotes a point lower than or equal to the point which ψ denotes. The second part formalises the position of the abstract interpretation of a λ-term in the appropriate abstract domain and has formulae of the form $\Gamma \vdash e : \phi$, meaning that the λ-term e with its free variables taking values in the appropriate abstract domains (syntactically, conjunctive types) given by the environment Γ denotes a point lower than or equal to the point which ϕ denotes.

Jensen's inference system contains a transitivity rule in the subtypes $(\phi \leq \psi)$ part and a weakening rule and application rule in the type inference $(\Gamma \vdash e : \phi)$ part so it does not immediately yield an algorithm for answering queries.

Hankin and Le Métayer [HLM94] modified Jensen's system to get the 'lazy types system' and then went on to derive an algorithm from this. It is the lazy types *inference* system rather than the algorithm with which I am concerned here.

The modifications made by Hankin and Le Métayer can be considered in two stages. In stage one they modified the subtypes system to remove the transitivity rule and the type inference system to remove the weakening rule. This results in the weakening free inference system (Definition 3.8). In stage two they introduced 'laziness' into the inference system to deal with the application rule. This results in the lazy types system discussed below.

In my MSc dissertation [Dol94] I proved that the weakening free inference system is sound and complete with respect to the simplified semantics mentioned above, that is, with respect to abstract interpretation. The soundness proof was routine. Completeness was easy to prove too because the operation of the inference system follows the structure of the semantics in the sense that a query of the form $\Gamma \vdash e : \phi$ is solved by first reducing the structure of e using the type inference system until only variables remain then using the VAR rule $\frac{\phi \leq \psi}{\Gamma[x^\sigma \mapsto \phi] \vdash_{wf} x^\sigma : \psi}$ to solve a query about the type of a variable by going into the subtypes system and finally solving a query of the form $\phi \leq \psi$ by removing all the $\wedge$'s and $\rightarrow$'s from the formulae until, arriving at last at the base type, we can just check whether or not $f \leq f$, $f \leq t$, $t \leq f$, $t \leq t$ match the base axioms $f \leq \phi$ and $\phi \leq t$. Hence the completeness proof splits neatly into two parts. We show by induction on the 'arrow structure' of the conjunctive types that the subtype system is complete and by induction on the structure of λ-terms that *if* the subtype system is complete *then* the type inference system is complete.

When Hankin and Le Métayer introduce 'laziness' into the weakening free system to get the lazy types system the soundness proof goes through much as before but the completeness proof is wrecked. To see why let us look at the change made to the system. The APP rule $\frac{\Gamma \vdash_{wf} e_1 : (\phi \rightarrow \psi) \quad \Gamma \vdash_{wf} e_2 : \phi}{\Gamma \vdash_{wf} e_1 e_2 : \psi}$ is replaced by $\frac{\Gamma \vdash_{lt} e_1 : ((\Gamma, e_2) \rightarrow \psi)}{\Gamma \vdash_{lt} e_1 e_2 : \psi}$ and two new rules for 'evaluating closures' CLOS-RIGHT $\frac{\psi \leq expand(\Gamma, e)}{\psi \leq (\Gamma, e)}$ and CLOS-LEFT $\frac{\Gamma \vdash_{lt} e : \phi}{(\Gamma, e) \leq \phi}$.

The idea is that since we do not know what we should take for ϕ in the original APP rule, we replaced the ϕ by the 'closure' (Γ, e_2) and only 'evaluate' it when it is needed. The second premise of the APP rule would become $\Gamma \vdash_{lt} e_2 : (\Gamma, e_2)$ but this can be discarded because it means *'the position in the abstract domain of the λ-term e_2 with variables interpreted as given by the environment Γ is less than or equal to the position in the abstract domain of the λ-term e_2 with variables interpreted as given by the environment Γ'* which is always true!

The CLOS-RIGHT rule reduces the query $\psi \leq (\Gamma, e)$ to $\psi \leq expand(\Gamma, e)$ where *expand* is a computable (but expensive) function which essentially finds the abstract interpretation of e in Γ and finds a name of the result in the conjunctive types system, that is, it 'totally evaluates' the closure. The CLOS-LEFT rule reduces the query $(\Gamma, e) \leq \phi$ to $\Gamma \vdash e : \phi$ from which the 'evaluation' continues.

Now we can see the problem with the lazy types system: in reducing a query of the form $\phi \leq \psi$ we may come to a query of the form $(\Gamma, e) \leq \phi$ which is reduced to $\Gamma \vdash e : \phi$, taking us back into the type inference system. It is therefore not clear whether the reduction process terminates.

The result presented here is that given any query $e \leq \psi$ where e is a closed λ-term and ψ is a conjunctive type the system with 3 restrictions *does* terminate.

The idea behind the proof stems from the following observation. If we start with the query $\Gamma \vdash (\lambda x.e_1)e_2 : \phi$ the system reduces it using the APP rule then the ABS rule as follows

$$\cfrac{\cfrac{\Gamma[x \mapsto (\Gamma, e_2)] \vdash_{lt} e_1 : \phi}{\Gamma \vdash_{lt} \lambda x.e_1 : ((\Gamma, e_2) \rightarrow \phi)}}{\Gamma \vdash_{lt} (\lambda x.e_1)\ e_2 : \phi}$$

The λ-term in the top premise here is in effect e_1 with (Γ, e_2) substituted for x, that is, it is the β-reduct of $(\lambda x.e_1)e_2$. Hence there is some similarity between solving a query in the lazy types system and running the program. This gives us the clue that we may be able to modify Tait's notion of 'convertibility' [Tai67] to show that the lazy types system terminates.

In modifying Tait's method, I found it inconvenient to deal with the environment Γ so I changed Hankin and Le Métayer's system so that rather than store the values of variables in an environment and only 'substitute them for the variable' in an application of the VAR rule, I substitute values for variables immediately. I also found it inconvenient to have two types of query $e : \phi$ and $e \leq \phi$ which have the same semantics so I rewrote the type inference system translating expressions of the form $e : \phi$ into $e \leq \phi$. This makes the rule which translates the query $e : \phi$ into $e \leq \phi$ redundant and eliminates one of the rules for removing conjunction. Finally, when the FIX rule is used to reduce a query in Hankin and Le Métayer's system it must be followed by a use of CONJ then ABS so I combine FIX, CONJ and ABS to get a new rule to replace FIX. The result is Definition 3.11.

There are two main differences between Tait's problem and the termination problem for the lazy types system. Firstly it is formulae of the form $e \leq \psi$ which are reduced in our system rather than terms and secondly our system has a fixed point operator. Tait's notion of 'convertibility' must be adapted for this new situation.

The fixed point operator does not actually *act* as a fixed point operator but it complicates matters because it switches terms between 'co-variant' and 'contra-variant', so I will first explain the definition which would suffice in the absence of fix.

The first two restrictions ensure that any query $e_1 \leq e_2$ is first reduced to queries of the form $e_1 \leq e_1' \rightarrow \cdots \rightarrow e_n' \rightarrow X$ where $X \in \{t, f\}$. Now, $e_1 \leq e_1' \rightarrow \cdots \rightarrow e_n' \rightarrow X$ says in effect that if the term e_1 is given inputs $e_1', \ldots, e_n'$ then the output will be $\leq X$. It then makes sense to say that e_1 is convertible if for all convertible $e_1', \ldots, e_n'$ the query $e_1 \leq e_1' \rightarrow \cdots \rightarrow e_n' \rightarrow X$ terminates. If there were no fixed point operator in the system this definition would work.

The problem with fix is that a query of the form $fix(\lambda x.e) \leq \phi_k$ is reduced to queries of the form $e[\bigwedge_{j\in\{1,\ldots,n\}} \phi_j/x] \leq \phi_j$ so that the term substituted for a variable is a conjunction of terms of the form $e_1 \to \cdots \to e_n \to X$ and is not itself convertible so we cannot apply the induction hypothesis. To get round this I define (Definition 3.16) 'left convertible' and 'right convertible' terms (where left and right refer to the position relative to $\leq$ in a formula). This is just a formalisation of the definition proposed above apart from the additional clause in ARROW LC 'whenever $e \equiv (e_1 \wedge \cdots \wedge e_n)$ with each $e_i \in T_S^L(\alpha \to \beta)$ we have each $e_i \in RC(\alpha \to \beta)$'. The point of the new clause is that it is exactly what is needed to show that all right convertible terms are left convertible.

The definitions and proofs follow. The interesting cases in Theorem 4.5 are ARROW and FIX because they involve switching terms between 'co-variant' and 'contra-variant'.

3 Definitions

Definition 3.1 (Standard Types) *The set, T, of (standard) types is the smallest set closed under*

BOOL $Bool \in T$

INT $Int \in T$

ARROW *if* $\sigma, \tau \in T$ *then* $(\sigma \to \tau) \in T$

where Bool Int ( ) and $\to$ are symbols.

Definition 3.2 (λ-terms) *Each member of the family $(\Lambda_T(\sigma))_{\sigma\in T}$ of sets of well typed λ-terms indexed by (standard) types in T is the smallest set closed under*

VAR $x^\sigma \in \Lambda_T(\sigma)$ *(a countable supply of variables of each type)*

CONST $c \in \Lambda_T(\sigma_c)$ *(constants for true, false and the integers)*

ABS *if* $e \in \Lambda_T(\tau)$ *then* $\lambda x^\sigma.e \in \Lambda_T(\sigma \to \tau)$

APP *if* $e_1 \in \Lambda_T(\sigma \to \tau)$ *and* $e_2 \in \Lambda_T(\sigma)$ *then* $e_1 e_2 \in \Lambda_T(\tau)$

FIX *if* $e \in \Lambda_T(\sigma)$ *then* $fix(\lambda x^\sigma.e) \in \Lambda_T(\sigma)$

COND *if* $b \in \Lambda_T(Bool)$ *and* $e_1, e_2 \in \Lambda_T(\sigma)$ *then* $cond(b, e_1, e_2) \in \Lambda_T(\sigma)$.

Definition 3.3 (Abstract Domains) *The set, $T^\#$, of abstract domains is the smallest set closed under*

BASE $2 \in T^\#$

ARROW *if* $B_1, B_2 \in T^\#$ *then* $B_1 \to B_2 \in T^\#$

where 2 is the complete lattice $\{0_2, 1_2\}$ with $0_2 \leq 1_2$ and, for complete lattices B_1 and B_2, $B_1 \to B_2$ is the complete lattice of continuous functions from B_1 to B_2.

Definition 3.4 (Syntactic Abstract Types) *The set, $\hat{T^\#}$, of syntactic abstract types is the smallest set closed under*

BASE $2 \in \hat{T^\#}$

ARROW *if* $\alpha, \beta \in T^{\hat{\#}}$ *then* $(\alpha \to \beta) \in T^{\hat{\#}}$

where 2 ( ) and $\to$ *are symbols.*

Definition 3.5 *The abstract domain,* $\sigma^{\#}$, *corresponding to a (standard) type,* σ, *is defined via the function* $-^{\#} : T \to T^{\#}$ *which is defined by structural recursion on the definition of* T

BOOL $Bool^{\#} = 2$

INT $Int^{\#} = 2$

ARROW $(\sigma \to \tau)^{\#} = \sigma^{\#} \to \tau^{\#}$.

Definition 3.6 *The syntactic abstract type,* $\sigma^{\hat{\#}}$, *corresponding to a (standard) type,* σ, *is defined via the function* $-^{\hat{\#}} : T \to T^{\hat{\#}}$ *which is defined by structural recursion on the definition of* T

BOOL $Bool^{\hat{\#}} = 2$

INT $Int^{\hat{\#}} = 2$

ARROW $(\sigma \to \tau)^{\hat{\#}} = (\sigma^{\hat{\#}} \to \tau^{\hat{\#}})$.

Definition 3.7 (Conjunctive Types) *Each member of each of the families* $(T_S^C(\alpha))_{\alpha \in T^{\hat{\#}}}$, $(T_C^C(\alpha))_{\alpha \in T^{\hat{\#}}}$ *of sets of non standard types indexed by syntactic abstract types in* $T^{\hat{\#}}$ *is the smallest set closed under*

BOT $f \in T_S^C(2)$

TOP $t \in T_S^C(2)$

CONJ *if* $\phi_1, \ldots, \phi_n \in T_S^C(\alpha)$ *then* $(\phi_1 \wedge \cdots \wedge \phi_n) \in T_C^C(\alpha)$

ARROW *if* $\phi \in T_C^C(\alpha)$ *and* $\psi \in T_S^C(\beta)$ *then* $(\phi \to \psi) \in T_S^C(\alpha \to \beta)$.

Definition 3.8 (Weakening Free Inference) *The non standard type inference system for inferring non standard types of well typed* λ*-terms has two types of well formed formulas. Firstly, if* $\phi, \psi \in T_C^C(\alpha)$ *then* $\phi \leq \psi$ *is well formed. Secondly, if* Γ *is an environment which maps variables,* x^τ, *of (standard) type* τ *to values in* $T_C^C(\tau^{\hat{\#}})$ *for each* τ, *and e is a well typed* λ*-term and* ϕ *is a non standard type in* $T_C^C(\sigma^{\hat{\#}})$ *where* σ *is the (standard) type of e, then* $\Gamma \vdash_{wf} e : \phi$ *is well formed.* $\Gamma[x^\sigma \mapsto \phi]$ *is the environment* Γ *but with* x^σ *mapped to* ϕ. *The axioms and rules of inference are*

$$\text{BOT}\, f \leq \phi \qquad \text{TOP}\, \phi \leq t \qquad \text{TOP-ARROW}\, \phi \leq \psi_1 \to \cdots \to \psi_n \to t$$

$$\text{CONJ-}\leq \frac{\theta_1 \leq \psi_1 \ \ldots \ \theta_m \leq \psi_m}{(\phi_1 \wedge \cdots \wedge \phi_n) \leq (\psi_1 \wedge \cdots \wedge \psi_m)} \qquad \text{ARROW} \frac{\phi_2 \leq \phi_1 \quad \psi_1 \leq \psi_2}{(\phi_1 \to \psi_1) \leq (\phi_2 \to \psi_2)}$$

$$provided \{\theta_1, \ldots, \theta_m\} \subseteq \{\phi_1, \ldots, \phi_n\}$$

$$\text{CONJ} \frac{\Gamma \vdash_{wf} e : \phi \quad \Gamma \vdash_{wf} e : \psi}{\Gamma \vdash_{wf} e : \phi \wedge \psi} \qquad \text{VAR} \frac{\phi \leq \psi}{\Gamma[x^\sigma \mapsto \phi] \vdash_{wf} x^\sigma : \psi} \qquad \text{CONST}\, \Gamma \vdash_{wf} c : t$$

$$\text{ABS} \frac{\Gamma[x^\sigma \mapsto \phi] \vdash_{wf} e : \psi}{\Gamma \vdash_{wf} \lambda x^\sigma . e : (\phi \to \psi)} \qquad \text{APP} \frac{\Gamma \vdash_{wf} e_1 : (\phi \to \psi) \quad \Gamma \vdash_{wf} e_2 : \phi}{\Gamma \vdash_{wf} e_1 e_2 : \psi}$$

$$\text{FIX}\frac{\Gamma \vdash_{wf} \lambda x^{\sigma}.e : (\bigwedge_{j\in\{1,\ldots,n\}} \phi_j \to \phi_1) \wedge \cdots \wedge (\bigwedge_{j\in\{1,\ldots,n\}} \phi_j \to \phi_n)}{\Gamma \vdash_{wf} fix(\lambda x^{\sigma}.e) : \phi_k} k \in \{1,\ldots,n\}$$

$$\text{COND-1}\frac{\Gamma \vdash_{wf} b : f}{\Gamma \vdash_{wf} cond(b, e_1, e_2) : \phi} \quad \text{COND-2}\frac{\Gamma \vdash_{wf} e_1 : \phi \quad \Gamma \vdash_{wf} e_2 : \phi}{\Gamma \vdash_{wf} cond(b, e_1, e_2) : \phi}.$$

Definition 3.9 (Lazy Types) *Each member of each of the families* $(T_S^L(\alpha))_{\alpha\in T^{\#}}$, $(T_C^L(\alpha))_{\alpha\in T^{\#}}$ *of sets of non standard types indexed by syntactic abstract types in* $T^{\#}$ *is the smallest set closed under*

BOT $f \in T_S^L(2)$

TOP $t \in T_S^L(2)$

CONJ *if* $\phi_1, \ldots, \phi_n \in T_S^L(\alpha)$ *then* $(\phi_1 \wedge \cdots \wedge \phi_n) \in T_C^L(\alpha)$

ARROW *if* $e \in T_C^L(\alpha)$ *and* $\psi \in T_S^L(\beta)$ *and e is closed then* $(e \to \psi) \in T_S^L(\alpha \to \beta)$

VAR *if* x^{σ} *is a variable then* $x^{\sigma} \in T_C^L(\sigma^{\#})$

CONST *if c is a constant then* $c \in T_C^L(2)$

ABS *if* $e \in T_C^L(\alpha)$ *and* x^{σ} *is a variable then* $\lambda x^{\sigma}.e \in T_C^L(\sigma^{\#} \to \alpha)$

APP *if* $e_1 \in T_C^L(\alpha \to \beta)$ *and* $e_2 \in T_C^L(\alpha)$ *then* $e_1e_2 \in T_C^L(\beta)$

FIX *if* $e \in T_C^L(\alpha)$ *and* x^{σ} *is a variable and* $\sigma^{\#} = \alpha$ *then* $fix(\lambda x^{\sigma}.e) \in T_C^L(\alpha)$

COND *if* $b \in T_C^L(2)$ *and* $e_1, e_2 \in T_C^L(\alpha)$ *then* $cond(b, e_1, e_2) \in T_C^L(\alpha)$.

Definition 3.10 (Expand) *The family* $(expand_{\alpha})_{\alpha\in T^{\#}}$ *of functions from the sets of closed non standard types in the family* $(T_C^L(\alpha))_{\alpha\in T^{\#}}$ *to the sets of non standard types in the family* $(T_C^C(\alpha))_{\alpha\in T^{\#}}$ *can be defined in any way subject only to the conditions that it be computable and semantically sound in the sense that for all* $\alpha \in T^{\#}$ *and all closed* $e \in T_C^L(\alpha)$, $[\![expand_{\alpha} e]\!]_{\alpha} = [\![e]\!]_{\alpha}$.

Definition 3.11 (Lazy Type Inference System) *If* $\alpha \in T^{\#}$, $e_1, e_2 \in T_C^L(\alpha)$ *and* e_1 *and* e_2 *are closed then* $e_1 \leq e_2$ *is a well formed formula of the lazy types inference system. The axioms and rules of inference of the lazy types system are*

BOT$f \leq \phi$ TOP$\phi \leq t$ TOP-ARROW$\phi \leq \psi_1 \to \cdots \to \psi_n \to t$

$$\text{CONJ}\frac{\theta_1 \leq \psi_1 \ \ldots \ \theta_m \leq \psi_m}{(\phi_1 \wedge \cdots \wedge \phi_n) \leq (\psi_1 \wedge \cdots \wedge \psi_m)} \quad \text{ARROW}\frac{\phi_2 \leq \phi_1 \quad \psi_1 \leq \psi_2}{(\phi_1 \to \psi_1) \leq (\phi_2 \to \psi_2)}$$

provided$\{\theta_1, \ldots, \theta_m\} \subseteq \{\phi_1, \ldots, \phi_n\}$

$$\text{EXP}\frac{\phi \leq expand\ e}{\phi \leq e} \quad \text{ABS}\frac{e[\phi/x^{\sigma}] \leq \psi}{\lambda x^{\sigma}.e \leq (\phi \to \psi)} \quad \text{APP}\frac{e_1 \leq (e_2 \to \psi)}{e_1e_2 \leq \psi}$$

$$\text{FIX}\frac{e[\bigwedge_{j\in\{1,\ldots,n\}} \phi_j/x^{\sigma}] \leq \phi_1 \cdots e[\bigwedge_{j\in\{1,\ldots,n\}} \phi_j/x^{\sigma}] \leq \phi_n}{fix(\lambda x^{\sigma}.e) \leq \phi_k} k \in \{1,\ldots,n\}$$

$$\text{COND-1}\frac{b \leq f}{cond(b, e_1, e_2) \leq \phi} \quad \text{COND-2}\frac{e_1 \leq \phi \quad e_2 \leq \phi}{cond(b, e_1, e_2) \leq \phi}.$$

Restriction 3.12 *If a query is of the form* $e \leq (\phi_1 \wedge \cdots \wedge \phi_n)$ *then the conjunction is reduced using CONJ before any reduction which applies to e, even if e is itself a conjunction, giving* $e \leq \phi_1, \ldots, e \leq \phi_n$.

Restriction 3.13 *If a query is of the form* $e_1 \leq e_2$ *with* $e_2 \in T_C^L(\alpha) \setminus T_S^L(\alpha)$ *and* e_2 *is not a conjunction then it must be reduced to* $e_1 \leq expand(e_2)$ *before any other reductions can take place and the EXP rule is only used for such* e_2.

Restriction 3.14 *If a query is of the form* $fix(\lambda x^\sigma.e) \leq \psi$ *then it must be reduced to* $e[(\bigwedge_{j\in\{1,\ldots,n\}} \psi_j)\wedge\psi/x^\sigma] \leq \psi_1, \ldots, e[(\bigwedge_{j\in\{1,\ldots,n\}} \psi_j)\wedge\psi/x^\sigma] \leq \psi_n$, $e[(\bigwedge_{j\in\{1,\ldots,n\}} \psi_j)\wedge \psi/x^\sigma] \leq \psi$ *where* $\bigwedge_{j\in\{1,\ldots,n\}} \psi_j \equiv expand(fix(\lambda x^\sigma.e))$.

Definition 3.15 (Terminate) *A well formed formula is said to terminate if all trees grown over it by backwards application of rules of inference of the lazy types system with the 3 restrictions are finite (without regard to whether the trees are proofs).*

Definition 3.16 (Left- and Right-Convertible) *Each member of each of the families* $(LC(\alpha))_{\alpha\in T^{\hat{\#}}}$, $(RC(\alpha))_{\alpha\in T^{\hat{\#}}}$ *of sets of left convertible and right convertible non standard types indexed by syntactic abstract types in* $T^{\hat{\#}}$ *is the smallest set closed under*

BASE RC $t, f \in RC(2)$

LC *if* $e \in T_C^L(2)$ *and* $\forall\psi \in RC(2)$ $e \leq \psi$ *terminates then* $e \in LC(2)$

ARROW RC *if* $e \in LC(\alpha)$ *and* $\psi \in RC(\beta)$ *and* e *is closed then* $(e \to \psi) \in RC(\alpha \to \beta)$

LC *if* $e \in T_C^L(\alpha \to \beta)$ *and* $\forall\psi \in RC(\alpha \to \beta)$ $e \leq \psi$ *terminates and whenever* $e \equiv (e_1\wedge\cdots\wedge e_n)$ *with each* $e_i \in T_S^L(\alpha \to \beta)$ *we have each* $e_i \in RC(\alpha \to \beta)$ *then* $e \in LC(\alpha \to \beta)$.

4 Proofs

Lemma 4.1 *For all* $\alpha \in T^{\hat{\#}}$, $RC(\alpha) \subseteq T_S^L(\alpha)$ *and* $LC(\alpha) \subseteq T_C^L(\alpha)$.

Proof

By induction on the definition of $T^{\hat{\#}}$.

BASE *By Definition 3.16* $RC(2) = \{t, f\}$ *and by Definition 3.9 BOT and TOP* $\{t, f\} \subseteq T_S^L(2)$.

If $e \in LC(2)$ *then by Definition 3.16* $e \in T_C^L(2)$.

ARROW *If* $(e \to \psi) \in RC(\alpha \to \beta)$ *then by Definition 3.16 we must have* $e \in LC(\alpha), \psi \in RC(\beta)$ *and* e *closed. By induction hypothesis* $e \in T_C^L(\alpha)$ *and* $\psi \in T_S^L(\beta)$ *so by Definition 3.9 ARROW* $(e \to \psi) \in T_S^L(\alpha \to \beta)$.

If $e \in LC(\alpha \to \beta)$ *then by Definition 3.16* $e \in T_C^L(\alpha \to \beta)$. □

Lemma 4.2 *For all* $\alpha \in T^{\hat{\#}}$, $LC(\alpha) \cap T_S^L(\alpha) \subseteq RC(\alpha)$.

Proof

By cases following the definition of $T^{\hat{\#}}$.

BASE *By Definition 3.16* $RC(2) = \{t, f\}$ *and by Definition 3.9* $T_S^L(2) = \{t, f\}$ *so* $T_S^L(2) \subseteq RC(2)$.

ARROW *if* $e \in LC(\alpha \to \beta)$ *and* $e \in T_S^L(\alpha \to \beta)$ *then by Definition 3.16 with* $n = 1$ $e \in RC(\alpha \to \beta)$. □

Lemma 4.3 *For all* $\alpha \in T^{\#}$, $T_S^C(\alpha) \subseteq RC(\alpha)$ *and* $T_C^C(\alpha) \subseteq LC(\alpha)$.

Proof

By induction on the definition of $T^{\#}$.

BASE *By Definition 3.7* $T_S^C(2) = \{t, f\}$ *so* $T_S^C(2) \subseteq RC(2)$.

Suppose $\phi \in T_C^C(2)$. *Then by Definition 3.7* ϕ *is of the form* $(\phi_1 \wedge \cdots \wedge \phi_n)$ *where each* ϕ_i *is either* t *or* f. *Let* $\psi \in RC(2)$. *Then by Definition 3.11 the only reduction which applies to* $\phi \le \psi$ *is CONJ giving* $\phi_i \le \psi$ *for* $i \in \{1, \ldots, n\}$. *Now* $\phi_i \le \psi$ *is one of* $f \le f, f \le t, t \le f, t \le t$ *so no reduction applies. Hence, for all* $\psi \in RC(2)$, $\phi \le \psi$ *terminates so* $\phi \in LC(2)$.

ARROW *If* $\theta \in T_S^C(\alpha \to \beta)$ *then, by Definition 3.7 ARROW,* θ *is of the form* $(\phi \to \psi)$ *with* $\phi \in T_C^C(\alpha)$ *and* $\psi \in T_S^C(\beta)$. *By induction hypothesis,* $\phi \in LC(\alpha)$ *and* $\psi \in RC(\beta)$ *so* $(\phi \to \psi) \in RC(\alpha \to \beta)$.

Suppose $\phi \in T_C^C(\alpha \to \beta)$. *Then, by Definition 3.7,* ϕ *is of the form* $(\phi_1 \wedge \cdots \wedge \phi_n)$ *where each* $\phi_i \in T_S^C(\alpha \to \beta)$. *As above, each* $\phi_i \in RC(\alpha \to \beta)$. *We must show that* $\forall \psi \in RC(\alpha \to \beta)$ $\phi \le \psi$ *terminates. Let* $\psi \in RC(\alpha \to \beta)$. ψ *is of the form* $(e \to \psi')$ *for* $e \in LC(\alpha)$ *and* $\psi' \in RC(\beta)$. *If* $n > 1$ *then the only reduction rule which applies to* $\phi \le \psi$ *is CONJ reducing it to* $\phi_i \le \psi$ *for* $i \in \{1, \ldots, n\}$ *(if* $n = 1$ *then continue the argument with* ϕ *for* ϕ_i*). Since* $\phi_i \in T_S^C(\alpha \to \beta)$, *by Definition 3.7 it is* $(\theta_i \to \psi_i)$ *for some* $\theta_i \in T_C^C(\alpha)$ *and* $\psi_i \in T_S^C(\beta)$. *By induction hypothesis* $\theta_i \in LC(\alpha)$ *and* $\psi_i \in RC(\beta)$. *Now,* $\phi_i \le \psi$ *is* $(\theta_i \to \psi_i) \le (e \to \psi')$ *so the only reduction which applies is ARROW giving* $e \le \theta_i$ *and* $\psi_i \le \psi'$. $\psi_i \in T_S^C(\beta) \subseteq T_C^C(\beta)$ *so by induction hypothesis* $\psi_i \in LC(\beta)$. *Also,* $\psi' \in RC(\beta)$ *so* $\psi_i \le \psi'$ *terminates. Since* $\theta_i \in T_C^C(\alpha)$ *it is* $({\phi'}_1 \wedge \cdots \wedge {\phi'}_m)$ *where each* $\phi'_j \in T_S^C(\alpha) \subseteq RC(\alpha)$. *By Restriction 3.12* $e \le \theta_i$ *must be reduced to* $e \le \phi'_1, \ldots, e \le \phi'_m$ *but since* $e \in LC(\alpha)$ *and each* $\phi'_j \in RC(\alpha)$ *each of these terminates. Hence* $\phi \le \psi$ *terminates so* $\phi \in LC(\alpha \to \beta)$. □

Lemma 4.4 *For all* $\alpha \in T^{\#}$, $RC(\alpha) \subseteq LC(\alpha)$.

Proof

By induction on the definition of $T^{\#}$.

BASE $RC(2) = \{t, f\}$. *Each of* $f \le f, f \le t, t \le f, t \le t$ *terminates since no reduction applies to it so for all* $\psi \in RC(2)$, $f \le \psi$ *and* $t \le \psi$ *terminate so* $f, t \in LC(2)$ *so* $RC(2) \subseteq LC(2)$.

ARROW *Suppose* $\theta \in RC(\alpha \to \beta)$. *Then* θ *is* $(e \to \psi)$ *for some* $e \in LC(\alpha)$ *and* $\psi \in RC(\beta)$. *By induction hypothesis* $\psi \in LC(\beta)$. *We must show that* $\forall \theta' \in RC(\alpha \to \beta)$ $\theta \le \theta'$ *terminates. Let* $\theta' \in RC(\alpha \to \beta)$. *Then* θ' *is* $(e' \to \psi')$ *for some* $e' \in LC(\alpha)$ *and* $\psi' \in RC(\beta)$. $\theta \le \theta'$ *is* $(e \to \psi) \le (e' \to \psi')$ *so only the reduction rule ARROW applies, reducing it to* $e' \le e$ *and* $\psi \le \psi'$. *Since* $\psi \in LC(\beta)$ *and* $\psi' \in RC(\beta)$, $\psi \le \psi'$ *terminates. We must show that*

$e' \leq e$ also terminates. If $e \in T_S^L(\alpha)$ then by Lemma 4.2 $e \in RC(\alpha)$ so, since $e' \in LC(\alpha)$, $e' \leq e$ terminates. If $e \notin T_S^L(\alpha)$ then there are two cases.

If *$e \equiv (e_1 \wedge \cdots \wedge e_n)$ with $e_i \in T_S^L(\alpha)$ then since $e \in LC(\alpha)$ we have by Definition 3.16 that each $e_i \in RC(\alpha)$ (if $\alpha \equiv 2$, each $e_i \in RC(2)$ since $T_S^L(2) = RC(2)$). By Restriction 3.12 we must reduce $e' \leq e$ to $e' \leq e_1, \ldots, e' \leq e_n$. Since $e' \in LC(\alpha)$ and each $e_i \in RC(\alpha)$ each of these terminates so $e' \leq e$ terminates.*

Otherwise *$e \in T_C^L(\alpha) \setminus T_S^L(\alpha)$ and e is not a conjunction so by Restriction 3.13 $e' \leq e$ is reduced to $e' \leq expand(e)$. Now, $expand(e) \equiv (\psi_1 \wedge \cdots \wedge \psi_m)$ for some $\psi_i \in T_S^C(\alpha)$. By Lemma 4.3 each $\psi_i \in RC(\alpha)$. So $e' \leq e$ is reduced to $e' \leq (\psi_1 \wedge \cdots \wedge \psi_m)$ which by Restriction 3.12 must be reduced to $e' \leq \psi_1, \ldots, e' \leq \psi_m$. Since $e' \in LC(\alpha)$ and each $\psi_i \in RC(\alpha)$ each of these terminates so $e' \leq e$ terminates.*

In either case $e' \leq e$ terminates so $\theta \leq \theta'$ terminates so $\theta \in LC(\alpha \to \beta)$. □

Theorem 4.5 *For all $\alpha \in T^{\hat{\#}}$, $e \in T_C^L(\alpha)$, variables $x_1^{\sigma_1}, \ldots, x_n^{\sigma_n}$, $e_1 \in LC({\sigma_1}^{\#})$, $\ldots, e_n \in LC({\sigma_n}^{\hat{\#}})$, if $e^* = e[e_1/x_1]\ldots[e_n/x_n]$ is closed then it is in $LC(\alpha)$.*

Proof

By induction on the structure of e following Definition 3.9.

BOT *If e is f then e^* is f and $f \in LC(2)$.*

TOP *If e is t then e^* is t and $t \in LC(2)$.*

CONJ *If e is $(\phi_1 \wedge \cdots \wedge \phi_m)$ then e^* is $({\phi^*}_1 \wedge \cdots \wedge {\phi^*}_m)$. If e^* is closed then each ϕ_i^* is closed so, by induction hypothesis, each $\phi_i^* \in LC(\alpha)$. Also, each $\phi_i^* \in T_S^L(\alpha)$ so by Lemma 4.2 each $\phi_i^* \in RC(\alpha)$. It only remains to show that, for all $\psi \in RC(\alpha)$, $e^* \leq \psi$ terminates. The only reduction which applies is CONJ reducing it to $\phi_i^* \leq \psi$ for $i \in \{1, \ldots, m\}$. Since $\phi_i^* \in LC(\alpha)$ and $\psi \in RC(\alpha)$ this terminates so $e^* \leq \psi$ terminates.*

ARROW *If e is $(e' \to \psi)$ then e^* is $(e'^* \to \psi^*)$. If e^* is closed then e'^* and ψ^* are closed so by induction hypothesis $e'^* \in LC(\alpha)$ and $\psi^* \in LC(\beta)$. Now $\psi^* \in T_S^L(\beta)$ so by Lemma 4.2 $\psi^* \in RC(\beta)$. So, since $e'^* \in LC(\alpha)$ and $\psi^* \in RC(\beta)$, $(e'^* \to \psi^*) \in RC(\alpha \to \beta)$ so by Lemma 4.4 $(e'^* \to \psi^*) \in LC(\alpha \to \beta)$.*

VAR If *e is $x_i^{\sigma_i}$ for some $i \in \{1, \ldots, n\}$ then e^* is e_i which is in $LC({\sigma_i}^{\hat{\#}})$ by assumption.*

Otherwise *e is some other variable and e^* is not closed.*

CONST *If e is the constant $c \in T_S^L(2)$ then e^* is c. No reduction rules apply to $c \leq t$ or $c \leq f$ so, for all $\psi \in RC(2)$, $c \leq \psi$ terminates so $c \in LC(2)$.*

ABS *If e is $\lambda x^\sigma.e'$ then we may assume x^σ is not one of $x_1^{\sigma_1}, \ldots, x_n^{\sigma_n}$ (else rename the bound variable) so that e^* is $\lambda x^\sigma.e'^*$. If e^* is closed then e'^* contains at most the variable x^σ free. We must show that for all $\psi \in RC(\sigma^{\hat{\#}} \to \alpha)$ $\lambda x^\sigma.e'^* \leq \psi$ terminates. Since ψ is of arrow type, it must be $(e_1 \to \psi_1)$ with*

$e_1 \in LC(\hat{\sigma^\#})$ *and* $\psi_1 \in RC(\alpha)$. *Only the rule ABS applies to* $\lambda x^\sigma.e'^* \leq (e_1 \rightarrow \psi_1)$ *and reduces it to* $e'^*[e_1/x^\sigma] \leq \psi_1$. *Now* $e_1 \in LC(\hat{\sigma^\#})$ *and* $e'^*[e_1/x^\sigma]$ *is closed so by induction hypothesis* $e'^*[e_1/x^\sigma] \in LC(\alpha)$ *so, since* $\psi_1 \in RC(\alpha)$, $e'^*[e_1/x^\sigma] \leq \psi_1$ *terminates so* $\lambda x^\sigma.e'^* \leq \psi$ *terminates.*

APP *If* e *is* e_1e_2 *then* e^* *is* $e_1^*e_2^*$. *If* e^* *is closed then each of* e_1^* *and* e_2^* *is closed so by induction hypothesis* $e_1^* \in LC(\alpha \rightarrow \beta)$ *and* $e_2^* \in LC(\alpha)$. *We must show that for all* $\psi \in RC(\beta)$ $e_1^*e_2^* \leq \psi$ *terminates. Only the rule APP applies to* $e_1^*e_2^* \leq \psi$ *and reduces it to* $e_1^* \leq (e_2^* \rightarrow \psi)$. *Now* $e_2^* \in LC(\alpha)$ *and* $\psi \in RC(\beta)$ *so* $(e_2^* \rightarrow \psi) \in RC(\alpha \rightarrow \beta)$ *so, since* $e_1^* \in LC(\alpha \rightarrow \beta)$, $e_1^* \leq (e_2^* \rightarrow \psi)$ *terminates so* $e_1^*e_2^* \leq \psi$ *terminates.*

FIX *If* e *is* $fix(\lambda x^\sigma.e_1)$ *then we may assume* x^σ *is not one of* $x_1^{\sigma_1}, \ldots, x_n^{\sigma_n}$ *(else rename the bound variable) so that* e^* *is* $fix(\lambda x^\sigma.e_1^*)$. *If* e^* *is closed then* e_1^* *contains at most the variable* x^σ *free. We must show that for all* $\psi \in RC(\hat{\sigma^\#})$ $fix(\lambda x^\sigma.e_1^*) \leq \psi$ *terminates. By Restriction 3.14* $fix(\lambda x^\sigma.e_1^*) \leq \psi$ *can only be reduced to* $e_1^*[(\bigwedge_{i\in\{1,\ldots,m\}} \psi_i) \wedge \psi/x^\sigma] \leq \psi_1$,..., $e_1^*[(\bigwedge_{i\in\{1,\ldots,m\}} \psi_i) \wedge \psi/x^\sigma] \leq \psi_m$, $e_1^*[(\bigwedge_{i\in\{1,\ldots,m\}} \psi_i) \wedge \psi/x^\sigma] \leq \psi$ *where* $\bigwedge_{i\in\{1,\ldots,m\}} \psi_i \equiv expand(fix(\lambda x^\sigma.e_1^*))$. *Now each* $\psi_i \in T_S^C(\sigma^\#)$ *so by Lemma 4.3* $\psi_i \in RC(\hat{\sigma^\#})$ *and* $\psi_i \in LC(\hat{\sigma^\#})$. *Also,* $\psi \in RC(\hat{\sigma^\#})$ *so by Lemma 4.4* $\psi \in LC(\hat{\sigma^\#})$. *In order to apply the induction hypothesis we must show that* $(\bigwedge_{i\in\{1,\ldots,m\}} \psi_i) \wedge \psi \in LC(\hat{\sigma^\#})$. *Let* $\psi' \in RC(\hat{\sigma^\#})$, *we must show that* $(\bigwedge_{i\in\{1,\ldots,m\}} \psi_i) \wedge \psi \leq \psi'$ *terminates. The only rule which applies to it is CONJ which reduces it to* $\psi_i \leq \psi'$ *or* $\psi \leq \psi'$. $\psi_i, \psi \in LC(\hat{\sigma^\#})$ *and* $\psi' \in RC(\hat{\sigma^\#})$ *so each of these terminates so* $(\bigwedge_{i\in\{1,\ldots,m\}} \psi_i) \wedge \psi \leq \psi'$ *terminates so we have* $(\bigwedge_{i\in\{1,\ldots,m\}} \psi_i) \wedge \psi \in LC(\hat{\sigma^\#})$. *Hence, by induction hypothesis,* $e_1^*[(\bigwedge_{i\in\{1,\ldots,m\}} \psi_i) \wedge \psi/x^\sigma] \in LC(\hat{\sigma^\#})$ *so, since each* $\psi_i \in RC(\hat{\sigma^\#})$ *and* $\psi \in RC(\hat{\sigma^\#})$, *each of* $e_1^*[(\bigwedge_{i\in\{1,\ldots,m\}} \psi_i) \wedge \psi/x^\sigma] \leq \psi_1, \ldots, e_1^*[(\bigwedge_{i\in\{1,\ldots,m\}} \psi_i) \wedge \psi/x^\sigma] \leq \psi_m, e_1^*[(\bigwedge_{i\in\{1,\ldots,m\}} \psi_i) \wedge \psi/x^\sigma] \leq \psi$ *terminates so* $fix(\lambda x^\sigma.e_1^*) \leq \psi$ *terminates.*

COND *If* e *is* $cond(b, e_1, e_2)$ *then* e^* *is* $cond(b^*, e_1^*, e_2^*)$. *If* e^* *is closed then* b^*, e_1^* *and* e_2^* *are closed so by induction hypothesis* $b^* \in LC(2)$, $e_1^* \in LC(\alpha)$ *and* $e_2^* \in LC(\alpha)$. *We must show that for all* $\psi \in RC(\alpha)$ $cond(b^*, e_1^*, e_2^*) \leq \psi$ *terminates. Two rules can apply, COND-1 and COND-2. If COND-1 is used the formula reduces to* $b^* \leq f$ *which terminates since* $b^* \in LC(2)$ *and* $f \in RC(2)$. *If COND-2 is used the formula reduces to* $e_1^* \leq \psi$ *and* $e_2^* \leq \psi$ *both of which terminate since* $e_1^*, e_2^* \in LC(\alpha)$ *and* $\psi \in RC(\alpha)$. *Hence* $cond(b^*, e_1^*, e_2^*) \leq \psi$ *terminates.* □

Corollary 4.6 *For all* $\alpha \in T^\#$, *if* $e \in T_C^L(\alpha)$ *is closed then* $e \in LC(\alpha)$ *and if* $\psi \in T_S^L(\alpha)$ *then* $\psi \in RC(\alpha)$.

Proof

If $e \in T_C^L(\alpha)$ *is closed then by Theorem 4.5 with* $n = 0$ $e \in LC(\alpha)$. *If* $\psi \in T_S^L(\alpha)$

then by Definition 3.9 ψ is closed so by Theorem 4.5 with $n = 0$ $\psi \in LC(\alpha)$ so by Lemma 4.2 $\psi \in RC(\alpha)$. □

Corollary 4.7 *If e is a closed λ-term of standard type σ and $\psi \in T_S^C(\hat{\sigma^{\#}})$ then the query $e \leq \psi$ terminates.*

Proof

Since e is a closed λ-term, $e \in T_C^L(\hat{\sigma^{\#}})$ so by Corollary 4.6 $e \in LC(\hat{\sigma^{\#}})$. Since $\psi \in T_S^C(\hat{\sigma^{\#}})$, $\psi \in T_S^L(\hat{\sigma^{\#}})$ so by Corollary 4.6 $\psi \in RC(\hat{\sigma^{\#}})$. Since $e \in LC(\hat{\sigma^{\#}})$ and $\psi \in RC(\hat{\sigma^{\#}})$, $e \leq \psi$ terminates. □

Acknowledgements

This work was funded by the UK EPSRC award number 94314806. I would like to thank Prof. Chris Hankin for explaining the lazy types system to me and encouraging me to try what turned out to be a very interesting problem; Michael Iossif for a helpful conversation about Tait's paper; Dr. David Sands for some helpful comments on an earlier draft; Martin Berger and Gautham Radhakrishnan for getting me started with LaTeX and the organisers of this workshop for giving me the opportunity to present my work.

References

[Abr91] S. Abramsky. *Domain theory in logical form.* Annals of Pure and Applied Logic, 51:1–77, 1991.

[BHA86] G. L. Burn, C. L. Hankin and S. Abramsky. *Strictness Analysis for Higher Order Functions.* Science of Computer Programming, 7:249–278, 1986.

[Dol94] A. P. G. Dolan. *Lazy Types for Strictness Analysis.* MSc Dissertation, Department of Computing, Imperial College of Science, Technology and Medicine, Univ. of London, 1994.

[HLM94] C. L. Hankin and D. Le Métayer. *Deriving Algorithms from Type Inference Systems: Application to Strictness Analysis.* Proc. of POPL'94. ACM Press, 1994.

[Jen92] T. P. Jensen. *Abstract Interpretation in Logical Form.* PhD Thesis, Department of Computing, Imperial College of Science, Technology and Medicine, Univ. of London, 1992. Available as DIKU Report 93/11.

[Sin97] A. P. G. Sinnadurai. *Not yet titled.* PhD Thesis, Department of Computing, Imperial College of Science, Technology and Medicine, Univ. of London, 1997.

[Tai67] W. W. Tait. *Intensional Interpretations of Functionals of Finite Type I.* Journal of Symbolic Logic, 32:198–212, 1967.

ORDERED SOS RULES AND WEAK BISIMULATION

IAIN PHILLIPS
Department of Computing, Imperial College, London SW7 2BZ.

IREK ULIDOWSKI
Research Institute for Mathematical Sciences, Kyoto University, Kyoto, Japan

One of the main reasons for developing formats of rules with negative antecedents, for example the GSOS format, was to enable natural description of process operators like the sequential composition, priority and broadcast parallel. We propose an alternative method for defining these and similar operators, which does not rely on rules with negative antecedents. Instead, we use ordinary rules but with an ordering on them which indicates the order of their application. We show that operators which are definable by our method preserve a version of weak bisimulation.

1 Introduction

Structured Operational Semantics (SOS) is considered to be the standard method for defining operational meaning of process operators in an arbitrary process language. It was originated by Milner for CCS [1, 2] and formalised by Plotkin [3]. The meaning of each operator on processes is given by a set of transition rules. Each of the rules describes how the behaviour of a process, constructed with the operator and some subprocesses, depends on the behaviour of these subprocesses. For example, the following is one of the rules for $\boxplus$, the CSP external choice operator,

$$\frac{X \xrightarrow{a} X'}{X \boxplus Y \xrightarrow{a} X'.}$$

The rule allows to infer that a process $a.\mathbf{0} \boxplus b.\mathbf{0}$ may perform action a since its subprocess $a.\mathbf{0}$ may itself perform a.

Process operators can be classified accordingly to the form of rules defining their operational meaning. A format of rules is a collection of forms of rules. We say that an operator is in a certain format if its rules belong to that format. Most of the popular process operators are in the De Simone format [4].

However, there is a number of process operators which cannot be adequately defined by De Simone rules alone. The most important examples of these are the sequential composition, priority and broadcast parallel operators. These operators are usually defined by rules with *negative antecedents*, i.e. expressions like $X \stackrel{a}{\nrightarrow}$. Consider, for example, the rules for the sequential composition operator ;

$$\frac{X \xrightarrow{\alpha} X'}{X;Y \xrightarrow{\alpha} X';Y} \qquad \frac{\forall \alpha.\, X \stackrel{\alpha}{\nrightarrow} \quad Y \xrightarrow{\beta} Y'}{X;Y \xrightarrow{\beta} Y',}$$

where α and β are any visible or silent actions. Given a process $\mathbf{0}; a.\mathbf{0}$ we can deduce, using the second rule for a and the fact that $a.\mathbf{0}$ can perform a, that the process itself can perform a.

Transition rules with negative antecedents as means to give operational semantics to general process operators were originally considered by Bloom, Istrail and Meyer [5, 6, 7]. They proposed a general format of rules called the GSOS format. Groote [22] proposed a more general format called the *ntyft/nxyft* format.

Another issue concerning the formats of transition rules is the use of silent actions. The original De Simone and GSOS formats treated both silent and visible actions in the same way, i.e. as visible. This resulted in many difficulties when *weak equivalences* over De Simone or GSOS process languages were considered. The problem was studied by Bloom [8, 9], Vaandrager [10] and the second author [11, 12]. He proposed the ISOS format, which offers a sound and intuitive treatment of silent actions as well as use of negative antecedents and copying.

In this paper we will only consider those formats of rules which treat silent actions as invisible; for example the formats in [8, 10, 11, 9, 12]. A number of important results were established for these formats. Firstly, certain weak equivalences were shown to be preserved by all process operators in these formats [10, 9, 12]. Secondly, (completed) trace congruences with respect to these formats were discovered [10, 11]. Thirdly, algorithms for generating complete axiomatisations of some weak equivalences were developed [13, 14, 15].

The main conceptual contribution of the paper is a new method for defining process operators, including the sequential composition and priority operators, by transition rules with *no* negative antecedents. Our method is based on a simple idea of *ordering* the transition rules for each operator. The behaviour of a process can then be determined by examining the rules of its main operator, starting with the rules highest in the ordering and then considering the rules lower in the ordering. As a result, a rule lower in the ordering can only be applied if none of the rules above it can. Intuitively, this has the effect of applying a rule with negative antecedents. A simple example is given to illustrate our method. Consider a priority operator θ, which gives a a priority over b, defined by the following rules.

$$\frac{X \xrightarrow{a} X'}{\theta(X) \xrightarrow{a} \theta(X')} \qquad \frac{X \stackrel{a}{\nrightarrow} \quad X \xrightarrow{b} X'}{\theta(X) \xrightarrow{b} \theta(X')}$$

We easily deduce $\theta(b.\mathbf{0} \boxplus c.\mathbf{0}) \xrightarrow{b} \theta(\mathbf{0})$. Employing our method we only need the first rule and a similar rule for b (but with no negative antecedents) together with an ordering which puts the first rule above the second. Clearly, the first rule cannot be applied to the process $\theta(b.\mathbf{0} \boxplus c.\mathbf{0})$. But, since $b.\mathbf{0} \boxplus c.\mathbf{0} \xrightarrow{b} \mathbf{0}$, we obtain $\theta(b.\mathbf{0} \boxplus c.\mathbf{0}) \xrightarrow{b} \theta(\mathbf{0})$ by the second rule.

The main technical problem we address is how to combine orderings on rules with the intended use of silent actions. It is known that all ISOS operators, which include most of popular process operators, preserve a version of weak bisimulation [12]. However, it is not difficult, as will be shown in the forthcoming sections, to come up with a positive ISOS operator and a careless ordering on its rules such that the operator does not preserve weak bisimulation. In order to avoid such operators we propose a number of conditions on orderings such that if they are satisfied then the defined operator is guaranteed to preserve weak bisimulation.

2 Preliminaries

Let Var be a countable set of variables ranged by $X, X_i, Y, Y_i, \ldots$. A signature Σ is a set of pairs (f, n), where $n \in \mathbb{N}$ is an arity of f. An element $(g, 0)$ of Σ is called a constant symbol and it is abbreviated as g. The set of open terms over Σ with variables in $V \subseteq \mathsf{Var}$, denoted by $\mathbb{T}(\Sigma, V)$, is ranged by $P, Q, \ldots$. The set of closed terms, written as $\mathrm{T}(\Sigma)$, is ranged by $p, q, \ldots$. $var(T)$ denotes the set of variables appearing in a term T. We use $\equiv$ for syntactic equality. Σ context with n holes $C[X_1, \ldots, X_n]$ is a member of $\mathbb{T}(\Sigma, \{X_1, \ldots, X_n\})$. A *proper* context is a context where each variable occurs at most once. If $t_1, \ldots, t_n$ are Σ terms then $C[t_1, \ldots, t_n]$ is a term obtained by substituting X_i by t_i, $1 \le i \le n$. An equivalence $\sim$ on $\mathrm{T}(\Sigma)$ is the congruence if for all Σ contexts $C[\boldsymbol{X}]$ we have $\boldsymbol{t} \sim \boldsymbol{t}'$ implies $C[\boldsymbol{t}] \sim C[\boldsymbol{t}']$. Similarly, an operator (f, n) preserves $\sim$ if for all n-ary vectors of closed terms $\boldsymbol{t}$ and $\boldsymbol{t}'$ with $\boldsymbol{t} \sim \boldsymbol{t}'$ we have $f(\boldsymbol{t}) \sim f(\boldsymbol{t}')$. A *substitution* ρ is a mapping from Var to $\mathbb{T}(\Sigma)$. The substitution ρ extends to a mapping $\mathbb{T}(\Sigma) \rightarrow \mathbb{T}(\Sigma)$ in a standard way. $\mathsf{Act} = \mathsf{Vis} \cup \{\tau\}$, ranged by $\alpha, \ldots$, is a finite set of actions, where Vis is the set of visible actions, ranged by $a, b, \ldots$, and τ is a silent, internal action which is not in Vis.

In this paper we only consider *weak* equivalence on processes. The main characteristic of weak equivalences is the type of process behaviour which is used to determine which processes are related—only visible behaviour is taken into account. In particular this means that only the visible actions of processes are recorded and the silent actions are abstracted away. If one is interested in using weak equivalences and if one searches for a general format of rules with a suitable treatment of silent actions then, we believe, it is reasonable to have the following minimal requirement concerning the form of rules: *All operators defined in the format should preserve the chosen weak equivalence.*

The first attempt to accommodate silent actions in formats of rules is due to Bloom [8]. The important idea of silent rules, called there *patience* rules, was introduced there but the overall treatment of silent actions was not completely satisfactory: one could define operators which would count the number of silent actions processes can perform. Vaandrager in [10] modified the original De Simone format [4] by using the silent rules and showed that failure equivalence is preserved by all operators definable in the modified format. Then, the second author introduced in [11] the ISOS format—a general format of rules with negative antecedents and a suitable treatment of silent actions. He proved that ISOS operators preserve a version of weak bisimulation [12] (sometime called delay bisimulation) and refusal simulation preorder [11]. Also, similar modifications to those used in the ISOS format and some new ideas were applied to positive GSOS rules in [9]. As a result a number of formats were proposed and a number of weak equivalences, including rooted branching and weak bisimulations, were shown to be preserved by the operators in these formats. Finally, the second author showed in [15] that testing preorder of De Nicola & Hennessy [16] is preserved by De Simone (with silent rules) operators.

In this paper we shall consider only those rules which belong to (a slightly extended) ISOS format as described in [11, 12]. The ISOS rules have two distinctive forms. We will use the following notational agreement: we write $X \widetilde{\overset{\alpha}{\to}} X$ instead of $X \overset{\tau}{\not\to}\overset{\alpha}{\not\to}$.

Definition 1 An *action rule* has the following form

$$\frac{\{\ X_i \overset{a_i}{\to} X'_i\ \}_{i\in I} \qquad \{\ X_j \widetilde{\overset{\beta_{jk}}{\to}} X_j\ \}_{j\in J, k\in K_j}}{f(X_1,\ldots,X_n) \overset{\alpha}{\to} C[\mathbf{Y}],}$$

where X_i, X'_i are all different variables, I and $J \subseteq \{1,\ldots,n\}$, all K_j are finite subsets of natural numbers and $C[\mathbf{Y}]$ contains at most the variables $Y_1,\ldots,Y_n$, where $Y_i = X'_i$ if $i \in I$ and $Y_i = X_i$ otherwise. Note that each Y_i may appear in $C[\mathbf{Y}]$ a number of time or not at all. The notions of the *operator* of the rule, the *action, positive* and *negative antecedents* and the *consequent* are as usual. The action rule is *positive* if $J = \emptyset$ or, in other words, if it does not have any negative antecedents. We say that (f, n) *tests* its m-th argument and the

m-th argument for (f, n) is *active* if there is an action rule for (f, n) with X_m in the antecedents. The antecedents and the consequent of a rule r are written as $ante(r)$ and $cons(r)$ respectively.

A *silent rule*, or τ-rule, for an operator f is any of the following rules for $1 \leq i \leq n$, hereafter written as τ_{f_i} or simply as τ_i when f is known from the context,

$$\frac{X_i \xrightarrow{\tau} X_i'}{f(X_1, \ldots, X_i, \ldots, X_n) \xrightarrow{\tau} f(X_1, \ldots, X_i', \ldots, X_n).}$$

An action rule is τ-producing if $\alpha = \tau$, otherwise it is Vis-producing. Let $rules(f)$ be the set of all action rules and τ-rules with $f(\boldsymbol{X})$ in the consequent. The ith argument is *active* in some action rule r if X_i appears in the antecedents of r, and it is active in a set $S \subseteq rules(f)$ if it is active in some action rule in S. Denote the set of such i by $active(S)$, and write $active(f)$ instead of $active(rules(f))$. Let $tau(S)$ be $\{i \mid \tau_i \in S\}$, and write $tau(f)$ instead of $tau(rules(f))$. A τ-rule τ_i is *associated* with f if the ith argument of f is active.

Definition 2 With the notations as in the previous definition, a set of rules $S \subseteq rules(f)$ is in the *ISOS* format (*positive ISOS* format) if it satisfies $active(S) = tau(S)$ (and all its action rules are positive). A process operator is an ISOS (positive ISOS) operator if the set of its defining rules is in the ISOS (positive ISOS) format. An ISOS (positive ISOS) process language is a triple $(\Sigma, \mathsf{A} \cup \{\tau\}, R)$, where Σ is a finite set of ISOS (positive ISOS) operators, $\mathsf{A} \subseteq \mathsf{Vis}$, A is finite and R is a finite set of rules for operators in Σ.

Most of the operators in commonly used process languages are positive ISOS except, for example, for the CCS and ACP choice operator $+$ and the ACP left-merge operator. They are not positive ISOS because they do not have the associated τ-rules. But, there are positive ISOS versions of these operators which are appropriate for most of the purposes. For example, the CSP external choice operator $\boxplus$ is one of the positive ISOS choice operators. It is defined by the following rule schema

$$\frac{X \xrightarrow{a} X'}{X \boxplus Y \xrightarrow{a} X'} \qquad \frac{Y \xrightarrow{a} Y'}{X \boxplus Y \xrightarrow{a} Y'}$$

together with two appropriate τ-rules. Also, the CSP internal choice operator and the mixed choice defined in [12] are positive ISOS operators.

Given an ISOS process language $(\Sigma, \mathsf{A} \cup \{\tau\}, R)$, a *labeled transition system* can be defined in a standard way; the details can be found, for example, in [5, 17, 7, 12]. A labeled transition system for the above language is a structure

$(\mathrm{T}(\Sigma), \mathsf{A} \cup \{\tau\}, \rightarrow)$, where $\mathrm{T}(\Sigma)$ is a set of *process terms* or *processes* and $\rightarrow \subseteq \mathrm{T}(\Sigma) \times \mathsf{A} \cup \{\tau\} \times (\mathrm{T}(\Sigma)$ is the unique *transition relation* generated by the language. We will often call this transition system the basic transition system for a given language. Expressions of the form $t \xrightarrow{\alpha} t'$, where $t, t' \in \mathrm{T}(\Sigma)$ and $\alpha \in \mathsf{A} \cup \{\tau\}$, are called *transitions*. They are varied by T, T'. With the notation as above, we say that transition $t \xrightarrow{\alpha} t'$ is *valid* (*holds*) in $\rightarrow$ if $(t, \alpha, t') \in \rightarrow$.

We will use some standard notation: for $(p, a, q) \in \rightarrow$ we write $p \xrightarrow{a} q$ and interpret it as process p performs a and in doing so becomes q. The abbreviations we will use are $p \xrightarrow{a}$ for $\exists q \in \mathrm{T}(\Sigma).\ p \xrightarrow{a} q$ and $p \not\xrightarrow{a}$ for $\neg \exists q \in \mathrm{T}(\Sigma).\ p \xrightarrow{a} q$. Also, $p \stackrel{\tau}{\Rightarrow} q$ means $p = q$ or $\exists p_1, \ldots, p_n$ such that $p = p_1$, $p_1 \xrightarrow{\tau} \ldots \xrightarrow{\tau} p_n$ and $p_n = q$. Using the above we write $p \stackrel{\underline{a}}{\Rightarrow} q$ to mean $p \stackrel{\tau}{\Rightarrow} p' \xrightarrow{a} q$ for some p'.

Next, we define a version of weak bisimulation relation which is based on weak bisimulation (or observation equivalence) discussed in [18, 19, 12]. This version is often called *delay* bisimulation [20, 21].

Definition 3 Assume the basic transition systems for a given ISOS process language with the set of actions $\mathsf{A} \cup \{\tau\}$.

1. A binary relation R on processes is a *weak bisimulation* if pRq implies, for all $\alpha \in \mathsf{A} \cup \{\tau\}$,

$$\begin{array}{l} \forall p'.\ p \xrightarrow{\alpha} p' \ \text{ implies } \ (\exists q'.\ q \stackrel{\underline{\alpha}}{\Rightarrow} q' \ \text{ and } \ p'Rq'), \\ \forall q'.\ q \xrightarrow{\alpha} q' \ \text{ implies } \ (\exists p'.\ p \stackrel{\underline{\alpha}}{\Rightarrow} p' \ \text{ and } \ p'Rq'). \end{array}$$

2. $p \approx q$ if there exists a weak bisimulation R such that pRq.

The difference between our definition of weak bisimulation and the standard notion as defined, for example, in [2] and denoted here by $\approx_B$ lies in the meaning of $p \stackrel{\underline{a}}{\Rightarrow} q$: in [2] $p \stackrel{\underline{a}}{\Rightarrow} q$ means $p \stackrel{\tau}{\Rightarrow} p' \xrightarrow{a} q' \stackrel{\tau}{\Rightarrow} q$, for some p', q'. It is worth noting that $\approx$ is strictly finer than $\approx_B$ since the third τ-law is not sound for $\approx$. One of the reasons for choosing this version of weak bisimulation is that the standard version is not preserved by many simple positive ISOS operators. In fact, there are much simpler De Simone operators [15], for example action refinement-like operators, which fail to preserve the standard version.

Finally, we state the congruence result for $\approx$ and ISOS operators.

Proposition 4 Let $G = (\Sigma, \mathsf{A} \cup \{\tau\}, R)$ be any (positive) ISOS process language. Then $\approx$ is preserved by all Σ operators, that is for all $(f, n) \in \Sigma$ we have

$$\forall 1 \leq i \leq n.\ p_i \approx q_i \ \text{ implies } \ f(p_1, \ldots, p_n) \approx f(q_1, \ldots, q_n).$$

The proof is similar to that of Theorem 9.5.1 in [12], thus it is omitted.

3 Ordering on Rules

The antecedents of ISOS rules, unlike those of positive ISOS rules, refer to both the positive and negative behaviour of subprocesses. We will use a priority ordering on positive ISOS rules in order to achieve the effect of rules with negative antecedents. The ordering specifies the order in which the rules are to be applied when deriving transitions of terms.

Example 5 Consider an operator f such that $f(p)$ behaves like p except that whenever p cannot perform b then $f(p)$ can perform a new action $\tilde{b}$. Operator f can be defined by the following ISOS rules.

$$\frac{X \xrightarrow{\alpha} X'}{f(X) \xrightarrow{\alpha} f(X')} \qquad \frac{X \overset{\tau}{\not\rightarrow} \overset{b}{\not\rightarrow}}{f(X) \xrightarrow{\tilde{b}} f(X)}$$

But, f can also be defined as follows, for $\alpha \neq b$,

$$\frac{X \xrightarrow{\alpha} X'}{f(X) \xrightarrow{\alpha} f(X')}\ r_1 \qquad \frac{X \xrightarrow{\tau} X'}{f(X) \xrightarrow{\tau} f(X')}\ r_1$$

$$\frac{X \xrightarrow{b} X'}{f(X) \xrightarrow{b} f(X')}\ r_2 \qquad f(X) \xrightarrow{\tilde{b}} f(X) \quad r_3$$

with the ordering $r_3 < r_1, r_3 < r_2$. We notice that, using ISOS rules, $f(p) \xrightarrow{\tilde{b}}$ if and only if $p \overset{\tau}{\not\rightarrow} \overset{b}{\not\rightarrow}$. Applying the positive ISOS rules with the above ordering we can deduce $f(p) \xrightarrow{\tilde{b}}$ only if rules r_1 and r_2 cannot be applied for $f(p)$: that is when $p \overset{\tau}{\not\rightarrow}$ and $p \overset{b}{\not\rightarrow}$.

Let $<_f$ be a relation on $rules(f)$. $r <_f r'$ means that r has a lower priority than r' (and r' has a higher priority than r) when deriving the transitions of $f(p)$, any p. By this we mean that a rule can only be applied when no rules with higher priority can be applied. We do not assume irreflexivity or transitivity of the relation $<_f$. Given positive ISOS language G $<_G$, or simply $<$ if G is clear from the context, is $\bigcup_{f \in \Sigma_G} <_f$.

Definition 6 An ordered process language is a pair $(G, <)$, where G is a positive ISOS process language and $<$ is the ordering on its rules as described above.

Next, we describe how to associate a transition relation with $(G, <)$. Our method is based on that originated in [22]. We will need a function $d : \mathrm{T}(\Sigma) \rightarrow$

$\mathbb{N}$ to specify the depth of operator names in a ground term over a signature Σ. Function d is defined inductively:

- $d(t) = 0$ if t is a constant,

- $d(g(t_1, \ldots, t_r)) = 1 + \max\{d(t_i) \mid 1 \leq i \leq r\}$.

The extension of d to transitions is defined as expected: $d(t \xrightarrow{*} t') = d(t)$. Also, the following will be useful: $higher(r) = \{r' \in rules(f) \mid r <_f r'\}$, and correspondingly $lower(r)$.

Definition 7 Given $(G, <)$ we associate a transition relation, $\rightarrow \subseteq \mathrm{T}(\Sigma) \times \mathsf{A} \cup \{\tau\} \times \mathrm{T}(\Sigma)$, defined as follows: $\rightarrow = \bigcup_{l<\omega} \rightarrow^l$, where transition relations $\rightarrow^l \subseteq \mathrm{T}(\Sigma) \times \mathsf{A} \cup \{\tau\} \times \mathrm{T}(\Sigma)$ are:

$$\begin{aligned} T \in \rightarrow^l \text{ iff } \; d(T) = l \;\&\; \exists\, r \in R,\ \rho : V \rightarrow \mathrm{T}(\Sigma).\ [\, &\rho(cons(r)) = T \\ &\&\ \rho(ante(r)) \in \textstyle\bigcup_{k<l} \rightarrow^k \\ &\&\ \forall r' \in higher(r).\ \rho(ante(r')) \notin \textstyle\bigcup_{k<l} \rightarrow^k \,]. \end{aligned}$$

Similarly as in [22] it is easy to show that the transition relation $\rightarrow$ associated with a given $(G, <)$ *agrees* with it. Intuitively, it means that all transitions in $\rightarrow$ are derivable by rules of G under the ordering $<$. In general, there may be a number of transition relations which agree with $(G, <)$. But, we claim that the transition relation associated with $(G, <)$ is the unique transition relation which agrees with $(G, <)$. The definitions of the basic and derived transition systems for $(G, <)$ are then straightforward.

4 Ordered Rules with Silent Actions

One may wonder if all process operators which are defined by ordered positive ISOS rules preserve our version of weak bisimulation. The answer is negative. We will give a number of examples to prove our claim. Moreover, these examples will help us to find a number of conditions such that all operators, which can be defined by rules satisfying these conditions, preserve $\approx$.

Notation: In order to shorten the presentation of the forthcoming conditions we will leave out the outermost universal quantifiers binding $f \in \Sigma$ and $r \in rules(f)$. Also, all the rules mentioned in the conditions, i.e. τ_i, r and r', are understood to belong to $rules(f)$.

Consider an interleaving parallel operator $\|$ defined as follows:

$$\frac{X \xrightarrow{a} X'}{X \| Y \xrightarrow{a} X' \| Y} \; r_{a*} \qquad \frac{X \xrightarrow{\tau} X'}{X \| Y \xrightarrow{\tau} X' \| Y} \; \tau_1$$

$$\frac{Y \xrightarrow{a} Y'}{X \| Y \xrightarrow{a} X \| Y'} \; r_{*a} \qquad \frac{Y \xrightarrow{\tau} Y'}{X \| Y \xrightarrow{\tau} X \| Y'} \; \tau_2$$

The names of rules and rule schemas accompany them on the right. The ordering is $r_{a*} > \tau_2$. Now we have $b \approx \tau b$ and $a \| b \stackrel{b}{\Rightarrow}$, but $a \| \tau b \stackrel{b}{\not\Rightarrow}$.

Thus, we need to find a conditions on the ordering relation which would not allow the above ordering. The first condition might be as follows.

$$\text{if } r \text{ is a } \tau\text{-rule then } higher(r) = \emptyset$$

The intuition is that τ-rules should not have lower priority. But, although the condition is quite natural it is also restrictive. For example, let f be a binary operator. When deriving the behaviour of $f(p, q)$ one may want to give priority to the first subprocess (like with the sequential composition operator). This may result in some rules associated with the first subprocess being above τ_2. We can allow such orderings provided that all the rules, which are above τ_2, are above all the rules with active second argument. This can be written as follows.

$$\begin{array}{lll} \text{if } r \in higher(\tau_i) & \text{then} & lower(\tau_i) = \emptyset \text{ and} \\ & & \forall r'.\ \text{if } i \in active(r') \text{ then } r \in higher(r') \end{array} \quad (1)$$

The condition implies that no action rule can be above any of its τ-rules.

There are operators, definable by positive ISOS rules satisfying condition (1), which do not preserve weak bisimulation. Consider the priority operator θ which gives d priority over b. It is defined by the following rule schema, for $\alpha \in \{b, d, \tau\}$,

$$\frac{X \xrightarrow{\alpha} X'}{\theta(X) \xrightarrow{\alpha} \theta(X').}$$

The action rules are denoted by r_b and r_d, and the τ-rule is τ_1. Suppose $r_d > r_b$. Let $p = b \| \tau d$ and $q = b \| d$, where $\|$ is the usual interleaved parallel composition operator. Then, $p \approx q$ and $\theta(p) \stackrel{b}{\Rightarrow}$, but $\theta(q) \stackrel{b}{\not\Rightarrow}$. To repair this we additionally require $\tau_1 > r_b$.

This example leads to the following condition.

$$\text{if } i \in \mathit{active}(\mathit{higher}(r)) \text{ then } \tau_i \in \mathit{higher}(r) \tag{2}$$

The intuition here is that in order to apply the rule r we need to make sure that no other rules with higher priority (and thus their τ-rules) can be applied.

Next, we claim our main result.

Theorem 8 Let $(G,<)$ be an ordered process language, where $G = (\Sigma, \mathsf{A} \cup \{\tau\}, R)$ is any positive ISOS process language and the ordering $<$ satisfies conditions (1) and (2). Then $\approx$ defined over the derived transition system for $(G,<)$ is preserved by all Σ operators.

The theorem is proved similarly as, for example, in [17, 6, 12]. Due to the lack of space the proof is omitted.

5 Applications

Sequential composition is often defined by rules with negative antecedents as, for example in [5, 7]. However, it can be defined by the following ordered rule schemas, where $a, b \in \mathsf{A}$:

$$\frac{X \xrightarrow{a} X'}{X;Y \xrightarrow{a} X';Y}\; r_{a*} \qquad\qquad \frac{Y \xrightarrow{b} Y'}{X;Y \xrightarrow{b} Y'}\; r_{*b}$$

together with the appropriate τ-rules τ_1 and τ_2. The ordering on the rules satisfies $r_{a*} > r_{*b}, \tau_2$ for all a, b and the conditions (1) and (2).

Priorities are employed in process languages to represent such phenomena as time-outs and interrupts. For a given partial order $<$ on visible actions $\theta(X)$ is a restriction of X such that action a can only happen only if no $b > a$ is possible. This can be defined operationally by the first of the following rules.

$$\frac{X \xrightarrow{\alpha} X' \quad X \stackrel{\beta}{\not\rightarrow} \; (\forall \beta > \alpha)}{\theta(X) \xrightarrow{\alpha} \theta(X')} \qquad\qquad \frac{X \xrightarrow{a} X'}{\theta(X) \xrightarrow{a} \theta(X')}\; r_a$$

However, θ can be defined by a set of ordered positive ISOS rules, like the second rule above for each $a \in \mathsf{A}$ and the τ-rule τ_1. The ordering requires $r_a < r_b$ whenever $a < b$, and $\tau_1 > r_b$ whenever there exist an action rule r_a such that $r_a \in \mathit{higher}(r_b)$. In [23], the first author surveyed a number of approaches to priorities in process algebras. He showed how these approaches might be fitted into a common operational framework based on ordered rules.

The **broadcast parallel** operator $\|$ can be defined by the following positive ISOS rules

$$\frac{X \xrightarrow{a} X' \quad Y \xrightarrow{a} Y'}{X \| Y \xrightarrow{a} X' \| Y'} \qquad \frac{X \xrightarrow{a} X'}{X \| Y \xrightarrow{a} X' \| Y} \qquad \frac{Y \xrightarrow{a} Y'}{X \| Y \xrightarrow{a} X \| Y'},$$

denoted by r_{aa}, r_{a*} and r_{*a} respectively, with the ordering $r_{aa} > r_{a*}, r_{*a}$.

6 Conclusions

We have introduced a new method for operationally defining arbitrary process operators which are normally defined by transition rules with negative antecedents. Our method relies on rules without negative antecedents but we equip the rules with an ordering. It specifies the order in which the rules are applied when deriving transitions of process terms. We have also proposed two conditions on rule orderings which guarantee that all operators definable by rules satisfying these conditions preserve weak bisimulation.

References

1. R. Milner. *A Calculus for Communicating Systems.* Springer-Verlag, Berlin, 1980. LNCS 92.
2. R. Milner. *Communication and Concurrency.* Prentice Hall, 1989.
3. G. Plotkin. A structural approach to operational semantics. Technical Report DAIMI FN-19, Aarhus University, 1981.
4. R. de Simone. Higher-level synchronising devices in MEIJE-SCCS. *Theoretical Computer Science*, Vol. 37, pp. 245–267, 1985.
5. B. Bloom, S. Istrail, and A.R. Meyer. Bisimulation can't be traced: preliminary report. In *Conference Record of the 15th ACM Symposium on Principles of Programming Languages*, San Diego, California, 1988.
6. B. Bloom. *Ready simulation, bisimulation, and the semantics of CCS-like languages.* PhD thesis, MIT, 1990.
7. B. Bloom, S. Istrail, and A.R. Meyer. Bisimulation can't be traced. *Journal of ACM*, Vol. 42(1),, 1995. Also appeared as Technical Report TR 90-1150, Cornell, 1990.
8. B. Bloom. Strong process equivalence in the presence of hidden moves. Preliminary report, MIT, 1990.
9. B. Bloom. Structural operational semantics for weak bisimulations. *Theoretical Computer Science*, Vol. 146, pp. 27–68, 1995. Also appeared as Technical Report TR 93-1373, Cornell, 1993.

10. F.W. Vaandrager. On the relationship between process algebra and input/output automata. In *Proceedings of the 6th Annual IEEE Symposium on Logic in Computer Science*, Amsterdam, 1991.
11. I. Ulidowski. Equivalences on observable processes. In *Proceedings of the 7th Annual IEEE Symposium on Logic in Computer Science*, Santa Cruz, California, 1992.
12. I. Ulidowski. *Local Testing and Implementable Concurrent Processes.* PhD thesis, Imperial College, University of London, 1994.
13. L. Aceto, B. Bloom, and F.W. Vaandrager. Turning SOS rules into equations. In *Proceedings of the 7th Annual IEEE Symposium on Logic in Computer Science*, Santa Cruz, California, 1992.
14. I. Ulidowski. Axiomatisations of weak equivalences for De Simone languages. In I. Lee and S.A. Smolka, editors, *Proceedings of the 6th International Conference on Concurrency Theory* CONCUR'95, Philadelphia, 1995. Springer-Verlag. LNCS 962.
15. I. Ulidowski. Finite axiom systems for testing preorder and De Simone process languages. In *Proceedings of the 5th International Conference on Algebraic Methodology and Software Technology AMAST'96*, München, Germany, 1996.
16. R. De Nicola and M. Hennessy. Testing equivalences for processes. *Theoretical Computer Science*, Vol. 34, pp. 83–133, 1984.
17. J.F. Groote and F. Vaandrager. Structured operational semantics and bisimulation as a congruence. *Information and Computation*, Vol. 100, pp. 202–260, 1990.
18. R. Milner. A modal characterisation of observable machine behaviours. In G. Astesiano and C. Böhm, editors, *CAAP 81*, pp. 25–34, Berlin, 1981. Springer-Verlag. LNCS 112.
19. S. Abramsky. Observation equivalence as a testing equivalence. *Theoretical Computer Science*, Vol. 53, pp. 225–241, 1987.
20. W.P. Weijland. *Synchrony and Asynchrony in Process Algebra.* PhD thesis, University of Amsterdam, 1989.
21. R.J. van Glabbeek and W.P. Weijland. Branching time and abstraction in bisimulation semantics. In G.X. Ritter, editor, *Information Processing 89*, pp. 613–618. Elsevier Science Publishers B. V. (North-Holland), 1989. To appear in JACM.
22. J.F. Groote. Transition system specifications with negative premises. In J.C.M. Baeten and J.W. Klop, editors, *Proceedings of* CONCUR'90, Amsterdam, 1990. Springer-Verlag. LNCS 458.
23. I.C.C. Phillips. Approaches to priority in process algebras. Unpublished manuscript, 1994.

FINITE BUT UNBOUNDED DELAY IN SYNCHRONOUS CCS

M. HUTH, M. KWIATKOWSKA
School of Computer Science, University of Birmingham, Edgbaston, B15 2TT, UK

We recast Milner's work on SCCSϵ, a calculus for finite but unbounded delay based on SCCS, by giving a denotational semantics for admissibility of infinite computations on a bifinite domain $\mathcal{K}$. Using Abramsky's SFP domain $\mathcal{D}$ for bisimulation we obtain a fully abstract model in $\mathcal{D} \times \mathcal{K}$ for an operational preorder which includes divergence and, if restricted to finite behaviour, corresponds to Abramsky's finitary preorder. We use finite but unbounded delay, choice and the synchronous product to derive a fair parallel operator in SCCSϵ.

1 Introduction

This paper mainly builds upon two pieces of work: Milner's calculus SCCSϵ, an extension of SCCS with finite but unbounded delay [1] and Abramsky's domain equation for bisimulation [2]. The importance of synchronous CCS with finite delay stems from its ability to make fine-grained distinctions between *passive* resources, like an accessible register, and *active* ones, like agents that need to initiate some action in finite time. To clarify this point, consider an active agent δp which behaves like p, but can also delay by performing any number of silent actions 1. This can be defined by means of the equation $\delta p \equiv \mathsf{rec}\ x.1x+p$ but, unfortunately, δp admits the infinite computation consisting entirely of delay steps (1^ω), and thus it cannot be guaranteed that p is *eventually* evoked. So, while δp models *passive* resources well, one still has to cater for the case of active agents. For that purpose, Milner introduced the operator ϵ, where ϵp behaves like δp except that it *prevents* the infinite delay of p. Using finite delay, one can also provide a more expressive coding of an asynchronous calculus within the synchronous one [3]. The presence of finite but unbounded delay further allows for very natural solutions to certain fairness problems arising from the synchronous parallel operation. For example, one can use ϵ to define a fair parallel in SCCSϵ. In fact, one may think of such a delay as a special *liveness property* [4].

Milner developed a theory of finite but unbounded delay with an accompanying notion of operational preorder (called *fortification*), an asymmetric and conservative extension of (strong) bisimulation in SCCS. For guarded recursion he showed that recursive equations have least (but not always unique) fixed points with respect to this operational preorder, and that it is preserved by all the combinators of the calculus. The notion of fortification crucially depends on that of an *admissible infinite computation* u for a process p. In [1] this had been formalized using prevention ordinals. However, Milner's paper does not give a denotational semantics for SCCSϵ, and it is not at all clear what such a semantics should look like. For example, should it somehow be derived as a sort of limit from a denotational semantics for the finite computations as done in [5, 6][a] following an idea in [8]? And if so, would we be able to "turn the handle" and extract a sound and complete program logic from a fully abstract denotational model? Unfortunately, the models in [5, 6] leave the realm of SFP domains for which there exists such a mechanical method for transforming a denotational semantics into an equivalent program logic [9].

In this extended abstract we sketch the details of a fully abstract denotational model for an extension of fortification, more precisely, an extension of fortification *plus divergence*, in a bifinite domain, which then allows us to use the machinery of [9] at the level of objects. Our model is a product $\mathcal{D} \times \mathcal{K}$ where $\mathcal{D}$ is the initial solution for Abramsky's domain equation for bisimulation in [2]. The bifinite domain $\mathcal{K}$ is a complete lattice and the semantics on $\mathcal{K}$ is monotone, whereas the semantics on $\mathcal{D}$ is continuous. The semantics on $\mathcal{D} \times \mathcal{K}$ is then realised as a pairing of these semantics. Since the category SFP and the category of complete lattices and monotone maps are cartesian closed [10, 11] this opens up the possibility of future work on finite delay in a higher-order setting.

The significance of this work lies foremost in giving a fully abstract denotational semantics for SCCSϵ and in giving it in a *bifinite*, and in particular, *algebraic* lattice (i.e., an inverse limit of finite lattices with respect to continuous projection-embedding pairs). This lattice has a Stone dual from which one may "read off" the corresponding program logic. Another main contribution is the logical separation of finitely observable and truly infinite, "fair", behaviour in the model resulting in a very elegant representation of the *environment* as $\mathcal{K}$, the infinite part of the model. By the same token, our model lets us "recycle" the full abstraction results of [2] for SCCS on $\mathcal{D}$, the finitely observable part of the model. Our results improve on the work in [12, 5], for we specify a *bifinite* model and we develop an asynchronous fair parallel from *finer* building blocks (synchronous product, sum and finite but unbounded delay). Our results also go well beyond those in [6]; their model is *not* fully abstract and there proofs require substantial book-keeping of the synchronous product for synchronization algebras [13].

[a] Such a derivation as a limit process has in fact *intrinsic* limitations [7].

2 The Calculus SCCSϵ and its Operational Semantics

We study Milner's SCCSϵ, synchronous CCS with finite delay [1, 14] with the standard signature, the only exception being its restriction to *finite sums*, as done in [2], in order to secure full abstraction of our denotational semantics.

Definition 1 *We define a language $\mathcal{L}$ by the following grammar in* BNF *form:*

$$p ::= \mathsf{nil} \mid a{:}p \mid p\lceil A \mid p[S] \mid \epsilon p \mid p+p \mid p \times p \mid x \mid \mathsf{rec}\ x.p$$

where x is out of a countable set of variables Var, *a is an element of a countable abelian group* Act *with identity* 1, *A is a subset of* Act *containing* 1 *and S:* Act $\rightarrow$ Act *is a group homomorphism. The binding operations* rec x, $x \in$ Var, *introduce the usual notions of free and bound variables. Let* SCCSϵ *denote the set of all closed terms of $\mathcal{L}$. We can define an additional operation δ within $\mathcal{L}$ by setting $\delta p \equiv \mathsf{rec}\ x.1x + p$. We write ap instead of $a{:}p$ whenever this is unambiguous.*

The structural operational semantics for SCCSϵ is standard as in [14]:

$$\frac{}{ap \rightarrow^{a} p} \qquad \frac{p \rightarrow^{a} p',\ a \in A}{p\lceil A \rightarrow^{a} p'\lceil A} \qquad \frac{p \rightarrow^{a} p'}{p[S] \rightarrow^{Sa} p'[S]}$$

$$\frac{p_1 \rightarrow^{a} p_1',\ p_2 \rightarrow^{b} p_2'}{p_1 \times p_2 \rightarrow^{ab} p_1' \times p_2'} \qquad \frac{p_1 \rightarrow^{a} p_1'}{p_1 + p_2 \rightarrow^{a} p_1'} \qquad \frac{p_2 \rightarrow^{a} p_2'}{p_1 + p_2 \rightarrow^{a} p_2'}$$

$$\frac{p[x{:=}\mathsf{rec}\ x.p] \rightarrow^{a} p'}{\mathsf{rec}\ x.p \rightarrow^{a} p'}$$

with the two additional rules (WAIT) and (FULFILL) of [1]:

$$\frac{}{\epsilon p \rightarrow^{1} \epsilon p}\ (\mathtt{WAIT}) \qquad \frac{p \rightarrow^{a} p'}{\epsilon p \rightarrow^{a} p'}\ (\mathtt{FULFILL})$$

The last two rules *attempt* to express the operational intuition that ϵp has the same dynamic capacity as the process p (FULFILL) but that it may choose to postpone its dynamics unboundedly but finitely often (WAIT). This attempt, however, fails as such: using the operational rule for recursion, one readily notices that $\delta p \equiv \mathsf{rec}\ x.1x + p$ has the same *finite* behaviour as ϵp; these processes are in fact bisimilar. However, if p is some process in SCCSϵ which cannot compute an infinite sequence of 1's then δp is allowed to delay forever, whereas ϵp is not. So we need to refine the notion of bisimulation in order to express such different capacities of performing *infinite* computations. Essentially, we need to rule out infinite computations $\epsilon p \rightarrow^{1} \epsilon p \rightarrow^{1} \epsilon p \rightarrow \ldots$ where each transition is justified by an instance of the (WAIT) rule. This will require a precise book-keeping of such undesired *subcomputations* in a general context $C(p_1, \ldots, p_n)$ which is built from the only static combinators of this process calculus: synchronous product, relabeling and restriction. In [1] this is achieved via *prevention ordinals*; we extend his definition to include relabeling.

Definition 2 *[1] We define a partial function* $\mathrm{o}: \mathsf{SCCS}\epsilon \times \mathsf{Act}^\omega \rightharpoonup \mathsf{Ord}$ *into the class of ordinals. We then say that* p admits the infinite computation $u \in \mathsf{Act}^\omega$ *if and only if the ordinal* $\mathrm{o}(p,u)$ *is undefined. We define* $\mathrm{o}(p,u)$ *to be the least ordinal* λ *such that* (p,u) *is contained in the set* M_λ. *The sets* $M_\lambda \subseteq \mathsf{SCCS}\epsilon \times \mathsf{Act}^\omega$ *are defined by transfinite induction, setting* $M_0 = \{(\mathsf{nil}, u) : u \in \mathsf{Act}^\omega\}$ *and for* $\lambda > 0$

- $(ap, bu) \in M_\lambda$ *if* $a \neq b$ *or* $(a = b$ *&* $(p,u) \in M_\mu$ *for some* $\mu < \lambda)$*;*
- $(p\lceil A, u) \in M_\lambda$ *if* $u \notin A^\omega$ *or* $(p,u) \in M_\mu$ *for some* $\mu < \lambda$*;*
- $(p[S], u) \in M_\lambda$ *if* $u \neq S^\omega v$ *for all* $v \in \mathsf{Act}^\omega$ *or for all* $v \in \mathsf{Act}^\omega$ *with* $u = S^\omega v$ *we have* $(p,v) \in M_\mu$ *for some* $\mu < \lambda$*;*[b]
- $(\epsilon p, u) \in M_\lambda$ *if for all* $m \in \omega$ *such that* $u = 1^m v$ *we have* $(p,v) \in M_\mu$ *for some* $\mu < \lambda$*;*
- $(p_1 + p_2, u) \in M_\lambda$ *if* $(p_i, u) \in M_{\mu_i}$ *for some* $\mu_i < \lambda$, $(i = 1,2)$*;*
- $(p_1 \times p_2, u) \in M_\lambda$ *if for all* $v, w \in \mathsf{Act}^\omega$ *with* $u = v \cdot w$ *we have* $(p_1, v) \in M_\mu$ *or* $(p_2, w) \in M_\mu$ *for some* $\mu < \lambda$*;*[c]
- $(\mathsf{rec}\ x.p, u) \in M_\lambda$ *if* $(p[x := \mathsf{rec}\ x.p], u) \in M_\mu$ *for some* $\mu < \lambda$.

Given a process $p \in \mathsf{SCCS}\epsilon$ *we associate with it its set of admissible infinite computations* $\mathrm{k}(p) = \{u \in \mathsf{Act}^\omega \colon\ \mathrm{o}(p,u)$ *is undefined*$\}$.

For example, one may now prove that $\mathrm{k}(\delta\, \mathsf{rec}\ x.ax) = \{1^\omega\} \cup \{1^m a^\omega : m \in \omega\}$ and $\mathrm{k}(\epsilon\, \mathsf{rec}\ x.ax) = \mathrm{k}(\delta\, \mathsf{rec}\ x.ax) \setminus \{1^\omega\}$ as expected. It should be pointed out that this formal definition exactly captures Milner's informal notion of admissibility for *guarded* terms in $\mathsf{SCCS}\epsilon$ [1, Theorem 5.3]. We therefore take this formal definition as applying to *unguarded* terms in $\mathsf{SCCS}\epsilon$ as well.[d] Our full abstraction results will indeed be formulated for this larger class of processes.

---

[b] The map $S^\omega : \mathsf{Act}^\omega \to \mathsf{Act}^\omega$ is defined by $S^\omega u = Su_0 Su_1 \cdots$.

[c] Given $v, w \in \mathsf{Act}^\omega$ we define $v \cdot w$ as the infinite word $u \in \mathsf{Act}^\omega$ where u_i is the product $v_i w_i$ in the group Act, $(i \geq 0)$.

[d] Recall that a term p is guarded if all free occurrences of its free variables occur in some subexpression of the form ap'.

Before we introduce operational preorders for processes in SCCSϵ we state the usual definition of a *divergence predicate* [2]:

$$\frac{x \in \mathsf{Var}}{\mathsf{rec}\ x.x\uparrow} \qquad \frac{p\uparrow}{p\lceil A\uparrow} \qquad \frac{p\uparrow}{p[S]\uparrow}$$

$$\frac{p_1\uparrow}{p_1+p_2\uparrow} \qquad \frac{p_2\uparrow}{p_1+p_2\uparrow} \qquad \frac{p_1\uparrow \text{ or } p_2\uparrow}{p_1 \times p_2\uparrow}$$

$$\frac{p[x{:=}\mathsf{rec}\ x.x]\uparrow}{\mathsf{rec}\ x.p\uparrow} \qquad \frac{p\uparrow}{\epsilon p\uparrow}$$

where we needed to add the rule for ϵ above. Note that this last rule matches the combined ones for $+$ and recursion if we identify ϵp with rec $x.1x + p$, for $1q$ converges for all processes q. This is to be expected since syntactic divergence is a *finitary* property. We write $p \rightarrow p'$ if $p \rightarrow^a p'$ is provable from the rules of the structural semantics for $a \in$ Act. The triple (SCCS$\epsilon, \rightarrow, \uparrow$) is a transition system in the sense of [2]. Following Hennessy's and Stirling's ideas of generalized transition systems [15], we define such a notion which suitably represents admissible infinite computations.

Definition 3 *A* generalized transition system $\mathcal{G}$ over Act *is a quadruple* $(S, \rightarrow, k, \uparrow)$ *where* S *is a set of states,* $\rightarrow$ *associates to every* $a \in$ Act *a binary relation* $\rightarrow^a \ \subseteq S \times S$ *and* $\uparrow \subseteq S$ *is a predicate of divergence. Finally,* $k\colon S \rightarrow \mathcal{K}$ *is a function, where* $\mathcal{K}$ *is the bifinite domain of subsets of* Act^ω *ordered under* reverse *inclusion:*[e] $\mathcal{K} = \mathcal{P}(\mathsf{Act}^\omega)$ *with* $F \sqsubseteq G$ *in* $\mathcal{K}$ *if and only if* $G \subseteq F$.

Notice that $\mathcal{K}$ has uncountably many compact elements as the set Act^ω is uncountable. Further, generalized transition systems depend on Act and its derived parameter $\mathcal{K}$. The intuition behind a generalized transition system is that it provides an operational semantics for abstract states in terms of transitions labeled by elements of Act and that $k(s)$ represents the set of admissible *infinite* computations beginning in state s. We define natural co-inductive relations on generalized transition systems and we list their usual properties.

Definition 4 *Let* $\mathcal{G} = (S, \rightarrow, k, \uparrow)$ *be a generalized transition system over* Act. *A* partial fortification *on* $\mathcal{G}$ *is a binary relation* $R \subseteq S \times S$ *such that* xRy *implies*

- $k(x) \supseteq k(y)$
- $\forall a \in$ Act $x \rightarrow^a x'$ *implies the existence of some* y' *such that* $y \rightarrow^a y'$ *and* $x'Ry'$
- $x\downarrow$ *implies* $[y\downarrow$ *&* $(\forall a \in$ Act $y \rightarrow^a y'$ *implies the existence of some* x' *such that* $x \rightarrow^a x'$ *and* $x'Ry'$)$]$[f]

[e] Of course, Act^ω denotes the set of infinite strings over Act.

[f] Convergence $\downarrow$ is defined as $S\backslash\uparrow$.

For general reasons there exists the greatest partial fortification on $\mathcal{G}$, denoted by $\prec_{\mathcal{G}}$ or $\prec$ if $\mathcal{G}$ is clear from the context; moreover, $\prec$ is a preorder. A relation R satisfying just the latter two clauses above is called a partial bisimulation *[2]; the greatest partial bisimulation always exists and is a preorder denoted by $\leq^{\mathsf{B}}$; it is contained in Abramsky's* finitary preorder $\leq^{\mathsf{F}}$ *[2]. The operational preorder we consider is $p \lhd q$ if and only if $p \leq^{\mathsf{F}} q$ & $k(p) \supseteq k(q)$, the intersection of the finitary preorder with refinement with respect to admissibility. Also define $p \blacktriangleleft q$ if and only if $p \leq^{\mathsf{B}} q$ & $k(p) \supseteq k(q)$.*[g]

We take $\lhd$ as the basis for this work since it is based on the notion of *observability* in its finitely observable behaviour; it further contains $\prec$ and $\blacktriangleleft$ while still enjoying all the nice properties of $\prec$, such as being a congruence and having least fixed points. The possibility of considering several plausible operational preorders seems to be inherent in studying transition systems with infinite computations. For example, in [16], we find two operational preorders for a simple language based on finite automata with three different delay operators. Hennessy is able to specify a complete axiomatization for one of them, but only a sound one for the other.[h] This is to be compared with our full abstraction results in section 3.3.

By adjusting the parameters k and $\uparrow$ of generalized transition systems we may *unify* operational concepts as particular instances of partial fortifications. First, if $k(s) = \mathsf{Act}^{\omega}$ for all $s \in S$, we simply arrive at the notion of 'partial bisimulation'. Second, if k is arbitrary and $\uparrow = \emptyset$ then we obtain Milner's 'fortification relation' [1], which he defined for the concrete instance $\mathbf{k}$.

2.1 Admissibility Denotationally

Definition 5

$$
\begin{array}{ll}
\mathsf{nil}^{\mathcal{K}} = \emptyset & a^{\mathcal{K}} F = \{au \colon u \in F\} \\
F \lceil A^{\mathcal{K}} = F \cap A^{\omega} & F[S]^{\mathcal{K}} = \{S^{\omega} u \colon u \in F\} \\
F +^{\mathcal{K}} G = F \cup G & F \times^{\mathcal{K}} G = \{v \cdot w \in \mathsf{Act}^{\omega} \colon v \in F \text{ and } w \in G\} \\
\epsilon^{\mathcal{K}} F = \{1^n u \colon n \in \omega, u \in F\} & \delta^{\mathcal{K}} F = \{1^{\omega}\} +^{\mathcal{K}} \epsilon^{\mathcal{K}} F.
\end{array}
$$

Lemma 1 *The functions $\mathsf{nil}^{\mathcal{K}}$, $a^{\mathcal{K}}$, $\lceil A^{\mathcal{K}}$, $+^{\mathcal{K}}$, $\epsilon^{\mathcal{K}}$ and $\delta^{\mathcal{K}}$ are continuous. The functions $[S]^{\mathcal{K}}$ and $\times^{\mathcal{K}}$ are monotone. If S is injective then $[S]^{\mathcal{K}}$ is continuous as well.*

[g] One readily sees that $p \prec q$ implies $p \blacktriangleleft q$, for $\prec$ is a partial bisimulation and so $p \prec q$ implies $p \leq^{\mathsf{B}} q$ and $k(p) \supseteq k(q)$, but we do not know whether the converse is true as well. Clearly, $\blacktriangleleft$ is *properly* contained in $\lhd$ [2].

[h] Hennessy does not define a denotational semantics.

The denotational semantics of admissible infinite computations is specified in the standard way:

Definition 6 *Let* $\mathsf{Env}_{\mathcal{K}}$ *be* $\mathcal{K}^{\mathsf{Var}}$*. The signature* Σ *of* $\mathcal{L}$ *has only one constant* nil*, unary operations* $a\_$*,* $\_\lceil A$*,* $\_[S]$ *and* $\epsilon\_$*, and binary operations* $+$ *and* $\times$*. The semantics* $[\![\,]\!]^{\mathcal{K}}: \mathcal{L} \to \mathsf{Env}_{\mathcal{K}} \to \mathcal{K}$ *is defined as the standard least fixed point semantics[17].*

The map $\times^{\mathcal{K}}$ is not continuous in general. There exists a process $q \in$ SCCSϵ and a chain of processes $p_0 \prec p_1 \prec p_2 \prec \ldots$ in SCCSϵ such that $\bigcap_{k\geq 0}([\![p_k]\!]^{\mathcal{K}} \times^{\mathcal{K}} [\![q]\!]^{\mathcal{K}})$ differs from $(\bigcap_{k\geq 0}[\![p_k]\!]^{\mathcal{K}}) \times^{\mathcal{K}} [\![q]\!]^{\mathcal{K}}$. Therefore, the least fixed point will not, in general, be reached in ω many steps. Since we want to show that $\mathtt{k}(p) = [\![p]\!]^{\mathcal{K}}$ for all processes $p \in$ SCCSϵ, we need to realize $[\![\,]\!]^{\mathcal{K}}$ as the *transfinite* limit of approximating semantics as done in [18, 12]:

Definition 7 *We define a family of functions* $[\![\,]\!]^{\mathcal{K}}_{\alpha}: \mathcal{L} \to \mathsf{Env}_{\mathcal{K}} \to \mathcal{K}$*,* $\alpha \in \mathsf{Ord}$*, by transfinite induction on* α*:*

$$
\begin{aligned}
[\![p]\!]^{\mathcal{K}}_{0}\rho &= \mathsf{Act}^{\omega} \\
[\![\mathsf{nil}]\!]^{\mathcal{K}}_{\alpha+1}\rho &= \mathsf{nil}^{\mathcal{K}}, \quad \alpha \in \mathsf{Ord} \\
[\![x]\!]^{\mathcal{K}}_{\alpha+1}\rho &= \rho(x), \qquad x \in \mathsf{Var} \\
[\![\mathsf{op}(p_1, \ldots p_k)]\!]^{\mathcal{K}}_{\alpha+1}\rho &= \mathsf{op}^{\mathcal{K}}([\![p_1]\!]^{\mathcal{K}}_{\alpha}\rho, \ldots, [\![p_k]\!]^{\mathcal{K}}_{\alpha}\rho), \quad \mathsf{op}\ k\text{-ary in } \Sigma \\
[\![\mathsf{rec}\ x.p]\!]^{\mathcal{K}}_{\alpha+1}\rho &= [\![p[x := \mathsf{rec}\ x.p]]\!]^{\mathcal{K}}_{\alpha}\rho \\
[\![p]\!]^{\mathcal{K}}_{\lambda}\rho &= \bigcap_{\alpha<\lambda} [\![p]\!]^{\mathcal{K}}_{\alpha}\rho, \quad \lambda \text{ limit ordinal.}
\end{aligned}
$$

Proposition 1 *[12] We have* $[\![\,]\!]^{\mathcal{K}} = [\![\,]\!]^{\mathcal{K}}_{\lambda_0}$ *for some (limit ordinal)* $\lambda_0 \in \mathsf{Ord}$.

Before we compare $[\![p]\!]^{\mathcal{K}}$ with $\mathtt{k}(p)$, let us gain some intuition about the meaning of $[\![\mathsf{rec}\ x.p]\!]^{\mathcal{K}}$. Here is an example that shows how finite terms are being dealt with using the logical nature of $\emptyset$ for the Σ-algebra $\mathcal{K}$: we compute $[\![\mathsf{rec}\ x.a(\epsilon x + b\,\mathsf{nil})]\!]^{\mathcal{K}}$. If $p \equiv a(\epsilon x + b\,\mathsf{nil})$ we have $[\![\mathsf{rec}\ x.a(\epsilon x + b\,\mathsf{nil})]\!]^{\mathcal{K}} = \mu F \in \mathcal{K}.[\![p]\!]^{\mathcal{K}}[x \mapsto F] = \bigcap_{n\in\omega} f_p^n(\mathsf{Act}^{\omega})$ where $f_p(F) = a^{\mathcal{K}}(\epsilon^{\mathcal{K}}F +^{\mathcal{K}} b^{\mathcal{K}}\mathsf{nil}^{\mathcal{K}}) = a^{\mathcal{K}}(\epsilon^{\mathcal{K}}F +^{\mathcal{K}} b^{\mathcal{K}}\emptyset) = a^{\mathcal{K}}(\epsilon^{\mathcal{K}}F +^{\mathcal{K}}\emptyset) = a^{\mathcal{K}}\epsilon^{\mathcal{K}}F$. Therefore, $[\![\mathsf{rec}\ x.a(\epsilon x + b\,\mathsf{nil})]\!]^{\mathcal{K}} = \bigcap_{n\in\omega}(a^{\mathcal{K}}\epsilon^{\mathcal{K}})^n\mathsf{Act}^{\omega}$ and so $u \in [\![\mathsf{rec}\ x.a(\epsilon x + b\,\mathsf{nil})]\!]^{\mathcal{K}}$ if and only if there exists a family of natural numbers $(k_n)_{n\in\omega}$ such that $u = a1^{k_0}a1^{k_1}\cdots a1^{k_m}\cdots$ as one would expect. Another example is $\mathsf{rec}\ x.(a\,\mathsf{nil}+x)$ and $a\,\mathsf{nil}$. Clearly, these terms are bisimilar. We also have $\mathsf{rec}\ x.(a\,\mathsf{nil} + x) \lhd a\,\mathsf{nil}$, but $a\,\mathsf{nil} \not\lhd \mathsf{rec}\ x.(a\,\mathsf{nil} + x)$ as $[\![a\,\mathsf{nil}]\!]^{\mathcal{K}} = \emptyset$ and $[\![\mathsf{rec}\ x.(a\,\mathsf{nil} + x)]\!]^{\mathcal{K}} = \mathsf{Act}^{\omega}$.[i]

---

[i] Strictly speaking, we need to compute $\mathtt{k}(a\,\mathsf{nil})$ and $\mathtt{k}(\mathsf{rec}\ x.(a\,\mathsf{nil} + x))$ but we already make use of Theorem 1 since computing the meaning is easier than proving it.

Full Abstraction for $\mathcal{K}$

Theorem 1 *For all processes $p \in \mathsf{SCCS}\epsilon$ we have $\mathtt{k}(p) = [\![p]\!]^{\mathcal{K}}$.*

Proof. First, it suffices to show that $u \notin [\![p]\!]^{\mathcal{K}}$ if $\mathsf{o}(p,u)$ is defined. We prove the statement H_λ[j] "$\forall u \in \mathsf{Act}^\omega\ \forall p \in \mathsf{SCCS}\epsilon\ \mathsf{o}(p,u) < \lambda \Rightarrow u \notin [\![p]\!]^{\mathcal{K}}$" for all λ. Second, since $[\![p]\!]^{\mathcal{K}} = [\![p]\!]^{\mathcal{K}}_{\lambda_0} = \bigcap_{\lambda<\lambda_0} [\![p]\!]^{\mathcal{K}}_\lambda$ it suffices to prove H_α "$\forall p \in \mathsf{SCCS}\epsilon\ \forall u \in \mathsf{Act}^\omega\ u \notin [\![p]\!]^{\mathcal{K}}_\alpha$ implies $u \notin \mathtt{k}(p)$" for all $\alpha \leq \lambda_0$. □

A closer inspection of the proof above reveals that the rules for delay, relabeling and synchronous product are responsible for the blowup of the ordinals $\mathsf{o}(p,u)$, where the synchronous product takes the lion's share, for there are, in general, uncountably many ways of decomposing u into $v \cdot w$.

3 Our Fully Abstract Model

3.1 Denotational Semantics

We make substantial use of Abramsky's paper [2] and briefly recall his powerdomain construction. For an SFP domain D let $P^o[D]$ be $P[D] \cup \{\emptyset\}$, where $P[D]$ is the standard Plotkin powerdomain of D, see e.g. [10]. The domain $P^o[D]$ is ordered by $X \sqsubseteq Y$ if and only if $X = \{\perp\}$ or $X \sqsubseteq_{EM} Y$, where the latter is the Egli-Milner order denoting that $(\forall x \in X\, \exists y \in Y\ x \leq y)$ & $(\forall y \in Y\, \exists x \in X\ x \leq y)$. Note that $\emptyset$ is above $\{\perp\}$ but incomparable with all the other elements in $P^0[D]$. Thus we can view $P^0[D]$ as a coalesced sum of the two-point domain and the Plotkin powerdomain of D. This view will readily give us a locally-continuous functor $P^0[\,]$ which, given a strict, continuous map $f\colon D \to E$, renders a continuous function $P^0[f]\colon P^0[D] \to P^0[E]$ with $P^0[f](\emptyset) = \emptyset$. The separated sum (or co-power) $\Sigma_{a\in\mathsf{Act}}$ is locally-continuous and maps strict maps to strict maps. Using the standard machinery for solving recursive domain equations in SFP, Abramsky obtains an initial solution $\mathcal{D}$ for the domain equation $D \cong P^0[\Sigma_{a\in\mathsf{Act}} D]$. Following Abramsky's *principle of specification structures* [19], we completely separate the finitely observable part (safety specification) from the infinite one (liveness) by considering $\mathcal{E} = \mathcal{D} \times \mathcal{K}$. We have already made $\mathcal{K}$ into a monotone Σ-algebra. Since ϵp and δp have the same operational semantics with respect to their finitely observable behaviour, we are compelled to define $\epsilon^{\mathcal{D}} = \delta^{\mathcal{D}}\colon \mathcal{D} \to \mathcal{D}$ where the latter is expressible as $\delta^{\mathcal{D}} d = \mu e \in \mathcal{D}.1^{\mathcal{D}} x +^{\mathcal{D}} d\,\rho[x \mapsto e]$. Since $1^{\mathcal{D}}$ and $+^{\mathcal{D}}$ are continuous, this least solution $\delta^{\mathcal{D}} d$ will depend on d in a continuous way, i.e., $\delta^{\mathcal{D}}\colon \mathcal{D} \to \mathcal{D}$ is a continuous map. Thus we can think of $\mathcal{D}$ as a continuous Σ-algebra, which is essentially the one in [2], to which we just added a new function symbol ϵ mod-

[j] The relation $\mathsf{o}(p,u) < \lambda$ means that $\mathsf{o}(p,u)$ is defined and strictly less than λ.

eled by the denotation of δ, i.e., via recursion. Therefore we can understand $\mathcal{D} \times \mathcal{K}$ as the *product* of the two Σ-algebras $\mathcal{D}$ and $\mathcal{K}$. In particular, we have a unique denotational semantics $[\![]\!]^{\mathcal{D}}: \mathsf{SCCS}\epsilon \to \mathcal{D}$ induced by the standard denotational least fixed point semantics $[\![]\!]^{\mathcal{D}}: \mathcal{L} \to \mathsf{Env}_{\mathcal{D}} \to \mathcal{D}$; the latter equals $[\![]\!]$ in [2] if we interpret ϵp as $\mathsf{rec}\ x.1x + p$. To give some concrete examples for $\mathsf{op}^{\mathcal{D}}$ with $\mathsf{op} \in \Sigma \setminus \{\epsilon, \delta\}$ let $d, e \in \mathcal{D}$, $a \in \mathsf{Act}$ and $F, G \in \mathcal{K}$. Then we have $\mathsf{nil}^{\mathcal{E}} = (\emptyset, \emptyset)$, $(d, F) +^{\mathcal{E}} (e, G) = (d \uplus e, F +^{\mathcal{K}} G)$ and $a^{\mathcal{E}}(d, F) = (\{\!|\langle a, d\rangle|\!\}, a^{\mathcal{K}} F)$. See [2] for the remaining, more complex, Σ-operations on $\mathcal{D}$.

Definition 8 *Let* $\mathsf{Env}_{\mathcal{E}} = \mathcal{E}^{\mathsf{Var}}$. *For all* $p \in \mathcal{L}$ *and all* $\langle \rho_1, \rho_2 \rangle \in \mathsf{Env}_{\mathcal{E}}$ *we set* $[\![p]\!]^{\mathcal{E}} \langle \rho_1, \rho_2 \rangle = \langle [\![p]\!]^{\mathcal{D}} \rho_1, [\![p]\!]^{\mathcal{K}} \rho_2 \rangle$.

3.2 $\mathcal{D} \times \mathcal{K}$ as a Generalized Transition System

We make $\mathcal{D}$ and $\mathcal{K}$ into generalized transition systems and view $\mathcal{D} \times \mathcal{K}$ as a product of such systems. In [2] we have the transition system $(\mathcal{D}, \to, \uparrow)$ where $d \to^a d'$ if and only if $\langle a, d' \rangle \in d$, and $d\uparrow$ if and only if $\bot \in d$. We think of this as a generalized transition system by considering $(\mathcal{D}, \to, k, \uparrow)$ where $k(d) = \mathsf{Act}^{\omega}$ for all $d \in \mathcal{D}$. This reflects our stance that $\mathcal{D}$ solely models *finitely observable* behaviour—in $\mathcal{D}$ we make no assertions about admissible infinite computations.

As for $\mathcal{K}$, we choose $(\mathcal{K}, \to, \mathrm{id}_{\mathcal{K}}, \emptyset)$ where we decree that for all $a \in \mathsf{Act}$ and all $F, G \in \mathcal{K}$ we have $F \to^a G$ if and only if $G = \{u \in \mathsf{Act}^{\omega} : au \in F\}$. This is a rigid consistency condition on the infinite and finite behaviour of a process. The choice of $\mathrm{id}_{\mathcal{K}}$ reflects that these sets 'denote themselves'. The choice of $\emptyset$ means that we can't specify divergence without having terms available. This is *orthogonal* to the situation in $\mathcal{D}$. Also note that the transition relations on $\mathcal{K}$ nicely model the *environment*, for every state in $\mathcal{K}$ may respond with any action $a \in \mathsf{Act}$ in the most general way possible.[k] The map $a^{\mathcal{K}}: \mathcal{K} \to \mathcal{K}$ preserves all infima (=unions), so it has a left adjoint $(a^{\mathcal{K}})_*$ which preserves all suprema (co-limits). It is easy to see that the generalized transition system $(\mathcal{K}, \to, \mathrm{id}_{\mathcal{K}}, \emptyset)$ satisfies $F \to^a G$ if and only if $G = (a^{\mathcal{K}})_* F$. This gives a nice categorical explanation of the transitions on $\mathcal{K}$ as left adjoints of semantic prefixing.

We make $\mathcal{E} = \mathcal{D} \times \mathcal{K}$ into a generalized transition system by setting $(d, F) \to^a (e, G)$ if and only if $d \to^a e$ in $\mathcal{D}$ and $F \to^a G$ in $\mathcal{K}$, $k((d, F)) = F$, and $(d, F) \uparrow$ if and only if $d \uparrow$.[l] The product above separates the finitely ob-

[k] By abuse of notation, we will refer to these generalized transition systems as $\mathcal{D}$ and $\mathcal{K}$. The reader is invited to check that the greatest partial fortification on $(\mathcal{K}, \to, \mathrm{id}_{\mathcal{K}}, \emptyset)$ equals $\supseteq$.

[l] This can be seen as a product of the generalized transition systems $\mathcal{D}$ and $\mathcal{K}$ in the sense

servable from the infinite behaviour. This logical separation will be faithfully reflected in its greatest partial fortification.

Remark 1 *Let* $(S, \rightarrow, k, \uparrow)$ *be a generalized transition system with* $k(s) = \mathsf{Act}^\omega$ *for all* $s \in S$ *and let* $\leq^{\mathsf{B}}$ *denote the greatest partial bisimulation on the transition system* $(S, \rightarrow, \uparrow)$. *The greatest partial fortification relation on the product* $(S, \rightarrow, k, \uparrow) \times \mathcal{K}$ *equals* $\{\langle (p, F), (q, G)\rangle \in (S \times \mathcal{K}) \times (S \times \mathcal{K}) \mid p \leq^{\mathsf{B}} q \;\&\; F \supseteq G\}$.

The proof of this remark crucially depends on the nature of our transition system on $\mathcal{K}$: all states $F \in \mathcal{K}$ may respond with every action $a \in \mathsf{Act}$ in a most liberal but deterministic way.

3.3 Full Abstraction

Using the full abstraction results for Abramsky's finitary preorder together with Theorem 1, we can prove full abstraction of our model with respect to $\lhd$.

Theorem 2 *The model* $\mathcal{D} \times \mathcal{K}$ *is fully abstract with respect to* $\lhd$; *it is further sound with respect to* $\prec$.

4 Further Properties of our Model

4.1 A Fair Parallel

In [3] it has been shown that the composition operator '$|$' of the original asynchronous CCS in [20] could be modeled in the synchronous calculus as $p \,|\, q \equiv p \times \delta q + \delta p \times q$.[m] The discussion of *passive* versus *active* asynchronous agents in [1] suggests the shortcomings of this definition and the need for introducing finite but unbounded delay syntactically via ϵ. Our model naturally supports a fair parallel $p \,||\, q \equiv p \times \epsilon q + \epsilon p \times q$. The equational properties of $||$ may be deduced from the properties of $+$ and ϵ in our fully abstract model. Since our semantics is a pairing, the equations have to be satisfied by $\mathcal{D}$ *and* by $\mathcal{K}$; the theory of $\mathcal{D} \times \mathcal{K}$ is the intersection of the theories of $\mathcal{D}$ and $\mathcal{K}$. In fact, $\mathcal{K}$ alone is a poor model (one for automata on infinite sequences), for $a(p + q) = ap + aq$ holds in it.

4.2 $\mathcal{D} \times \mathcal{K}$ *in Logical Form*

In [2] we find a complete account of the domain $\mathcal{D}$ in logical form. For a definition of $\times$ on domain pre-locales see [9]. We therefore restrict ourselves to expressing the domain $\mathcal{K}$ as a domain pre-locale A. Strictly speaking, we

of model theory.

[m] This further requires a re-interpretation of prefixing.

leave the category SFP in [9], for $\mathcal{K}$ is uncountably based, but as long as we allow our language to have uncountably many generators, the results in [9] will readily generalize to bifinite domains, which are *coherent algebraic spaces* [10]. For illustration it suffices to specify the predicate C of [9]. A typical element in C_A is of the form $\{H \in \mathcal{K}: F \cap H = \emptyset\}$ for some finite set $F \subseteq \mathsf{Act}^\omega$. This set corresponds to the property of not being allowed to do any infinite computations from a given finite set $F \subseteq \mathsf{Act}^\omega$.

Since our denotational semantics is actually only continuous in the first coordinate, we cannot extend the Stone duality on the level of objects to a duality on the level of morphisms in the usual way. There is a definite need for establishing a theory of domains in logical form as in [9] which extends this framework to larger categories of topological spaces.

5 Future Work

One can readily check that $\delta^{\mathcal{K}}[\![p]\!]^{\mathcal{K}}\rho$ is the least and $\epsilon^{\mathcal{K}}[\![p]\!]^{\mathcal{K}}\rho$ the greatest fixed point of the function $f: \mathcal{K} \to \mathcal{K}$ with $f(F) = [\![1x + p]\!]^{\mathcal{K}}\rho[x \mapsto F]$ where x is not free in p. This suggests enriching SCCS with another syntactic clause $\mathsf{frec}\ x$, $x \in \mathsf{Var}$, which behaves like $\mathsf{rec}\ x$ in the finitely observable part (structural operational semantics, divergence, semantics in $\mathcal{D}$ etc.) but which is evaluated as a *greatest* fixed point in $\mathcal{K}$. The language $\mathsf{SCCS}\epsilon$ can then be canonically interpreted into this new calculus by interpreting ϵp as $\mathsf{frec}\ x.1x + Tp$ where Tp is the interpretation of p.

Acknowledgements

This work was supported in part by EPSRC grant GR/K42028. Samson Abramsky, Matthew Hennessy, Alan Jeffrey, Achim Jung and Robin Milner have been extremely helpful and encouraging by providing detailed comments during various phases of this work. Iain Phillips and David Sands kindly reviewed this paper.

References

1. R. Milner. A finite delay operator in Synchronous CCS. Technical Report CSR-116-82, University of Edinburgh, 1982.
2. S. Abramsky. A domain equation for bisimulation. *Information and Computation*, 92:161–218, 1991.
3. R. Milner. Calculi for synchrony and asynchrony. *Theoretical Computer Science*, (25):267–310, 1983.

4. N. Francez. *Fairness*. Springer Verlag, 1986.
5. M. C. B. Hennessy. An Algebraic Theory Of Fair Asynchronous Communicating Processes. *Theoretical Computer Science*, 49:121–143, 1987.
6. C. Hartonas and M. Kwiatkowska. Synchronization Trees and Fairness: A case study. In C. Hankin et al., editor, *Theory and Formal Methods 1994*. Imperial College Press, 1995. pp.181–198.
7. M. Mislove. Denotational Models for Unbounded Nondeterminism. In A. Melton S. Brookes and M. Mislove (guest editors); Maurice Nivat, editors, *Mathematical Foundations of Programming Semantics. Eleventh Annual Conference*, Electronic Notes in Theoretical Computer Science, pages 193–210, March 29–April 1 1995.
8. G. Winskel. Generalized trees to give denotational semantics to finite delay. Unpublished Manuscript, 1983.
9. S. Abramsky. Domain theory in logical form. *Annals of Pure and Applied Logic*, 51:1–77, 1991.
10. S. Abramsky and A. Jung. Domain theory. In S. Abramsky, D. M. Gabbay, and T. S. E. Maibaum, editors, *Handbook of Logic in Computer Science*, volume 3, pages 1–168. Clarendon Press, 1994.
11. S. Mac Lane. *Categories for the Working Mathematician*. Springer Verlag, 1971.
12. M. C. B. Hennessy. Modelling Finite Delay Operators. Technical Report CSR-153-83, University of Edinburgh. Department of Computer Science, 1983.
13. G. Winskel. Synchronization trees. *Theoretical Computer Science*, 34:33–82, 1984.
14. R. Milner. *Communication and Concurrency*. Series in Computer Science. Prentice-Hall International, 1989.
15. M. C. B. Hennessy and C. Stirling. The Power of the Future Perfect in Program Logics. *Information and Control*, 67(1–3):23–52, 1985.
16. M. C. B. Hennessy. Axiomatizing Finite Delay Operators. *Acta Informatica*, 21:61–88, 1984.
17. P. D. Mosses. Denotational semantics. In J. van Leeuwen, editor, *Handbook of Theoretical Computer Science*, pages 577–632. North Holland, 1990.
18. D. M. Park. On the Semantics of Fair Parallelism. In D. Bjorner, editor, *Abstract Software Specifications*, volume 86 of *Lecture Notes in Computer Science*, pages 504–526. Springer Verlag, 1980.
19. S. Abramsky. Semantics of interaction. Lecture Notes for the Summer School on Semantics and Logics of Computation, 25–29 September, Isaac Newton Institute, Cambridge University, 1995.
20. R. Milner. *A Calculus for Communicating Systems*, volume 92 of *Lecture Notes in Computer Science*. Springer Verlag, 1980.

Hausdorff Systems

Chris Townsend
Department of Computing, Imperial College, London SW7 2BZ.

The open/proper parallel is stated. Hausdorff systems (**HausSys**) are introduced as the proper parallel to Vickers' continuous information systems (**Infosys**) [10] and just as **Infosys** corresponds to the completely distributive lattices we prove that there is a well known class of locales which correspond to the Hausdorff systems: they are the stably locally compact locales. We prove this fact by simplifying Banaschewski and Brümmer's proof that the stably locally compact locales are equivalent to the compact regular biframes [1].

1 Introduction

A poset is called a *SUP-lattice* if and only if it has all joins. A SUP-lattice homomorphism preserves all joins. A poset is called a *preframe* if and only if it has directed joins, finite meets and the directed joins distribute over the finite meets. A preframe homomorphism preserves finite meets and directed joins. A poset is called a *frame* if and only if it has all joins, finite meets and arbitrary joins distribute over finite meets. A frame homomorphism preserves all joins and finite meets. We define the category of locales (**Loc**) to be the opposite of the category **Frm** of frames. The category of locales can be treated as if it is a category of topological spaces (see [2] and [9]). If $f : X \to Y$ is a locale map then we write $\Omega f : \Omega Y \to \Omega X$ for the corresponding frame homomorphism. f is said to be *open* if Ωf has a left adjoint $\exists_f$ which is a SUP-lattice homomorphism and this adjoint pair satisfies the Frobenius condition

$$\exists_f(a \wedge \Omega f(b)) = \exists_f(a) \wedge b \qquad \forall a \in \Omega X, b \in \Omega Y.$$

Spatially we are thinking of the open continuous functions. It is easy to check that a sublocale $i : X \hookrightarrow Y$ is open if and only if i is an open map. The open locale maps were investigated in Joyal and Tierney ([3]) where they show that for any locale X, X is discrete (i.e. $\Omega X = PA$ for some set A) if and only if

$$X \xrightarrow{!} 1$$
$$X \xrightarrow{\Delta} X \times X$$

are both open.

We say $f : X \to Y$ is *proper* if and only if Ωf has a right adjoint $\forall_f$ which is a preframe homomorphism and $\forall a \in \Omega X, b \in \Omega Y$,

$$\forall_f(a \vee \Omega f(b)) = \forall_f(a) \vee b$$

Spatially we are thinking of the proper continuous functions. It is easy to check that a sublocale $i : X \hookrightarrow Y$ is closed if and only if i is a proper. A locale X is compact regular if and only if it is compact and for every $a \in \Omega X$ we have that

$$a = \bigvee^{\uparrow}\{b | b \lhd a\}$$

where $b \lhd a$ iff there exists $c \in \Omega X$ such that $b \wedge c = 0$ and $a \vee c = 1$. Spatially the compact regular locales are the well known compact Hausdorff spaces. It can be shown ([7], [5]) that a locale X is compact regular if and only if

$$X \stackrel{!}{\rightarrow} 1$$
$$X \stackrel{\Delta}{\rightarrow} X \times X$$

are both proper. Consequently, since $X \hookrightarrow X \times X$ is proper if and only if it is a closed sublocale map, it is natural to use the expression *compact Hausdorff locale* when referring to a compact regular locale. The proper maps have been investigated in [8],[5].

It should now appear reasonable to make the statement 'compact Hausdorff locales are parallel to discrete locales' given that the definition of open map is 'parallel' to the definition of proper map. This parallel is investigated in [5]. There is a pair of parallel results which we will need in this paper. The open result can be checked as an easy exercise:

Lemma 1.1 *There is a bijection between relations on a pair of sets X, Y (i.e. subsets of $X \times Y$) and SUP-lattice homomorphisms from PY to PX. Furthermore, relational composition corresponds to function composition under this bijection.* □

It is not immediately clear how this lemma can be viewed as a statement about locales. However, since the subsets of a set A are the same thing as the open sublocales of the corresponding discrete locale (i.e. the locale X where $\Omega X = PA$), we have the following restating:

Lemma 1.2 *There is a bijection between the open sublocales of $X \times Y$ for discrete X, Y and SUP-lattice homomorphisms from ΩY to ΩX. Relational composition is sent to function composition under this bijection.* □

The proper parallel is a little harder to prove (see Chapter 5 of [5] for details). Before we state it note that since the category of compact Hausdorff locales is regular a relational composition of closed relations on compact Hausdorff locales can be defined.

Lemma 1.3 *There is a bijection between the closed sublocales of $X \times Y$ (i.e. relations on $X \times Y$) for compact Hausdorff X, Y and preframe homomorphisms from ΩY to ΩX. Relational composition is sent to function composition under this bijection.* □

In [10] Vickers introduces the category of continuous information systems (**Infosys**). These are pairs (X, R) where X is a set and R is a relation on X which is idempotent with respect to relational composition. There are many morphisms possible between continuous information systems. The most general are relations:

$$R : (X, R_X) \to (Y, R_Y)$$

$R \subseteq X \times Y$ such that $R = R_Y \circ R \circ R_X$ where $\circ$ is relational composition. These are called the lower approximable semi-mappings.

So it is natural to introduce the parallel of continuous information systems as follows: a Hausdorff system is a pair (X, R) where X is a compact Hausdorff locale and R is a closed relation such that $R \circ R = R$. If (X, R) is an infosys, then we know from Lemma 1.1 that there is a SUP-lattice homomorphism $\downarrow^R: PX \to PX$ corresponding to R. $\downarrow^R$ is idempotent since R is. The set

$$\{T | T \in PX \quad \downarrow^R T = T\}$$

can then easily be seen to be a completely distributive lattice. The essence of [10] is a proof that all completely distributive lattices arise in this way.
Given a Hausdorff system (X, R) we know that there is a preframe morphism $\Downarrow^{op}: \Omega X \to \Omega X$ corresponding to R which is idempotent (lemma 1.3). Hence

$$\{a | a \in \Omega X \quad \Downarrow^{op} a = a\}$$

is a subpreframe of ΩX. It has finite joins: $\Downarrow^{op} 0$ is least and the join of a, b is given by $\Downarrow^{op} (a \vee b)$. Further,
Lemma 1.4 $\Omega \bar{X} \equiv \{a | a \in \Omega X \quad \Downarrow^{op} a = a\}$ *is a stably locally compact locale.*
Although it is well known what the class of completely distributive lattices is (intuitively all joins distribute over all meets), it is less well known what the stably locally compact locales are. Banschewski and Brümmer describe them as corresponding to the 'most reasonable not necessarily compact Hausdorff spaces'. Johnstone ([2]) captures them as exactly the retracts in **Loc** of the coherent locales. The standard definition is a locale whose frame of opens is a stably continuous lattice, i.e. the directed join map from the ideal completion of the frame to itself has a left adjoint, and that left adjoint preserves finite meets. Or, to put this another way, every open is the join of opens way below ($\ll$) it, and (i) $1 \ll 1$, (ii) $a \ll b_1, b_2$ implies $a \ll b_1 \wedge b_2$. Where, as usual, $a \ll b$ if and only if for all directed $S \subseteq \Omega X$ if $b \leq \bigvee^{\uparrow} S$ then there exists $s \in S$ such that $a \leq s$. For more information about stably locally compact locales look at [4].

Proof of lemma: First we check that the frame is continuous i.e. that $\forall a \in \Omega \bar{X}$

$$a = \bigvee{}^{\uparrow} \{b | b \ll_{\Omega \bar{X}} a\} \qquad (*)$$

Since ΩX is compact regular we know that $(\forall a, b \in \Omega X)$

$$a \lhd b \quad \Leftrightarrow \quad a \ll b$$

hence to conlude (*) all we need do is check that

$$b \ll a \quad \Rightarrow \quad \Downarrow^{op} b \ll_{\Omega \bar{X}} a$$

if $a \in \Omega\bar{X}$. Say $b \ll a$ and $a \leq \bigvee^{\uparrow} S \quad S \subseteq^{\uparrow} \Omega\bar{X}$ then $\exists s \in S \quad b \leq s \quad \Rightarrow$ $\Downarrow^{op} b \leq \Downarrow^{op} s = s$.
As for stability we need to check that $1 \ll_{\Omega\bar{X}} 1$ (trivial by compactness of ΩX) and $a \ll_{\Omega\bar{X}} b_1, b_2$ implies $a \ll_{\Omega\bar{X}} b_1 \wedge b_2$. Since $b_i \in \Omega\bar{X}$, ΩX is regular and $\Downarrow^{op}$ is a preframe homomorphism we know that

$$b_i = \bigvee^{\uparrow} \{\Downarrow^{op} c | c \lhd b_i\}$$

Hence $a \leq \Downarrow^{op} c_i$ for some c_1, c_2 with $c_i \lhd b_i$. Hence $a \leq \Downarrow^{op} (c_1 \wedge c_2)$. But $c_1 \wedge c_2 \lhd b_1 \wedge b_2$ and so $c_1 \wedge c_2 \ll b_1 \wedge b_2$. Hence $a \ll_{\Omega\bar{X}} b_1 \wedge b_2$. $\square$.

The aim of this paper is to prove that every stably locally compact locale arises in this way. The proof is essentially a manipulation of Banaschewski and Brümmer's proof that stably locally compact locales are dual to compact regular biframes [1].

2 Stably locally compact locales

Bearing in mind the correspondence between preframe homomorphisms on the frame of opens of compact Hausdorff locales and closed relations on these locales then, provided we generalize our definition of morphism in **StLocKLoc** to include all (formally reversed) preframe homomorphisms it should be clear that there is a functor:

$$\begin{aligned} \mathcal{C} : \textbf{HausSys} &\rightarrow \textbf{StLocKLoc} \\ (X, R) &\mapsto \bar{X} \end{aligned}$$

where $\Omega\bar{X} = \{a \in \Omega X | \Downarrow^{op} a = a\}$.
It is also easy to verify (given Lemma 1.3) that $\mathcal{C}$ is full and faithful.

We want to define

$$\mathcal{B} : \textbf{StLocKLoc} \rightarrow \textbf{HausSys}$$

Say X is a stably locally compact locale. Define $\Lambda\Omega X$ to be the set of Scott open filters of ΩX. So for all $F \subseteq \Omega X$, $F \in \Lambda\Omega X$ iff

(i)	F is upper closed
(ii)	$a, b \in F \quad \Rightarrow \quad a \wedge b \in F$
(iii)	$1 \in F$
(iv)	$a \in F \quad \Rightarrow \quad \exists b \in F \quad b \ll a$

Lemma 2.1 *$\Lambda\Omega X$ is a stably locally compact locale.* □

Now since X is stably locally compact we know that there is a frame injection $\Downarrow: \Omega X \to Idl\Omega X$. Now define $B_{\Omega X}$ to be the free Boolean algebra on ΩX qua distributive lattice. There is a frame injection of $Idl\Omega X$ into $IdlB_{\Omega X}$ which we will denote by Ωl. So if we compose this injection with $\Downarrow$ we find that ΩX can be embedded in $IdlB_{\Omega X}$.

Lemma 2.2 *$\Lambda\Omega X$ can be embedded into $IdlB_{\Omega X}$.*

Proof: Send F to $\bigvee^{\uparrow}_{b \in F} \downarrow \neg b$. It is routine to check that this is a frame injection. □

Define: Y=the subframe of $IdlB_{\Omega X}$ generated by the image of the above two embeddings.

Theorem 2.1 *Y is a compact Hausdorff locale.*

Proof: Compactness is immediate since ΩY is a subframe of the compact frame $IdlB_{\Omega X}$. As for regularity it is clearly sufficient to check that

$$\Omega l\Downarrow a = \bigvee^{\uparrow}\{I | I \lhd \Omega l\Downarrow a\}$$

for every $a \in \Omega X$ and

$$\bigvee^{\uparrow}_{b \in F} \downarrow \neg b = \bigvee^{\uparrow}\{I | I \lhd \bigvee^{\uparrow}_{b \in F} \downarrow \neg b\}$$

$\forall F \in \Lambda\Omega X$.

However $a = \bigvee^{\uparrow}\{x | x \ll a\}$ and $F = \bigvee^{\uparrow}\{G | G \ll F\}$ since both ΩX and $\Lambda\Omega X$ are continuous posets. So it is sufficient to prove that

$$x \ll a \quad \Rightarrow \quad \Omega l\Downarrow x \lhd \Omega l\Downarrow a \qquad \text{(I)}$$

$$G \ll F \quad \Rightarrow \quad \bigvee^{\uparrow}_{b \in G} \downarrow \neg b \lhd \bigvee^{\uparrow}_{b \in F} \downarrow \neg b \qquad \text{(II)}$$

(I): Say $x \ll a$. Set $F = \Uparrow x$ (a Scott open filter). Then $\bigvee^{\uparrow}_{b \in F} \downarrow \neg b \in \Omega Y$. But clearly

$$\Omega l\Downarrow x \wedge \bigvee^{\uparrow}_{b \in F} \downarrow \neg b = 0$$

Further $x \ll a \quad \Rightarrow \quad \exists \bar{a} \quad x \ll \bar{a} \ll a$. Hence

$$\Omega l\Downarrow a \vee \bigvee^{\uparrow}_{b \in F} \downarrow \neg b \;\geq\; \Omega l\Downarrow a \vee \downarrow \neg \bar{a}$$

$$\geq\; \downarrow \bar{a} \vee \downarrow \neg \bar{a} = 1$$

Hence $\Omega l\Downarrow x \lhd \Omega l\Downarrow a$

(II): Say $G \ll F$. So $\exists x \in F \quad G \subseteq \Uparrow x \subseteq F$ (since $F = \bigvee^{\uparrow}\{\Uparrow x | x \in F\}$). Then

$$\bigvee^{\uparrow}_{b \in G} \downarrow \neg b \wedge \Omega l\Downarrow x = 0$$

Now $x \in F \quad \Rightarrow \quad \exists \bar{x} \in F \quad \bar{x} \ll x$ and so

$$\Omega l\Downarrow x \vee \bigvee^{\uparrow}_{b \in F} \downarrow \neg b \geq \downarrow \bar{x} \vee \downarrow \neg \bar{x} = 1 \qquad \square$$

We want a closed idempotent relation on Y and so we need to find a preframe endomorphism $\epsilon : \Omega Y \to \Omega Y$ such that $\epsilon^2 = \epsilon$. If $I, J \in \Omega Y$ we write $I \bar{\lhd} J$ if and only if $\exists F \in \Lambda\Omega X$ such that

$$I \wedge \bigvee\nolimits^{\uparrow}_{b \in F} \downarrow \neg b = 0$$
$$J \vee \bigvee\nolimits^{\uparrow}_{b \in F} \downarrow \neg b = 1$$

Clearly $\bar{\lhd} \subseteq \lhd$ and the last proof has shown us that $x \ll a$ implies $\Omega l{\downarrow}x \bar{\lhd} \Omega l{\downarrow}a$. Define

$$\begin{array}{rcl} \epsilon : \Omega Y & \to & \Omega Y \\ J & \mapsto & \bigvee^{\uparrow}\{I \mid I = \Omega l{\downarrow}a \text{ some } a, I \bar{\lhd} J\} \end{array}$$

Facts about ϵ:

- ⋆ $\forall J, \quad \epsilon(J) = \Omega l{\downarrow}a$ for some $a \in \Omega X$
- ⋆ $\epsilon(\Omega l{\downarrow}a) = \Omega l{\downarrow}a \quad \forall a$
- ⋆ $\epsilon^2 = \epsilon$
- ⋆ ϵ is a preframe homomorphism.

Hence define $\mathcal{B}$: **StLocKLoc** $\to$ **HausSys** by $\mathcal{B}(X) = (Y, R_\epsilon)$, where R_ϵ is the closed relation corresponding to ϵ. It should be quite clear from contruction that $\mathcal{CB}(X) \cong X$.

3 Morphisms

Given our observation that $\mathcal{C}$ is full and faithful and that $\mathcal{CB}(X) \cong X$ it is easy to see how to make $\mathcal{B}$ functorial. We have thus established an equivalence between stably locally compact locales with formally reversed preframe maps and Hausdorff systems. This result can be refined in order to define an equivalence between the stably locally compact locales (as a full subcategory of **Loc**) and the Hausdorff systems (with suitable morphisms): see Chapter 7 of [5]. However the purpose of this paper has been to show how the construction of a compact Hausdorff locale from a stably locally compact locale does not need to go via an embedding into the coframe of congruences ([1]) but can be carried out quite simply by taking the Boolean completion (qua distributive lattice) of the frame corresponding to the stably locally compact locale and then embedding into its ideal completion.

Acknowledgements

This work is funded by an Engineering and Physical Science Research Council grant.

References

[1] B. Banaschewski and G.C.L. Brümmer. Stably continuous frames. *Math. Proc. Cam. Phil. Soc.*, (7):7–19, 1988.

[2] Peter T. Johnstone. *Stone Spaces*, volume 3 of *Cambridge Studies in Advanced Mathematics*. Cambridge University Press, Cambridge, 1982.

[3] André Joyal and Miles Tierney. *An Extension of the Galois Theory of Grothendieck*, volume 309. 1984.

[4] Mike Smyth. *Stable Compactification I.* J. London Math. Soc. **2**. 45. 1992. pp321-340.

[5] Chris Townsend. Preframe Techniques in Constructive Locale Theory. *Phd thesis* Dept. Computing Imperial College London. 1996.

[6] Chris Townsend. Localic Priestley Duality. *manuscript* Dept. Computing Imperial College London. 1996.

[7] J.J.C. Vermeulen. Some constructive results related to compactness and the (strong) Hausdorff property for locales. *Lecture Notes in Mathematics*, **1488**, (Springer, Berlin, 1991) pp401-409.

[8] J.J.C. Vermeulen. Proper maps of locales. *Journal of Pure and Applied Algebra*, 92:79–107, 1994.

[9] Steven Vickers. Topology via Logic *Cambridge Tracts in Theoretical Computer Science* **5**. Cambridge University Press. 1989.

[10] Steven Vickers. Information systems for continuous posets. *Theoretical Computer Science*, 114:201–229, August 1993.